# Forensic Medicine and Toxicology

# FORENSIC MEDICINE

AND

TOXICOLOGY.

# CHARLES GRIFFIN & CO.'S MEDICAL SERIES.

## STANDARD WORKS OF REFERENCE FOR PRACTITIONERS AND STUDENTS.

Issued in Library Style, Large 8vo, Handsome Cloth, very fully Illustrated

### NEW VOLUMES.

**Diseases of the Heart** (Diagnosis of). By A. E. SANSOM, M.D., F.R.C.P., Physician to the London Hospital, &c. With Illustrations and 13 Plates. 28s

**Clinical Diagnosis:** the Chemical, Microscopical, and Bacteriological Evidence of Disease. By Dr. von JAKSCH, of Prague. Translated from the Third German Edition by JAS. CAGNEY, M.A., M.D. With all the Original Illustrations, many printed in colours. SECOND EDITION. 28s

**Peripheral Neuritis** (A Treatise on). By Dr. JAS. ROSS and JUDSON BURY, M.D., Senior Assistant-Physician Manchester Royal Infirmary. 21s

**Ruptures** (A Treatise on). By J. F. C. MACREADY, F.R.C.S., Surgeon, City of London Truss Society. With Illustrations and 24 Plates.

**The Diseases of Children** (MEDICAL). By H. BRYAN DONKIN, M.D., F.R.C.P., Physician, E London Hospital for Children.

**Human Anatomy.** By ALEXANDER MACALISTER, M.A., M.D., F.R.S., F.S.A., Professor of Anatomy in the University of Cambridge and Fellow of St John's College. With 816 Illustrations. 36s

**Human Physiology.** By Prof. LANDOIS and W. STIRLING, M.D., Sc.D., Brackenbury Professor of Physiology in Owens College and Victoria University, Manchester Examiner in the University of Oxford. With 845 Illustrations (a number in colours). In Two Volumes. FOURTH EDITION. 42s.

**Embryology** (An Introduction to). By ALFRED C. HADDON, M.A., M.R.I.A., Professor of Zoology in the Royal College of Science, Dublin. 18s

**The Brain and Spinal Cord:** The Structure and Functions of. By VICTOR HORSLEY, F.R.S., Prof of Pathology, University College. 10s 6d

**The Central Nervous Organs** (The Anatomy of) in Health and Disease. By Prof. OBERSTEINER, of Vienna. Translated, with Annotations and Additions by ALEX. HILL, M.A., M.D., Master of Downing College, Cambridge. 25s

**Mental Diseases:** with Special Reference to the Pathological Aspects of Insanity. By W. BEVAN LEWIS, L.R.C.P. Lond., M.R.C.S. Eng. Medical Director of the West Riding Asylum, Wakefield. With Illustrations and 18 Plates. 28s

**Gout** (A Treatise on). By Sir DYCE DUCKWORTH, M.D. Edin., F.R.C.P., Physician to, and Lecturer on Clinical Medicine at, St Bartholomew's Hospital. 25s

**Rheumatism and Rheumatoid Arthritis.** By A. E. GARROD, M.A., M.D. Oxon., Assistant-Physician to the West London Hospital, &c. 21s

**Diseases of the Skin.** By T. M'CALL ANDERSON, M.D., Professor of Clinical Medicine in the University of Glasgow. 25s

**Diseases of the Eye.** By Dr. ED. MEYER, of Paris. Translated from the Third French Edition by A. FREELAND FERGUS, M.B. Ophthalmic Surgeon, Glasgow Royal Infirmary. 25s

**Railway Injuries:** with Special Reference to those of the BACK and NERVOUS SYSTEM. By H. W. PAGE, F.R.C.S. Eng. 6s

**The Surgery of the Spinal Cord.** By WILLIAM THORBURN, B.S., B.Sc., M.D., Assistant-Surgeon to the Manchester Royal Infirmary. 12s 6d

**The Surgery of the Kidneys,** being the Harveian Lectures for 1889. By J. KNOWSLEY THORNTON, M.B., M.C., Surgeon to the Samaritan Free Hospital, &c. 5s

\*<sub></sub>\* Volumes on other Subjects in active preparation

An Illustrated List of the Series post free on application.

LONDON: CHAS GRIFFIN & CO., LTD., EXETER STREET, STRAND.

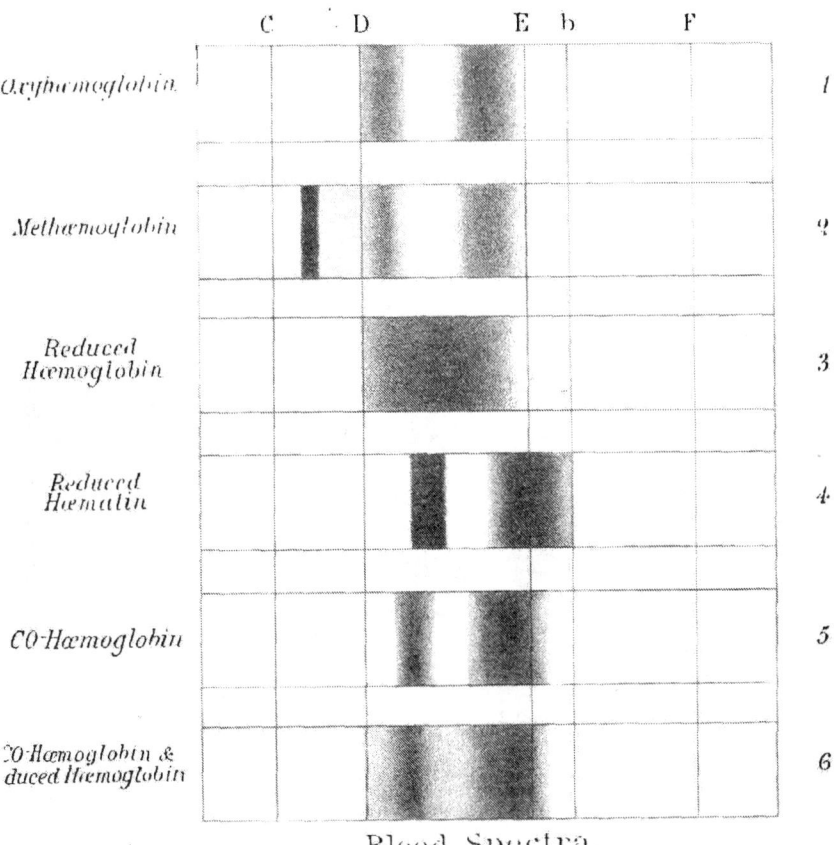

Blood Spectra.

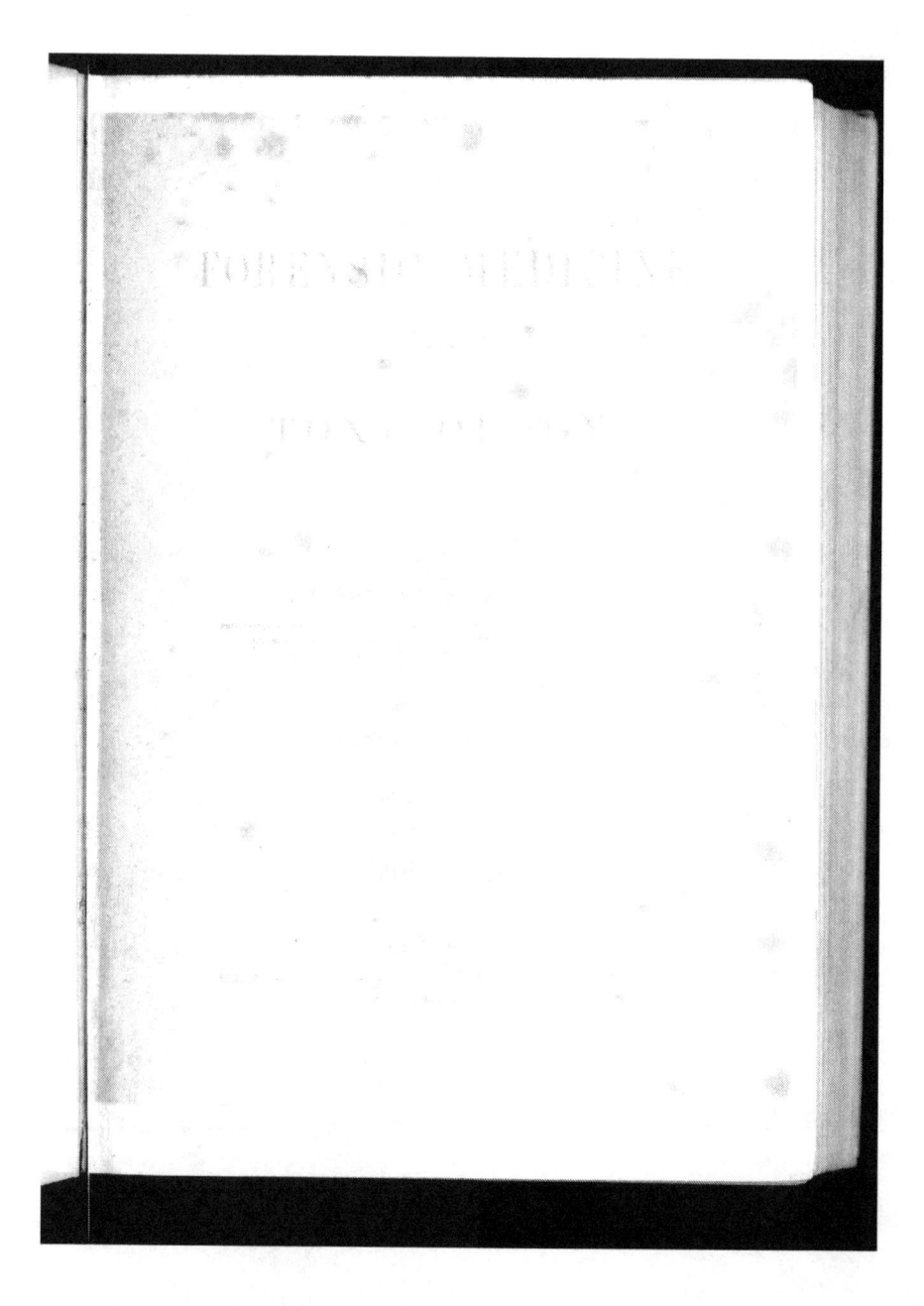

# FORENSIC MEDICINE

AND

# TOXICOLOGY.

BY

J DIXON MANN, M.D, F.R.C.P.,

PROFESSOR OF MEDICAL JURISPRUDENCE AND TOXICOLOGY IN OWENS COLLEGE MANCHESTER
EXAMINER IN FORENSIC MEDICINE IN THE UNIVERSITY OF LONDON, AND IN THE
VICTORIA UNIVERSITY, PHYSICIAN TO THE SALFORD ROYAL HOSPITAL

LONDON
CHARLES GRIFFIN & COMPANY, LIMITED,
EXETER STREET, STRAND.
1893.

[All Rights Reserved]

M3 5371
1803

# PREFACE.

This work has been written chiefly as a Text-Book for Students of Medicine it is hoped that it may also prove useful to Practitioners and others who are interested in the subject of Forensic Medicine Since Medical Practitioners in general acquire much of their expert medico-legal knowledge from the study of reported cases, no pains have been spared in the selection, from a wide field of English and Foreign periodical literature, of typical examples illustrative of the subjects dealt with

The section on Toxicology has been arranged with a view to simplicity and convenience of reference rather than to the attainment of an ideal classification

I have to thank my friend and colleague Professor A H Young for valued assistance and advice on anatomical and morphological subjects

In addition to the authorities referred to in the text, the following works have been consulted —Spiegelberg's *Lehrbuch der Geburtshulfe*, Holmes and Hulke's *System of Surgery*, Dixon's *Law, Practice, and Procedure in Divorce*, Brunton's *Pharmacology, Therapeutics, and Materia Medica*, and Dragendorff's *Ermittelung von Giften.*

J. DIXON MANN

Owens College,
Manchester, *April, 1893.*

# CONTENTS.

## PART I—FORENSIC MEDICINE

| CHAPTER | PAGES |
|---|---|
| I.—Introduction, Coroner's Court, Assizes, | 1-7 |
| II.—Medical Evidence, Oral and Documentary | 7-15 |
| III.—Legal Procedure in Scotland, | 15-17 |
| IV.—Examination of the Dead Body, | 17-21 |
| V.—Age in its Medico-legal Relations, | 21-32 |
| VI.—Modes of Dying, | 33-36 |
| VII.—Signs of Death, | 36-58 |
| VIII.—Personal Identity, | 58-63 |
| IX.—Blood and other Stains, | 63-72 |
| X.—Identity of the Dead, | 72-78 |
| XI.—Sexual Abnormalities, | 78-88 |
| XII.—Rape and Unnatural Offences, | 89-112 |
| XIII.—Signs of Pregnancy and of Delivery, | 112-119 |
| XIV.—Criminal Abortion, | 119-129 |
| XV.—Infanticide, | 130-166 |
| XVI.—Birth in Relation to the Civil Law | 166-177 |
| XVII.—Life Assurance, | 178-182 |
| XVIII.—Medico-legal Bearings of Divorce, | 182-185 |
| XIX.—Modes of Death resulting chiefly from Asphyxia, | 185-232 |
| XX.—Death from Extremes of Temperature and from Lightning, | 233-242 |
| XXI.—Death caused by Burns and Scalds, | 242-255 |
| XXII.—Mechanical Injuries and Wounds | 256-309 |
| XXIII.—Starvation, | 309-315 |

## PART II—INSANITY.

| | |
|---|---|
| XXIV.—Types and Medico-legal Bearings of Insanity, | 316-380 |

## PART III.—TOXICOLOGY

| | |
|---|---|
| XXV.—Poisons in their General Aspect, | 381-406 |
| XXVI.—Corrosive Poisons, | 407-422 |
| XXVII.—Metallic Irritant Poisons | 423-476 |
| XXVIII.—Non-metallic Elements, | 476-491 |
| XXIX.—Gaseous Compounds, | 491-507 |
| XXX.—Alcohols, | 507-521 |
| XXXI.—Benzene and its Derivatives, | 522-540 |
| XXXII.—Alkaloids and Vegetable Poisons, | 540-611 |
| XXXIII.—Animal Poisons, | 612-622 |

# PART I.—FORENSIC MEDICINE.

## CHAPTER I

### INTRODUCTION—CORONER'S COURT—ASSIZES.

FORENSIC MEDICINE is a many-sided subject. A knowledge of it demands more or less acquaintance with medicine in all its branches, and with the collateral sciences. It has been said that any medical practitioner who has a fair knowledge of his profession only requires common sense to qualify him as a medical jurist. This is a specious but fallacious statement. A knowledge of surgery, or of obstetrics, for example, limited to that required for the relief of suffering would be of little use in unravelling many of the complex questions with which the medical jurist has to deal, although the branches of medicine named may be those which are appealed to for that purpose. Much of the knowledge and skill possessed by the surgeon is useless to the medical jurist, and that knowledge of a surgical character which is important to the medical jurist is all but useless to the surgeon. Take the case of a wounded man: the surgeon examines the wound in order to determine the best treatment for its cure. To him it is of minor moment as to whether the wound was self-inflicted or not, or as to whether it might have been produced by a certain weapon, or could not have been thus produced. The attention of the medical jurist, on the other hand, is chiefly directed to these points. Something more is required for forensic purposes than a knowledge of the various departments of medicine in relation to the healing of the sick, and this additional knowledge cannot be replaced by common sense; it necessitates special training. If a medical man were to commence his career as a medical jurist with no other preparation than a knowledge of medicine and surgery and the allied sciences solely as regards the art of healing, without being acquainted with the connecting links by which they are made subservient to forensic practice, he would inevitably overlook those features of a case which, correctly interpreted, yield the required information.

A many-sided subject like forensic medicine has this disadvantage it has no real starting-point. At whatever point the writer begins, he is conscious of assuming the possession of knowledge on the part of the reader which has not yet been imparted, and further, the sequence of subjects is determined by convenience rather than by evolution, many of them being simply grouped together without inter-relation.

It is customary to commence with a description of the modes of procedure in the courts of law, and of the duties, and the obligations of medical witnesses. This, in most respects the most convenient plan, will now be adopted, and, following the usual mode of procedure in criminal cases, the first court to claim attention is—

## THE CORONER'S COURT

The office of **Coroner** has existed from very early times. Formerly it was of much dignity and importance, and entailed the fulfilment of many duties now in abeyance. At the present time, the chief duties of the coroner are to enquire into the cause of death in those cases in which there is reason for doubting that death resulted from natural causes. In the ordinary course of events, when death occurs from natural causes and under ordinary conditions, the medical attendant certifies as to the cause of death; this he is bound to do under a penalty of forty shillings. Such a certificate signed by a duly qualified and registered medical practitioner, together with oral evidence given by a person present at the time of death, is accepted by the registrar of deaths, who issues a certificate authorising the interment of the deceased.

If, however, there is reason to doubt the naturalness of the cause of death, or if death resulted directly or indirectly from an accident, or injury, the medical attendant should not certify; the case should be referred to the coroner. A heavy responsibility thus devolves on the medical practitioner: on the one hand he is bound under a penalty to certify to the cause of death, and on the other he renders himself liable—under certain contingencies—to censure, and possibly to legal proceedings, if he does so. If a medical attendant has reasonable grounds for suspicion that the death of his patient did not result from natural causes, he should decline to certify, and should communicate with the coroner, or the police authorities. The second reason for declining to certify—death resulting from or after an accident—not unfrequently brings medical practitioners unwittingly into collision with the coroner. There are two ways in which this may occur.—When death takes place at a remote period after the occurrence of the accident, especially when intercurrent disease—such as an attack of acute bronchitis—is the ultimate cause of death. In such a case the medical attendant naturally regards the disease, and not the accident, as the cause of death, and certifies accordingly. The second way in which a medical man may inadvertently place himself in the power of the coroner is by certifying the death of a patient who suffered from some chronic, but ultimately fatal, malady, in the course of which an accident not directly affecting life—such as fracture of one of the bones of a limb—happens to the sick person. Death may not occur for several weeks after the accident, and the medical attendant certifies as though it had not happened. In both these instances the coroner should be informed in place of giving a certificate. It frequently happens in such cases that pressure is brought to bear on the medical attendant to induce him to certify, and thus spare the deceased's family the publicity of an inquest. It is to be borne in mind, however, that a worse thing may happen to the relatives than an ordinary inquest. If a certificate is given, and it is accepted by the registrar with the result that interment takes place in due course, the coroner, on hearing of the matter, may order the body to be exhumed for the purpose of holding an inquest over it.

Many coroners, on receiving information of the death of an individual under suspicious circumstances, after satisfying themselves—as a rule, by hearsay evidence obtained through their officer or other policeman—as to the absence of criminal causation, or other reason for holding an inquest, intimate to the registrar that he may authorise interment without an inquest being held. This is not strictly in accordance with the law, which provides, that, "except upon holding an inquest, no order, warrant, or other document for the burial of a body shall be given by the coroner." (50 and 51 Vict.)

> When a coroner is informed that the dead body of a person is lying within his jurisdiction, and there is reasonable cause to suspect that such person has died either a violent or an unnatural death, or has died a sudden death, of which the cause is unknown, or that such a person has died in prison, the coroner shall summon a jury of not less than twelve, nor more than twenty-three, men to enquire touching the death of such persons aforesaid. When it appears to the coroner that the deceased was attended at his death, or during his last illness, by any legally qualified medical practitioner, the coroner may summon such practitioner as a witness. If the deceased was not so attended in his last illness the coroner may summon any legally qualified medical practitioner in actual practice, in or near the place where the death happened, to give evidence as to cause of death. In either case the medical witness may be required by the coroner to make a post mortem examination of the body, with or

without analysis of the contents of the stomach or intestines. If, however, anyone states on oath before the coroner that, in his belief, the death of the deceased was caused partly or entirely by the improper or negligent treatment of a medical practitioner, such medical practitioner shall not make nor assist at the post-mortem If a majority of the jury are not satisfied with the medical evidence, they may require the coroner, in writing, to summon some other legally qualified medical practitioner named by them to make a post-mortem examination (whether a post-mortem examination has been previously made or not) with or without analysis of contents of stomach or intestines, and to give evidence as to cause of death With such a requisition the coroner is bound to comply. Where a medical practitioner fails to obey a summons of a coroner issued in pursuance of the Coroner's Act, he shall, unless he shows good and sufficient cause for not having obeyed the same, be liable to a fine not exceeding five pounds.

It will be seen from the above paragraph, which is a condensed quotation from the Coroner's Act (50 and 51 Vict ), that no restriction is placed on the coroner as to whom he shall summon as a medical witness, beyond the definition "a legally qualified medical practitioner in actual practice in or near the place where the death happened" This constitutes a serious defect in the present legal mode of investigating the cause of death in suspicious cases

For the efficient performance of the duties involved, it is obvious that the medical man who gives evidence as to the cause of death in cases demanding careful and skilled investigation should be a person experienced in such duties, to select the practitioner nearest at hand is by no means the way to secure this A medical man occupied in general practice has neither time nor opportunity to acquire the necessary skill and experience It is desirable in the interest of justice, that special pathologists should be appointed in various parts of the country, whose duty it should be to make the necessary investigations on the bodies of those whose mode of death is the subject of legal enquiry Until this is done, any medical man is liable to be summoned by the coroner to undertake this very special duty. A further defect in the Coroner's Act consists in requiring the medical practitioner to make an analysis of the contents of the stomach if necessary This is obviously the result of ignorance on the part of the framer of the Act as to the functions of a practitioner of medicine and, probably, also as to the nature of "an analysis" The isolation and identification of a poison which is combined with a relatively large amount of organic matter, is a task sufficiently exacting for the expert chemist, and should never have been allotted to an ordinary medical practitioner. It is always understood, notwithstanding the wording of the summons, that the duty of the medical practitioner is limited to making the post-mortem examination, and to removing and securing in appropriate vessels, with precautions which will subsequently be described, the parts selected for analysis. The coroner has it in his power to obtain the services of a chemical expert, to whom the substances destined for analysis are sent.

The medical witness should remember that almost all the criminal cases which attain the notoriety of *causes célèbres* are initiated in the Coroner's Court, and that the evidence he there gives may subsequently be subjected to the keenest scrutiny, by subtle intellects specially trained for the purpose. The fact that the majority of the cases which come before the Coroner's Court end there, too often conduces to carelessness on the part of the medical witness in the preparation of the evidence he is about to give. Trusting to the impulse of the moment, he expresses opinions which he subsequently regrets having uttered. All statements there made are committed to paper in the form of depositions, to which the witness appends his signature, copies of these depositions are in the hands of both judge and counsel when the case comes before the assizes.

The object of a coroner's inquest is to ascertain whether the individual over whose body the inquest is held died from natural causes or not. As the proceedings are not directed against any one—that is, no one is being tried—it is not necessary that a suspected person should be present. Witnesses are not subjected to cross-examination by counsel, the coroner and the jury alone have the right to interrogate them. Occasionally, as in fatal railway accidents, counsel representing the railway company, or a servant of the company who is supposed to be responsible for the occurrence of the accident, is present at the inquest. The counsel is present in the interest of his client, but not as his defender. He has no *locus standi* and can only question a witness by permission of and through the coroner. The Coal Mines Regulation Act of 1887 provides for the examination of witnesses by counsel representing persons whose interests are affected, subject nevertheless to the order of the coroner.

The procedure in the Coroner's Court is very simple. Witnesses are examined on oath, their evidence is recorded, and in event of further proceedings being taken, they are bound under a pecuniary penalty to appear at the superior court to which the case is transferred. If the evidence is incomplete, and there is a prospect of additional evidence forthcoming, the coroner may adjourn the inquest.

## MAGISTRATES' COURT.

Another preliminary court of enquiry is the **Magistrates' Court of Petty Sessions**. In this court the proceedings take the form of an investigation as to the culpability or non-culpability of a person accused of some act of criminality, or negligence of a criminal nature As it is now a question of guilt or innocence, the accused person must be present, for the same reason witnesses may be examined and cross-examined by counsel, if no arrest has been made the magisterial investigation cannot take place Unimportant cases—such as simple assaults—may be dealt with summarily In cases of suspected manslaughter or murder it frequently happens that the magisterial investigation is held immediately after the inquest, and the medical witnesses who have there appeared are called upon to repeat their evidence before the magistrates If the evidence is deemed sufficiently conclusive of culpability the prisoner is committed for trial to a superior court, the witnesses being bound over to appear there and give evidence. The summons to attend at the assizes is called a **subpœna**, which every witness in a criminal case is bound to obey when tendered with reasonable travelling expenses The relative obligations of common and expert witnesses will be subsequently discussed.

## ASSIZES

The **Assizes** are courts in which both criminal and civil cases are tried Usually two judges are present, one presides over the **Crown Court**, where the criminal cases are tried; and the other over the **Civil Court**, where suits between two individuals or parties are tried It is with the former we are at present concerned

Before a case that has been sent up for trial from a lower court can come before the judge and petty jury, it undergoes an investigation by the **grand jury**. The function of the grand jury is to ascertain whether the cases brought before it are proper cases to go to trial. This the grand jurymen do by hearing the evidence of such witnesses as they think fit, without the intervention of counsel If they are satisfied that a case should go before the judge and petty jury they find a "true bill," if not, they "cut the bill"—that is, they quash the proceedings and the accused is discharged Medical witnesses under subpœna may be required to give evidence before the grand jury

The **Crown Court of Assize** is constituted by a judge and a sworn jury of twelve men who are called the petty jury The duty of the petty jury is to hear the evidence, and, guided by the summing up of the judge, to deliver a verdict by which the prisoner is found guilty or not guilty The judge receives the verdict, and when it is one of guilty, allots the punishment he deems adequate. Before Courts of Assize barristers only can plead In the Magistrates' Courts of Petty Sessions both barristers and solicitors can plead.

The evidence of witnesses in Courts of Assize is delivered in the following manner:—First comes the **examination-in-chief**. This consists of a series of questions put to the witness by the counsel who represents the side on which the witness appears. Previously informed by the statements contained in his brief, which consists of a full account of the case prepared by the solicitor who has charge of it, the counsel interrogates the witness so as to place before the court a clear account of all that the witness knows with regard to the case. Frequently many successive questions are so couched that they can be answered by simple negatives or affirmatives. When the examination-in-chief is concluded, a counsel for the opposite side cross-examines the witness. The object of the **cross-examination** is to lessen the value of the previously given evidence so far as it is adverse to the cross-examiner's client.

Evidence is rarely, if ever, of uniform value. It is like a chain, some of the links of which are strong, others are weak. The object of the examiner-in-chief is to place the strong links in a high light and to keep the weak ones in obscurity. The cross-examiner reverses the process, placing the strong links in the back ground, and bringing out to the fullest the unreliability of the weaker links. Proportionally to his success is the force of the evidence reduced.

After the cross-examination, the counsel on the same side as the witness may re-examine him. The object of **re-examination** is to put straight any part of the evidence that has been distorted by cross-examination, and to clear up doubtful points. An observant counsel will have noticed any answers given by the witness during cross-examination which were inconclusive or ambiguous, and will put such questions as will enable the witness fully to explain his meaning. In the re-examination the counsel may not introduce any new matter unless by permission of the judge, and, if allowed to do so, a supplementary cross-examination on the new matter may be made.

It is competent for the judge and the members of the jury to question witnesses.

The procedure in the other higher courts of justice are conducted on the same lines as those described.

# CHAPTER II

## MEDICAL EVIDENCE ORAL AND DOCUMENTARY.

**Evidence** may be of two kinds:—(1) Evidence as to facts that have come under the observation of the witness, (2) evidence as to the interpretation of facts, founded on a knowledge possessed by the witness of a special subject. Witnesses of the first kind are called "common witnesses," those of the second are known as "expert witnesses."

**The Common Witness**, or witness to facts.—A medical man acts as a common witness when he gives evidence as to the condition of a wounded person examined by him. In such a case his duty is to describe the nature of the wounds, the general condition of the patient, and other circumstances that he observed at the time he made the examination. A common witness is obliged to give evidence if legally summoned to do so.

**The Expert Witness.**—When giving evidence solely as an expert, the witness acts as an interpreter of facts without having personal knowledge of them. Usually, a medical witness acts both as a common and as an expert witness, his skilled or expert opinion being founded on facts that he himself has observed. To continue the illustration above given of the duties of a common witness.—After describing the actual condition of the wounded person he may be asked if the wound was of such a nature as to be dangerous to life. In answering this question the witness is no longer giving evidence to facts, he is acting as an expert, and thus combining the functions of a common and an expert witness. Before giving purely expert evidence—that is, evidence founded on facts of which he has no personal cognisance—it is necessary that the witness should have heard the facts on which he expresses an opinion stated on oath before the court.

The obligations of the expert witness are not so easily defined as those of the common witness. Hypothetically the knowledge possessed by an expert, who has no personal acquaintance with facts relating to a given case, is his own property, and, therefore, he ought not to be obliged to part with it against his will. This view has been taken by more than one judge. Lord Campbell ruled that a scientific witness was not bound to attend on being served with a subpœna. Justice Maule ruled that an expert is under no obligation to give evidence before a court of law. Unfortunately for experts the difference of opinion with which they are proverbially accused pervades the judicial bench. Other judges have ruled that wilful neglect of a properly served subpœna constitutes contempt of court. In the face of decisions so adverse it is difficult to determine what the law on the subject really is. It is probable that an expert who had no personal acquaintance with a case might neglect a subpœna without rendering himself liable to attachment for contempt of court, but he might render himself liable to an action for damages. Such an action, though futile so far as obtaining a verdict goes, would subject the defendant to much trouble and to some pecuniary loss in defending it. Having regard to the uncertainty of the results the safest course would be to obey the subpœna under protest

Previous personal knowledge of the facts of a case preclude a witness from taking any possible advantage of the *status* of an expert witness. There is no doubt as to the obligations of a witness so situated; he must obey a subpœna in his capacity as a common witness, although the evidence he is going to give may be of an expert character.

**Professional Secrets.**—It is an honourable law of the medical profession that confidential statements made by a patient to a medical adviser are held to be inviolable secrets. In a court of law this inviolability is overruled, a medical witness, if asked, is bound to reveal any secrets that have come to his knowledge whilst in attendance on a patient. However repugnant it may be to the feelings of a medical man to violate the confidences of the consulting-room, he has no option. If, when in the witness-box, he refuses to answer a question involving the betrayal of a secret which is really the property of his patient—it having been revealed to him in trust and under the conviction of absolute confidence—he renders himself liable to committal for contempt of court. It is conceivable that a medical man might feel the obligation to secrecy so great as to compel him to decline to answer a question involving betrayal of the confidence of his patient. Such a step, however, should not be taken without a profound conviction of duty. A good citizen obeys the law, although he may have scruples in doing so; therefore, a witness should not set his private judgment against authority without very searching self inquiry; an obstinate conviction must not be mistaken for a sense of duty. In the majority of cases it will probably be compatible with his sense of duty, if the witness enters a protest against answering the question and then bows to the requirements of the law.

When giving evidence, the witness may refresh his memory by referring to notes made by him at the time of, or immediately after, the events or proceedings to which he is testifying. Such notes must have been written by himself and must be the original copy, he must not copy the original notes and use the copy in the witness-box, or, if he does so, he must keep the rough copy so that it may be compared with the transcript, the two must agree word for word. It is much better to use the original notes, and thus save explanation and discussion. In using notes in the witness-box, the witness is only allowed to refer to them from time to time in order to refresh his memory for figures, dates, names of persons, or of places, &c., he may not read his notes in consecutive sentences. The law requires that the evidence tendered by a witness in court, should be oral and not documentary.

In the course of a trial it is not unusual for a counsel to quote from a text-book on forensic medicine, or from some other book containing matter germane to the question at issue. If the witness disagrees with the quotation it is well for him to ask to be allowed to look at the book; possibly by reading the context he may find that the difference of opinion is only apparent; in any case, before accepting or denying a quotation, the meaning of which he does not fully comprehend, it is advisable for the witness to read the passage himself. A book should not be quoted if the author is living. The objection is founded on the principle that evidence should be oral and delivered on oath in the witness-box, so that the giver of it may be cross-examined; this of course is impossible if the author is dead, and, therefore, his writings are admissible. The witness himself should not quote authorities to substantiate his opinions unless asked; the opinions he expresses are supposed to be the outcome of his own knowledge and experience.

Medical and expert witnesses are usually allowed to be present in court whilst the trial in which they are going to give evidence is proceeding. It is often absolutely necessary for the expert to become acquainted with the evidence tendered by the witnesses to fact seeing that the opinions he forms are founded on this evidence. Merely having a transcript of the evidence delivered by the witnesses to fact read to him, in place of hearing it delivered, is liable to lead to error of interpretation on the part of the expert. Further, if the evidence to a certain fact is lacking in some detail which is necessary to be brought out in order to arrive at a correct conclusion, the expert witness, if in court, has the opportunity of communicating with his counsel so that questions may be asked and the doubtful point cleared up.

A few words as to the giving of evidence before courts of law will be of assistance to the inexperienced medical witness. One of the most important points to remember is that, although the medical witness to a great extent deals with technical matters, he is addressing an audience which may be regarded as ignorant of technical terms. The judge and the counsel, although men of the highest intelligence and education, are not for the most part versed in the technical expressions by which medical men are accustomed to describe anatomical and pathological details. The medical witness has only to listen to lawyers discussing some point of law to appreciate the difficulty interposed to members of another profession by the use of technical words and phrases. If the judge and bar are not in a position to follow medical evidence couched in technical terms, much less are the jury—men of very ordinary intelligence and education—able to do so. The description of an injury which would be perfectly suitable if given before a medical society might be just as unsuitable if delivered in the witness-box. The avoidance of technical terms necessitates a good deal of paraphrasing, as such terms are necessarily the most concise in which the speaker can convey his thoughts. It is obviously more convenient to speak of the "peritoneum" than to say ' the membrane that covers the bowels,' but the latter expression would, and the former would not, convey information to the occupants of the jury-box. It may be received as an axiom that it is absolutely necessary for a medical witness so to express himself that anyone of ordinary intelligence can understand him.

Next in importance to the avoidance of technical expressions is the avoidance of superlatives and hyperbole. All evidence should be given with exactitude and without any attempt at dramatic effect—the style to aim at is a matter-of-fact style. Every object or condition should be described in the simplest terms consistent with perspicuity. As already stated, many of the questions asked require simply affirmative or negative responses. When a long string of such questions is asked there is often a tendency on the part of the witness to anticipate one or more of the succeeding questions which he divines are coming. This draws upon him a sharp reproof from the counsel, who has planned his interrogations and means to follow them out in his own way.

If a witness is doubtful about the answer to a question it is better to say frankly that he does not know than to seek to escape the difficulty by giving an ambiguous answer. When a counsel insists on "yes or no" to a question that the witness feels cannot be properly so answered, he should ask to be allowed to qualify his answer, always avoiding such appeals unless the obligation of the oath he has taken to tell "the whole truth" is in danger of being violated. No witness is required to answer a question if the answer would incriminate him.

All answers should be uttered in a sufficiently audible voice as to reach the judge and the jury, and sufficiently slowly as to enable the former to take notes. A witness should avoid a reserved or defiant manner, as though giving evidence under protest. Questions relating to facts should be promptly answered, those involving interpretation of facts demand caution. Too ready acquiescence should not be given to an apparently careless inquiry which half assumes the answer. A guarded reply to a question the answer to which involves a certain amount of discrimination is equally desirable as is a frank and open reply to a question relating to a fact observed by the witness.

## FEES ALLOWED TO MEDICAL WITNESSES.

**Coroner's Court.**—The Coroner's Act states that the fees for medical witnesses attending an inquest shall be :—For attending to give evidence at any inquest whereat no post-mortem examination has been made by the witness, one guinea. For making a post-mortem and attending to give evidence, two guineas. No fee shall be paid to a medical practitioner for making a post-mortem without the previous direction of the coroner. No extra fees are provided for if the inquest is adjourned. When an inquest is held over the body of a person who has died in a lunatic asylum, or in a public hospital, infirmary, or other medical institution, whether supported by endowments or by voluntary contributions, the medical officer of such institution shall not be entitled to any fee. It has been recently decided that workhouse infirmaries are included in this classification. If the dead body of a person is brought into a hospital or other public institution, and the medical officer of that institution is summoned to give evidence, he is entitled to the usual fee. The Act provides that immediately after the termination of the inquest the coroner shall pay the medical witness his fee.

**Magistrates' Court.**—If the witness resides within three miles of the Court, ten shillings and sixpence; if at a greater distance, one guinea.

**Assize Court.**—One guinea per day, with two shillings for every night away from home, and second class railway fare, or threepence a mile each way if there is no railway. Sundays are not counted.

**Court of Probate and Divorce.**—One guinea per day if resident within five miles of the General Post Office; if at a greater distance, two or three guineas per day, with expenses out of pocket in coming and returning.

**Court of Appeal.**—One guinea if resident in London; two or three guineas if from a distance, with reasonable travelling expenses.

In civil cases an arrangement is usually made with the solicitor as to the amount of fee before accepting the subpœna. In default of this, if the witness has not received what he deems a reasonable fee, he may appeal from the witness-box before being sworn; after taking the oath objections are futile, he is bound to give evidence. It is well to have a written agreement from the solicitor binding him to pay the fee, otherwise he is not responsible, and may refer the witness to his client, which often means loss of the fee.

If a witness is summoned to attend at two Courts at the same time, he must obey the summons to the higher Court. If one summons is for a Criminal Court and the other for a Civil Court, that for the Criminal Court must have the preference.

## DOCUMENTARY EVIDENCE

Documentary evidence includes **dying declarations** and **medico-legal reports**.

A **dying declaration** is a record of the evidence given by a person who is dying, or who believes that he is dying, from the results of an injury sustained, or a poison administered, at the hands of some person or persons. For a dying declaration to be valid it is necessary that the person who makes it should feel convinced that he is about to die. It is further necessary that this should be definitely stated in the written declaration. As the individual is incapable of writing down his deposition it is taken by a second person, and this duty may devolve on a medical man. If the condition of the patient, though critical, is such as to permit of a short delay, the police should be informed; it is their duty to secure the attendance of a magistrate, who will take down the declaration. In such a case all that the medical practitioner has to do, if required, is to pronounce as to the mental fitness of the deponent to make the declaration. Should the condition of the dying person be such that there is not time to procure the attendance of a magistrate, the medical attendant himself must write down the declaration. In doing this the following rules should be observed:—If possible, the attendance of one or more intelligent persons should be procured to act as witnesses; this is not necessary, but when important issues are at stake it is advisable to omit no precautions that can possibly be taken. The medical man should then satisfy himself that the person making the declaration is convinced that he is about to die, and the declaration should commence with a statement to that effect. Such a statement must be unqualified; on one occasion the addition of two words was sufficient to invalidate a dying declaration, thus:—"No hope of my recovery at present," the last two words destroyed the expression of certainty that death was imminent, and the declaration was rejected at the trial. *The exact words uttered by the dying person should be written down.* No questions should be asked, except such as are necessary to clear up any obscurity. The declaration should be limited to a statement of what was done to the deponent at the time the injuries were inflicted, his own actions are not relevant. When completed, the declaration should be read over to the deponent, and, if possible, he should then append his signature. In any case, the witnesses present, together with the writer of the declaration, should sign it.

In some cases death occurs so rapidly, that even the medical attendant may not be able to take down the dying man's words in writing before he dies. The duty of the medical man in such cases is to listen to anything voluntarily said by the patient, and to take an early opportunity of writing down the exact words, and signing the statement. If others were present when the words were uttered, the statement should be read over to them, and their signatures should also be appended.

Considerable responsibility devolves upon medical men who are in attendance on persons who have been criminally injured and are in danger of death. No time should be lost in communicating with the police, as, apart from the occurrence of unexpectedly rapid death, the patient may become delirious or comatose.

If a person who has made a dying declaration recovers, the document ceases to have any legal force. The law only admits evidence when tendered on oath; in the case of a dying person an exception is made. It is believed that an individual who is convinced that he is about to die, will feel himself equally under an obligation to tell the truth, as though he was in the witness-box, and had taken the oath. If, after making a dying declaration, the deponent recovers, he reverts to his normal condition as regards the law and must tender his evidence before the court in the usual way. Dying declarations are not admissible in civil cases.

**Medico-legal reports** in criminal cases are more used in Scotland than in England. A medical report is divisible into two sections.— (1) The result of the examination of the case, or, in other words, the facts that have been observed. (2) The deductions drawn from a consideration of such facts.

It is absolutely necessary in a well ordered medical report that this division should be rigidly adhered to. Every fact should be recorded before the inferential part of the report is begun. Short of absolute inaccuracy, nothing vitiates a medical report so much as the mixing of facts with deductions; first state the facts and then the conclusions drawn from them. The legal authorities for whom the report is made may know nothing of the case, and they require to become acquainted with all the facts before they are in a position to appreciate the deductions drawn from them.

The facts to be observed in the living are limited to those which fall within the scope of medical observation. A good report, while containing all that is necessary, will be free from extraneous matter. Nothing should be included in a report that does not come under the personal observation of the reporter; indirect or hearsay evidence is as much out of place in a report as in the witness-box. To avoid error of reading, all dates should be written in full. Every detail that can possibly have a direct bearing on the case should be noted, it is impossible to foresee what questions may subsequently arise. When making a report concerning a dead body, everything, both as regards the body and its surroundings, should be scrupulously noted. When the autopsy is completed, and, consequently, all the available facts are obtained, the inferential part of the report is to be undertaken.

If the report refers to a living person a careful study of the facts is to be made in order to arrive at a conclusion as to the way in which an injury has been inflicted, whether the statements of the wounded person are or are not borne out by the actual condition of the injured parts. If it refers to a dead body the questions are:—How was death caused? Did it immediately follow the infliction of the injuries? If not, what interval intervened? Were the injuries of such a nature as to incapacitate the deceased from moving after they were inflicted?—with other observations to which attention will be directed when the mode of conducting a post-mortem examination for medico-legal purposes is described.

The advice previously given as to oral evidence is equally applicable to documentary evidence. The language in which a report is drawn up should be free from technical terms and exaggerated expressions. The report should not be too long; when giving oral evidence in court the judge and the counsel will take care that the witness does not err in this respect; when writing a report he has unlimited scope, and is sometimes apt to be verbose. It is to be remembered that the writer of a report has not done with it when he has despatched it to its destination. Copies are placed in the hands of counsel, who will insist on an explanation of every ambiguous phrase; the longer the report, the more likely are ambiguous phrases to occur, for it is in the inferential part that verbosity asserts itself.

## CHAPTER III

### LEGAL PROCEDURE IN SCOTLAND.

There are certain differences with regard to legal proceedings in Scotland as compared with England.

Public prosecutors are appointed by the Crown, who conduct criminal prosecutions in both higher and lower courts. The Lord Advocate and the Deputy Advocates take charge of cases which come before the High Courts of Justiciary; the Procurator Fiscal appears before the lower courts.

The first step in a criminal prosecution is taken by the Procurator Fiscal, who, on information supplied by the police or by private persons, makes such inquiries as satisfy him with regard to the necessity or not for legal proceedings. Any person who is supposed to know anything about the case is interrogated privately before the Sheriff, or, to use the legal term, is "precognosed." The examination is not made on oath, unless the witness is suspected not to be telling the truth. The evidence obtained is written down and forms the precognitions. The counsel for the accused, as well as the counsel for the Crown, has the power of precognosing the witnesses.

The Sheriff or Justice, before whom the preliminary examination has been conducted, liberates the accused, or commits him for trial in accordance with the nature of the evidence obtained. If the accused is committed, the precognitions are forwarded to the Crown Counsel in Edinburgh, who have the power either to stop the proceedings, or to send the accused before the High Court, or one of the Circuit Courts of Justiciary, or before the Sheriff with or without jury. The Courts of Justiciary correspond to the Courts of Assize in England. Should the case be sent for trial, the persons who have been precognosed, or such of them as the Crown Counsel select, are summoned by writ as witnesses. Neglect of such citation, unless sufficient cause be shown, is punishable by a fine of £5, and also by imprisonment from which the offender is only released on expressing his regret before the Court and tendering bail to appear to give evidence.

Common witnesses are not allowed to be in Court except when giving evidence; this applies to medical witnesses also, who appear as witnesses to fact. Expert witnesses are generally allowed, by mutual consent of the opposing counsel, to remain in Court. When an expert is giving his evidence, the other experts are usually required to leave the Court. An expert witness who has been in Court during the delivery of evidence by common witnesses, cannot be examined as a witness to facts.

The Procurator Fiscal performs the duties undertaken by the Coroner in England, but without a jury. If a dead body is found, or a case of suspicious death occurs, the Procurator Fiscal, on being informed, has the power of directing a medical man to make an examination of the body, and to forward him a report dealing with the case, all such reports being certified by the reporter "on soul and conscience." If the medical examiner is satisfied with an external examination, he may certify to the Procurator Fiscal without making an internal examination. If a complete examination is requisite, the Procurator Fiscal issues a warrant to the medical practitioner who has already seen the case, and usually associates with him another practitioner of experience. The warrant is countersigned by the Sheriff or Justice, and empowers the holders of it to take charge of the body, and to make such examination as the law requires. The warrant also enables the inspectors to exclude improper persons from the room where the examination is being made. If, notwithstanding this authorisation, the relatives of the deceased refuse to allow the examination to take place, the authorities granting it (on being informed) will take steps to remove opposition. To ensure completeness of examination, the Crown Office in Scotland issues a form of instructions to medical inspectors, which contains elaborate directions for making the necropsy.

A medical practitioner, whether previously acquainted with a given case or not, cannot refuse to be precognosed if duly cited to that effect. Refusal is met by a further warrant, and, in case of contumacy, by imprisonment.

The fee for attendance at High Courts of Judiciary, or the Sheriff Criminal Court, is a guinea per day, if the court is held in the town in which the medical witness lives. If the witness comes from a distance, he is allowed two guineas per day, both for the actual attendance at court and also for each day occupied in travelling to and fro, with a guinea per day for travelling expenses.

## CHAPTER IV

### EXAMINATION OF THE DEAD BODY.

**Post-mortem Examinations for Medico-legal Purposes.**—There are several important points to be observed when making a medico-legal necropsy over and above the requirements of ordinary pathological investigations.

**External Inspection.**—The examination should be made in daylight, colour changes are often invisible by artificial light. If the body is seen on the spot where it was first discovered, attention should be paid to the following points:—The exact posture in which it lies, the expression and colour of the face, the position of the hands whether clenched or not, if clenched, they should be examined for any substance possibly grasped by them. The fingers should be examined for cuts or wounds. The condition of the dress if disordered, indicating a struggle, or if it is soiled or stained with blood. Attention should be directed to the ground on which the body lies and to that immediately around it for signs of struggling and for objects that may have dropped, as fragments of clothing, &c. Any discovery should at once be recorded in writing. The presence or absence of body heat, of cadaveric rigidity, or of putrefactive changes are to be observed. When an exhaustive investigation of the body *in situ* has been made, it may be removed to some place convenient for further examination.

The clothes are now to be removed and any cuts or injuries sustained by the clothing carefully compared with the underlying surface of the body. Marks resembling bruises should be sponged so as to make sure that they are not due to dirt or other external stain. Indications for identification are to be sought for in surface marks —nævi, moles, tattoo-marks, cicatrices, external abnormalities or loss of fingers or limbs, absence of natural, or presence of artificial, teeth, colour of the hair, height, weight, sex, age, state of nutrition, and indications of social position, or of occupation. In women and female children the presence or absence of the hymen, any signs of recent violence to the genital organs, together with the presence of foreign substances in any of the natural apertures of the body should be ascertained.

If there are wounds, examine them carefully as to their length and depth and the structures divided or injured, whether they could have been self inflicted, and the kind of weapon that could have produced them. Examine the neck for marks of strangulation. If there is a gunshot wound, look for blackening or tattooing of the surrounding skin, and also for blackening of the hand.

The internal inspection must be complete, all the cavities of the body should be opened, even though sufficient cause for death is found in the cavity first opened. If this is not done, the counsel for the defence may assume the presence of disease in an important organ which has not been investigated, or it may be necessary to have a second examination made to clear up a doubtful point which ought to have been settled by the first examination. The cavity supposed to be implicated in the cause of death should be opened first. In cases where there is no reason for selecting one cavity before another, the order from above downwards may be followed. If there are any penetrating wounds produced by cutting instruments or by firearms, ascertain their direction, and, in case they are not self-inflicted, try to form an opinion as to the relative position of the deceased and his assailant. When bones, cartilages, or intervertebral substances are injured, it is well to remove the injured parts and preserve them as evidence. Look carefully for any acute or chronic morbid changes in the organs, especially in cases of suspected poisoning, or when there is no gross traumatic lesion which would account for death. When the head has been injured the use of the chisel and hammer to open the cranium is to be avoided for fear of producing a fracture of the skull, or of causing one already existing to spread the saw only should be used The vagina and the uterus are to be examined for signs of recent delivery and for mechanical injuries, or for injuries produced by the introduction per vaginam of caustic or irritant substances. The vertebral canal should be opened and the condition of the cord ascertained

Cases of suspected poisoning —Several large glass jars, preferably new, but in any case thoroughly cleansed, should be provided If they are furnished with glass stoppers so much the better, if not, some bladder or gutta-percha tissue should be obtained which may be secured by string over the mouths of the jars It is convenient to have a large dish—a photographer's square porcelain dish is the best—for placing the stomach in when opening it.

Before opening the body, examine the mouth and lips for injuries caused by a corrosive, and ascertain if there is any peculiar odour given off from the mouth After making the primary incision through the abdominal parietes, again try if any special odour can be distinguished, and if so obtain corroboratory evidence from those who are present; the same proceeding should be adopted when the stomach and intestines are opened When the abdominal cavity is opened, look for signs of inflammation of the peritoneum or of any of the viscera, especially of the peritoneal aspect of the stomach Then place a ligature round the lower end of the œsophagus, and a double one at the commencement of the duodenum Divide the œsophagus above its ligature, and the duodenum between the two, and remove the stomach On a dish, as already described, open the stomach along the lesser curvature, taking care that none of the contents are lost The contents may be poured into one of the jars, and the inner coat of the stomach examined forthwith, its colour when first opened being noted Search should be made with the aid of a lens for crystals, fragments of leaves, berries, and other parts of plants, and for particles of pigments, (such as indigo) which are mixed with certain poisons—as arsenic when sold in small quantities, and strychnine in the form of vermin-killer Any suspicious substances found should be carefully collected and examined under the microscope. The intestines, large and small, separately ligatured, are to be removed and treated in the same way In the case of corrosive and irritant poisons, the œsophagus should also be removed, opened, and its internal appearance noted, the effects of the poison being traced from the mouth down the digestive tract as far as any can be observed. The presence or absence of solid motions in the lower bowel is to be recorded.

The colour of the blood, its condition as regards fluidity, and the colour of the solid organs generally, should be observed. Indications of fatty degeneration in liver, kidneys, and heart, of injection, especially of the kidneys, and of ecchymoses must be looked for. In addition to the stomach and intestines with their contents, the liver, kidneys, spleen, as much of the blood as can be collected, with the contents of the urinary and gall bladders, should be severally removed and placed separately in appropriate vessels for analysis. It is well to remove the brain with any fluid that is present within the cranium, especially in the case of volatile poisons, and to preserve it as above described. All vessels should be closed so as to be as nearly air-tight as possible, and the mouths finally covered with paper securely tied, the knot of the string being well covered with sealing-wax impressed with the private seal of the medical man who makes the examination. Labels should be attached to the jars and bottles, on each of which a description of the respective contents, with the name of the individual from whom they were derived, and the date of the necropsy, should be clearly written. Two lists of the jars and contents should be made; one being forwarded along with the jars to the analyst, or to the authorities who take charge of them meanwhile, the other being retained by the sender. The jars should pass through as few hands as possible; when feasible, the person who makes the post-mortem should himself deliver them to the analyst. They should be kept in a cool place, but no preservative should be added to their contents.

It is convenient and advisable that two practitioners should conjointly make the post-mortem examination. In case of doubtful or of obscure indications, the advice and countenance of a colleague is advantageous, and the division of labour—one practitioner making the section, and the other recording the results—adds to the completeness of the investigation and to the facility with which it is made. Every step should be accurately recorded at the time, or in event of the examination being made by one medical man only, immediately after its completion. If the notes are made by a colleague they should be read over on the spot by the operator, and then signed by both medical men. No other persons than those concerned in making the necropsy should be present. If a medical man is implicated, he must not be permitted to be present; he may depute another medical practitioner to represent him at the necropsy, but his representative must not take any active part in the proceedings. In all cases in which a legal inquiry is likely to take place, the medical practitioner in charge should refrain from making an examination until he receives an order from the coroner to do so. When an inquest is going to be held, the dead body is technically in the possession of the coroner until he has issued his order for burial, and, consequently, it may not be interfered with without his permission. In other cases the Anatomy Act of 1832 (2 & 3 Wm IV, c 75, sec 7) provides that the executors, or other party having lawful possession of the body, may permit an anatomical examination to be made.

**Exhumation**—When suspicion of foul play arises after the body of the supposed victim has been interred, the coroner and the authorities at the Home Office may order the body to be exhumed and a medical inspection made. The medical man deputed to examine the body should be present at the exhumation, and should previously see that adequate provision is made for making a full investigation. A relative or friend of the deceased should be present at the exhumation in order to identify the body. When the interment has been recent an ordinary post-mortem examination can be made, but if the body has lain long underground decomposition will be more or less advanced and the usual post-mortem appearances destroyed. In such cases injuries to the bones, especially those of the skull, and in women the uterus (which resists putrefaction longer than the other soft organs) may afford valuable evidence. Most frequently, exhumations are undertaken in cases of suspected poisoning; in such cases, the stomach and intestines are to be removed—if recent, they should be ligatured as described in the directions for the ordinary examination and placed in clean glass vessels well secured. The liver, spleen, and kidneys should also be removed. When the presence of a metallic poison is suspected, as mercury or arsenic, some of the bones should also be taken, the shaft of the femur, for example. If the interment was remote, so that the coffin is decayed, it is advisable in cases of mineral poisoning to remove a little of the surrounding earth for chemical examination. However far putrefaction is advanced, neither preservative fluid nor disinfectant must be used when making the post-mortem, nor added to the parts removed. The stage of the putrefactive changes in relation to the length of time the body has been interred should be noted.

## CHAPTER V

## AGE IN ITS MEDICO-LEGAL RELATIONS

The question of age in the living may come under the notice of the medical jurist in relation to criminal responsibility, marriage, fecundity, viability, rape, and personal identity. In the dead, in relation to infanticide, criminal abortion, and personal identity.

A child under seven years of age is held by the law to be incapable of committing a crime, and, consequently, is exempt from punishment. Above that age, but below fourteen years, a child is still deemed irresponsible, unless proof of such a degree of intelligence is forthcoming as to show that he understood the criminal character of the act committed by him. An "infant" under the age of fourteen years is presumed by law to be incapable of committing a rape, and, therefore, cannot be found guilty of the crime, nor of an attempt to commit it. At and after the age of fourteen a youth is held responsible for his actions, but he does not attain the full privileges of an adult until he reaches the age of twenty-one years. It is not until he attains his majority (twenty-one years) that he can make a valid will (1 Vict., 26). The day of birth is included in computing the age, and, therefore, a valid will may be made on the day before the twenty-first "birthday," as the law does not recognise a division of time less than one complete day. The obligation to serve on a jury does not affect a man until he has reached his majority. In courts of law evidence may be given irrespective of age, provided that a sufficient degree of intelligence is manifested by the child when interrogated by the judge as to his or her capacity to understand the necessity of speaking the truth. The marriageable age in this country is fourteen years for the male sex, and twelve years for the female.

In determining age in the living, no reliable criteria are available after adult life is reached. In the young, the teeth yield evidence up to the thirteenth or fourteenth year. General indications, of course, exist, but their variability—from idiosyncrasy, mode of life, personal attention, &c.—is so great, that to estimate the age of a living person between the two extremes of life is little more than guess-work.

In the dead, the case is different. There are developmental signs which, when found, limit the age of the individual in both directions sufficiently narrowly to enable a fairly accurate estimate to be made. No single sign, as a rule, is determinative; but when several are found to be in accord the expert is warranted in giving a decided opinion.

The most reliable information in the later fœtal months, and in the earlier years of life, is afforded by the ossification of the bones. The length and weight of the body during intra-uterine life afford important data, as do also the degree of development of the nails on the fingers and the toes, the size of the external ear, the presence or absence of meconium in the intestines, of lanugo on the skin, and of the pupillary membrane in the eye, and, in the male, the position of the testicles. It is not necessary for our present purpose to go further back than the sixth month of intra-uterine life, at this period viability may be said to begin. The dead body of a fœtus that can be proved not to have reached the sixth month of utero-gestation, may be regarded as having been still-born, which would, of course, negative the charge of infanticide. Concealment of birth, apart from infanticide, is a crime independent of the age of the fœtus.

To avoid error, the period of utero-gestation in the following tabulation is stated in complete months; for example, of six months duration, not in the sixth month. The latter mode of expression is ambiguous. Gestation of six months duration means that the full period named has been accomplished. Gestation in the sixth month means any time from the commencement to the end of the sixth month, and, therefore, may mean five months and one day.

## DEVELOPMENT OF THE FŒTUS FROM THE SIXTH MONTH TO THE FULL TERM OF UTERO-GESTATION

**Six Months.**—Length, 9 to 13 inches. Weight, 1 to 2 pounds. The head of the fœtus is large in proportion to the body. The insertion of the funis is considerably below the middle of the body. The skin is red and wrinkled, the underlying fat, which subsequently imparts rotundity to the body and limbs, is only now commencing to form. The body is covered with downy hair or lanugo, and also with a thin layer of vernix caseosa—a white substance consisting of sebaceous matter derived from the skin, mixed with epithelium and lanugo. The bones of the head are widely separated at the sutures, the anterior and posterior fontanelles being open. The sylvian fissure is formed. The precentral, inferior frontal, and intra-parietal sulci of the cerebral cortex appear.[1] The eyebrows and the eyelashes are beginning to form. The eyelids are adherent. The pupillary membrane, which is formed in the third month, is present. The external auricle measures 16 to 24 millimetres.[2] The finger nails are forming, but are quite soft; the toe-nails are less developed. The scrotum is smooth and empty. The testicles are on the psoas muscles, below the kidneys. In the small intestine there is a little mucoid secretion, which may be coloured with bile-pigment. Centres of ossification are present in the os calcis, the manubrium, and in the bodies and laminæ of the sacral vertebræ.

**Seven Months.**—Length, 12 to 15 inches. Weight, 2 to 4 pounds. The skin is rather paler, and is well covered with lanugo and vernix

[1] Cunningham, *Contribution to the Surface Anatomy of the Cerebral Hemispheres*, 1892.
[2] von Troeltsch, *Die Anatomie des Ohres*.

caseosa. The lanugo is beginning to disappear from the face, that of the scalp is taking on the character of hair and is becoming darker. The superior precentral and the superior frontal sulci appear. The eyelids are not adherent. The pupillary membrane, which reaches its highest development during this month, begins to disappear. The external auricle measures 26 millimetres. The finger-nails do not quite reach the ends of the fingers. The testicles are near the abdominal ring. Meconium is found in the large intestine. Examined microscopically, this substance is seen to consist of mucous corpuscles, epithelium from the intestine, small crystals of bilirubin (very like hæmatoidin crystals), crystals of stearic acid, and vernix caseosa. Centres of ossification are present in the first piece of the body of the sternum and in the astragalus.

Eight Months.—Length, 15 to 17 inches. Weight, 4 to 5 pounds. The insertion of the funis is only slightly below the mid-point of the body. The skin is a little paler, and is more filled out by increased amount of fat beneath it. The face retains a wrinkled appearance. The lanugo is disappearing. The pupillary membrane has generally disappeared. The external auricle measures 26 to 28 millimetres. The nails feel harder, and have reached the ends of the fingers, but probably not the ends of the toes. The testicles are in the inguinal canal, or they may have reached the upper part of the scrotum, especially the left testicle. Valvulæ conniventes are formed in the small intestine. The kidneys are now larger than the adrenals, and the bladder may contain urine. A centre of ossification is present in the second piece of the body of the sternum.

Nine Months, at term.—Length, 18 to 20 inches. Weight, 5 to 8 pounds. The head measures transversely 3¾ to 4 inches; sagittally, 4½ to 5 inches. The shoulders measure 4¾ inches across; the hips, 4 inches. The umbilicus is only three-quarters of an inch below the mid-point of the body. The skin has lost its rosy tint, and resembles more in colour that of the adult. The limbs and body are plump, and the face has lost its wrinkles. The lanugo has almost disappeared. Vernix caseosa is only present in quantity on the back and on the flexor aspect of the limbs. The hair on the head is mostly dark and is about an inch long. Along the lines of the sutures the bones of the skull are close together, but the parietal and occipital bones are only united by membrane and are freely movable. The posterior fontanelle is closed; the anterior fontanelle is not closed. The secondary sulci of the brain appear, and the surface is more highly convoluted. The eyelashes and the eyelids are well-formed. The external auricle measures 33 to 36 millimetres. The cartilages of the nose and the ears feel hard. The nails project beyond the tips of the fingers, and they reach the tips of the toes. The testicles are in the scrotum, which is well corrugated. Meconium is present in the large intestine only. The breasts in both sexes are well-formed, and contain some secretion. In the lower end of the femur there is a centre of ossification which measures 0.2 inch in diameter. This centre of ossification is of great importance to the medical jurist when investigating the development of the fœtus in cases of infanticide. It appears with tolerable constancy about a fortnight before full term, the epiphysis in which it is developed being the only one in which ossification begins before birth. Centres of ossification are also present in the cuboid, in the first coccygeal vertebra, and in the third piece of the body of the sternum.

The above criteria of the stage of development of the fœtus are subject to considerable variation, and consequently a decided opinion should not be given unless, in a given case, several of the most important reasonably coincide. As regards dimensions and weight, it is to be remembered that male children usually exceed female children in both respects. The variation in weight of children at term is considerable. Ortega[1] delivered a woman of a still-born child which measured 27 inches in length and weighed 24¾ pounds; it measured 7½ inches across the shoulders. Playfair[2] quotes the case of a child born of parents of gigantic stature—the mother being 7 feet 9 inches in height, and the father 7 feet 7 inches. The child was still-born; it measured 30 inches in length and weighed 23¾ pounds. The weight of the fœtus at term being more influenced by the state of nutrition is less constant than the length. Rickets retards ossification, and thus interferes with the closure of the fontanelles and with the development of the various centres of ossification normally existing at term.

In the newly-born, putrefactive changes take place with great rapidity and seriously interfere with the indications afforded by the weight, the condition of the skin, hair, nails, cartilages of the nose and ears, and by producing opacity of the cornea, with evidence afforded by the pupillary membrane. It is to be observed that the absence of the pupillary membrane does not in itself determine the maturity of the fœtus, nor is the absence of the testicles from the scrotum to be accepted as an indication of immaturity; they not unfrequently remain in or above the inguinal canal until or beyond puberty. The presence or absence of the centre of ossification in the lower epiphysis of the femur, although not infallible, is perhaps the most reliable means of enabling an opinion to be formed as to the maturity or otherwise of a fœtus, even when putrefactive changes are so far advanced as to render other indications valueless. It is to be remembered that the difference

[1] *Nouvelles Arch. d'Obstét. et de Gynécol.*, 1891.
[2] *Science and Practice of Midwifery.*

between a fœtus at eight months and one at full term is not sufficiently pronounced as to enable a positive opinion to be given. This, however, does not affect the issue in the greater number of cases that come before the medical jurist, seeing that in either case the child might have been born alive.

The following table shows the more important developmental changes which take place in the fœtus from six months to full term :—

TABLE OF DEVELOPMENTAL CHANGES IN THE FŒTUS.

| Months. | Length in inches. | Weight in pounds. | Nails. | Pupillary membrane. | Testicles. | Centres of ossification. |
|---|---|---|---|---|---|---|
| 6 | 9-13 | 1-2 | Forming. | Present. Eyelids adherent. | On psoas muscles below kidneys. | Os calcis. Manubrium. Bodies and laminæ of sacral vertebræ. |
| 7 | 12-15 | 2-4 | Not reached ends of fingers. | Partly present. Eyelids open. | About abdominal rings. | First piece of body of sternum. Astragalus. |
| 8 | 15-17 | 4-5 | Ends of fingers, but probably not of toes. | Disappeared. | Inguinal canal; may be in scrotum. Left often before right. | Second piece of body of sternum. |
| 9 | 17-20 | 5-8 | On fingers perfectly formed: not necessarily on toes. | ... | Usually both in scrotum which is corrugated. | Cuboid. Third piece of body of sternum. First coccygeal vertebra. Lower epiphysis of femur. |

After birth, the circulation soon becomes of the adult type. The epiderm begins to desquamate about the third day. The skin, at first hyperæmic and red in colour, subsequently acquires a yellowish tinge. When desquamation is finished—the time occupied varying from one to two weeks or more, according to the vigour of the child—the skin assumes its permanently normal colour. During the first three days the child loses weight. A few hours after birth the intestines relieve themselves of the meconium which accumulated during intra-uterine life. At birth, the normal umbilical cord is plump, spiral, and of an opal colour; in weakly children it is flaccid and is much thinner. After division of the cord, the portion attached to the child becomes flabby and begins to shrivel up on the first or second day: desiccation commences at the free end, advances towards the point of insertion, and is completed about the third or fourth day. The cord is then flattened, and has a parchment-like, translucent appearance, exhibiting the arteries and vein as red lines. If a cord that has undergone mummification is soaked in water, it does not return to its previous condition. About the fourth or fifth day the cord separates by ulceration close to the abdominal wall. Around the point of detachment is an inflammatory zone, which persists some time after separation. The usual purulent secretion which accompanies ulcerative processes is more or less present. The degree of, and the time occupied by, the inflammatory processes which attend separation of the cord vary with the development and vital activity of the child: the feebler the child, the longer the process of detachment. Cicatrisation of the navel is usually completed in about eight to twelve days.

After separation of the funis and completion of desquamation of the epiderm, the progress of dentition and the development of the various centres of ossification that form after birth afford the most reliable criteria of age. There are, however, other indications which may be of use.

The capacity of the stomach rapidly increases after birth. Ashby and Wright[1] estimate the rate of increase as follows:—

| | |
|---|---|
| At term, | about 2 fluid ounces |
| Fourth week, | ,, 3-4 ,, |
| Three months, | ,, 5 ,, |
| Twelve months, | ,, 10 ,, |

The cubic capacity of the skull at term equals 500 cc. In the second year, it has increased to 1000 cc. In adult life, it averages 1500 cc.

The increase in the child's **weight** during the first twelve months of its life is very pronounced. Pfeiffer gives the following table (abridged):—

| | Pounds | Ounces |
|---|---|---|
| In the first month, | 8 | 5½ |
| ,, third ,, | 11 | 15 |
| ,, sixth ,, | 16 | 3½ |
| ,, ninth ,, | 20 | 1 |
| ,, twelfth ,, | 22 | 7 |

The weight does not increase so rapidly after the end of the first year. It is again doubled at the end of the sixth year, and also at the end of the fourteenth year. These figures obviously presuppose that the nutrition of the child is progressively maintained.

The average length of a child at the end of the fourth year is double the average length at term.

At birth, the angle formed by the ramus and the body of the lower jaw is obtuse, being equal to about 110°. The body is almost semi-

[1] *Diseases of Children*, 1892.

circular in form; it is shallow and chiefly consists of the alveolar portion; the basal part is but little developed. The permanent teeth

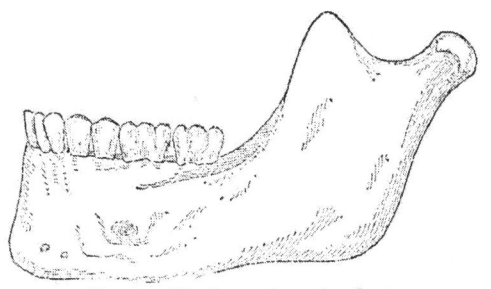

Fig. 1.—The lower jaw at puberty.

being more numerous than the temporary teeth require additional space; this is provided by growth of the body of the jaw posteriorly,

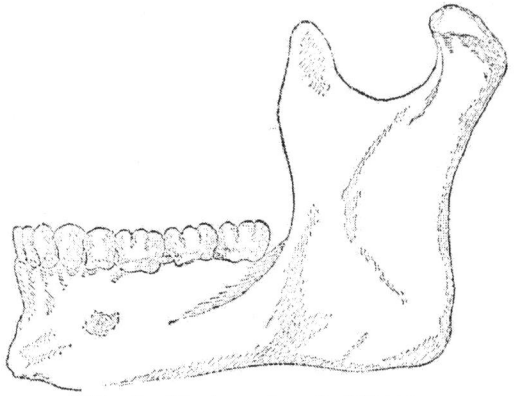

Fig. 2.—The lower jaw of adult age.

which changes its form from a semi-circle to that of a horse-shoe. Coincident with its increase in length, the body becomes deeper and

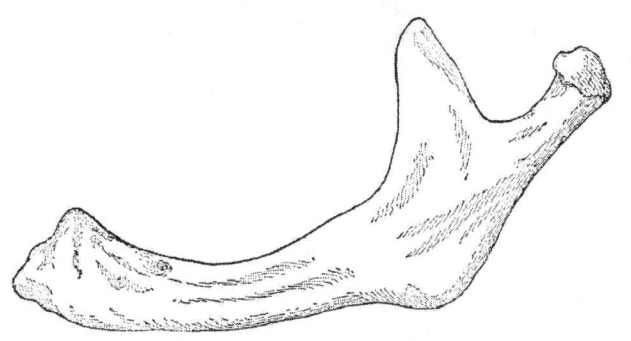

Fig. 3.—The lower jaw of old age.

THE TEETH.

thicker. The ramus lengthens, and the angle formed by it with the body becomes less obtuse, so that in adult life it approaches a right angle. In advanced old age the teeth are lost, and the alveolar portion of the jaw atrophies, consequently the body is again shallow, and the angle formed by it with the ramus is once more obtuse. It will be seen from this description that the shallow jaw of infancy and that of old age are anatomically complementary the one to the other: the body of the infantile jaw is almost exclusively alveolar, that of old age is exclusively basal. This is demonstrated by the position of the mental foramen in the infantile and senile jaw respectively—in the former, the foramen is low down; in the latter, it opens at the upper border.

## THE TEETH.

The **temporary** or milk teeth are twenty in number. They appear in the following order:—

| | | |
|---|---|---|
| 7th month, | . . . | lower central incisors. |
| 8th ,, | . . . | upper central incisors. |
| 7th to 9th ,, | . . . | upper lateral incisors. |
| 10th to 12th ,, | . . . | lower lateral incisors. |
| 14th ,, | . . . | first temporary molars. |
| 17th ,, | . . . | canines. |
| 22nd to 24th ,, | . . . | second temporary molars. |

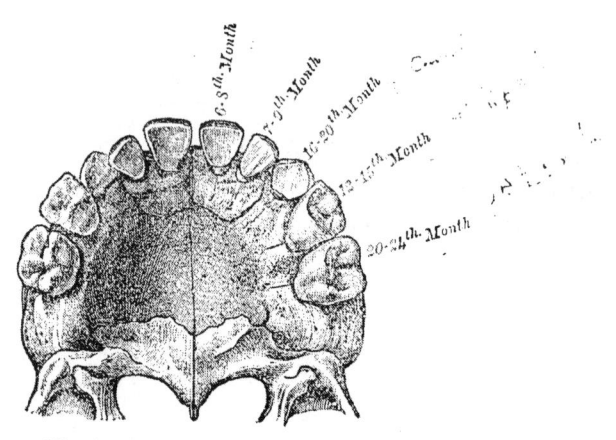

Fig. 4.—Temporary teeth (upper jaw).
(Macalister's *Human Anatomy*).

In weakly children, especially in those suffering from rickets, dentition is retarded. The converse of this occurs at rare intervals: children have been born with the incisors cut.

The **permanent** teeth are thirty-two in number. They appear in the following order:—

| | | |
|---|---|---|
| 7th year, | . . | first molars. |
| 8th ,, | . . | central incisors. |
| 9th ,, | . . | lateral incisors. |
| 10th ,, | . . | anterior premolars, or bicuspids, } these replace the |
| 11th to 15th ,, | . . | posterior premolars, } temporary molars. |
| 11th to 13th ,, | . . | canines. |
| 13th to 16th ,, | . . | second molars. |
| 18th to 30th ,, | . . | third molars, or wisdom teeth. |

The first of the permanent teeth appear on ground previously unoccupied—behind the rearmost of the temporary set. As a rule, they appear before any of the temporary teeth are lost, so that, on counting the teeth in one jaw from the central line backwards, if there are only five, they belong to the temporary set; if there is a sixth, it belongs to the permanent set. The rest of the permanent teeth replace the temporary teeth in the same order in which the temporary teeth appeared. The permanent molars appear at intervals of about six years. A child, nine years of age, will have twelve permanent teeth; at thirteen or fourteen, it will have twenty-eight—that is, all except the four wisdom teeth.

In advanced life, the bones of the head tend to become thinner from absorption of the diploë. The long bones become lighter and more fragile, the inorganic components being in excess. Many of the teeth are absent, and those which remain are worn down and discoloured.

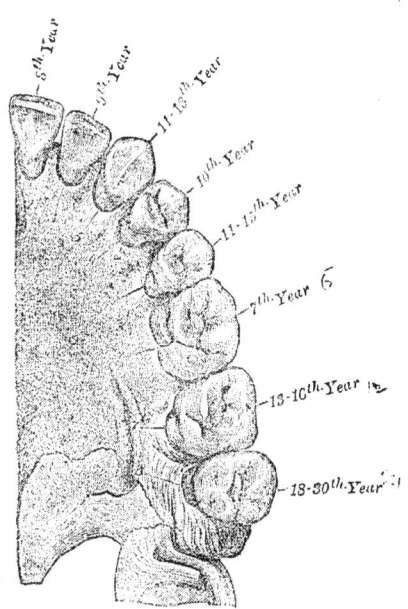

Fig. 5.—Permanent teeth.
(Macalister's *Human Anatomy*).

The following Tables are arranged (mostly from Quain's *Osteology* by Thane) with the view of showing the probable age of a body or skeleton up to puberty, from the presence of the principal centres of ossification, and to later adult age from the union of epiphyses with bones, or of one bone with another:—

## Table Showing the Periods at which Points of Ossification Appear after Birth.

| Years of Life. | Bones in which the Ossific Points Appear. |
|---|---|
| 1st | Fourth piece of the body of the sternum. |
| ,, | Coracoid process of the scapula. |
| ,, | Head of the humerus. |
| ,, | Os magnum (carpus). |
| ,, | Head of femur. |
| ,, | Upper end of tibia. |
| ,, | External cuneiform (tarsus). |
| 2nd | Lower end of radius. |
| ,, | Unciform (carpus). |
| ,, | Lower end of tibia. |
| ,, | Lower end of fibula. |
| 3rd | Great tuberosity of humerus. |
| ,, | Patella. |
| ,, | Internal cuneiform (tarsus). |
| 3rd to 4th | Upper end of fibula. |
| 4th | Great trochanter (femur). |
| ,, | Middle cuneiform (tarsus). |
| 4th to 5th | Scaphoid (tarsus). |
| ,, | Lower end of ulna. |
| 5th | Lesser tuberosity (humerus). |
| ,, | Internal condyle (humerus). |
| ,, | Trapezium and semilunar (carpus). |
| 5th to 6th | Upper end of radius. |
| 6th | Scaphoid (carpus). |
| 7th | Trapezoid (carpus). |
| 10th | Upper end of ulna. |
| 12th | Pisiform (carpus). |
| 13th to 14th | External condyle (humerus). |
| ,, | Small trochanter (femur). |

## Table Showing the Periods of Union of Epiphyses with Shafts of Bones, and of Bones with each other.

| Years of Life. | Epiphyses and Bones. |
| --- | --- |
| 1st or 2nd | Symphysis of lower jaw. |
| 2nd | Frontal suture; unites from below upwards; may persist. |
| ,, | Anterior fontanelle filled up. |
| 7th or 8th | Rami of ischium and pubis. |
| 17th | Epiphysis of upper end of ulna. |
| ,, | ,,  small trochanter (femur). |
| 17th to 18th | ,,  condyles (humerus). |
| ,, | ,,  upper end of radius. |
| 18th | ,,  great trochanter (femur). |
| ,, | ,,  lower end of tibia. |
| ,, | Lower sacral vertebræ. |
|  | Portions of acetabulum united. |
| 19th | Epiphysis of head of the femur. |
| 20th | ,,  ,,  humerus. |
| ,, | ,,  lower end of radius. |
| ,, | ,,  ,,  ,,  ulna. |
| 21st | ,,  upper end of tibia. |
| ,, | ,,  lower end of fibula. |
| 24th | ,,  upper end of fibula. |
| 25th | Second and third pieces of sternum. |
| ,, | First and second sacral vertebræ. |
| ,, | Epiphysis of clavicle. |
| ,, | ,,  lower end of femur. |
| 40th | Manubrium with body of sternum. |

## CHAPTER VI.

### MODES OF DYING.

It is customary and convenient to speak of death as beginning in one of the three essential organs concerned in the maintenance of life—the brain, the lungs, and the heart; failure of action on the part of any one of these organs speedily interferes with the functions of the other two. If the blood is insufficiently aërated in the lungs, the vasomotor centres are irritated, and consequently the heart's action is impeded by the narrowing of the blood-channels, the musculature of the heart itself being enfeebled by impure blood-supply. If the heart does not propel the blood with sufficient activity through the lungs, the respiratory centres are ultimately paralysed. Again, if a blood-clot presses on the centres in the medulla, both heart and lungs succumb. If the final obvious indications of life are to be accepted, the heart and the lungs are the organs which, by cessation of function, actually bring about somatic death. From this aspect the mention of death beginning in the head may be regarded as unnecessary; it is convenient, however, to retain Bichat's classification. It is to be borne in mind that, chiefly, the medical jurist is only concerned in the investigation of deaths which have resulted from violence; but not unfrequently he is called upon to investigate cases in which death was the result of disease—the manner of death, or the circumstances under which it took place, being suspicious of foul play.

The three modes of dying are—*Asphyxia, Syncope, Coma.*

### ASPHYXIA.

When the respiratory function is arrested beyond a certain limit asphyxia is the result. There are various ways in which the interchange may be interrupted which normally takes place in the lungs between the blood and the air, viz. :—

The nervous supply to the respiratory muscles may be abolished either centrally (medulla), or peripherally (pneumogastrics or phrenics). Fixation of the respiratory muscles (tetanus or strychnine); mechanical pressure on thorax; collapse of lungs (pneumothorax); foreign bodies in the air passages, or closure of them by external compression

3

(strangulation); drowning; respiring air deficient in oxygen; spasm of glottis from mechanical irritation (particles of food), or from irritant gases (Cl, $SO_2$), are each capable of producing death from asphyxia.

**Symptoms.**—The phenomena of asphyxia may be divided into three stages. In the first, the respirations are deeper, more frequent, and more laboured than in the normal condition. The extraordinary muscles of respiration are called into action, and the struggle for air becomes more and more severe. The blood becomes more venous, and stimulates the respiratory centres, evoking violent attempts at respiration. In the second stage, the inspiratory muscles are less active, whilst the expiratory muscles contract energetically, as do also almost all the muscles of the body, producing general convulsions. In the third stage, the respiratory centres are paralysed. The pupils are widely dilated, consciousness is abolished, and the reflexes are absent. A few gasps at long intervals, and all is over. Hughlings-Jackson[1] directs attention to absence of the knee-jerk when the blood is highly venous. In the earlier stages of asphyxia the knee-jerks are exaggerated, but when the third stage is reached they are entirely lost.

**Post-mortem Appearances.**—The right side of the heart, the pulmonary artery, the venæ cavæ, and the veins of the neck are gorged with dark venous blood. The left side is comparatively empty from post-mortem contraction (see under "Cadaveric Rigidity"). The blood, nearly black, contains a large amount of $CO_2$, and, therefore, coagulates slowly. The hæmoglobin is almost entirely reduced; ordinary venous blood contains a considerable amount of $O_2 Hb$ as well as reduced Hb. (Landois and Stirling.)

## SYNCOPE.

When the circulation suddenly fails, syncope is the result. The circulation may fail from cessation of the heart's action, the result of disease (aortic regurgitation, fatty heart, &c.), of inhibition (psychical shock, blow on the head, or reflexly from blow on epigastrium). The circulation may also fail from loss of blood (wounds of the large blood-vessels, or of the heart itself, profuse hæmatemesis, &c.) or from sudden withdrawal of blood from the circulation without loss (blows on the abdomen by paralysing the splanchnics may enlarge the vascular area of the abdomen to such an extent as to deplete the rest of the system).

**Symptoms.**—Pallor of the face, including the lips, dimness of vision, cold clammy sweat, sense of impending dissolution, craving for more

[1] *British Med. Journ.,* 1892.

air, great restlessness, gasping for breath, nausea, possibly vomiting, rushing sounds in the ears, momentary delirium quickly passing on to insensibility, followed by convulsions precede death. The whole of these symptoms are not always present. In simple fainting there may be only immediate loss of consciousness with cold surface and sighing respiration. In all cases the pulse is weak, irregular, or imperceptible. The condition called collapse, though attended by failure of the heart's action, differs from syncope inasmuch as the patient retains consciousness.

**Post-mortem Appearances.**—When death has resulted from insufficient supply of blood to the heart, that organ has been found contracted and empty. When the cause of death has been heart-paralysis both sides have been found to contain blood. (See "**Cadaveric Rigidity**")

## COMA

When from any cause affecting the brain insensibility is produced which terminates in death, the individual is said to die from coma. Increase of intra-cranial pressure, or dynamic disturbance of the cerebrum or of its circulation, may produce coma (concussion, hæmorrhage, tumour, abscess, embolism, thrombosis, depressed fracture of the skull). Inflammatory processes (meningitis, &c.) Abnormal condition of the blood circulating through the brain (uræmia, certain poisons, as opium, alcohol, and that which produces the complication attending diabetes known as diabetic coma).

**Symptoms.**—The symptoms produced by many of the causes of coma above enumerated may take the initial form of stupor, from which the patient may be partially roused for a few seconds or more. This condition subsequently deepens into profound insensibility, from which the patient cannot be roused. Some of the causes enumerated produce sudden coma without any antecedent stupor. In stupor the reflexes may be retained or even exaggerated, in coma they are usually diminished or lost. Power to swallow fluids is consistent with stupor, but not with coma. A comatose person is utterly insensible to all external impressions; he lies powerless, breathing heavily, with stertor from paralysis of the soft palate. The surface is usually covered with a cold sweat, the temperature being at or below normal, except in lesions of the pons and a few other conditions. The pulse may vary, but is often full and laboured. The breathing becomes more and more embarrassed from diminished activity of the respiratory centres, and mucus collects in the air-passages, causing the form of breathing known as "the death rattle." The pupils either dilated or contracted, are insensitive to light, and the conjunctival reflex is lost.

**Post-mortem Appearances**—In some of the conditions which produce coma, examination of the brain reveals the cause. From what has been already said it will be apparent that the condition of heart and lungs is not constant. As a rule, they resemble more or less the condition found in death from asphyxia.

---

## CHAPTER VII

### SIGNS OF DEATH.

THE movements which accompany respiration and circulation are the two most obvious indications of the existence of animal life. If signs of movement of the lungs and of the heart are present, it is clear that death has not yet occurred. If the lungs cease acting, the heart may continue to beat for many minutes, which, also, is conclusive that death has not yet taken place. When both heart and lungs have ceased to act, the tissues retain "vitality" for some time, during the continuance of which it cannot be truly asserted that the individual is dead. To this lingering "vitality" of components is due the potentiality of resuscitation of the entity they compose, after temporary cessation of the main functions by which life is sustained. If the heart persistently ceases to beat, the vitality of the tissues progressively diminishes, until at last a point is reached when death is absolute and universal; when this point is reached, but not before, resuscitation is impossible.

It is very necessary for the medical jurist thoroughly to appreciate the importance of the distinction between *systemic* or *somatic death*, and *death of the tissues* or *molecular death*. In profound syncope, for example, there is every external appearance of death; but, if the heart resumes its function, the patient recovers. Hence the necessity of careful study of the phenomena which succeed death, in order to be able to distinguish between real and apparent death.

Auscultation, carefully conducted and repeated if necessary at intervals, will enable an opinion to be formed as to whether the heart and lungs have or have not ceased to act. Absolute silence should be maintained during the investigation, which should be conducted with all deliberation. Error on the part of the practitioner, should he wrongly pronounce that death has taken place, is so obviously capable of refutation that his reputation is damaged, and, what is of infinitely greater importance, such an error might lead to that most ghastly of all blunders—the treatment of a living being as though he were dead.

After the occurrence of somatic death—that is, after permanent cessation of respiration and circulation—certain phenomena occur in definite order. The time occupied by many of these phenomena, although variable, is limited, and consequently, by ascertaining the stage at which they have arrived, an opportunity is afforded of approximatively estimating the interval that has elapsed between death and the period of investigation. These phenomena are manifestations of the occurrence of molecular death. The rapidity of their onset is, to some extent, determined by conditions which exercise an influence on the amount of vital energy with which the tissues are endowed immediately before somatic death. Such conditions comprise disease, poison, violent exercise, and other exhausting influences. If the tissues are depressed in vitality at the moment of somatic death, they rapidly succumb to molecular death, and the course of the succeeding phenomena is hastened. If, on the other hand, they are in full activity when somatic death takes place, they resist the advent of processes which are really the antecedents of decomposition.

## CESSATION OF RESPIRATION AND CIRCULATION

At the moment of somatic death, the skeletal muscles lose their tonus and become flaccid. When death takes place whilst the body is in the recumbent posture, the loss of tonus is immediately manifested by dropping of the lower jaw, the eyelids remain open, or partially so, and the limbs are flexible. The pinched look of the face—facies hippocratica—that frequently manifests itself at the time of death, changes to a more or less peaceful expression, often—in the case of persons above middle age not much emaciated—evoking the comment from the bystanders that the deceased now resembles the appearance he presented in youth. This alteration in facial expression is due to relaxation of the muscles smoothing away the sharp contour of the features. The eyes lose their lustre and acquire the peculiar ghastly stare so characteristic of death. The pupils dilate at the time of death, and do not respond to light. Marshall[1] states that contraction of the pupils subsequently takes place for a period varying from one to forty-eight hours after death; that atropine dilates the pupils after death, in some instances as long as four hours after, and that esserine contracts the pupils, but not for so long after death. The surface of the body, including the lips, becomes pallid; people of florid complexion often retain

[1] *The Lancet*, 1885.

their colour for several days after death. Ten or twelve hours after death, the eyeballs sink in the orbits and become flaccid, so that the cornea retains the dint caused by pressure of the finger-nail or other hard substance.

Death abolishes the distinction between living and dead matter, and, consequently, the human body after death becomes subject to the laws which govern inanimate matter. That remarkable property with which man in common with other animals is endowed—the power of maintaining an equable internal temperature, whatever may be the temperature of the surrounding air—is now lost. The consequence is, that the body yields up its heat and slowly but progressively cools down to the temperature of the surrounding media.

### POST-MORTEM COOLING

From fifteen to twenty hours is the time usually required for the body to cool to the temperature of its surroundings. It is obvious that this can only be accepted as a general statement. The actual time taken by a cadaver to become cold is determined by conditions, some of which are of internal and others of external relation.

**Conditions of Internal Relation.**—At the time of death resulting from some diseases, and from certain other modes of death, the body-heat greatly exceeds the normal. This has been observed in cholera, acute rheumatism, poisoning by strychnine, tetanus, and some forms of apoplexy. After death from cholera, yellow fever, and some other diseases, post-mortem elevation of temperature has been observed. Under like external conditions, a cadaver having at the moment of death a temperature 8° or 10° F above normal, would take longer to cool than one at the normal temperature. Certain modes of death, without necessarily causing any elevation of temperature, retard the rate of cooling death from suffocation, and some other kinds of sudden death from violence may have this effect. The state of nutrition at the time of death also exercises a considerable influence, bodies loaded with fat do not cool so rapidly as those which are emaciated. The bodies of persons in the prime of life do not cool so rapidly as those of very young or of very old people. Those who have died from lingering or wasting diseases cool rapidly, the temperature probably being subnormal before death.

**Conditions of External Relation.**—The temperature of the surrounding media and their capacity for heat-conduction exercise an important influence, a body submerged in water will cool more rapidly than in air, because water is colder and is a better conductor of heat than the air above it, a body lying naked on the flags will cool quicker than one protected by clothing and lying on a bed. Without particularising further, it may be accepted that the greater the difference of temperature between the dead body and the surrounding media, the more rapidly is its heat lost in a given unit of time; therefore, the rate of post-mortem cooling is not uniform, but is proportional to the difference in temperature existing at any given period between the body and its surroundings. From this it follows that the cooling rate will be quicker in the earlier than in the later hours, because in the later hours the temperature of the body more nearly approximates to that of its surroundings; during the first few hours it may average 2° or 3° F per hour, subsequently it will not exceed 1° F per hour. The longer of the two periods—twenty hours—stated as sufficient in ordinary cases to allow the body to cool, may be accepted as practically, but not absolutely, correct. For the reason just given, the cooling-rate is exceedingly slow when the temperature of the body differs but slightly from that of its surroundings; therefore, the last few degrees of body-heat take a long time to disappear, the body in the meantime being cold for all practical purposes.

## POST-MORTEM STAINS

Coincident with cooling is the formation of certain discolorations on the dependent parts of the body. Various terms are used to indicate these stains, as—cadaveric hypostases, cadaveric ecchymoses, post-mortem lividities, sugillations. When the subject of giving evidence was dealt with, the necessity of avoiding technical terms in the witness-box was emphasised; in furtherance of this advice it is recommended that the words which head this section should invariably be used when discussing the subject, as conveying a clearer idea of what is meant to the ordinary hearer than any of the synonyms. Post-mortem stains are produced by gravitation of the still fluid blood into the capillaries and the venous radicles of the lower parts of the body which are obviously determined by the position in which it rests. If the body is lying on its back the lobes of the ears, the shoulders, the lumbar region, the buttocks, and the posterior parts of the legs and arms will constitute the lower parts. If the body is in the prone posture, the face, chest, abdomen, and the anterior parts of the legs and arms will be the lower parts. In addition to the results produced by gravity, are those due to loss of tonus of the walls of the capillaries which occurs at the time of death. The effects produced by the gravitation of the fluid blood are not limited to the surface of the body, the internal organs are also subject to them.

As the formation of post-mortem stains is dependent on the fluidity of the blood, the question arises—how long does the blood remain fluid within the body after death ? Coagulation within the dead body commences later, and takes place much more slowly than is the case with blood withdrawn from the living organism. It is impossible to state with exactitude the time that elapses between death and the commencement of coagulation ; about four hours is the period allotted Clots may form within the large veins at this interval after death, but the progress of coagulation is so slow—especially in the smaller veins—that the great bulk of the blood is probably still fluid for many subsequent hours This being the case, the exact period after death when the blood begins to coagulate is of little importance. The time occupied in coagulation may be further prolonged by the condition of the blood at the time of death The presence in it of excess of carbon dioxide retards coagulation ; therefore, the blood of persons who have died from suffocation coagulates very slowly.

The salient features of slow coagulation outside the body are distinguishable in the blood-clots formed within the cadaver These features are sinking of the red blood corpuscles to the lower stratum before solidification takes place, and the consequent formation of a more or less colourless layer at the upper part of the clot This division of the clot into two layers is of importance to the medical jurist On examination of a dead body in which coagulation has taken place, the clots ought to correspond with the position of the body, the coloured layer being furthest from the upper surface of the body If this is not the case—if the *colourless* part of the clot is found at the *undermost* part of the body—proof is afforded that the position of the body has been reversed after coagulation took place. The blood-clot formed within the body after death is not nearly so firm as one formed from blood withdrawn from the circulation during life Apart from death from suffocation, it does not appear that the reluctance of the blood to coagulate within the vessels depends upon the presence of $CO_2$, as blood which has remained fluid within the body for some hours after death will coagulate when received over mercury without exposure to air

To return to post-mortem stains They begin to appear on the undermost parts of the body from four to twelve hours after death; not unfrequently they may be seen earlier than the first-mentioned period They consist of patches of a dull red, or they may be of a bluish-slate colour At first they impart a mottled appearance to the skin, later on the individual patches coalesce and form large areas of discoloration The outline of the patches is irregular but is well-defined, the margins stand out in bold relief against the neighbouring uncoloured skin The stained portions are not elevated above

## POST-MORTEM STAINS

the level of the surrounding skin. Although post-mortem stains occur on the undermost parts of the cadaver, they are absent from those parts which are in contact with the substance on which the body lies. If a body lies in the ordinary position—on its back—the shoulders, buttocks, calves, and heels will be unstained. The reason for this is that the compression of the parts named, caused by the body-weight on the one hand and the resistance of the unyielding surface which supports the weight on the other, prevents the gravitation of the blood into the vessels of the skin. An amount of compression much less than that produced by the weight of the body is sufficient to exclude the blood from the part thus compressed. A tight collar or neckerchief may act in this way, and so produce a mark round or partly round the neck that might resemble to some extent the mark left by a cord after death by strangulation. Post-mortem stains continue to form so long as the blood, or a part of the blood, remains uncoagulated. Whilst the blood remains fluid, the post-mortem stains are only permanent provided the position of the body at the time of their formation remains unaltered. If post-mortem stains have made their appearance on the posterior part of a body which lies on its back, and whilst the blood is still fluid the position of the body is reversed, the stains on the back part will disappear and fresh ones will be formed on the now dependent parts in front. Permanency of position in post-mortem stains is only secured by coagulation of the blood; after it has taken place, any alteration in the position of the body produces no effect on them, nor are new ones formed. For this reason, if the position of a body is materially changed after coagulation, it will be found that the post-mortem stains do not correspond with the altered position, and consequently afford evidence of the body having been interfered with. Casper states that they are invariably present after death from hæmorrhage; other authorities have found them absent, or but feebly indicated in such cases, and also when anæmia from disease was the cause of death.

The distinction of post-mortem stains from bruises made during life is of great importance. Mistakes in this relation may be, and have been, the cause of doing serious injustice to innocent persons. The difference is very marked and easy of recognition. In post-mortem stains the blood which produces them is still within the blood-vessels—it is contained in the flaccid, dilated venous radicles and capillaries of the rete, above the papillæ. The surface is uninjured; if examined in an oblique direction, or with an oblique light, no trace of disturbance of the epiderm is found. The parts stained are not elevated, they are practically on the same level with the surrounding skin. The stains are always on the most dependent parts of the body, with the exception of such parts as are subject, or have been subjected, to compression. The margins of the stains are well defined, they do not fade away into the surrounding skin. The depth of colour of the patches of stain is uniform, or nearly so. The stains when in patches (such as might, by the ignorant, be mistaken for bruises) rapidly increase in size, mostly in a direction determined by gravity.

In bruises made during life, the discoloration of the skin is caused by extravasation of blood in and under the papillæ of the true skin from vessels which have been ruptured by violence. The surface of the skin will generally be found disturbed, the result of impact with the object that produced the bruise. Except in the case of very slight injuries, the bruised part will be found more or less elevated. The position of the mark of a bruise is not determined by gravity, it may be on any part of the body, and instead of having a well-defined irregular outline, it will correspond somewhat in shape with the causal agent, or with that part of it which came in contact with the surface, and the margin will be ill-defined, fading away into the surrounding skin. The colour of a bruise is not uniform; if the injury has existed for a day or two a zone of yellow or green may be seen round the outer parts.

Such are the differences observable on the surface between post-mortem stains and bruises. **The critical distinction is made by incising the part.** In a post-mortem stain no blood escapes except from a few minute points which represent the divided vessels of the rete previously distended with blood. On the other hand, an incision into a bruise reveals the presence of effused blood, either clotted or fluid, below the rete, or when the bruise has been the result of great violence, still deeper down.

So far for external post-mortem stains. The same conditions that produce the stains on the skin influence the internal organs. When the body has been lying on the back, the veins of the pia mater at the posterior part, and the lateral and occipital sinuses will be found filled with blood. This is even the case after death from hæmorrhage, a fact to be borne in mind lest the presence of so much blood in the highest part of the body (during life) should be regarded as inconsistent with that cause of death. The posterior fourth of each lung is almost invariably filled with blood, here also is some risk of attributing the condition to pathological causes. The posterior parts of the stomach and of the intestines, especially those in the pelvis, are also stained. The absence of inflammatory exudation, and the fact that on stretching out the bowels the colouration will be found absent at parts lying between the discoloured portions, is sufficient to prevent error of interpretation. The posterior halves of the kidneys are usually gorged. The veins in the pia of the cord often present an appearance not unlike that resulting from meningitis. The heart is free from staining, but fibrinous clots—the so-called cardiac polypi—are common.

## CADAVERIC RIGIDITY.

The flaccidity of the muscles which occurs immediately after death gives place to an opposite condition of extreme hardness. So long as the muscles remain flaccid they retain their irritability, and respond to electrical stimuli in the same way that they do in life. This is due to the persistence of molecular or tissue life after the cessation of somatic life. At a variable period after death, the muscles of the lower jaw begin to stiffen; this is the first indication of the onset of cadaveric rigidity or, as it is also called, rigor mortis. Under ordinary circumstances, the skeletal muscles begin to stiffen in from four to ten hours after death. The stiffening spreads from the muscles of the jaw to those of the face, neck, and trunk, and lastly to the limbs. It is fully developed in from two to three hours, when the entire body is firm and stiff. The limbs cannot be flexed at their joints without considerable force, and the body when moved behaves as though it was devoid of articulations. This condition lasts for a period varying from a few hours to six or eight days. Twenty-four to forty-eight hours may be regarded as the average duration of cadaveric rigidity. In addition to the hardness, a certain amount of contraction of the muscles takes place during the onset of cadaveric rigidity. The muscles become shorter and thicker, and the limbs, if left to themselves, stiffen in a position of partial flexion. Experimentally it is found that a muscle in the act of stiffening will lift a weight, showing that actual contraction takes place. This question will be fully discussed later on. When cadaveric rigidity is present, the muscular electrical current is either abolished, or there is a feeble current in the opposite direction to the normal. The muscles have also lost the power of responding to electrical stimuli. The chemical reaction of the living muscle at rest is neutral or slightly alkaline; that of muscle doing work is acid. Muscles in which cadaveric rigidity is present have a strongly acid reaction, said to be due to the presence of sarcolactic acid, and, possibly, also of glycero-phosphoric acid; in addition, a large amount of carbon dioxide is set free. The actual cause of the muscles becoming hard and stiff is the coagulation of the myosin within the sarcolemmas of the muscular fibres (Kühne). Rigidity does not occur in the body of a fœtus of under seven months. Preyer[1] doubts this generally accepted statement.

[1] *Specielle Physiologie des Embryo.*

The rigidity seems to exist in two conditions, the first passing on to the second by simple lapse of time. In the first condition, it is supposed that the myosin is only partially coagulated, being of a jelly-like consistence; in this stage the muscle has not yet lost its irritability. If, whilst the muscle is in the first state of rigidity, fresh arterial blood is transfused into the blood-vessels, the semi-coagulated myosin is dissolved, and it is then found that the muscles are still irritable and respond to electrical stimuli (Brown-Séquard).[1] When the second stage is reached the coagulation of the myosin is complete, and the irritability of the muscles has permanently disappeared. This coincides with the period of death of the muscular elements, and of the tissues of the body generally. When cadaveric rigidity is fully developed, if one of the limbs is forcibly flexed at a joint, the rigidity does not return, the joint remains supple, and the limb in the position in which it is left. In this way *post-mortem* rigidity may be distinguished from *ante-mortem* rigidity as occasionally met with in hysterical or cataleptic subjects. In the latter condition, if the limb is forcibly bent it tends to return to its previous position, and again becomes rigid. In the first stage of cadaveric rigidity, however — when the myosin is only partially coagulated — a certain degree of stiffening again occurs after a joint is forcibly flexed.

The conditions which hasten the onset of cadaveric rigidity are those which have an exhausting or depressing influence on the muscles immediately before death; hence, after violent muscular exercise, death is speedily followed by rigidity. It has been observed that the bodies of soldiers killed at the commencement of a battle, before they have undergone much fatigue, do not become rigid so soon as those of their fellow-combatants who succumb at a later period, after many hours' arduous fighting. After death from diseases or poisons, which depress or exhaust the system (especially if attended with clonic spasm of the muscles) rigidity comes on early. Finlayson[2] records a case of chronic Bright's disease in which cadaveric rigidity exceptionally commenced within fifteen minutes after death. Animals that have been hunted for some time before death stiffen almost at once, and within a few minutes may be held out by the hind legs perfectly rigid. On the other hand, in speedy death (with exceptions presently to be mentioned) occurring to individuals in vigorous health the onset of cadaveric rigidity is delayed. Even in those who are in full vigour, if death is immediately preceded by convulsions, rigidity comes on early, because the vital energy of

[1] See also Heubel on "Die Wiederbelebung des Herzens nach dem Eintritt vollkommener Herzmuskelstarre." Pflüger's *Archiv*, 1889.
[2] *Brit. Med. Journ.*, 1884.

the muscles is lowered. It has been found that the muscle-currents disappear, and the electrical irritability of the muscles is diminished before the development of rigidity. All these facts point to one conclusion: that cadaveric rigidity is a consequence of death of the muscles, that it creeps on as the muscles are dying, and is, therefore, partially present before they are dead, but it is not fully developed until molecular death has taken place.

It may be asserted as a general proposition that the sooner rigidity comes on after death, the sooner will it pass away. The converse is equally true: the longer it is in appearing, the longer will it last. An unexhausted condition enables the muscles, within limits, to resist disintegration when deprived of further aid from the nutrient supply and the eliminative agencies by which their vigour was maintained during systemic life. A high state of vigour is resistant of change, not only up to the period when change commences, but for a time after. Hence it is, that both the onset and the duration of cadaveric rigidity (other conditions being equal) are dependent on the store of vitality possessed by the muscles at the moment of somatic death.

**Heat-Stiffening.**—The rigidity of a cadaver that is fully under the influence of ordinary cadaveric rigidity may be increased by subjecting the body to a temperature of 75° C. The explanation is, that other albuminates present in the muscles besides myosin are thus coagulated. Myosin coagulates (in mammals) about 50° C., another albuminate coagulates at 47° C., and serum-albumin coagulates at 73° C. If, therefore, either before or after the full development of cadaveric rigidity, the body is subjected to a temperature exceeding 73° C., but short of causing disintegration, all these albuminates are coagulated, and a higher degree of rigidity is produced than that dependent on natural causes.

The **Involuntary Muscles** are also affected by cadaveric rigidity; the only internal organ necessary to consider in this respect is the heart. Very soon after death, before the skeletal muscles begin to stiffen, the heart-muscles become rigid. It has long been observed that when the heart is in the condition of cadaveric rigidity, the ventricular walls, especially the left, are firm and contracted, and present an appearance totally different to that which obtains after rigidity has passed off. It has also been observed by physiologists that certain changes in the condition of the heart-muscles take place during the development of cadaveric rigidity. The heart, like the skeletal muscles, not only stiffens, but it undergoes contraction sufficient to entirely alter the relative capacity of its cavities after death. This fact is of great importance to the medical jurist, since a decision as to the mode of death is not unfrequently based on the condition of the heart as found at the necropsy. When the post-mortem appearances of death from syncope were described, the condition of the heart was represented as being contracted, which is often the case at a necropsy on the body of one who has died from syncope, the result of want of blood to supply the heart. The question arises—is this the condition of the heart at the time of death; or, in other words—did death take place with the heart in systole? Strassmann's[1] experiments are very instructive in relation to this question. In a number of animals which had been killed by sudden paralysis of the heart, he opened the thorax as soon as circulation and respiration had ceased. In some the heart was examined immediately; others, after superficial investigation, were covered over and left until the next day. When the heart was examined immediately after death, the left ventricle was found to contain more blood than the right. When the examination was made on the following day, the left ventricle was almost invariably found firmly contracted, and its contents for the most part, or entirely, expelled either into the left auricle or into the aorta. In animals that had been killed by rapid suffocation, when the heart was examined immediately after death, the right ventricle contained on the average twice as much blood as the left; at a subsequent examination, the left ventricle was found contracted and empty, or nearly so. In all cases, when the heart was examined immediately after death, even after death from strychnine, both right and left ventricles were found in diastole, relaxed and filled with blood; in no case was the heart found to have stopped in systole. Strassmann directs attention to the extremely early development of cadaveric rigidity in the heart: in animals poisoned with hydrocyanic acid it was observable one hour after death. Even so early as this, the left ventricle did not contain nearly so much blood as it did immediately after death. Post-mortem contraction of the right ventricle is much feebler than that of the left; only in cases where hæmorrhage has taken place is it found empty. These investigations indicate that the condition of the heart at the necropsy affords no certain proof of its condition at the moment of death. Only when left and right sides are both found to be filled with blood can it be said that the original condition has been maintained.

In post-mortem examinations on the human subject, it is usual to allow an interval of at least twenty-four hours to elapse before the examination is made. During this time the heart will have become rigid, and whether examined whilst in this state, or subsequently when the rigidity has departed, it is dangerous to assume that the organ is then in the condition which existed at the moment of death.

[1] *Vierteljahrsschr. f. ger. Med.*, 1889.

The post-mortem condition of the heart is by no means so plainly indicative of the mode of death as is frequently taught

The subject of post-mortem contraction of the heart leads to further consideration of the cadaveric contraction of the skeletal muscles previously mentioned

Coagulation of the myosin alone is not sufficient to account for all the phenomena which accompany the development of cadaveric rigidity; the shortening undergone by the muscles indicates something more than mere stiffening. Many physiologists are of the opinion that after-death rigidity is accompanied by, if not caused by, a true muscular contraction. L Hermann[1] points out that the chemical processes in vital muscular contraction and in cadaveric rigidity are analogous, with the exception of the formation of myosin from myosinogen. In both, $CO_2$, sarcolactic, and other acids are formed, heat is evolved, and the muscle-current is reversed. He holds that cadaveric rigidity is a contraction of the muscles, occasioned by some unknown stimulation, the contraction lasting longer and passing off much more slowly than an ordinary contraction. Bierfreund[2] divided one ischiatic nerve in recently killed animals and invariably found that rigidity was delayed on the injured side. Hemisection of the spinal cord below the pyramidal decussation was also followed by delayed rigidity of the side on which the cord was divided. The effect of cutting off the communication with the nerve centres was strikingly displayed in a dog in which the left cerebral cortex was stimulated during life, producing right-sided convulsions; the right half of the cervical cord was subsequently divided, and the animal was then killed. The effect of the convulsions would have been to hasten the onset of rigidity on the side on which they occurred, if no subsequent steps had been taken. The result of cutting off the communication with the brain on that side, however, was that, on examining the extremities four and a-half hours after, the left side was pronouncedly stiff, whilst the right side was almost as movable as at the time of death. Two hours later there was still a marked difference between the two sides. The body of a man who died forty-eight hours after an attack of apoplexy, also showed delayed rigor on the paralysed side. It was formerly asserted (Nysten) that in hemiplegia there was no difference in the cadaveric rigidity of the two sides so long as the nutrition of the affected muscles had not suffered

We are now in a position to consider that abnormal occurrence of cadaveric rigidity to which the designation **Cadaveric spasm**, or **Instantaneous rigor**, has been given

[1] *Lehrbuch der Physiologie.*
[2] *Arch für die ges Physiologie*, 1888.

When this phenomenon occurs the last act of life is crystallised in death. It does not consist of an abnormally speedy onset of rigidity after a brief interval of relaxation of the muscles, such as has already been described, but in an absolute prolongation of the last vital contraction of the muscle into the rigidity of death. A few examples will indicate the nature of the phenomenon, and may possibly afford a clue to its interpretation. Seydel[1] narrates the following cases:—(1) A man alighted from a railway carriage in order to procure refreshment; whilst obtaining something to eat, he was disturbed by what he took to be the signal for departure, and ran across the line to his train, not noticing that the locomotive was being backed towards the first carriage. He probably saw the danger when it was too late, and in stooping to avoid it his head was caught between the buffers, and he was immediately killed. His arm was outstretched at the moment, and grasped in his hand were some provisions he had just obtained; some hours after, the arm was still extended in the air, and the hand was firmly clasped on the food. (2) By the giving way of a bridge, thirteen persons were suddenly precipitated into the water and drowned. Twelve hours after, when the bodies were recovered, in most of them the extremities were so firmly outstretched as to render it difficult to lay them in their coffins. (3) A man was standing on the ice in the act of lighting a cigar, he fell through, and when the body was recovered, it was found in the upright posture with the cigar and match between the fingers. (4) A man poisoned by carbon monoxide gas in his bedroom was found dead in a kneeling posture at the bedside. Again, Regnard and Loge,[2] giving an account of some experiments made by them on the body of a recently-decapitated criminal, state that two seconds after the head was severed from the trunk, the jaws were firmly clenched; four minutes after the mouth was still firmly closed. Rigidity did not appear in the body until three hours after decapitation, when it began to develop in the lower extremities; six hours after decapitation the arms were still free from any trace of rigidity. The heart—ventricles and auricles—continued to beat rhythmically and strongly for twenty-five minutes after decapitation, and the auricles for forty minutes more. One hour after execution the heart was opened, and the left ventricle was found hard and contracted, the right remaining soft.

The coagulation of myosin, unaccompanied by any other agency, fails to account for this immediate onset of cadaveric rigidity. Some observers have assumed that there is invariably a period of muscular relaxation after death, a line of demarcation between vital action and

[1] *Vierteljahrsschr. f. ger. Med.*, 1889.
[2] *Le Progrès Médical*, 1887.

cadaveric inertia. A glance at the examples just given will show that this assumption is contradicted by facts; the most fugitive muscular relaxation after death would be sufficient to have prevented the occurrence of several of the cases cited. The experiments of Bierfreund tend to prove that some causal relation exists between cadaveric rigidity and the nervous system—that the latter exercises an influence on the onset of the former. Falk and Schroff have demonstrated experimentally that irritation of the medulla produces instantaneous cadaveric rigidity. Seydel groups the cases that have occurred in medico-legal practice into two classes—(a) injuries to the head, with probable irritation of the medulla; (b) toxic action of gases, either $CO$, or, in those suffocated or drowned, $CO_2$. It is suggested that the hypothetical spasm and respiratory centres are in close relation in the medulla, and that instantaneous rigidity may result from irritation of these centres. One objection to this hypothesis is that instantaneous rigidity by no means invariably follows death from suffocation by drowning or by hanging. It has been observed that when it does occur from this cause, the individuals have been endowed with powerful muscular development. Whatever the true explanation may be, there is strong reason to believe that the nervous system plays an important part in the causation of instantaneous rigidity. The subject is of great interest to the medical jurist, since the grip of the fingers of a dead body on the handle of a pistol is often the sole evidence in favour of suicide as against homicide.

The ordinary type of cadaveric rigidity, as before stated, commences in the muscles of the jaw, and spreads over those of the face, neck, trunk, and limbs. It passes off in the same order—that is to say, the muscles which first become rigid are the first to lose their rigidity. Rigidity disappears about the period of the commencement of putrefaction, and it has been supposed that the disappearance of rigidity is due to the solvent action of ammonia resulting from decomposition of the nitrogenous structures. Myosin is soluble in alkalies, and, according to this view, the ammonia evolved by putrefactive processes dissolves the myosin and thus liberates the muscles. Hermann and Bierfreund, with other physiologists, oppose this view, and state that cadaveric rigidity disappears, or begins to disappear, before any putrefactive changes take place. Hermann attributes its disappearance to solution of the myosin by excess of acid which is formed in the muscles during the continuance of rigidity. In favour of this view, disappearance of rigidity has been observed in muscles retaining a strong acid reaction. It is also urged that an advanced stage of putrefaction would be necessary for the evolution of sufficient ammonia to dissolve the myosin, whereas rigidity often passes off before any observable degree of decomposition has taken place. Bierfreund examined the muscles microscopically when rigidity had passed off, and found no micro-organisms of putrefaction present, or only isolatedly in the outer layers of the muscles. The inference is that cadaveric rigidity passes off about the time that putrefaction begins, but it is not certain that putrefaction is a necessary factor in causing its disappearance.

When cadaveric rigidity has passed away the muscles are soft and flabby; they are now dead, and no longer react to electrical stimulation. However short may be the duration of rigidity, when it has disappeared it never returns. There are thus two periods of muscular relaxation after death, separated by a period of rigidity. During the first period of relaxation the muscles still live, and demonstrate their vitality by responding to stimulation. During the early part of the period of rigidity they also retain their vitality, but it is latent, or masked. They then lose their vitality, and when rigidity has passed off, and the second period of relaxation is arrived at, they are found to be divested of all the characteristics of living matter; in other words, they are in the state of molecular death.

## PUTREFACTION

The last of the phenomena which, under ordinary conditions, follows death, is the resolution of the organised tissues into their elementary constituents. Complex organic bodies are, step by step, resolved into simpler forms, until, ultimately, they are split up into inorganic substances. The agencies concerned in the causation of putrefaction are—*micro-organisms, moisture, air*, and *warmth*.

**Micro-Organisms.**—*Bacterium termo*, the micro-organism of putrefaction, may be accepted as a generic name for a number of different forms not yet differentiated. These bacteria are ubiquitous, and unless special means are taken either to prevent their access, or to render the tissues unfitted for their use, the dead body invariably succumbs to them.

**Moisture** favours the progress of putrefaction. The human body contains a large amount of water in the various fluids and soft tissues, amply sufficient for putrefactive purposes, provided it is not dissipated by rapid evaporation. The addition of moisture from without, especially if accompanied by warmth, greatly accelerates decomposition. The most favourable conditions under which putrefaction takes place are warmth and moisture, with free access of air. The oxygen of the air plays its part, but if the air is sterilised it cannot of itself produce putrefaction; as, however, the air invariably contains micro-organisms in abundance, access of air means importation of bacteria. The differing rapidity with which a corpse putrefies in accordance as to whether it is unclad, partially clothed, or completely so, demonstrates the influence exercised by the air in this respect. If a dead body has lain for some time in the open, it will be found that the parts best protected from the air—as the feet are when enclosed in boots—have undergone the least change. **Temperature** is an important factor in determining the rate of putrefaction. A temperature of from 60° to 70° F is favourable to its progress, hence putrefactive changes advance much more rapidly in summer than in winter. When a corpse is interred in the ordinary way, the depth of the grave has an influence on the rate of putrefaction, because the nearer the surface, the greater the effect of the diurnal and seasonal changes of temperature. Excess in any of the conditions specified as conducing to putrefaction—except, perhaps, in the case of micro-organisms—has an opposite effect.— Total submersion of the body in water retards putrefactive changes. Excess of air, in the form of a continuous current of air, by promoting desiccation, tends to dry up the tissues, and thus impedes decomposition. Excess of temperature, in either direction, is also unfavourable; a high temperature tends to mummify the soft parts, whilst a very low temperature—below the freezing point—absolutely and indefinitely prevents any putrefactive changes whatever.

Thus far the influences considered—which accelerate, and which retard putrefaction—have been of external relation; there remain for consideration those conditions of the body itself which tend to render it more or less prone to decay.

**Age.**—The bodies of infants putrefy more rapidly than those of adults. The bodies of spare, old people, putrefy slowly. Obesity, generally, predisposes the body to putrefaction. The mode of death is an important factor. **Diseases** of an adynamic type as enteric, all septic diseases, and dropsy, death resulting from extensive **mechanical injuries**, from lightning, and from sewer gas, all have a tendency to produce early putrefaction. On the other hand, death from arsenical or from sulphuric acid poisoning tends to be followed by delayed putrefaction.

## SIGNS OF PUTREFACTION

**External putrefactive appearances** displayed by bodies which have been exposed to the air. The first outward indication of putrefaction appears about the second or third day after death, in the form of a greenish discoloration on the middle of the abdomen, which spreads to the genital organs. Other centres of discoloration of the same character appear on the legs, neck, and back. The eyeball yields to pressure, the cornea is more or less corrugated, and has a milky appearance. At or before this period—four to five days after death—blood-stained fluid oozes from the mouth, together with froth and air bubbles. The gases resulting from decomposition collect in the abdomen, and under the skin, and distend the whole body, the features being unrecognisable. The tongue may be forced between the lips, and the eyeballs protruded. About eight or ten days after death the cornea falls in and appears concave. Still later, bullæ filled with blood-stained serum form on various parts of the surface, the whole body is reddish-brown or greenish, and is still further distended with gas. Large areas are devoid of skin, and maggots without number cover the body. The further processes are simply those attending the final dissolution of the soft parts, and are not to be recognised in stages.

The earlier **gases of decomposition**, according to Tidy,[1] are chiefly sulphuretted and carburetted hydrogen, ammonia, phosphuretted hydrogen, nitrogen, and the two oxides of carbon. Later, the sulphuretted hydrogen and ammonia decrease, the predominating gases being carburetted hydrogen and carbon monoxide. Several of these gases being inflammable will ignite, if a light is applied to a small puncture from which they are issuing.

The colour changes seen in the cadaver are due to decomposition of the hæmoglobin, the result of the chemical action of the $H_2S$ and other gases. The altered colouring matter transudes the tissues and tints them accordingly, the veins as dark lines may be traced by their anatomical distribution.

If the body is buried, the protection from air afforded by the coffin and the earth in which the coffin is placed has a considerably retarding influence on the rate of putrefaction. The stronger and more air-tight the coffin the longer is the body preserved. This, however, is only markedly the case if the body is placed in the coffin and closed up soon after death, before putrefactive changes have commenced. The retarding influence of sealing up the body in an air-tight receptacle whilst putrefaction is in progress is not nearly so potent as is the case with a fresh corpse. Some kinds of soil preserve bodies which are interred in them, even without coffins, in a remarkable way. Dry sandy soil, especially if associated with warmth, promotes desiccation rather than putrefaction. Peaty soil retards putrefaction, probably from the presence in it of acids (tannic and others) derived from the vegetable matter of which it is largely composed.

After death from drowning, and also in the case of bodies placed in water immediately after death from other causes than drowning, putrefaction takes place slower than in air, due to the relatively lower

[1] *Legal Medicine*, 1883.

## SIGNS OF PUTREFACTION

temperature of water as compared with the air above it, and to the exclusion of air from the body. For the first few days little change takes place. Before the end of the first week, the skin on the fingers, the palms of the hands, and the soles of the feet becomes sodden and white, and the face acquires an ashy pallor. The first discoloration takes place on the face, which is swollen and of a reddish-brown, with patches of green on the eyelids and lips. The discoloration descends to the neck and sternum, sometimes the surface over the latter shows a little redness before the face. The skin is now very wrinkled. In about six or eight weeks, the skin of the hands and feet with the nails comes away, and the hair falls off, or is quite loose. The abdomen is greatly distended with the gases of decomposition, which usually find exit by the natural apertures. The inflation may recur more than once, the body floating with each recurrence, and sinking again when the gases escape. After two to three months, the skin of the arms, thorax, and legs is green. Patches of adipocere will probably be formed on the cheeks and other parts of the body. A month or two later, the soft parts are detached, the bones separating subsequently.

It will be observed that the sequence of colour-changes due to putrefaction in water, is different from that which takes place in air. In water the colour-changes begin on the face and spread downwards. In air they begin on the abdomen, and spread downwards and upwards. The order in water obtains whether the body was that of a person drowned (which remains continuously in the water), or whether it was thrown into the water after death, provided that decomposition in air had not previously commenced. If a body is removed from the water in which it has lain for a week or so, it will probably show few signs of putrefaction. A very short subsequent exposure to the air will cause putrefaction to advance at a rapid rate, so that one day in air will be productive of greater change than several weeks further submersion. The rate of putrefaction in water is governed by several conditions, the temperature of the water, the covering of the body, the degree and continuousness of the submersion are all so many factors. Shallow stagnant water is more conducive to putrefaction than deep water, or than shallow water in which there is a current. The influence of the sun-heat is obviously greatest under the first-named conditions. If the body is well protected by clothing, the progress of putrefaction will be delayed. Complete and continuous submersion in deep water is equivalent to low temperature and absence of air, and, therefore, to retarded putrefaction. Dead bodies usually float with the head and extremities below the water-level; the bodies of men in the prone posture, those of women—on account of the adipose tissue of the breasts and abdomen—in the recumbent posture. In the one case the back, and in the other the abdomen is at or above the water-level. When the body is buoyed up to the surface, the rate of putrefaction is accelerated, especially if the sun's rays are hot. On the other hand, if from any cause, such as the presence of a thick layer of tenacious mud at the bottom of the water, or the entanglement produced by sea-weed, ropes, or other impediments, the body is prevented from floating, the contrary effect is produced.

Casper gives the following time-ratio for putrefactive changes in *air*, *water*, and in *earth*. Assuming that an equal average temperature obtains in all three cases—one week in air equals two weeks in water, and eight weeks buried in earth in the usual manner.

**Internal Putrefactive Appearances.**—The internal organs—on account of their inherent differences in density, firmness, proportion of fluid entering into their structure, and in their accessibility to air—undergo putrefaction in a more or less regular order. Casper's long experience enabled him to formulate the order as follows:—

| Putrefy rapidly. | Putrefy slowly. |
|---|---|
| 1. Larynx and Trachea | 9. Heart |
| 2. Brain of infants. | 10. Lungs |
| 3. Stomach | 11. Kidneys |
| 4. Intestines. | 12. Bladder |
| 5. Spleen | 13. Œsophagus |
| 6. Omentum and Mesentery | 14. Pancreas |
| 7. Liver | 15. Diaphragm |
| 8. Adult brain | 16. Blood-vessels |
|  | 17. Uterus. |

The mucous membrane of the larynx and trachea is found to be bright or brownish-red or greenish in from three to five days in summer, and in from six to eight days in winter. The only external colour-change at this period will be that of the abdomen. The absence of bony union of the bones of the skull permits easy access of air to an organ feebly resistant to decomposition, hence the earlier decay of the infantile brain in comparison with that of the adult. About the fifth or sixth day after death the stomach exhibits indications of incipient putrefaction in the form of isolated patches of a dirty-red at the fundus; they are first seen in the most dependent part where the post-mortem staining exists. Great caution is necessary in order to avoid mistaking post-mortem changes in the stomach for indications of inflammation, the result of irritant poisons. The spleen may putrefy before the stomach. The liver is usually found firm for several weeks after death. The gall-bladder resists putrefaction much longer. The adult brain shrinks, and the hemispheres soften soon after death, but it takes months, under ordinary conditions, for the brain to melt into the reddish pulp so early seen in the infantile brain. The remaining organs putrefy relatively late. The heart is found fairly fresh when the stomach and liver are in an advanced stage of putrefaction; several months are required to produce in the heart an equal degree of decomposition. The lungs usually show putrefactive changes about the same time as the heart. They may be found in good condition when the external signs of putrefaction are well advanced. The first indication consists of pale red spots of varying size on the surface of the lung, the pleura being raised at these points by the gases of decomposition. These small bullæ are not unfrequently met with even in relatively fresh corpses, but further changes scarcely ever occur until general putrefaction is far advanced, when the colour of the lungs changes to dark bottle-green, and eventually to black, and they subsequently soften and dwindle away. The kidneys resist long; at a considerable interval after death they soften, and become of a blackish-green. The bladder is still more resistant. The œsophagus is much more durable than the rest of the digestive tract. The pancreas does not decay until the body as a whole is much decomposed. The diaphragm may be seen, and its muscular and aponeurotic structures distinguished, four to six months after death. The large arteries last very long; Devergie found the aorta quite recognisable in a body that had been buried fourteen months. The uterus resists the longest of all the soft organs of the body; this enables not only the sex of a cadaver to be ascertained when the external parts are destroyed by putrefaction, but also the occurrence or not of pregnancy or of recent delivery, as was done by Casper in a foully decomposed body which had lain nine months in a cesspool.

The interval that has elapsed between death and the time that a body undergoing putrefaction is examined, cannot be estimated, even approximatively, by the stage that the putrefaction has reached. The variations in the degree of putrefaction met with at stated periods after death are so extreme, that the attempt to establish a mean is futile. To take one instance out of many of unusually early putrefaction, the following recorded by Taylor and Wilks[1] will serve as an illustration:—A man, aged twenty-six, died in the month of November of typhoid fever and perforation of ileum. Sixteen hours after death there was no cadaveric rigidity. The whole body was bloated, the cellular tissue was so emphysematous that, when the skin was pierced, gas escaped which was easily ignited. The colour of the surface was

[1] *Guy's Hospital Reports*, 1863.

reddish. The internal organs were dark, soft, and much decomposed, and they emitted a very putrid odour. The liver was full of gas.

Abnormally early putrefactive changes do not follow the usual sequence, which, as stated, commences with a green patch on the abdomen. The whole of the surface of the body at once assumes a red colour, with dark lines which show the course of the superficial veins. The appearance is much as though the earlier stages of putrefaction were omitted, or hurried over, so that a condition which usually requires ten or twelve days for its production is arrived at in as many hours.

An illustration of the opposite extreme is related by Taylor and Stevenson.[1] A youth died suddenly, and the body retained such a natural appearance that the friends thought he was in a trance. It was not till thirty-five days after death that they would allow an inspection to be made, when, in spite of the long interval during which the body had been exposed to a warm atmosphere, it was found that putrefaction had made but little progress.

In the face of such extremes, it is clearly impossible to estimate the duration of the interval which has elapsed since death, from the stage of putrefaction present in the body.

Some of the putrefactive changes in the viscera require to be distinguished from the changes due to inflammation. In the stomach and intestines, for example, appearances may be seen which, though due to putrefaction, might be mistaken for the effects of an irritant poison. The first thing to notice is that the reddening of putrefaction invades the whole of the tissues of which the organ is composed; any variation in this respect is due to the differing density of the structures which enter into the formation of the viscus. Reddening of the stomach due to the action of an irritant during life is limited to the mucous membrane, that due to putrefaction invades the muscular coats as well. After acute gastritis the mucous membrane will easily separate from the structures on which it rests, a condition not met with as a result of putrefaction. The course of post-mortem reddening more clearly follows the distribution of the blood-vessels than is the case in inflammatory discolorations. After death the blood-vessels of an inflamed part are filled with blood, the vessels of a patch of putrefactive reddening are empty, or are distended with gas. In serous cavities, fluid may be found which is distinguishable from *intra vitam* exudation by the absence of inflammatory products—pus corpuscles, shreds of membrane, exudation corpuscles, and also by absence of thickening of the membrane itself.

There are two exceptional processes which may replace ordinary

[1] *Principles and Practice of Medical Jurisprudence.*

putrefaction—**Mummification**, and conversion of the soft parts into **Adipocere**.

## MUMMIFICATION.

This term is applied to desiccation of the soft parts of the body, so that instead of disappearing by colliquative putrefaction, they are dried up and preserved as hard leathery masses, or they may become brittle. In a climate like that of England it is only under exceptional circumstances that mummification takes place. The requirements are dry, warm air, which is most effective when in movement. Mummification under ground is more common in hot countries, in sandy parts. The mummified bodies of newly-born infants have been found in boxes, or lying exposed to currents of dry air between the rafters of a house and the ceiling of the room below. The length of time required for mummification to take place varies with the conditions of each case. It has occurred in three months.

## ADIPOCERE.

The substance to which this name—derived from *adeps, cera*—is applied is an impure ammoniacal soap. The basis is a compound of oleic and stearic acids with ammonia, admixed with which are fibres, and other debris, from organic tissues, with a varying amount of the salts of potash, soda, lime, and iron. In some cases lime replaces ammonia as the base, probably from the presence of much lime in the medium in which the body is placed. The two principal components—fat and ammonia—are derived from the soft parts of the body, the latter resulting from decomposition of the nitrogenous tissues. The bodies of obese subjects and those of children (who usually have much fatty tissue) are more likely to be converted into adipocere than those of spare people. The external conditions which favour the formation of adipocere are submersion of the body in water, and burial in damp soil, or in well-filled graveyards. Cesspools promote either saponification or ordinary putrefaction, sometimes one and sometimes the other.

Adipocere is a waxy-looking substance, having an unctuous feel. It varies in colour from almost white to dark brown; it has a disagreeable odour, especially when heated. If broken, traces of fibres are seen, between the meshes of which the soap is deposited. Adipocere is of less specific gravity than water; it is a very permanent body, and may last for twenty years and upwards.

The time required for the formation of adipocere is naturally variable, depending, as it does, on so many internal and external conditions. It has been held that two or three months' submersion in water is about the shortest time in which it is formed. Traces however, have, been found in from four to five weeks. In moist earth it takes longer to form—eight to twelve months. It may be accepted that in temperate climes indications of saponification, in bodies placed under circumstances favourable to its production, may be met with in one month after death. For the whole of the soft parts to be converted into adipocere would take many years.

In hot climates the process may be marvellously rapid. The following cases reported by Mackenzie[1] occurred in Calcutta:—(1) A male Hindoo was killed by the kick of a horse, and was buried the following day. Four days after burial, the body was exhumed in order that an inquest might be held. It was in an advanced state of saponification externally, the heart and liver being also saponified. (2) A young Chinese woman, alleged to have died in child-birth, was buried, circumstances necessitated an inquest, and the body was exhumed seventy-six hours after interment, when it was found to be considerably saponified. These bodies were buried in a soft, porous soil, saturated with moisture, the temperature being high, the body last mentioned was enclosed in a wooden coffin. (3) Another case was that of an European sailor who fell into the river Hooghly and was drowned, eight days and ten hours after the body was recovered. The external parts, the heart, liver, spleen, kidneys, stomach, intestines, and bladder were saponified. (4) Another young European was drowned in the same river, his body being recovered seven days after. It was in an advanced state of saponification externally, the lungs, heart, liver, kidneys, stomach, and intestines were also saponified, and what is very curious is that the stomach contained undigested food—flesh and potatoes—of which the flesh was entirely saponified, the potatoes not being altered in the least. Other instances of early conversion into adipocere are recorded as occurring in India, in one case, the body was saponified externally and internally in two days.

## CHAPTER VIII

### PERSONAL IDENTITY.

THE question of identity may arise both with regard to a living person and also in respect to a dead body. Certain indications serve as clues in both cases, but it is convenient to consider the subject separately under the heads of *identity of the living* and *identity of the dead.*

[1] *The Indian Med. Gazette*, 1889.

## PERSONAL IDENTITY OF THE LIVING

The identification of a living person may come before the Criminal Courts of Law in respect to accusations of murder, assault, and rape, and in the case of escaped prisoners, or of lunatics who have evaded restraint. In the Civil Courts the identity of the claimant to an estate, or of a man who has been long absent from the country, and who, on his return, seeks to resume his family relations, may become the subject of legal investigation. Many of the points which can be utilised in civil cases—as family resemblance in features, voice, manner of walking, and other similar characteristics—do not come within the cognisance of the medical expert. His aid is chiefly required to determine the presence or absence of birth-marks, of marks that have been subsequently produced, of deformities, congenital or acquired, of artificial change in the colour of the hair, and other similar matters. He may also be called on to give an opinion as to the possibility of scars or marks on the skin disappearing in the course of time, or by artificial means, without leaving traces, and also as to the alterations in general appearance that may be produced by time, exposure to climatic influence, hardship, and the like. In criminal cases the expert's attention is usually directed to recent wounds, scratches, foot-prints, and other indications of a struggle, in addition to marks or signs of longer standing, and also to the presence of hairs, or to stains of blood or other colouring-matter, on the person or clothing.

**Cicatrices.**—The scars left by the healing of wounds differ in size, shape, and character, in accordance with the nature of the injury which gave rise to them. If there has been no loss of tissue, as in the case of a linear incision, and the wound was small and it healed by primary union, the resulting cicatrix may, after a time, be almost, if not quite, invisible. If the entire thickness of the skin has been cut through, it is doubtful whether the scar ever absolutely disappears; the scars left by venesection and by cupping are, as a rule, permanent, and quite evident to the eye.

If a portion of skin throughout its entire thickness is destroyed it is never renewed, the cicatricial tissue which replaces it is permanent and is wanting in all the characteristics of true skin. It is furnished neither with sebaceous nor sweat glands, nor with hair follicles, and it is sparingly supplied with blood-vessels. In the early stage a cicatrix is of a red colour, changing to brown. Subsequently the brown fades, and in course of time the cicatrix becomes white and more or less glistening, which is the characteristic and permanent appearance of old cicatrices. There is no time-limit within which these changes take place, a cicatrix may remain coloured for years all that can be said is that a red cicatrix is probably not an old one, and that a white cicatrix is not recent, the intermediate stage is of uncertain duration. The visibility of an old linear cicatrix is to some extent dependent on the colour of the surrounding skin. If the skin is white the cicatrix will be little, if at all, different in tint from its surroundings, and may, therefore, escape cursory observation. Advantage may be taken of its relatively feeble blood-supply to demonstrate the existence of the scar. On stimulating the vascular activity of the part by friction, or by slapping it with the hand or with a wet cloth, the normal skin becomes reddened, and the scar, retaining its blanched appearance, now stands out in marked contrast. When searching for a small linear cicatrix, allow the light to fall obliquely on the part, and examine with a lens. The attempt to obliterate a cicatrix will obviously be unsuccessful. As the skin of the part is absent, and is replaced by another tissue, the removal of that tissue will not restore the skin. A puckered cicatrix may sometimes be dissected out and the edges of the wound brought together, thus forming a linear cicatrix, which materially reduces the amount of disfiguration; the size and shape of the cicatrix will be altered, but it will not be obliterated. It is to be noted that cicatrices made in infancy increase in size with the growth of the body. If produced later, they sometimes seem to diminish in distinctness in the lapse of years.

**Birth-marks.**—The removal of birth-marks, such as moles and nævi, is usually possible, but not without leaving some trace behind, except in the case of very small and superficial nævi. If the entire thickness of the skin is not implicated, skilful treatment may cause a small nævus to disappear without leaving a mark. It is rarely, however, that careful examination with oblique light and a lens fails to yield some trace, although in a general way all indication of the nævus may be said to have disappeared. If in the process of removal, whether by electrolysis or by the injection of some fluid, one or more of the papillæ under the rete is injured, a corresponding depression will be produced on the surface, which, though small enough to escape the unaided eye, will probably be visible if examined, as described, with a lens. Larger or deeper-seated nævi, or moles, may be removed by excision, but for the reasons already given, a scar will remain, although different in shape from the original mark.

**Tattoo-marks.**—It is a favourite habit of sailors and soldiers, and also of others, to have various devices tattooed on the skin of the chest, arms, or other parts of the body. The procedure consists in pricking out the device, or a portion of it, with needles, and then rubbing in some colouring agent, the operation being repeated until the design is complete. A good deal of swelling and inflammation is produced, and on its subsidence the design is found to be more or less permanently depicted.

The durability of tattoo marks depends on two factors—the character of the colouring-matter, and the depth to which it is carried.

The colouring agents used are carbon in various conditions—as gunpowder, soot, Indian ink, or lamp black—and vermilion, indigo-blue, writing-ink, and other substances. Carbon is permanent as a colouring agent; it is insoluble in all fluids, and its colour does not fade. The other substances named are less likely to be permanent, although they may be so. I have seen a tattoo-mark which was produced forty years ago with ordinary writing ink, and which is still visible. The tattooing in which carbon is used is not black, but is blue-black.

The position in which the colouring matter is located is equally important as regards permanency. If it is superficial, there is the possibility of its removal in time by wear and tear or by artificial means. The reported cases in which tattoo-marks have been erased without leaving any trace, were most probably of this class, as shown by the mode in which the obliteration was effected. The application of acetic acid, dilute hydrochloric acid, cantharides, and the like, would remove the epiderm, and dissolve out the colouring matter or, if it was insoluble, would cause it to be washed out with the exudation from the cutis. Another mode of obliteration of superficial tattoo-marks is to pick out the coloured particles with a needle. In the case of superficial tattooing, it might be possible to obliterate the mark in some such way without leaving any or but very little trace of its former existence. If on the other hand, a permanent colouring-matter is carried down to, or into, the papillæ, it will remain undisturbed for an indefinite period and cannot be removed without leaving indelible scars. Any attempt to obliterate such a mark by means of acetic acid, or of blistering fluid would be futile, and removal with a needle (if practicable) would injure the papillæ and so lead to depressions on the surface of the skin, which would betray what had been done. Of course, a tattoo-mark, of however permanent a nature, may be removed by excision, or by the application of caustic substances, or of a red-hot iron, but a depressed cicatrix of a size larger than the tattoo will result; in the Tichborne case (1873) some such attempt at obliterating a tattoo-mark above the left wrist had been made. It may be accepted that when tattoo-marks disappear in the lapse of time, or when they can be artificially removed without leaving a trace, either the tattooer, or the colouring agent, or both, are in fault.

IV. The colour of the hair may be changed either to a darker or to a lighter shade. Hair dyes are usually composed of a solution of a salt of silver, lead, or bismuth; when a speedy result is desired, sulphuretted hydrogen is subsequently used to produce a black sulphide. The metals may be tested for by digesting the hair in nitric acid with the aid of heat, driving off the acid, and then adding the appropriate reagent to a solution of the nitrate in water. Hair may be bleached by means of chlorine, but those who habitually assume light coloured hair usually resort to an aqueous solution of peroxide of hydrogen. Any mode of bleaching the hair causes it to become lustreless and brittle. The indications by which an opinion may be formed in regard to the naturalness or otherwise of the colour of the hair are—that artificially coloured hair has an unnatural hue whether dark or light, and the colour is not uniform, as may be seen by turning the hair over. On careful scrutiny of the hair towards its roots, there will generally be found a difference in tint, especially if the dye has not been applied for a few days. A comparison between the colour of the hair on the head and that on the rest of the body may help in deciding, but too much confidence must not be placed on this, as there is often, naturally, a considerable difference. If no decision can be arrived at for the moment, a day or two passed without the opportunity of applying a dye will place it out of the power of a suspected person, to keep up the imposition. Sudden complete blanching of the hair from grief or dread is reported to have occurred, but the evidence is scarcely conclusive. The hair that grows subsequently, however, may be devoid of pigment.

When one or more hairs are found on the person of the accused which resemble the hair of the victim, or *vice versâ*—hair on the victim resembling that of the accused—a careful comparative examination has to be made. The points to observe are the tint, diameter, length, and any peculiarities such as are caused by the use of pomade or dye. Hair from the head of a woman is slightly thinner than that from the head of a man. The hairs from different parts of the body vary in thickness. Those from the axilla and from the pubes of both sexes are respectively stouter than from other parts of the body, except from the beard. Hairs that have never been cut, as those of the eyelids and eyebrows, taper to a point; hairs that have been cut are either stumpy at the ends, or are split into several branches. The student is strongly recommended to examine microscopically, hairs from the commoner domestic animals—the cat, the dog, the horse, the cow, and the sheep, so as to become familiar with their appearance. The same advice applies to fibres from various fabrics—cotton, wool, silk, linen, &c.

**Footprints** sometimes afford evidence of identity. The impression may be that produced by the naked foot, or by the boot or shoe. In the case of the bare foot, the evidence afforded is rarely conclusive, unless there is some distinct peculiarity or deformity. Nevertheless, if the impression is sufficiently well-marked, a cast should be taken, or in the case of a foot-stain on a hard surface—as when an individual treads with the naked foot into a pool of blood, and then produces a print on the neighbouring unstained part of the floor—a tracing should be obtained by laying a piece of tracing-paper over the dried stain, and carefully going over the outline of it with pen and ink. If possible, the board or flag with the print entire should be removed, as affording still more direct evidence. More reliable is the evidence obtained from the impression produced by the tread of a foot wearing a boot or shoe. Even in this case it is only when the identical boot or shoe is forthcoming that convincing proof is afforded. Conclusions drawn from comparison between the impression and a boot belonging to the accused other than the one that produced the impression are open to serious objections. If the impression is sufficiently distinct as to yield a cast one of two methods may be adopted. The impression may be carefully smeared with a flexible feather dipped in oil, and then filled in with plaster of Paris mixed with water to the consistency of cream. Ample time must be allowed for the plaster to set before attempting to remove the cast. The other method is to hold a large piece of red-hot iron (a cook's salamander is convenient) over the impression, without touching it, until it is well warmed, and then to gently sprinkle the impression with paraffin wax chopped up into a coarse powder. The hot iron should be re-applied after each addition of paraffin, so as to render it fluid, until a sufficiently thick cast is obtained. When the paraffin is set, which takes place almost immediately, the cast is carefully removed and any adhering soil gently detached with a soft brush.

The marks on an accused person resulting from scratches, cuts &c., will be dealt with when discussing the question of homicidal violence.

## CHAPTER IX

## BLOOD AND OTHER STAINS.

IN medico-legal investigations it is frequently of the greatest importance to determine whether stains on the clothing of the accused, or on a knife or other weapon found in his possession, are or are not due to blood. The question may have to be solved under difficulties, such as result from the stain being very small, very old, or on foul linen. The opinion of the expert only becomes necessary when the stain is of ambiguous appearance, or of microscopic dimensions, the appearance of a fabric which has been drenched with blood is usually sufficiently characteristic as to need little critical examination  For this reason the medical jurist has to select, from the methods used in the physiological laboratory, those which yield the most reliable results with mere traces of blood  the intention is not to demonstrate all the properties of blood, but simply to identify it

Blood-stains may be examined by three methods—**Microscopical, Spectroscopical,** and **Chemical.**

## MICROSCOPICAL EXAMINATION OF BLOOD-STAINS

If a blood stain is <u>recent</u> it will present a bright red, or reddish-brown colour, and the fabric on which it exists will be <u>stiffened</u>  The stain should first be carefully examined with a short focus lens, or with the low power of the microscope  The fabric will be found to have red filaments, and minute clots interspersed in the meshes of its fibres, which present all the outward appearances of coagulated blood.  In old blood-stains no coloured substance is seen lying on the fabric as in recent stains  the appearance under the lens is simply that of a fabric that has been stained by some dye  If a small piece of recently stained fabric is cut out and placed in a watch-glass with a few drops of glycerine and water (1 to 10), the colouring matter will rapidly tinge the solution, and in a short time a few drops may be squeezed out of the cloth on to a microscope slide, covered with a thin glass, and examined under a power of 300 to 400 diameters  Red corpuscles will be seen in various conditions in accordance with the age of the stain.  If quite recent, many of them will present a fairly normal appearance; others will be contracted and out of shape, irregular in outline, or milled at the edges like coins  With increasing age of the stain the blood corpuscles shrivel up, and become more difficult of recognition, until at last they are completely disintegrated

**The distinction of human blood from that of animals** is a question that has long exercised the minds of medical jurists  The blood of <u>birds</u>, fishes, and <u>reptiles</u> presents sufficiently marked differences as to render differentiation between it and human blood possible  The red corpuscles are larger than those in human blood, they are oval in shape, and are nucleated  The only mammals which have blood corpuscles characteristically different in shape from those of man belong to the <u>camel tribe</u>, which also have oval red corpuscles, but they are not nucleated  The difference in size between the red corpuscles of man and those of the commoner mammals is so slight that even with fresh blood a witness would not be justified in deposing positively that a given specimen was derived from a human being, and not from one of the lower animals, much less when the corpuscles have been dried, and subsequently immersed in an artificially prepared substitute for serum. Of the commoner animals the sheep presents the most marked difference in size of red corpuscles as compared with those of man: the proportion is as 5 to 7·7. Differences in size, which may be of considerable interest from the histological standpoint, are not necessarily sufficiently distinctive for medico-legal purposes. In questions where the life of a possibly innocent man is at stake, all expert evidence must be free from doubt, it may, therefore, be stated in the witness-box that, with the exceptions mentioned, it is impossible positively to distinguish human blood from that of the lower animals. The same attitude is to be taken when the subject of menstrual blood is under discussion; such blood, although possessing certain characteristics as regards coagulability, and reaction to indicators of alkalinity or acidity, is not capable of being differentiated absolutely from blood derived from other parts of the body.

Whether the result of the microscopical examination is in favour of the stain being due to blood or not, further investigation is to be made. It is convenient in the first place to have recourse to what is known as the Guaiacum Test.

If the suspected stain is on a fabric, a fragment should be cut off and placed on a colour-slab, or other white non-absorbent surface. To it add one or two drops of a freshly-prepared solution of guaiacum in alcohol and promote admixture by manipulation with the point of a glass rod. Then drop on a little ozonic ether, or aqueous solution of peroxide of hydrogen. If the stain consists of blood, a blue colour is produced; if not, no colour-change takes place. When the stain is on dark-coloured cloth—e.g., from a black coat—the blue colour may be seen on the white surface around the fabric, or a piece of white filtering paper may be superimposed and pressure applied, in which case the paper will be tinted blue. This test is only to be accepted when it yields a negative reaction—that is to say, when no colour-change results, blood is not present. In its positive phase—the production of a blue colour—the indication is only to be accepted provisionally; the substance tested *may* be blood, but corroboration is required before a decision is given. Other substances than blood possess the property of striking a blue colour with guaiacum and peroxide of hydrogen, therefore on no account must a positive opinion be expressed from the indications obtained by this test. Even a negative result with this test must not be considered final. It is an axiom in forensic medicine that every detail demands every possible

5

corroboration. The guaiacum test, therefore, is only a preliminary test which is easy of application, and requires but a fragment of material. Its use is to pave the way for further inquiry.

The next step is to cut out a portion of the stained fabric close round its margin, and to place it in a watch-glass with a few drops of distilled water. The colouring matter from a fresh stain will be readily dissolved out. If the stain is old the colouring matter will have been converted into hæmatin and will be much less soluble. The appearance of the stain, if it is on linen, or other light-coloured fabric, will afford an indication of its age. Fresh stains are of a more or less bright red; with the lapse of time the colour becomes browner, but retains a trace of red in its composition for years. The rapidity with which the colour of a blood-stain undergoes this change depends on the freedom with which it is exposed to the air, and upon the presence or absence of chemical impurities in the air, such as the oxides of sulphur, hydrochloric acid, ozone, and the like. For this reason blood-stains change more rapidly when exposed to the air in large manufacturing towns than in agricultural districts. It is futile to attempt to infer the age of a blood-stain from its appearance, since it is due to external conditions of unknown activity. If the stain appears old, the watch-glass with the portion of fabric covered with water should be protected by an inverted watch-glass, so as to retard evaporation, and left for half an hour or more; it may be preferable to use a test-tube instead of the watch-glass. Some amount of manipulation with a glass-rod may be resorted to in order to facilitate solution of the colouring matter, but it is well to avoid mechanical interference as much as possible, lest the resulting solution is rendered turbid. Filtration will remedy this, but if the quantity of coloured fluid is small, the loss from absorption by the filter paper is of importance. Decantation, after allowing the matter in suspension to subside, is open to the same objection—loss of fluid; moreover the suspended matter is often reluctant to subside. Should the stain resist the solvent action of water a saturated solution of borax in cold water may be used, and if very insoluble a few drops of ammonia water may be added, in which case the solution obtained will be one of hæmatin. Alkalies convert hæmoglobin into hæmatin, but if the blood colouring-matter is insoluble in water, it has already undergone this change.

### SPECTROSCOPICAL EXAMINATION OF BLOOD-STAINS.

The fluid thus obtained (after filtration, if necessary) is placed in a small test-tube, or, preferably, in a glass cell with parallel walls, and examined with the **spectroscope**. A small direct-vision spectroscope is convenient, but more exact results are obtained with a single prism table-spectroscope.

Should the amount of fluid for examination be very small, the adaptation of the spectroscope to the microscope, known as the **microspectroscope**, must be employed. In this case, it is best to use one of Sorby's cells, which consists of a short length of barometer tubing—about half or three-quarters of an inch—ground to parallel surfaces at the ends, one of which is cemented on to an ordinary microscope slide. A couple of drops of the fluid to be examined will fill the cell, and thus expose a layer of half or three quarters of an inch in thickness between the source of light and the prisms. It is well completely to fill the cell with the fluid to be examined, and to slide a thin coverglass on to the upper end of it, avoiding air-bubbles. The cell is then placed on the stage of the microscope, the eye-piece of the instrument being replaced by a direct-vision spectroscope with focusing arrangement. The spectroscopic eye-piece is furnished with a reflecting prism at one side, so that a solution containing blood colouring matter in a known condition can be made to throw its spectrum alongside that of the blood under examination for the purpose of comparison. When using the microspectroscope, the mirror of the microscope is so adjusted as to project the rays of light through the tubular cell into the instrument, as in ordinary microscopic work. A bright source of artificial light is preferable to daylight, as the presence of Frauenhofer's lines may be embarrassing. The position of the D line can readily be ascertained by bringing a platinum wire, which has been previously dipped in a solution of a sodium salt, into the flame.

The **spectra** of hæmoglobin and its derivatives are so characteristic that, when obtained, their evidence may be considered conclusive of the presence of blood. For this assertion to hold good, it is essential that the alterations about to be described in the position of the absorption bands should be produced; a final opinion must not be given from an examination of blood colouring matter in one condition only. There are other substances which yield spectra closely resembling the spectrum of oxyhæmoglobin, but no substance other than blood will give in addition the bands of reduced hæmoglobin, and of reduced hæmatin. If all these spectroscopic reactions are produced from a single specimen of colouring matter, that colouring matter is derived from blood without the possibility of doubt.

The **spectrum of oxyhæmoglobin** is characterised by the presence of two absorption bands between the D and E lines of the solar spectrum. The first band commences at the D line, and extends towards E. The second band commences after a slight gap, and terminates at the E line. Some absorption also takes place at both ends of the spectrum, especially at the violet end. It is to be remembered that the appearance of the spectrum, as to breadth of bands and general amount of absorption, varies with the concentration of the solution under examination. A good plan is to begin with a strong solution, and gradually to dilute it until the best results are obtained. The spectrum described is the one met with in recent blood-stains. As before stated, the "age" of a blood-stain is not entirely determined by the time that has elapsed since the blood escaped from the body. It may be prematurely aged by the presence of acid vapours in the air, or it may retain its freshness in a pure atmosphere for a considerable time. It is important to bear this in mind.

Very frequently the blood colouring matter will have passed from the condition of oxyhæmoglobin into that of **methæmoglobin** before the stain comes to be examined. The exact constitution of methæmoglobin has not yet been determined. Perhaps the prevailing view is that it consists of hæmoglobin in combination with the same amount of oxygen as that of oxyhæmoglobin, but that the combination is closer. A current of neutral gas—as hydrogen or nitrogen—will not disassociate the oxygen of methæmoglobin as it does that of oxyhæmoglobin. When the stain has passed into the condition of methæmoglobin, it will have acquired a brownish hue, and will probably yield an acid reaction. The solution obtained from a stain in this state is less red and more brown than one obtained from a fresh stain, there is, however, no great diminution in solubility.

The **spectrum of methæmoglobin** for all practical purposes may be said to resemble that of $O_2Hb$ with the addition of a thin band in the red, nearer the C line than the D. There is also more absorption of the violet end of the spectrum than is the case with $O_2Hb$. The methæmoglobin spectrum then consists of three bands—two in the same position as those of $O_2Hb$ but paler, and one thin band in the red.

If to a solution of either oxyhæmoglobin, or of methæmoglobin, a reducing agent, such as Stoke's reagent [an aqueous solution of ferrous sulphate with a little tartaric acid, alkalised with ammonia], or, what is preferable, ammonium sulphide is added, the spectrum of reduced hæmoglobin is obtained. This spectrum consists of a broad, ill-defined band, occupying very nearly the same position as the two bands of $O_2Hb$—that is to say, covering almost all the spectrum between the D and E lines. The absorption of the violet end of the spectrum is about the same as with $O_2Hb$; the red end is rather more absorbed.

After identifying hæmoglobin in its two states—in combination with oxygen and deprived of it—some of it is to be converted into hæmatin. Hæmoglobin is decomposed by acids and alkalies into two substances, hæmatin—acid or alkaline—which retains the iron of hæmoglobin, and globin. Acid hæmatin has a spectrum not unlike that of methæmoglobin; it is not so easily seen as some of the other spectra of blood, and for its recognition requires a good instrument and a solution of a definite density. Alkaline hæmatin also has a spectrum of its own, more difficult to obtain than that of acid hæmatin. It is not necessary for the identification of blood colouring matter that the two last-mentioned spectra should be examined. It is sufficient if, in addition to the spectra of hæmoglobin or methæmoglobin and of reduced hæmoglobin, the spectrum of reduced hæmatin, or as some prefer to call it hæmochromogen, is obtained and identified.

To a little of the original solution of hæmoglobin or methæmoglobin add a few drops of a 20 per cent solution of sodium hydrate. A change in colour is seen and the original spectrum disappears. Then add a few drops of ammonium sulphide to the solution of alkaline hæmatin thus obtained, a further change of colour is at once apparent, the solution becomes somewhat claret-coloured. On examining with the spectroscope the spectrum of reduced hæmatin, the most pronounced of all the blood-spectra, is seen. It consists of two bands slightly nearer the violet end of the spectrum than the bands of $O_2Hb$. The first band is dark and is exceedingly well defined at the edges; it is situated about midway between the D and the E lines. The second and broader band, not quite so well defined, commences before the E line and extends as far as the $b$ line; the violet end of the spectrum is more absorbed than is the case with $O_2Hb$. The reducing power of ammonium sulphide is not so active as that of Stokes' fluid, and in consequence, when ammonium sulphide is used, the second band of reduced hæmatin is not, as a rule, fully developed for some time (5 or 10 minutes) after the first, which appears at once. Reduction may be hastened by gently warming the solution after the addition of ammonium sulphide.

If the colouring matter of the blood-stain has been converted into hæmatin before the fabric is submitted to examination, the first solution obtained from it will yield the spectrum of acid hæmatin. The resemblance between the bands of methæmoglobin and those of acid hæmatin has already been pointed out. The addition of a reducing agent at once distinguishes the one from the other—the methæmoglobin spectrum changes to that of reduced hæmoglobin, the acid hæmatin spectrum to that of reduced hæmatin. When acid hæmatin has been produced by natural causes (without the addition of acid), the use of ammonium sulphide, as reducing agent, obviates the necessity of previous alkalisation.

Both hæmoglobin and hæmatin after being reduced can again be oxidised by shaking up the respective solutions with air. To enable this to be done easily, the smallest quantity of the reducing agent must be used that will effect its purpose.

### CHEMICAL EXAMINATION OF BLOOD-STAINS.

If there is sufficient material at command the most conclusive of the chemical tests for blood may be resorted to—the production of **Hæmin crystals.** Cut out a piece of the stained fabric about the size of a postage stamp; much less is sufficient with skilful manipulation. Divide this piece into three equal sized slips and place them one over the other on a microscope slide. Add a minute crystal of sodium chloride, and sufficient glacial acetic acid to thoroughly saturate the fabric and then a few drops more. Roll a glass rod backwards and forwards over the fabric for a minute or two, so as thoroughly to incorporate the acid with the colouring matter. A dirty brown fluid can now be pressed out of the fabric by a final passage of the rod, the fabric itself being at the same time withdrawn with a pair of forceps. Bring the fluid to the middle of the slide by stroking it up at each side with the shaft of the rod, and drop on a thin cover-glass. Hold the slide by one end, and pass the centre of it to and fro over the flame of a Bunsen burner; continue until active ebullition, manifested by bubbles rapidly forming under the cover, takes place. Then allow the slide to cool gradually. When cold examine under a power of 300 diameters.

In the production of hæmin crystals there are one or two precautions to be observed. The amount of sodium chloride must be very small— a crystal the size of a small pin's head is sufficient; if more is added the field, when examined with the microscope, is seen to be covered with cubes of sodium chloride crystals. Plenty of acid must be used. The boiling demands care: it must be thoroughly done, but if heat is too suddenly applied the glass will probably crack; if excess of caution is observed—the heat being applied very gradually—the fluid round the circumference of the thin glass will be evaporated, and the dried up residue will seal in the fluid beneath the cover, so that when ebullition takes place the cover-glass will be projected to a distance.

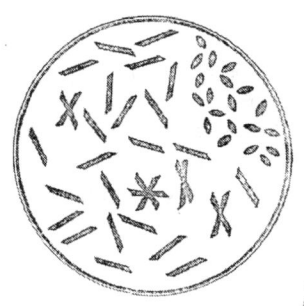

Fig. 6.—Hæmin crystals.

Hæmin crystals (*Teichmann's crystals*) are composed of hydrochlorate of hæmatin. They are insoluble in water, alcohol, and dilute acetic and hydrochloric acids. They are soluble in boiling acetic and hydrochloric acids, and in the caustic alkalies. They yield the blue reaction with the guaiacum test, and when incinerated, and the ash is treated with a drop of hydrochloric acid and a solution of potassium sulphocyanide, the presence of iron is demonstrated by the red colour produced. Under the microscope they appear as brown or claret coloured crystals which have a steely-blue (watch spring) lustre by reflected light. They usually take the form of rhombic plates which are frequently superimposed so as to form crosses or stars. The size of the crystals varies; sometimes they are exceptionally large and well formed, at others they are scarcely recognisable with a power of 500 diameters. When small they occasionally resemble the so-called whetstone crystals of uric acid, but are much smaller. Crystals obtained in the manner described, and possessing the above-mentioned physical and chemical characteristics, afford conclusive proof of the presence of blood.

**Blood-stains on knives**, or other steel weapons are frequently very difficult to deal with if the stain is not quite fresh; the colouring matter has a tendency to combine with the oxide of iron, and thus become very insoluble. The saturated borax solution with a few drops of ammonia water will dissolve out sufficient hæmatin for spectrum analysis. The deposit is scraped off the weapon, and digested with a little of the solution, and then decanted or filtered off the iron oxide. Fresh blood stains on metal are easily dealt with, except when the stain is very thin and in small patches, as after a knife that has been used for homicidal purposes has been wiped with a cloth. Careful pencilling of the stained portions with a small camel-hair brush dipped in distilled water, or borax solution, will generally procure enough colouring matter for recognition by the microspectroscope. If a clasp knife is undergoing investigation, special attention should be paid to the joint, and if on examination with a lens it appears to contain colouring matter, the pivots must be withdrawn, and the parts of the knife separated; in this way ample evidence may not unfrequently be obtained.

When blood has been projected from a divided small artery, it may reach a neighbouring wall, or article of furniture. The appearance will probably be that of small splashes or spots; sometimes they take the form of notes of exclamation when the jet falls obliquely on the surface. Distinction between arterial and venous blood found on clothing, or on furniture, cannot well be made except when a very small artery has sprinkled its contents to a distance in a fine spray.

## STAINS OTHER THAN BLOOD

**Rust-stains on knives**, but more especially stains produced by their use in cutting fruit, as oranges or apples—the stain then consisting of citrate or malate of iron respectively—often present a strong resemblance to blood-stains. Rust-stains are insoluble in water, and the solutions obtained from the stains produced by vegetable acids on steel yield none of the reactions of blood. Fabrics may be stained with *vegetable, mineral,* or *anilin* colouring matters. Most fruit stains that resemble blood are altered by ammonia water to a greenish tint, other vegetable stains are made crimson by the same reagent, some, as logwood, are turned to a bluish-black. Dilute acids often alter the colour of vegetable stains.

Mineral stains are often due to the oxide, or some of the salts of iron. Ammonium sulphide usually blackens such stains, but as the ammonia of this reagent darkens some vegetable stains, as archil and logwood, it is necessary to make a control experiment with ammonia-water alone. In the case of the oxide, or of ferric salts, a drop of HCl, followed by a drop of potassium ferrocyanide solution, will yield Prussian blue. Most of the anilin stains resembling blood when treated with dilute $HNO_3$, become yellow, or tinge the excess of acid yellow. In addition to these tests, the absence of hæmoglobin and its derivatives must be proved.

## CHAPTER X

### IDENTITY OF THE DEAD.

THE identification of the dead is required when the body of an unknown person who has died from violence, starvation, or disease is found in the open air, or in an out-house, or other uninhabited premises, after a fire in an inhabited house or hotel where strangers are temporarily residing, or after the occurrence of an explosion, or of a railway accident.

The difficulties of the investigation are increased if the body is much mutilated, or is far advanced in putrefaction. Perhaps the most difficult cases are those in which dismemberment and mutilation have been effected with the special object of preventing recognition of characteristics that might lead to identification.

There are certain points to which attention must be directed, which constitute the basis of an investigation having for its object the identification of the body of an unknown person. **The stature, age, sex, general state of nutrition, colour of hair, scars, skin-marks of any kind,** deformities, indications of past injury to the bones, and the presence of false teeth, with absence of the natural teeth, all claim attention. In the unmutilated fresh body most of these points can be cleared up, the age, as a rule, being the most difficult.

When an opinion has to be founded on an investigation of fragments of a body, with the flesh and skin remaining, much depends on the nature of the parts. An entire hand, for example, would convey more information as to the social condition and occupation than a foot. If the body has been very much mutilated, and but a few fragments are forthcoming, a part of the thorax or abdomen would probably reveal the sex of the victim. Close attention to details is necessary to secure success in all inquiries of this kind. When fragments of a body are examined, special attention should be paid to the parts where separation from the rest of the body has been effected. An exact description should be written down at the time, and if possible a photograph taken, or a drawing made, so that at a future time, if other fragments are found, it may be ascertained whether they belong to the same body or not.

The presence of scars, however small, should be noted. It may subsequently turn out that the individual whose body is under examination had been bled from the arm, or had received a small wound, the scar of which was known to have been present up to the time of his disappearance. It has been recommended in cases where there is suspicion of the previous existence of tattoo-marks, to take out the neighbouring lymphatic glands, and to examine them for traces of the colouring matter.

## THE STATURE

Within somewhat wide limits, the stature may be determined from the measurement of single limbs, or even of some bones. The length of the arm multiplied by two, with six inches added for each clavicle, and an inch and a half for the width of the sternum, gives the distance between the tips of the middle fingers when the arms are stretched out, and approximatively the height of the body (Taylor). The femur equals about .275 of the body height (Quain). Calculations have been made, and tables drawn up with the view of establishing a relation between the length of some of the long bones, and the stature of the individual to whom they belonged, but the mean ratio is obtained from measurements ranging over extremes too widely apart to permit of its general application. Estimations of stature from the measurements yielded by one or two bones are very unreliable; if they are given at all it must be in a qualified manner, as they partake largely of the nature of guess-work. When the entire skeleton is available, 1½ inches is to be added to its length to represent the soft structures.

Criteria for the estimation of **age** have already been given.

If the body is entire, but in an advanced stage of putrefaction, there may be difficulty in ascertaining even the sex. The points to be noted are the hair of the head, that of the pubes, and the development of the breasts. In women the hair of the head is, as a rule, longer and finer than in men. The pubic hair does not usually advance so near the umbilicus in women as in men. The breasts are fuller in women. In female children all but the first indication will be absent. The clothing will help identification, even if only fragments remain attached to the body. Metallic articles, as rings and other ornaments, may afford a clue. The resistance offered by the uterus to putrefactive changes is to be borne in mind.

If the soft parts have disappeared, the **bones** will afford indications as to age and sex. When isolated bones, or fragments of bones only, are forthcoming, the first question to be answered is:—Are they **human**, or do they belong to one of the **lower animals**? A bone that is intact does not usually present insuperable difficulty, a due acquaintance with human osteology will enable a satisfactory conclusion to be arrived at, for or against. If a bone is not human, it is by no means easy for an ordinary medical man to determine the animal from which it is derived; unless well versed in comparative osteology, it is best for a witness to content himself with the statement that the bone in question is not a human bone. Fragments of the shafts of the long bones may present great difficulties, and demand corresponding cautiousness on the part of the witness. The fragment may be so small and anomalous in appearance, that the question becomes—Is it bone or not? The microscope will determine the question by demonstrating the presence or absence of the structural characteristics of bone.

From time to time collections of bones are discovered under circumstances which give rise to suspicion that a **murder** has been perpetrated. If such a collection is referred to the expert for a report, the first step is to determine whether they are human or not. If they are human, they should be arranged in order, so as to build up a skeleton as completely as possible. It sometimes happens that duplicate bones are present, which, of course, indicate the dual nature of the remains. A full report should be drawn up, and a drawing or photograph taken when the arrangement is complete. Any abnormality or trace of injury should be noted, taking care not to include under this head the results of violence produced by the implements used in the process of disinterment. The questions to be answered are:—What was the **age**, stature, and sex of the individual or individuals to whom the bones belonged, and are there any indications of the cause of death? Each question must be considered separately.

The age is to be inferred from the condition of the teeth, and that of the epiphyses of the long bones, together with the other indications previously tabulated. The stature can only be arrived at approximately, especially if the skeleton is not complete. The question of sex, as regards the skeleton, remains to be considered.

## SEXUAL CHARACTERISTICS OF THE SKELETON

The **female skeleton** is smaller and of slighter build than that of the male, the individual bones weighing less than the corresponding bones of the male. The following account of the chief distinctions between the bones of the male and female skeleton is taken from Macalister's *Human Anatomy*:—

The male skull is larger, heavier, and more ridged than the female, with more prominent mastoid processes, occipital protuberance, zygomatic and superciliary ridges, and a larger capacity (11–10), especially in the frontal and occipital regions. The female skull preserves a look of immaturity, and such characters of immaturity as the preponderance of temporal length over frontal, the prominence of the parietal tubera and the concomitant narrowness of the base. The average maximum length from the glabella (the smooth spot between and below the superciliary arches) to the most prominent point of the occiput is 19.6 cm in the male, and 18.3 cm in the female. The **capacity** of the skull—ascertained by filling it through the foramen magnum with No. 8 shot (the other foramina being plugged with cotton wool) and then measuring the shot in a graduated vessel—averages, in the European male, 1570 cc, the European female 1378 cc. The female **lower jaw** has a less prominent chin, and a weaker, shorter coronoid process than the male, the angle formed by the ramus and body is greater. The **thorax** is shorter and wider in the female when not distorted by stays. The ribs are more oblique. The twelfth male rib averages 103 mm in length, that of the female 83.8 mm. The **mesosternum** (body) is more than twice the length of the **presternum** (manubrium) in the male, but less in the female. The **lumbar curve** in the female vertebral column is of greater length, and the lumbo-sacral angle is greater than in the male. The normal adult male sacrum is about 105 mm high and about 117 broad, the female about 101 high and 118 broad; these relations are expressed by the sacral index $\dfrac{\text{breadth} \times 100}{\text{height}}$. Sacra, such as those of Europeans, in

76                    FORENSIC MEDICINE.

which this index exceeds 100, are called *platyhieric*, those under 100 are *dolichohieric*, as is the case in most of the black races. The sacral index of British males is about 112·4, of females 116. As a rule, all females are *platyhieric*.

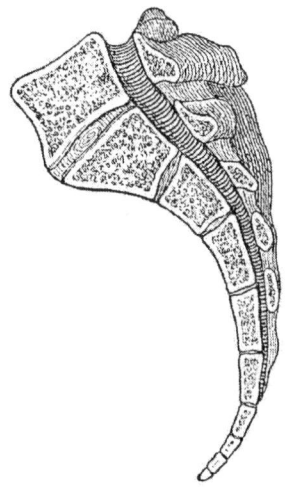

Fig. 7.—Male sacrum.            Fig. 8.—Female sacrum.

Ward[1] gives the following characteristics of the curve of the male and female sacrum respectively :—The curvature of the female sacrum occurs chiefly at the lower half of the bone. The upper half is nearly straight. The male sacrum is on an average more curved than that

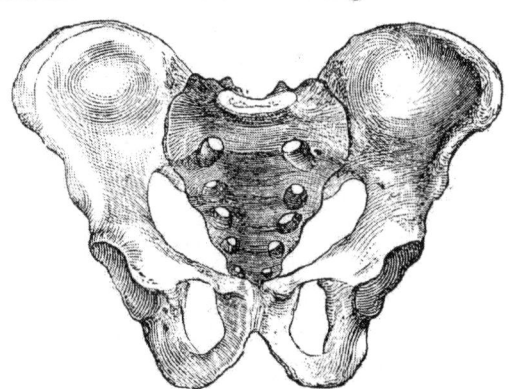

Fig. 9.—Male pelvis (from Macalister's *Anatomy*).

of the female, and its curvature is more equally distributed over its whole length. The male sacrum, in many instances, approximates in

[1] *Outlines of Human Osteology.*

## SEXUAL CHARACTERISTICS OF THE SKELETON.

form to that of the female, but the female sacrum rarely presents the characters proper to the male. Thus it is much more common to find a straight sacrum in a male subject than one that is very much curved in a female.

The pelvis, as a whole, is the most characteristic part of the skeleton in the two sexes respectively. The **male pelvis** is deeper, rougher, with deeper iliac fossæ and symphysis, a smaller pubic angle, a vertically ovate obturator foramen, and inflexed tubera ischii. The female pelvis

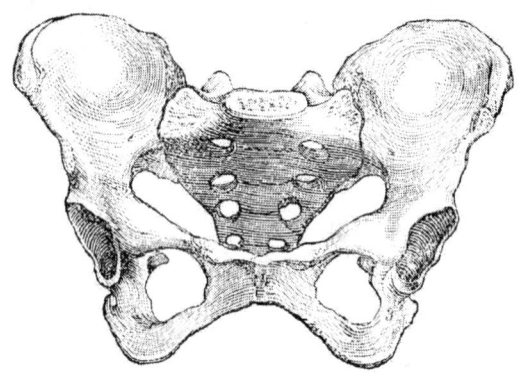

Fig. 10.—Female pelvis (from Macalister's *Anatomy*).

is shallower, wider, smoother, with shallower symphysis, and wider pubic arch, everted ischia, and a triangular obturator foramen. These sex characters are discernible at birth. The sagittal diameter of the brim from sacral promontory to upper edge of symphysis pubis is 100 mm. in the male, 116 in the female. The transverse, 124 in male, 135 in female. The oblique from the sacro-iliac joint to the ilio-pubal eminence, 110 in the male, 126 in the female. The index of the pelvic brim, $\frac{\text{sagittal} \times 100}{\text{transv. diam.}}$, varies in different races. The neck of the femur has a lower angle in the adult female than in the male, averaging 118°, the male being 125°.

The skeleton may bear traces of **violence inflicted during life.** Injuries to the skull caused by firearms are usually too obvious to escape notice. Fractures, especially of the base, might be overlooked except a careful examination is made. Injuries to the **cervical vertebræ,** from excessive violence due to death by strangulation or by hanging, are to be looked for, also fractures of the ribs. If such injuries have been produced immediately before death there will be no evidence of attempt at repair. The presence of callus shows that an interval elapsed between the receipt of the injury and death. Indications of old fractures should be sought for. The remains of the

African traveller Livingstone were identified by the presence of an old ununited fracture of the humerus, the existence of which was known to his friends

# SUBJECTS INVOLVING SEXUAL RELATIONS.

## CHAPTER XI

### SEXUAL ABNORMALITIES.

The subject of sex is one that frequently comes under the notice of the medical jurist Questions relating to it may arise in regard to newly-born children, as when a woman gives birth to an infant whose sex is doubtful, but which, if a male, is heir to an estate Later in life sexual development or capacity has to be considered in relation to impotency, rape, impregnation, and allied subjects

In order that an infant shall be capable of inheriting an estate the law demands that it shall have "the shape of mankind," if the estate is entailed on male heirs the question of sex is added. It is impossible to define the limit at which deformity is so excessive as to deprive the subject of it of the right to be considered a human being The various types of monsters which may be born alive are so diverse that although they may be capable of scientific classification each case has to be separately considered The law leaves the question open without determining the degree of deviation from the normal which would constitute absence of human shape Under these circumstances it is useless to attempt any abstract differentiation, all that the expert can do is to make a very careful and detailed examination of the infant, and to report what he has found to the court It may be observed parenthetically that, contrary to popular opinion, it is criminal to hasten the death of an abnormally formed fœtus or monster, although it may obviously be incapable of long survival.

The question of sex in an infant is sometimes equally impossible of determination Here, however, the morphology of the sexual organs serves as a guide to interpretation In a living infant, the external generative organs only are available for examination As an aid to the interpretation of abnormal appearances a glance at the condition of matters at the period of development when the sexes differentiate will be of service. The accompanying two figures diagrammatically represent the male and female external organs in this stage.

In Fig. 11 the genital tubercle (*c*) forms the clitoris, the genital folds (*l*) become the labia minora, and the cutaneous folds of the cloacal lips (*L*) remain separate and form the labia majora. The urogenital sinus remains as the vestibule. In Fig. 12 the genital folds have approximated and united in the median line, closing on the urethra as far as the glands of the penis, *P*. Those cutaneous folds of the cloaca, which in the female remain separate as the labia majora, coalesce and by their union form the scrotum (*S*). If the genital folds do not unite, the urethra remains open at the raphé (*R*), producing the condition called **hypospadias**.

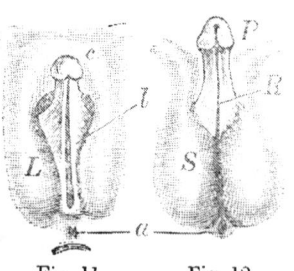

The conditions which obtain in the fully developed external organs of the female are approximatively those which exist before differentiation of the sexes. Further growth and development in a new direction is required to form the male organs, and during its progress most of the conditions arise which cause ambiguity of sex. It is easy to see that hypospadias may be so extensive as to cause the male organs to appear like abnormally formed female organs. If the testicles have not descended, and the scrotum is cleft, there exists a condition resembling that before differentiation. In such a case it would not be easy to determine the sex from external inspection only. If one or both *testicles* can be found and identified the sex of the infant is thereby determined—it is a *male*. The detection of an *ovary* is equally determinative of the *female* sex. If a glandular organ is accessible it must be carefully examined by the touch, the harder it is the more likely it is to be an ovary. The virgin ovary is largely composed of fibrous tissue, hence it is hard—more so than the testicle. In the adult, compression of the glandular body, if the subject is a male, produces the peculiar sickly, faintly feeling which is experienced when the testicles are thus treated. The representative of the penis may or may not be perforate; its prepuce may be free, or it may be continuous with the genital folds or labia minora, the two last-named conditions being in favour of the female sex. If the opening of a cul-de-sac exists below the mouth of the urethra and in front of the bowel, it will probably represent the Müllerian ducts or vagina, and, therefore, is indicative of the female sex, a similar opening, however, may exist in the masculine type of hermaphrodism being that of the vesicula prostatica—the homologue of the uterus. **Epispadias** consists in the existence of an opening on the dorsal aspect of the penis which is often accompanied by general malformation of the other external genitals. It may be associated with extroversion of the bladder

After puberty indications may be afforded by the occurrence of functional activity of the sexual apparatus If periodic discharges of blood take place, they are indicative of the female sex; seminal discharges indicate the male sex The **bodily conformation** may be taken into consideration—the growth of hair, the general contour, the mammary development together with the vocal intonation Moral characteristics are not of much value as determinatives, since long custom exercises a powerful influence as regards the sexual proclivities and the habits of the individual

Developmental malformations of the internal as well as of the external organs of generation are also met with Individuals so deformed are often, though improperly, called **Hermaphrodites** The union of the sexes in one being is an old myth having for its basis the assumed power of self reproduction In this sense hermaphrodism has no existence; but so far as the linking together in one person of the male and female generative organs, or of parts of them is concerned, a goodly array of examples are to hand It is customary to speak of cases of simple malformation of the external genitals which impart a false or ambiguous sexual identity, as cases of *spurious* or *false* hermaphrodism Such cases have already been described A few words remain to be said on the subject of so-called true **hermaphrodism**

The normal sequence in the male subject is for the Wolffian ducts to persist, whilst the Mullerian ducts almost entirely disappear, in the female the converse takes place It happens from time to time that this order is not followed, and in place of it both the Wolffian ducts with the primitive reproductive gland, and the Mullerian ducts, develop in one and the same individual, into the organs of which they are the antecedents in the embryonic state

Watson[1] tabulates the sexual homologies thus:—

| Female. | Sinus uro-genitalis | Male. |
| --- | --- | --- |
| Urethra | Upper part of urinary pedicle | Upper portion of prostatic urethra |
| Vestibule | Lower part of urinary pedicle | Lower portion of prostatic and membranous urethra. |
| Glands of Bartholini. | Blastema | Glands of Cowper |
| Crura and corpus clitoridis | Corpora cavernosa | Crura and corpus penis |
| Glans clitoridis and vaginal bulbs | Corpora spongiosa | Glans penis and corpus spongiosum urethræ |
| Labia majora. | Genital ridges | Scrotum and raphé. |

[1] *Journ of Anat. and Phys.ol*, 1879.

Sir J Y Simpson[1] classified the so-called true hermaphrodism into —

Lateral —Testicle on one side, and ovary on the other

Transverse.—External organs male and internal female, or the reverse

Vertical, or double.—
  (a) Ovaries with combined male and female passages
  (b) Testicles with combined male and female passages
  (c) Ovaries and testicles coexisting on one or both sides

Watson considers the lateral to be the only true kind of hermaphrodism, and thinks that the others ought to be included in the class of spurious hermaphrodism, except (c), which ought probably to be placed in the category of double monsters

The following are examples of different forms of hermaphrodism — Schmorl[2] describes a case of lateral and transverse hermaphrodism in which the external organs had a general resemblance to the male form — there was a well-developed, but imperforate penis  The scrotum was divided  in the right half there was an organ of the same structure as the testicle, the left half was empty  The internal organs were of the female type —a vagina, which did not open externally, a uterus with cervix and Fallopian tubes, and an ovary on the left side  Hutchinson, Junior,[3] dissected the body of a full grown fœtus, the subject of transverse hermaphrodism  The penis was well formed but for a slight hypospadias, the raphé of the scrotum was very well marked  The bulb and prostate extremely well developed, into the latter opened a vagina, above which were perfectly formed uterus, ovaries, and Fallopian tubes  Heppner[4] examined the body of a child two months old, which presented the appearance of vertical hermaphrodism  The external organs were of the male type, there was a hypospadic penis with glans and prepuce, an empty scrotum with raphe, and a prostate gland, but no vasa deferentia nor vesicula seminalis  A vagina, a uterus with arbor vitæ in the cervical canal, round and broad ligaments, well formed Fallopian tubes and ovaries existed on both sides  Under each ovary was a testicle, and near each testicle was an organ resembling the parovarium  Ceccherelli[5] describes a living example of vertical hermaphrodism, the subject being fourteen years of age  The mammæ were well developed  There was a hypospadic penis  The scrotum was divided and contained only one testicle, between the folds of the split scrotum, or labia, the neck of the uterus could be felt  The female organs appeared complete  Menstruation had occurred regularly since the twelfth year of age, and the individual had copulated as a woman  From the opening in the penis semen was ejected, a specimen of which was examined by Virchow and found to contain spermatozoa

[1] Todd's *Cyclopædia of Anatomy*     [2] Virchow's *Arch*, 1888
[3] *The Lancet*, 1885     [4] Du Bois-Reymond's *Arch*, 1870
[5] *Lo sperimentale*, 1874

**Abnormalities of the Male Organs**—Individuals in whom one testicle only is in the scrotum, are known as **monorchids**. This condition, whether the result of imperfect development, or of operative interference, is no bar to procreation. Non-descent of both testicles does not necessarily deprive the individual of procreative power, although it probably lessens it, and may be a positive barrier; the subjects of this abnormality are called **cryptorchids**. Many post-mortem examinations of individuals labouring under this defect have demonstrated the absence of spermatozoa in the spermatic fluid, but a number of cases in the living have been recorded in which procreative power has existed, so that the positive evidence outweighs the negative. Even absence of both testicles—at least for a time after removal—does not entirely destroy fertility. This however can only be due to imperfect ablation, or to the existence of a reserve of spermatic fluid after the organs which secreted it had been removed.

Absence of the **penis**, or of the whole of the external genital organs, may occur either from defective development, injury, or disease. In some cases the penis is united in its whole length to the scrotum; if the organ itself is fully formed, the abnormality is capable of being remedied by surgical operation.

The female external organs may be wanting, with or without absence of the internal organs. Sometimes the vulva presents a normal appearance, but there is no vagina. The vagina may be either congenitally deficient, or it may have been closed by inflammatory processes, not unfrequently from diphtheritic disease in childhood. Surgical procedure can only be resorted to when structures representing the vagina are present. The external organs may be complete, the ovaries and the uterus—one or both—being wanting. The capacity of the vagina may be inadequate for the reception of the penis; usually this condition is capable of being remedied by appropriate treatment. The condition named **Vaginismus**, especially if associated with pronounced hysteria, may as effectively bar sexual intercourse as structural atresia of the vagina. Large hernias in both sexes may prevent intercourse.

### IMPOTENCE AND STERILITY

By **impotence** is meant incapacity for sexual intercourse, by **sterility** incapacity for procreation of children. The first term is usually used in reference to the male sex, the second to the female sex; they are, however, respectively referable to both sexes: a man may be sterile as well as a woman, and a woman may be impotent as well as a man. A man may be incapable of procreation, either in consequence of impotence, or, though competent for intercourse, in consequence of absence of the impregnating elements of the semen. A woman may be sterile from absence of the external generative organs rendering her incompetent for sexual intercourse, or, with the presence of these organs, from absence of the ovaries or uterus; in the latter case she would be sterile without being impotent. It will be necessary to discuss the subject with respect to the two sexes separately, and, for convenience, to take impotence and sterility together. In medico-legal practice the subject of impotence and sterility arises in relation to cases of divorce, legitimacy, and criminal assaults.

## SEXUAL DEFECTS IN MALES.

Impotence and sterility in the male may be due to organic defect or to functional disorder, the organs being anatomically perfect. *Age, malformation*, and *constitutional causes* may severally be causal factors.

**Age.**—The two extremes of life may render the individual incompetent for sexual intercourse; no limits can be stated, however, when this occurs.

**Extreme Youth.**—At the age of puberty, which is usually about the fifteenth or sixteenth year, the sexual powers normally begin to develop, capacity for intercourse preceding procreative power. Considerable latitude occurs in this respect. The earliest recorded[1] age at which the power for procreation existed in the male is thirteen years; a boy at this age impregnated a young woman. Many cases are recorded of boys becoming fathers at fourteen years of age. Puberty does not consist in a change that takes place at a certain fixed period of life, it is dependent for its early or late occurrence upon hereditary influence, and upon the conditions which surround the individual, morally and physically. For this reason, when examining a case of reputed sexual capacity, the medical man should not be influenced so much by the age of the individual as by his physical and moral development. There are boys of fifteen or sixteen who are sexually mere children, whilst at a much earlier age other boys have the powers and the instincts of adults. The presence of hair on the pubes, and of a developed penis, with or without the general conditions which indicate incipient manhood—as the tone of voice and bodily conformation—are strongly indicative of sexual capacity. It is to be noted that, although advanced corporeal development is found in most cases of hereditary sexual precocity, when premature puberty has been brought about through evil example and vicious habits, the bodily appearance is often the reverse of manly. In addition to observing the development of the penis, the condition of the prepuce is to be noted. In boys accustomed to sexual grati-

[1] *Brit. Med. Journ.*, 1887.

fication in any form, the glans will be more or less uncovered, unless the prepuce is abnormally long.

**Advanced age** is no barrier to procreative power. It is true that the sexual capacity diminishes with age, and, consequently, an old man is less likely than a youth to impregnate a woman, this however is only stating probability, the medical jurist has to depose to possibility. Active spermatic filaments have been found in the seminal fluid of men of 70 and 80 years of age, and even older; numerous instances have occurred in which men who have married at this time of life have had children. So long as there are active spermatozoa present in the seminal fluid, the possibility of impregnation must be admitted. It may therefore be stated that advanced age is not incompatible with the possible retention of procreative power.

The **imaginative faculties** occasionally completely inhibit the sexual emotions. A man from this cause may be utterly unable to have intercourse with one woman although quite competent with another; a perverted sentiment causes the mental attitude to be one of extreme disgust at the idea of coitus with the woman towards whom this sentiment is entertained.

**Debility** due to disease may produce temporary or permanent loss of the sexual functions, most acute diseases of a severe type—as fevers, pneumonia, and the like lead to temporary loss. Of chronic diseases diabetes is one that commonly abolishes sexual energy. Diseases of the nervous system have a special tendency to derange the sexual functions. Tabes at first increases capacity and later on abolishes it. In chronic myelitis the sexual power is usually impaired at an early period, it diminishes more or less rapidly and is finally lost. Ross[1] states that in incomplete paraplegia the sexual power may be preserved for a long time. In the many toxic conditions producing peripheral neuritis, the virile power is more or less impaired, and in some there is complete impotence. **Mumps** sometimes results in metastatic inflammation of one or both testicles, which may lead to atrophy and consequent abolition of procreative power. A common nervous disorder of anomalous character to which the term **neurasthenia** is applied is frequently accompanied by sexual debility, and those who suffer from this complaint often attribute the origin of their troubles to loss of virility. This tendency is caused or increased by previous habits of masturbation.

**Blows on the head** have been followed by temporary or even permanent loss of the virile power.

The **malformations of the male sexual organs**, described in the previous section, may or may not produce impotence or sterility in

[1] *Diseases of the Nervous System*, 1883.

accordance with their character and degree. The first consideration is—does the condition prevent the secretion of normal spermatic fluid? and, secondly, if not, is there any absolute mechanical impediment to its being conveyed to the vagina?

**Complete absence** of both testicles renders a man sterile. If they are removed whilst the individual is in full sexual activity, it is possible that one or more fruitful intercourses might take place afterwards, but the power of impregnation is eventually lost. Massazza,[1] experimenting on animals, found that castration does not immediately abolish procreative power; active spermatozoa were discovered in the spermatic ducts nine days after removal of the testicles. The removal of the testicles does not necessarily render a man impotent, although it deprives him of procreative power. History relates that the ladies of imperial Rome were in the habit of taking advantage of this fact by indulging in illicit pleasure with eunuchs as the act entailed no risk of impregnation. In more recent times the male sopranos (*castrati*), who as a class are barely extinct, have often given rise to scandal. When the testicles exist, although not in their normal situation, the condition imposes no absolute barrier to fertility. Cryptorchids have been known to be fruitful.

**Malformations of the penis** are the chief cause of mechanical impediment to impregnation. Epispadias almost invariably makes a man sterile, because the condition renders it next to impossible that the seminal fluid can reach the vagina. Hypospadias is or is not a barrier to impregnation in accordance with the degree of malformation and its position; if the penis and scrotum are cleft, or even if the penis only is open at the root, the difficulty is insurmountable by natural means; artificial transference of the semen to the vagina has resulted in impregnation. Since impregnation may result from deposition of semen on the vulva, without propulsion of it into the vagina, great reticence must be observed in expressing an opinion as to the *possibility* of impregnation under adverse conditions on the part of the male. Cases of hypospadias have to be considered on their individual merits; the malformation itself is not a fixed condition, and therefore it may or may not render a man sterile. Binding down of the penis to the scrotum is another impediment of varying significance. The same question obtains as with hypospadias—is the deformity of such a character as to totally forbid the possibility of the deposition of semen within the vulva? A curious anomaly may occur with respect to the question of impotence and sterility in the male: the rule is that the former includes the latter, but that the converse is not the case. If a man, by accident or disease, loses the whole of the

[1] *Riforma Medica*, 1891.

penis, the testicles remaining, he is obviously impotent, but from what has just been said, he is not necessarily sterile, cases have occurred in which a man thus mutilated has succeeded in effecting impregnation

### SEXUAL DEFECTS IN FEMALES.

Impotence and Sterility in the female may also be due to organic defect, or to functional disorder.

Age.—In the female sex puberty usually occurs in this country at fourteen or fifteen years of age. At this age a change takes place in the bodily conformation—the girl becomes more womanly. The commencement of menstruation is the index by which the advent of puberty is recognised, showing that the individual has arrived at the period of life when the capacity for procreation exists. As the development of the virile power in the male may be accelerated or retarded, so in the female may the menses appear early or late. Cases of abnormally early menstruation are not unfrequently recorded, but, as pointed out by Cullingworth,[1] all discharges of blood from the genital organs of young children are not to be regarded as instances of precocious menstruation. In many cases the discharge is not periodic, and there are no corresponding signs of abnormally early development of the breasts and external genital organs. Exceptionally, however, puberty commences at a very early age, and the reality of the condition is vouched for by the occurrence of pregnancy. The earliest recorded age at which pregnancy occurred in this country is reported by Dodd.[2] A girl began to menstruate at the age of twelve months, became pregnant when eight years and ten months old, and was delivered of a living child which weighed seven pounds. Allen[3] reports a case in which a girl commenced to menstruate at eleven years of age, and at the age of thirteen years and six months gave birth to a fine healthy boy weighing nine pounds; the father of the child was only fourteen years old. In another case, reported by Dobson,[4] a girl began to menstruate when only eleven years old; she became pregnant at twelve years and nine months, and gave birth to a male child at the age of thirteen and a half. Lefebvre[5] records the case of a girl who was born fully developed with hair on the pubes, she began to menstruate at four years of age, and became pregnant at eight by a man aged thirty-seven, the pregnancy terminating by the expulsion of a mole containing a well characterised

---

[1] *Liverpool and Manchester Med and Surg Reports*, 1876.
[2] *Lancet*, 1881.
[3] *Brit. Med. Journ.*, 1885.
[4] *Brit. Med. Journ.*, 1884.
[5] *Gaz Hebdom*, 1878.

human embryo. Curtis[1] records a case and after inquiry vouches for the facts, in which a girl became pregnant (by a boy of fifteen) twenty-four days before she was ten years old; she was delivered at the age of ten years eight months and seven days of a healthy child at full term. These cases illustrate the necessity for the medical jurist to determine the presence or absence of puberty by the degree of sexual development attained by the individual rather than by the age. The condition of the breasts, the presence or otherwise of hair on the pubes, and the general contour of the external sexual organs are the indications by which an opinion is to be formed.

**Advanced Age.**—Unlike men, women, with few exceptions, are limited in the duration of their procreative capacity. The menopause is usually an indication that the period of fertility is at an end. The average age at which menstruation ceases is forty-five years; it may cease earlier, or it may be prolonged to fifty; exceptional cases of still later menstruation are recorded as far as and beyond seventy. It is to be observed, however, that as in preternaturally early menstruation, all hæmorrhages from the vagina in advanced life are not to be accepted as evidence of the existence of the monthly function. Uterine polypi and malignant disease of the uterus are conditions which may give rise to hæmorrhage occurring with more or less periodicity. A most extraordinary case of delayed menstruation is recorded by Marx[2] —A woman forty-eight years old, who had been married twenty years, had never menstruated; at that age she was treated for oophoritis by periodic local abstractions of blood, and subsequently she commenced menstruating at monthly intervals. When the account was published she was fifty-two years old and continued to menstruate regularly.

Women rarely have children after about forty-five years of age, but exceptions to this rule, and also to the rule that the procreative powers cease at the menopause, are occasionally met with. Davis[3] relates the case of a woman who was delivered at fifty-five years of age; the baptismal certificate of the woman was seen, and her statement of age thus corroborated. Underhill[4] delivered a woman in her forty-ninth year who had not menstruated for two years. Lavasseur[5] records the case of a woman, aged fifty, who had ceased to menstruate for two years, and who gave birth to a living child at full term. Depasse[6] relates the case of a woman who had ceased menstruating nine years previously, and who had a married daughter forty years old. At the age of fifty-nine years she was delivered of a healthy

[1] *Boston Med. and Surg. Journ.*, 1863
[2] *Przegląd lekarski*, 1889
[3] *Lond. Med. Gaz.*, 1847
[4] *American Journ. of Obstet.*, 1879
[5] *Gaz. Hebdomadaire*, 1873.
[6] *Gaz. de Gynécol*, 1891

child which she suckled, weaning it on her sixtieth birthday  Piiou[1] states that a woman who had ceased menstruating at the age of forty-eight years, recommenced twenty four years after and menstruated regularly at monthly intervals for six periods, and then ceased, two months afterwards she gave birth to a two months' fœtus. The woman was seventy-two years old when this took place!

The form of impotence in men due to psychical causes has its complementary condition in women  In men the state is negative—one of pure passivity  in women the impediment is of an active character. It arises from a highly emotional type of hysteria which is associated with vaginismus  A woman in this condition is incompetent for the sexual act, the slightest approach evokes a paroxysm of dread, and of consequent resistance which defies all efforts  Anæsthetics have been used to enable intercourse to be effected, sometimes with permanent success  In other cases the irritability of the vaginal orifice is so intense that the least contact throws the sphincter vaginæ into such powerful contraction as to prevent the introduction even of the finger. In such cases the condition may be more local and physical than general and psychical, and is consequently amenable to surgical treatment.

As intercourse may be accomplished if the woman is entirely passive, it follows that general disease—paralysis and the like—does not produce impotence in the female, as it does in the male sex  Extreme bodily deformity is not necessarily a barrier to intercourse, as women with limbs ankylosed in positions that apparently would forbid all approaches have borne children

The local abnormalities previously mentioned may or may not prevent intercourse. Absence of external genitals, excessive narrowing or absence of the vagina, the presence of a very firm hymen with small aperture, or quite imperforate, adhesion of the labia, tumours filling the vagina, large incarcerated hernias, and other analogous conditions will impede or entirely prevent coitus in accordance with their character and degree  Absence of uterus and ovaries, the external organs being complete, will not prevent intercourse, though it will obviously prevent conception  A not infrequent cause of sterility is the so-called chronic uterine catarrh, in this condition the mucous membrane of the uterus is spongy, and secretes an abnormal amount of clear mucus which may be blood-stained  Some vaginal discharges by their marked acid reaction render impregnation difficult, spermatozoa are rapidly killed in fluids having a very acid reaction, and also in those which have a very alkaline reaction.

[1] *Bulletin de la Société de Méd d'Angers*, 1865.

## CHAPTER XII

## RAPE AND UNNATURAL OFFENCES.

Rape may be defined as carnal knowledge of an individual by one of the opposite sex without consent; in practice it is understood to refer to carnal knowledge by a male of a female of adult age against her will, or of a girl under a certain age with or without her consent. As the law at present stands:—

> "Any person who unlawfully and carnally knows any girl under the age of thirteen years shall be guilty of felony. Any person who attempts to have unlawful carnal knowledge of any girl under the age of thirteen years shall be guilty of a misdemeanour. Any person who unlawfully and carnally knows or attempts to have unlawful carnal knowledge of any girl being of or above the age of thirteen years and under the age of sixteen years, or unlawfully and carnally knows, or attempts to have unlawful carnal knowledge of any female idiot or imbecile woman or girl, under circumstances which do not amount to rape, but which prove that the offender knew at the time of the commission of the offence that the woman or girl was an idiot or imbecile, shall be guilty of a misdemeanour. Provided that it shall be sufficient defence to any charge under subsection one of this section" [referring to the age of the girl being above thirteen and under sixteen] "if it shall be made to appear to the Court or jury before whom the charge shall be brought that the person so charged had reasonable cause to believe that the girl was of or above the age of sixteen years. Provided also that no prosecution shall be commenced for an offence under sub-section one of this section" [referring to the ages between thirteen and sixteen] "more than three months after the commission of the offence."—Criminal Law Amendment Act, 1885 (48 and 49 Vict., ch. 69).

It is to be noted that the question of age, parenthetically explained, does not refer to idiots nor imbeciles, also that between the ages of thirteen and sixteen an accusation of rape must be made within three months after the alleged offence was committed. Although not stated, it is probable that this time-limit is intended to apply to all ages above thirteen.

A definition of the term "**carnal knowledge**" is necessary for a full comprehension of the above quotation from the Act. By carnal knowledge the law includes any degree of sexual intercourse from mere introduction of the penis within the vulva, with or without emission, to complete penetration with emission. If this is done to an adult woman without her consent and against her will, or to a child under any circumstances, it constitutes rape. Formerly both penetration into the vagina and emission were required, and subsequently (24 and 25 Vict., ch. 100) penetration only, with or without emission, was deemed sufficient to constitute the crime. It has been decided by the Courts that introduction of the penis within the vulva, without causing any injury to the hymen, constitutes rape under the conditions above stated. The relation between age and volition is to be noted.—If a girl of or above the age of sixteen years consents to the act, rape is not committed. If a girl of or above the age of thirteen and under the age of sixteen consents or not, the act on the part of the man is nevertheless criminal, and he is liable to imprisonment for misdemeanour, with or without hard labour, for a term not exceeding two years. If a girl under the age of thirteen years consents or not, the aggressor is guilty of felony if he effects his purpose, and of a misdemeanour if he attempts only. In the former case the allotted punishment ranges, at the discretion of the Court, from imprisonment for a term not exceeding two years to penal servitude for life; in the latter case the imprisonment must not exceed two years. Therefore, below the age of sixteen years, consent or even solicitation on the part of the girl does not do away with the criminality of the act. The same statement applies to women who are idiots or imbeciles; consent on their part does not absolve the accused—he is guilty of a misdemeanour. The restrictions of the law apply to prostitutes as well as to women of chaste life: if a man has forcible intercourse with a prostitute against her will, he is guilty of rape, and is liable to be punished accordingly.

If a man, by personating the husband, has intercourse with a married woman with her free consent, he is guilty of rape (48 and 49 Vict., c. 69). Formerly this question was left to the judgment of the court in each case, the consequence being that some judges pronounced the act to be rape, others held that the consent, although obtained by fraud, did away with the criminality of the act. To obviate this want of uniformity the law definitely decides the question as above.

Cases have occurred from time to time that have given rise to the question—Can rape be committed on a woman without her knowledge during sleep? According to the present interpretation of the law, an affirmative answer must be given. The mere introduction of the penis within the vulva would not necessarily cause pain enough to awake a sound sleeper; the act, however, would constitute rape according to the definition of the crime above given. The question was originally propounded when penetration was necessary to establish rape, and at the present time it usually arises in respect to cases in which intromission is alleged to have taken place, when this is the case a qualified answer is required. It would be quite possible for a woman accustomed to sexual intercourse to be violated with complete intromission during sleep. Instances have occurred in which this has taken place, one such is reported in the *Edinburgh Monthly Journal*, 1862. Guy[1] mentions the case of a married woman who slept so heavily that her husband frequently had connection with her during sleep. The conditions are quite different, however, when the victim is alleged to have been a virgin up to the time the violence was used. It may be confidently stated that an adult man of average sexual development could not fully penetrate a woman who was a virgin, without her knowledge, during natural sleep. Cases in which it is alleged that this has taken place, are *ipso facto* to be treated with grave suspicion, if not with absolute incredulity.

In abnormal states of sleep, or stupor, as for example *post epileptic coma*, it is not impossible that a virgin might be ravished without being conscious of the violence at the time. It is to be expected, however, that on recovery of consciousness she would experience soreness in the private parts, and most probably would find that her underclothing was stained with blood. In Casper Liman's *Handbuch* a case is narrated of a girl who was subject to epileptic seizures which always left her unconscious for some hours after. A man who was acquainted with this fact on one such occasion took advantage of it, and had intercourse with her without her cognisance. The probability of the occurrence of violation under these conditions would greatly depend on reliable evidence being obtained that the alleged victim was subject to epilepsy followed by stupor.

**Hysteria** or **catalepsy**, as causes of unconsciousness, or of a condition of subjugation to the will of the person accused, are to be received with much caution. It is to be admitted that a girl, or a woman, of a certain neurotic type may for a time be deprived of volition by so-called hypnotism, and whilst in such a condition might be violated without offering effective resistance, or even any resistance whatever. All such accounts, however, are very suspicious, and are—without convincing evidence to the contrary—to be regarded as plausible excuses for non-resistance rather than genuine statements. In giving an opinion respecting such a case, the possibility of the occurrence of hypnotic sleep, or of mental and bodily subjugation induced by suggestion, is to be admitted hypothetically, but great reserve should be maintained in accepting any such condition as accounting for the absence of resistance or of outcry, whilst the act was being perpetrated.

[1] *Forensic Medicine.*

Extreme terror may undoubtedly deprive a girl or woman for the moment of the power of offering effective resistance to her violator; volition and physical energy may be temporarily paralysed by the outrageously violent demeanour of an assailant, so that he may accomplish his purpose without any opposition. It is not necessary that the threatened general violence should be directed to the intended victim. In one case recorded by Maschka,[1] the ravisher seized the infant of the woman he desired to violate, and threatened to dash its brains out unless she submitted; the terror thus induced by the appeal to her maternal instincts made the woman submit. In this case, although no physical force was resorted to, the woman was effectively constrained by moral coercion. The law makes no distinction between moral and physical coercion, intercourse against the victim's will, effected after passivity produced by a blow on the head or by threats, is equally criminal. It must be quite clear, however, that the alleged mental and physical paralysis through fright was actually experienced by the woman, and not feigned as an excuse for offering no opposition. If a woman in the act of illicit intercourse only begins to cry out and struggle when she becomes conscious of the approach of a third person, and states that the reason she did not do so before was because she was paralysed by fear, the probability is that she was a consenting party, and that her outcry was prompted by the desire to save her character when detection seemed inevitable. Amos[2] relates a droll case, in which a man was charged with violating a girl who gave as the excuse for not screaming, that she was afraid of wakening her mother, who slept in the next room.

Narcotics or anæsthetics are occasionally used, and probably much more frequently alleged to have been used, with the object of rendering a woman unconscious and thus placing her at the mercy of her would-be ravisher. The substances usually resorted to for this purpose are—*alcoholic beverages, chloroform,* and *opium,* or some of its preparations. It is probably much more common than is publicly known for women to be intentionally intoxicated with wine or spirits, which may be drugged with opium or not, in order to deprive them of consciousness and power of resistance, with the object of facilitating violation. A woman profoundly intoxicated would be quite incapable of effective resistance, even if she retained sufficient perception as to be aware of what was taking place. In forming an opinion respecting a case of this kind, the difficulty is to determine whether the woman was as much under the influence of the intoxicant as she professes to have been. A woman who voluntarily drinks an alcoholic beverage until discretion is

[1] *Handbuch,* Bd 3      [2] *Lond. Med. Gaz.,* 1831

vanquished by desire, and then yields to the embraces of her male companion, on return to her ordinary state of mind may regret her fall to such an extent as to attempt to visit him with the entire culpability of the act, and so exonerate herself—at least in the eyes of the world—from all fault. In such a case the points for consideration are:—The previous character of the woman, her age (a young woman would be more likely to adopt this course than one of middle age), the kind and amount of intoxicant, together with accidental evidence, such as a too clear and detailed account of the transaction being given by the prosecutrix to be consistent with a progressively increasing loss of consciousness. For the reason last named, the time that the man and woman spent together if ascertainable might be suspiciously short for an intoxicant of the kind partaken of to produce profound unconsciousness.

With regard to the administration of chloroform vapour for the purpose of rendering a woman incapable of resistance, it is to be observed that there are probably only two ways in which this could be done. The first is when a woman *voluntarily inhales* the vapour (which for this purpose includes all anæsthetics capable of being thus administered) for a proper object—as the extraction of a tooth—and when under the influence of the anæsthetic is violated by the administrator. The other way is when the vapour is administered to a woman who is *asleep*. A case of the first kind is quoted at length by Wharton and Stillé.[1] A young lady went to a dentist to have a tooth filled, the operation being painful, ether was administered, and, according to the deposition of the prosecutrix, violation was effected whilst she was under its influence. The peculiarity of the case consists in the statement made by the prosecutrix that though unable to resist she was conscious of what occurred to the minutest detail, and moreover could see the disordered state of her clothes when she opened her eyes after the offence had been committed, the dentist having for a moment retired to another part of the room. The young lady discreetly closed her eyes before the dentist returned and allowed him to readjust her clothing; a few minutes after she was sufficiently conscious as to discuss the advisability of having the offending tooth extracted; on being informed that it was too far decayed to be filled, more ether was given, and the extraction performed. When the effects of the anæsthetic had passed off, she left the house without reproaching the dentist, and did not mention the occurrence until some hours after. To complete the story, the dentist was sentenced to four and a-half (?) years' imprisonment, but was subsequently released on representation being made to the authorities that it was quite possible that the whole

[1] *Medical Jurisprudence.*

affair was an hallucination. On reading the detailed account, it is difficult to determine the exact degree of admiration relatively due to the presence of mind displayed by the young lady on the one hand, and the nicely adjusted sentence of the court on the other. This case has been narrated with the object of emphasising a rule that has been many times urged—that a medical man, or dentist, should never administer an anæsthetic to a female patient without the presence of a third person. This should be one of those rules that has no exception. It is well known that a partial degree of unconsciousness produced by an anæsthetic is not unfrequently attended by delusions, and in the case of females such delusions occasionally take an erotic type. The vividness of the subjective impression is so great that the person on whom the impression is made thoroughly believes in its objectivity. On an occasion, which it is to be hoped will be unique, such an impression was apparently transferred to a second person. A married lady, to whom a dentist administered chloroform, afterwards accused him of violating her whilst under the influence of the anæsthetic, and her husband, who was present during the whole time she was unconscious, testified that his wife was under the strongest impression that she had been violated. The jury found the dentist guilty of an attempt to commit a rape, with a recommendation to mercy.[1]

The administration of chloroform to sleeping persons in order to prepare them for surgical operations has been tried on many occasions; in some instances the individual passes into the condition of chloroform narcosis without awakening from natural sleep, in others, in spite of very gradual administration, the vapour produces such irritation of the glottis that the subject of the experiment awakes. Dolbeau[2] records some experiments made by him in relation to a case in which it was alleged that a girl had been chloroformed during sleep and afterwards violated. Out of twenty-nine attempts to bring sleeping persons under the influence of chloroform, he succeeded in ten and failed in nineteen.

There is no doubt that a woman once under the influence of an anæsthetic is at the mercy of any one who chooses to take advantage of her helpless condition. The two ways in which a woman might be thus rendered insensible—by voluntary inhalation and by surprising her whilst asleep—probably comprise all the cases in which violation has been effected with the aid of anæsthetics administered in the form of vapour or gas. Those cases of alleged chloroform narcosis effected by waving a pocket handkerchief impregnated with an odorous substance before the face, the proceeding being followed by

[1] *Boston Med. and Surg. Journ.*, 1858.
[2] *Annales d'Hygiène*, 1874.

sudden insensibility, are from the nature of things untrue. It is a matter of common experience that the chloroformist at a surgical operation frequently requires the aid of an assistant during the earlier stages of the administration, to restrain the struggles of a patient who submits voluntarily. Except in the case of a weakly person, it would be no easy matter to administer chloroform single handed to a woman against her will; the difficulty would probably be quite as great as to commit the rape without the aid of the anæsthetic. A practitioner who is called upon to examine the prosecutrix in such a case should carefully examine the face, neck, shoulders, and wrists for finger-marks or bruises, which would be very likely to be produced (in a genuine case) in overcoming the attempts made by the victim to evade the anæsthetic.

The use of other narcotics to facilitate violation is not common, but the drugging of alcoholic beverages with *opium* or *morphine* has been recorded. The following case of alleged administration of *chloral hydrate* came under my cognisance two years after the trial. A married man, in consequence of the absence of his wife who was a monthly nurse, was left in his house one night with a servant girl, fourteen years of age. The girl's statement of what happened was that in the evening she complained of toothache and her master dropped something that tasted like peppermint out of a bottle on to a little cotton-wool, and applied it to the tooth; she then went to bed and immediately fell fast asleep. At daybreak she awoke and found her master in bed with her, but he at once got up and left the room. She discovered that she was bleeding from her private parts, which felt painful; she went to sleep again, awoke at the usual time in the morning, got up and did a hard day's work at washing clothes. Although her mistress returned in the morning she made no complaint until evening, when she told her sister the above story. No medical examination was made for five days after the alleged violence had been perpetrated. The following is copied verbatim from the deposition before the magistrates of the medical man who examined the girl :—" There had been penetration, and the nymphæ (?) had been destroyed. There was some inflammation of the private parts. She winced on my touching her. There must have been violence. Chloral would taste like peppermint and would produce a deep sleep such as would enable any one to commit an act of this sort without the girl knowing." Unfortunately for the accused no rebutting medical evidence was forthcoming. The trial took place at the Manchester Assizes at a time when the public mind was greatly agitated with regard to criminal assaults on young children, an agitation which led to the passing of the Criminal Law Amendment Act of 1885. In spite of the utter improbability of the girl's tale, and of the self-contradictory nature of the medical evidence, the prisoner was sentenced to ten years penal servitude. Two years after, in consequence of representations from several medical men to the Home Secretary, the convict was released. This case admirably illustrates the value and importance of reliable expert medical evidence, and the necessity for every medical witness to know what he is talking about when he is in the witness-box. Any well-informed medical man would at once have made it clear to the jury that a few drops of a solution of chloral hydrate on cotton wool could not possibly have produced immediate and profound insensibility, lasting for hours, which would enable an adult man to fully penetrate a young girl of fourteen (presumably a virgin) without her knowing. In this way the medical evidence would have served its proper purpose as intended by the law, especially in cases of criminal assault—to corroborate that which is true, and to confute that which is false in the evidence relating to technical subjects given by the prosecutrix.

By Vict. 48 and 49, the administration of any drug, matter, or thing to a girl or woman with intent to stupefy or overpower, so as thereby to enable any person to have unlawful carnal connection with such woman or girl, constitutes a misdemeanour.

It has been doubted whether a man unaided could fully consummate sexual intercourse with a woman against her will, the woman not being disabled by blows or other violence nor by drugs. The fact that a woman by continued movements of her body could effectively prevent intromission, has led some to deny the possibility of an adult female being violated without aid other than the directly applied physical strength of the man. The question is one which depends on the relative physical strength of the two individuals. A strong man would be likely to succeed with an old or weakly woman, or with a child; a puny man, on the other hand, could be held at bay by a vigorous woman without much difficulty. When the respective muscular developments of the man and woman are more nearly balanced, some discrimination is required in giving an opinion. There is one point with respect to this subject that is often lost sight of—the social position and habits, and the temperament of the woman. Women of the lower classes are accustomed to rough play with individuals both of their own and of the opposite sex, and thus acquire the habit of defending themselves against sportive violence. In the majority of cases such a capacity for defence would enable a desperate woman to frustrate the attempts of her intentioned ravisher. A delicately nurtured woman, on the other hand, is so appalled by the unwonted violence that her faculties may be partially benumbed, and her powers of resistance correspondingly enfeebled.

Under exceptional circumstances the woman's movements may be so hampered as to make her an easy victim Casper[1] mentions the case of a strong well-developed woman who was rendered powerless by having her dress thrown over her head, and whilst thus enveloped was violated by a man single-handed

It was formerly a matter of debate as to whether rape could be followed by pregnancy The question needs no discussion, as the impregnation of an ovule is not influenced by volition—it may be accomplished without the participation and against the will of the woman.

Another question has arisen may injuries to the genital organs produced by rape be sufficient to cause death? An affirmative answer is unfortunately afforded by the occurrence from time to time of cases in which death was directly due to mischief inflicted on the immature sexual organs of young girls by brutal attempts to effect intromission of the penis, apart from injuries otherwise inflicted. Colles[2] reports the case of a girl aged eight years who was violated by an adult. She died from peritonitis in six days At the autopsy the perineum was found torn and the vagina gangrenous As a result of the early age at which marriage is consummated in India, death of immature girls has not unfrequently occurred from attempts at marital intercourse.

## THE PHYSICAL SIGNS OF VIRGINITY.

In the young adult virgin the breasts are hemispherical in form, and are firm and elastic to the touch. The nipples are small, and are surrounded by areolæ, which are rose-coloured in blondes and darker in brunettes. Occasionally a slight secretion of a fluid having some of the characteristics of milk may be found in the virgin breasts, this may be due to sexual activity without unchaste habits

The labia majora are more or less rounded at their free edges, are firm and elastic, and approximate each other closely; the labia minora are small and pale in colour The posterior commissure is intact Except in rare cases of defective development, the hymen in one of its varied forms is always present. Its most usual appearance is that of a crescent placed transversely across the entrance of the vagina, with the crescental horns towards the urethra Sometimes the hymen extends all round the orifice of the vagina, and is perforated by a circular or irregularly formed aperture, or by a vertical slit There may be more than one aperture or there may be no aperture at all, constituting the condition known as imperforate hymen. The rigidity

[1] *Handbuch*, Bd. 1.   [2] *Med Times and Gaz*, 1860.

of the hymen varies as well as its form. In some virgins it is patulous and yielding, so that the opening will admit of the introduction of the finger without injury to the hymeneal margin, in others it is firm and unyielding, in which case the passage of any object slightly larger than the opening will tear its free border. The vagina is narrow, especially in the very young, and its walls are more or less rugose. The rugæ, however, may be replaced by a smooth, non-corrugated surface, due to various conditions which arise from the state of the general health.

## PHYSICAL SIGNS OF THE LOSS OF VIRGINITY.

The breasts undergo no alteration by a single coitus, and, in the absence of impregnation, little if any by habitual intercourse. The labia majora et minora only afford corroborative evidence, in the form of an inflammatory condition in recent cases, when much violence has been used. The posterior commissure is not affected by complete and habitual ordinary intercourse, except in the very young, and in adults when unwonted violence has been resorted to. The hymen yields the most reliable evidence of loss of virginity, the appearance presented varying with the interval that has elapsed between defloration and the period of examination; it also varies with the age of the individual, the original character of the membrane as to size of aperture and degree of rigidity, the dimensions of the male organ which inflicted the injuries, and the amount of violence brought to bear at the time they were inflicted. Recent injuries appear as sharped-edged tears or slits which may traverse the entire hymen, and may be continued through the mucous membrane of the vulva and vagina. In the ordinary crescentic hymen there is usually one slit in a backward direction towards the commissure; there may be others. In exceptional cases a new aperture is made, usually below the normal opening, leaving a strip of membrane stretching across the mouth of the vagina. From the torn hymen there is usually some hæmorrhage, which is occasionally excessive, in any case if the examination is conducted soon after the infliction of the injuries, blood-clots or stains will be found on the parts. There will also be an inflammatory condition of the ostium vaginæ and adjacent structures, rendering them painful to the touch, a little later, especially in young children, the inflammatory processes will cause a muco-purulent discharge of a yellow or greenish-yellow colour. This discharge is not to be mistaken for the result of gonorrhœal infection which it closely resembles, nor yet for a previously existing leucorrhœa, the distinction is by no means easy, and many false accusations have been made solely on the strength of a discharge which, though due to pathological causes, has been attributed to criminal violence. The discharge which is due to inflammation caused by mechanical irritation, is usually not so copious as that resulting from gonorrhœal infection; from leucorrhœal discharge it is distinguished by indications of an acute inflammatory condition of the mucous membrane which secretes it. Threadworms may cause a discharge from the vagina. Spitzer[1] relates the case of a girl of fourteen who was suspected to have been violated; she had a profuse discharge from the vagina, and on syringing the passage out, threadworms came away, showing the true nature of the case. The presence or the absence of gonococci have been regarded as respectively indicative of the specific or the innocent character of the discharge. Lober[2] obtained cultivations of gonococci from stains on the clothing in a case of rape. Kratter[3] found gonococci in the vaginal discharge in one out of two cases of rape in which he searched for them, and he attaches much importance to bacteriological investigations in such cases. Vibert and Bordas[4] believe that the distinction between gonorrhœa and leucorrhœa cannot be determined with absolute certainty by bacteriological examinations even of the most complete kind, and, therefore, that an expert is not justified in affirming the nature of a discharge on this ground; these views were accepted by the Société de Médecine Légale de France before which body the statements were made. In the present state of bacteriology we are not in a position to say that the presence or absence of gonococci would justify a statement on oath either for or against specific infection. The rugose condition of the virginal vaginal mucous membrane is not changed by isolated acts of intercourse, and it may be absent in virgins.

If an interval of four or five days intervenes between defloration and the period of examination, the appearance of the parts will differ from that above described, especially if the violence has not been excessive. At this period there will be no blood-clots found, and all inflammatory appearance may have disappeared. The sharp edges of the rents in the hymen will be rounded off and the raw surface probably healed. The result is the formation of *carunculæ myrtiformes* which consist of irregularly rounded nodules formed by the remains of the hymen. If recent, the carunculæ are swollen, tender, and of a deep red colour; if more remotely formed, they are firmer, harder, and lighter in colour. It is to be observed that, unless the male organ is disproportionately large, a single intercourse does not result in the formation of a number

---

[1] *Wiener med. Wochenschr*, 1892.
[2] *Bulletin medical du Nord de la France*, 1887.
[3] *Vierteljahrsschr. f. ger. Med. Supplement*, 1891.
[4] *Annales d'Hygiène*, 1891.

of nodules representing the pre-existence of correspondingly numerous rents in the hymen; if all the damage sustained by the hymen consists in a single tear, the subsequent appearance will not correspond with what is usually understood by the term carunculæ myrtiformes; complete transformation of the hymen into carunculæ is, as a rule, only accomplished by repeated acts of intercourse. Tears in the hymen never unite again, the injury to the membrane is permanent.

The Physical Signs of Virginity or of Non-Virginity in relation to Rape.—For the following reasons the signs of loss of virginity do not in themselves constitute proof of rape, nor do the signs of the presence of virginity disprove its occurrence:—

Absence of the physical signs of virginity may be due to lawful marital intercourse, to illicit but voluntary intercourse, to accidental rupture of the hymen, and, in very rare cases, to congenital absence or imperfect development of the hymen.

The physical signs of virginity may persist in a female on whom a rape has been perpetrated:—from the presence of a patulous hymen with large aperture, especially if the penis of the assailant was of small size; from extreme youth of the victim, the sexual organs being too small to permit of vaginal penetration (excluding tearing of the parts asunder); and lastly, it is to be borne in mind that mere vulval penetration without the infliction of any injury is sufficient to constitute rape.

The hymen may be ruptured by an adequate force of any kind, apart from sexual intercourse. It is reported to have given way from the presence of blood-clots during menstruation, from ulceration following diphtheria or other diseases, from jumping, riding on horseback, or falls on a hard projection. Masturbation has been stated, but probably without sufficient grounds, to be a cause of rupture of the hymen; in the majority of cases of habitual masturbation the hymen will be found intact, the manipulations being limited to the parts anterior to it. Medical examinations or applications may cause injury to the hymen. Some of these reasons for the absence of, or injury to, the hymen are quite feasible, others are far-fetched; each case has to be judged on its own merits.

Complete intromission of the penis may take place without injury to the hymen. The conditions necessary are those previously mentioned, a patulous or elastic hymen, and a not too voluminous penis. Repeated acts of intercourse may take place with no other results than slightly enlarging the aperture through or above the hymen. No inference can be drawn from the presence of a large aperture, the margins of the membrane being intact, as it may be the natural condition of the part. Distinction must be made between complete intercourse through a patulous hymen, and that form of intercourse which results in impregnation through a small aperture in a tough hymen, which, though a fruitful intercourse, is an imperfect one. Exceptionally, the hymen is both tough and elastic; Maschka mentions the case of a prostitute in whom an uninjured hymen of this kind was present, although complete intercourse had repeatedly taken place.

Rape, including emission, may be perpetrated on **very young children** without injuring the hymen in the least. The external genitals are too small to admit the adult male organ, and the hymen is deeply seated, so that unless sufficient violence is used as to tear open the parts, the assault may be accomplished without leaving more than superficial traces of its commission. A degree of violence may be used on a young child that stops short of lacerating the parts, and is yet sufficiently great as to cause subsequent sloughing of the external genitals. Pathological sloughing of the vulva from noma, or from diphtheria, enterica, variola, &c., must be borne in mind in relation to cases of this kind. Anomalous injuries are occasionally produced by sexual violence to young girls. Dorffmeister[1] relates the case of a girl, aged eight years and three quarters, in whom complete prolapse of the mucous membrane of the urethra was caused by coitus with a boy fourteen and a-half years old.

In married women there may be absence of the signs of rape, so far as the genital organs are concerned, from conditions the converse of those which obtain in young children. In a woman habituated to sexual intercourse the parts do not sustain injury from a subsequent coitus, even, as a rule, when the act is accomplished with violence. The indications of criminal assault in married women are to be sought for in the presence of spermatozoa in the vagina, and more particularly of the marks of bruising on various parts of the body.

The circumstances under which the crime is usually committed are such as to render it easy for a designing person to make a charge of rape, and difficult for the accused to rebut the accusation. The crime is one so thoroughly and so universally detested that the victim, or supposed victim, obtains immediate sympathy. It is unfortunately a fact that accusations of rape are very frequently groundless, and in such cases the accused and innocent person suffers from this proneness on the part of the public to accept without question the statements of the prosecutrix. False accusations are not only made by women, and by girls of responsible age, but cases occur from time to time in which mere children are instructed by their mothers to accuse an individual selected for some special reason — extortion of money, or for the sake of revenge — and are not only taught what tale to tell, but are

[1] *Friedreich's Blätter f. ger. Med.*, 1887.

manipulated in such a way as to produce physical indications resembling those caused by criminal assaults, so as to bear out their statements. Fournier[1] relates the case of a girl, aged eight years, who was said to be the victim of a criminal assault, the person accused being under arrest. Examination of the child showed the presence of violent inflammation of the vulva with erosions of the labia, all the parts being bathed with green pus, the hymen was intact. Several of the glands in the groins were enlarged. After some difficulty it was eventually found out that the mother of the child had produced the injuries by friction with a blacking-brush, an appropriate accusation having been put into the child's mouth to account for them. In cases of this class it is astonishing with what consistency and pertinacity the child repeats her tale, the threats of severe punishment held out by the mother if she betrays the secret exercise a profound influence in keeping her to the point. If hard pressed the child will burst into tears and nothing more can be got out of her for the time. In the case just narrated it was only by bribing the child with the promise of a doll that the truth came out, the mother on being confronted with the child's final statement confessed the imposture.

When a rape is committed, as a rule no one is present except the victim and her ravisher, the administrators of the law therefore seek for corroborative evidence in addition to the direct evidence of the prosecutrix. The most important corroborative evidence is afforded by medical examination of the prosecutrix, the value of such evidence varies considerably. An early examination of the person of a girl who was intact up to the time the assault was committed, yields much more information than one made several days after the commission of the offence on a woman habituated to sexual intercourse. Seeing that vulval penetration (which does not necessarily leave any trace behind) without emission is sufficient to constitute rape, it might be supposed that medical inspection would be futile; in the great majority of cases, however, more than simple contact between the penis and the parts anterior of the hymen takes place, and, consequently, traces of violence are discoverable. Although emission is not necessary to constitute rape, it usually occurs, and traces of the deed are thus left behind. Again, most valuable information is afforded by the discovery of bruises on the body generally, caused by the efforts of the ravisher to overcome the resistance of his victim. Stains of blood or of semen on the clothing are also of importance. Lastly, the presence of gonorrhœa or of syphilis may form a link in the chain of evidence.

[1] *Bull. Acad. de Méd.*, 1880.

## MEDICAL EXAMINATION IN CASES OF SUSPECTED RAPE.

The first duty of the medical practitioner who is required to examine a woman in relation to all matters involving inspection of the sexual organs, is to obtain her free consent. The law holds a woman's person to be inviolable—*an examination made without consent constitutes an indecent assault*. No authority can overrule this privilege; consequently, a medical practitioner who errs with regard to it *cannot shield himself behind an order* received from a magistrate, police authority, or any other person; no one has a right to order an examination of a woman's person against her will, and, therefore, any medical practitioner who carries out such an order without obtaining consent is guilty of an indecent assault, and is liable to be punished accordingly. A civil action for damages will also lie, as many medical men have discovered to their cost. If a magistrate or other authority orders a medical practitioner to examine a woman without consent, and the order is carried out, both parties are liable to prosecution. This question is here emphasised, because medical practitioners on the whole are ignorant of the risks they run with regard to the examination of women. It is to be observed that passive submission does not constitute free consent; a woman who simply submits and utters no protest, may afterwards deny having consented. The proper way is to make the woman understand the nature of the required examination, and then to ask if she consents to its being made, and on no account to persuade or urge her to submit—her consent must be given of her own free will. When dealing with persons with whom the medical man is unacquainted, and in all medico-legal cases, a respectable witness should hear the consent given. If the prosecutrix in a case of rape will not consent to an examination, the medical practitioner must inform the authority of the fact from whom he received the order.

An examination of the genitals of a female in a case of alleged rape must be very complete. It is to be remembered that the evidence to be given consists not only in a statement of what was obvious, but questions may be asked in relation to what might and ought to have been observed. To enable a thorough examination to be made, the female must be placed in such a position that the thighs may be widely separated; slight injuries to the hymen are rarely sufficiently evident without the membrane being put on the stretch by freely separating the labia, the lithotomy position is the best for this purpose. In young children especially, the hymen is deeply situated, and cannot be inspected unless the anterior parts are well stretched open. In recent cases, the parts are so tender that the necessary separation causes much pain, and evokes spastic rigidity of the adjacent muscles, which may seriously embarrass the proceeding; in children this is almost always the case. To wait until the tenderness has subsided is to lose the opportunity of seeing the injured parts in the condition in which they yield the most exact information. A good plan is to apply freely a 20 per cent solution of cocaine hydrochlorate five or ten minutes before making the examination, one or two applications, at intervals of three or four minutes, will produce a degree of local anæsthesia which will make an examination possible. If the parts are much lacerated, the cocaine must not be applied too long nor too freely lest toxic effects be produced — *raw surfaces are very absorbent.*

In cases of recent injury to the hymen the conditions previously described will be found. The presence of carunculæ myrtiformes in a woman recently violated indicates previous acts of intercourse. All injuries must be carefully noted, and their extent fully determined — as, for example, rupture of the perineum in children, and occasionally in adult virgins to whom excessive violence has been used. The probable amount of blood effused should be estimated from the condition of the underclothing. Specimens of the contents of the vagina should be removed with a glass rod and examined with the microscope for spermatozoa. The surface of the entire body, but especially the thighs, wrists, and neck, should be examined for bruises, scratches, and other marks of violence. Tears, stains produced by mud, paint, or other substances should be sought for on the outer clothing, and, if present, their position noted. The underclothing should be carefully inspected for stains of blood and semen; if the linen is moderately clean, stains produced by semen appear as patches without distinct colour, but of a slightly different tint to the rest of the fabric, which is stiffened at the part stained; a drop of weak gum-water would produce to the naked eye a very similar appearance. After noting their position on the garment all suspicious looking spots should be carefully cut out and preserved for future investigation; friction or other mechanical disturbance of the stained portion is to be avoided. Amongst the lower orders the underclothing is often exceedingly filthy, being stained with fæcal matter, urine, and possibly menstrual blood, in addition to the foulness due to prolonged wear; when this is the case the recognition of seminal stains is difficult. Stains resembling blood-stains should also be cut out for identification. Information should be obtained as to present or recent menstruation. The presence or absence of venereal disease is to be noted.

The examination of the **dead body** of a female on whom a rape is suspected to have been committed is conducted on similar lines to those followed in the case of the living. The medical witness must be prepared for cross-examination as to the possibility of the appearance indicating bruises being due to post-mortem stains, also as to whether the injuries produced by the rape were sufficient to cause death, whether certain injuries, or wounds, were inflicted before or after death, as well as the means probably used to inflict them. If first examined on the spot where it was found, attention must be paid to the position of the body as a whole, to that of the limbs and of the clothing. The surroundings must be investigated for indications of a struggle, especially if the body was found out of doors, foot marks scrutinised, and, if necessary, casts of them taken in the manner described on p. 63. Any peculiarities of the soil—as sandy, clayey, and the like—are to be noted, and if of a markedly characteristic appearance, a specimen should be preserved for comparison with the soil possibly present on the boots of an accused person. The state of the weather at the time the crime was committed is also to be ascertained as affording a possible clue in case of the arrest of a suspected person. The subsequent examination of the body should be of such completeness as to enable the witness to testify to the presence or absence of fractures of the bones (especially of those of the skull), the condition of the internal organs, and of the natural apertures of the body as regards the presence in them of foreign bodies.

If the accused is in custody a medical examination will probably be required of his person and clothing. That which has already been said as to the necessity for consent on the part of a woman for an examination of this kind, applies with equal relevance to a man. No one has the legal right to make an examination of the generative organs of a man against his will, nor to order such an examination to be made.

Except when venereal disease has been communicated to the violated female, and the discovery of a similar disease on the accused would constitute a link in the chain of evidence, examination of the male, as a rule, yields little information. If spermatozoa are found in the urethra, or on the shirt, their presence may be accounted for by the avowal of recent intercourse with another woman than the one violated, or of an emission without intercourse. If, as is most likely, no spermatozoa are found in the urethra, recent emission would not be disproved, since the act of urination would wash all traces away. The points to notice on the male are—the presence of spermatozoa on the person or clothing, of blood-stains (in a case of recent rape on a virgin, traces of blood should be specially sought for under the prepuce, and about the frænum), the condition of the outer clothing as to tears and stains of various kinds, the boots with any adherent soil or mud, recent scratches on the face or other parts of the body, the presence of long hairs on the coat or trousers (if found they should be preserved for comparison with the hair of the victim), together with a careful observation of the general build of the man, so as to enable an estimate to be made of his physical strength—whether he appears strong enough to have overcome a woman such as the prosecutrix.

## EXAMINATION OF SEMINAL STAINS.

If a drop of mucus is taken from the vagina in order to ascertain whether spermatozoa are present or not, all that is necessary is to place the mucus on a slide, to cover it with a thin cover glass and examine with a power of 300 to 400 diameters. If semen has been deposited on a fabric and has dried, the spermatozoa require softening and liberating from the surface to which they are attached by the inspissated albumen of the fluid. If pure water is used the spermatozoa tend to swell out to such an extent as to cause them to disintegrate, the heads separating from the filaments. To justify a statement on oath that a given specimen contains spermatozoa it is essential that one or more should be seen in a complete form, for although the appearance presented by the heads and the filaments apart is very suggestive, it does not constitute positive evidence, it is essential, therefore, that precautions should be taken to minimise the risk of separation of head and filament. The first precaution is to avoid handling the fabric more than necessary, and to keep the stained portions flat, without creasing them; the next is to use a fluid for softening that will not cause the spermatozoa to swell too much. Ungar[1] recommends for this purpose a very dilute solution of hydrochloric acid in distilled water—one drop to 40 cubic centimetres, a few drops of the acidulated water is placed in a watch-glass with a small strip of the stained fabric so that its lower end dips into the fluid. The time requisite for softening varies from a few minutes to several hours in accordance with the age of the stain. It is well thoroughly to soften the albumen before attempting to detach the spermatozoa or else they will be broken. If only the lower end of the strip of cloth dips into the acidulated water, there is little risk of the spermatozoa being detached prematurely, therefore it is better to allow too much rather than too little time. Old stains require four or five hours. When the softening is complete, the fragment of fabric is removed with a pair of dressing forceps and gently dabbed on a microscope slide. The deposit thus obtained

[1] *Vierteljahrsschr. f. ger. Med.*, 1886.

is covered with a thin glass cover and examined as previously directed. As the spermatozoa are very translucent objects, it has been proposed to stain them with the view of making them more visible; either the dry or the moist process may be adopted. Ungar recommends a double stain for the dry process, which may be thus used:—After the strip of fabric has undergone the requisite softening in the acidulated water, it is withdrawn with the forceps, allowed to drain a little, and then dabbed on a thin glass cover so as to leave a deposit, which is allowed to dry at the temperature of the surrounding air. When dry the cover is taken up with the forceps and rapidly passed—deposit side upwards—over a Bunsen flame so as to thoroughly harden the deposit. When cold, the cover-glass is floated—deposit side downwards—on a solution of eosine in a watch-glass, the solution is composed of eosine 2.5 c.grm., alcohol 30 cc., and distilled water 70 cc. The watch glass with its contents should be protected so as to retard evaporation, and allowed to remain one hour, after which the cover-glass is removed, drained, exposed until dry, and then lightly washed with one part alcohol to two parts water. The next step is to place the cover-glass in a solution of logwood (Friedlander's) for a period varying from a few minutes to an hour or more, the time depending upon the action of the stain, which is variable. The preparation is then washed and examined in the usual way. The results obtained are—that the back part of the head is stained dark blue, and the front part, with the middle piece and filament, an intense red. A simpler and more practicable method is to combine the softening and staining solutions in one. A solution of methyl green 1.5 to 3 in 100 parts of water, to which from 3 to 6 drops of hydrochloric acid are added, in accordance with the amount of colouring material used, will serve this purpose. The strip of fabric with the seminal stain is allowed to dip into a few drops of this dye in a watch-glass and to remain for several hours. It is then removed with the forceps and dabbed on a slide, the deposit may be examined at once in the moist state.

A human **spermatozoon** consists of a head, to which is attached a short rod-like piece continued by a long slender filament, the whole measuring 0.05 mm. in length. The head is egg-shaped when viewed in one direction, and more pointed—like the outline of the flame of a candle—when viewed sideways. The whole spermatozoon is composed of transparent protoplasm with a delicate fibrillous outline. With the amplifying power used for the purpose of identification—300 to 400 diameters—no trace of structure is visible. Spermatozoa retain their activity within the sexual organs of women for many hours, they have been found active in the vagina seven to eight days after emission. They preserve their form after cessation of activity for almost an indefinite time, and may be recognised by the methods above described in a seminal stain several years old.

The parts of the female underclothing on which a seminal stain is most likely to be found after violation are the front and back of the chemise in the neighbourhood of the genital organs. It is to be noted that a stain may be due to seminal fluid and yet no spermatozoa may be present; spermatozoa are sometimes absent in the semen of an individual at one time and present at another. Very exceptionally certain tricomonads, known as *tricomonas vaginæ*, have been found in the vaginal mucus, and the fact of their existence has been utilised to weaken evidence given as to the presence of spermatozoa in cases of alleged rape. A glance at the representations of spermatozoa and these tricomonads (Figs. 13 and 14) is sufficient to show the difference between the two, which is so great that one could not possibly be mistaken for the other by any competent observer. The head of the tricomonad is circular in outline, it is very much larger than the head of a spermatozoon, it is granular in place of being structureless, and the filament or tail is proportionally very much shorter. The form of a spermatozoon is so characteristic that if one only is found intact—that is, head and filament continuous, the one with the other—the stain from which it was derived may be pronounced without hesitation to be due to seminal fluid.

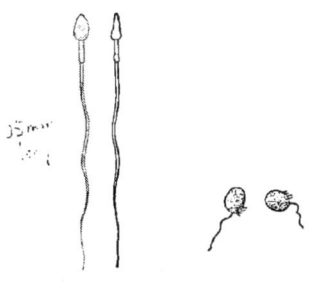

Fig. 13.—Human Spermatozoa.

Fig. 14.—Tricomonas Vaginæ.

**Blood-stains** on the underclothing of females alleged to have been violated are to be examined after the methods described on p. 64. When blood-stains are present, the blood may not have entirely permeated the fabric on which it was deposited; should this be the case, note whether the stain is on the *inner* or the *outer* surface of the fabric in relation to the body of the wearer. Bayard[1] records a case in which the falsity of a charge of rape was demonstrated by the blood-stains having been smeared on the outer surface of the child's linen, thus proving that the blood was not derived from the genital organs of the alleged victim. Maschka[2] mentions a case of a similar nature, in which he found the stains to have been produced by the blood of a bird, the imposture being subsequently confessed. Romberg[3] mentions an extraordinary blunder made by a medical man, who stated

[1] *Annales d'Hygiène*, 1847.   [2] *Handbuch*, Bd. 3.
[3] Casper-Liman, Bd. 1.

that certain stains on a little girl's chemise were respectively caused by blood and semen, although they really resulted from the child having eaten a plum tart in bed—the supposed blood-stains being due to plum juice, and the seminal stains to fatty matter derived from the pastry!

## UNNATURAL SEXUAL OFFENCES

Under this head are comprised *Sodomy*, *Pederastia*, and *Bestiality*.

**Sodomy** means unnatural sexual intercourse between two human beings usually of the male sex. The converse form Tribadism—gratification of the sexual instinct between two human beings of the female sex—is not publicly known in this country, at least so far as the law courts are concerned. **Pederastia** is that form of sodomy in which the passive rôle is played by a boy, the active agent being man or boy. **Bestiality** means sexual intercourse between mankind and the lower animals.

The desire for unnatural sexual intercourse between mankind may be acquired, or it may be innate. In the acquired form it may be due to unrestrained luxury and depravity, or to example and habit, as in eastern countries where pederastia is common. Westphal[1] was one of the first to discuss the subject from the neuropathic standpoint in his monograph on "Die conträre Sexualempfindung." In some cases there is no doubt that a congenitally abnormal condition of the sexual instinct exists—it is perverted in a sense contrary to nature. In this way a woman may be physically a woman and psychically a man, and a man may be physically a man and psychically a woman. The condition is not always perfectly defined, there may be various combinations of sexual feelings which produce complex results. If the condition is paramount in one direction—say that a man is psychically a woman, although his sexual organs may be anatomically perfect, such a man has no sexual proclivity towards a woman and is utterly incapable of coitus with her, any forced attempts to accomplish the act are attended by such a feeling of disgust that an erection is impossible. Such individuals from their childhood manifest a perverted sexual condition. Charcot and Magnan[2] report the case of a man, aged twenty-eight years, who when he was a boy of six had a violent desire to see naked boys and men, and for this purpose used to frequent the banks of a river in which some soldiers were in the habit of bathing. When at adult age he had not the least inclination towards women sexually, but he took keen pleasure in dressing himself as a woman, and displayed great taste in the matter of feminine articles of toilet. In cases of a less pronounced nature, there may be a penchant for the male sex and still a capacity for coitus with women. In cases of acquired pederastia, it

[1] *Arch. f. Psychiatrie*, 1870.  [2] *Archives de Neurologie*, 1882.

is probable that some few fibres of abnormal passion were originally present, since many men given to the most unbridled debauchery never develop any tendency to unnatural intercourse, the idea of it being as repugnant to them as to men who have their passions under normal control

The development of latent perverted instinct may within limits be dependent on external relations. It is quite probable that many men in whom some infinitesimal potential element of sexual perversion exists escape its development, and neither to themselves, nor to those who know them best, is there ever any indication of its presence. Many papers have lately been written on the subject, chiefly in the French and German journals; amongst the writers are Krafft-Ebing,[1] Savage,[2] Leonpacher,[3] Krueg,[4] Tamassia,[5] and others Chevalier's *De l'inversion de l'instinct sexuel au point de vue médico-légal* contains a *résumé* of the subject up to the year 1885

It is probable that inverted sexual feeling is much more widely spread than is supposed, the cases that come before the courts of law being but the shadow of the reality. Not many years ago the police of a town in the north of England took possession of a public room in which a ball of a very exclusive character was taking place. It was found that the company consisted wholly of men, half of them being dressed as women, in order that their proceedings should not be observed, they had provided themselves with blind musicians.

The passive as well as the active agent in the commission of sodomy is amenable to the law, except when overcome by force, or by being drugged, or when under fourteen years of age The act is criminal when committed with a woman as well as with a man. As in rape, the passive agent can give evidence as to the perpetration of the crime The medical evidence in cases of sodomy is not nearly so important as it is in cases of rape The active agent shows no indications of the habit, although the contrary has been asserted The passive agent if long habituated to the act, may display certain indications which are by no means constant. There may be an involution of the soft parts at the anus, producing an appearance resembling the bell of a trumpet; the sphincter ani may be relaxed, and the anal opening more patent than normal, a condition which may be accompanied by prolapse of the mucous membrane A smooth condition of the skin round the anus is sometimes met with Tears in the sphincter ani, or of the mucous membrane of the rectum, are only found in recent cases, and are more common in young boys than in adults, in such cases there may be

---

[1] *Arch f. Psychiat*, 1877; and *Allgemeine Zeitsch f Psychiat*, 1881
[2] *Journ of Mental Science*, 1884  [3] *Friederich's Blatter f ger Med*, 1887.
[4] *Brain*, 1881  [5] *Revista Sperimentale*, 1878

swelling and inflammation present. The discovery of spermatozoa is only important if the passive agent is very young, or if they are obtained from within the anus, as of course they might otherwise be derived from the individual himself. With regard to the distinction between the active and the passive agents it is to be remembered that the rôles are interchangeable—the agent that on one occasion takes the passive, may on the next take the active part. For this reason, when making an examination in a case of alleged sodomy, it is well to investigate the condition of both the parts concerned in each of the agents. A medical man recently told me that when acting as assistant to a police surgeon, he was on one occasion required to examine a man and a boy who were in custody on the charge of sodomy. He examined the man solely as the active agent, and the boy as the passive agent, without finding any indications; at the trial it turned out that the boy and not the man was the active agent.

The possibility of sodomy being perpetrated on a man against his will, or during sleep, is contrary to common sense. With regard to young boys, it is possible that they might be overcome by force. The same remarks apply to this crime as to drugging and other modes of taking away the power of resistance, as were made with regard to rape.

Medical evidence in cases of bestiality is limited to a search for hairs (derived from the abused animal) on the clothes and person of the accused.

**Indecent exposure** of the person is a criminal offence which does not come under the notice of the medical jurist in the way that the above-mentioned offences do, but his opinion may be asked as to the criminal responsibility of the offender. Certain forms of cerebral degeneration dispose those who are subject to them to exhibit their persons in public. In this country the cases have been mostly those of elderly men developing senile dementia, or in younger men, the subjects of epileptic automatism, of alcoholism, or of the initial stage of general paralysis. Recently Krafft-Ebing[1] has directed attention to a form of sexual psychopathy in which there is a special psychical degeneration occurring in the early years of life, mostly referable to hereditary influence, or to pathological conditions, such as rachitis. He gives illustrative cases in which there is an apparently uncontrollable tendency on the part of the subjects to expose their persons to others. Among these is one by Freyer[2] of a man, thirty-five years of age, who was arrested for lingering about a girls' school, and when he succeeded in attracting the attention of the pupils exhibiting his person. For the same offence he had been in prison more than half-a-dozen times before, for periods of from

[1] *Wiener med. Blätter*, 1892.  [2] *Zeitschr. f. Medizinalbeamte*, 3 Jahrg.

three months to three years, on the last occasion he was very properly sent to a lunatic asylum instead of to prison. He had been subject to epileptic seizures, and it is worthy of remark that when the impulse to expose himself developed, the epileptic attacks ceased.

## CHAPTER XIII

### THE SIGNS OF PREGNANCY AND OF DELIVERY.

MEDICAL practitioners may be called on by legal authorities to ascertain the occurrence or non-occurrence of pregnancy under the following circumstances:—(a) When a woman sentenced to death pleads pregnancy as a bar to execution; (b) when a woman whose husband is recently dead asserts that she is pregnant with an heir to the estate, the heir-at-law, to protect himself from fraud by the importation of a spurious heir, may demand proof of pregnancy. In both these instances the ancient proceeding, which is only now dying out, was to empannel a jury of twelve matrons or discreet women to make the necessary investigation and to report to the court. This duty is now fulfilled by one or more medical practitioners. (c) When a woman who has been seduced claims increased damages on account of being with child; (d) when an unmarried woman, or widow, or a married woman living apart from her husband, is, as she alleges, libellously accused of being pregnant; or (e) when a woman who has lost her husband through culpable neglect of some person or persons, claims damages for his loss and for the future support of an unborn child.

#### SIGNS OF PREGNANCY.

An exhaustive description of all the various indications of the existence of pregnancy which are of value to obstetricians, is out of place in a treatise on Forensic Medicine. What the medical jurist has to depose to on oath, is not the probability or otherwise of a certain woman being pregnant, but the fact that she is or is not pregnant. Most of the signs of pregnancy are only conjectural, and although an obstetrician of great experience might probably form a fairly accurate forecast in the absence of the really diagnostic signs, he would hesitate to make a positive statement on oath, unless the infallible signs were present.

The two signs of pregnancy usually depended on by married women to determine their condition are—the temporary cessation of the

## SIGNS OF PREGNANCY. 113

menses, and the sensation of quickening. Neither of these signs are of value to the medical jurist seeing that the woman he interrogates is an unfriendly witness. It is usually her object to impress the medical examiner with the idea that she is pregnant (in some cases the converse obtains), and therefore no reliance can be placed on her statements in this respect. If a truthful statement as to these signs is given, it is of little value, since the stoppage of menstruation may be due to other causes than pregnancy, and the sensation of quickening is a subjective indication and is unreliable even in the case of women who have experienced it in former pregnancies. In the earliest months of pregnancy the **breasts** enlarge and become firmer. They are more sensitive to the touch, and knotty cords can be felt in the region of the nipples; the areolæ surrounding the nipples appear swollen and shiny and acquire a darker hue from increase of pigment, especially in dark-skinned women. A number of elevated nodules form round the periphery of the areolæ indicating the presence of active sebaceous glands. When the breasts are gently squeezed a milk-like secretion exudes from the nipples. The **abdomen** begins to show indications of distension about the third month; the uterus at this period lies in the hypogastrium. During the first three months the organ retains its pear-shaped outline, afterwards it develops laterally and becomes more ovoid. If the abdominal walls permit of an accurate examination of the shape of the uterus, its form when gravid, together with its mobility and elasticity to the touch, enables the experienced practitioner to arrive at a fairly accurate diagnosis during the earlier months. At or soon after this period alternate contraction and relaxation of the uterine walls may be detected by palpation. The vaginal portion of the **cervix becomes soft** and yielding from infiltration with serum, the edges of the os being rounded; owing to the general tumefaction of the surrounding parts the cervix seems shortened. The mucous membrane of the vagina acquires a cyanotic appearance, and the small veins of the vulva are enlarged and prominent. Bimanual examination—one hand grasping the fundus, and the first and middle fingers of the other applied within the vagina to the os—enables the operator to ascertain the size of the uterus, and probably, in the earlier months—by means of reciprocal movements of the two hands—to feel the sensation of a mobile body within it. The **uterine souffle** is a blowing sound synchronous with the maternal pulse; it chiefly arises in the arteries which run up the cervix, but extends to various parts of the uterus. It may be heard about the fourth month or even earlier.

The signs so far enumerated are suggestive but not conclusive. There are but *two incontrovertible signs* of pregnancy—the **sounds of the fœtal heart,** and the presence and movement of the **fœtal members**

8

as felt through the abdominal walls. The fœtal heart beats at the rate of 120 to 160 in the minute, the sounds resemble the tick of a watch at some distance from the ear. When the fœtus is in the usual position they are best heard to the left of the umbilicus, a little below it. They become audible about the 18th or 20th week, but at times they may be heard earlier. If the child is surrounded by an unusually large amount of liquor amnii, or if there is a very thick layer of fat on the maternal abdomen, the fœtal heart-sounds are heard with difficulty, if at all. By careful palpation the parts of the child's body that are accessible through the abdominal parietes of the mother may be distinguished, and in the living child movements may be felt. Here also the conditions which impede recognition of the fœtal heart-sounds will probably prevent manipulation of the fœtal members; unless the contour of the child's body can be detected, the perception of movements cannot be relied on as a proof of pregnancy, since erratic contraction of the recti muscles of the maternal abdomen might be mistaken for them. If the child is dead the recognition of the fœtal members is the only positive sign of pregnancy.

Since the infallible signs of pregnancy are not available during the first eighteen weeks of pregnancy, no positive statement on oath can be made until this time has expired, which is equivalent to saying that the occurrence of pregnancy cannot be positively determined until quickening has taken place. A negative result yielded by an examination made after a supposed pregnancy of eighteen weeks' duration affords no proof that the woman is not pregnant; the difficulties already mentioned may prevent recognition of the signs of pregnancy, and a further difficulty may be interposed by the child being small and of feeble vitality. As in all other propositions it is easier to prove a positive than a negative; if the fœtal heart-sounds are heard, whether the body can be felt or not, the fact of pregnancy is established; if neither one nor the other are discoverable, no positive conclusion for the moment can be arrived at. It is under conditions like these that the suggestive signs of pregnancy are of value, as affording grounds for delay and subsequent re-examination or not, as the case may be. Usually a woman pleading pregnancy will state that she is several months advanced, so that some indications of the alleged condition will be present. Should she state that she has been only recently impregnated, further examination must be postponed whether there are any indications of pregnancy or not.

## POST-MORTEM APPEARANCES OF PREGNANCY.

Little need be said under this head. In addition to many of the objective signs of pregnancy in the living, two further indications are described, of which the first only is of importance. (a) The presence of an ovum with villi, or of a fœtus with placental attachment. (b) The presence of a so-called true corpus luteum in one of the ovaries. If an impregnated ovum, sufficiently developed as to be recognised as such, is found in the uterus after death (or, in case of ectopic gestation, elsewhere) the fact of pregnancy is established. Certain abnormal products of conception may replace the ovum or fœtus; it is, therefore, necessary to distinguish between such abnormal products and other pathological conditions which occur independently of impregnation. These abnormal products of conception are called moles. They are of two kinds— the *sanguineous mole* and the *vesicular mole*.

The sanguineous mole is the result of hæmorrhage into the fœtal membranes. The embryo perishes in consequence of pressure produced either by bulging of the chorion and amnion into the fœtal cavity, or the chorion is ruptured and the fœtal cavity is distended with blood; the embryo undergoes maceration and disappears, or it escapes if the ovum ruptures. If the membranes with the blood-clots remain long in the uterus, calcareous deposits may occur in them. In some cases the distended chorion and amnion form what are known as blood-cysts. The sanguineous mole rarely exceeds the size of an orange. A mole may exist along with a fœtus which undergoes normal development, twin conception having taken place: one of the ova develops, the other degenerates.

The vesicular mole is formed by vesicular degeneration of the villi of the chorion. The appearance is that of a vast number of vesicles varying from the size of a pin's head to that of a pigeon's egg. The vesicles are, as it were, threaded in rows, cysts forming along the length of the villi. The cysts are filled with a fluid containing mucin and albumin in varying proportions. The embryo perishes; and if the degenerative process commences at an early period of pregnancy all traces of it may have disappeared when the mole is examined; if it commences at a later period remains of the embryo or fœtus may be found.

It is unfortunate that the term 'hydatid mole' has been applied to the results of vesicular degeneration of the chorionic villi, a condition which has no relation with the true hydatid. The distinction is not so much a matter of pathological accuracy; it concerns the important question—Can a "hydatid mole" be formed without impregnation? From the description given, it will be seen that the so-called "hydatid" or vesicular mole results from degeneration of a product of conception; therefore, it can only occur as the result of impregnation. The true hydatid (echinococcus) is very rarely found in the uterus. Gunsburg[1] reports a case in which labour was impeded by a true hydatid growing

[1] *Centralblatt für Gynæcologie*, 1884.

from the lower part of the uterus, and states that he found only four cases recorded of hydatid tumour in the cavity of the pelvis

**Corpus Luteum**—The difference between the so-called *true* and *false* corpora lutea was formerly regarded as, in itself, constituting proof of the pregnant or non-pregnant condition having obtained during life.

The false corpus luteum, or, as it is also called, the corpus luteum of menstruation, does not undergo development under the usual conditions

The true corpus luteum, or corpus luteum of pregnancy, develops for several months after impregnation, and attains a very much larger size. This increased development is due to greater activity of the circulation, and probably also to trophic nerve influences resulting from the presence of the ovum in the uterus. Such increased development, however, may take place in consequence of myomata and other pathological conditions of the uterus. On the other hand, pregnancy may occur without the formation of a true corpus luteum. It may be accepted for medico-legal purposes that corpora lutea, as indications of pregnancy or of non-pregnancy, are of no diagnostic value

## SIGNS OF DELIVERY.

The question of recent delivery most frequently comes under the notice of the medical jurist in relation to infanticide, or to concealment of birth. In civil cases feigned delivery may require investigation. In respect to imputations against the chastity of unmarried women, and under other circumstances, an opinion as to the occurrence of remote delivery may be required

Taking recent delivery first, the subject is divisible into the signs observable in the living, and those observable in the dead

### SIGNS IN THE LIVING OF RECENT DELIVERY AT TERM

A woman who has been delivered at term within two or three days of the period of examination presents more or less the following appearances. There is usually a certain languid look, like that of a person recovering from an illness. The lower eyelid and its surroundings are pigmented to an extent which varies with the complexion of the individual. The **temperature** may be slightly elevated. The **pulse** slows immediately after labour, and then quickens, and again slows, and remains so for several days; it is full, but there is no increase in arterial tension. The **skin** is moist. The **breasts** are full and elastic, or they may be hard and nodulated; the superficial veins are visible. The nipples are as described in the pregnant condition. The fluid—**colostrum**—at first secreted is not true milk; it is viscid, and contains yellow particles visible to the naked eye. Microscopical examination shows the presence of large corpuscles called **colostrum corpuscles**, which are composed of a number of fat granules bound together by a hyaline substance. According to Heidenhain, these corpuscles are cells of alveolar epithelium, which become round and faintly granular, and eventually take up fat granules from the alveoli. When treated with acetic acid they display nuclei. True milk contains very few colostrum corpuscles, and less albumin than is present in colostrum. The abdominal walls are flaccid and wrinkled; beneath them the **uterus** is felt as a hard round ball. The **cervix** is soft, and open at the internal os, the external os is patulous, the lips being bruised, and they may be torn. The internal os begins to close during the first twenty-four hours; the external os remains patulous for a long time. The **vagina** is dilated and relaxed, the rugæ being absent. The mucous membrane at the mouth of the vagina usually exhibits some slight tears, especially in primiparæ; in them also any remains of the hymen are completely destroyed, as evinced by the presence of recent tumefied nodules (*caruncular myrtiformes*). The **vulva** are tumid and open, especially at their perineal aspect. The **posterior commissure** is usually ruptured, the perineum in some cases being lacerated. The lochia, at first almost pure blood, change about the third day to a serous fluid more or less tinged with blood, containing epithelium, mucus, exudation-corpuscles, and shreds of membrane. Subsequently, the blood diminishes, and its place is taken by fatty granules and pus, the colour changing to yellowish or greenish. The amount and the duration of the lochia are variable. The signs of recent delivery are well-marked for the first few days; after the lapse of a week they are more difficult of recognition, and in a fortnight will have so far disappeared as to render absolute diagnosis of *recent* delivery impossible. It is to be understood that the signs enumerated refer to those which follow delivery at term.

## SIGNS IN THE DEAD OF RECENT DELIVERY AT TERM

In addition to the indications available in the living, ocular inspection of the uterus and its appendages becomes feasible when a necropsy is made of the body of a woman recently delivered. If death has taken place soon after delivery, before the commencement of involution, the **uterus** will present the appearance of a flabby bag nine or ten inches long, with widely open mouth. Within, the surface is irregular and is covered with coagula of blood, with portions of decidua and with flakes of lymph. At the part where the placenta was attached the muscular structure is devoid of covering, and is darker in colour than the rest of the organ. Here may be seen as large lacunæ the openings of the dilated veins (*uterine sinuses*). The cervix is drawn out and is much thinner than the walls of the body of the uterus, it often presents a bruised and ecchymosed appearance The vagina is dilated, relaxed, and devoid of rugæ. A so-called true corpus luteum will probably be found in one of the ovaries

### SIGNS IN THE LIVING OF REMOTE DELIVERY AT TERM.

In women who have given birth to a child at some remote period the breasts are more pendulous and flaccid, and the nipples usually more prominent, the areolæ being deeper in tint than in nulliparous women The abdominal walls also are not so firm and elastic, and the skin of the abdomen is usually marked with streaks of a silvery lustre These marks are not invariably found after pregnancy, they are wanting in about 8 per cent of cases that have gone on to full term. They occur from other causes than pregnancy—from peritoneal tumours, ascites, ovarian tumours, and on the legs from typhoid and typhus fevers, in pregnant women they also occur on the breasts Although often called cicatrices they do not result from replacement of one tissue by another, which is the characteristic of a cicatrix They are due to partial absorption of some of the elements of the skin, and to modification of others The fibrous tissue of the chorium, which is normally arranged in a kind of dense network, is re-arranged in parallel lines which traverse the streaks from side to side the papillæ are diminished in size by atrophy, and are spread wider apart. The labia are more open and the posterior commissure is usually represented by a cicatrix which may extend to the perineum The hymen will not only be replaced by carunculæ myrtiformes, but the continuousness of the nodules composing the carunculæ will be destroyed The formation of carunculæ results from coitus, but the base of the hymen remains—where the mucous membrane of the vagina is folded over to form it—and is only completely destroyed by the passage of the child's head The vagina is more open and smoother than before child-bearing, its anterior wall may project into the lumen of the canal The cervix uteri is irregular, the os is puckered, fissured, and more circular and patent than in nulliparous women, admitting the tip of the finger

These signs are best marked in women who have born many children When a woman has born but one child at a period remote from the time of examination, many of the signs may be wanting The most deceptive appearance is presented by women who have given birth to a single child short of the full term In such cases, after the lapse of a few years there may be no indication that the woman has been delivered Even two or three deliveries of this kind may leave no trace, the woman presenting all the characteristics of a nullipara.

### SIGNS IN THE DEAD OF REMOTE DELIVERY AT TERM

The only additional evidence to that afforded by the signs of delivery in the living is obtained from inspection of the walls and cavity of the uterus. The uterus that has contained a child remains permanently larger and heavier than in the virgin state. The walls are thicker, and the cavity is not so triangular in outline, the angles where the Fallopian tubes enter being rounded off. Evidence of past rents of the external os may be seen as cicatricial irregularities. The difference between a parous and a nulliparous uterus, however, may not be sufficiently well marked in a given case as to enable a decision to be arrived at.[1]

---

## CHAPTER XIV

### CRIMINAL ABORTION.

IN Medical language the term abortion refers to the expulsion of a fœtus, or embryo, before the viable period—i.e., before the sixth month of gestation; the term miscarriage is used synonymously. Delivery after the sixth month, but before full term, is called premature labour. Under the term abortion, the law includes both these periods, therefore criminal abortion consists in unlawfully procuring the expulsion of the contents of the gravid uterus at *any period of gestation short of full term*. It will be observed that this definition does not provide for the induction of premature labour by medical men. The law does not recognise this proceeding by making any exception in its favour, hence the necessity for medical men to protect themselves when about to induce labour prematurely, for the purpose of saving the mother's life, or from other proper motives, by explaining the object and necessity of the operation to all concerned, and, if possible, obtaining the moral support of a colleague. Under certain conditions the necessity for the operation is universally admitted, and if the practitioner under such conditions acts openly, he is held to be exonerated from the penalties imposed by the law. This does not mean that legal proceedings cannot be instituted, but that no conviction would ensue.

[1] See *Trans. of the Obstetrical Society*, vols. XVII and XVIII.

The law is thus expressed—

> "Every woman being with child, who, with intent to procure her own miscarriage, shall unlawfully administer to herself any poison or other noxious thing, or shall unlawfully use any instrument or other means whatsoever, with like intent, and whosoever with intent to procure the miscarriage of any woman, whether she be or be not with child, shall unlawfully administer, &c., shall be guilty of felony."

> "Whosoever shall unlawfully supply or procure any poison or other noxious thing, or any instrument or thing whatsoever, knowing that the same is intended to be unlawfully used or employed with the intent to procure the miscarriage of any woman, whether she be or be not with child, shall be guilty of a misdemeanour." (24 and 25 Vict., ch. 100, ss. 58 and 59.)

Attention is first directed to the statement that the intention of the act constitutes the crime. If means are taken to produce abortion it matters not whether the woman is or is not pregnant; and further, if the woman is pregnant, it is not necessary that abortion should follow the attempt to procure it, in order to constitute the crime. If a woman places herself in the hands of any one with the object of having abortion criminally induced, and she dies in consequence, the operator or administrator is guilty of murder, although he or she had no intention of causing the woman's death. If the means employed were of such a nature as not to be dangerous to life, the crime may be reduced to manslaughter. This throws great responsibility on medical witnesses. In the first of the two sections of the act quoted, it is stated that the administration of "any poison or other noxious thing" with intent to procure abortion is felony. The question becomes what is a noxious thing? Any substance, however harmless, under certain conditions or in certain amount may be injurious. Much depends also on the intent with which it is administered. For example, if a large dose of jalap is secretly administered as a practical joke, or in some alcoholic beverage, with the object of punishing a surreptitious drinker of the same, the law regards such a proceeding as a venial offence. If the same drug is administered to a pregnant woman, or to a woman whom the administrator believes to be pregnant, with the object of procuring abortion, it would probably be regarded as a "noxious thing;" not because the administration is of necessity likely to be followed by abortion, but on account of the criminal intention it displays (see Section 58 above quoted). It might be supposed that the word "noxious" was redundant in relation to the phrase "other means whatsoever," inasmuch as the latter covers all the ground; it is not improbable, however, that the framer of the Act had in his mind a reference to mechanical or local means of procuring abortion. The first clause specifies poison, and then strengthens or enlarges the term by adding "or other noxious thing." The second clause specifies "any instrument," and to prevent quibbling adds "or other means whatsoever." One judge, however (Brett), ruled in a case of criminal abortion, that the word "noxious" should be omitted in the indictment, as the comprehensive phrase "other means whatsoever" included any substance administered whether noxious or not (*Reg. v. Willis*, 1871). As this ruling does not universally obtain, it is necessary for the medical witness to be prepared to express an opinion in the witness-box as to the properties, noxious or otherwise, of some of the drugs most commonly used with the object of procuring criminal abortion.

## MODES OF PROCURING CRIMINAL ABORTION.

Criminal abortion is attempted in one or more of three ways —By the *administrations of drugs* by the mouth, by acts of *general violence*, by *mechanical means* used directly to the uterus or its contents.

Two classes of **drugs** which are reputed to act directly on the uterus, include many of the substances used for procuring abortion criminally —they are *emmenagogues* and *ecbolics*. The former are supposed to promote menstruation, or to re-establish it after its arrest from causes other than pregnancy, the latter are supposed to cause the expulsion of the contents of the gravid uterus. Whatever value this distinction may have in therapeutics, it is not without importance to the medical jurist. In the case of those who have even a limited acquaintance with the properties of drugs, the administration of a drug supposed to possess ecbolic properties would have much more significance than if it was known merely as an emmenagogue. The accused may state that he did not know the woman was pregnant, he was only told that there was a temporary absence of menstruation; the administration of an emmenagogue would be consistent with such a statement, but not that of a reputed ecbolic. Such a drug would only be given when the object of the administrator was to empty a gravid uterus. Unfortunately the distinction between these two classes of drugs is not well defined, many drugs are included in both. There are, however, two or three that would not be administered for simple stoppage of menstruation.

A favourite emmenagogue of the working classes is **pennyroyal** (*Mentha pulegium*), usually given as pennyroyal tea; it has also been used for procuring abortion, and is about as efficacious in one direction as in the other. This is a substance that might be innocently administered to a woman in the early stage of pregnancy, the administrator regarding the case as one of simple arrest of menstruation. **Savin** (*Juniperus sabina*) is another so-called emmenagogue, but with a different reputation; it is better known as an abortive. The selection of this drug for the purpose of restoring arrested menstruation would be suspicious of criminal intent. Savin is an irritant, and possesses no real emmenagogue nor ecbolic properties. The like may be said of a number of substances popularly regarded as abortifacients, as rue, tansy, yew, saffron, &c. In addition to reputed ecbolics, powerful purgatives as colocynth, aloes, and gamboge, emetics as tartar emetic, general irritants as arsenic, cantharides, and hellebore, have from time to time been resorted to. Apparently as the result of association of ideas, the salts of iron, which are frequently prescribed for anæmic amenorrhœa, have thus acquired the reputation of being active ecbolics. It is astonishing what a tenacious hold this superstition has on the medical profession; many medical men would not prescribe iron to a pregnant woman, however much it was indicated. I have heard it stated in evidence that five-drop doses of tincture of the perchloride of iron was a dangerous and highly improper medicine to give to a woman with child. This is the outcome of sheer ignorance, any medicinal preparation of iron has no pretentions whatever to ecbolic properties. Taylor and Stevenson[1] record a case in which the tincture of the perchloride was given in large doses daily to a pregnant woman, for the purpose of procuring abortion; the health of the woman was seriously injured, without abortion being produced.

The drug which has the most claim to be regarded as an ecbolic is ergot (*secale cornutum*). When labour at term has commenced, the contractions of the uterus can both be increased, and altered in character—becoming more tetanic—by the administration of ergot. This specific action on the uterus has led to the use of the drug for the purpose of initiating contraction of the gravid, but quiescent organ. Experiments on animals justify, but experience of its use with the human female negatives the views held by many as to its efficiency in procuring abortion. Kobert[2] states that two constituents of ergot, cornutine and sphacelinic acid, produce abortion in dogs and cats. In the earlier months of pregnancy (the period when abortion is resorted to) the administration of ergot will not induce miscarriage in the quiescent human uterus, except the organ is predisposed to part with its contents on account of a diseased state of the membranes of the ovum, such as occurs in syphilitic subjects, or from general disturbance of the system caused by the toxic action of the drug. Even when abortion is threatened—as evinced by hæmorrhage—the action of ergot does not necessarily stimulate the uterus to expulsive efforts. Atthill[3] gave it in such a case with the object of emptying the uterus; the hæmorrhage was arrested, but no abortion resulted, the patient gave birth in due

[1] *Manual of Med. Jurisprudence.*  [2] *Practitioner*, 1885.
[3] *Brit. Med. Journ.*, 1889.

time to a living child. Even when full term is approaching, ergot will rarely initiate labour. Atthill[1] states that he has frequently given ergot as a preventive of post-partem hæmorrhage, commencing its administration a week or ten days before the expected advent of labour, and never once had reason to suppose that it hastened that event. Saxinger[2] records a case in which a woman with contracted pelvis, on two occasions had premature labour induced by means of the introduction of a bougie. On the third occasion—four or five weeks before term—powdered ergot was tried in place of mechanical means. Four grms (62 grains) of the fresh powder were given daily for three days. The pulse fell from 88 to 60 beats per minute, and the patient was attacked with vomiting and feebleness, but the uterus did not respond. The experience of many other obstetricians corroborates the conclusion that ergot in non-poisonous doses has not the power of developing uterine action in the quiescent gravid state, in the absence of predisposing conditions.

When abortion has resulted from the use of ergot it has been due to the general toxic effects produced. Richter[3] reports the case of a girl, six to seven months pregnant, who took from 2 to 4 ounces. She suffered from the symptoms of acute ergot-poisoning—quick pulse, thirst, pain in stomach and abdomen, stoppage of urine, great restlessness—and, half an hour after giving birth to a dead child, died from profuse hæmorrhage. Tardieu[4] reports the case of a woman four months pregnant who aborted in consequence of taking ergot, and died from peritonitis twenty-four hours afterwards. In another case reported by Otto,[5] death took place shortly after the expulsion of an embryo five inches in length. Death may result from ergot without abortion having occurred; illustrations of this will be found in the toxicological section on ergot-poisoning.

It may be inferred, from a consideration of the cases recorded in which abortion has been attempted by resort to drugs, that no infallible ecbolic is known. When abortion has resulted from the uses of drugs, it has been due either to a predisposing condition of the uterus or of its contents, or to the general toxic effects of the substance taken.

**General Violence as a Cause of Criminal Abortion.**—The universal experience of medical practitioners is, that under certain conditions pregnant women may suffer from general mechanical violence of an extreme kind without causing miscarriage, and under other conditions the uterus rids itself of its contents on the slightest provocation.

---

[1] *Dublin Journ. of Med. Science*, 1888.   [2] *Maschka's Handbuch*, Bd. 3.
[3] *Vierteljahrsschr. f. ger. Med.*, 1861.   [4] *Annales d'Hygiène*, 1855.
[5] *Maschka's Handbuch*, Bd. 3.

Since excessive violence to one woman fails to produce results which follow the occurrence of a mere shadow of it to another, it is obvious that the result is determined by intrinsic rather than by extrinsic relations. So long as the gravid uterus and its contents maintain their normal healthy relations towards each other, general violence is not usually successful unless the mother's life is endangered, and not always then.

When general violence is resorted to with the intention of causing abortion, one or more of the following methods may be adopted — Purposely falling down stairs, or from a height, the use of excessively tight stays, allowing the abdomen to be violently kneaded, walking, or riding on horseback, for many successive hours until the bodily powers are quite exhausted, and other means, all of which are singularly futile. Such are usually the prelude to more direct and efficacious procedures.

**Local Violence as a Cause of Criminal Abortion.**—It has been shown that drugs and general violence, as a rule, fail to bring about miscarriage. Greater success attends the use of mechanical means, applied in such a way as to disturb the relation between the uterus and its contents. To accomplish this the force must be applied directly to the parts in question, the usual method is to pass up the vagina, in the direction of the womb, some pointed instrument, such as a piece of wire or of wood. The direction actually taken depends upon the knowledge and skill of the operator. An abortionist who has some slight acquaintance with the anatomy of the parts, and has had sufficient practical experience to enable him to utilise it, will at least endeavour to pass the implement through the os uteri, with the object of puncturing the membranes of the ovum. A less informed person, who has probably only heard the method described as "passing a piece of wire up the private parts till blood comes," will perforate the cervix, or the body of the uterus, in the endeavour to reach its contents. Unqualified practitioners of a low type, and some who are qualified, use male metallic catheters, and by taking care not to wound the uterus, are not unfrequently successful in accomplishing their object without much disturbance of the woman's health. There are reasons for believing that abortion is criminally procured in a vast number of cases in which the proceedings are undertaken by men who have, or who have had, some relation with the medical profession, and who are therefore capable of exercising such a degree of skill in puncturing the membranes, as to avoid injuring the uterus; this materially diminishes the risk of the operation, and consequently lessens the probability of the crime being detected.

Cases in which criminal abortion has been procured rarely come before the court of law except when the result of the proceeding has been fatal to the mother. As the woman solicits the crime, and is a culpable party, it is only natural that she should strive to conceal it. In this she is usually successful unless her life is endangered, when the necessity for legitimate medical advice puts others in possession of the secret. Fatal results are mostly due to ignorance or to recklessness on the part of the operator, and to carelessness on the part of the patient. It is well known to obstetricians that puncturing the fœtal membranes is not always followed by immediate expulsion of the uterine contents; days of inaction may intervene. Under such circumstances the woman becomes impatient, and urges the abortionist to take more active measures. In this way even a practised hand may be induced to resort to unnecessary violence by which he perforates or lacerates the uterine mucous membrane, and so gives rise to septicæmia. Abortionists are not unfrequently of intemperate habits, and under the influence of drink they lose their usual cautiousness, and do more damage than they intended. The patient also being obliged to comport herself as though nothing was the matter, goes about her daily work, and thus adds another element of risk.

The procurers of criminal abortion sometimes adopt more heroic means than simple puncture of the membranes. Wherry[1] records the case of a woman three months pregnant who had the fœtus cut in pieces *in utero* by an abortionist with what she described as a "silver hook." The legs, the arms, and the head were separated from the trunk, the fragments coming away piecemeal. They showed no signs of decomposition, the skin being rosy and firm. Peritonitis ensued, but the woman recovered.

Attempts are not unfrequently made by unscrupulous women to avail themselves by fraud of the skill of honourable members of the medical profession in order to procure abortion. Such women will go to the consulting-room of a medical man, or to the out-patients' room of a hospital, and state that they are suffering from displacement of the womb, adding that the present is not the first time that the organ has become displaced, and that on previous occasions the doctor they consulted straightened or replaced it with the aid of the uterine sound. It is needless to say that inquiries as to the possibility of pregnancy are skilfully evaded, and as the fraud is attempted in the earliest months, a medical man off his guard is easily deceived. Miscarriage may be induced by passing a bougie between the ovum and the uterine walls and allowing it to remain until expulsion takes place, by vaginal douches of warm water, and by dilatation of the cervical canal by means of elastic dilators, methods usually only adopted by skilled persons.

[1] *Brit. Med. Journal*, 1881.

Occasionally the woman herself attempts to procure her own miscarriage by direct mechanical means. Various implements have been used with this object. Partridge[1] relates the case of a woman in the seventh month of pregnancy who introduced a hair-pin, points downward, into the uterus and allowed it to remain. No abortion took place for three weeks. The woman then became ill and sought medical advice when the hair-pin was found to have penetrated the walls of the uterus. The os was dilated and the hair-pin and ovum were extracted twenty-three days after the introduction of the former. The woman died of peritonitis.

The attempt to procure criminal abortion is usually made in the earlier months of pregnancy before the enlargement of the abdomen becomes obvious. Young, inexperienced girls as a rule resort to drugs first, and, after proving their inefficacy, apply to the professional abortionist; in this way the actual abortion may be delayed until the third or fourth month or later. Women of more experience seek mechanical aid as soon as they suspect their condition—after the omission of one menstrual period. It is to be remembered that married women, as well as those who are single, have recourse to forced miscarriage. In the earliest months the attachment of the ovum to the uterus is but feeble, and consequently direct mechanical disturbance is almost certain to cause miscarriage; if effective, the uterus expels its contents in from a few hours to three or four days after the operation. It is quite possible, however, for a uterine sound (or other similar instrument) to be introduced into the cavity of the gravid uterus without causing miscarriage. In such cases the membranes are not ruptured; the blunt sound passes between them and the uterine wall, and produces but slight separation. Many gynecologists have unwittingly passed a sound into a gravid womb without ill effects. Säxinger[2] relates a case in which a medical man (under the impression that he had to deal with a pathological condition of the organ) on two separate occasions passed a sound into the uterus of a pregnant woman in the early months without interfering with the normal course of gestation.

The induction of criminal abortion imperils the patient's life in two ways—by causing *profuse hæmorrhage*, the result of retention of the placenta or some other product of conception, or by *septic inflammatory processes*. Lesser[3] states that in instrumentally induced abortion the extent of injury to the uterus does not materially influence the length of time the woman survives, the cause of death being always puerperal fever. Septicæmia following abortion is a suspicious symptom, pointing

[1] *New York Med. Journ.*, 1884.   [2] Maschka's *Handbuch*, Bd. 3.
[3] *Atlas der ger. Med.* (zweite Abtheilung), 1891.

to mechanical interference as the cause. Little surprise can be felt at the frequency with which septic inflammation follows criminal abortion when the absence of all attempts to render the instruments used aseptic is taken into account. It is not to be forgotten, however, that death of the ovum from pathological causes may determine septic inflammation from absorption of the products of putrefaction. The retention of the placenta, or part of it, after spontaneous abortion also frequently gives rise to septicæmia.

### SIGNS OF ABORTION IN THE LIVING

The indications that abortion has taken place vary with the period of gestation at which it occurred, and the interval that elapses between the event and the examination. If pregnancy is cut short in the first or the second month, even on early examination, very little will be found different from that which accompanies an ordinary menstrual period; when a few days have elapsed the parts will have entirely recovered their usual condition. Abortion at three or four months leaves immediate traces behind in the form of a more or less patulous condition of the vagina, and possibly the vulva may be swollen. Spiegelberg[1] describes a funnel-shaped condition of the cervix uteri, which grows narrower from below upwards, as being very characteristic of the recent occurrence of abortion. The condition of the breasts should be investigated. The further pregnancy is advanced, so much the more will the signs of abortion resemble those already described as attending delivery at term. As the signs of abortion are less pronounced than those of delivery at term, so do they disappear sooner. The examination of a woman after the alleged occurrence of abortion should be conducted within twenty-four hours, otherwise little information will be yielded by it. Pathological indications in the form of metritis or peritonitis may be present.

### SIGNS OF ABORTION IN THE DEAD

In making the preliminary incisions and in removing the uterus with the vagina attached, great care must be taken not to injure it in any way. If the vagina is slit open some indications may be afforded as to the best direction in which to dissect the uterus, in order to trace out any punctures in its walls. Any such puncture, or laceration, should be carefully measured, and its position and direction ascertained. The length and the breadth of the cavity and the thickness of the uterine walls should be measured. The presence in the substance of the uterus of products of inflammation, the position of any perimetric

---

[1] *Lehrbuch der Geburtshulfe*

inflammation, the presence or absence of mucous membrane in the cavity, and the appearance of its walls are respectively to be noted. If the third month of gestation has been accomplished the site of the placenta will probably be distinguishable. Those who have not previously examined the cavity of a uterus recently delivered in the natural way are liable to draw erroneous conclusions from the appearances presented, more especially when the later months of gestation have been reached. The walls of the cavity are black and irregular—as though bruised—and convey the idea that violence has been resorted to; care must be taken to distinguish between the physiological condition and one that results from mechanical ill-usage. The ovaries should be examined for corpora lutea, not that the information thus obtained is of importance, but because questions on the subject may be asked by counsel. In addition to ascertaining the condition of the generative organs, the state of the stomach and the intestines must be investigated for possible indications of irritant poisoning resulting from the administration of one or more of the so-called ecbolics. For the same reason the kidneys should also be examined. In exceptional cases a caustic fluid has been injected into the vagina for the purpose of inducing abortion; the condition of its mucous membrane is, therefore, to be observed. Lastly, if an embryo is found in the generative tract its probable age is to be ascertained.

The following is an epitome of the **stages of development of the** fœtus during the first five months of intra-uterine life:—

**One Month.**—The embryo measures about one-third of an inch in a straight line from cephalic to caudal curve, and three-quarters along the curve; the ovum is about three-quarters of an inch long. The presence of the limbs is indicated. The nasal pits, a cleft indicating the position of the mouth, and two black dots representing the eyes, with the umbilical vesicle and the blood-vessels are present. The amnion is close to the embryo, and is separated from the villous chorion by a clear cavity.

**Two Months.**—The embryo measures half an inch in a straight line from highest point of cephalic curve to caudal curve; along the curve about an inch. It weighs 60 grains. The nasal and oral openings are separated. The head is becoming distinct from the body. The Sylvian fossa is distinguishable. The primitive kidneys (Wolffian bodies) have almost disappeared, and have become divided into urinary and generative organs. The first centres of ossification have appeared in the lower jaw, the clavicle, ribs, and bodies of the vertebræ. The amnion is in contact with the chorion, the amniotic cavity contains more fluid. The villi of the chorion are especially well developed at one spot. The umbilical vessels passing to the chorion are the only visible remains of the allantois.

**Three Months.**—The embryo is 2¾ to 3½ inches long, and weighs from 300 to 450 grams. The head is separated from the trunk by the neck. The ribs are sufficiently developed as to differentiate the chest and abdomen. The pupillary membrane is present. The eyelids and the lips are closed. The teeth begin to form. The fingers and toes can be distinguished, also the rudiments of the nails. The penis and clitoris are of equal length; sexual differentiation is commencing. The chorion has lost most of its villi. The placenta is distinct. The umbilical cord is spiral, about 2¾ inches long, and is inserted into the lower fourth of the linea alba. The decidua vera and reflexa are in contact.

**Four Months.**—The fœtus is 4 to 6½ inches long, and weighs from 2 to 4 ounces. The head equals one-fourth of the body length. The mouth is open, the nose, eyes, and ears are distinct. The length of the external ear is from 5.5 to 7.5 mm. The skin is firmer. Hairs (lanugo) are beginning to form. The pupillary membrane is quite distinct. The eyelids are closed. The occipital lobe is mapped-out. Points of ossification are present in lower segments of sacrum. The placenta is larger, and weighs about 2¾ ounces. The umbilical cord measures 7½ inches, is more spiral, and is thicker from the formation of Wharton's jelly; it is inserted above the lower fourth of the linea alba. The sex is distinguishable. The chorion and amnion are in contact. Movements of the limbs have been observed.

**Five Months.**—The fœtus is 7 to 10½ inches long, and weighs 10 ounces. The head is still disproportionately large; hair commences to appear on it. Lanugo begins to form along the eyebrows and on the forehead. The skin is red, and its surface is covered with *vernix caseosa*. The eyelids are closed; the pupillary membrane is still present. The external ear measures 8 to 12 mm in length. The nails are forming. The temporal and frontal opercula grow during this month, and the Sylvian fossa becomes triangular. The surface of the Island of Reil is marked by sulci. The fissure of Rolando appears, or it may not be present until later.[1] Points of ossification are present in pubes and os calcis. Bile-stained fluid is in the small intestines. The placenta weighs 6 ounces. The umbilical cord measures 12 inches in length. The movements of the fœtus are perceptible to the mother.

The subsequent stages of development will be found described on p. 23.

[1] Cunningham, *l. c.*

## CHAPTER XV.

### INFANTICIDE.

In its restricted and technical signification infanticide means the murder of an infant at the time of, or soon after, its birth. To kill an infant a few weeks old would also be infanticide, but such a case presents a different aspect to the medical jurist, inasmuch as it demands only the same kind of evidence as in ordinary cases of murder in older persons; much more is required from the medical witness in a case of true infanticide. In order that murder can be perpetrated the victim must have had a separate existence. In the legal sense a partially-born infant has not a separate existence, although it may breathe and has consequently acquired the power of maintaining life as a distinct individual. For this reason the medical witness in a case of infanticide has not only to give evidence as to cause of death as in ordinary cases of murder, but has further to endeavour to ascertain if the infant breathed, and whether it was or was not born alive. Since infanticide is usually committed with the object of concealing the occurrence of delivery, the deed is done in secret, and in most instances without the aid of a second person, the burden of proof of live birth, therefore, falls on the medical witness. The questions to be considered in cases of infanticide relate to the mother on the one hand, and to the child on the other.

As regards the accused woman the question is—Has she been delivered of a child recently, or at a period consistent with the time that apparently has elapsed since the birth of the infant? The signs of delivery already discussed afford criteria for the solution of this question.

As regards the child the questions relate to—1 Its maturity. 2 Whether it has or has not breathed. 3 Whether it was born alive, and, if so, the length of time it lived. 4. The cause of death. 5 The length of time it has been dead.

### 1. THE MATURITY OF THE CHILD.

This is to be determined by a minute investigation of the body with reference to the appropriate indications of age which are described in the section devoted to that subject.

## 2 HAS THE CHILD BREATHED?

An answer to this question has to be sought for by examining the lungs with respect to—(*a*) volume, (*b*) colour; (*c*) consistence, (*d*) specific gravity (*hydrostatic test*). Corroborative evidence may be afforded by the presence or absence of air in the stomach and intestines.

(*a*) The Volume of the Lungs before and after Respiration.—When the thorax of a newly-born infant that has not breathed is opened the lungs are scarcely visible, the thoracic cavity is chiefly occupied by the heart and thymus gland. If these organs are drawn on one side, or the margins of the opening through the thoracic wall are stretched wide apart, the lungs may be seen lying near the vertebral column, their sharp borders reaching forwards to about one-third of the length of the ribs. The diaphragm is only covered by them at its posterior part. If the child has fully breathed the lungs more or less fill the thorax and partly cover the pericardium. The right lung is usually more prominent than the left. The thin sharp margins of the lungs have become rounded, and their under surface covers most of the arch of the diaphragm. If the difference in volume between the lungs of an infant that had breathed and one that had not was invariably as pronounced as above described there would be little need for further evidence. The descriptions given, however, represent the two extremes—absolutely no respiration in contrast with fully established respiration; in such cases there is little probability of error. When the infant has but feebly or imperfectly breathed, the volume of the lungs may be only slightly different—and possibly not at all—from that which obtains in the fœtal condition. In these cases nothing is learnt from an inspection of the size of the lungs.

The Position of the Diaphragm.—The increase in the volume of the lungs causes them not only to spread forward but also downward, the result being that the arch of the diaphragm is depressed. Usually in infants that have not breathed the highest part of the arch is on a level with the fourth or fifth ribs; after respiration it sinks to the level of the sixth or seventh ribs. It is obvious from what has already been said in reference to imperfect respiration that the height of the diaphragm can only be distinctive in well marked cases; it is, therefore, of little use as a means of determining doubtful cases. Even in cases in which infants have fully respired, the diaphragm has been found nearly as high as before the occurrence of respiration. The presence of gases or of fluids from putrefactive processes in the abdomen or thorax alters the curvature of the diaphragm.

(*b*) The Colour of the Lungs before and after Respiration.—Before respiration the colour of the lungs is pale brown, resembling that of the liver, but paler. It has been likened by Casper and Liman to strong chocolate and water, sometimes being lighter, more like chocolate with milk; at the borders the colour is a little brighter. The tint varies with the amount of blood present in the lung. The lobes are indicated by lines of a lighter colour. A marked characteristic of lungs that have not respired is that, with insignificant exceptions, the colour is uniform over the entire surface; the posterior portion may be a little darker than the anterior, but there is no mottling.

After full respiration the lungs assume a lighter colour, which partakes of many shades from light red to dark bluish-red. When there is much blood in the lungs, dark bluish red forms the ground-tone on which spots and patches of bright red are seen; when there is less blood the ground-tone is light red, the patches then taking the darker hue. This marbled or mottled appearance is very characteristic of the occurrence of respiration; it is never found in the fœtal lung. The shaded patches and spots project slightly above the rest of the lung surface, being formed by distension of the alveoli with air. The pleura of the lung that has breathed is very transparent, and imparts brilliancy to the underlying tints, the fœtal lung, on the contrary, has a dull non-transparent surface. It is absolutely necessary to observe the colour of the lungs, both fœtal and respired, soon after the thorax is opened, as exposure to air quickly alters the tints, making them lighter.

When the infant has feebly respired for a short time only, indications in the form of spots or patches of a different colour to the rest of the lung may or may not be present on its surface. They usually appear first on the border of the upper lobe of the right lung, and may be found there when absent from the rest of the surface of both lungs. They appear as red, or bluish-red spots on the otherwise uniform brownish tint of the unrespired part of the lung. The spots are irregularly coloured, having a mottled look. The presence of these spots —inflated alveoli—is a sure indication that air has entered the lungs. They may be absent, however, in exceptional cases, even when the child has for a short time survived birth, respiration having been imperfectly carried on.

Artificial inflation may cause the surface of the lungs to assume a bright red colour, which, according to Casper, is uniformly distributed over the surface without any trace of mottling. Taylor and Stevenson mention a case in which Braxton Hicks performed artificial inflation in a still-born infant, the attempt at resuscitation being unsuccessful. On opening the thorax it was found that the air cells in about three-fourths of the lungs had received air, but the colour of the lungs was different from that which obtains after natural respiration, being of a pale fawn tint. On the other hand, Runge[1] and Oblonsky[2] assert that a mottled appearance may be produced by the method of artificial inflation called Schultze's-swinging.

When death results from hæmorrhage in the newly-born infant, the lungs are pale and reddish-grey; if respiration has taken place, bluish-black marbling is to be seen on the light-coloured ground.

To epitomise: a uniform brownish colour of the lungs is indicative of the fœtal state, a mottled or marbled appearance, of various tints as described, is peculiar to lungs that have breathed. The possibility of artificial inflation must be taken into account.

(*c*) The Consistence of the Lungs before and after Respiration.—Before respiration the fœtal lung resembles liver, not only in colour but also in texture, it is compact and firm, and on pressure offers resistance to the finger. After respiration the lung is elastic and yielding, and when compressed between the finger and thumb produces a feeling of crepitation. The difference in consistence between fœtal lungs and those which have respired is respectively due to the absence and to the presence of air in the alveoli; therefore, when respiration has been imperfectly performed, the characteristic feel of a lung that has breathed will be only partially present, or, it may be, entirely absent; if partially present, some portions of the lung will crepitate, others will not.

Coincident with the establishment of respiration is the commencement of the pulmonary circulation. During fœtal life the blood that reaches the lungs is limited to the amount required for their nutrition. When respiration is established, the whole of the blood in the body passes through the lungs which, consequently, at any given moment, contain an amount greatly in excess of that which was present in the fœtal state. If an incision is made into the fœtal lung it cuts like liver, and from the cut surfaces—the colour of which is uniform—only here and there a little blood appears when slight pressure is made. Lungs that have breathed are less easily cut, as the tissues, on account of their elasticity, recede before the knife, the stroke of which produces a crepitant sound; the cut surface is irregularly coloured, and if scraped with the blade of the knife, blood-stained froth is obtained.

The increased amount of blood that passes through the lungs after respiration is established adds to their weight. On this fact is founded the so-called **static test**. The average weight of lungs before respiration is stated to be from 450 to 600 grains, after respiration 960 grains; numerous observations have proved that these figures are far from representing the actual lung-weights respectively. As the lungs of the infant under inspection cannot be weighed both before and after

[1] *Berliner klin. Wochenschr.*, 1882.   [2] *Vierteljahrsschr. f. ger. Med.*, 1888.

respiration, a reliable average weight would be necessary for the utilisation of the static test. This, however, is unattainable, the lung-weights, both before and after respiration respectively, being so extremely variable. Ploucquet proposed to obviate the difficulty introduced by the varying weight of the lungs in newly-born infants, by assuming a certain proportion between the lung-weight and the total body-weight. The assumption is fallacious, as no such ratio exists. The static test in any form is useless as a means of determining the occurrence or not of respiration.

(*d*) The Specific Gravity of the Lungs before and after Respiration.— Although the lungs as a whole are heavier after the child has breathed, they are specifically lighter, the increase in weight caused by the influx of blood is more than counterbalanced by the air that is present in the alveoli.

On the difference in specific gravity of lungs which have and which have not respired, is founded the hydrostatic test. Advantage is taken of the fact that the specific gravity of unrespired lung tissue is greater than that of water, whilst the specific gravity of respired lung-tissue is less than that of water. If, therefore, unrespired lungs are placed in water they sink; if respired lungs are placed in water they float.

The Hydrostatic Test is thus Performed.—The lungs with the bronchi, as far as their junction at the trachea, are placed in some water contained in a suitable vessel. They either float or sink. If they float, observe whether the bulk of them remains above the water-level, or whether they float almost or quite submerged. The bronchi should then be divided, and each lung tied separately, the respective degree of buoyancy being observed as before. Each lung is now cut into about a dozen pieces, and each piece tested separately. If they float, they are to be taken out of the water and subjected to firm compression, in order, if possible, to drive out the air or gas that causes them to float. If the air has entered the lungs in the act of natural respiration, no degree of force, unless sufficient to cause disintegration of the lung-tissue, will expel it, and, consequently, on again placing the fragments in water they still float. If the lungs sink, it should be noticed whether one or both sink, and whether slowly or rapidly. They are then divided into a dozen or twenty pieces, each of which is tested separately. If the lungs, when whole and when cut in pieces, sink, presumptive evidence is thereby afforded that the child has not breathed.

The possible fallacies of the hydrostatic test are—that the lungs may float (α) from *artificial inflation*, (β) from the presence of the *gases of putrefaction*. That they may sink (γ) from the effects of *disease*, (δ) from *imperfect respiration* (*atelectasis*), or from absolute persistence of the fœtal condition, although the child has breathed and lived for some time

(α) Artificial Inflation.—This may be performed in several ways—by the direct application of the operator's mouth to that of the child, by forcing air into the lungs through a silver catheter, or other similar instrument passed by the mouth into the trachea, or by the method known as Schultze's swinging. Inflation of the lungs in a new-born infant is no easy matter, the air being apt to find its way into the stomach rather than into the lungs. When the attempt at resuscitation is not successful, *post-mortem* examination shows that the lungs are rarely more than partially inflated. As already described, the appearance of lungs artificially inflated is stated by some to be very different from that displayed by lungs in which complete natural respiration has taken place. It has also been asserted that a further difference exists—that the air contained by lungs artificially inflated can be expelled by pressure. This is contradicted by experience, and is opposed to physiological experiment. In Braxton Hicks' case of artificial inflation, previously mentioned, no amount of pressure short of destruction of tissue caused the divided pieces to sink. An explanation of these contradictory statements may probably be found in the position occupied by the air artificially introduced. If it arrives in the alveoli without rupturing their walls, there is no reason to suppose that it can be more easily expelled by pressure than air which has been naturally inspired. If, however, the air has not penetrated beyond the lobular bronchi, or (as readily occurs in artificial inflation) it has been propelled with sufficient pressure to rupture the septa between the alveoli, and to obtain access to the sub-pleural connective tissue, there is nothing to prevent its expulsion on compression of the lung fragments.

When artificial inflation is only *partially successful* in distending the lungs, it has been stated that no additional blood enters them, so that, although they may be more voluminous than in the fœtal state, they are not heavier, and that an incision into the lung-substance does not yield blood, as in the case of a lung that has naturally respired. This view, supported by Casper and other leading experts, has of late years been proved to be incorrect. Runge,[1] Sommer,[2] and Oblonsky[3] have all recorded cases in which the lungs of still-born children, by means of Schultze's-swinging, have acquired all the properties of lungs that have partially respired in the natural way. Oblonsky removed, by Cæsarean section, a nine months' fœtus from the body of a woman who

---

[1] *Berliner klin. Wochenschr.*, 1882.  [2] *Vierteljahrsschr. f. ger. Med.*, Bd. 43.
[3] *Vierteljahrsschr. f. ger. Med.*, Bd. 48.

died suddenly, the operation being performed about ten minutes after death The child was dead, and attempts at resuscitation were made by Schultze's-swinging. The attempts were unsuccessful, and on examining the body the thoracic cavity was found almost entirely filled with the lungs The apices of both lungs, and the edges of the lobes were rosy-red in colour, and the rest of the lung surface was purple-red with rose-coloured spots, presenting a mottled or marbled appearance The lungs floated on the surface of water, and when divided all the pieces floated except those derived from the posterior aspect From the edges of an incision in the apices blood stained froth exuded. Other cases are also recorded by the same writer in which blood-stained froth was obtained by the incision of lungs artificially inflated

The distinction formerly made between the effects of natural respiration and artificial inflation is no longer to be received in an absolute sense In many cases it doubtless holds good, but since exceptions have been proved it is to be admitted that *no known test* will enable an infallible opinion to be expressed as to whether lungs have respired incompletely, or have been artificially inflated

Apart from physical evidence, the occurrence of artificial inflation in cases of suspected infanticide is opposed to reason In the newly-born infant the performance of artificial respiration is a difficult task for the expert, and without special knowledge it would be barely possible for an ordinary woman to put it into practice. Schultze's method, by which lungs have been inflated to a degree comparable with the effects of imperfect respiration, is little used in this country, and demands expert knowledge and practice for its performance If the inflation is done by a second person who was in attendance at the labour, evidence of the fact would be forthcoming

(β) **The Gases of Decomposition**—The lungs belong to the class of organs which putrefy slowly The thorax being intact, if there are no external signs of putrefaction, or only those of the early stage, it may be accepted that the lungs will not be influenced by the gases of decomposition so far as the hydrostatic test goes The earliest indication of putrefaction in the lungs consists in the appearance of small vesicles filled with gas between the lung substance and the pleura, the pressure of the gas lifting the pleura in detached spots They first appear at the free borders of the lobes, and at the base of the lungs; subsequently, the deeper seated tissues of the lungs are infiltrated with gas The vesicles under the pleura vary in size from that of a pin's head to that of a bean, in the early stage they are small and are often found clustered together, or in rows By pressure of the finger the gas can be displaced, and if small the vesicle disappears as the gas travels under the pleura; if such a vesicle is pricked with a needle so as to allow the gas to escape, the pleura falls flat. Air within the alveoli is not expelled, neither by pressure nor by simple pricking with a needle. It is to be noted that an appearance similar to the small vesicles of putrefaction might be caused by rupture of the alveoli from too vigorous attempts at artificial inflation. In the early stage of putrefaction of the lungs the organs retain their appearance sufficiently to enable distinction to be made between the colour of the foetal lung and of that which has breathed. When a more advanced stage is reached the colour is dark green, sometimes almost black, or dirty-brown. The lung-substance is softened, and on section a dirty-red fluid escapes—the odour is then highly offensive. Foetal lungs do not decompose so rapidly as those which have breathed.

When foetal lung-tissue is infiltrated with the gases of decomposition its specific gravity is lessened, therefore in this state it will float. A piece of lung in this condition compressed by the finger and thumb under water gives off a number of relatively large and irregularly formed air-bubbles which ascend through the water. A piece of fresh lung that has breathed when similarly treated yields a stream of fine, equal sized bubbles. Pressure drives out the gas from decomposed lungs, so that pieces which float in their original condition sink after compression; this result, however, may ensue in the case of lungs which have breathed when the lung-substance is softened by putrefaction. Foetal lungs which have been rendered buoyant by putrefaction spontaneously lose that property in a still more advanced stage of decomposition, and sink as they would before being attacked by putrefaction.

It may be accepted that when the lungs are in an advanced stage of putrefaction, no trustworthy evidence can be yielded by the hydrostatic test. The fact mentioned at the beginning of this section, however, is to be remembered—that the lungs putrefy slowly, therefore an advanced stage of external putrefaction does not preclude the necessity of testing the lungs. Ogston[1] found no putrefactive buoyancy of the lungs from the body of an infant which had been dead five months. Casper examined two new-born infants whose bodies were in an advanced stage of decomposition; the heart and the liver floated from the presence of gas, whilst the lungs sank. If a distinction is to be made, the evidence afforded by the lungs *floating* is quite unreliable when the organs are undergoing putrefaction; that afforded by the lungs *sinking*, if an advanced stage of putrefaction is not reached, may be taken into account.

(7) **The Effects of Disease.**—Pulmonary disease in the first days of life is rare; certain forms—as pneumonia, pleurisy with effusion, and

[1] *Lectures on Medical Jurisprudence.*

so-called pulmonary apoplexy—are capable of depriving the lung of its buoyancy after the occurrence of respiration. If the disease began during intra-uterine life, it might either completely or partially prevent the entry of air into the lungs. Death from suffocation may produce such a degree of hyperæmia of the lungs as to cause them to sink in water. In none of these conditions would there be any real difficulty, as the pathological appearances caused by the diseases would be apparent either to the naked eye or with the aid of the microscope. With the exception of excessive hyperæmia produced by suffocation, it is unlikely, but not impossible, that the whole of both lungs would be so affected by disease as to sink when subdivided. If sinking of the lungs is due to consolidation after the occurrence of respiration, any attempt to inflate them by blowing down the trachea will be unsuccessful; but if due to persistence of the foetal condition, inflation can be thus accomplished.

(*b*) **Imperfect Respiration.**—It is a remarkable fact that very exceptionally an infant may survive its birth for many hours, during which period the chest may rise and fall as in ordinary respiration, and what is even more remarkable, the child may cry, and yet after death the lungs are found to have completely retained their foetal condition—the colour, volume, consistence, and specific gravity being respectively the same as in the unrespired lung. From this total absence of aeration, all degrees of alveolar distention may occur up to that which accompanies fully developed respiration. The term atelectasis has been applied to such conditions, the meaning of the word being imperfect expansion; medical jurists use the word in order to indicate defective performance of a physiological function; it is used by others to indicate an acquired pathological condition—partial consolidation of the lungs. The word is unnecessary and inconvenient. The expression "imperfect expansion" is sufficiently distinctive, and admits of change to "non-expansion" to signify absolute persistence of the foetal condition, whereas atelectasis being itself a comparative expression cannot correctly be thus used.

There are three ways in which it is sought to explain the anomaly of a child living and breathing for many hours without a trace of the occurrence of respiration being present in the lungs after death. Maschka and others deny that air enters the lungs at all in such cases, the passage of air along the trachea and bronchi is regarded as sufficient to account for the signs manifested during life. Others accept the theory first propounded by Simon Thomas[1]—that in feeble infants the respiratory movements may gradually subside in such a way that the passive elasticity of the lung-tissue, at every expiration,

[1] *Nederl. Tydschr. v. Geneesk.*, 1864.

drives out more air than is drawn in at the inspirations, in this way the lungs after having breathed gradually return to the fœtal condition. As the result of experimental investigation Ungar[1] states that the air which has entered the lungs may be entirely absorbed after respiration has ceased by the blood circulating through them.

When from immaturity or from extreme feebleness a newly-born infant barely exists, its demand for oxygen will be very slight, and it is conceivable that the necessary interchange might take place in the air tubes without the help of the alveoli. The rising and falling of the chest, as in ordinary respiration, is not inconsistent with retention of the fœtal condition of the lungs. Hermann[2] showed experimentally that the lungs in the fœtal condition require more pressure to expand them than those which contain air on account of the adhesion of the bronchial and alveolar epithelium. If the lungs are once expanded, however feeble the infant may be, there will be some movement of air in them, but, if the initial unfolding of the lung-tissue has not already taken place, the movements of the chest wall may be inadequate to overcome the resistance. It is, however, difficult to understand how sufficient air could be inspired under these conditions as to enable the child to cry to the extent that has occurred in many cases. Vernon[3] heard a newly-delivered child cry, whilst under the bed-clothes, sufficiently loud as to be audible to him as he entered the adjoining room. The child lived five hours, and after death the lungs sank, whole and divided, and showed no trace of air-vesicles under the microscope. The second hypothesis—gradual expulsion of all the air by the elasticity of the lung-tissue is in accord, neither with physiological experiments nor with clinical experience. Hermann (l.c.) proved that the elastic power of the lung that has once contained air cannot expel the air and restore the lung to the fœtal state. Children are frequently born immature and feeble, and die shortly after birth, but the occurrence of lungs in a fœtal condition under such circumstances is exceptionally rare. Ungar's hypothesis is not improbable, seeing that in these cases of low vitality the heart may continue to beat some time after the cessation of respiration, in this way it is feasible that the residual air might be entirely absorbed by the blood. Caussé[4] records the case of a seven months' infant which survived several days. After death the right lung was found more expanded than the left, and when cut into yielded dark coloured blood, but it was not crepitant. Both lungs, whole and divided, sank in water. In this case it seems probable that modified respiration took place in the right lung as it was

[1] *Vierteljahrsschr. f. ger. Med.*, 1883. [2] *Pfluger's Archiv*, 1879.
[3] *The Lancet*, 1855. [4] *Annales d'Hygiène*, 1878.

more expanded than the left (which remained fœtal), and yielded blood on being cut into. Still it sank whole and divided when placed in water, showing that after death it contained no air.

Whatever may be the true explanation, the fact must not be lost sight of—that under exceptional conditions an infant may breathe, and even cry at intervals, for many hours after its birth, and yet after death the lungs may absolutely resemble those of a still-born child. A less extreme condition, in which a portion of the lung contains air, does not present the same difficulty, as the hydrostatic test is capable of demonstrating the fact. It has been asserted that air which has entered the lungs during imperfect respiration can be driven out by compression of the detached pieces of lung so that they will sink in water. If the air has arrived in the alveoli (as it presumably has) it is difficult to see how this can be. When a piece of lung is compressed the bronchioles are compressed as well as the air cells, the result being that the air contained in the bronchioles is expelled, but not that in the alveoli; the stronger the pressure the more firmly is the air pent up in the alveoli, unless such force is used as to rupture them.

The inferences to be drawn from the results obtained from the hydrostatic test are:—That if the whole of the lungs float, both entire, when cut in pieces, and after the application of pressure, proof is afforded that the child has breathed, the possibility of artificial inflation being borne in mind. If the lungs sink both whole and divided, the probability is that the child has not respired. This qualified statement is rendered necessary by the occasional occurrence of an imperfect type of respiration, which leaves the lungs in the fœtal condition. Absence of buoyancy from disease is also to be remembered, though not so conducive to error. It is obvious that no lung-test can distinguish between lungs that retain the fœtal type, notwithstanding the occurrence of a modified form of respiration; the stomach-bowel test may be of service in such cases. Less importance is to be attached to negative evidence in this direction, as no injustice to the individual results; at the most, a guilty person may escape, an innocent one cannot suffer. When putrefactive processes have invaded the lungs, the greatest reticence is to be displayed in accepting the evidence afforded by the hydrostatic test; in such cases it is better to state that the condition of the lungs does not admit of an opinion being given as to whether the child did or did not breathe.

A detailed bibliography up to date of the various tests used to ascertain the occurrence or non-occurrence of respiration in the newly-born infant, will be found in a series of articles by Mueller in the *Wiener medicinische Wochenschrift* for 1891.

**The Presence of Air in the Stomach and Intestines.**—Breslau,[1] in the year 1865, drew attention to the fact that the stomach and intestines in still-born infants sink when placed in water, whilst in infants which have survived birth a sufficient amount of air is present within one or both of these viscera as respectively to render them buoyant. In 1886 Ungar[2] began to advocate the importance of this distinction, which, meanwhile, had not been practically utilised to any great extent. Since then the subject has received much attention, especially in Germany, and numerous observations have been made with the view of ascertaining how far the presence or the absence of air in the stomach and intestines can be depended on as proof of live birth, or of the occurrence of respiration. The advocates of this test have designated it "the second life-test."

The air that is contained in the digestive tract of a newly-born infant finds its way there in the act of swallowing during the first and subsequent respiratory movements. If the child does not survive the first few respirations, the stomach only is more or less inflated, but if the child breathes for some time, the air finds its way into the duodenum and, subsequently, lower down the intestinal canal. The test is performed by placing double ligatures at the cardiac and pyloric ends of the stomach, and also at the lower part of the duodenum. The stomach, separated from the œsophagus, is, with the intestine, then placed in water; if the united viscera float, they are detached and tested separately. The results of many experiments tend to show that this test is of considerable importance in determining the occurrence or absence of respiration. The advocates of the test state that it is not only capable of substantiating the result obtained from the hydrostatic lung-test, but that it is capable of determining whether breathing has or has not occurred in those cases of imperfect respiration in which, after the child has survived several hours, the lungs retain the fœtal condition and, consequently, yield negative results with the hydrostatic test. There are two ways in which the stomach bowel test may be rendered untrustworthy—by attempts at artificial inflation, and by the occurrence of putrefaction. Artificial inflation, whether attempted by the direct application of the operator's mouth to that of the child, or by means of a catheter or other tube, or by Schultze's-swinging, is almost certain to cause air to enter the stomach, whether it enters the lungs or not. It is obvious that putrefaction will vitiate the test. In the *absence of artificial inflation*, and of *putrefaction*, if the stomach, and especially if the duodenum also floats, the fact affords strong evidence that the infant breathed. Under the same conditions, if the stomach sinks it is *no* proof that the child was still-born.

[1] *Monatsschr. f. Geburtskunde*, Bd. 25.  [2] *Vierteljahr-schr. f. ger. Med.*, 1887.

Nikitin[1] gives a table of a hundred cases in which the evidence obtained from the hydrostatic test and the stomach-bowel test are placed side by side. The results show that the latter test is likely to occupy an important position amongst the means resorted to in order to ascertain whether an infant has or has not breathed. Ungar's[2] last communication gives a full bibliography of the subject up to the present time.

### 3. WAS THE CHILD BORN ALIVE?

It is ever to be borne in mind that the lung-test at the most can but prove that the child has or has not breathed. When the medical witness gives evidence based on the lung-test, if the lungs float he must limit himself to the statement that his investigations prove that the child breathed; he must not say that the child was born alive. The reason for this limitation is that, although the written law contains no definition of live birth, the judges do not recognise the birth of a child to be accomplished until the whole of its body is external to the maternal organism. It is not necessary that the umbilical cord should have been divided. As is well-known, a child may breathe after its head is extruded from the vagina, whilst the rest of its body still remains within the maternal passages. To kill a child in this stage of its birth is not murder, since the administrators of the law deny that it then has any separate existence. It will be seen from this that proof of complete respiration is not in itself proof of live birth. If the child is killed immediately after its birth, in the legal acceptation of the term, medical evidence cannot prove that it was born alive; no evidence except that of an eye-witness is competent to do so. Again, it is not even necessary for the child's head to be born in order that it may breathe. There are numerous cases on record in which infants breathed, and demonstrated the fact by crying, whilst still within the uterus. M'Lean[3] records the case of a child that cried for four or five minutes whilst within the uterus; "the voice sounding as if coming from the cellar." Delivery was effected with the forceps. In the recorded cases in which respiration took place whilst the child was inside the maternal passages, the admission of air resulted from their dilatation either by the hand of the accoucheur, or the instruments used by him, so that a channel of communication was established between the external atmosphere and the child's mouth. If this was invariably so, the occurrence of respiration whilst the child is within the vagina or uterus, would be of no importance in cases of suspected infanticide, as the accoucheur could give evidence as an eye-witness

---

[1] *Vierteljahrsschr. f. ger. Med.*, 1888.    [2] Virchow's *Archiv.*, 1891.
[3] *American Journal of Obstetrics*, 1889.

as to whether the child was or was not born alive, it appears just possible however, that air might find admission to the child's mouth without adventitious aid

It is to be noted in any of these modes in which respiration occurs before legal birth that, if death takes place immediately afterwards, the expansion of the lungs will probably be incomplete For the reasons already given, the initial expansion of the lungs is a gradual process The adhesiveness of the contiguous layers of epithelium in the bronchioles and the alveoli does not yield to the first few inhalations, step by step the air penetrates until at last the entire respiratory tract is opened up According to Dohrn,[1] under normal conditions the alveoli are not fully dilated until the second or third day, in weakly children still longer time is required fully to expand the lungs and to remove all trace of their fœtal state If, therefore, the lungs are found completely expanded, it is probable that the child was fully born, as the difficulty of access of air whilst the head is within the vagina, and the probably short delay in the completion of delivery when the head is outside (the body being within), would render the accomplishment of perfect expansion of the lungs unlikely At the risk of reiteration, attention is directed to the difference in the quality of the evidence afforded by the hydrostatic test as regards proof of respiration and of live birth respectively —If the lungs are fully expanded, so that every separate piece floats after being subjected to pressure, the occurrence of respiration (allowing for the remote contingency of artificial respiration) is proved, the same state of the lungs affords only *presumptive* evidence of live birth In the one case, with due observance of experimental precautions, there can be no doubt as to the truth of the assertion, in the other, it is a mere surmise, for though improbable, it is not impossible for the child to remain with the body unborn (the head being expelled) until the lungs are fully distended

The Stomach-bowel Test affords circumstantial evidence of survival of birth If the intestines as well as the stomach contain air, and in consequence float when placed on water—the absence of attempts at artificial inflation and of putrefaction being understood—the probability is that the child did not die immediately after birth The lower the air permeates the intestinal canal the greater the probability that the child survived birth

The Middle Ear Test —In the fœtal state the middle ear is filled with an embryonic gelatinous mass Wreden[2] and afterwards Wendt[3] found that when respiration has fully taken place, this mass is re-

[1] *Archiv f Gynacologie*, 1889   [2] *Otitis neonatorum*, 1868
[3] *Arch f Heilkund*, 1873

placed with air. Wendt further states that if attempts at respiration are made whilst the infant is immersed in the amniotic, or in any other fluid, such fluid will be found replacing the gelatinous mass. Ogston,[1] junior, found that the mass disappeared in from a few hours to two or three weeks after birth. Schmaltz[2] states that the mass begins to disappear during fœtal life, and that although the influence of respiration on it is recognisable, the absence of the mass is no certain proof that respiration has taken place; he often found the mass in infants that had breathed, and in some instances it was absent in the fœtal state. Lesser[3] states that a few respirations produce little effect on the contents of the middle ear, but that after several hours' respiration they are displaced. Lesser also states that in premature children the fœtal condition of the middle ear may persist for more than twenty hours after birth. Stevenson[4] found the middle ear test useful in several cases.

**Changes in the Umbilical Cord.**—Much difference of opinion exists as to the value of mummification of the cord as an indication of live birth. Casper denies that it has any value, Billard and others hold that its occurrence is an indication of extra-uterine life. Under certain conditions it may undoubtedly be of importance as a diagnostic sign. Lowndes[5] relates the case of a new-born child which had probably been dead eleven or twelve days. For half an inch from the navel the cord was perfectly fresh, then came the usual line of demarcation, and the remainder of the cord, about $2\frac{1}{2}$ inches, was completely mummified. There was no appearance of ligature. The inference was that the child had lived at least twenty-four hours. Such a case is rare, but it serves to show that mummification of the cord is not to be overlooked in suspected infanticide. Normal **separation** of the cord, with the accompanying signs of reaction—the line of capillary congestion and the inflammatory exudation products—are unmistakable indications that the child has survived birth; unfortunately such signs are not available until, at the least, four or five days after birth. Care must be taken not to confound a red line, which at birth surrounds the spot where the cord is inserted, with the line of separation. The former is simply a coloured ring without any swelling or indications of inflammation; the latter is a true reactionary area, of a distinctly inflammatory character. If the body of an infant in an advanced stage of putrefaction is found with no remains of the umbilical cord attached it is not therefore to be assumed that natural separation has taken place. The

---

[1] *Brit. and For. Med. Chirurg. Review.*, 1875.
[2] *Arch. J. Heilkund*, 1877.   [3] *Vierteljahrsschr. f. ger. Med.*, 1879.
[4] Taylor and Stevenson, *Manual of Med. Jurisprudence*, 1891.
[5] *Liverpool Med. and Chir. Journ.*, 1889.

cord may have been detached close to the abdomen by violence, either during life or after death, and the signs which ordinarily serve to differentiate between normal and violent separation will be destroyed by the putrefactive processes.

The alterations which take place in the skin of an infant after birth, described on p. 26, may be utilised as indications of survival of birth.

The changes which take place in the heart and vessels after the cessation of the fœtal circulation are of no value in determining whether the child was born alive or was still-born. Elsasser[1] by careful examination proved that the processes by which the foramen ovale, the ductus venosus and ductus arteriosus are closed, do not commence for several days after birth; they take weeks to accomplish, and they do not follow any regular order.

Occasionally the presence of milk or other nutrient substance in the stomach may be discovered, and survival of birth thus proved. Anything found in the stomach should be submitted to microscopical examination. Fluids in the stomach derived from either the maternal or the fœtal organism—as blood, or meconium—prove nothing except that the infant was living about the time of birth. The absence of meconium from the large intestines, though not affording proof of survival after birth is suggestive of it; the presence of meconium, however, does not indicate still-birth, as frequently it is not expelled for a day or more after birth.

It is from a consideration of such of the above described signs of live birth as are available that an opinion is to be formed as to whether the child was born alive, and, if so, how long it lived. In some cases there is no difficulty in determining the former point, and but little in approximately estimating the latter; others present features of extreme difficulty, and demand both painstaking investigation and a display of due reserve in the statement of opinions based on such investigations. If the child died immediately after birth it is out of the power of medical evidence to *prove* that it was born alive, whatever reasons there may be for inclining to that opinion. The reliable signs of survival of birth only come into play after the lapse of several days.

### 4. THE CAUSE OF DEATH

The first consideration is—Did the child die from natural causes? It is a well ascertained fact that among illegitimate children the mortality is much greater than it is with those born in wedlock. Newsholme[2] states that in twelve urban districts the mean mortality

---

[1] Henke's *Zeitschr*, Bd 64.     [2] *Elements of Vital Statistics.*

for infants in the years 1871–75 was, for legitimate children 192 per 1,000 legitimate births; for illegitimate 388 per 1,000 illegitimate births. In Glasgow during 1873–75, the annual deaths of legitimate infants to every 1,000 legitimate births were 152; of illegitimate infants to every 1,000 illegitimate births 286. Tatham states in his annual report for the Borough of Salford in 1887, that the proportion of deaths under the age of one year per 1,000 births was 187 for legitimate and 371 for illegitimate children.

## DEATH OF THE INFANT FROM NATURAL OR ACCIDENTAL CAUSES.

A large percentage of infants are either still-born or die from natural causes shortly after birth; first pregnancies are more likely to yield still-born children than subsequent pregnancies. In a great many of the cases in which medical examination of the bodies of infants found under suspicious circumstances is required to be made, the mothers are young women who have not previously had children. The necessity for concealing their condition during pregnancy leads to actions which are detrimental to the well-being of the infant *in utero*. The labour also takes place under disadvantageous conditions; the woman has no help, and, if parturition is prolonged, or the umbilical cord prolapses, or is coiled round the child's neck, or any other lethal complication capable of being rectified by skilled assistance occurs, the child may be still born from absence of help, but without any criminal intent on the part of the mother. The infant, from immaturity or intra-uterine malnutrition, may perish during or immediately after birth simply from deficient vitality. Malformations of the heart, of the intestinal tract, or of the central organs of the nervous system, are capable of easy recognition as causes of the infant's death. Disease, as apoplexy, pneumonia, hydrothorax, gastro-intestinal hæmorrhage and the like, may occasion death. Asphyxia, from non-expansion of the lungs, or from the introduction of blood, meconium, or liquor amnii into the air passages, is another cause of death.

It will be necessary to describe some of these modes of **natural or accidental death** in detail.

Prolapse of the umbilical cord is lethal if the prolapsed part of the cord is subjected to firm and continuous compression sufficient to interrupt the blood current. The percentage of deaths in prolapse has been variously estimated, Hohl[1] states it to be about 11 per cent., Scanzoni[1] puts it at 55 per cent. Lloyd Roberts[2] records the case of a woman in whom prolapse of the funis occurred in nine consecutive labours.

---

[1] *Lehrbuch der Geburtshulfe.*  [2] *The Lancet*, 1868.

When the circulation through the cord is arrested, the fœtal blood becomes venous and stimulates the respiratory centres into action, the infant makes attempts at respiration, and access of air being prevented, suffocation ensues. The post-mortem signs of suffocation will be found to be present on examination of the body—capillary ecchymoses, injection of the tracheal mucous membrane, distension of the heart with blood, and the presence of blood, meconium, particles of vernix caseosa and mucus in the air-passages and stomach. The contents of the bowels are usually voided during the attempts at respiration, and the body of the child is consequently befouled. The discovery of particles of vernix caseosa in the bronchial tubes affords strong evidence in favour of intra-uterine suffocation. Strassmann[1] takes advantage of the fact that weak solutions of anilin dyes stain keratin-tissues. A section of the lung-tissue may be stained in a solution composed of one drop of a one per cent. solution of gentian-violet to a watch-glass of water; allow to remain five minutes; wash with alcohol, and clear with oil. A simpler way is to take a little of the contents of a bronchial tube, spread it on a cover-glass, dry over a Bunsen flame, and stain. The stain is taken by the particles of vernix caseosa, and their presence is then easily detected.

**Accidental strangulation with the umbilical cord** is frequently stated to have been the cause of death in cases of alleged infanticide; the fact that during birth the child's neck is not unfrequently surrounded by the cord gives colour to the statement. It occurs in about 25 per cent. of deliveries; the mortality being estimated at from 1·1 per cent. to 2·7 per cent. Sänger[2] relates a case that was delivered in hospital. When the head was expelled, the face was deeply cyanosed; the funis was coiled once round the neck, in the first instance too tightly stretched to be released, and when subsequently removed no pulsation was perceptible—the child was still-born. The skin of the face and neck was of a dark bluish-red colour, sprinkled with numerous petechiæ, very dark, almost black. The eye-balls were prominent, the conjunctivæ swollen and marked with petechiæ. The tongue protruded between the teeth. The superficial veins appeared as dark lines. On the front of the neck were two firm ridges extending to the angle of the lower jaw, resembling the "double chin" in stout people. These ridges were covered with large ecchymoses, and between them, over the sternum, was a shallow, blackish groove a few centimetres long. The skin of the trunk was livid and cyanotic. There was a layer of blood 1 cm. thick under the scalp. Internally the brain was anæmic, but œdematous. The meninges were pale, and the sinuses only moderately filled with blood; there was fluid in the

[1] *Vierteljahrsschr. f. ger. Med.*, 1887.   [2] ***Archiv. f. Gynäcologie***, 1879.

lateral ventricles. The veins of the skin and of the muscles of the head and neck above the mark of the cord were very hyperæmic; both skin and muscles showed numerous ecchymoses. The larynx and vocal cords were very œdematous, the air passages were empty. The lungs retained their fœtal condition, the colour being pale blue-red; there were numerous sub-pleural ecchymoses. The pericardium contained some fluid, and the heart was ecchymosed. (Nothing is said about the amount of blood contained by the heart.) The compression chiefly affected the jugulars, carotids, and vagi. Hyperæmia of the brain and membranes is not a necessary accompaniment of death by strangulation, the compression of the carotids impedes access of blood. The funis measured 66 cm. (26 inches) in length. The portion from the navel to the neck 15 cm. (6 inches), round the neck 15 cm. and from the neck to placenta 36 cm. (14 inches).

The condition of the brain and membranes is not constant neither in death from strangulation with the funis, nor from compression of the funis occasioned by prolapse; out of twelve cases, Scanzoni found cerebral hyperæmia in four. The mark produced by strangulation with the umbilical cord is usually continuous round the neck, its breadth corresponds to the thickness of the cord. The groove is rounded in transverse section, it is soft, and what is very important, the skin is not excoriated.

Marks resembling those produced by the cord surrounding the neck may be caused by forcible bending of the head forwards during labour, especially in fat children. Careful examination will show the absence of the signs of real compression, such as are produced by the application of a constricting medium. Forcible stretching of the neck may produce red stripes on the front or back of it. Kaltenbach[1] directs attention to these marks as resembling those due to strangulation, they disappear in two or three days with exfoliation of the epiderm. When the child's head has passed the os uteri, the pressure of the contracted cervix round its neck may leave a mark which will be broad, and not so well defined as marks produced by other modes of construction. The fœtal membranes may get twisted round the child's neck and leave a suspicious looking mark.

**Prolonged labour** is not an unfrequent cause of death to the child; the compression produced by a spastically contracted uterus after rupture of the membranes, if long continued, not only kills the child but produces conditions of the body which may easily be mistaken for the results of intentional violence. Ashby,[2] in making post-mortem examinations of the bodies of recently born infants, found meningeal hæmorrhage as a frequent result of asphyxia produced by prolonged

[1] *Centralbl. f. Gynacologie*, 1888.   [2] *Brit. Med. Journ.*, 1890.

labour Stadtfeldt[1] states that hæmorrhage in the cranium is liable to be regarded as a sign of criminal suffocation, whereas it is chiefly due to injury received in labour. The spine also may be injured by extreme bending, and blood found alongside it; in one case Stadtfeldt found blood poured out about the kidneys without any obvious injury to the spine or any of the neighbouring organs. Effusion of blood is not uncommon when death of the child results from protracted labour, and this need occasion no surprise when the power of the uterine muscles, and the delicate nature of the tissues of an infant at or before term are taken into consideration. In some cases the child lives several days after birth, although the injury which eventually caused death was then received. Keser[2] met with such a case in which he found eight ounces of blood in the peritoneum.

A remarkable case is recorded by Monteith[3] of a child, born after natural labour, with a depressed fracture in the middle of the right parietal bone, which was split from the sagittal suture on the one side of the depression to the coronal suture on the other; spiculæ projected from the inner surface of the fractured bone.

**Immaturity** or **malnutrition** during intra-uterine life may lead to death of the infant shortly after birth; the latter is frequently due to placental degeneration, often of syphilitic origin, which interferes with the supply of blood to the fœtus; if the placental blood supply is very gradually diminished, as in progressive degeneration, there may be no signs of asphyxia in the fœtus, it is simply enfeebled from insufficient nutrition; if the circulation is more speedily interrupted by premature detachment of the placenta from the uterus, the signs of asphyxia will probably be present. The blood supply to the fœtus may be cut off by spontaneous rupture of the funis. Rivet[4] records a case in which a stream of blood from spontaneous rupture of the umbilical vessels followed breaking of the membranes.

Sudden death in new-born infants has resulted apparently from **hyperplasia of the thymus gland**. Grawitz[5] records two such cases, in one the gland covered the greatest part of the pericardium. Scheele[6] records another case in a child sixteen months old. The mode in which death is occasioned is not clear, although the postmortem signs of asphyxia are present; it is possible, in some cases at least, that spasm of the larynx may have caused the asphyxia. Paltauf[7] states that there is no proof of compression of the trachea by hyperplastic enlargement of the thymus gland, which is simply one

[1] *Nord Medicin Arka*, Bd. 17.   [2] *The Lancet*, 1886.
[3] *The Lancet*, 1874.   [4] *Arch de Tocologie*, 1883.
[5] *Deutsche med. Wochenschr*, 1888.   [6] *Zeitsch f. klin Med*, 1890.
[7] *Wiener k'in Wochenschr*, 1890.

of the appearances due to general disease of the lymphatic system and is not a direct cause of sudden death

Lethal malformations and disease, as pneumonia or hydrothorax, are usually sufficiently obvious as to occasion no difficulty in arriving at a conclusion as to the cause of death. Defective ossification of the bones of the skull increases the risk of fatal compression during labour, and may be mistaken for injuries produced by violence. Taylor and Stevenson[1] mention the case of an infant whose body was discovered in a pond, presenting the appearance of injury to the skull in the form of two holes in one of the parietal bones; on careful examination it was found that the bone at the edges of the apertures was thinned down, and that originally the spaces had been covered with membrane which had disappeared with maceration.

Delayed parturition has been mentioned as a cause of mortality to the child; the opposite extreme — hasty parturition — is also attended with risk. The modes in which death may be thus caused are various. If the child is expelled head downwards on a hard surface the bones of the skull may be fractured. If the woman is standing upright when the child comes away the parietal bones are broken if any; when but one is broken it is usually the left, on account of the rotation of the child in passing through the pelvis; the fractures may extend to the frontal or the occipital bones. The child may be precipitated into a night commode or other utensil, and may be drowned in the liquor amnii or other fluid into which it may fall. When the child falls into such a receptacle it usually arrives head downwards, and, consequently, if not quickly removed, a small quantity of fluid is sufficient to produce asphyxia. Mere falling to the floor without fracture of the skull may produce a fatal result from the injury sustained. Simple exposure to the cold air without covering and without any injury whatever, especially in the case of a weakly child, may be sufficient to cause death. In all these instances when lethal traumatic injuries are not produced by the fall, death results because the child receives no attention. If it is removed from the source of danger — drowning, or exposure to cold — it does not die. In fatal cases the usual explanation why the child was left to die is that the mother became unconscious at the moment of delivery.

This is a question of considerable importance, as it arises in a large number of cases of infanticide. Much scepticism is displayed by many experts as to the occurrence of unconsciousness during delivery. Heidenhain[2] relates the case of a woman who was seized with labour pains in the middle of the night and got out of bed to obtain a light,

[1] *Principles and Practice of Med. Jurisprudence*
[2] *Vierteljahrsschr. f. ger. Med.*, 1889

whilst doing so she alleged that the child was suddenly born and fell to the ground, the umbilical cord being torn at the moment the child fell. The mother returned to bed and fainted; on regaining consciousness the child was dead. Death was caused by intra-cranial hæmorrhage, the result of injury to the left parietal bone. Heidenhain looks with suspicion on the frequency of fainting after the birth of illegitimate children, and regards sudden labours in primiparæ as very unusual. Both these objections have considerable weight, but cases beyond suspicion have occurred which prove the possibility of rapid delivery with simultaneous or subsequent insensibility. Pullmann[1] records an instructive case of this kind. A married lady of good position, who anticipated with much pleasure the expected birth of a child, had some pains in the back but did not regard them as labour pains. An hour or two after bearing-down pains began, and the membranes ruptured; the doctor and nurse were immediately sent for. Meanwhile the patient felt a strong desire to urinate and got out of bed to pass water. She placed herself on the vessel, but feeling a peculiar quick movement in the genital organs, she sprang up, and at the same moment the child fell into the vessel, the placenta following. The mother immediately lost consciousness, and if the nurse at that moment had not entered and removed the child from its perilous position—head downwards in the vessel—it would undoubtedly have died. The child was about the thirty-first week of development; there was no *caput succedaneum*. The mother had an extensive rupture of the perineum in consequence of the quick expulsion. If this had occurred to a servant girl, and in obedience to her desire to urinate she had gone to the closet, the child would have been dead long before she had recovered her senses, but her account of the event would probably have been regarded as a pure fabrication. Brunon[2] relates the case of a primipara near term, who felt some pain in the back and a desire to defecate, she essayed to do so and then returned to bed. On feeling a still more imperative desire she again raised herself in order to go to the commode but was surprised to find something between her thighs, which was the head of the child. She knew nothing of what had taken place until she became aware of the presence of something externally. In another case reported by Langier,[3] a woman eight months advanced in pregnancy was seized with an irresistible desire to relieve the bowels, and on getting out of bed the child was suddenly expelled into the utensil, the funis was not torn, and the placenta had to be removed subsequently; the child was resuscitated. The woman felt nothing until a quarter of an hour

[1] *Vierteljahrsschr. f. ger. Med.*, 1891. [2] *Journ. de Méd. et de Chirurg.*, 1890.
[3] *Annales d'Hygiène*, 1891.

before expulsion. These cases show that statements made under circumstances of great suspicion are not, therefore, to be summarily rejected as being all but impossible.

When a woman becomes unconscious at the moment of expulsion, she must on regaining consciousness perceive what has taken place, and consequently imparts a guilty appearance to the event if she conceals the dead child and keeps the matter secret. The body of the child should be carefully examined for signs of injury inconsistent with the statement made, and the contents of the air passages should be examined for fluid, or other substance of the nature of that into which it is alleged the child fell. The funis, if torn, should be examined for indications of artificial separation, either with a cutting instrument or by being pulled asunder with the hands. If the infant was vigorous it might inspire sufficient air to make the lungs partially buoyant, in the act of falling into the receptacle, in any case indications of asphyxia would be present. In homicidal cases the child is usually suffocated or strangled, and consequently the body should be specially examined about the mouth, nostrils, and throat.

Hæmorrhage from the funis, divided after being ligatured, may cause death, apparently from indisposition of the blood to coagulate, or from insufficient tightness of the ligature.

## DEATH OF THE INFANT FROM CRIMINAL VIOLENCE.

The modes of death now to be considered are those which constitute the crime of infanticide. It is obvious that an infant is entirely at the mercy of any one disposed to take its life, there is scarcely any limit, therefore, to the ways by which this may be accomplished. Certain methods however preponderate in frequency as easy of execution, and because they most nearly simulate the appearances which are met with after death from accident or from natural causes.

**Suffocation** is the commonest mode of committing infanticide. A newly-born infant is easily suffocated by the application to the mouth and nostrils of any soft substance—as the bare hand, or a folded piece of cloth. Although very slight pressure is sufficient for the purpose, the tender tissues of the infant usually yield evidence of its occurrence, if the pressure is applied directly to the mouth. It is very rare that the minimum amount of violence necessary to accomplish the object is used, it may be accepted as an axiom that in almost all homicidal attempts more violence is used than is sufficient to cause death. This applies with exceptional force to child murder, the perpetrator is usually a woman who is under the influence of strong emotion at the time she commits the crime, and, therefore, is not in a condition to nicely gauge the degree of violence requisite to cause death. Another reason why excessive violence is often used is the necessity of immediately silencing the cries of the infant. The external appearances after death vary with the mode in which suffocation was effected—whether by pressure directly applied to the mouth or by enveloping the infant in some soft material which prevents access of air. Fiehtz[1] relates three cases of infanticide by suffocation. The first was accomplished by covering the child with a feather bed, in this case no external signs of violence were present. In the second case the mother suffocated the child by placing her hand over its mouth and nose. At the inspection the mouth was found closed, the lips white, with the point of the tongue between them. Four marks corresponding with the finger nails were found on the right side of the neck just above the shoulder, and a single mark on the left side in a similar position; the internal signs of asphyxia were present. Immediately after the child was born the mother placed her left hand over its mouth and thus prevented respiration—the marks on the throat being caused by the finger and thumb nails resting on the neck, the fingers and thumb having been flexed so as to adapt the hand to the convexity of the child's face. The third case showed no trace of violence in the neighbourhood of mouth and neck, nor on any other part of the body; internally the signs of asphyxia were visible. Suffocation had been induced by enveloping the child in an apron. Schiller[2] made an examination of the body of a new-born infant, and found, in addition to the signs of asphyxia, a quantity of blood in the finer bronchi. At the back of the pharynx he found injuries which had been inflicted by the mother having pushed her forefinger into the child's mouth with the object of producing suffocation. The finger had been firmly held there for some time, and the finger nail had excoriated the pharyngeal wall and so produced the haemorrhage. Suffocation was due to the presence of the finger rather than to the blood in the bronchi, as the latter was unmixed with air.

The body of an infant that has died from suffocation may be found in a medium capable of causing suffocation, death having been produced before immersion, hence the necessity of not accepting a probable cause of death without due investigation. The body may be found in a pond, or in a cesspool, but the child may have been dead when it was deposited there. Scrupulous care should be taken to search both air passages and intestinal tract for traces of the medium in which the body was found, if traces are present, they afford evidence of life at the time of immersion. A solid medium in a divided state—as sand

[1] Vierteljahrsschr. f. ger. Med., 1891.  [2] Ibid., 1887.

or loose earth—may yield similar evidence of burial alive. Maschka[1] records a case in which the body of an infant was found buried about a foot deep in a field. The mouth contained a mass of mud-like consistence composed of sand and earth such as surrounded the body, some of which had penetrated as far as the pharynx and larynx, but could not be traced further neither into trachea nor œsophagus. The stomach contained no trace of it, but in the duodenum a small fragment was found. The lungs afforded proof of respiration, and presumptive indications of death from asphyxia were present. The opinion given was that the child breathed before being placed in the earth, and that by subsequent attempts at inspiration some of the soil was drawn into the mouth, but was too coherent to pass further. In the movements of swallowing which accompanied the attempts at breathing, a fragment of the soil found its way into the stomach, and was carried forward into the duodenum by peristaltic movements which do not immediately cease at the moment of somatic death. Tardieu[2] records the discovery of an infant's dead body in a box, the child having died from suffocation but not from being shut up in the box. The under lip was everted and imprinted with the texture of a woven fabric, a fragment of which adhered to it; suffocation had been effected by pressure of a linen cloth on the child's mouth.

As previously stated, a new-born infant is easily suffocated. Leaving it under the bed-clothes is sufficient to extinguish life, without producing any of the external signs of suffocation; in such cases, due reserve must be exercised in attributing death to criminal intent. The mother may have fainted or otherwise have become unconscious, or irresponsible for her actions, for a period sufficiently long as to allow of the death of the infant without having entertained any design of taking its life. No hard and fast rule can be laid down. In married women who have just undergone the pangs of labour, the capacity for appreciating external conditions varies to an almost unlimited extent. Some women become maniacal at the moment of delivery, and subsequently lapse into a semi-unconscious state; others are apathetic as to the fate of their offspring, for a time quite sufficient to allow of death from neglect if the requisite attention is not forthcoming, and subsequently display the liveliest interest in its well-being. The opposite extreme, usually met with in unmarried women, is equally well marked. It is no uncommon event for a servant girl to be delivered of a child in the same room with her fellow-servant, and to dispose of its body without exciting any suspicion at the time. In one case a servant girl at the

---

[1] *Vierteljahrsschr. f. ger. Med.*, 1886
[2] *Etude Medico-légale sur l'Infanticide*

moment the child was born heard the front-door bell ring, she attended to the door and let her mistress in. It was subsequently found that at the time the placenta was still within the uterus, and that hæmorrhage was taking place. In another case a servant girl went a distance from home, and when returning she asked the boy who drove the cart in which she rode to stop. She got out, went to a recess in the hedge, and five minutes after was seen walking home, a distance of a mile and a half; the day following she went about her work as usual. In the five minutes' interval she had given birth to a living child. The external influences which affect married and unmarried women respectively, as to their behaviour during and after labour, are to be taken into consideration in forming an opinion as to the probability or otherwise of intentional neglect on the part of the mother of anything necessary for the well-being of the infant. As regards unmarried women, there are *prima facie* grounds for suspecting them to be desirous of the death of the infant to which they have given birth, but in the absence of incriminating circumstances it is unjust to turn a deaf ear to the woman's statement—that she lost consciousness at the moment of delivery. Since it is a fact that married women who desire their children to live not unfrequently succumb for a time to the violence of their emotions, or of their sufferings, and imperil the life of their offspring, the possibility of a like condition attacking an unmarried woman is not to be denied.

**Strangulation** is frequently resorted to as a means of infanticide. It may be carried out either by compression of the child's throat with the unaided hands, or by means of a cord, ribbon, or other similar object.

When strangulation is effected with the **unaided hand**, marks produced by the pressure of the fingers are usually to be seen. It frequently happens that two or more impressions produced by the finger nails are found on the left side of the child's neck, and a single impression on the right side; this arises from the throat being clutched between the fingers and thumb of the right hand. The nail marks may be further back than might be expected, on account of the whole neck being grasped instead of the air passage only. In addition to the marks of the nails there may be superficial ecchymoses more or less corresponding to the lines of pressure produced by the fingers, the ecchymoses often spread to the ears and along the sides of the face. Excoriations of the epiderm produced by scratches of the finger nails may be present. In some instances no external signs are visible, although death has been produced by throttling, in these cases it is probable that the web between the thumb and first finger was applied to the front of the throat, the back of the neck being supported by the palm of the other hand. The intervention of a soft fabric between the hand and throat materially lessens the amount of external marking Although no superficial ecchymoses are visible, the deep structures may be infiltrated with blood If great violence has been used the muscles are bruised, the cartilages of the larynx probably fractured, and even the vertebræ may be injured

Marks resembling those produced by criminal violence may result from attempts on the part of the mother to aid her delivery Scratches produced by the finger nails may be found in the neighbourhood of the nose, mouth and ears, with possibly indications of pressure by the finger tips on the under part of the lower jaw and side of the neck It is exceedingly unlikely that the mother could endanger the child's life by attempts to expedite delivery, when severe injuries have been inflicted, the presumption is against this explanation In arm or leg presentation, fracture or dislocation might be caused by improper traction on the part of the mother in her attempt to drag out the child.

Suffocation may be produced by firm, prolonged compression of chest and abdomen so as to prevent inspiration Unless a soft fabric protected the child's body, the marks of the finger and finger nails would probably be distinguishable Tardieu mentions such a case in which there was a depression of the chest and abdomen

When a piece of cord or ribbon, or other similar medium, has been used to strangle the child, a more or less distinct groove will be found round, or partly round, the neck The breadth and depth of the groove, within limits, is governed by the kind of material used, and the degree of force applied. A thin cord applied with the same degree of force would produce a narrower, deeper furrow than a handkerchief The bottom of the groove is usually white or grey, the borders being livid or of a violet colour There will probably be some superficial ecchymoses visible in parts of the groove or its borders, but not invariably so Excoriations of the epiderm are likely to occur, unless the strangulating medium was very smooth and soft in texture Deep extravasations of blood below the groove and around it are almost invariable, and if great violence has been used there may be injuries to the larynx or trachea, and even to the cervical vertebræ with laceration of the muscles. Internal examination reveals the signs of death from asphyxia.

The usual defence in accusations of infanticide by strangulation is— that death was caused by the funis surrounding the neck during labour. The indications of accidental strangulation produced in this way have already been described, one or two additional points remain for discussion. First, as to the appearance of the mark round the neck. It has been erroneously assumed that local ecchymoses are not present when the funis is the constricting medium, but the results of post-mortem examinations in undoubted cases of accidental strangulation with the funis prove the contrary. There is a distinction (previously mentioned) which is of considerable moment as a diagnostic sign—the smooth, soft funis does not excoriate the skin. Excoriation of the skin is not invariable in homicidal strangulation, but its presence points in that direction. When the funis encircles the child's neck at birth it not unfrequently goes more than once round, which will be indicated by the mark on the neck. As a rule, in cases of accidental strangulation caused by the coiling of the funis round the child's neck, the lungs will be found in the fœtal state—they will sink when placed in water. This rule is subject to exceptions. The asphyxia which causes death in these cases may result from arrest of circulation in the umbilical vessels as well as from constriction of the child's neck. When the head is expelled the constriction may be just insufficient to cause strangulation, although the tension on the funis may be sufficient to arrest the circulation through it, which would determine the commencement of respiration. Very little additional tension would arrest the breathing, and in the absence of skilled assistance the child would die during birth. On examination the neck would show signs of strangulation, and the lungs would yield evidence of having respired. Winter[1] records a case illustrating this complication. A woman, aged twenty-one, with normal pelvis, was attended in labour by a midwife. The funis surrounded the child's neck too tightly to be removed, and the head was expelled but the shoulders impeded further progress; a medical man arrived in five minutes and he tied and divided the funis. The child was delivered with considerable difficulty in a deeply asphyxiated condition, and only with prolonged efforts was it brought to life; a distinct strangulation-mark ran round the neck. The child died in eight hours after. At the necropsy a clot of blood was found under the pia mater flattening the cerebral convolutions; blood was also found in the lateral ventricles and at the base of the brain. Ecchymoses were present on the pleura and pericardium, and extravasation of blood under the mucous membrane of the larynx, the lungs were partially distended with air. In the absence of any history it would probably have been assumed that the child was born alive and was afterwards strangled.

The average length of the funis is about 20 inches, it may not exceed 6 inches, or it may reach 70 inches or more. When both fœtal and placental portions of the funis are forthcoming they should

[1] *Bericht uber d Sitz d Ges f Geb u Gyn*, 1885.

be measured, the total length might be insufficient to allow of the child's neck being encircled by it; further, the tension-limit of the funis should be tested, it might be unable to bear the strain necessary to strangle the child. The funis has been used as a medium for criminal strangulation, the allegation made being that it surrounded the child's neck at birth. In such cases the cord will be stretched, and will probably show traces of local displacement of the Wharton's jelly from being twisted round the fingers in the act of strangulation; the funis is so smooth and slippery that simply grasping it with the hand scarcely affords the necessary hold. The lungs would probably show signs of having partially respired, although in one case of criminal strangulation with the funis the lungs were found in their fœtal state.

Strangulation-marks round the child's neck are sometimes alleged to have been produced by a handkerchief or piece of tape with which the mother attempted to aid her delivery. This is an improbable supposition, and in any case very little force could be thus applied, so that careful examination of the marks externally, and dissection of the deeper structures underlying them, would probably enable a conclusion to be arrived at.

Intentional neglect in tying the funis may lead to death from hæmorrhage. The absence of a ligature does not prove that the cord was not tied; it may have been removed, or the funis may have separated at the site of the ligature. This warning is specially appropriate in the case of infants whose bodies are not examined until a week or two after death; post-mortem softening may easily cause detachment of the distal end of the funis along with the ligature. Devergie[1] relates a case in which an infant with cord and placenta was being removed from a river where it had remained for about a fortnight; the funis was so tender that it gave way, and the placenta was carried down the stream. A medical man, not knowing these facts, examined the body, and concluded that the funis had been torn at the birth, and that death had resulted from hæmorrhage. The free end of the funis should be examined as to the condition of the structures which enter into its composition. If it has been divided with a sharp cutting instrument, the transverse section will be clean and even; if it has been torn the section will be jagged and irregular, some of the structures being more elastic and less yielding than others; if division has been effected by means of a blunt knife, it will probably be difficult to determine the mode of separation, in which case it is well to avoid giving a decided opinion.

The importance of the question as to how the funis was divided is

[1] *Annales d'Hygiène*, 1873.

well illustrated by the following case narrated by Koch[1].—A servant girl, advanced in pregnancy, felt a desire to relieve the bowels. She went to the closet and was suddenly delivered, the child falling through the opening, the girl explained the event as being accidental. The placenta subsequently came away, and the child was removed from the closet asphyxiated. The funis was nearly 20 inches long, it was of moderate thickness and was separated about the mid portion of its length—10 inches from the navel. On the fœtal portion there were three injuries, two of which affected the amniotic sheath only, the arteries not being injured; the third went through half the funis, one artery and the vein being divided; the injuries were comparatively smooth, except the one through the amniotic sheath, which was rather ragged. The vessels were irregularly divided, and they partially projected beyond the other structures. Two experts pronounced that the funis had been divided with a sharp-cutting instrument, basing their opinion on the presence of the injuries described, and on the unusual position of the point of separation, accidental rupture usually taking place either close to the placenta, or close to the navel. Re-examination led to a change of opinion—that the injuries were not produced by a cutting instrument, but by the sudden tug of the falling child. Winckel states that he has often seen injuries of this kind produced by sudden tension of the funis. The medical expert witness should ever be alive to the importance of not accepting what appears at first sight to be an evident explanation of the cause of injury, without considering whether there may not be another and correct, though less obvious, interpretation. In the above case the first opinion, if accepted, would have condemned the girl as a murderess; the second to some extent confirmed her story, and established the possibility of the affair being really accidental. According to Winckel,[2] rupture of the funis from precipitate labour, in more than three-fourths of the cases, takes place within 6 inches from the umbilicus, in 12 per cent, close to or within the umbilicus, still less frequently in the middle of the cord or near the placenta.

Fractures of the skull are frequently found to have been inflicted on new-born infants when death is suspected to be due to infanticide. When either the mother or her paramour kills the child by blows on the head, or by dashing it against a wall, the injuries inflicted are usually excessive. It is a mode of killing which does not admit of the attempt to attribute death to natural, and scarcely to accidental causes; the sole object is to deprive the child of life as quickly as possible, and to trust to concealment of its body in order to escape the consequences, the result almost invariably is that the bones of

[1] *Arch. f. Gynæcologie*, 1886.    [2] *Lehrbuch d. Geburtshulfe*, 1889.

the skull are literally smashed in. When the deed is perpetrated by the mother she is usually at the time in a state of maniacal excitement, and is therefore in no condition to pay heed to the amount of damage she inflicts. After the child is dead it is generally thrown into a pond or midden, or buried in the ground.

The defence usually is that the injuries were caused at birth from difficult or from precipitate labour. As previously shown, fractures of the bones of the skull may be caused during ordinary difficult labour—without the use of instruments or of manual interference—and, further, they may present an appearance not unlike that which results from modified criminal violence. When the injuries have been intentionally inflicted there will be more or less damage done to the external soft parts. The scalp will show signs of the force resorted to, in the form of excoriations, rents, or complete disintegration of structure, which are not seen when the injury to the skull has been caused during ordinary non-instrumental labour. If fracture has resulted from the head being forced through a contracted pelvis, the shape of the head and the presence of a well developed cephalhæmatoma will afford evidence of the fact. The presence of blood under the scalp or the pericranium, or even within the skull, is quite consistent with natural causation. When criminal violence has been resorted to, there will probably be slight injuries visible on other parts of the body besides the head, such as finger-marks, scratches, and bruises, from rough handling during commission of the crime. If, on the other hand, the defence is that the woman was suddenly delivered whilst in the erect posture, attention should be directed to the point of separation of the funis, usually, but not invariably, it is near the navel, in order to determine whether it was cut or torn asunder, the free end of the funis is to be carefully examined with a lens. The injuries sustained by the skull will probably be much less than those criminally produced. Whilst it is undoubtedly true that the child's skull may be fractured by the mother being delivered in the upright posture, the child falling head downwards on to a hard surface, yet hasty delivery has frequently taken place under these conditions without the child receiving material damage. Snell[1] records the case of a woman who in the upright posture was unexpectedly delivered of a child at term. The child fell head downwards on a stone floor, rupturing the funis in its fall, yet it sustained no injury, not even a bruise being apparent. If the injuries to the skull are extensive, homicide is indicated; lesser degrees of violence are compatible with either criminal or accidental causation, and consequently demand careful consideration of all

[1] *Brit. Med. Journ.*, 1891.

available indications, and frequently no slight discrimination in order to interpret them aright.

Another defence may be made—that the injuries to the skull were accidentally inflicted by the mother in attempting to expedite her delivery. It would be difficult to fracture the skull in this way though it would not be impossible. The degree of injury inflicted on the skull, together with the absence of marks of violence on the rest of the body, are the indications from which an opinion is to be formed.

Sometimes the dead body of an infant is found in a waste piece of ground surrounded by a wall, and it becomes a question as to whether any injuries sustained by the head may not have been caused after death by the body being thrown over the wall; the same consideration is involved if the body is found under a heap of stones or in a coal-heap, or if it has been forced down a soil-pipe or drain. The great difficulty in answering this question arises from the fact that any injury caused *immediately* after death is not characteristically different from one inflicted during life. It was formerly assumed that a blood-stained appearance of the edges of the fractured bones indicated that the injuries had been inflicted during life, but if the injuries are produced soon after death a like appearance ensues; if some hours elapse between death and the production of the fractures the absence of such signs is to be expected. No positive opinion can be formed if the edges of the fractured bones are blood-stained, as to whether the fractures were made before or immediately after death; if there is no staining of the edges, and but little effusion of blood within or without the skull, the inference to be drawn is that the injuries were caused after death.

Violence inflicted on the child's neck, producing subluxation, or fracture of the cervical vertebræ may have caused death; evidence of the injury will be observable on examination of the body.

**Wounds** produced by cutting or pointed instruments are frequently met with on the bodies of infants found dead. They vary in extent from minute punctures penetrating vital organs, to extensive wounds such as result from decapitation, or even complete dismemberment. Punctures through the fontanelles, the orbital plate, between the vertebræ, and between the ribs into the heart, have been discovered after death. These less apparent methods of causing death should be borne in mind when no obvious injury can be discovered. The more formidable injuries reveal themselves at first sight; the difficulty in dealing with them arises from the usual defence—that they were inflicted after death, with the object of facilitating the disposal of the body. The signs by which a diagnosis is to be made as to whether wounds have been inflicted before or after death are elsewhere described. In the case of smaller wounds it may be asked whether they were sufficient to cause death. Next to injury of a vital organ, hæmorrhage has to be considered as a cause of death, an exsanguineous condition of the body and internal organs generally, points to hæmorrhage. The condition of the funis—whether it has been tied or not—should be seen to before an opinion is formed as to the probability of death having occurred through loss of blood from wounds. If it is alleged that the child was still-born, and that it was mutilated with the object of more easily concealing its body, the presence or absence of the signs of respiration, as far as they are available, must be ascertained.

An instance of mutilation of the child during birth is given by Barbour.[1] An unmarried woman travelling alone in a railway carriage was suddenly seized with labour-pains. Feeling something protruding from the vagina, she attempted with some force to deliver herself, and in so doing broke the presenting limb—an arm—which in a moment of pain and frenzy she then severed with a table-knife and threw out of the window. On reaching home she was delivered by version of a still-born well-nourished male child, with the right arm missing two inches above the elbow. A considerable quantity of blood had escaped from the vagina after the amputation of the arm, and the child's body was pallid, so that hæmorrhage was doubtless the cause of death.

Drowning is not frequently resorted to as a means of infanticide, but the bodies of infants already dead are often thrown into ponds, canals, or rivers to get rid of them. An infant's body, if well nourished contains a large proportion of fat, and consequently does not readily sink. If the body is found in water with a mummified funis it is certain that the child, living or dead, remained in air sufficiently long for mummification to take place; a funis once mummified does not return to its original condition on being placed in water. On the other hand, if the child is submerged, either living or dead, while the funis is fresh and plump, mummification does not occur. The signs of death from drowning do not differ in the infant from those found in the adult; they will be described elsewhere. If still-birth is alleged with the object of reducing the crime to concealment of birth, an examination of the lungs will determine the question, unless putrefaction prevents; in the absence of clear evidence of death from drowning careful search should be made for other causes of death. When the body is found in a night commode or closet, and hasty parturition is tendered as an explanation, the

[1] *The Lancet*, 1892

funis must be carefully examined with the object of ascertaining whether it has been torn asunder or divided with a cutting instrument. It has been stated that in the act of falling the child may make an inspiration sufficiently vigorous as to fully inflate the lungs, but from what has been already said on this subject, it may be inferred that complete inflation could not take place under such circumstances; it is not to be denied, however, that partial inflation might occur. Any fluid or other matter found in the air-passages or stomach should be compared with the medium in which it is alleged the child was drowned.

A superficial glance at a section of the lung might lead to the assumption that no fluid was present, as it is not always found in the larger bronchi. There is an absence of frothy mucus in the lungs of new-born children that have been plunged into a liquid before breathing; under these conditions an infant makes attempts at respiration and inspires some of the liquid, but as no air is already in the lungs, and none enters with the liquid, the bronchi do not contain froth such as is met with after drowning in the lungs of those who have respired. Dittrich[1] records the case of a pregnant woman who suddenly felt a desire to defæcate, and in consequence placed herself over a small tub containing waste water, coffee grounds, dust, and the like; she immediately gave birth to an infant at or near term, and tore the funis without tying it. On section of the child's body the lungs were found in the fœtal state, except that they contained much blood; they sank both whole and divided. In the trachea and larger bronchi no foreign substance was visible, but on careful examination the lumena of the small bronchi were seen to be filled with a mixture which corresponded with the medium in which the infant was drowned; on microscopical examination the finest bronchioles were found to be choked up with it. The stomach and intestines sank when placed on water.

Intra-uterine maceration must not be lost sight of as a possible cause of changes resembling those produced by prolonged submersion in water.

Destruction of the body of a new-born infant is sometimes attempted by incremation. The questions in such cases are—Was the child stillborn? If not, was it alive or dead when subjected to the action of fire? The first question is to be answered in accordance with the signs already given, and the second with those described in the chapter on death by burning.

Exposure to cold and deprivation of food, if sufficiently prolonged, will, of course, cause death of the infant. Deliberate infanticide is

[1] *Prager med. Wochenschr.*, 1890.

not often attempted in this way; when a child is exposed so as to endanger its life it is with the object of getting rid of it without actively committing murder. The defence usually offered is—that the child was born unexpectedly (hasty parturition), and that it was still-born; or if living, that it was exposed so as to attract attention (before the door of a house, for example) in order that it might be rescued. In like manner a new-born living infant has been placed in a hamper with a feeding bottle and sent by train to the putative father.

Poisoning is rarely resorted to in the newly born as a means of infanticide; if suspected, an analysis of the digestive organs and their contents must be made.

#### 5. THE LENGTH OF TIME THE CHILD HAS BEEN DEAD.

This is to be estimated by the stage at which the post-mortem phenomena have arrived. The tendency is for animal heat and cadaveric rigidity to pass away, and for putrefaction to occur sooner than is the case with the adult body. When the putrefactive stage is reached no positive opinion is justifiable as to how long the child has been dead.

#### POST-MORTEM EXAMINATIONS IN CASES OF SUSPECTED INFANTICIDE.

When making a *post-mortem* examination of the body of an infant suspected to have been murdered, it is necessary to investigate very closely the external appearances. The presence of body-warmth, cadaveric rigidity, or of the signs of putrefaction should first be noted. If the body has been found without any history, a preliminary search should be made for marks or other indications which might lead to identification, and notes should be made of articles of clothing, or of the box, paper, or other envelope within which the body was found. Vernix caseosa is to be sought for, its presence demonstrating absence of the usual attentions at birth. The funis should be carefully examined as to the mode in which it has been separated; the portion attached to the child's abdomen should be measured. The whole of the surface of the body must be examined for scratches, bruises, and other slighter injuries; if any are found, attention should be directed as to their probable causation—from accidental causes during or after birth, or from criminal violence. Before touching the mouth the position of the tongue and lips should be observed—whether the tongue protrudes, and the lips are flattened or everted. Any other indications of pressure on the mouth and nostrils—such as might be produced by the bare hand, or by the application of a cloth—with the presence of punctiform ecchymoses on the face, and its general hue, whether pallid or livid, should be noted. The natural apertures of the body should be examined for foreign bodies. Any marks on or round the neck must be closely investigated, and the underlying structures subsequently examined by dissection. Should the whole body be extremely pallid observe if there is any external cause for haemorrhage other than an untied funis.

The internal examination is commenced by making the usual incision through the skin from the upper part of the manubrium to the pubes. After opening the abdominal cavity the forefinger of the right hand is introduced and its tip placed on the highest part of the arch of the diaphragm, with the forefinger of the left hand the intercostal spaces are counted from above downwards until the position of the two fingers corresponds: this determines the height of the diaphragm. The thorax is then opened and the condition of the heart ascertained *in situ*. It is convenient to continue the primary incision upwards through the skin of the neck and of the lower jaw, and to divide the symphysis by passing one blade of a sharp-pointed pair of scissors within the mouth, from above downwards in the middle line, immediately behind the alveolar process. Separate the soft structures and fold the two halves of the jaw outwards and backwards, in this way a complete view of the mouth and pharynx is obtained without disturbing any foreign body that may be present, the tongue can be drawn forwards or to one side as is most convenient. The lungs, stomach, and intestines are removed for testing as to specific gravity after their volume and general appearance have been noted. Before cutting through the scalp see if there is any trace of puncture, and after reflecting it examine the fontanelles with the same object, the possibility of puncture or other injury to the cervical cord should be borne in mind. The presence of meconium or of food-stuffs in the intestines is to be noted. The stage of development of the child must be estimated by an appeal to the various indications enumerated in the section which deals with the subject. The existence and size of the ossific centre in the inferior epiphysis of the femur is ascertained by slicing away thin sections from the lower end of the bone until the maximum diameter of the centre is reached. The possibility of poisoning must not be lost sight of, the organs necessary for chemical analysis should be removed for that purpose if deemed necessary.

**Concealment of Birth.**—"If any woman shall be delivered of a child, every person who shall by any secret disposition of the dead body of the said child, whether such child died before, at, or after its birth, endeavour to conceal the birth thereof, shall be guilty of a misdemeanour." (24 and 25 Vict., c. 100, sec. 60.)

In a great many accusations of infanticide the jury reduce the crime to that of concealment of birth. Concealment of a living child that does not die before it is discovered does not constitute the misdemeanour. In cases of concealment of birth the question of live birth does not arise, therefore medical evidence is simplified in comparison with that required in cases of infanticide. Medical evidence is limited to proof that the remains found are those of a child, and that the accused has or has not been recently delivered. The present state of the law leaves it uncertain whether a fœtus before quickening would come under the definition of "a child."

According to Scotch law concealment of pregnancy is a crime. It is not necessary that the dead body of the child should be found, nor need there be proof of infanticide; all that the law requires is that the woman must be proved to have been pregnant sufficiently long as to render possible the birth of a living child. If, during her pregnancy, the woman reveals the fact to another person, even if it is with the object of arranging for concealment of the child's birth, and evidence to this effect is tendered, the law is evaded—the pregnancy is no longer "concealed."

## CHAPTER XVI

### BIRTH IN RELATION TO THE CIVIL LAW.

**Live-birth,** in the legal acceptation of the term is determined by the same conditions in both criminal and civil cases. In criminal cases the character of the medical evidence differs from that which is usually tendered in civil cases, because in the majority of criminal cases the woman gives birth to the child in secrecy, so that no witness to the fact that the child was fully born at the time when signs of life were developed is forthcoming; consequently expert evidence founded entirely on the indications presented by the dead body of the newly-born infant has to be relied on. In civil cases witnesses are usually to hand—the accoucheur and the nurse—who were present when the child was born, and who therefore can testify to the fact of legal birth at the time the child displayed tokens of vitality; hence proofs of live birth are available in civil cases which, by circumstances, are excluded in criminal cases. The occurrence of respiration, to which so much significance is attached in cases of infanticide, constitutes but one indication of life, its importance arises from the fact that it leaves after death more or less permanent and reliable traces of its occurrence, with the exception of the stomach-bowel test, all other manifestations of a life that ceases almost immediately after it has demonstrated its existence vanish and leave no trace behind.

According to the law of England, the <u>most evanescent sign of life, provided that it is observed after the child is entirely outside the body of the mother,</u> constitutes proof of live birth. With this proviso the least muscular movement that may amount to a mere momentary twitching of the lips or of a limb, or a few beats of the heart, either heard with the stethoscope or felt in the cardiac region, or by pulsation in the undivided funis, or the more obvious evidence afforded by respiration, with or without crying are each, and severally, proofs of live birth. The duration of any of these signs is immaterial—one moment of life thus manifested avails, as proof of live birth, as much as though the child continued to live for days or months. According to the law of Scotland the commencement of respiration after expulsion must be proved to establish live birth.

In civil law, live birth comes into consideration in respect to the inheritance of property; in such cases much may depend on the fact that the child displayed, or did not display signs of life after birth, and in event of live birth, on proof of the exact time when it was born. If the head is born, and an interval elapses before the body is expelled during which the child is observed to breathe and cry, that is not the moment of birth. The delay may extend over some minutes, and, as the law does not recognise the fractional part of a day, if it occurs partly before and partly after midnight, a mistake in recording the exact time of birth might make a difference of twenty-four hours, and possibly alter the succession to an estate if the child continued to breathe until and after birth. It may die, however, during the delay, before the body is expelled; in which case the child is still-born, the law taking no cognisance of signs of life manifested before complete expulsion.

The question of live birth has to be considered in respect to **Tenancy by Courtesy.** " When a man marries a woman seized of an estate of inheritance, and has by her issue born alive, which was capable of inheriting her estate; in this case he shall, on the death of his wife, hold the lands for his life as tenant by the courtesy of England."

It will be seen that there are two obvious conditions to be fulfilled—(*a*) That the <u>issue must be born alive</u>, (*b*) that it was capable of inheriting. A third condition, which is not quite so obvious on glancing over the above quotation, is (*c*) that the <u>woman must be living at the time she gives birth to the child.</u>

(a) The proof of live birth is afforded by the evidence of the medical man, or of the nurse, or of both, who were in attendance at the labour. (b) Capacity for inheritance requires that the child shall have the shape of mankind. This question has been previously discussed under the head of sexual and other abnormalities (c) Death of either wife or husband dissolves their marriage If a married woman who is in possession of an estate held on the above named terms is pregnant with a living child and dies before the child is born, her estate at once descends to the heir-at-law, not being intercepted, as it were, by the birth of the child. If the birth of the child precedes the death of the mother by ever so little, the child being born alive but dying immediately, the husband acquires the estate for the rest of his life By Cæsarean section a child may be removed alive from the body of its *dead* mother, in such a case the husband would *not* become tenant. The point has been discussed as to whether a child extracted by Cæsarean section from the body of a *living* woman can be regarded in the legal sense as being born, it is probable that under these conditions the husband could enjoy the tenancy

## LEGITIMACY.

The law assumes every child born during marriage, or, if after the death of the husband, within limits consistent with the normal duration of gestation to be legitimate unless the contrary is proved

Proof that the husband is not the father of the child may be adduced on the ground that he is **physically incompetent**, or that he **has not had access** to his wife within a period consistent with the date of the child's birth. Physical incompetency resulting from the extremes of age, or from malformation or disease, has already been dealt with The plea of non-access, in addition to evidence as to fact—with which the medical witness has nothing to do—involves the consideration of the duration of (a) *normal gestation*, together with the questions how far may gestation be (b) *prolonged*, and how far may it be (c) *shortened* consistent with the birth of a living child

(a) **Normal Duration of Gestation**.—There is no means of absolutely determining the duration of gestation, hence the discrepancies in the time allotted by different authorities Of the many data from which the interval between impregnation of an ovum and the birth of an infant at term may be calculated, two only need be mentioned—the *cessation of menstruation*, and *a single coitus.*

The cessation of menstruation, apart from accidental interruption of the function, is an uncertain starting-point It is generally accepted that menstruation is not necessarily associated with ovulation it may take place without ovulation, and ovulation may occur without menstruation. The impregnated ovum may embed itself in the uterine mucous membrane during any part of the inter-menstrual period, and therefore the normal duration of pregnancy cannot be accurately determined from cessation of the menses. Matthews Duncan, reckoning from the last day of menstruation, computes the duration of gestation at 278 days. Other authorities give a lower or a slightly higher computation.

A single coitus affords no fixed datum, because impregnation is not necessarily synchronal with it. Spermatozoa retain their activity within the female organs for many days, during any of which they may reach the ovule and fecundate it. Computed from a single coitus, the duration of gestation is stated by Ahlfeld[1] to be 271 days, by Stadfeldt[2] 272 days, by Duncan[3] 275 days. According to Lowenhardt,[4] the average from statistics gives 272 days.

The normal duration of pregnancy is generally accepted as being about 280 days, with the possibility of exceeding this period. The duration of pregnancy should always be expressed in days; months may be either calendar or lunar, therefore the use of the word is conducive to error.

(b) **Abnormally Prolonged Gestation.**—Attempts to estimate the extreme limits of gestation in either direction are further embarrassed by the fact that, in almost all such cases, the evidence on which the estimations are based is liable to be tainted. In many cases the interests of the individuals concerned are profoundly involved, either from the moral or the pecuniary standpoint. Apart from wilful misrepresentation, women are very apt to be misled by their feelings and wishes. It may be premised that the usually accepted duration of gestation is undoubtedly capable of considerable extension, the difficulty lies in limiting the degree of extension. In some countries the limit is fixed by law; in France and Italy the limit is 300 days; in Germany a child born within 302 days after the death of the husband is regarded as legitimate; in Scotland a child born ten lunar months after the death of the husband is considered legitimate. In England and America no limit is fixed, and consequently the opinion of experts is taken, and the entire question is discussed at every trial into which the subject enters. The longest gestation yet allowed by the English courts was 301 days; in America 317 days have been allowed. Both these cases were indictments for seduction, and probably sentiment had something to do with the verdicts; a claimant to an estate might have fared differently.

[1] *Monatsschr. f. Geburtshulfe*, 1869.   [2] *Annales de Gynécol.*, 1877.
[3] *Fecundity, Fertility, Sterility*, 1866.   [4] *Arch. f. Gynaecol.*, 1872.

Many cases are recorded of gestation extending to 300 days and beyond, cases which approach, but do not exceed, 300 days, have a much greater air of probability about them than those which claim additional weeks. Acker[1] reports a case in which gestation lasted 305 days after a single coitus, the child not exceeding in development that of full term. Allowing for the uncertainty of the moment of impregnation after insemination, the duration of gestation in this case might be reduced to 290 days. In a case recorded by Purkhauer,[2] the woman menstruated in the non-pregnant state regularly every 28 days. She had her last period on the 28th of April, 1889, she felt the child first about the middle of September, which would make the end of the first week in February, 1890, the probable date of labour. On the 13th of March, 1890, she was delivered of a living boy weighing 8 lbs 12½ oz, and measuring nearly 21 inches in length. If conception is dated at seven days after the cessation of the last menstruation, the duration of gestation was 316 days. If seven days before the next anticipated period is taken—which, however, would not agree with the date of quickening—the duration of gestation would be 300 days. Thompson[3] records a case in which the duration of gestation, reckoned from the last day of menstruation, was 317 days, and from the last coitus 301 days. Duncan[4] records a case in which menstruation ceased on January 15th. The fœtal movements were perceived by the mother about the beginning or middle of May, she was of enormous bulk, and expected to be confined about the 15th to the 21st of October. Delivery was delayed until the 7th of December, 325 days from the cessation of the menses. The child, a male, was of much more than the usual size and weight. This was her fourth child; her first child she carried 300 days, and her second and third about 285 days. Armstrong[5] mentions the case of a woman who went 303 days in her second pregnancy, and 319 in her fourth. Murray[6] gives the following details of a woman he attended.—She ceased to menstruate on February 12th, 1888, on November 28th she thought she was in labour, but the symptoms passed off. She was delivered on January 12th, 1889, of a still-born child, weighing 7½ lbs and measuring 19½ inches in length. The interval between the cessation of menstruation and delivery was 330 days.

The theory that has been advanced—that protracted gestation is generally associated with unusually long inter-menstrual periods—is not supported by Purkhauer's case above recorded, as the woman when not pregnant menstruated regularly every 28 days.

[1] *Amer Journ of Obstetrics*, 1889  
[2] *Friedreich's Blatter f ger Med*, 1890  
[3] *Obstetrical Transactions*, 1885  
[4] *Medical Times and Gazette*, 1877  
[5] *The Lancet*, 1890  
[6] *Brit Med Journ*, 1889

It will be observed that the above cases illustrate the subject of protracted gestation in a progressively increasing ratio, until the formidable total of 330 days is reached. This is not final, so far as recorded cases go, but so far as the credulity of the reader goes it probably is. In many cases of apparently protracted gestation, it is more than likely that the menses were accidentally suppressed, and that impregnation subsequently occurred.

(*c*) **Abnormally shortened gestation** comprises the consideration of the stage of development of the fœtus at birth, and its viability or capacity to live after birth. There is more scope for medical evidence in shortened than in protracted gestation; in the latter, the child cannot be more than fully developed, although in some cases it has surpassed the usual size, but when full term is not reached indications of the fact are more or less obvious. In forming an opinion, too much emphasis must not be laid on the size and weight of an infant; they constitute two valuable signs of development, especially the length, which has a more fixed relation to age than the weight, but they must not be allowed to exclude other signs, nor can any reliable comparison be made between the healthy stoutness of the mother, or the converse, and the size and weight of the child, as some little women habitually produce large children, and women of large stature and imposing appearance not unfrequently give birth to ill-nourished infants at full term. As in all other questions of differentiation, extremes are easy of recognition; a child at term has characteristics that clearly distinguish it from a six or seven months' fœtus; on the other hand there is little difference between an eight and a nine months' fœtus, for fully a fortnight before term, the child has acquired all the distinguishing characteristics of maturity. The most reliable signs of fœtal development are only available in the dead body; they are the various points of ossification, and the superficial configuration of the brain. The external indications of immaturity, in addition to size and weight, are the dark-red hue and wrinkled condition of the skin, and the presence on it of lanugo, the size of the auricle, imperfect formation of the finger nails, disproportionate size of the head, absence of the testicles from the scrotum (in the male), together with general feebleness, indicated by deficiency of vigorous movements and clamorous cries, with inability to suck the proffered nipple. The body-heat of immature children is subnormal, and requires conserving by means of thick layers of cotton-wool and other surroundings, which lessen the loss from the surface.

**Viability.**—An infant may have arrived at a sufficiently advanced period of development as to be born alive, but not to be viable—that is, not to be endowed with the capacity of continuing to live. As a general statement it may be accepted that 180 days represent the lowest limit at which an infant is viable, but it is by no means to be inferred that all infants at this period of intra-uterine life are viable; on the contrary, prolonged survival is the exception and not the rule, consequently good evidence is required to establish the occurrence of viability at this age. Bonnar[1] tabulated a number of cases of premature birth, tracing the after life of the infants; of 22 which were born alive at 180 days of intra-uterine life, only 4 lived one year and upwards; six more of the same group lived twenty four-hours and upwards, but none of the rest longer than four months. Bailly[2] records the case of a child born at six months and twenty days. It was very feeble, and required much care to sustain the body-heat; as an illustration of its small size it is stated that the father's finger-ring could be passed over the child's foot nearly as far as the knee. Thirteen days after birth the child weighed 1,250 grammes (about $2\frac{3}{4}$ lbs.); twelve months after birth, when the case was reported, it was living and thriving. In a well authenticated case reported by Outrepout[3] the child was at about 27 weeks of intra-uterine life when born. It measured $13\frac{1}{2}$ inches, and weighed $1\frac{1}{2}$ lbs.; the skin was wrinkled and covered with down, the nails were like folds of skin, and the papillary membrane was entire; the limbs were small and were maintained in the fœtal attitude. The child was living at the age of 11 years, and had the appearance of a boy about 8 years old.

Instances are recorded in which infants born before 180 days have been reared; such cases are very exceptional and provoke scepticism as to correctness of data. Bonnar's list contains the case of one child born at 150 days which lived to the age of 19 years. A case is recorded by Moore[4] of a child born at the end of the fifth month, which measured 9 inches in length, and weighed $1\frac{1}{2}$ lbs.; at the age of 15 months the child was healthy and weighed 19 lbs. Illustrative of the risk encountered in estimating the stage of development from the size of the child is a case recorded by Hubbard.[5] The period of utero-gestation is stated to have been about the seventh month. The infant was 10 inches long; the circumference of the head round the ears was 8 inches, round the thighs $2\frac{1}{2}$ inches; the weight was 1 lb. 2 oz.; the child was well formed, the finger-nails being perfect; it lived eight hours. Reference to the Table on p. 26 shows that the finger-nails are not perfectly formed until utero-gestation has advanced eight months, but the length and weight of this child would indicate that it had not exceeded six months. Barker[6] relates the case of a

---

[1] *Edinburgh Med. Journ.*, 1865.   [2] *Arch. de Tocologie*, 1879.
[3] *Henke's Zeitschr.*, 1823.   [4] *Philadelphia Med. and Surg. Reporter*, 1880.
[5] *New York Med. Journ.*, 1890.   [6] *Med. Times*, 1850.

child born 158 days after intercourse. It measured 11 inches in length and weighed 1 pound; the nails were scarcely visible; the eyelids were closed until the second day after birth; the skin was wrinkled; three and a-half years after it was thriving and healthy, but only weighed 29½ lbs. A number of similar cases have been recorded but none of very recent date. Cullingworth[1] collected several, amongst which is included an instance of early viability (seventh month) that he met with in his own hospital practice.

Children born at the intra-uterine age of five months have lived for a few hours, but not much longer; it is needless to cite such cases as it is acknowledged that a fœtus may display signs of life when born at that period of development. Without impugning the veracity of those who have recorded such cases, it is nevertheless true that no instance, accompanied by absolutely convincing evidence of viability in a five months' fœtus, has yet been recorded.

In France and Italy a child born within 180 days after marriage can be repudiated by the husband if no intercourse has taken place between him and his wife before marriage. In Germany a husband can repudiate the parentage of a child given birth to by his wife when he can prove non-intercourse from the three hundredth to the one hundred and eightieth day before the birth of the child. In Scotland a child born six months after the marriage of the mother is considered legitimate. In England and America no limit is fixed: as with protracted gestation each case is determined on its own merits.

## SUPERFŒTATION.

The possibility of superfœtation is a disputed point amongst obstetricians; some allow that exceptionally it may occur, others regard it as being physiologically impossible. All allow the possibility of superfecundation—that is, the separate impregnation of two ova discharged during the same period of ovulation; the difficulty arises with respect to the possibility of an ovum derived from a subsequent ovulation being impregnated some months after the occurrence of gestation resulting from fecundation of an ovum discharged during a previous ovulation. It is now admitted on all sides that the condition of the impregnated uterus until the middle of the third month does not interpose any insurmountable obstacle to re-impregnation. The union of the decidua reflexa with the vera is not then complete, and therefore no absolute barrier exists between the ovum and the spermatozoa; the plug of viscid mucus in the cervical canal also offers no insurmountable obstacle. Those who deny the possibility

[1] *Obstetrical Journ. of Great Britain and Ireland*, 1878.

of superfœtation base their opposition on the non-occurrence of ovulation during gestation. If ovulation never takes place from the commencement of gestation until after delivery, it is clear that superfœtation is impossible. The rule is that ovulation is in abeyance during pregnancy; are there any grounds for assuming the occurrence of exceptions to the rule? Galabin[1] instances extra-uterine pregnancy as affording evidence that ovulation may exceptionally take place during pregnancy: a five months' fœtus has been found in the abdomen and one of three months in the uterus; the intra-uterine fœtus would be better situated for obtaining nourishment, and therefore its inferior development cannot be attributed to failure in this respect. The exceptional occurrence of menstruation during the early months of pregnancy does not afford more than an inferential support to the hypothesis of ovulation occurring at the same time since menstruation and ovulation are not interdependent.

Those who deny the possibility of superfœtation explain the cases in which its occurrence has been assumed as being instances of twin pregnancy in which, as is common, one fœtus develops more than the other. Spiegelberg,[2] in applying this fact, regards superfœtation as a physiologically untenable and exploded hypothesis, and considers those cases in which a fully developed child has been born, followed by another, also fully developed (within the limits attributed to superfœtation) as instances of twin fœtuses; one, much more developed than the other, being born first, and the one left behind making up for lost time and eventually appearing in as fully developed condition as the first. Cases of supposed superfœtation in which the births are more widely separated have been accounted for by the presence of a double uterus, with or without separate vaginæ. If only the body of the uterus is duplex, the abnormality is more likely to escape detection than when a double vagina is present. Ross[3] relates a case illustrative of this abnormality. On the 6th of July a woman was delivered of two fœtuses at about six months of utero-gestation; on the 31st October she was delivered of a child at full term; subsequent examination showed the existence of a double uterus. The explanation of the interval between the births of the two immature fœtuses and the child at term, is that one cavity of the uterus was prematurely delivered of twins, and that the other retained its contents up to the full period of utero-gestation. In this case there was no septum in the vagina, and unless a careful examination had been made, and the cause of the abnormal course of pregnancy

---

[1] *Manual of Midwifery*, 1886    [2] *Lehrbuch der Geburtshülfe*, 1880
[3] *The Lancet*, 1871

thus explained, another case of superfœtation would have been placed on record.

The occurrence of ordinary twin gestation with a prolonged interval between the births is well illustrated by a case recorded by Pincott.[1] A woman gave birth to a weakly female infant on the 18th of October, which died the same day; after delivery the placenta came away as in ordinary confinements. On the 19th of the following November—35 days after—she gave birth to a second and finely developed female child at full term; fœtal movements were felt before the membranes ruptured, but the child was still-born.

Of the cases adduced in favour of superfœtation, those in which an interval of not more than from two to three months apparently elapsed between the respective conceptions, may be explained on the supposition of ordinary twin impregnation with retention of the second fœtus after expulsion of the first. Even a longer interval is not impossible if the development of the fœtus which remains behind, has been greatly retarded by its more favourably placed companion. If, as supposed by some, maturity of the fœtus is the initiative cause of natural labour, it is easy to see how a backward fœtus, rendered so by no inherent defect, may remain in the uterus for a considerable time beyond the limit of the normal period of gestation. The cases which, from a still longer interval between the respective conceptions, are regarded as proving the occurrence of superfœtation, prove too much. Towards the end of the third month the union of the decidua reflexa and vera introduce an actual barrier to re-impregnation, and a further difficulty is interposed by the then or subsequent position of the ovaries and oviducts in relation to the uterus. These obstacles, in addition to the almost invariable cessation of ovulation during pregnancy, render cases of alleged superfœtation in which an interval of five and a-half months has occurred between the births of two viable children extremely difficult of acceptance. As with other negative propositions, the occurrence of superfœtation cannot well be disproved, but it may be regarded as being very close to the vanishing-point of probability.

Death of the Fœtus in Utero.—It occasionally happens that the fœtus dies *in utero* and is retained for a more or less prolonged period; if its surroundings remain intact the access of air and of micro-organisms is prevented, and either maceration or mummification of the body without putrefaction takes place. If the development of the fœtus has not advanced beyond the first month the recently formed tissues are disintegrated, so that when expelled no trace of structure is discernible. At a later period of utero-gestation there

[1] *Brit. Med. Journ.*, 1886.

may be simply maceration of the skin, which is raised in blisters, or is entirely peeled off, the fœtus being otherwise fairly well preserved; in other cases, the fœtus undergoes mummification, and presents a flattened dried-up appearance. Schellenberg[1] describes a case of this kind. A woman ceased menstruating on the 20th of June, 1876; she felt the child at the beginning of November; on the 12th of May, 1877, she was delivered of a six months' fœtus, which was pressed flat and in a mummified condition; it had remained in the uterus five months after death. Garrigues[2] describes a case occurring in a woman 37 years of age. Nine months after the last menstruation a fœtus and placenta in a perfectly fresh condition were expelled; the fœtus was at about the end of the fourth month of development; the epiderm had come off, and the soft parts were atrophied.

The medico-legal bearing of twin deliveries, separated by an interval of two or more months, and of retention of a dead fœtus, is of theoretical rather than practical value. The cases in which these conditions might come in question are where a woman gives birth to an apparently fully developed child—born alive, but dying soon after birth—within seven or eight months after the death or absence of her husband, and two or three months after is delivered of a second infant, also of full development, which lives; the heir-at-law might dispute the legitimacy of the second infant. Again, if a woman whose husband had been absent for eight or nine months, gave birth to a four months' fœtus eight months after her husband left her, her chastity might be called in question.

The earliest period at which a woman who has been delivered of a child can again be impregnated is usually understood to be about a month after delivery; Bonnar states that it may take place as early as the fourteenth day.

Paternity and Affiliation are determined by circumstantial evidence, and by resemblance to the father in appearance, voice, manner, gait, and other characteristics. Medical evidence is directed to the minute examination of deformities, birth-marks, or other bodily peculiarities. In the newly-born the questions discussed in the section on legitimacy might have to be considered.

When a child is alleged to be supposititious, it may become the duty of a medical man to examine the child with regard to the length of time it has survived birth, and the pretended mother for signs of recent delivery. If the fraud has been so successfully accomplished that suspicion is not aroused for some time after the feigned delivery (the woman having at some previous time given birth to a child at term), detection may not be easy. In recent cases the condition

[1] *Arch. f. Gynäcol.*, 1877.  [2] *American Journ. of Obstetrics*, 1884.

of mother and child will probably be found not to agree; it is difficult for a woman to obtain a new-born infant at the right moment, and consequently indications of its having survived birth longer than the alleged date of confinement will reveal the fraud. If the woman is examined within three or four days of the pretended parturition, the usual signs of recent delivery ought to be present. It is the duty of a medical man summoned to attend a woman in labour, if he arrives after the child is born, to assure himself that the woman has been just delivered, and that the child has been recently born; the placenta also should be examined. All this is perfectly natural from the purely obstetrical standpoint and cannot be reasonably objected to. Any attempts to hinder such investigations constitute grounds for suspicion, and are to be met by firm, though gentle persistence. This applies to both rich and poor: with the former the legitimate succession to an estate may be imperilled; with the latter the extortion of money from an alleged seducer may be the motive. In event of absolute refusal to permit the desired examination as being unnecessary, the contingencies that might arise should be explained; further objection would constitute reasonable ground for suspicion as to the *bona-fides* of the transaction.

## SURVIVORSHIP.

When two or more individuals, concerned either actually or presumptively in the succession of property, lose their lives by the same accident, it may be of great importance to others concerned in the succession to determine respectively the precedence of death. In the absence of eye-witnesses the determination is necessarily founded on conjecture; for this reason the later decisions of the courts of appeal are in favour of each case being determined by the balance of facts that can be substantiated, rather than on presumption of survivorship on account of difference in age or sex. In the absence of positive evidence as to which of two persons lived the longest who perished under like conditions and from the same cause, they are assumed to have died at the same time so far as succession to property is concerned.

A number of rules have been formulated as to probabilities of the survival of one person longer than another when menaced with a common death. Age, sex, physical strength, special resources (as the capacity to swim when the cause of death is drowning) have been regarded as affording presumptive evidence sufficiently strong to justify the determination of survivorship. The possible effects of these various conditions are described when dealing with the respective modes of death.

## CHAPTER XVII.

### LIFE ASSURANCE.

Insurance companies avail themselves of the services of medical men in two distinct capacities—as chief medical adviser, or as medical examiner. Each company has one chief adviser, and an unlimited number of medical examiners. The chief adviser, in addition to acting as examiner with regard to proposers who present themselves at the head office, reads through and criticises all reports from the medical examiners in various parts of the country. He acts as a medical assessor or referee to the Board of Directors, and advises them as to the importance of any indications of disease, or as to the significance of details of personal or of family history. When a life cannot be regarded as first-class on account of the presence of some disease, or tendency thereto, it is customary to add a certain number of years to the actual age of the applicant and to demand a correspondingly increased annual payment; under such circumstances the chief medical adviser has to estimate the probable duration of life, and to fix the age at which the proposal shall be accepted. He has to satisfy himself that there are no omissions nor obvious errors in the examiners' reports, and if he detects any discrepancy his duty is either directly or through the office to communicate with the examiner, and to request an explanation.

Medical Examiners are selected by the actuary or other officer of the company in those towns in which an agency is established; in large towns all the proposers are usually sent to one medical man, who in this way becomes an adviser of the company; in country places any medical man may be selected whose residence happens to be conveniently near to that of the proposer. When the policy is for a very large sum, the office may require the proposer to be examined by two medical men. The object evidently is to secure, as far as possible, a thorough investigation of the physical condition and functional activity of the various organs of the body; to accomplish this the two medical men should make the examinations separately, an arrangement however which is usually not specified, and as competition between rival offices is very close, the agents favour a conjoint examination by the medical men in order to avoid deterring the applicant by the prospect of having to undergo two distinct examinations.

Insurance offices vary in their requirements as to reports. some provide elaborately arranged printed forms which suggest all the necessary investigations, and contain a long string of questions relating to personal and family history to be answered by the applicant, which are severally asked, and the answers recorded by the medical man at the time the examination takes place. Printed forms of exhaustive questions have one distinct advantage: their routine character enables questions of a more or less delicate nature to be put without causing offence; this applies especially to syphilis, the possibility of the presence of which in a latent form is not to be lost sight of. Other offices, in the letter to the medical man requesting him to examine an applicant, direct attention to the chief subjects on which information is required, and ask him to furnish a report in the form of a letter to the actuary; when this is the case the applicant himself fills in his statement of family and personal history and sends it direct to the office. No one should be present at the examination except the applicant and the medical examiner. The first thing is to observe the general appearance of the applicant—the complexion, the healthy or cachectic colour of the skin, the presence of enlarged veins on the nose or cheeks, puffiness or redness about the eyes, together with the general expression, whether it affords indications of latent physical disease, or of mental anxiety. The gait of the applicant as regards spasticity, ataxia, or other deviation from the normal, and the state of the tongue, gums, teeth, and throat are to be noted. Inquiries are to be made as to the presence of hernia and other pathological conditions. The height and weight, the measurements of the chest at the level of the sixth rib, during full inspiration and deep expiration, should be ascertained. The expansion of the chest should also be observed with the eye and the respiration rate taken; this and the rate of the pulse, which should also be counted, is frequently influenced by nervousness of the applicant. The lungs and heart are to be examined in the usual way (the skin being bared) and the result recorded. Special attention should be devoted to the apices of the lungs, back and front, especially if the family history is indicative of phthisis. The character of the breath-sounds as regards harshness vesicular breathing, prolongation of the expiratory sound, and lessened audibility of the inspiratory sound, together with increased vocal resonance at the apices, are all of significance. If a heart murmur is present, the valves implicated and the character of the murmur is to be recorded; if the murmur is mitral-regurgitant listen how far posteriorly it can be heard, as affording some clue to the amount of regurgitation and consequently of the importance of the lesion. In some nervous people a sound resembling that of a murmur of organic origin may be heard on applying the stethoscope; such a sound disappears after the first impression produced on the nervous system by the momentous nature of the examination has passed off. It is to be borne in mind that even strong healthy men are often influenced to an extraordinary degree in this way, the very fact of not having undergone medical examination before, with the possibility presented to their minds that some deadly latent disease may be discovered, produces no little mental perturbation. If there is a gouty family or personal history the tension of the pulse and the daily amount and the colour of the urine should be ascertained. In all cases a specimen of urine voided in the presence of the examiner, or with such precautions as preclude the possibility of deception, should be examined as to naked-eye appearance, reaction, specific gravity, and presence or absence of albumen; if albumen is present a microscopical examination should be made for casts. In the case of applicants of or above middle age, especially if the urine is pale and of low specific gravity, more than a cursory examination for albumen should be made. As is well known the urine from cases of granular kidney is light coloured, of low specific gravity, and often contains a mere trace of albumen, and at times none at all; such urine examined off-hand, with nitric acid, may appear free although a little may be present, after adding the acid, it should be allowed to stand for ten or fifteen minutes, and then examined. It is preferable to add two drops of acetic acid to a test-tube nearly full of the urine and to boil the upper stratum; a slight haziness where the heat has been applied reveals the presence of a very small amount of albumen. If the specific gravity is above 1020 the urine should be examined for sugar, and in any case if there are reasons for suspecting diabetes.

Discussion as to the probable duration of life when albumen is present in the urine, or when auscultation reveals the presence of a heart-murmur, would be out of place in a book of this kind; the reader is referred to treatises on general medicine.

Insurance companies not unfrequently send a separate form to the usual medical attendant of the applicant requesting answers to the questions there printed. It is optional on the part of the medical attendant whether he answers the questions or not, but if he does so and accepts the fee, he is bound to answer fully and without reserve. Some offices ask the applicant's permission to interrogate his medical attendant; if given it is supposed to relieve the attendant from any obligation to professional secrecy in this particular instance.

Formerly it was customary for insurance offices to bar death from suicide, and this restriction gave rise to medico-legal discussions in relation to insanity as a cause of the suicidal act. At the present time it is the custom to take the risk of suicide along with other risks, provided that death from this cause does not occur within

## FORM OF MEDICAL REPORT IN LIFE ASSURANCE.

| | |
|---|---|
| Figure and general appearance? | ............................................................... |
| Weight? | ........................st....................lbs. |
| Height? | ..........................ft........................in. |
| Measurement of abdomen? | ..........................................................in. |
| Of the chest at full inspiration? | ..........................................................in. |
| At deep expiration? | ..........................................................in. |
| Number of respirations per minute? | ............................................................... |
| Is there anything abnormal in the character of the respirations? | ............................................................... |
| Is there any indication of disease, either acute or chronic, of the respiratory organs? | ............................................................... |
| State the rate and tension of the pulse? | ............................................................... |
| Is it intermittent or irregular? | ............................................................... |
| Is there any indication of disease of the heart or blood-vessels? | ............................................................... |
| Test the urine, voided at the time of examination, and state: | |
|   A. Specific gravity? | A..................B. Reaction?.................. |
|   C. Presence of albumen? | C..................D. Of Sugar?.................. |
|   E. Result of examination by the microscope? | E............................................................... |
| Do you know the party examined to be the person described in the application? | ............................................................... |
| How long have you known the applicant? | ............................................................... |
| Mention some physical mark of identification? | ............................................................... |
| Is the risk affected by anything in his residence or occupation? | ............................................................... |
| Where was this examination made, at applicant's place of business, residence, or examiner's consulting-room? | ............................................................... |
| Was there present at the examination any person other than the applicant and the examiner? | ............................................................... |
| Are you satisfied that there is nothing in his physical condition, habits, personal or family history not distinctly set forth tending to shorten his life? | ............................................................... |
| Do you unqualifiedly recommend the applicant for insurance? | ............................................................... |

a certain period, which has been fixed by most offices at one year after the payment of the first premium—that is to say, after the first renewal of the policy, by the payment of the premium due at the expiration of one year from the date on which the policy was granted, the risk of suicide is accepted by the office, and in event of its taking place, the sum insured for is paid. Some offices retain older customs, and simply return to the legal representatives of the holder of a policy who has committed suicide the money, without interest, paid in premiums.

## CHAPTER XVIII

### MEDICO-LEGAL BEARINGS OF DIVORCE.

MARRIAGE is of the nature of a contract and is not legally binding if one of the parties to it is incapable of consenting to, or fulfilling, the contract at the time it was entered into. In relation to divorce there are two questions which come within the province of the medical jurist. The first is one of **unsoundness of mind** preventing consent this constitutes a civil disability which invalidates marriage, the second is **impotency or physical incapacity** for sexual intercourse: this constitutes a canonical impediment to marriage.

The plea of insanity can only be offered in a suit for nullity of marriage when the mental disorder existed at the time the marriage took place; the fact that one of the contracting parties was insane at the time the contract was entered into renders the contract null and void, because insanity incapacitates the person subject to it from giving a rational assent to the terms of the contract. Insanity rarely develops without warning, but salient symptoms may suddenly show themselves after the mind has been some time diseased, the previous condition not being sufficiently marked as to give rise to suspicion of mental disorder; marriage, in such cases, not unfrequently kindles up the dormant state of mental disease into one of an acute character. In some instances the relatives and friends of the affected party conceal the disorder from the person with whom the marriage contract is to be made, with the forlorn hope that the new domestic relations will dissipate the existing trouble, the result almost invariably being disastrous to all concerned. When insanity is pleaded as a cause for nullity the diseased mental state is usually observed shortly after the marriage takes place. In the case of *Hunter* v *Edney* (Divorce Court, 1882) the wife refused to allow the marriage to be consummated, and an investigation of her mental condition showed that she was suffering from melancholia, and probably had been for some time. The judge in granting a decree, pointed out that the woman did not appear capable of understanding actions free from the influence of delusions, and was, therefore, incapable of entering into a contract like that of marriage.

The plea of insanity in relation to proceedings in the divorce court took a new departure in the case of *Hanbury* v *Hanbury* (Divorce Court, 1892.) The wife brought an action against the husband for dissolution of marriage because of his adultery and cruelty. The defence was that the respondent was suffering from insanity when the acts complained of were committed. The President, Sir C Butt, in summing up said that it had been argued that insanity was an answer in a suit for dissolution of marriage. He was far from asserting that it was not in any case, but he thought to make the plea a good one, the insanity must be lasting. It might be that the plea would be a good one if the insanity of the person were such as to necessitate his being placed in an asylum, from which there was no prospect of his discharge because there was no prospect of his recovery, or of amelioration of his malady. A decree *nisi* was granted. From this it seems that insanity might be admitted as a plea for irresponsibility. The case in point did not decide the question, because the respondent had given way to great excess in alcohol, a fact that weighed with the jury and confused the issue so far as precedent in relation to insanity itself is concerned.

In order that incapacity to take part in the performance of sexual intercourse can be regarded by the Court as a ground for a decree of nullity, it must be proved that the defect existed at the time of marriage and that it is of a permanent nature. It is not essential that the malformation should be of such a nature as absolutely to prevent coitus, if it interposes only a partial obstacle it constitutes a ground for a suit for nullity. The incapacity must be permanent, if a cure is at all possible, though it may be extremely improbable, it is sufficient reason for refusal of a decree, if however, an operation to effect a cure would be attended with great danger to life, the malformation is regarded as incurable. If the impediment did not exist at the time of marriage but has occurred since, it does not constitute a ground for nullity.

In cases where there is no apparent physical defect a cohabitation of three years' duration is required to ascertain with whom the fault lies. This rule is not invariable. If the Court deems that a sufficient time has elapsed for the difficulty to be overcome were it not of a permanent nature, a decree may be granted sooner. In one case, upon an apparently conclusive medical certificate that the impotence would be permanent, nullity was pronounced after a cohabitation of three months only. Triennial cohabitation is not required when the incapacity of husband or wife is of a visible and incurable nature which can be ascertained at once.

Wilful refusal of marital intercourse is not sufficient to obtain a decree, although persistent resistance on the part of the wife has been so regarded. Repeated attacks of hysteria in the wife brought on by the husband's attempts at intercourse has, after a cohabitation of three years without consummation, been deemed ground for a decree nisi.

Impotence does not render a marriage void, but only voidable—that is, the injured person must take active proceedings and sue for a decree. If sufficient grounds have existed, such as an absolute physical impediment to intercourse so that the marriage has not been consummated, and no proceedings are taken during the life-time of husband and wife, the marriage cannot be declared void after the death of one of them. This has been attempted in order to deprive the husband of benefits from a wife who died intestate, the next of kin claiming the estate.

It is incumbent on the petitioner for a decree of nullity of marriage on the ground of impotence to prove that marriage has not been consummated. The necessary evidence is obtained by medical examination of the generative organs of the respondent, which is made by two medical inspectors appointed by the Court. The husband and wife may conjointly select two medical men, or if they cannot agree each may nominate one; the petitioner then moves the Court for the appointment of the medical men chosen as inspectors, and at the same time moves for an order that the respondent submit to the inspection. The two medical inspectors after appointment have the following oath administered to them which sufficiently explains the duties they are called upon to fulfil.

"In the High Court of Justice Probate, Divorce, and Admiralty Division (Divorce)

"A B and C D, doctors of medicine

"You are produced as inspectors in a cause depending in the Probate, Divorce, and Admiralty Division of the High Court of Justice (Divorce), entitled      , falsely called      , to examine the parts and organs of generation of      , the petitioner in this cause, and also of      , falsely called      , the respondent in this cause

"You respectively swear that you will faithfully, and to the best of your skill, inspect the parts and organs of generation of each of them, the said      and      , and make a just and true report in writing, to the Right Honourable the President of the above Division, whether the said      [*the petitioner*] is capable of performing the act of generation, and, if incapable, whether such, his incapacity, can be cured by art or skill, and also, whether the said      is or is not a virgin, and whether she hath or hath not any impediment on her part to prevent the consummation of marriage, and that one of you will deliver such report under your hands and seals, closely sealed up, to one of the registrars of the above Division

" Sworn at the Principal Registry of the Probate, Divorce, and Admiralty Division of the High Court of Justice, this      day of      , 18  , Before me,   [Signatures of the medical inspectors]

                , Registrar "

Medical evidence will be received upon the question of incapacity, although no application has been made for an order for personal inspection of either of the parties

---

# MODES OF DEATH RESULTING CHIEFLY FROM ASPHYXIA.

## CHAPTER XIX

DEATH from hanging, strangulation, suffocation, and drowning, is chiefly due to asphyxia

### HANGING

Death from hanging is produced when the body is wholly or partially suspended by means of a cord or other ligature round the neck, until life is extinct  It is not necessary that the body should be in the upright posture, nor that it should cease to rest on the ground or other means of support, as will be presently shown, a very slight degree of tension on the ligature, such as that caused by partial suspension, is sufficient to produce death  Apart from judicial hanging the post-mortem appearances are those of death from asphyxia, together with indications of the manner in which asphyxia was produced

In by far the greatest number of cases of death from hanging the ligature surrounds the neck above the thyroid cartilage  Even if the noose is originally placed lower down, it is not in the first instance drawn tight enough to prevent the weight of the body dragging the neck as far through it as it can come  In 153 cases observed by Maschka (l.c.) the ligature was above the thyroid cartilage in 149, on it in 1, and below it in 3. When the ligature is above the thyroid cartilage slight constrictive force suffices to occlude the air-passages. Langreuter[1] investigated the mechanism of the closure of the air-passage on the dead body by removing the skull cap and brain in the ordinary manner, and cutting away the base of the skull so that the laryngo-pharyngeal region came into view. The subjects of the experiments had died from natural causes—they were not cases of death from strangulation. A cord was placed round the throat, between the thyroid cartilage and the hyoid bone, and carried up under the angle of the lower jaw. By moderate traction in the long axis of the body, as in hanging, the epiglottis was pushed against the back of the pharynx; by stronger traction the base of the tongue followed, and the free end of the epiglottis was pressed between the base of the tongue and the posterior pharyngeal wall, only moderate force was necessary to entirely close the air-passage. If the cord was placed below the thyroid cartilage, or horizontally upon it, and traction made as before, it slipped up above the cartilage; if retained on the cartilage with the hand, the vocal cords could not be completely approximated even when great force was used in pulling the constricting medium upwards and backwards. On suspending the body, the cord at once slipped up immediately under the lower jaw, and on looking from above, the tongue was seen to be displaced, upwards and backwards, and pressed into the opening in the base of the skull. Most of the experiments were repeated with a rolled-up handkerchief, the results were the same, but more force was required. Ecker[2] demonstrated like results with the body of a man which was found hanging from a tree in winter, frozen so hard as to be easily sawn into vertical sections. The soft structures at the posterior part of the floor of the mouth were doubled up into the cavity of the pharynx so as completely to fill and obliterate the naso-pharyngeal passage. Fig 15 is an exact representation of what was found.

When hanging causes complete occlusion of the air-passages, death results for the most part from asphyxia. Another factor, however, has to be considered, which may produce effects equal to or even exceeding those of asphyxia in prominence—compression of the large blood-vessels of the neck. These vessels, in any case, will undergo some compression, and, if the air-way escapes complete occlusion, arrest of the intra-cranial circulation may be the principal cause of death. When death begins in the brain, as the result of compression of the large vessels of the neck, it is not so much from excess of intra-cranial

[1] *Vierteljahrsschr. f. ger. Med.*, 1886.  [2] *Virchow's Arch.*, 1870.

blood pressure, as from arrest of the cerebral circulation; it is very exceptional for cerebral hæmorrhage to take place. If the air-way escapes occlusion, or is only partially occluded, a much longer time elapses before death takes place than if respiration is completely arrested. This has been shown experimentally with a dog—an opening was made in the lower part of the trachea, and the animal was hung by the neck with a cord, the noose being above the opening; a much longer time was required to cause death than is the case in ordinary hanging, and the post-mortem signs are different.

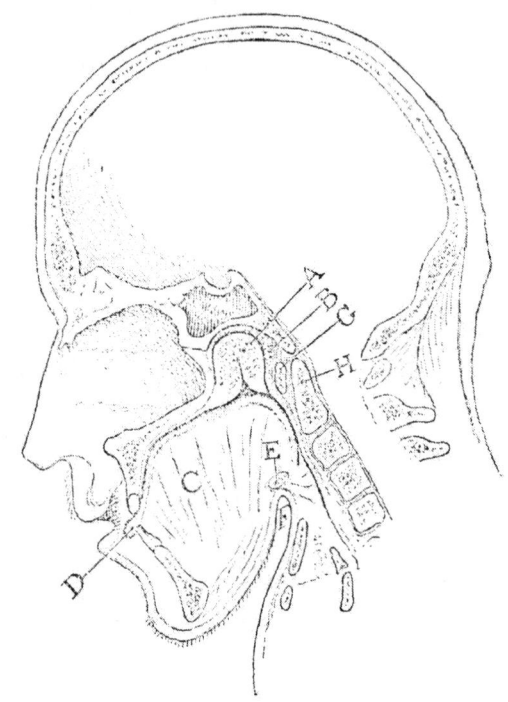

Fig. 15.—A, soft palate; B, wall of the pharynx; C, tongue; D, tip of the tongue pressed between the teeth; E, body of the hyoid bone; F, groove made by the rope; G, anterior portion of the atlas; H, odontoid process of the axis.

Great importance was formerly attributed to the respective influence of pure asphyxia and of what was called apoplexy as proximate causes of death from hanging. This resulted from the inconstant post-mortem appearances presented by the brain and by the lungs: sometimes the brain, sometimes the lungs, and sometimes both are found gorged with blood. It was inferred that if death took place from asphyxia the post-mortem signs ought to be invariable; as they were found not to be invariable, hypotheses were formulated to explain the discrepancy. It was assumed that death from hanging might be brought about in two distinct ways: by pure asphyxia and by apoplexy without asphyxia; seeing, however, that in a large number of deaths from hanging both lungs and brain are hyperæmic, a mixture of the two causes of death was described to suit this post-mortem condition. In consequence of these views the post-mortem appearances respectively produced by two closely allied modes of death were frequently treated as though they resulted from separate and distinct causes, and variable external conditions were regarded as necessary factors in the production of these dissimilar results.

Experiments, however, show that the preponderance of the signs of death from asphyxia over those indicating disturbance of the intracranial circulation, or the converse, are not solely dependent on the varying degrees of compression produced by the ligature on the air- and blood-channels respectively. Precisely similar external conditions may cause, in one case excess of blood in the lungs but not in the brain, and in another excess of blood in the brain but not in the lungs. It is probable that the state of the lungs, as regards inflation at the moment the air-passage is occluded, has a good deal to do with the relative hyperæmia of brain and lungs; some experiments made by Patenko[1] tend to prove this. A number of dogs were hung, some at the end of full inspiration, others at the end of full expiration, and the distribution of the blood in the various internal organs was observed after death. In those hung at the end of full *inspiration* the lungs contained little blood, but the sinuses of the skull, the membranes of the brain, and also the vessels of the abdominal organs, contained a great deal. In the animals hung at the end of full *expiration* the lungs contained much blood, and the cephalic and abdomen vessels little. When the air-passages are occluded at the end of full *expiration*, the blood flows from the periphery into the heart and—on account of the negative pressure developed in the thoracic cavity—from thence to the lungs; it cannot leave the lungs on account of the damming up that occurs in the dilated pulmonary vessels and from the want of intrapulmonary pressure. On the other hand, when occlusion takes place at the end of full *inspiration*, the pressure on the lungs causes expulsion of the blood they contain and consequent excess in the cranium and in the abdominal vessels. Hofmann (*l.c.*) considers that retraction of the abdominal walls, especially at the pit of the stomach—which occurs simultaneously with the efforts at respiration—compresses the lungs, and thus drives out the blood from them.

Strong corroborative evidence that the want of uniformity in post-

[1] *Annales d'Hygiène*, 1885.

mortem appearances of death from hanging is not dependent (or is so only under exceptional circumstances), upon external conditions, is afforded by an appeal to the statistics of deaths resulting from asphyxia in general. Out of 234 cases of death from asphyxia produced in various ways, Maschka found in 18, hyperæmia of the brain, membranes, and sinuses, in 30, a condition rather resembling anæmia, in 156, an ordinary moderate amount of blood.

It is thus evident that a clearly defined condition of the brain and lungs is not to be expected when making post-mortem examinations on cases of death from hanging, nor is it possible from inspection of these organs to determine the relative importance of stoppage of the air- and of the blood-channels, as the cause of death in any given case.

Another mode of death from hanging has been described, said to be due to compression of the vagi in the neck by the suspending cord or ligature. Hofmann[1] attributes the immediate loss of consciousness, and cessation of the action of the heart, to pressure on the vagi and the large vessels in the neck.

If pressure on the vagi produced any effect on the heart it would be suddenly to arrest it in diastole; there is abundant evidence, however, apart from physiological experiment, to prove that the heart continues to beat for a considerable time after stoppage of respiration by hanging. M'Causland[2] made some observations on a man executed by hanging, the rate of the pulse being taken every quarter of a minute after suspension. At the third quarter of the first minute it equalled 40 heart-beats per minute; at the last quarter of the fifth minute 152. The radial pulsation became less distinct until the end of the seventh minute, when it could no longer be felt. With the stethoscope the heart-beats could be heard during the eleventh minute at a rate of 120 per minute; at the end of the fourteenth minute it was still heard, but weak and fluttering; at the fifteenth minute it had ceased to beat. Schwab in a similar case found that the heart did not cease to beat until eight minutes after suspension. Maschka (l.c.) observed two similar cases, in one the heart-beats continued for four and in the other for five minutes after suspension. Balfour[3] gives three sphygmographic tracings taken from the radial artery of a criminal at intervals of 3½, 5½, and 7½ minutes after suspension; the heart continued to beat for twenty minutes. Misuraca[4] tied both vagi in dogs. Death did not take place

[1] *Journal de Medecine*, 1878.
[2] *Philadelphia Med. and Surg. Reporter*, 1883.
[3] *Clinical Lectures on Diseases of the Heart*, 1882.
[4] *Revista Sperimentale*, 1889.

until from fourteen hours to seven days afterwards. It is not probable, therefore, that pressure on the vagus has to do with the cause of death by hanging.

Compression of the large vessels of the neck by arresting the cerebral circulation induces very rapid loss of consciousness. The accounts given by those who have been rescued after a sufficiently long suspension to produce complete unconsciousness are mostly to the effect, that after a preliminary feeling of loss of power and ability to make any attempts to move the limbs, which is often preceded by subjective ocular and aural sensations (such as the appearance of sparks and a rushing sound), all becomes dark, and consciousness is abolished. The sudden onset of insensibility explains why in accidental and in suicidal hanging no attempts are made by the victim to save himself, in many instances the least movement would be enough to avert death. In other modes of committing suicide, voluntary or involuntary endeavours to escape the consequences of the act are not uncommon.

Post-mortem Appearances—External.—Cadaveric rigidity varies as to the time of its appearance. In one case subsequently mentioned it commenced within half an hour after death; in other cases it is delayed. If the body has been long suspended the post-mortem stains are most marked at the lower parts and there may be punctiform superficial ecchymoses. The face is usually pale and the expression tranquil, in some cases it is swollen and livid. The eyes are half open and not usually prominent, although in some cases they may be; the pupils vary as to dilatation. The tongue may be protruded between the teeth, but this is by no means invariable, it occurs in rather under 50 per cent of cases. Maschka directs attention to a bluish colour of the free border of the lips (which has been noticed by previous observers) as of frequent occurrence—in 98 cases out of 153. According to Adamkiewicz[1] cyanosis and swelling of face, ears, and lips only occur when the death agony is prolonged, this condition is more likely to be present in plethoric individuals. If the body is cut down at an early period the tumefaction and cyanosis disappear. Punctiform ecchymoses may be present on the face and neck, they are more likely to occur under the conjunctivæ—ocular and palpebral—and also on the outer surface of the lower eyelids; they are only present in 8 or 10 per cent of cases, therefore their absence is less significant than their presence. Turgescence of the genital organs of both sexes may or may not be present, it is due to hypostatic hyperæmia and is of no value as a sign of death from hanging. Escape of semen, urine, or fæces is of no diagnostic value, as it results from muscular

[1] *Vierteljahrsschr. f. ger. Med.*, Bd. 18.

relaxation, and is met with in many kinds of death both violent and natural. Sometimes saliva flows from the corner of the mouth and may be traced after death; this is not invariably the case, but when observed indicates suspension during life. The hands may be clenched, but this is at the most an indication of violent death; in suicidal hanging the hands, as a rule, are not clenched unless the act has been associated with more effort than is usually the case, or when the suicide has given himself a long drop.

The most important external appearance is the **mark round the neck** produced by the suspensory medium. Generally speaking, the breadth and depth of the mark depends upon the nature of the ligature used. If it is broad, soft, and yielding, only a superficial mark will be produced, and exceptionally there may be none at all; if it is thin, hard, and firm the mark will be deep and narrow. In either case any pattern or irregularity on the surface of the suspensory medium may be reproduced on the skin with which it has been in contact—the strands of a rope, or the texture of a handkerchief for example. The mark may entirely surround the neck, but is more frequently limited to the anterior half, and runs between the thyroid cartilage and the hyoid bone, taking an upward direction at the sides immediately behind the ears, where it usually ceases. If a cord with a running noose has been used, and sometimes even with a medium like a pocket-handkerchief, the mark may be continuous round the neck; in the latter case, probably on account of excessive weight of the body or the length of drop. From irregularity of pressure, or from some peculiarity in the nature of the suspensory ligament, the mark may be interrupted in a part where it is usually continuous. Exceptionally the mark may only exist at one side of the neck, the opposite side being free; this arises from the position of the noose which causes the head to fall sidewise instead of forwards as is usual. Occasionally the mark runs horizontally round the neck under the thyroid cartilage, the original position of the cord being maintained owing to the use of a noose that tightens easily and so keeps its hold, and also possibly to unusual prominence of the cartilage preventing the cord from slipping up.

The **colour and consistence** of the mark varies with the nature of the ligature. It may be pale and soft, with slightly reddened or livid borders, or it may be dusky red, or bluish-grey in colour with margins of a slightly deeper hue, or, finally, it may be yellowish-brown with darker margins, and of a horny or parchment-like consistence. The first two varieties are the result of soft or yielding ligatures; the last is produced by hard, rough ligatures which injure and partially rub off the epiderm, so that the underlying cutis becomes dry. More than one of these forms may be met with in a single mark it may be white and soft at one part, brown and hard at another.

Internal Appearances.—Hæmorrhage into the subcutaneous tissue in the neighbourhood of the mark produced by the ligature is comparatively rare, Maschka found it only in 10 cases out of 153. The adjacent muscles are not often injured, although Lesser[1] states that in 50 cases of hanging he found injuries to the muscles in 11, mostly in the sternomastoid. Fractures of the hyoid bone and thyroid cartilage are of exceptional occurrence, when present, they are mostly due to degenerative changes producing abnormal fragility. Fracture or separation of the vertebræ has only been seen in one or two cases, of which Lesser records one. Rupture of the inner or middle coats of the carotids sometimes happens, Lesser found it in 7 cases out of 50. It mostly occurs in individuals at or past middle life, the 7 cases just mentioned were all above forty years of age, although in none of them was endarteritis deformans present. The remaining internal appearances are common to all modes of death from asphyxia.

The appearance of the brain and lungs has already been described when discussing the modes of death from hanging. In rather over 50 per cent of cases the amount of blood present in the brain and cerebral vessels does not differ from the normal, in the remainder there is sometimes more and sometimes less than normal. Very rarely is there extravasation of blood, although in odd cases small ecchymoses may be present in the dura mater, their presence is significant of the mode of death. The mucous membrane of the trachea and epiglottis is generally injected. Maschka directs attention to a cyanotic or dark blue colour of the mucous membrane of the pharynx sharply limited below, which is rarely absent in death from asphyxia and seldom present in other modes of death. The lungs may exceptionally contain hæmorrhagic foci in their substance, sometimes they are œdematous, probably in consequence of slow death. The presence of small sub-pleural extravasations of blood is very suggestive of death from asphyxia, they are due to rupture of capillary vessels, occasioned by attempts at respiration after the air-passages are occluded. They are more likely to be formed when the occlusion takes place at the end of full expiration; increased blood pressure caused by stimulation of the vaso-motor centre has probably also to do with their formation. It is to be remembered, however, that they occur in other modes of death from violence—as from falling from a height, from burns, from CO and some other forms of poisoning, and in the course of certain diseases, such as scurvy. Their absence does *not* contra-indicate death from asphyxia. Ecchymoses sometimes

[1] *Vierteljahrsschr. f. ger. Med.*, 1881

occur in the heart, the right half of which is usually filled with dark fluid blood, but this appearance is by no means constant. The mucous membrane of the stomach is not unfrequently intensely injected, a condition which may be shared by that of the intestines; ecchymoses are occasionally found in both. The kidneys are often hyperæmic, sometimes ecchymoses are present. The liver may contain more blood than usual. The blood is usually dark coloured and fluid.

From the medico-legal standpoint three contingencies have to be considered in all cases of death from violence—Was death the result of Accident, Homicide, or Suicide?

Accidental hanging is of exceedingly rare occurrence. With one or two exceptions, the few instances recorded resulted either from playful attempts made by boys to imitate judicial hanging, or, in the case of still younger children, from swinging in the vicinity of a dependent rope, by which the child's neck was surrounded and its body suspended until death took place. Maschka records a case of fatal accidental hanging in which a man, slightly under the influence of alcohol, slipped off a ladder and was caught in the noose of a rope hanging from the ceiling. Kirkhead[1] relates a case which he regards as accidental rather than suicidal, in which the mode of suspension was peculiar. A young man eighteen years of age, who was a prisoner, was found dead in his cell, suspended by one of his braces round the neck, his feet touching the floor, the braces were made of frieze and lined with coarse calico. The deceased, with his back to the wall, had evidently stood on some hot-water pipes about 6 inches from the floor, placing the brace under the lower jaw he had passed the ends, without tying them, through a chain-loop which depended from the window of the cell, he had then either stepped or slipped off the pipe, when the sides of the chain loop came together sufficiently close as to grip the brace and hold it fast, with the body suspended by it. The brace was not knotted nor fastened to the chain in any way, and it appeared highly improbable that it could in this manner sustain the weight of the body; subsequent trial showed that the grip of the chain was sufficient to prevent the rough surfaced material from slipping under the strain placed upon it. The incompleteness of the preparations, with other circumstances, made it probable that the prisoner contemplated only a feigned attempt at suicide in order that he might be placed in a ward with company. Quick onset of cadaveric rigidity was observed in this case, the boy was seen alive at 2.20, the body was found at 2.30, and at 3 o'clock cadaveric rigidity had commenced in the neck.

A most exceptional case of accidental hanging was the occasion of a

[1] *The Lancet*, 1885.

trial for manslaughter, *Reg.* v. *Montague* (Com. Oyer and Term. Dub., 1892). The prisoner was accused of having caused the death of her daughter, a child three years old. As a punishment, she tied the child's arms above the elbows with a stocking, which was then passed round the body so as to pinion them to the sides. At the back one end of a cord was attached to the stocking, the other end being fastened —5 feet 8 inches from the ground, and, consequently, about 2½ feet above the child's head—to a ring in the wall of a dark closet. The child was left three hours, and when the mother went to liberate her, she found her dead and suspended by the cord in such a way that when it was loosened from the ring the body fell forward. There was a mark produced by pressure on the neck at the lower part of the windpipe. Either the stocking slipped up to the throat, or the cord got partially round the front of the neck, the result being death from hanging. The prisoner was found guilty, and was sentenced to twelve month's imprisonment.

Homicidal hanging is also infrequent. It would be exceedingly difficult to murder a man of average strength by hanging unless he was deprived of the power of resistance. In the case of the very old or very young it might be accomplished single handed, or even with a robust man if he was taken unawares. In the greatest number of cases, however—not the result of accident nor suicide—in which bodies are found hanging, death has been caused in some other way, and the body hung in order to simulate suicide. This leads to a consideration of the signs of death from hanging, with regard to the possibility of distinguishing between suspension during life and after death.

First, as to the punctiform ecchymoses that may be found on the lower parts of the body. Two antagonistic views are held as to their causation; one is that they are produced after death by the weight of the blood in the body rupturing the coats of some of the smaller vessels; the other is that they are formed during life from the increased blood-tension occasioned by the asphyxia. Observations are forthcoming which serve to support both views. Lesser[1] hung recently-dead bodies for twenty-four hours, and although the lower parts were as hyperæmic as they well could be, not a trace of extravasation was found; he also found extravasations in the non-dependent parts of bodies in which death had resulted from asphyxia. Strassmann[2] relates a case of suicidal hanging in which the body was found in a kneeling posture; the post-mortem stains were limited to the thighs where ecchymoses were found in abundance; the legs below the knees were pale and free from ecchymoses. Hofmann (*l.c.*) believes that the

[1] *Vierteljahrsschr. f. ger. Med.*, 1884.   [2] *Vierteljahrsschr. f. ger. Med.*, 1888.

extravasations are formed *intra-vitam*, but developed after death when the body is left suspended. Liman regards the ecchymoses solely as indicative of prolonged suspension after death. It may be accepted that ecchymoses on the lower parts of the body are of no value as indications of suspension during life.

A mark round the neck affords no *proof* that death was caused by hanging. Casper regarded the mark as purely a post-mortem phenomenon—probably a too sweeping assertion; still, it is perfectly true that a cord-mark may be produced after death that cannot be distinguished from one produced during life; this applies not only to a period immediately after death, but also to an interval of several hours after. Punctiform extravasations of blood are occasionally found when the cord-mark is cut into, but they cannot be relied on to indicate suspension during life, as they have been found in the bodies of those suspended after death; for the same reason the injected vessels along the borders of the mark are of no diagnostic value. Deeper seated injuries in the neck, such as fracture of the cartilages or hyoid bone, or rupture of the muscles, have also been found after post-mortem hanging. Rents in the inner coats of the carotids, when accompanied by extravasation of blood within the walls of the arteries, are indicative of suspension during life; they occur very rarely, however, and are easily caused accidentally when making the post-mortem examination. It is to be remembered, on the other hand, that death may result from hanging, and yet, for the reasons previously given, no trace of a mark round the neck may be visible. The presence on the chin of saliva which has flowed from the mouth points to suspension during life; but it is not a constant sign, nor one on which alone a decided opinion could be expressed. The remaining internal signs are at the most indications of death from asphyxia—they cannot be utilised as evidence of death from hanging.

The result of this inquiry as to the value of the signs of death by hanging in determining whether a body was suspended before or after death is, that they are *not* sufficiently conclusive as to justify the expression of an absolute opinion.

Other circumstances should be taken into consideration in attempting to solve the question. The body should be carefully examined for signs of struggling or of injuries other than those due to the assumed mode of death; the possibility of poisoning must not be overlooked. The absence of any such signs is more significant than their presence. It is not an unfrequent occurrence for a person who has determined to commit suicide to make the attempt in more than one way; such a person may ineffectually cut his throat, or take poison, or in some other way injure himself, and, finding that death is long in coming, may subsequently effect his purpose by hanging. If the injuries are of such a nature that they could not be self-inflicted, the fact of the body being suspended affords presumptive proof of homicide. The possibility of accidental post-mortem injuries caused by the body falling to the ground when cut down, or if examined at a distance from the place where it was found by rough handling during transport, should not be lost sight of.

Illustrations of self-inflicted wounds found on bodies in cases of suicidal hanging which might, at first sight, give rise to suspicion of homicide are given by Maschka. In one case, several incised wounds were found on the inner side of the left fore-arm, one of which divided the radial artery. In another case, a suicide discharged a fire-arm into his mouth, fracturing the hard palate, and lacerating the soft parts, and then hung himself. In a third, an old woman, sixty years of age, hung herself, and was cut down by her husband; on return to consciousness she seized a knife and cut her throat; at the necropsy an ordinary cut-throat wound was found above the thyroid cartilage and a cord-mark as well.

In some cases the balance of probability would be against that which actually occurred. Liman[1] records the case of a woman who inflicted on herself two wounds which penetrated the pericardium and afterwards hung herself; also that of a man who, in consequence of being shot in the back by another person, hung himself. In such cases it would be impossible to determine the question of suicide or homicide from the post-mortem appearances alone. Compare them with some cases of homicide, in which the dead body was subsequently hung, and the necessity for great caution is apparent. Deveaux relates the case of a woman who was found hung in a barn; on careful examination a small round wound was found under the left breast which transfixed the heart, the case being one of homicide. In another case, reported by Vrolik, a sailor was stabbed through the heart by a woman in a brothel; the body was afterwards washed, clad in a clean shirt and hung to make it appear that the death was suicidal.

Homicidal hanging is almost exclusively confined to young children; in adults, strangulation and suffocation—the analogous modes of death—are much more easy of accomplishment. One case is recorded by Ogston in which a woman tied a ligature round the neck of her husband while he was asleep and then pulled him up with it. Hofmann[2] relates the case of a man who, by hanging, killed five of his children, aged 8 months, 2, 6, 8, and 9 years respectively; and, finally, hanged himself. In another case a man hung his two children (girls), aged 6 and 13 years, probably whilst they were asleep.

[1] *Handbuch d. ger. Med.*  [2] *Lehrbuch d. ger. Med.*

In 1888 an exceptional and dramatic mode of homicidal hanging was put into execution in Paris by a man named Eyraud with the aid of a female accomplice named Bompard. The girl formed an illicit connection with one Gouffé, who was the selected victim. In the alcove of a room where an interview was to take place between Gouffé and Bompard, Eyraud fixed a compound-pulley over which a rope furnished with a strong hook was passed; the apparatus and the alcove were concealed by a curtain behind which Eyraud was placed; in front of the alcove was a sofa. Whilst Gouffé was sitting on the sofa the girl placed herself on his knee and in a playful manner adjusted the noose of a silk cord round his neck, and then passed the free end of the cord (which was furnished with an eye or small loop) to her accomplice who slipped the eye over the hook depending from the pulley, and pulled the rope to which it was attached until Gouffé was drawn up from the sitting posture and suspended by the neck; the rope was then made fast to the sofa so as to keep the body suspended. After robbing the corpse—which was the object of the murder—it was put into a box and taken to a distance and there left. The body was discovered fourteen days after and on examination it was found that both cornuae of the hyoid bone were fractured. The culprits were ultimately arrested, and from the confession of Bompard the actual mode in which the deed was perpetrated became known. The case is remarkable in itself, and, further, has an adventitious interest, because the question of hypnotic suggestion was raised in favour of the female prisoner; it was urged that she was subject to the will of her accomplice, and was not personally responsible for the part she took in the transaction. A full account of this case by A. Lacassagne is contained in the *Arch. de l'Anthropologie*, 1890.

Suicidal Hanging.—Hanging is the commonest of all modes of committing suicide; about twice as many people put an end to their lives in this way as by any other single means of self-destruction. Judicial hanging apart, suicide is accountable for about 95 per cent. of the total deaths by hanging. The proportion of men to women who commit suicide by hanging is about as 3.5 is to 1. The reason why this mode of self-destruction is relatively so frequently adopted is that the means for carrying it out are to be found in every house and but little skill or effort is required in its execution, and further the act of placing the head through a noose and allowing the body to depend from it partakes of a more passive character than using a knife to cut the throat, or a revolver to blow out the brains.

If the body of an adult of ordinary physical development is found hanging without any sign of injury or of struggling, and the general appearances are consistent with death from hanging, the probability of its being a case of suicide is very great. From what has been previously said the presence of wounds or of poison does not preclude suicide, but in such cases the contingency of homicide would be greater. In addition to making a thorough examination of the surface of the body for marks due to scratches, bruises, or blows, the clothing and immediate surroundings should be investigated. A few scratches on the neck are not necessarily indicative of homicide, occasionally they are inflicted by the victim himself involuntarily clutching at the noose. Care must be taken not to mistake signs of antecedent injuries for those caused at the time of death.

No conclusion can be arrived at as to the relative probability of suicide or homicide from the position in which the body is found. It is not necessary that the feet should cease to rest on the ground, sufficient pressure on the neck to cause death may be produced even in the sitting posture. Grant[1] relates how a man, aged 48 years, hung himself by tying the ends of a common cotton pocket-handkerchief together and suspending it from the handle of his bedroom door, which was only 2 feet 9 inches from the floor, he then sat down on the floor with his back to the door, put his head through the loop and bent forwards. This was proved by flattening of the nates—cadaveric rigidity having set in before the body was discovered—and by the post-mortem staining on the lower part of the back and legs. The mark on the neck was 1½ inches broad and extended from below the chin obliquely upwards and backwards over the occiput, the texture of the cloth being plainly impressed on the skin. Many cases of a more or less similar nature are recorded. Nobiling[2] reports the case of a man, aged 24, who also hung himself with a pocket-handkerchief attached to the latch of a door, which was 3 feet 7 inches from the floor. He adopted the kneeling posture and was found dead with the knees bent and the toes touching the floor, The handkerchief was folded broadly and left no mark behind.

In some cases the attitude is such that death can scarcely be said to be due to hanging, inasmuch as there is little or no suspension; such cases more nearly approach strangulation. Hurpy[3] records a case of this kind, of which the accompanying figure is an illustration.

A woman, 77 years of age, was found dead in the posture depicted. The arms were extended alongside the trunk, and the pronated hands touched the floor on their dorsal aspect, the legs and feet were also extended; the night-dress and chemise covered the body and showed no signs of disorder. The cord by which she hung herself was nearly 40 inches long, and was attached about 17 inches from the floor to the

---

[1] *The Lancet*, 1889.   [2] *Aerztliches Intelligenzblatt f. Baiern*, 1884.
[3] *Annales d'Hygiène*, 1881.

leg of a heavy table. The head half-rotated to the left rested with the right malar prominence on the floor, about 12 inches from the table foot. The woman was subject to delusions, and had committed suicide in this exceptional manner. In Tardieu's *Étude sur la Pendaison* a number of somewhat similar instances of hanging by incomplete suspension are illustrated.

The diagnosis between suicide and homicide is occasionally embarrassed by the hands or the legs of the deceased being found tied together; in such cases the way in which the limbs are secured, the position and the kind of knot, and the firmness with which it is tied are to be carefully noted. In some instances there is little difficulty in determining that the ligature round the limbs was tied by the victim himself; in other undoubted cases of suicide the position or the character of the knot is such as to make it appear almost impossible that it was self-tied. A striking illustration of the latter kind

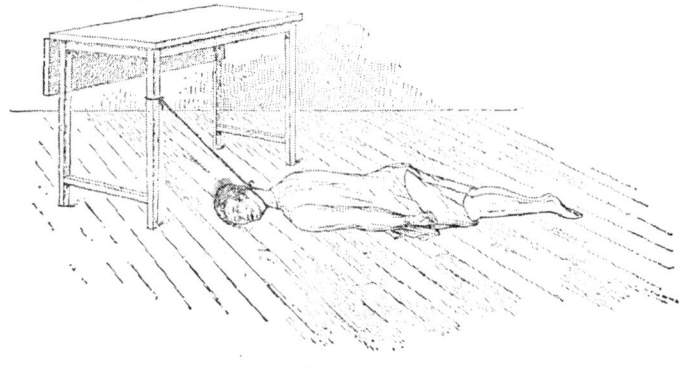

Fig. 16.

is given by Filippi, Severi, and Montalti.[1] The nude dead body of a man hanging by the neck was found in his office; the right foot touched the floor, the left was slightly lifted from it by flexion of the knee. The wrists were tied together behind the back in such a way that the knot of the cord was in front of them and rested on the back of the body. It was exceedingly improbable that the knot could have been tied as found, behind the back of the individual himself, and as every other indication pointed to suicide, the question arose—could he have tied them in front, and then passed his legs between the arms? Professor Filippi, to whom I am indebted for a copy of a photograph taken at the time, with permission to reproduce it, informs me that this was subsequently tested by enlisting the services of a young acrobat, who, with considerable difficulty,

[1] *Manuale di Med. Legale*, 1889.

succeeded in passing his legs between his arms, with the wrists tied together in front

**The after effects of Threatened Death from Hanging.**—When the body is cut down before life is extinct. efforts at resuscitation may be so far successful as to re-establish respiration, it is to be noted, however, that in some cases return of automatic respiration is not followed by ultimate recovery, the surface of the body remains cold, the circulation feeble, and insensibility persists, death taking place some hours subsequently When recovery takes place, certain neuroses or psychoses occasionally manifest themselves Terrien[1] met with one case, in which epileptiform convulsions with tetanic spasm drawing the head to one side occurred, the patient remained unconscious for several days, and on regaining consciousness was found to be amnesic In a second case, there were epileptiform convulsions with opisthotonos, and on return to consciousness the patient made movements for some time as though walking Petrina[2] records the case of a man who remained unconscious for twenty-four hours after attempted suicide by strangulation, during which time he had violent clonic convulsions of the whole body, but especially of the right side of the face and of the left arm, followed by a general condition of muscular rigidity. When he became conscious the speech was stammering, but deglutition was not difficult, there was paralysis of the right facial nerve and of the left side of the body, with diminished sensibility on the right side of the face and on the left side of the body, except on the front of the thorax, where there was some hyperæsthesia The paralysis gradually improved Ataxia subsequently occurred on the non-paralysed side, the inco-ordination spreading from the upper to the lower extremities, and then passing over to the paralysed arm This was probably a case of hæmorrhage into the pons Wagner[3] records the occurrence of acute dementia as a result of threatened death from hanging

### STRANGULATION

When death results from asphyxia caused by constriction of the neck by means of some form of ligature without suspension of the body, it is said to be due to strangulation The mode of death is the same as that which occurs in hanging

**Post-mortem Appearances—External**—The only appearance that needs special consideration is the mark produced by the ligature round the neck As a rule, the mark produced by strangulation differs from that produced by hanging in taking a more horizontal

---

[1] *Progrès Medical*, 1887.   [2] *Prag med Wochenschr.*, 1880
[3] *Jahrbucher f Psychiat*, 1889

direction, and in more completely encircling the neck; since the direction of the constrictive force does not necessarily tend to draw the ligature above the thyroid cartilage as in hanging, the mark is not unfrequently on the level of or below the cartilage.

Exceptions occur when the victim is thrown to the ground and the ligature is pulled upwards and backwards; the direction taken by the mark then resembles that due to hanging. On the other hand,

Fig. 17.

a horizontal mark may be produced by hanging when the position of the noose is different from that which is usual—*e.g.*, the knot being under the chin. The nature of the ligature influences the character of the resulting mark: if the ligature exercises unequal pressure as it surrounds the neck, the mark will be irregularly formed and may be interrupted in its course. Death has resulted from strangulation without the occurrence of any mark round the neck; in such cases it is probable that the ligature was of a yielding nature, was not applied with excessive force, and did not remain long round the neck.

The observations already made as to the absence of differential signs between marks round the neck produced by suspension of the body before death and after, apply equally to marks due to strangulation.

Internal Appearances resemble those described as due to death from hanging.

Accidental Strangulation is even a more rare mode of death than accidental hanging. Taylor and Stevenson record the case of a girl who was employed in carrying fish in a basket on her back, supported by a leathern strap passing above the shoulders round the front of her neck; she was found dead sitting on a stone wall, off which the basket probably slipped while she was resting, causing the strap to firmly compress the windpipe. Gordon Smith[1] gives a similar case of a boy who was in the habit of going about with a cord round his neck, to which a weight was attached; he was found dead in a chair, the weight having changed its position and drawn the cord tight round the front of the neck. Lesser[2] records the case of an epileptic, who was found dead with his feet on the bed and his face and breast on the floor; he was clad in his shirt only, which was gripped between his body and the lower part of the bed so that the collar was tightly drawn round the neck. On the lower part of the neck there was a shallow mark rather over half an inch broad, not depressed but sharply defined from the hæmorrhages and post-mortem staining in the surrounding skin; on the face and lower part of neck were punctiform ecchymoses. As Lesser admits, this is a doubtful case. Although there were indications of asphyxia, it is by no means clear that strangulation was the cause of it. The mouth and chest on the floor (which was covered with a carpet), and the epileptic seizure, are sufficient to account for the asphyxia and ecchymoses; the mark round the neck might be due to pressure from the collar, rendering the underlying skin bloodless without arresting breathing.

Homicidal Strangulation.—The relative frequency of homicidal and suicidal strangulation is the converse of that which occurs when hanging is the cause of death. On account of the rapidity with which insensibility supervenes when the throat is constricted, as is the case in strangulation, even a strong man, if taken unawares, is unable to defend himself or to cry for help. It is much easier to strangle a man than to hang him, because the constrictive force can be brought into play the moment the ligature is placed round the neck, whereas in homicidal hanging the victim has time to resist, because the constrictive force does not come into play until the body is lifted off the ground, and in the meantime he is put on the alert by feeling the cord

[1] *Principles of Forensic Med.*, 1827.
[2] *Atlas der ger. Med. (Zweite Abtheilung)*, 1890.

round his neck. A case described by Lesser[1] shows how easily homicidal strangulation may be effected even when the victim is a strong man. A man twenty-seven years of age, in complete possession of his bodily and mental powers, had a cord thrown round his neck from behind whilst sitting on a chair; the ends were drawn together, carried twice more round, tied once in a single knot in front, and a second time in a double knot at the angle of the right lower jaw; the victim fell senseless without making any attempt at resistance, the deed being perpetrated by one man. An adult has been strangled in a room divided only by a wooden partition from another room in which were persons who heard no suspicious sounds.

In accordance with the general principle that *a murderer uses more violence* to effect his purpose than is necessary, the distinctive feature of homicidal strangulation is—greater local injury than is found in strangulation from accident or suicide. A diagnosis is chiefly required between homicide and suicide; accidental strangulation is rarely alleged in defence in cases of suspected homicide, as the surroundings would probably determine the question off-hand. Mere extravasations of blood under the mark in the neck, though pointing to, are not indicative of homicide, nor are external injuries, such as scratches, excoriations of the skin, and slight bruises of more significance; they are suspicious indications, but nothing further. On the other hand, fractures of the thyroid or cricoid cartilages, or of the hyoid bone are distinctly indicative of homicide, as they are rarely, if ever, found in cases of suicidal strangulation; unfortunately for diagnostic purposes, such injuries are frequently absent in homicidal strangulation. Bleeding from the ears has been caused by strangulation accompanied with excessive violence, but it is of exceptionally rare occurrence. It is not necessary that the tympanum should be ruptured, although this has happened; the blood may be derived from the meatus, external to the tympanum, from bursting of some of the small superficial vessels in the same way that subcutaneous extravasations are formed, the effused blood obtaining exit through slight rents in the skin. Bleeding from the ears without rupture of the tympanum has however been observed in suicidal strangulation. Protrusion of the eyeballs, and of the tongue against or between the teeth, is more likely to occur in violent strangulation than in hanging, but it is not a constant sign. Turgescence of the face with a cyanotic or dusky-red hue may also occur, but, as with protrusion of the eyeballs, if present at the moment of death, on removal of the ligature it may afterwards disappear; even after strangulation with violence the face may be pallid. Blood has been observed to escape from both mouth and nostrils after homicidal

[1] *Atlas der ger. Med.* (*Zweite Abtheilung*), 1890.

strangulation; in such cases it is probable that the violence of the act is not the sole cause, but that extreme efforts at self-defence on the part of the victim unduly distend the blood-vessels of the head before the ligature is sufficiently tightened as to completely arrest the blood-current. In suicidal strangulation, bleeding from the nostrils has occurred from the violence of the efforts made by the suicide to tighten the ligature to the uttermost.

Signs of general violence are to be sought for as indicative of homicide. As previously stated, scratches or excoriations in the neighbourhood of the strangulation mark are suspicious, but do not constitute proofs of homicidal violence; they may have been produced by the ligature before it arrived at its final position, or by the suicide involuntarily plucking at it, especially if the finger nails are long. The rest of the body should be carefully examined for wounds and bruises; the back of the shoulders, for example, may show traces of counter pressure employed to steady the victim whilst the ligature was being tightened. When discussing the subject of supposed homicidal hanging, it was mentioned that death was not unfrequently caused by strangulation, and the body subsequently suspended by the neck to simulate suicide by hanging. In such cases there would probably be two marks on the neck; this, however, has occurred in suicidal hanging, from the neck slipping further through the noose after a period of suspension.

Homicidal strangulation occupies a prominent position among the modes of violent death that from time to time are feigned by an individual who wishes either to excite compassion; to account for the loss of a sum of money entrusted to his charge which he has embezzled, but which he alleges was stolen from him after he was rendered unconscious; to revenge himself on some one against whom he has a grudge, by accusing him of an homicidal act; or, in the case of hysterical women, without any obvious reason whatever. All cases of alleged attempted homicidal strangulation, in which the victim has sustained little external injury, should be approached with a certain amount of scepticism on the part of the medical man. This need not be displayed in the first instance; the mental attitude should be that of a man open to conviction, but who requires convincing. Many of these cases of imputed homicidal violence would scarcely be heard of were it not that the medical man who first sees the case does not approach it in a sufficiently judicial frame of mind; he accepts the statements of others who first discovered the supposed victim without sufficiently weighing their probability. Tardieu relates more than one instance of this description. In one, a man, stated to be in an almost lifeless condition, was found in a cellar with the hands and feet tied, and a cord three or four times round the neck, but not tied, in three hours he was himself again, except that he could not speak. According to the man's own statement subsequently made, he had been eleven hours in the condition as found. The whole affair was a palpable fraud, but there was not wanting medical evidence in favour of the account given, which was that the man's master had attempted to strangle him. Another case was that of a girl who asserted that she was the victim of a political conspiracy, and that a man had attempted to strangle her and at the same time had stabbed her with a dagger. Her dress was cut, but not her body. She was dumb when discovered after the alleged assault, but when Tardieu told her she would speak in a minute, she did so and confessed the imposture.

Suicidal Strangulation.—Although strangulation is an exceptional mode of committing suicide, instances are not so rare as formerly was assumed. Self-strangulation was regarded as next to impossible, except some contrivance of the nature of a tourniquet was adopted, such as passing a short stick between the cord and the neck, and twisting it round until asphyxia was produced. Numerous cases have proved, however, that the necessary constrictive force can be brought to bear by simply encircling the neck once or twice with a ligature and then tying it, or even without tying. The way in which the ligature is applied, together with the position and the formation of the knot, is of great importance in differentiating between suicidal and homicidal strangulation. Maschka considers that when the ligature goes several times round the neck, suicide is indicated rather than homicide, because quick and powerful tightening of it by a murderer would be more easily accomplished with a single turn than if there were several. On the other hand, there is nothing to prevent a murderer from using a single turn first, and, when unconsciousness has been produced, twisting the cord once or twice more round the neck, and tying it to make sure that the victim shall not recover. In Lesser's case of homicidal strangulation, previously mentioned, the cord went several times round. The position of the knot varies: it is most commonly found in front or to one side, usually the left, exceptionally it has been found on the back of the neck; the right- or left-handedness of the suicide may affect the position of the knot. More than one knot, especially if one is separated from the other by an extra turn of the cord round the neck, points to homicide. The more perfect the formation of the knot, the less likely is the case to be one of suicide. Anything peculiar about the construction of the knot must be noted, sometimes an indication is thus obtained as to the trade of the person who made it—sailors, for example, use knots of a different kind to those used by landsmen. The material of which the ligature consists may afford a clue.

The degree of violence inflicted by the ligature is a valuable indication. Fractures of the thyroid or cricoid cartilages or of the hyoid bone may almost be taken to exclude suicide; the like may be said of rupture of the muscles and of the inner coats of the carotids. Slight extravasations into the substance of the muscles underlying or near the cord-mark may occur in suicidal strangulation, but they are then limited in extent, being for the most part of the punctiform type. When the subject of homicidal strangulation was discussed, attention was drawn to the possibility of after-suspension of the body, in order to simulate suicide, and the consequent formation of a double mark round the neck; a like occurrence may be met with when a primary and unsuccessful attempt at suicide by strangulation has been followed by self-suspension. A careful comparison of the two marks would probably enable an opinion to be formed as to the real mode of death if by strangulation, the lower and more horizontal mark would be characterised by signs of greater violence than the mark due to suspension; if by hanging, the converse would hold good.

Signs of general violence would be absent, except such as might be produced in applying the ligature—scratches and slight abrasions about the neck. The possibility of unsuccessful attempts to put an end to life in other ways before adopting strangulation must not be lost sight of. When the body is examined before it has been disturbed, the state of the clothing and of the surrounding objects would show whether there had been any struggling or not. It is to be remembered, however, that a murderer might obliterate such indications, and also that suicides have been known to be affected with a kind of fury before putting an end to themselves, and have thrown all the surroundings into disorder.

The following cases are illustrative of the manner in which suicidal strangulation has been effected.—In a case reported by Filippi,[1] an insane man strangled himself by simply surrounding his neck twice with a strip of woollen material and tying it in front. Francis[2] records the case of a man, also a lunatic, who strangled himself by twisting some string round his neck, tying the ends to his wrists, and then extending his arms to the utmost; he was found dead, having fallen from his original kneeling posture on to one side. In a case related by Ogston,[3] the body of an old man was found in a wood with a neckcloth wound more than once round the neck, a walking stick had been passed through the loop of the neckcloth and twisted so as to tighten it. From the obliquity of the outer fold of the neckcloth, Ogston at first thought that the body had been dragged along

[1] *Revista sperimentale di fren. e med. legale*, 1879
[2] *Med. Times and Gazette*, 1876
[3] *Lectures on Med. Jurisp.*, 1878

the ground with the stick; on careful examination he concluded that the oblique direction of the neckcloth had been produced by a final convulsive struggle; the stick, entangled in a clump of young trees, had held the ligature fast, whilst the movements of the body had drawn it into the position in which it was found.

### STRANGULATION BY THROTTLING.

When strangulation is effected with the unaided hands, the act is called throttling.

The experiments made on the dead body by Langreuter (see section on *Hanging*) illustrate the facility with which the air-way may be occluded by external pressure. It was found that if the thumb and forefinger were placed externally on the two sides of the thyroid cartilage respectively, the least pressure was sufficient to close the aperture between the vocal cords; stronger pressure made the cords overlap each other. When strong pressure was made between the larynx and the hyoid bone, the air-passage was stopped, principally through approximation of the ary-epiglottic ligaments.

The only points to which attention need be specially directed in relation to throttling are the external and internal **appearances** produced by the **pressure of the fingers on the throat.** The general external and internal appearances are those common to other forms of strangulation.

Position of the Marks.—They are usually found on both sides of the front of the throat directly below the lower jaw; sometimes they are far back at the angle of the lower jaw. They may be sufficiently detached as to indicate the exact spot occupied by each finger, but not unfrequently they are too closely clustered together to be separately identified. They are distinguishable from an interrupted mark of a cord by not being on the same level. The marks may correspond more or less with the shape of the finger tips, but are often irregular in outline, from infiltration of extravasated blood round about. The impressions of the finger nails may be present as crescentic indents; and if there has been much struggling, the skin of the throat will be scratched and excoriated. There may be only one mark on one side and several on the other, respectively corresponding to the thumb and fingers; if the assailant was right-handed, the thumb mark will be on the right side of the neck; if the left hand was used, it will be on the left side. The appearance of the marks, if examined not long after death, is that of bruising; more or less blood escapes beneath the skin and produces the characteristic discoloration. If some time elapses before the examination is made, the marks may present the dry, horny, or parchment-like look and feel, described as occurring in one form of the cord-mark from hanging, this is due to injury sustained by the epiderm from rough contact with the fingers, which allows evaporation to take place from the denuded surface of the cutis

General signs of violence will probably be visible in some parts of the body, the attack is often made on a victim in the erect posture, and in falling injuries to the head are easily sustained

On section a considerable amount of extravasated blood is usually found in the underlying soft tissues. Fractures of the thyroid and cricoid cartilages and of the hyoid bone are frequently met with. The carotids escape injury. Lacerations of the inner surface of the cheeks from violent pressure against the teeth may occur.

It is usually asserted that throttling is necessarily and invariably a homicidal act. Accident as a mode of production may be ignored, and it has been held to be an impossibility for any one to commit suicide by compressing the throat with the unaided fingers. For all practical purposes throttling may be regarded solely from the homicidal standpoint. Still, one solitary case is recorded by Binner[1] of suicidal throttling. A woman, aged forty, suffering from melancholia, who had previously made several attempts to commit suicide, was found dead crouched in her bed with both hands compressing the throat; the elbows were supported on the knees, and the back leaned against the wall, there were marks of her finger nails on both sides of the throat. Death resulted from compression of the throat by the fingers.

A case of homicidal strangulation was tried at the Liverpool Winter Assizes in 1884. A man and his wife had been in the house a short time together when the man went out and sought assistance, "because his wife had fallen into the fireplace and he feared she was dead." She was found apparently dead sitting in a chair with the head supported by the wall, marks of blood were on the table, the wall, and the floor of the room. On examination of the body, a bruise was found immediately beneath the lobule of the left ear, and another three-quarters of an inch below the right ear, superficial extravasation was evident in both, together with a second and deeper extravasation half an inch below the surface of the right hand bruise. Other bruises were found over each eyebrow, at the back of the right wrist, over the knuckle of the left little finger, at the inner part of the left elbow, and at each angle of the mouth, within the mouth was a lacerated wound corresponding to the stump of a canine tooth. The tongue and gums were also injured, and one of the teeth in the upper jaw partly loosened. The deeper structures of the throat were not injured. The

[1] *Zeitschr. f. med. Beamte*, 1888

internal signs were those of death from asphyxia, the brain and membranes were intensely congested. The man was found guilty [1]

## SUFFOCATION.

When air is prevented from entering the lungs by other means than by external constriction of the throat, or by submersion in water, if death results, it is said to be due to suffocation

The modes of death from asphyxia which have previously been considered, are necessarily due solely to external influences brought to bear either accidentally or intentionally; from these suffocation differs, inasmuch as it may result from pathological causes apart from external agency  It is not necessary to enumerate all the morbid conditions which may lead to death from suffocation; a few will serve as illustrations —In children, spasm of the glottis or accumulation of exudative products in the air-passages; in adults, œdema of the glottis, paralysis of the vocal cords, bursting of a pharyngeal abscess, or of a thoracic aneurism into the trachea may suddenly cause death from suffocation. Nothing more need be said with regard to these and like conditions, except that the possible occurrence of those which leave no evidence after death must not be forgotten when searching for the cause of death in doubtful cases.

Suffocation may be produced from external causes by (*a*) the introduction of foreign bodies into the air-passages, (*b*) forcible compression of the chest, (*c*) covering over the mouth and nose (*smothering*)

(*a*) The introduction of foreign bodies into the air-passages from accidental causes may occur either in the case of children or of adults; the foreign substance is usually some kind of food, either solid or pultaceous; it may be introduced directly, as in the act of deglutition, or it may be regurgitated from the stomach, and find its way into the air-passages instead of being ejected from the mouth  When food enters the larynx, it is frequently the result of an involuntary movement of inspiration induced by sudden surprise or by a fit of laughter during the act of deglutition  A man who is intoxicated may vomit, and, through diminished reflex activity, no effort may be made to prevent the vomited matter from being drawn into the larynx  In some cases death occurs with exceeding rapidity, especially if the individual is advanced in years, and on post-mortem examination, the signs of death from asphyxia are found to be entirely absent· there is neither cyanosis during life, nor excess of blood in lungs, brain, or right heart after death  It is probable, in cases of this

[1] *Med. Chron*, 1885.

description, that death results from syncope. Perrin[1] directs attention to the absence of the post-mortem signs of death from asphyxia under conditions which are likely to produce them, and gives illustrative cases. An invalid, 62 years of age, in the midst of a meal suddenly fell on the knees of his neighbour quite dead. On examination, the epiglottis was erect and rigid, and a mass of food as large as a hazel-nut was found in the glosso-epiglottic fossa, at the fifth ring, the lumen of the trachea was obstructed by a cylindrical mass nearly 2½ inches long which reached down to the point of bifurcation. The lungs were normal and free from ecchymoses, the left side of the heart was empty and the right side only contained a few spoonfuls of partially fluid blood. In another case a man 68 years of age fell suddenly as though struck by lightning when leaving a café. At the necropsy, a mass composed of pancake was found to fill the posterior part of the pharynx, and to extend to the glottis, the epiglottis was raised.

It is not necessary that the air-passages should be blocked up with the foreign substance in order to induce suffocation; the introduction of a small extraneous body in such a way that it lodges on or between the vocal cords may be sufficient to excite spasmodic closure of the glottis and thus cause death. In the museum of Owens College there is a specimen taken from the body of a man who died under the following circumstances:—The man, when not quite sober, was turned out of a public-house; he tried to get in again, and in doing so his finger was caught in the door, shortly after he was found dead in the street. The body was taken to the Manchester Royal Infirmary, and Professor Young, who was then the pathologist, made a post-mortem examination but found no cause for death until on opening the larynx a small piece of skin was discovered just below the glottis. Further examination of the body showed that the fragment of skin had been detached from the index finger of the right hand. What probably happened was that on receiving the injury the man put his finger in his mouth to ease the pain, and the piece of skin in question, being all but detached, was carried away by a quick inspiration and lodged between the vocal cords.

Homicidal suffocation from the introduction of foreign bodies into the air-passages is rarely met with, except in infants or young children. In the case of children, various substances have been forced into the air-passages—such as rolled up pieces of cloth, pieces of newspaper, sand, earth, and artificial teats—the last-named to give colour to the assertion that death was accidental. Adults murdered by the introduction of foreign bodies into the air-passages have generally been under the influence of drink at the time

[1] *Poulet on Foreign Bodies in Surg. Practice*, 1881.

or have been aged and feeble persons. Littlejohn[1] records the case of a woman who died suddenly, and at the post-mortem examination a wine-bottle cork (most probably thrust into the throat when the woman was intoxicated) was found covered with frothy mucus and tightly inserted into the upper part of the larynx, the sealed end of the cork with the mark caused by the corkscrew was uppermost. The defence was that the woman had drawn the cork from a bottle with her teeth and that it was propelled down the throat accidentally; the fact of the sealed end being uppermost, however, disproved this. The frothy mucus which covered the cork indicated that it was introduced during life. The act was, doubtless, homicidal, but the accused was not found guilty, the Scotch verdict of 'not proven' being given.

Suicidal suffocation from the introduction of foreign bodies into the air-passages is limited to lunatics. A woman in an asylum aged 58, was found early one morning dead in bed with part of a stocking protruding from her mouth death having resulted from suffocation; no noise nor disturbance nor anything wrong was noticed by other patients who slept in the same ward. At the inquest a long stocking was exhibited which had been removed with great difficulty from the air-passages.[2] Sankey[3] mentions the case of a male epileptic who committed suicide in an asylum and was found dead lying on his back in bed with a round pebble in each nostril, and a strip of flannel rolled up and stuffed into the throat.

(b) **Suffocation from forcible compression of the chest** may be accidentally occasioned when large numbers of people are massed together on occasions of public rejoicing, or in panics, such as follow an alarm of fire raised in a crowded building. A lamentable instance occurred in 1883 in Sunderland. Some hundreds of children in the gallery of a public hall rushed down stairs and were arrested by a closed door; a block took place at the bottom of the stairs and about 300 children were piled up so as to form an inextricable mass some 7 or 8 feet high. About 200 were killed, for the most part from compression of the chest, although in very few instances were the ribs fractured, which may be accounted for by the flexibility of juvenile bones, and by the absence of powerful struggling, such as takes place in a crowd of adults. Lambert,[4] who examined many of the bodies, states that the appearances after death were almost uniformly:—congested puffy face, purple or blackish turgescence of the vessels of the neck, eyelids closed, eyeballs protruding and fixed, pupils dilated to the uttermost, and froth from the mouth and

[1] *Edin. Med. Journ.*, 1885.  [2] *Brit. Med. Journ.*, 1882.
[3] *Brit. Med. Journ.*, 1883.  [4] *Brit. Med. Journ.*, 1883.

nostrils. In twenty-four hours much of this had passed off, the face presenting the appearance of peaceful repose. Cadaveric rigidity was universally absent. In almost all the cases urine and fæces had been expelled.

Infants are but too frequently **accidentally suffocated by pressure** caused from overlaying; a heavily sleeping or, possibly, intoxicated mother encroaches on the infant lying by her side in such a way as to suffocate it. In these cases the cause of suffocation may be two-fold— pressure on the chest, and covering of the mouth and nostrils, each in itself being quite sufficient to quickly produce death. Of 258 deaths from overlaying Templeman[1] found that at the ages of one, two, and three months the numbers were 62, 67, and 66 respectively; at the fourth month the mortality sank to 21, at the fifth to 16, at the sixth to 13, at the seventh to 5, and at the eighth and ninth to 4 each. After nine or ten months old an infant is better able to struggle and to save itself from the risk of accidental suffocation.

**Homicidal suffocation from compression of the chest** has been effected in new-born infants. In adults, unless previously rendered incapable of resistance by intoxication or by debility from age, such a mode of homicide would be scarcely practicable. The oft quoted cases of Burke and of Bishop and Williams were examples of combined suffocation; they compressed the chests of their victims by allowing the weight of their bodies to rest on them, and at the same time covered the mouth and nostrils with the hands. Maschka met with the case of a girl of fourteen who was suffocated by pressure on the chest by one man, whilst another perpetrated a rape upon her.

(c) Suffocation by covering or compressing the mouth and nostrils is a mode of suffocation usually designated **smothering**. In the case of infants it may easily occur either **accidentally** or with **homicidal** intent by simply covering them over with a thick layer of clothing, such as the bed clothes; mere continued pressure of the child's face against the mother's breast in the act of suckling has proved sufficient. Adults may be accidentally smothered by immersion in substances composed of loose particles, such as grain, sand, flour, and the like. Falck[2] records the case of a man who was accidentally buried in a large quantity of flour. The mouth and œsophagus were filled with flour agglomerated with saliva, but none obtained access to the stomach; the lungs and the brain were hyperæmic; particles of flour were found in the bronchi as far as the smallest ramifications. Russo-Gilberti and Alessi[3] found loose particles of the surrounding material in the larynx, bronchi, and even in

[1] *Edin. Med. Journ.*, 1892.   [2] *Nordiskt med. Arkiv.*, 1891.
[3] *Archivio per la Scienze Mediche*, 1888.

the pulmonary alveoli of animals that had been buried alive. Epileptics are not unfrequently smothered during a seizure, either when in bed, from close approximation of the bed clothes to the face, or in the day time, from falling on to some yielding substance face downwards. Janeway records the case of an epileptic who had an attack in a stable-yard and was suffocated by the manure on which he fell, portions of which were found in the larynx after death.

Homicidal suffocation by smothering is, doubtless, of frequent occurrence as regards infants and young children; the modes which have been adopted are described in the section on infanticide. Older children, especially when surprised in sleep, easily succumb to smothering. A probable instance of this kind occurred in Manchester in the year 1862. Three children, aged 12, 8, and 5 years, were found dead, side by side, on the floor of a bedroom; they had probably been dead two days, rigidity had passed off, and the first putrefactive changes were developing. No external indications of violence were observed, except that in two of the children there were slight bruises, and in one there was a scratch on the face; internally there was an absence of apparent cause of death, and there was no trace of poison. Taylor, who investigated the case, concluded that death had resulted either from smothering or from chloroform vapour, and considered it most probable that the children had been smothered whilst in bed.

Adults have either to be taken unawares, or to be asleep, or intoxicated to permit of death being homicidally produced by smothering. Plasters made of pitch or other sticky substances have been used for the purpose of rendering persons helpless and incapable of raising an alarm whilst being robbed; if the plaster is not quickly removed death from suffocation results. Wald[1] records an instance of homicidal smothering of an adult. A man resolved to murder his wife, and took the opportunity while she was asleep in bed to cover her over with several heavy bed-covers, and then laid himself on the top; in a short time, the struggles she at first made ceased, and the woman was dead. The man then informed a doctor that his wife was attacked with cramps and desired his attendance, but before the doctor arrived he met him with the intelligence that she was dead; no suspicion was created, and the body was buried. Information was subsequently given to the authorities as to the real cause of death, and the body was exhumed and examined. Signs of death from asphyxia were present, and the murderer subsequently confessed to having perpetrated the crime in the way above described.

Suicidal smothering is almost unknown. A case[2] occurred in

[1] Gerichtliche Medicin, 1858.   [2] Wald, l c

France in which a woman got under the bed-clothes after desiring her little child to bring all the cushions, clothes, and other similar articles that were in the room and pile them on the top of her; the child did so, and some hours after when the woman was discovered she was dead. Signs of death from asphyxia were found at the necropsy.

The modes in which suffocation can be produced being so varied, the post-mortem signs within certain limits are correspondingly diversified.

Externally, the appearances comprise all degrees of significancy from those cases in which the mouth and nostrils are found filled with a foreign substance, down to those in which death has resulted from smothering by graduated pressure with a soft material—the first being obvious at a glance, the second yielding no external trace whatever of the cause of death. Apart from any special indication afforded by the presence of injuries about the mouth or nostrils, or of some of the material by means of which the air-passages were obstructed, one or more of the general signs of death from asphyxia may be visible, such as punctiform ecchymoses on the conjunctivæ and on the outer surface of the lower eyelids. Turgescence of the face and large vessels, with a cyanotic hue of the extremities, is suggestive of suffocation from compression of the thorax, but the condition disappears in a few hours after death.

Internally, there may or may not be the usual signs of death from asphyxia; the amount of blood contained by the lungs and heart is by no means constant, nor is the dark colour and fluidity of the blood invariable. Sub-pleural ecchymoses, which Tardieu erroneously regarded as exclusively due to asphyxia produced by suffocation, are usually present; the pericardium also may be ecchymosed. The degree of hyperæmia of the other organs—brain, stomach, intestines, spleen, liver, and kidneys—is subject to great irregularity. It is to be remembered that the absence of the so called signs of death from asphyxia do not exclude the possibility of death having resulted from suffocation.

When making an inspection of the dead body for medico-legal purposes the air-passages from the mouth down to the bronchi should always be examined, otherwise the real cause of death may remain undiscovered. It is too frequently assumed, if the conditions of the heart, the lungs, and the blood usually associated with death from asphyxia are absent, that there is no need to examine minutely into the state of the respiratory tract. More than once it has occurred that a medico-legal inspection which yielded negative results as to the cause of death has been proved to have been negligently made, by the discovery of a foreign substance in the air-passages on subsequent and more thorough examination. In addition to the detection of foreign bodies in the air-passages the state of the mucous membrane of the larynx and trachea requires investigation; it is sometimes found injected, and may be covered with frothy mucus, possibly blood-stained; this would point to an asphyxial mode of death, though its absence would not justify the opposite conclusion.

All signs of general violence, such as bruises, scratches, or ruffling of the epidermis are to be carefully looked for. The surroundings of the body, if the examination is made before it is disturbed, may afford valuable indications; if the body is clothed, careful inspection of every detail must be made and *notes taken before it is disturbed*. It not unfrequently happens that conditions subsequently discovered may receive important corroboration from some apparently trifling detail which, without this precaution, would have escaped notice, or from want of aid to the memory afforded by the notes would probably be imperfectly interpreted.

## DROWNING.

Drowning is a mode of death from asphyxia caused by continuous or by intermittent submersion of the mouth and nostrils under water or other fluid, so that access of air to the lungs is either at once or gradually cut off until life is extinct. When asphyxia is caused by hanging or by strangulation, access of air to the lungs is simply obstructed; when it is caused by drowning, an irrespirable medium is drawn into the air-passages by attempts at respiration, and in this way special changes are produced in the lungs beyond those which are due to uncomplicated asphyxia; these changes constitute one of the principal signs of death from drowning. Death may result from falling into the water and still not from asphyxia; fatal syncope may occur at the moment of submersion, or in rare instances the head or abdomen may strike against a rock or other solid body with sufficient violence as to cause immediate death from shock; in such cases the characteristic signs of death from drowning will be absent.

From experimental investigations Brouardel and Loye[1] consider that the mode of death from submersion usually attributed to syncope is due to inhibition. They emphasise the distinction between the manner in which the respiratory act is influenced by drowning on the one hand and by external constriction of the air-passages on the other. When asphyxia is produced by hanging, the entire muscular force of the respiratory apparatus is thrown into immediate action in the

[1] *Archives de Physiol. norm et Pathol.*, 1889.

endeavour to obtain oxygen. When submersion is the cause of asphyxia, there is at first an attempt on the part of the animal to breathe as usual, then, appreciating the danger, it struggles to escape and at the same time fixes the thorax, voluntarily suspending respiration in order to prevent the water from entering the air-passages; the respiratory centres, however, are soon stimulated beyond the control of volition, and involuntary respiratory movements are set up by which water is drawn into the lungs and penetrates the alveoli. In addition to the resistance offered by the will, the sensory nerves of the skin and of the air-passages play an important rôle.— If the trachea of an animal is opened and a tube inserted in the opening, the glottis no longer has control of the air-way, and it might be supposed on submerging the animal that water would at once be drawn into the lungs, the same suspension of respiration, however, takes place as before, from fixation of the thorax, so long as the centres can be kept in abeyance. But if both pneumogastrics are divided high up in the neck, and a tube placed in communication with a vessel of water is introduced into the trachea, the animal continues to breathe as usual for thirty seconds, although water is being received into the lungs in the place of air, then the animal becomes agitated, but still continues to breathe. If, after division of the pneumogastrics, an animal is plunged in water it fixes the thorax almost as though the nerves were intact, this demonstrates that the sensory nerves of the skin and of the naso-pharyngeal tract take part in the inhibition of respiratory movements; in the preceding experiment they were not called into play. When an animal, chloroformed until the cornea is insensitive, is submerged, it makes no attempt to prevent water entering the air-passages, but continues the movements of respiration as before submersion. From these experiments Brouardel and Loye infer that although volition has to do with the temporary arrest of respiration irritation of the nasal and laryngeal nerves exercises a still more powerful influence by inhibiting respiratory movements. A transient stage of interrupted respiration may exceptionally be replaced by one of permanent inhibition, and death from submersion thus caused with absence of the usual signs produced by the presence of water in the lungs.

When death takes place from drowning in the ordinary way, submersion is not usually continuous, even when the individual falls from a height above the water-level, and in consequence of the acquired momentum reaches a considerable depth, if not in some way prevented he generally returns at least momentarily to the surface. This is not due to the body being of lesser specific gravity than water, but to involuntary movements of the limbs—apart from skilled movements, such as are executed by practised swimmers. The specific gravity of the human body is slightly greater than that of water, being about as 1.08 to 1.005 or 1.03, according to the kind of water —fresh or salt. All the constituents of the body are specifically heavier than water, except fat and lungs which have breathed, and these do not suffice to counterpoise the heavier tissues; still, the difference is so slight that very little movement brings the body to the surface, if only for a moment. The greater the percentage of fat and of lung-capacity in relation to the body-weight, the greater the tendency to float; women as a rule float better than men because of the slighter build of the skeleton and large proportion of fat; new-born infants if well nourished will scarcely sink unless weighted.

The body of a person who has died from drowning is deprived of the buoyancy of the lungs, since the air they contained has been almost entirely replaced by water; this, together with the absence of movement, causes the body to sink and to remain submerged. Submersion continues until the gases of putrefaction are developed in sufficient quantity to reduce the specific gravity of the body below that of the surrounding medium; the body then rises to the surface unless prevented by some mechanical obstruction—such as being covered over with sand or mud, or being caught by weeds, ropes, or the like. Floatation generally occurs in temperate climes within the first week; the exact period after death depends upon the initial difference in specific gravity between the body and the medium in which it is submerged—chiefly determined by the amount of fat—by certain intrinsic conditions depending on the degree of vital exhaustion that preceded death and on the temperature and stillness of the water. A body submerged in deep water will not rise so soon as one lying in shallow water, because the latter will be warmer and will consequently promote an earlier formation of putrefactive gases. A body submerged in a pond is likely to rise earlier than one at the bottom of the river, because the still water acquires more heat from the sun's rays and from the stratum of air above it than the flowing water of a river.

**Post-mortem Appearances.**—When the body of a person who has been drowned is removed from the water within a few hours after death and is examined forthwith, there is usually little difficulty in determining that death was caused by drowning; on the other hand, when the body remains in the water until decomposition is advanced, insuperable difficulties are interposed which may render the formation of anything like a positive opinion impossible. The interval that elapses between the removal of the body from the water and the examination largely influences signs of great diagnostic value.— The froth visible about the mouth and nostrils in the recently drowned is soon dissipated on exposure to the air, the surface of the body—especially if the clothing is removed—in a short time becomes dry and discoloured  putrefactive changes in the body advance with great rapidity after its withdrawal from the water, and in a comparatively short time completely obliterate the indications which distinguish death by drowning from other modes of death with subsequent submersion of the body  The following description refers to the bodies of those recently drowned and examined shortly after removal from the water —

External Appearances —Cadaveric rigidity usually comes on early, in some cases immediately, so that the last position of the limbs during life is maintained after death  The surface is pallid, but not more so than that of a dead body under ordinary conditions  The face is tranquil and the eyes and mouth are partially open  There may be rosy patches on the face and neck, and in some instances the face is of a reddish-blue or violet hue, at a later period after death, its colour may be changed to a dirty red  The skin often presents the appearance known as "goose-skin," a condition met with in a variety of sudden deaths by violence, it is due to vital reaction, the manifestation of which persists after death from the occurrence of instantaneous cadaveric rigidity in the *arrectores pili* when in a state of contraction. The skin of the palms of the hands, the soles of the feet and the knees is bleached, sodden, and wrinkled, the result of imbibition ; it is of no significance other than showing that the body has lain in the water for twelve or more hours  The tongue has been described as being pressed forwards between the teeth ; it is only exceptionally that this occurs, and as the same condition is found after violent death from other causes it is a sign of little import  The most valuable of the external indications that death has resulted from drowning is the presence of a fine froth on the lips and nostrils  This froth or foam may be white or it may be blood-stained ; it has not been unaptly likened to the finely constituted lather produced by shaving-soap.  Draper[1] states that it is found after drowning under all circumstances and in all media, he has seen it in the case of an infant drowned in a cesspool  Its continuance however cannot be depended on for more than four days in winter and about three in summer—the body being under water; if it has disappeared from the lips, a little pressure on the chest may cause some to well out of the mouth  The presence of substances, such as weeds from the bed of a river, or of fragments of clothing, clutched in the fingers—due in the first instance to a vital act subsequently rendered permanent by instantaneous cadaveric rigidity— is evidence of submersion during life, in practice it is a sign not frequently met with.

[1] *Boston Med and Surg Reporter*, 1855

**Internal Appearances**—The lungs usually exceed their normal volume, so that they almost cover the pericardium, a condition sometimes described as "ballooning" of the lungs; instead of collapsing when the thorax is opened, they protrude so as to fill the aperture made by the removal of the sternum. The consistence of the lungs is doughy—they retain the pit produced by pressure of the finger. They are sometimes of a pale grey, with reddish stains produced by transudation of water tinged with blood-colouring matter; in other instances the entire surface of the lungs is of a reddish-blue. Draper, in the majority of cases examined by him, observed punctiform subpleural ecchymoses, though few in number and mostly at the lower part of the lobes. Most observers state that they are of very exceptional occurrence in death from drowning. Ogston, Junior, met with them in barely 7 per cent of the cases he examined. On section, the lung-substance is found to contain water which, along with froth, exudes from the cut surface on the slightest pressure; the bronchi, and possibly the alveoli contain fine froth of the same character as that on the lips and nostrils. The red stain, if visible on the surface of the lungs, is seen to pervade their entire substance.

Two views are held with regard to the condition of the parenchyma of the lungs after death from drowning. According to one, it is infiltrated with water or other medium in which drowning takes place, and this to a certain degree accounts for the increased volume of the lungs. According to the other view, there is but little fluid in the parenchyma, and any that is present is derived from exudation from the vessels producing œdema. Paltauf[1] states that the water which is drawn into the lungs in attempts at respiration enters the alveoli, and finds its way from thence by the lymph-spaces and occasionally through small lesions in the alveolar walls, into the interstitial alveolar, subpleural, peribronchial, and perivascular connective tissue. Lesser,[2] on the other hand, states that a secretion of mucus, which blocks the finer bronchi, is caused by aspiration of water into the air-passages, which therefore cannot reach the alveoli except in scarcely appreciable quantity. He denies that the parenchyma contains water; if any fluid is there it is derived from the blood-vessels and is a vital exudation product—a true œdema.

It is probable that a mucous secretion in the bronchi does occur during death from drowning, but only in quantity when the death-struggle is prolonged. Ceradini's[3] experiments on animals show this,

[1] *Ueber den Tod durch Ertrinken*, 1888.
[2] *Atlas d. ger. Med.*, 1891, and *Vierteljahrsschr. f. ger. Med.*, 1884.
[3] *L impaizzale*, 1873.

and also that blocking of the finer bronchi by the mucus is one reason why the lungs after death from drowning do not collapse when the thorax is opened—the alveolar contents cannot escape.

The fine froth contained in the air-passages is composed of a variable mixture of the drowning medium with air, mucus, and possibly blood. When the death-struggle has been prolonged more froth is produced and it is of a more lasting nature than when death occurs quickly; this results from the presence of a greater proportion of mucus, which imparts increased tenacity to the bubbles, and from more vigorous admixture of air, water, and mucus, which augments the total amount of froth. According to the observations of Brouardel and Vibert[1] staining of the froth is due to infiltration of blood-colouring matter derived from small extravasations in the parenchyma of the lungs.

If, after submersion, the body does not return to the surface until death has taken place, there will be less froth and more water in the air-passages than when the mouth and nostrils momentarily emerge once or more and additional air is inspired; this is supposing that death takes place from asphyxia; if from syncope or, what comes to the same thing, from permanent inhibition of the respiratory movements, no froth at all will be present. The pleural cavities usually contain a quantity of water with or without a certain admixture of mucus. The mucous membrane of the trachea may be injected, but this sign is more frequently absent after drowning than after other modes of death from asphyxia. The lumen of the trachea is usually filled with froth, which may reach the mouth unless the body has lain for some time in water or is not examined soon after withdrawal from it. The heart usually presents the appearance due to death from asphyxia; the left side is empty or thereabouts, and the right side filled with blood. The vascular condition of the brain and its membranes is not constant, and, therefore, is of no diagnostic value as regards death from drowning. Draper, in 149 examinations, found that injection of the membranes with hyperæmia of the brain was present in about half the number of cases. The blood, dark in colour and containing but little oxygen, is diluted with water, sometimes to the extent of one-third or one-fourth of its total weight (Brouardel and Vibert). The dilution is greater in the left side of the heart than in the right side, because the blood arriving by the pulmonary veins has received a fresh addition of water in passing through the lungs; the blood in the portal vein may also be much diluted from imbibition by its branches from the stomach, which, as will be presently explained, usually contains a quantity of water. The dilution of the blood is proportional to the duration of life after submersion:—slow drowning

[1] *Annales d'Hygiène*, 1880.

equals much dilution; quick drowning equals less; when death from submersion results from syncope, or inhibition of respiration, the blood does not contain any excess of water, unless the body remains long submerged. After death from drowning the blood is usually *fluid*, as is the case in other modes of death from asphyxia. Brouardel and Loye found when the body is examined soon after death from rapid drowning that the blood for the most part is coagulated—dark coloured clots are seen both in right and left sides of the heart, dilution of the blood which occurs during submersion is no obstacle to coagulation. If an interval of one or two days elapses after death before the examination is made, the blood is again fluid. The liquefaction of the coagulated blood occurs in a certain order—first, that in the right heart liquefies, afterwards, that in the thoracic vena cava, the left heart, the abdominal vena cava, and, lastly, long after the rest, that in the portal vein. From this, it appears that the fluidity of the blood found after death from drowning is not due to absence of coagulation, but to post-mortem decoagulation.

There is nothing distinctive in the condition of the mucous membrane of the stomach, its vascularity being variable; occasionally ecchymoses may be seen, as in other modes of asphyxial death. In another respect, however, the stomach and intestines yield valuable evidence as regards the occurrence of death from drowning. When submersion in the living takes place, a portion of the water drawn into the mouth is frequently involuntarily swallowed; hence the presence of water in the stomach has been regarded as a sign of death from drowning. In estimating the value of this sign, two questions naturally present themselves—(*a*) Is water invariably found in the stomach after death from drowning? (*b*) Is it possible for water to find its way into the stomach of a submerged dead body? Answers to these questions have been sought for by experimental investigations on animals, and by statistical observations of human bodies in which death took place from drowning.

(*a*) Experiments on animals drowned in water artificially coloured, show, for the most part, that water is swallowed in the act of drowning. In sixteen experiments by Fagerlund[1] some of the coloured water was invariably found in the stomach after death. Misuraca[2] almost always found water in the stomach of animals that had been drowned.

Observations made on human bodies as to the presence of water in the stomach after death from drowning yield less decisive results. Some observers state that water in characteristic amount was almost

[1] *Vierteljahrsschr. f. ger. Med.*, 1890.
[2] *L'aspissia meccanica e le sue varie forme*, 1888.

invariably present, others found it in a limited number of cases, and often in such small quantities as to be worthless from the diagnostic standpoint. Amongst recent observers v. Hofmann[1] found the amount to vary considerably, only exceptionally was it present in bulk. Ogston, Junior,[2] found it present in 74.6 per cent of cases. Tourdes[3] out of 93 cases found a considerable amount of water in the stomach in 37, but little in 34, and none at all in 22. Diaper in many of 149 cases states that the stomach was either empty or contained remains of food with a very small quantity of fluid. Lesser out of 30 cases found no appreciable amount in 9, a variable amount in 14, a layer of water distinct from the other contents of the stomach in 3, and in 4 water alone or mixed with a little mucus. Paltauf frequently found water in the stomach after death from drowning.

(b) Obolonsky[4] placed in coloured water the bodies of 18 children of from two weeks to two months old, weighted so that they could not float, they were allowed to remain submerged for from one to three days. In three of the bodies a considerable quantity of the coloured water was found in the stomach, in two others only a small quantity—these five bodies had lain seventy-two hours in the water, in the remaining thirteen no trace of water was found in the stomach. Misuraca never found water in the stomachs of animals submerged after death. Fagerlund experimented with a large number of dead bodies of children and animals by placing them in various positions —on the back, on the side, face downwards, &c.—under water, in some cases the mouth was kept open with pieces of wood, and the tongue was drawn forward and fixed. The results showed that water finds its way with great difficulty into the stomach after death. Bougier[5] placed the dead bodies of twenty-three human beings and seventeen animals in various coloured fluids without water entering the stomach in any one case.

From these experiments and observations the answers to the two questions will be :—(a) That *water is not invariably found in the stomach* after death from drowning. (b) That it *is possible* for water to find its way into the stomach of a *dead* body lying in water.

The amount of water found in the stomach is to be noted. when small it is of doubtful import, in some cases clear water is found in a separate layer above the other contents of the stomach. Fine froth may also be found in the stomach or œsophagus. The occurrence of fluid in the stomach possessing special characteristics corresponding with the medium in which the body is found may be of importance,

---

[1] *Lehrbuch der ger. Med.*, 1887
[2] *Edin. Med. Journ.*, 1882
[3] *Dictionnaire Ency. des Sciences Méd.*
[4] *Vierteljahrsschr. f. ger. Med.*, 1888
[5] *Thèse*, Paris, 1885

but it is not a proof of submersion during life. When submersion is followed by death from syncope no water is found in the stomach. Absence of water in the stomach after death does *not* exclude drowning as the cause of death.

In some cases a portion of the water that has entered the stomach during death from drowning is forwarded by vital contraction into the intestines, and its presence there has been regarded as almost certain proof of submersion whilst living. The questions put in relation to water found in the stomach are equally relevant in the case of the intestines. Fagerlund's very comprehensive experiments as to the conditions under which water may reach the intestines, afford valuable evidence. The outcome of them is that, occasionally during death from drowning peristaltic movements cause water to pass from the stomach into the bowels; that the pylorus offers a certain amount of resistance to the onward passage of the water; that the water passes into the bowels more easily from an empty stomach than from one filled with food; and that slow drowning appears to favour its ingress. In the dead body water only finds its way from the stomach into the bowels when excessive pressure is brought to bear.

As premised, the signs of death from drowning described in the preceding pages are those found in recently dead bodies which are examined shortly—within twelve or, at the most, twenty-four hours—after removal from the water; in warm weather even this interval will be sufficient to obscure the more significant indications. When putrefactive changes are advanced beyond the early stages, the frothy contents of the bronchi and trachea will have disappeared; there may be fluid and a number of air-bubbles, but no lathery-froth. At a certain stage of putrefaction the lungs collapse on opening the thorax, or are already collapsed: in the former case, the softening undergone by the lung tissue and by the mucus of the finer bronchi permits the alveolar contents to escape under the pressure of the atmosphere; in the latter, the pressure will have been already produced by transudation of water into the pleural cavities. The colour-changes, both external and internal, resulting from putrefaction are very deceptive, especially in relation to the possible occurrence of bruises, contusions and the like. After withdrawal of a body from water in which it has lain for twenty-four hours or more, bruises though present, may not be visible on account of imbibition by the skin; when the skin dries they become apparent.

The longer the body has been submerged the less valuable is the presence of water in the stomach or intestines as a sign of death from drowning. Water may find its way to a limited extent into the au-

passages of a body submerged after death, along with mud, or particles of sea-weed, grains of sand have been found even in the alveoli, but there is no great increase in the volume of the lungs nor fine froth in the bronchi. Transudation of water into the pleural cavities may buoy up the lungs in the dead body and make them look prominent on removal of the sternum without there being any "ballooning."

**Epitome of the Important Signs of Death from Drowning.**—The only external sign of import is the presence of a fine froth or lather on the lips and nostrils; this sign is of great significance, but its duration after death is limited. An adventitious sign constituted by the presence of weeds or other local objects grasped in the hands is also indicative of submersion during life, but its occurrence is not frequent.

The internal signs are—increased volume of the lungs with doughy consistence, water in the pleural cavities, exudation of water and froth on section of the lungs, <u>fine froth</u> in the bronchi and trachea, dilution of the blood, and water (or the fluid in which the individual was drowned) in the stomach, especially if some has reached the intestines.

In the event of an investigation made on a dead body removed from water being determinative of death from drowning, the next question is—Was drowning the result of accident, homicide, or suicide?

First, as to probabilities. In the year 1890 the deaths from drowning in the United Kingdom are thus apportioned in the Registrar General's report:—The total number of deaths from drowning was 2,997. Of these **accident** is accountable for 2,485—2,065 males and 420 females; **homicide,** 8—3 males (all infants under the age of one month) and 5 females; **suicide,** 504—304 males and 200 females.

Reference to these figures shows that by far the largest number of deaths from drowning are due to accident, the male sex contributing nearly five times as many as the female sex; this is to be accounted for by occupation-risks, which affect men much more than women. Amongst the very small number of deaths from homicidal drowning, all the male victims were infants. Under ordinary circumstances it would be difficult to murder a man by drowning, unless he was in some way rendered incapable of resistance; with women the difficulty is not so great, as they are more helpless when unexpectedly plunged into water.

When suicidal is compared with accidental drowning, a marked change is obvious in the proportion of the sexes—females being to males as 2 to 3. With women drowning is the preferred mode of committing suicide, probably because it requires no mechanical contrivance for its accomplishment, the simple act of falling into water is sufficient. In a certain proportion of suicides among women, the act is the result of sudden impulse, and, in many such cases, the necessity of preparing some means of carrying out their intention would be sufficient to allow of such a revulsion of feeling as to cause them to abandon their purpose, a neighbouring sheet of water solves the difficulty.

As a means of ascertaining whether drowning was due to accident, homicide, or suicide, the external relations are of increased importance as compared with those attending other modes of death from violence. If the body is clothed in the usual manner, the condition is consistent with any one of the three, but if the body is without clothing, and the signs of death from drowning are present, either accident or suicide is indicated—the former, if the place and the season of the year are suitable for bathing, the latter, when one or both are unsuitable. A hasty conclusion is not to be arrived at, even when circumstances seem exclusively in its favour; and, above all, no opinion should be expressed until a full examination of the body has been made. Illustrative of the necessity of this is a case related by Winsor.[1] The body of a woman was found naked in water about two feet deep; at first it was thought to be a case of accidental drowning, as the woman had been heard to express a desire to bathe in this particular place. On examination, however, an extravasation of blood was found in the right pectoral muscle, but none of the usual signs of death from drowning were present—no water was found in either lungs or stomach. The conclusion arrived at was that death had been caused by suffocation from pressure on the chest (probably by some one kneeling on it), and that the dead body had been placed where it was found.

Bruises and wounds on the body give rise to suspicion of foul play, but they may result from previous accident or suicidal attempt, or from injuries produced after death by the body being tossed against rocks, posts, or other objects by the current or movement of the water. Diaper (*l c*) relates two instructive cases of antecedent accidental injuries which complicated the diagnosis as to the mode of death. The dead body of a brewer was found in a large reservoir of water in the basement of a brewery; the sole access to the reservoir was through a shaft, barely two feet square in transverse section, the opening of which was in an upper storey of the building. The body showed undoubted signs of death from drowning, along with contusions on the face and top of the head, which did not seem likely to have been produced by falling down the shaft; it looked as though the deceased had been rendered unconscious by a blow on the head and then thrown down the shaft. On inquiry it

*Boston Med. and Surg. Journ.*, 1889

turned out that the bruises had been produced two days before death in a drunken brawl, and a letter was found on the body in which the deceased signified his intention to commit suicide. The second case was that of a man whose body was found in a river, with a lacerated and contused wound behind one ear which laid bare the skull, it had the appearance of having been caused, during life, by a sharp stone or other similar object. The signs of death from drowning were present. Here also the indications pointed to a blow on the head having been inflicted by some one, who afterwards threw the unconscious victim into the river. The body was ultimately recognised as that of a man who had fallen down a flight of steps whilst intoxicated, and who, being without means of sustenance, had subsequently committed suicide.

Injuries may be sustained in the act of jumping into the water, in this way fractures of the vertebræ, of the bones of the limbs, and also of the skull have been occasioned. Ogston states that in a woman who leaped over the parapet of a bridge the perineum was lacerated by forcible separation of the thighs on coming in contact with the water.

As previously stated in relation to another mode of violent death, suicides not unfrequently make more than one attempt to terminate their existence which may vary in kind a man may put a bullet into his chest and then drown himself, or he may cut his throat before doing so. It is by no means an exceptional occurrence for a man or woman to take poison and then to throw themselves into water; such cases demand great perspicacity in their interpretation, for the unlikely frequently happens. For example, the combination of poison with drowning is suggestive of suicide, but it has been due to homicide. A woman took advantage of another woman's liking for brandy to give her some which she had previously mixed with arsenic, the brandy was drunk in the open air, and, whilst the victim was sitting on the bank of a river with her back towards the water, her companion losing patience at the slow action of the poison, pushed her in, the body being found three days after. Such a case is clearly beyond the scope of medical evidence, so far as determining whether death was due to homicide or suicide is concerned; the lesson to be learnt from it is, not to express a decided opinion on a probability, which in this instance was very great, since the combination of poison and drowning is so rarely the result of an homicidal act that Bělohradsky,[1] who relates the above case, only met with it twice in more than a thousand cases. Whilst the *probability* of such combination is in favour of suicide, the *possibility* of homicide must not be ignored.

Strangulation is an exceptional method of committing suicide; therefore, if a dead body is found in water with signs of strangulation

[1] Maschka's *Handbuch*.

and with absence of the signs of drowning, the probability is in favour of homicide by strangulation and subsequent disposal of the body in water. A case recorded by Hofmann [1] constitutes an exception to this statement:—A girl, about twenty years of age, was found dead in a bath with a piece of thick pack-thread tied round the neck; the naked body was in a kneeling posture, the head being under water; examination showed that death resulted from strangulation. The bath was in a public institution, and the deceased locked herself in the bath-room, the door of which was under the observation of the attendant; there could, therefore, be no doubt that the girl had taken her own life. It might be inferred, had the case been one of homicide, that a murderer would have removed the evidence of strangulation before placing the body in the water, but Bĕlohradsky relates an instance which affords a further illustration of the risk of error which is inseparable from inferences founded on probabilities:— a dead body, the neck of which was surrounded three times with a cord, was found in water, but no signs of death by drowning were present; the case was one of homicide by strangulation, the body having been placed in the water after death. Care must be exercised not to mistake marks produced on the neck at the time of or soon after death for indications of foul play; in one such case the string of a cloak, and in another the branch of a tree produced deceptive appearances.

Indications of severe blows on the head, having the appearance of injuries sustained during life, may give rise to suspicion of homicide; the suspicion is strengthened if the signs of death from drowning are absent. The possibility of the injuries being independently produced within a limited period before death has to be taken into account. Except in the case of young children, cut-throat wounds on bodies found in water are strongly indicative of suicide.

When a dead body is found in water with a wound caused by a firearm, attention must be paid to the position of the wound: the inference usually is, that death resulted from suicide, but, to make this probable, the wound should be on the front of the body, in the head or chest. If the body is found in still water—as in a pond—the firearm should be near it; if in a river or in the sea, the body may have floated to a considerable distance from the spot where the shot was fired. There is obviously nothing to prevent a murderer from leaving the weapon near the body in order to suggest suicide; but such a proceeding would be risky, unless he had possessed himself of a firearm belonging to the deceased.

Injuries produced after death occur mostly in moving water—in

[1] *Wiener med. Presse*, 1879.

rivers with swift currents, in harbours, or in the locks of canals. Sometimes the injuries strangely simulate in position and extent wounds such as are frequently inflicted during life; in other instances, the body is smashed in a way that is incompatible with even extreme homicidal violence. As a rule, there is no difficulty, but care is occasionally necessary to distinguish between wounds inflicted at the time of death and injuries produced afterwards which co-exist on the same body. The characteristic appearance of wounds made before and after death are described in a succeeding chapter. When injuries to vital organs are found, which from their nature would necessarily be immediately fatal, and the body shows distinct signs of death from drowning, there can be no doubt that the injuries were produced after death. On the other hand, the absence of the signs of death from drowning and the presence of injuries of this type would be suspicious of foul play, unless, from the nature of the surroundings, it might be supposed that the body had fallen into the water unaided after the victim himself had inflicted the injuries — a man has been known to blow his brains out on the bank of a river and to fall dead into the water. A suicide who throws himself into the water from a great height, by striking some object may fracture and dislocate the spine in the cervical region; in such a case the signs of death from drowning would be absent, the manner in which death was brought about would have to be inferred from the surroundings. The possibility of death occurring from syncope on submersion with the subsequent production of injuries by the body being thrown violently against projecting objects must be borne in mind, as in this case there would be the combination of injuries, which, from their nature, might be expected to be immediately fatal, with absence of signs of death from drowning.

A case reported by Richardson[1] illustrates some of the points mentioned. The dead body of a man, of about 60 to 70 years of age, was found in the sea; decomposition was taking place, and was more advanced in the head than in the abdomen. The nasal bones were broken and loose, the scalp was torn away on each side of the head at the junction of the temporal and parietal bones, the bare skull was rough as though it had been rubbed against some hard substance, but the bone was not fractured. The spine was dislocated between the third and fourth cervical vertebræ, the spinous process of the latter being broken, and the cord crushed. The lungs were distended and spongy, they overlapped the heart, and when cut into exuded bloody froth. The blood was fluid and dark. The stomach

[1] *Brit. Med Journ.*, 1889.

contained a pint and a half of fluid, chiefly sea water. It was correctly inferred that death took place from drowning, and that the injuries were caused after death. The cardinal signs of drowning were found associated with an injury to the cervical cord which, had it been produced during life, would have been immediately fatal. Suicide was indicated by the month—November—together with the fact that the body had stockings on and also the waistband of a flannel shirt.

Occasionally a body presenting the signs of death from drowning is found in water only a few inches deep; such cases are usually suicidal, but they may be accidental, the deceased being intoxicated or under the influence of an epileptic seizure which caused him to fall into the water face downwards in a helpless condition. Except in the case of very young or very old subjects, it would be difficult to murder any one in this way, unless the victim was previously rendered incapable. Bruises or superficial marks of violence on the body having the characteristics of those produced during life are to be interpreted with caution, as a drunken man may have previously fallen more than once and thus occasioned the injuries, or they may have been produced by clonic epileptic spasms.

Drowning has been caused by placing the head only under water contained in a tub or other receptacle; in the case of adults the act is usually suicidal, the exceptions are when helplessness, occasioned by previous intoxication or other causes, has been taken advantage of to commit homicide. Infants have been drowned in this way, and their bodies afterwards thrown into a pond or river; in one such case, the fluid found in the air-passages consisted of dirty water containing soap, which demonstrated that the child was not drowned in the medium in which the body was found. Occasionally death may be due to accident, as when a workman falls head downwards into a cistern and is drowned with the rest of the body unsubmerged.

The hands and the feet may be found tied together with, or without, weights attached to the cords. The indication is suicide in the event of the signs of death from drowning being present; the body, however, should be carefully examined for marks of violence suggestive of foul play.

It sometimes happens that a person taking an ordinary warm bath for ablution is found dead without any external injuries. If the signs of death from drowning are present, the case will be either one of suicide or of accident, the latter being probably the result of an epileptic seizure; if they are absent, death will have been accidental from syncope; in one case it was due to thrombosis of the pulmonary vein. The question of homicide in these cases arises when there is ground for suspicion as to the motives and actions of a second person. The medical evidence would be expected to prove the cause of death, which might be due to asphyxia produced in some other way than by drowning, and to give an account of the general condition of the body with regard to indications of a struggle having taken place.

Men in embarrassed pecuniary circumstances have been known to commit suicide by drowning in such a way as to suggest accident, in order that their families might be benefited by money payable at death under an insurance policy; at the present time there is no necessity for this subterfuge, for reasons explained in the chapter on life assurance. Still, from time to time, suicide is committed in this way, it may be with the object of sparing the suicide's family any reflected odium. Medical evidence can do little beyond proving the cause of death; the distinction between suicide and accident will have to be determined by circumstantial evidence.

## RESUSCITATION FROM DROWNING

Since drowning usually results from asphyxia, with certain alterations in the physical condition of the lungs, the possibility of recovery after submersion is dependent upon two contingencies—the duration of the asphyxia, and the stage which the changes in the lung-tissue have reached.

In experiments with dogs in which the trachea is suddenly obstructed, it is found that the movements of respiration continue for about four minutes, the pulsation of the heart persisting for two to three minutes longer, recovery being possible at any period short of that when the heart ceases to beat. The experiments conducted by a committee of the Royal Medical and Chirurgical Society[1] show that the period within which recovery is possible is very much curtailed if drowning is the mode by which asphyxia is produced. Two dogs, one with the trachea plugged and the other not, were submerged for two minutes and then withdrawn from the water, the one in which the trachea was plugged recovered, the other did not. The reason for this difference lies in the condition of the lungs.—When the trachea is plugged neither air nor water can enter them, and consequently on removal of the obstruction, they are in a relatively fit state to resume their function; when the trachea is free water is drawn into the finer bronchi and the alveoli in the attempts at respiration, and consequently the lung-tissue becomes sodden and loses its elasticity.

In human beings asphyxia supervenes in from one to two minutes after submersion, and death usually before five to six minutes,

[1] *Med. Chirurg. Trans.*, 1862.

cases of recovery after longer submersion are recorded, but it is probable that in them some condition obtained which prevented water being drawn into the lungs. By practice, possibly aided by some exceptional inherent condition, individuals have acquired the capacity of enduring a longer period of submersion than ordinary without injurious results; in such cases there is obviously no attempt at breathing whilst under water, so that the question resolves itself into a capacity to postpone the asphyxial limit beyond that which is usual. In the description given of the condition of the lungs in drowning, it was stated that the aspiration of water causes a secretion of mucus in the bronchial tubes which tends to block the finer bronchi. After prolonged submersion, although the heart may continue to beat, and the vital condition (so far as the degree of asphyxia is concerned) is not hopeless, yet this blocking of the finer bronchi may prevent air reaching the alveoli after removal of the body from water, so that attempts at artificial respiration merely churn the mucus and froth to and fro in the air-passages without furthering respiration.

It is very encouraging to know, however, that with proper treatment perseveringly carried out recovery not unfrequently occurs after prolonged submersion, even when the case appears hopeless. On one occasion a boatman towed the body of a man ashore, and pronounced life to be extinct. A medical man corroborated this opinion, but two more sanguine bystanders began vigorous treatment, with the result that the apparently drowned man entirely recovered from the effects of the submersion. A good deal depends on prompt treatment; unfortunately, it often happens that among those present no one has a sufficiently practical acquaintance with the method of carrying on artificial respiration as to put it into execution in an efficient manner. The absence of means of supplying artificial warmth on the spot is another cause of failure; the success which has attended the establishment in Paris of places of succour for the drowned demonstrates the difference between immediate and delayed treatment. Formerly, submersion for two minutes was considered the limit of the probability of success; at present, prompt treatment, with means of applying warmth in the form of hot baths and blankets always to hand, enlarges the limit to five minutes, at which recovery is stated to be certain.

The following remarkable instance of recovery after prolonged submersion is recorded by Pope[1] —A man was sailing in a boat when it capsized and he fell into the water with some weights on the top of him, so that with the exception of his left arm he was entirely and continuously submerged for from twelve to fifteen minutes; he was resuscitated with considerable difficulty and eventually recovered.

[1] *The Lancet*, 1881.

The favourable issue was attributed to the weights pressing on the chest, which, together with concussion, so interfered with respiration, as to prevent any water from entering the lungs.

### ARTIFICIAL RESPIRATION

Silvester's Method.—After emptying the mouth and throat by turning the patient face downwards for a few seconds place him on his back with the head a little higher than the feet, the head and shoulders being supported on a compactly-folded article of clothing; remove everything tight about the chest and neck, draw the tongue forwards and maintain it in that position. Grasp the arms just above the elbows and draw them steadily above the head, keeping them on the stretch for two seconds, then reverse the movement, and press the arms firmly downwards against the sides of the chest for two seconds; repeat these manœuvres about fifteen times per minute until natural breathing is initiated, or as long as there is any hope of resuscitation. In the meantime friction and warmth are to be applied to the body.

Howard's Method.—Turn the patient face downwards with a firm roll of clothing under the stomach and chest, press with the whole weight on the patient's back two or three times for about four seconds each time, so as to drain the mouth and the air-passages as much as possible of the accumulated water. Then turn the patient face upwards, so that the roll of clothing is just below the shoulder blades, the head hanging back. Place the patient's hands above his head, kneel across his hips, fix your elbows against your hips, grasp the lower part of the patient's chest, and squeeze the sides together, pressing gradually forwards with all your weight for about three seconds until your mouth is nearly over that of the patient, and with a push suddenly jerk yourself backwards. Pause for three seconds, and then repeat the process, which should be performed about eight or ten times a minute.

It occasionally happens that, although automatic respiration is established, the patient succumbs shortly afterwards, or remains in a moribund condition for several hours, and then dies without having regained consciousness. In other cases, a temporary recovery of a more complete character takes place which may last for twenty-four or more hours, followed by death, apparently from exhaustion. The treatment subsequent to re-establishment of respiration will depend on the symptoms manifested; in some cases venesection may be indicated to relieve the heart, in others, stimulants and external warmth will be more efficacious.

# DEATH FROM EXTREMES OF TEMPERATURE AND FROM LIGHTNING.

## CHAPTER XX.

### DEATH FROM COLD.

Exposure to extreme cold in the first instance causes contraction of the vessels of the skin, the blood being driven into the internal organs; subsequently, if the exposure continues, the superficial blood-vessels are paralysed, giving rise to patches of localised erythema.

The symptoms are loss of energy, both physical and mental, followed by drowsiness and disinclination to move. The mental faculties become torpid, the special senses numbed, and the victim is seized with an irresistible desire to lie down and sleep; if this is yielded to, and help is not forthcoming, the lethargy passes into profound sleep, which deepens into stupor, and finally death takes place from general depression of the systemic powers. In some cases special disturbances of the nervous system manifest themselves in the form of clonic spasms or of psychical derangement.

It is probable that death results primarily from diminished supply of oxygen to the various organs, especially to the nerve-centres. A very low temperature interferes with the capacity of hæmoglobin to give up its oxygen; Pflüger[1] found that at 0° C. oxygen cannot be liberated from combination with hæmoglobin by removing the atmospheric pressure with the air-pump. As Bunge[2] puts it, the disassociation of oxygen from hæmoglobin is due to heat and not to the vacuum. At a low temperature the ordinary reducing agents, such as ammonium sulphide, take a much longer time than usual to abstract oxygen from hæmoglobin. Given, then, a diminished capacity of the hæmoglobin to yield up its oxygen and a coincident lowering of the activity of the tissues as regards their power to utilise it (internal respiration), an explanation is afforded of the gradual and general depression of the systemic powers and, also, of the occasional manifestations of disturbance of the nerve-centres.

In addition to these essential conditions certain influences of external relation frequently came into play:—Preliminary fatigue, with or without deprivation of food and sufficient clothing, renders the victim more susceptible to the effects of exposure to cold; recourse to alcohol in order to stimulate the jaded powers increases the desire

[1] *Arch. f. gesammte Physiologie*, Bd. 1.
[2] *Lehrbuch d. phy. u. path. Chemie.*, 1889.

for sleep; the extremes of age and feeble health diminish the capacity of resistance to cold.

The post-mortem appearances of death from exposure to cold with one exception, are not characteristic. The appearance alluded to is a cherry-red hue of the post-mortem stains on those parts of the surface of the body which are exposed to the air; they strongly resemble the stains met with in cases of poisoning by carbon monoxide. Falk[1] gives the most probable explanation of the way in which they are produced:— When hæmoglobin is exposed to an extremely low temperature it loses its property of parting with oxygen, but not that of combining with it; this applies to the blood both of the living and of the dead subject. The consequence is that, when a body is exposed to a temperature below the freezing point, the blood in the superficial vessels of those parts which are exposed to the air acquires oxygen by diffusion through the skin, and, retaining it, assumes the bright-red hue of arterial blood; within certain limits, if the temperature remains at or below zero, the cherry-red colour persists. When a body which displays this appearance is exposed to a higher temperature the hæmoglobin parts with its oxygen, and is reduced by the oxidising properties of the surrounding tissues which now come into play— the stains darken and become like those after death from ordinary causes.

The cherry-red hue of the post-mortem stains on those parts of the body exposed to air at a low temperature is not a proof of death from cold; a similar appearance may be produced after death from other causes if the body is subsequently thus exposed. It is only on the parts of the body exposed to the air that the blood assumes this peculiar colour; the parts which are covered, either by the clothing or by contact with the surface on which the body rests, present the usual appearance.

The internal appearances are limited to hyperæmia of the vessels of the brain and its membranes, with occasionally a similar condition of those of the abdominal viscera. On account of the access of oxygen, the lungs are often bright in colour like that of the exposed post-mortem stains on the surface of the body. The heart may be distended with blood, which is usually dark, but has been found bright in colour. From experimental researches on animals, Falk is disposed to regard a bright-red hue of the blood in the heart as a sign of death from cold; it is not produced by exposing dead bodies to the influence of a low temperature, because the atmospheric oxygen cannot diffuse itself so far internally as the heart. In animals that have died from exposure to a very low temperature which is continued

[1] *Vierteljahrsschr. f. ger. Med.*, 1887 u. 1880.

after death, the blood in the heart acquires the same hue as that in the lungs and on the surface, hence, whilst dark-coloured blood in the heart is consistent with death from cold, if bright coloured it is indicative of it

If putrefactive changes have commenced before the body is exposed to a low temperature, the characteristic stains do not appear, because tissues undergoing decomposition are active deoxidisers, even at the freezing point, decomposing tissues take up all the oxygen that is diffused through the skin to the neglect of the hæmoglobin which thus remains in the condition of reduced hæmoglobin From this it appears that although putrefaction in the broad sense is arrested at and below the freezing-point, a slow process of oxidation goes on in the parts which are accessible to air in cadavers in which decomposition has already set in

When an individual dies from exposure to a low temperature (at or below the freezing point), to which the body has been continuously exposed after death, the changes due to putrefaction will be absent The same absence of putrefaction occurs when death has resulted from other causes than cold, if the dead body is immediately and continuously subjected to a temperature below 0 C, under these conditions bodies have been preserved without apparent change for an indefinite time An interesting account is given in *d Arves Histoire du Mont Blanc* of the discovery of the remains of some guides who were swept down a crevasse by an avalanche in the year 1820, where they remained buried in ice at a great depth In the year 1861—after an interval of forty-one years—they were discovered Amongst the rest, a forearm and hand with the fingers intact were found, the flesh was white and fresh looking, and the finger nails were rosy-red when first seen, but the colour rapidly faded, on the ring-finger was a slight abrasion, the blood-stain from which was quite visible The joints of the arm and of the hand were flexible when thawed, as is the case in a body recently dead

If a dead body is found in the frozen condition with signs of putrefaction present, the assumption is that death was not caused by cold, there exists, of course, the remote possibility of an elevation of the surrounding temperature after death—during which, putrefactive changes might have taken place—followed by renewed cold

A frozen dead body is perfectly rigid, like a marble statue When the body is thawed, it is not unfrequently found that cadaveric rigidity is present, although the period after death when it usually ceases has long since passed, this applies to the bodies of those who have died from the effects of cold, and also of those who have died from other causes if they have been immediately subjected to a temperature below 0° C. After a frozen cadaver has been thawed, putrefaction quickly commences and advances very rapidly.

## DEATH FROM HEAT-STROKE.

This cause of death, which rarely comes under the notice of the medical jurist, is also called sunstroke; but since death frequently occurs without the direct action of the sun's rays, the latter term is too restrictive. Heat-stroke is probably due to derangement of the heat-regulating centres by continued high temperature of the surrounding air under circumstances which place the individual attacked in an unfavourable condition for resistance. It mostly occurs in tropical countries, especially where large bodies of men are massed together (as in barracks). Soldiers on march, or civilians taking an unwonted amount of exercise in the open air when the rays of the sun are excessively powerful, are liable to be attacked, either in a few hours, or suddenly, whilst the exercise is being taken. When the weather is excessively hot, patients are not unfrequently attacked during the night.

**Symptoms.**—In one form there is simply temporary hyperpyrexia with head-ache; in another and more severe form, the individual attacked falls down suddenly as though in a state of collapse. There is dimness of vision, vertigo, dilated pupils, and subsequently, drowsiness; the surface is pale, the pulse feeble and slow, and the respirations are of the sighing type; a sinking feeling at the pit of the stomach, with nausea or vomiting, is experienced. The symptoms resemble those of vagus inhibition—slowed heart, altered respiration, and irritability of the stomach. Another form more closely resembles cerebral compression; the patient becomes rapidly comatose, the pupils are contracted, the conjunctivæ congested, and the temperature is very high; it has been known to reach 110° F.; although the symptoms resemble compression, the pulse is quick. Sometimes an initial stage of cortical irritation manifests itself in the form of delirium and maniacal excitement.

The post-mortem appearances are—early onset and disappearance of cadaveric rigidity, with rapid advance of putrefaction; hyperæmia of many of the internal organs, such as the brain (which may be œdematous), the lungs and the vessels of the splanchnic area. Destruction of red blood-corpuscles has been observed.

## DEATH FROM LIGHTNING.

Attempts have been made to classify the various modes in which lightning causes death, but beyond dividing them into those in which more or less severe mechanical injuries and burns are produced, and those in which death occurs without any trace of injury, nothing is gained, nor is there much profit in speculating as to the relative conductivity of the different tissues and fluids of the body. When the "current" of a voltaic battery or of a dynamo is in question, Ohm's law holds good; with lightning it does not. The enormous difference in potential between cloud and cloud, or cloud and earth, overrides the law of conductivity as applied to voltaic electricity experimentally produced. Unlike a voltaic current, lightning does not invariably take the path of the least resistance; it will forsake a relatively good conductor and spring across a stratum of air, which offers a resistance many thousand times greater. This occasions no surprise when the enormous potential—which has been calculated at 3,604,000 volts for a flash of lightning a mile long—is taken into consideration. Whatever is the nature of the molecular changes which take place in a conductor along which a "current" of electricity is passing, it is obvious that time is involved. The duration of a flash of lightning has been computed at the twenty-thousandth part of a second; it is easy therefore to understand that the molecules of a substance which serves as a pathway to such a discharge must be placed under an excessive strain, which will for the moment vastly increase the resistance; the molecules are, as it were, taken unawares, and before they can adjust themselves to the stress, the resistance is probably augmented to that of the lateral path across which the lightning leaps. The erratic course frequently taken by lightning may be thus accounted for, both as regards the human body and, also, in respect to articles of furniture in rooms.

When a great difference in potential exists between the earth and a cloud above it, the intervening stratum of the atmosphere acts as a dielectric, the whole forming an inductive circuit; the tension increases until the resistance of the dielectric (the air) is overcome and then a discharge takes place. Any object raised above the earth's surface diminishes the resistance of the dielectric at that point to the extent to which it projects beyond the ground-level, and will anticipate the occurrence and determine the direction of the discharge, which would have been delayed until a still higher tension accumulated, had the ground-level been uniform. If a large area of the earth's surface is free from inanimate projections—as is the case in a plain devoid of trees or buildings—the body of a man in the erect posture may determine the line of discharge.

Although a flash of lightning appears to the eye as a mere line, and is in reality only a spark passing with immense velocity from point to point, its influence is not limited to its apparent path. What is visible is, so to speak, but the core of the discharge—where its influence is at the maximum; on every side of this line is a wide track, within the limits of which damage may be done; hence, during a thunderstorm the proximity to a tree is dangerous—the tree determines the occurrence and receives the central part of the discharge, and the immediately surrounding objects receive portions of its encircling zone.

The thermic power of a flash of lightning is very intense, but is very limited in duration, so that burns caused by lightning are frequently extensive without being deep. Although burns of considerable depth may occur on parts of the body with which the clothing is in contact, they are usually limited to those parts underlying metallic objects—as buckles and bracelets. The sudden high temperature acquired by metallic bodies surrounded by relatively imperfect conductors is probably due to their acting as condensers, and also to their molecular constitution being of such a nature as to readily transform the electricity they receive into heat. Burns may also occur on the unclothed parts of the body, as, for example, the face. Clothing saturated with rain will to a limited extent act as a conducting envelope, and will tend to divert a portion of the discharge and so lessen the amount of mischief to the body which might otherwise be produced.

The clothing, whether dry or wet, is frequently torn, in some cases to shreds, and stripped off the body. One or both of the boots may be forced off the feet, or the soles may be stripped away from the upper leathers; sometimes a hole is simply punched through part of the boot. This mechanical effect is due to the molecular disturbance which invariably attends an electric discharge:—When a discharge passes along a good homogeneous conductor, such as a piece of metal, if it is connected with the earth and is of sufficient sectional dimension, no obvious change is produced; if such a conductor, not in connection with the earth, receives a powerful discharge, it will either be damaged itself, or objects between its lower end and the earth will be damaged. A solid dielectric so interposed is either pierced or shattered when the potential exceeds the inductive capacity; a sheet of thick glass, for example, can be perforated by a strong discharge from a Leyden battery concentrated upon a limited area. When the conductor is composed of a number of varying resistances, the sum of which is relatively great, it will be torn or injured by the passage of a discharge at a potential like that of lightning. This results from unequal strain, which to some extent resembles that caused by the intercalation of a series of dielectrics in the path of a discharge, at each of which it becomes disruptive, mechanically breaking them down *seriatim*, and tearing apart the structures or fabrics along which it passes. After doing a certain amount of damage the discharge may

DEATH FROM LIGHTNING. 239

leap a distance; in the intervening space there will be absence of mechanical injury.

It is possible that the intense heat developed along the path of the discharge may also cause mechanical violence by suddenly converting water, or fluid into the composition of which water enters, into steam; in this case the chief factor would be the extreme rapidity with which the liquid is made to acquire the gaseous form.

A peculiar appearance due to arborescent markings is not unfre-

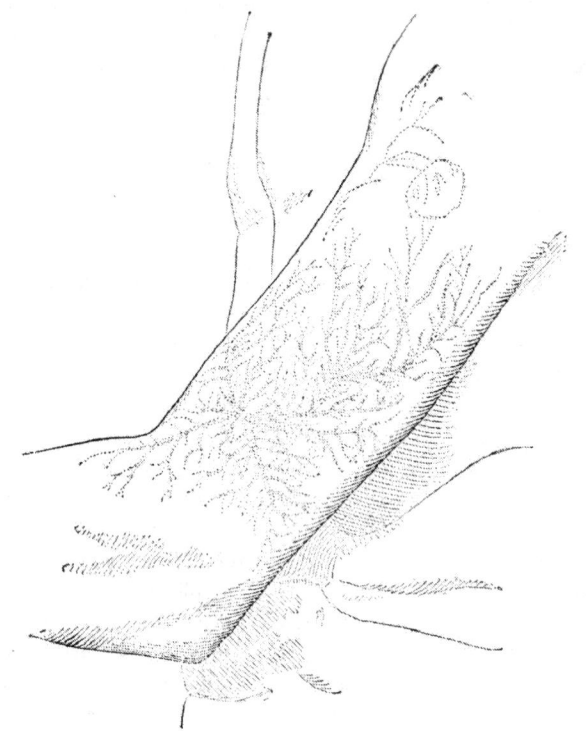

Fig. 18.

quently observed on the surface of the bodies of those who have been struck by lightning. These marks are not determined by the course of capillary vessels or other anatomical structures, but are caused by divarications of portions of the discharge producing a kind of specialised erythema, which indicates the paths taken by the discharge; they resemble, both in appearance and in causation, the well-known Lichtenberg figures of experimental electricity. Distinction must be drawn between them and marks due to superficial burns, which occasionally present peculiar outlines; the latter sometimes take the form of metallic objects worn on the body, which, heated by the discharge, produce burns of corresponding shapes. The foregoing figure, taken from the *Lancet* (1883), gives a good idea of the arborescent markings produced by lightning.

In those cases of death from lightning in which no sign of injury is found, neither on the surface of the body nor on the clothing, it is possible that the result may be due to the victim having been just outside the path of the main discharge, but sufficiently near as to receive a shock violent enough to permanently paralyse the central organs of the nervous system. In some such cases internal examination fails to demonstrate the proximate cause of death; in others there are indications of cerebral haemorrhage, or of diffuse disorganisation of the brain structure. Hennessy[1] relates the case of a man who was killed by lightning without there being any trace of burning or injury to body or clothing. On removing the calvarium, about half a pint of blood escaped from below the dura, but the brain itself appeared healthy. In contrast to this case is one related by Wilks[2]. A man struck by lightning whilst in the act of urinating in the open air, was thrown to the ground, but was not rendered unconscious. Although completely clothed before being struck, when found a few minutes after he was naked, with absolutely nothing on except part of the left arm of his flannel vest, the field around was strewn with fragments of clothing. The clothes, which were wet with rain, were split from top to bottom, and the edges torn into fringe-like shreds; they only showed marks of burning where they had been in contact with metallic objects. The hair on the face was burnt, and the body was covered with burns, which were superficial on the chest, but deeper on the abdomen and the right thigh. The right tibia was fractured—the ends of the bones projecting through the skin. There was a lacerated wound on the right heel, and a comminuted fracture of the os calcis. The man's watch had a hole fused through it, and the chain was almost entirely destroyed, only a few partially melted links remained. A highly interesting statement was made by the patient to the effect, that when urinating he habitually lifted the right heel from the ground; had it rested on the wet earth it would probably have escaped. Complete recovery took place.

The post-mortem appearances of death from lightning. External.—Cadaveric rigidity not unfrequently occurs at the usual period, sometimes it comes on immediately after death, and in this case is evanescent. The pupils may be dilated, contracted, or unequal. Arborescent markings, burns, singeing of the hair, ecchymoses,

[1] *Brit. Med. Journ.*, 1889.  [2] *Trans. of the Clinical Soc. Lond.*, 1880.

lacerations, or other indications of injury, may, or may not, be present. The clothing may be intact or it may be torn and stripped off the body; it may show signs of burning. Partial fusion of coins or other metallic objects on the person of the deceased is very significant of the mode of death. Kratter[1] directs attention to this means of diagnosis when other indications are wanting. Steel implements, such as pocket-knives, are often magnetised.

The internal signs are not characteristic. The blood has been described as dark and fluid; it is so sometimes, but it may coagulate as usual after death. The membranes and vessels of the brain have been found hyperæmic, and, in some cases, blood was extravasated. Fractures of the bones have occurred, but only exceptionally. Putrefaction usually commences early.

When an individual who is struck by lightning escapes death, it is not unusual for anomalous nerve symptoms to manifest themselves; the symptoms may take the form of sensory or of motor disturbances, with or without derangement of the special senses. In a case related by Paige, Buller, and Mills,[2] a woman was rendered insensible by being struck by lightning which had apparently touched the left side of the forehead above the eyebrow. A few minutes after she was found motionless, unconscious, and in a state of muscular relaxation, with the left eye closed, the right eye open, the face purple, and the pulse imperceptible; neither heart nor respiratory sounds were audible. On recovery of consciousness, it was found that the pharyngeal muscles were paralysed as well as those of the upper part of the body, including the arms; the right eye could not be moved; the patient could hear, but not speak. It was two weeks before the pharyngeal paralysis had passed off sufficiently to allow solid food to be swallowed. For five or six weeks the left eye was turned inwards and upwards, occasioning diplopia; ophthalmoscopic examination showed pallor of the optic nerve, but nothing indicative of neuritis past nor present; the field of vision was uniformly restricted for all colours. All the symptoms eventually disappeared, except that the left eye remained weak.

Sometimes the spinal cord is rendered functionless for a time, producing paraplegia, with anæsthesia of the paralysed parts, the bladder sharing in the paralysis; in other cases, the psychical powers are disordered, the patient being intellectually infeebled, or melancholic. A common condition is that of timorousness, especially during thunderstorms, which is probably simply the result of psychical shock, such as is caused by other alarming occurrences.

When examining a body found under circumstances which render

[1] *Vierteljahrsschr. f. ger. Med.*, 1891.   [2] *Montreal Med. News*, 1888.

death from lightning probable, the possibility of it having resulted from other causes must not be overlooked. Schauenburg[1] states that the dead body of a woman was found in a wood, at first it was thought that she had been struck by lightning, but examination showed that death was due to accidental strangulation caused by the bonnet-strings being drawn tightly round the throat in consequence of a fall. v. Hofmann[2] relates the case of a girl who was in a room during a violent storm which blew in the casement of a window. The shock broke a pane of the glass, and a fragment the shape of a knife-blade penetrated her chest, and caused death from internal hæmorrhage. Although no one had heard any thunder, the sudden death was attributed to lightning, and the body was buried; it was not until three weeks after that the actual cause of death was explained.

Since the introduction of electricity as a means of illumination fatal results have happened from time to time in consequence of individuals coming in contact with the circuit wires, all the deaths have been accidental with one exception, constituted by a man who is said to have committed suicide by taking hold of the terminals of a dynamo. Shield and Delepine[3] examined the skin in the region of a blister on the finger of a man who was accidentally killed by touching a dynamo, and give a detailed account of the microscopic appearances, which differ from those of ordinary burns.

## CHAPTER XXI.

### DEATHS CAUSED BY BURNS AND SCALDS.

Burns are caused by the action of a temperature considerably above that of the human body which is brought to bear upon it in the form of radiant heat or flame, or from contact with heated solid bodies. Injuries caused by solid bodies which become liquid at an elevated temperature—such as metals in a state of fusion—are classified as burns. Substances which act chemically and produce corrosion are also said to cause burns; injuries of this kind will be considered apart from the rest.

[1] Casper's *Vierteljahrsschr.*, 1855.    [2] *Lehrbuch.*
[3] *Brit. Med. Journ.*, 1885.

Scalds are caused by the action of steam or heated fluids on the surface, or in the mouth or other cavities of the body.

The injuries produced are proportionate to the temperature, the dimensions, and the period of action of the causal agent. The danger to life depends upon the severity of the injuries produced, both as regards the depth to which the tissues are disorganised and also as to the extent of the superficial area involved, and to some degree upon the localisation of the lesions.

A severe burn or scald of small superficial area, provided that its localisation is not exceptionally dangerous, is less risky to life than one which implicates a large superficial area, but does not penetrate so deeply. If a superficial area equal to one-third of the entire body-surface is destroyed, death is almost certain to ensue. This leads to the consideration of the cause of death from burns and scalds.

Death from burning may take place immediately the injuries are inflicted, within a short time after—from a few hours to several days, or at a more remote period when inflammation and suppuration have set in. The cause of death during the last-mentioned stage is self-explanatory; that involved in the two preceding stages is not yet determined; it is, therefore, necessary to consider briefly the most important of the many theories that have been advanced in its elucidation.

Some of these theories are based on assumptions mutually opposed. One[1] is that the vessels of the skin being destroyed by the heat, the blood that under normal conditions would circulate in them is driven into the internal organs, causing hyperæmia and ecchymoses, which lead to death. Another[2] and contradictory interpretation is that the vessels of the skin are dilated, and that death is occasioned by the resulting excessive cooling of the body, such as is supposed to occur when the surface of the body is experimentally covered with an impervious varnish; according to this view the hyperæmia of the internal organs is accounted for by loss of tonus of the blood-vessels. Another[3] theory, also founded on the loss of skin function, assumes the retention of certain excretory products which cause death by auto-intoxication. These products are regarded by some to be physiological, by others, pathological—that is, abnormally constituted excretory products, or toxines, which partake of the nature of alkaloids—i.e., derivatives of ammonia.

Most of the more recent theories are founded on changes which the blood itself undergoes, as a direct consequence of the elevated temperature to which it is subjected at the time the injuries are sustained.

[1] Follin, *Traité de path externe*.  [2] Falk, Virchow's *Arch*, Bd. 53.
[3] Catiano, Virchow's *Arch*, Bd. 87.

An early view, recently re-advanced,[1] was, that owing to loss of serum, the blood was so much thickened as to be unable to pass through the capillary vessels into the venous radicles. Overheating of the blood,[2] with associated paralysis of the heart, due to shock from irritation of a large area of nerves, is by some held accountable for immediate death, and reflex diminution of vascular tonus for death which, though not immediate, is not long delayed

A number of observers attribute early death from burning and scalding to destruction of, or to interference with, the function of the red blood-corpuscles by the heat, but they differ in their interpretation of the mode in which the injury to the corpuscles occasions death Some hold that destruction of the blood-corpuscles liberates fibrin-ferment[3] which causes coagulation of the blood in the heart and other organs, and so gives rise to infarcts in the kidneys, liver, and bowels, causing subsequent erosions in the latter Others[4] trace these changes to the debris of the broken-down corpuscles, in support of which theory they instance the presence in the blood of numberless small coloured particles derived from the hæmoglobin, and of "shadows" which represent the stroma of the red corpuscles, and, further, that the kidneys demonstrate the existence of free hæmoglobin by excreting it in the urine along with peculiarly coloured casts Death is supposed to result from acute nephritis with uræmic poisoning Part of the débris of the blood-corpuscles is supposed to disappear in the pulp of the spleen and in the marrow of the bones. Against[5] this view it has been urged that the actual number of red corpuscles is not greatly diminished after severe burns, but that loss of functional activity of a large percentage of them is thus occasioned, death resulting from the red corpuscles for the most part being rendered incapable of conveying oxygen to the tissues, the condition being that of acute functional oligocythæmia In opposition to this is the statement that blood supposed to be thus disabled, on being shaken with air, takes up oxygen as easily and as copiously as normal blood[6]

Still more recent views[7] corroborate and enlarge the theory of blocking of the blood-vessels, especially of the small arteries, veins, and capillaries, which is not due to embolism, but to thrombosis, from clinging of the altered red corpuscles to each other and to the walls of

[1] Tappeiner, *Centralb f d med Wissensch*, 1881
[2] Sonnenburg, *Verbrennungen Deutsche Chir*, 1879
[3] Foà, *Rivista sperimentale*, 1881
[4] Ponfick, *Berlin klin Wochenschr*, 1876-77, 1883
[5] Lesser, *Virchow s Arch*, Bd 79
[6] Hoppe-Seyler, *Zeitschr f physiol Chemie*, Bd 5
[7] Welti, *Beitrage zur path Anat*, *Ziegler u Nauwerck*, 1889, Silbermann, *Virchow s Arch*, 1890, Bd 119, Kleb's *Handbuch d. path Anat.*

the vessels, aided by the presence of a vast number of blood-plates and débris of disorganised corpuscles. Salvioli,[1] whilst agreeing with this view, explains the formation of the thrombi in a different manner. He states as the result of experimental observation that the blood-plates are so affected by the heat to which they have been subjected, that they deposit themselves on the walls of the vessels and give rise to the formation of minute thrombi, which are subsequently detached and are carried along by the blood, forming an enormous number of embolic nuclei. The ultimate pathological condition is due to three causes :—the presence of the minute emboli; narrowing of the smaller vessels from excessive local heat; and, from the same cause, to an adhesive condition of the red corpuscles. According to Salvioli, the blood-plates are not derived from other altered elements of the blood, but are normal and pre-existing. As proof of the important part played by the blood-plates in the formation of thrombi, he states that by repeatedly defibrinating the blood in a living dog, it is rendered poor in blood-plates, and that animals so treated survive the severest scalds, because no embolic nuclei are formed.

The preponderating opinion as to the cause of early death from burns and scalds is that it is a primary blood disorder, which chiefly results from injuries received by the red corpuscles when subjected to intense heat. Silbermann draws an analogy between the pathological changes which are caused by burning, and those produced by certain poisons—such as potassium chlorate, toluylenediamin, pyrogallol, and anilin.

It has frequently been observed that children succumb to burns and scalds more easily than adults. This is explainable on the ground that the child's skin is thinner, and, consequently, exposes the blood more freely to the action of the heat, and also that the resistance of the red corpuscles to any adverse influence is less in childhood than in adult life.

When death takes place immediately in the presence of fire, especially within a building, it may result from poisoning by CO or $CO_2$ developed by combustion. If from CO the blood and muscles will present the characteristic cherry-red appearance, and the blood will yield the absorption spectrum indicative of COHb; if from $CO_2$, the blood and the muscles will be dark in colour.

**Post-mortem Appearances—External.**—The appearances vary according to the severity of the injuries and the length of time the patient has survived them. In many cases the manner in which the injuries were caused produces characteristic indications:—A burn caused by radiant heat leaves a white appearance of the skin. Contact with

[1] *Arch. per le scienze mediche*, 1891.

flame blackens the skin from deposition of carbon, and singes the hairs; if not of great severity, there may be blisters at or around the site of the burn. The flame of an explosive, such as a mixture of coal-gas and air, scorches and mummifies the skin.

Gun-powder explosions not only blacken the surface from deposit of carbon, but, unless the patient is too far removed from the explosive, particles of unexploded powder are driven into the skin. The same observation applies to coal-mine explosions, after which the body is frequently blackened all over and profusely tattooed.

Red-hot solids or molten metals produce effects which vary according to the length of time they remain in contact with the surface. If for a short time the skin only may be disorganised, in which case there will probably be blisters or the remains of blisters close to the burn. If the burn is very severe the soft structures will be roasted or carbonised like over-cooked meat; in such cases there will probably be an entire absence of blisters. From this degree up to combustion of the entire body—nothing but a few fragments of bones being left—all stages may be met with.

**Scalds** caused by steam or boiling water are characterised by the formation of blisters, which may be absent at parts owing to stripping of the cuticle. The hairs are not affected by scalds. Superheated steam produces a dirty-white, boiled appearance of the surface, which has lost all elasticity and feels sodden; in such cases blisters may not be seen. Scalds caused by liquids which have higher boiling points than water are proportionally more severe.

The parts of the body protected by clothing are less injured by fire than those which are exposed; in slighter cases the covered parts escape altogether. The converse may occur if the clothing itself takes fire, which is notably the case when it is saturated with an inflammable liquid, such as petroleum; burns thus caused are of exceptional severity, and are further characterised by the distinctive odour of petroleum.

If the patient has lived some days, there will probably be signs of reaction, which modify the original appearances.

The bodies of those who are found dead from exposure to great heat are usually contorted, the limbs being in a state of flexion, so that, when the body is lying on the back, the arms project either upwards in a defensive attitude, or across the chest. This condition is due to heat-rigidity, the causation of which was explained when the subject of cadaveric rigidity was discussed.

**Internal Appearances.**—The brain is often shrunk to little more than one-fourth of its original volume, its form being fairly well maintained. The heart is usually filled with blood. The lungs are shrunk, and often of a reddish colour. Particles of soot may be found in the larynx, trachea, and bronchi, sometimes the mucous membrane is found injected and covered with froth, which may exist in amount sufficient to fill the air-passages. The kidneys may show signs of nephritis, and on section may present the appearance of reddish-brown markings, due to filling of the straight tubules with débris from the blood; this sign is not constant, but is sometimes very well marked. Frankel[1] records three cases of death from burning in which it was present, together with degenerative changes in the epithelium of the glomeruli and convoluted tubules. The mucous membrane of the stomach and bowels has been found to present a reddened appearance with swelling of the follicles. Curling[2] was the first to direct attention to the occurrence of ulcers of the duodenum in cases of death from burning when the patient had survived some time; they have been frequently observed, although they are not present in the greater number of cases. Wilks,[3] out of 37 cases, observed no symptoms of the duodenum being affected in any; of these cases 12 were examined post-mortem. These ulcers are probably due to thrombosis of the small artery that supplies the part.

The liver shows nothing distinctive. The uterus may be found but little changed, although the corpse is almost consumed. The testicles also resist the action of fire. The blood frequently presents a peculiar and characteristic appearance, being of a cherry-red colour, exactly like that of blood from a case of carbon monoxide poisoning. As previously stated, it is not uncommon for the blood of persons who have been burnt to death to contain carbon monoxide; but the condition now under consideration, although the naked-eye appearances resemble those due to COHb, has nothing to do with it; the absorption bands are those of $O_2Hb$, and reduction can be effected with the usual reagents. Falk[4] attributes the light-red colour to coagulation of some of the albumen of the blood in microscopic coagula, which reflect light after it has traversed only a thin superficial layer of blood, and, consequently, less light is absorbed. The colour, therefore, appears brighter from a purely physical cause; no chemical change in the colouring matter takes place. In fresh blood, this coagulation occurs at 62°-63° C. In blood that is undergoing decomposition, it either does not occur at all or else requires a higher temperature, due to complete or to partial conversion of the albumen into peptone, which does not coagulate with heat. Cherry-red blood from this cause is produced both in the bodies of those who have died from burning and also in dead bodies which have been exposed to a

---

[1] *Deutsche med. Wochenschr.*, 1889.
[2] *Med. Chir. Trans.*, 1842.   [3] *Guy's Hospital Reports*, 1856.
[4] *Vierteljahrsschr. f. ger. Med.*, 1888.

sufficiently high temperature; on the other hand, cherry-red blood due to the presence of COHb, indicates that the individual in whose body it is found was alive whilst the fire was in progress.

The most important question that the medical jurist has to answer after having examined a body injured by fire is—Did the burning take place during life or after death? The external signs, to which attention is directed with the view of answering this question, are limited to those displayed by the skin. When the injury is slight and is confined to the surface (a large area of the skin being affected) it presents the appearance during life of a diffuse erythema with patches where the epiderm has been detached. This appearance, produced equally by dry heat and by boiling water, is due to active hyperæmia and can only occur during life; it is never found on a dead body that has been exposed to fire. Unfortunately, it disappears, as a rule, after death, leaving the skin either pale or discoloured with post-mortem stains; it may sometimes be found, however, near parts that have suffered more severely. With certain reservations the presence of blisters indicates that the injuries were received during life; to fulfil the indication the blister should contain fluid rich in albumen, and it should be surrounded by an injected margin either limited to its immediate circumference or blending into the diffuse erythema above mentioned. When the epiderm is detached the base of the blister, if examined soon after death, will be red; it is to be noted, however, that, on the one hand, this redness of the base often disappears after death, and, on the other, that a slight reddening of the base of a blister produced after death may take place in consequence of exposure to air; it is, therefore, an indication of no positive value.

According to Hofmann, a blister having *all* the characteristics of those produced during life cannot be produced ten minutes after death. If an appropriate degree of heat is applied to the dead body a blister may be raised, but it will be filled either with aqueous vapour, which condenses after withdrawal of the heat—the epiderm collapsing— or with fluid which contains little or no albumen, at the most only sufficient to cause opalescence on boiling in a test tube; whereas the fluid from a blister raised during life affords evidence of abundance of albumen on being similarly treated. Blisters are more easily produced on dead bodies that are œdematous; but, of course, the signs of vital reaction are wanting. Taylor and Stevenson record the case of a man who was drowned, whose body (with the object of resuscitation) was placed in a hot bath within a few minutes of the accident, no pulsation being perceptible; blisters containing bloody serum were produced by the high temperature of the water although the man was apparently dead when placed in the bath, and the attempts at resuscitation were unsuccessful. With regard to the occurrence of blisters on the bodies of those who have been exposed to the action of dry or moist heat, the inference to be drawn is — that if the fluid contained in the blisters is rich in albumen, and the blister is surrounded by an injected margin, it was either produced during life or *immediately* after death.

When the body has been subjected to a still higher temperature there will be no blisters. In this case, the margins of the burns may afford some clue, if with the aid of a lens, or microscope, the capillaries of the corium can be distinguished as a blackish-brown network, the inference is that the burns were produced during life; burns produced in the dead body do not *usually* exhibit this network. The indication, however, is to be utilised with reserve, as a similar appearance may be produced by burns on those parts of the surface of the body where post-mortem staining is present; and it has been proved to be absent in undoubted cases of burning in the living. When the soft parts are completely charred it is impossible to say whether the burns were produced before or after death.

The internal differential signs of burns on the body produced before or after death are few in number, and not very distinctive in character. The condition of the blood may afford a clue, if it contains a large amount of CO, the presumption is that the individual from whose body it is derived was living at the time that the injuries were sustained. The hæmoglobin within the body only combines with CO by being passed through the lungs when they are respiring the gas, therefore the conditions necessary for producing the combination are wanting in the dead body. The naked-eye appearance of the blood must not be accepted as proof of the presence of COHb, direct comparison of its spectrum with that of $O_2Hb$ and evidence of non-reduction, or only partial reduction, after the addition of a reducing agent are required to substantiate its existence. Particles of soot or carbon in the larynx or the trachea are indicative of respiration having taken place whilst the fire was in progress.

Death by burning is usually accidental. This results either from isolated causation limited to the individual, as when the clothing catches fire, or from general causation, such as occurs when an inhabited building takes fire. From the nature of their clothing, women are more liable than men to fall victims to accidental burning of the first named type; the fabrics of which dresses are frequently made are very inflammable, and a passing contact with fire is sufficient to kindle them into a blaze, when the victim with an instinctive impulse to flee from danger rushes about and thus fans the flames. Accidents of this kind have not unfrequently happened to girls in ball-dresses, which usually are of exceptionally inflammable material, and before the flame is spent, or is extinguished, fatal mischief generally results. The upsetting or the explosion of paraffin lamps is another source of danger. Children are frequently burnt by playing with fire or with lucifer matches.

Accidental scalding is not uncommon in children of a tender age, caused by the child pulling over a tea-kettle or pot containing boiling water, the contents of which are discharged over its body. Internal scalding is occasionally produced by children drinking directly from a tea-pot, the contained fluid being very hot.

Isolated cases of accidental burning and scalding in male adults occur chiefly in the pursuit of occupations attended with special risk—such as metal founders and brewers.

Accidental fatal burning of general causation is more frequent in hotels, theatres, and other public buildings than in private houses. When theatres and public halls full of people take fire, a large percentage of deaths is due to suffocation from mechanical compression of the chest, mutually produced by a number of people seeking exit at the same door, and from the inhalation of the oxides of carbon.

When homicide has to be taken into consideration in respect to a dead body that is found partially consumed, the victim almost invariably has been killed by other means; fire is only made use of to conceal the crime. If the question, "Was death caused by the fire?" can be answered in the negative, suspicion of homicide is aroused, unless evidence to the contrary is forthcoming. When the body is not too far consumed, indications of violence may be visible—such as wounds produced by firearms, fractures of the skull, incised wounds, and marks of strangulation. It must be remembered, however, that stones, bricks, or slates not unfrequently fall from buildings which are on fire, and they may strike the head of a living or dead person and fracture the skull; the fire itself also may produce fissures or fractures of the cranial bones. Injuries closely resembling incised wounds may be produced by extreme heat; usually, but not invariably, they occur at the flexures of the joints. In a case observed by Curling, the clefts in the skin and underlying structures were traversed by vessels and nerves in such a way as to preclude their causation by a cutting instrument. A strangulation-mark on more than one occasion has been clearly visible on a body that was almost carbonised. Schüppel[1] examined the carbonised remains of a boy ten years old, whose body was found in a burning cottage, and discovered a distinct groove encircling the greater part of the neck, well differentiated from the blistered and charred surface above and below it, due to homicidal strangulation. The preservation of the mark is owing to the constrict-

[1] *Vierteljahrsschr. f. ger. Med.*, 1870.

ing medium being allowed to remain round the neck—it protects the skin underneath it, if the cord is removed before exposing the body to the fire, the mark will probably be destroyed

The identification of bodies partially consumed by fire is easy or difficult in proportion to the degree of injury they have sustained. The lines on which such an investigation is to be conducted are laid down in the section on personal identity in the dead. Attention is specially directed to the very considerable diminution in size and weight undergone by a body that has been partially carbonised. The remains should be carefully searched for metallic objects which may afford evidence for identification—such as keys, rings, watches, and, more especially, gold plates to which artificial teeth are attached.

## PRETERNATURAL COMBUSTIBILITY.

Under ordinary conditions the human body is with difficulty consumed by fire; a high temperature has to be maintained for a considerable time before the soft structures are carbonised. Exceptionally, an exactly opposite condition exists—the body is so easily consumed that the term "spontaneous combustion" has been applied to it. It may be premised at once that there is no evidence whatever to justify the use of the word "spontaneous," but there can be no doubt that an extraordinarily high degree of combustibility occurs in rare instances to which the term preternatural combustibility would more correctly apply. The peculiarity of the phenomenon consists in the fact that bodies which acquire this unnatural combustibility burn without the aid of heat derived from the consumption of combustible matter other than that afforded by the tissues themselves; the wooden floor on which such a body consumes is merely charred over the area that is in contact with it. This is totally opposed to the normal condition, in which the soft structures of the body not only refuse to burn of themselves—that is, by the simple application of a light—but they demand the consumption of an amount of fuel many times in excess of their weight before they can be destroyed, and when partly consumed soon cease to burn if the fire is withdrawn. It is to be inferred, therefore, that in preternatural combustibility some exceptional chemical change takes place, by which products of higher combustibility are developed than those which normally exist in the human body.

The subjects of this exceptional condition are usually fat, bloated, and much addicted to alcohol; exceptions have been met with in which the victims were spare and temperate of habit. They are almost invariably beyond middle age. The usual history is that the individual was in the midst of a debauch when the event took place, and that he was last seen some hours before, more or less profoundly under the influence of drink. The close relation between alcohol and preternatural combustibility of the body has led to the supposition that it might be the immediate cause, but this has been proved by experiment to be impossible. Chassagniol[1] steeped dead bodies in alcohol, and injected it into dog's veins without increasing the combustibility of the tissues. Any one who has thrown into the fire an old pathological specimen, which has been preserved in spirit, may have noticed that after the alcohol is burnt off, the solid tissues frizzle and burn slowly away, much as they would do in the recent state. Preternatural combustibility is evidently due to the formation in the body of some substance which is capable of burning alone when once ignited, not in a smouldering way, but with a luminous flame, as is proved by several cases in which flames were seen to proceed from bodies thus burning. It is exceedingly improbable that this substance can be any of the solid tissues, or fluids which have undergone chemical change; there is no analogy for such a complete alteration of property taking place within the living or dead body.

It seems most likely either that exceptionally early and abnormal processes of decomposition of the tissues set in, or that, in some other way, inflammable gaseous products are formed, which, on escaping, become accidentally ignited, and the heat produced by their combustion consumes the tissues. A suggestive case is reported by Gull[2] of a large, fat, bloated drayman of intemperate habits, who during cool weather was admitted into Guy's Hospital at nine o'clock one evening, and died an hour or two after admission. On the following day at one o'clock no signs of ordinary putrefaction were present, but the body was remarkably distended all over, the skin and the parts beneath being filled with gas, which, in the absence of any signs of decomposition, was suspected to have been exhaled from the blood. When punctures were made through the skin, the gas escaped and burnt with a flame like that of carburetted hydrogen; as many as a dozen flames were burning at the same time over the distended body. If this man had died in his own house, he would probably have passed his last hours alone, in a small room with a fire in it, and what so likely as that the gaseous emanations from his body should become ignited, with the result that another case of "spontaneous combustion" would have been reported.

In cases of so-called spontaneous combustion, there is nothing to show that the subject was alive at the time the burning commenced; on the contrary, the indications are rather against such

[1] *Bull. Soc. de Chirurgie de Paris*, 1874.  [2] *Med. Times and Gaz.*, 1885.

a supposition, if alive, the victim must be in a profound state of alcoholic coma, or else there would be instances recorded of cries for help, which are wanting. The formation of inflammable gases in the body, moreover, is not incompatible with life. Beatson[1] records the case of a man, who had foul eructations; he got out of bed one night and struck a match in order to see the time; whilst blowing out the match his breath took fire, and exploded with a report sufficiently loud as to awaken his wife. This is by no means a solitary case. The formation of inflammable gases in the digestive tract has been demonstrated by M'Naught[2] to be due to bacillary fermentation, and a like explanation appears probable in relation to the abnormal formation of gases in the dead body possessing similar properties. It has been noticed in all cases of preternatural combustibility, that the trunk is the original site of the combustion, the head and the extremities usually escaping, or, at the most suffering from the contiguous heat. In a case reported, with a history of the subject, by Reynolds,[3] the abdominal wall was charred completely, and there was a large hole about eight inches long in the middle line; the face was crimson as from fire, but not blistered; the hands, stretched above the head, were unburnt; the arms were burnt and blistered, but not blackened; the thighs were burnt to the bone as far as the knees, where the burning abruptly ceased. It is evident that the combustion started in the abdomen, and in this instance spread further down than is frequently the case. The woman was lying on her back with the thighs and knees well flexed, so that the former would be brought into close contact with the abdomen and would, therefore, be subject to the full play of the flames; the effect of the heat on the anterior muscles of the thighs would be to shorten them, and thus, in the first instance, to draw the thighs more closely towards the abdomen. The burning had taken place either before or immediately after death, as blistering with signs of inflammation was present on the surrounding parts.

It seems probable, that in cases of preternatural combustibility, inflammable gases are formed in the abdomen, either during life or from abnormal changes which commence immediately after death; that the gas is accidentally ignited, and that its combustion raises the temperature of the soft tissues, especially the fat, so high that they become carbonised, and give off gases of an inflammable nature which also take fire.

The part played by alcohol in the process has yet to be determined — whether its prolonged abuse leads to abnormal metabolic processes or post-mortem changes in the tissues, more especially in those of the

---

[1] *Brit. Med. Journ.*, 1886.   [2] *Brit. Med. Journ.*, 1890.
[3] *Med. Chron.*, 1891.

digestive tract, by which inflammable products are formed, or whether it undergoes some peculiar decomposition and itself furnishes the inflammable gas, is a matter of conjecture. The close alliance, shown by statistics, between the prolonged abuse of alcohol and an unnatural degree of combustibility of the body, makes it very probable that they stand in nearer relation to each other, as cause and effect, than that which has been allotted to them by some authorities, namely—that the alcohol simply stupefies the victim and makes him incapable of self-rescue.

The subject has an important medico-legal bearing. A murderer after killing his victim may endeavour to conceal his crime by burning, or partially burning the body, in some instances the surroundings might lend colour to the supposition that the case was one of preternatural combustibility, and of absence of criminal intervention—an allegation which has been made under these circumstances. The points to be remembered are—that in cases of true "self" combustion, there is rarely much indication of the effects of fire beyond that displayed by the body itself, and that the trunk chiefly suffers, the extremities for the most part being preserved. The complete destruction of tissue occasioned by "self" combustion could not be accomplished, in the case of an ordinary cadaver, without the expenditure of a considerable amount of extraneous fuel, evidences of which would be forthcoming, and in this case the effects would scarcely be limited to, or most apparent in the trunk.

## BURNS PRODUCED BY CORROSIVE FLUIDS.

Burns produced by corrosive fluids which come under the observation of the medical jurist are the result of malicious throwing of the fluid on to the face or other part of the body of the victim, the substances used are the mineral acids and strong solutions of the caustic alkalies, of these sulphuric acid holds the first rank, so much so that a special name is given to the act—"vitriol throwing." None of these substances will directly occasion death when thrown upon the body, unless under very exceptional circumstances, they may produce great disfigurement, however, and may indirectly conduce to a fatal issue.

As regards efficacy it is not without reason that sulphuric acid is the substance usually made use of, it attacks organic matter energetically, and its corrosive action is only partially arrested by wiping the surface on to which it has fallen—which is usually the only counteractive treatment available for the moment. **Sulphuric acid** in a concentrated form produces a **brownish-blackish** eschar if thrown on to the surface of the body, it is not necessary, however, for the acid to be of full commercial strength to effect this. If it is much diluted, the mark produced will be grey. Nitric acid leaves a yellow stain or slough, the colour being caused by the action of the acid on albuminoid bodies, forming xanthoproteic acid; the stains of nitric acid sometimes appear brownish on the dead body. Hydrochloric acid leaves a whitish-grey stain, and is not so destructive to tissue as are sulphuric and nitric acids.

There are certain appearances common to the eschars produced by all three acids. The surface is smooth and soft in contradistinction to the irregular and hard surface of a heat-burn, and the surrounding zone produced by congestion of the small vessels of the cutis, which encircles the eschar produced by fire, is wanting in that caused by acids.

The caustic alkalies have a solvent action on albuminoids and fats. Potash-ley is especially corrosive in its action on the tissues; under its influence they become tumid, and the skin communicates a greasy feeling to the touch; subsequently, the part becomes dry and resistant, the colour being dark, especially on the dead body. As is the case with the acids, the eschars produced by alkalies have no encircling zone of reaction.

If the surface is examined immediately after the receipt of the injury, direct evidence may possibly be obtained as to the nature of the corrosive, by brushing the surface with a small camel-hair brush (quill-mounted) dipped in distilled water, and then pressing the fluid out of the brush into a test-tube. The proceeding may be repeated once or twice, and the resulting fluid tested, first as to reaction, and then, if acid, as to the kind of acid; the appearance of the mark on the skin and the stains on the clothing will probably give a clue as to which acid should be sought for in the first instance. This plan however is rarely successful, as the part in all probability will have been well laved with water before an opportunity is afforded of trying it. The same remarks apply to injuries produced by alkalies, except of course as regards reaction and subsequent testing. The character of the stains severally produced on fabrics, with the method of testing, will be found described in the section on Toxicology.

In the absence of direct proof obtained from the injured part, it is of the highest importance to ascertain the nature of the substance thrown from evidence yielded by the clothing, as the *attempt* to injure by throwing a corrosive even should no bodily injury be sustained, constitutes felony. In the absence of bodily injury, the evidence required from the medical witness is an answer to the question—was the substance thrown of a corrosive nature?

## CHAPTER XXII.

## MECHANICAL INJURIES AND WOUNDS.

Almost all injuries to the body produced by mechanical violence are comprehended, in the legal sense, under the title of "wounds." The definition is enlarged beyond that given by the surgeon by the words which follow in the statute:—"Whosoever shall, by any means whatsoever, wound or *cause any grievous bodily harm* to a person." The last clause of this sentence obviates the necessity for defining whether a given injury is or is not a wound, which was a question that formerly led to much discussion at almost every trial relating to matters of personal violence, and which not unfrequently facilitated the escape of a guilty person.

If the injury is not obviously of a very severe kind, medical evidence will probably be required to determine whether the life of the injured person is in danger or not, and whether "grievous bodily harm" has been inflicted. These questions can only be answered after a thorough examination of the injuries has been made, the appearances found being interpreted with the aid of an appeal to general experience. The subject involves the consideration of injuries, both in their general aspect, and also as to special characteristics dependent upon the kind of instrument with which they were produced.

### CONTUSIONS.

This is a comprehensive term, embracing all degrees of injury produced by blows or sudden pressure with objects that do not divide the skin, from a simple bruise that merely causes rupture of a few blood-vessels in the corium, up to complete disorganisation of the soft structures underlying the seat of injury. One result common to all contusions is the extravasation of blood. The amount effused is not exclusively determined by the severity of the blow—the anatomical structure of the parts injured exercises a considerable influence; those which are open in texture allow the blood from the ruptured vessels to distribute itself more freely than those which are firm. A blow in the region of the eye causes wider spread extravasation than one of equal force on the palm of the hand. The condition of the blood-vessels is another factor; when diseased, as in purpura, subcutaneous hæmorrhages occur spontaneously or on the slightest pressure. In the absence of disease, many women develop bruises with the least possible pressure. This is a point to be remembered when estimating the degree of violence that has been exercised in the case of women of flabby constitution with soft skins, in whom a comparatively gentle grasp of the arm will produce bruises indicating the points of pressure caused by the thumb and fingers that might easily be attributed to excessive violence. When blood is effused in, or immediately beneath, the skin the discoloration produced is blue-black in colour. Pepper[1] directs attention to a change in colour not unfrequently undergone after death by superficial subcutaneous extravasations, which at first are bluish-black and subsequently become pink or scarlet.

**Superficial ecchymoses** make their appearance within a **few minutes** after their causation. **Deep-seated ecchymoses** may not appear for **days**, and then not always directly over the seat of the injury. If blood is effused from one or two relatively large vessels at some distance from the surface there may be no discoloration of the skin, but only a sense of fluctuation on palpation.

In certain parts of the body injuries of the severest kind may be inflicted without producing external signs of bruising. The wheel of a cart may pass over a man's abdomen and rupture the liver and other internal organs without the least trace of ecchymosis being visible in the skin, either before or after death. A kick or blow may rupture the bladder or intestines without leaving any external mark.

Superficial ecchymoses that are undergoing absorption, display a surrounding zone of colours: brown, green, and yellow, fading into the normal skin-tint, are usually present. These appearances, due to modifications undergone by the hæmoglobin, are initiated at the periphery, and gradually advance towards the centre of the discoloured spot, affording evidence of further distribution of the effused blood than at first was apparent — at some distance from the ecchymosis, the skin, which was not discoloured when the bruise was first produced, takes a lemon tint, which is continuous with the deeper shades of the original discoloration. Ecchymoses under the conjunctiva being very superficial, and being backed up by the white sclerotic, are of a bright red colour, and when fading pass through no chromatic changes except to yellow. **Deep-seated extravasations** of blood show no superficial colour changes other than a gradual diminution in intensity.

[1] *The Lancet*, 1887.

## WOUNDS

Under this head are comprised incised wounds, punctured wounds, and lacerated wounds

**Incised wounds** are those made with cutting instruments or with objects presenting more or less sharp edges, such as pieces of broken glass or crockery-ware. The chief characteristic of an incised wound made during life is that its edges retract and curve outwards, causing the wound to gape. This is to a great extent due to the elasticity of the skin, aided or counteracted, within limits, by the direction of the underlying fibres of the connective tissue and muscles, in accordance as to whether they run parallel with, or transversely to, the line taken by the incision; in the limbs the course of the fibres runs lengthwise, except near the joints. The cleanness and evenness of the edges of an incised wound are determined by the manner in which it was produced, and to a still greater extent by the nature of the object that produced it. A sharp knife will divide the skin in a clean regular way very different from the cut made by a sharp-edged stone. When a sharp knife is resolutely used for the purpose of inflicting a bodily injury, the conditions most favourable for the production of a clean incision are fulfilled—a suitable instrument appropriately handled. By falling on a sharp-edged stone, it is quite possible for a man to cut himself very severely, but the conditions are much less favourable as regards the regularity of the wound, especially of its margins. The skin being very elastic tends to recede before the edge of a cutting instrument, necessitating a sweeping or sawing movement in order to divide it; any such application of the edge of a stone or broken piece of earthenware would be of fortuitous occurrence. When incised wounds are really caused by falling on broken pottery, or the like, the broken edge is driven through the skin with but little, if any, of the movement necessary to divide it cleanly; the consequence being that the margins of the wound have a more or less contused appearance. To enable this to be distinguished the wound must be examined shortly after its infliction before any inflammatory changes take place. The distinction between an incised wound made with a dull edged knife with notched blade and one made with a sharp stone may not be so easy.

Some emphasis has been laid on the appearance of wounds made by sharp cutting instruments as compared with those caused by the wounded person falling on broken pottery and the like, because in cases of alleged criminal wounding with cutting instruments, the defence usually advanced is that the prisoner with his fist struck the prosecutor, who fell on a sharp stone which inflicted the wound. It is true that in either case the prisoner would be guilty of wounding, but the use of a knife is held to greatly increase the culpability of the act.

In certain parts of the body where the skin is somewhat stretched, with little between it and the bone underneath—as is the case over the malar bone, for example—the violent tangential impact of a rounded hard body, such as a cricket ball or even the clenched fist, may cause a wound scarcely, if at all, distinguishable from one made by a cutting instrument. Such wounds are due to sudden, forcible stretching of the integument, splitting or tearing it open. Due reserve should be displayed in attributing wounds in this and other similar parts of the body to the use of a cutting instrument; the possibility of the above described causation should ever be borne in mind. When such a wound is seen immediately after it is made, minute examination with a lens may reveal irregularities of the margins inconsistent with production by a cutting instrument.

The amount of hæmorrhage from incised wounds depends on the number and size of the vessels divided; it is usually considerable. In a recent wound blood-clots will be found, and the connective tissue laid bare will be infiltrated with blood.

Punctured Wounds.—The risk to life caused by punctured wounds is determined by their situation, the depth to which they penetrate, and the size and shape of the weapon by which they are produced. A fine exploring needle may be repeatedly introduced into certain organs—such as the liver—with impunity, whereas a still finer instrument introduced elsewhere may produce fatal results. Magnan[1] relates the case of a woman who committed suicide by passing an ordinary pin, barely an inch and a quarter long, into the left side below the breast at the sixth intercostal space. On examination after death seven small punctures were found in the apex of the heart, and the pericardium contained between seven and eight ounces of blood.

A punctured wound made with a sharp-edged and pointed knife, leaves a wound through the skin having almost parallel, but slightly concave margins which meet at acute angles at the two extremities. This is invariably the case if the knife or dagger is double-edged, and usually so with an ordinary blade—that is, sharp on one edge only—unless it is of considerable thickness at the back. When the blade is thick at the back throughout its entire length, or, when not so thick, if plunged in up to the hilt where the back is thickest, the opening is wedge-shaped; one extremity forms the apex, and the other the base of an exceedingly acute triangle. With either a double- or single-edged weapon, if it is

[1] *Comptes rendus de la Société de Biologie*, 1890.

thrust in and withdrawn in the same plane, without lateral movement, the aperture will be slightly less in length than the breadth of the instrument that produced it; this must be borne in mind when comparing the size of a punctured wound with a suspected weapon. For the same reason it is risky to express a decided opinion as to the depth of a stab-wound in the living subject, from a comparison between the length of the wound through the skin and the width of the blade at a given distance from the point. The discrepancy in size between the wound and the instrument that produced it is due to the elasticity of the skin. For the same reason, the edges of the skin in a wound produced by the thrust of a knife or dagger may be everted—the skin gripping the blade as it is withdrawn. If the weapon is not thrust in and withdrawn in the same plane the wound through the skin will be longer than the breadth of the blade, as any movement of an oscillating nature divides more skin than is necessary for its direct passage. If a part of the body is transfixed by a long-bladed weapon, the secondary orifice will be smaller than the primary, and its edges will be everted.

Punctured wounds made with pointed weapons of circular transverse section—such as a butcher's steel—are not circular in outline. Such instruments act as conical wedges; they do not cut but they split the tissues, the consequence being that instead of a round aperture, one resembling a slit is produced, the direction of the long axis of which is determined by the course of the fibres which enter into the structure of the tissues perforated. It is to be noted that the course of the fibres in the superficial structure of an organ does not take the same direction over its entire surface; in some organs the fibres radiate; in others they are arranged somewhat circularly from one or more centres. Punctured wounds caused by sharp-pointed fragments of glass and similar objects are characterised by a combination of cutting and splitting of the skin and the tissues perforated. The margins of the wound will be jagged, and will bear traces of bruising, the appearance being different from that of a wound produced with a sharp-pointed knife. Punctured wounds of a similar type are sometimes caused by certain artizan's tools; the pointed end of a file that is intended to be driven into a wooden handle has blunt cutting edges, which, when the implement is used as a dagger, or is accidentally thrust through the skin, tear open rather than cut the tissues. Sometimes the wound made by an instrument which has a special form is sufficiently distinctive as to betray the kind of weapon used.

The danger to life from punctured wounds is determined by their depth and by the structures they perforate. External hæmorrhage may or may not be profuse, but when only a little blood flows out of the wound, severe internal hæmorrhage may be taking place, and may speedily cause death.

Lacerated wounds are those which are produced by objects that tear the tissues in place of cutting them. Such a wound may be sustained by an individual who falls violently on a hard projection—as the corner of a box or step, or by catching against a nail or pointed hook with a sudden movement that rips open the surface. Lacerated wounds may be produced by blows with an obtuse-angled weapon, as a hammer or poker, also by the teeth of men or of the lower animals, and in a variety of other ways.

The characteristics of lacerated wounds are their irregularity and the jagged, swollen appearance of the margins. When produced by violent impact with a blunt-edged object, the skin in the neighbourhood of the wound is ecchymosed, the underlying tissues are more or less disorganised, and if a bone is near the surface, it is likely to be fractured. Heavy falls on a flat surface, such as the flags, a macadamised road, frozen ground, or the ice, may cause lacerated wounds—a causation frequently alleged to account for those suspected to be due to criminal violence. Some parts of the body are more likely than others to be lacerated in this manner: the scalp over the eyebrows, the tissues over the malar bone, or those over a flexed joint, as the knee for example. It is often difficult or impossible to say whether such wounds were directly caused by a blow or indirectly by the fall which resulted from the blow. The site of the wound may enable a decision to be arrived at; if it is at the vertex it is more likely to have been caused by a blow than by a fall, unless the wounded person fell from a height; the presence of soil or grit in the wound lends probability to the supposition that it resulted from a fall. Not only is the wound to be carefully examined, but the clothing also, especially the hat if the head is the part injured. When the head-covering shows a tear corresponding to the wound, and the margins of the tear are coated with grit or other substance derived from the ground, the wound being similarly coated, strong evidence is afforded that the injury was the result of a fall.

If a weapon is forthcoming by which the wound is alleged to have been made, it should be examined for marks of blood, for hairs, and for fibres derived from the clothing of the injured person. A minute comparison must be made of the weapon with the wound in order to determine whether such a weapon could have caused the wound. Sometimes the implement used leaves special indications in or about the wound—as, for instance, soot off a poker, and rust off a hammer or an iron bar.

Lacerated wounds do not, as a rule, bleed so freely as incised wounds; but if the structures lacerated are very vascular, bleeding to a fatal extent may occur. This is especially the case with regard to the external female genital organs; death from hæmorrhage has resulted from a lacerated wound of the vulva caused by a violent kick from a foot armed with an iron-bound clog, or even with a thickly-soled boot.

**The distinction between wounds inflicted before and after death.**—The characteristics of bruises produced during life have already been described. Marks of a similar kind may be produced immediately after death, and, further, local violence inflicted in the last moments of life, may not produce any obvious change in the colour of the skin until after death has occurred; therefore, it must not be assumed that the presence of a bruise-mark proves survival for a time after the causal violence was inflicted. There is no practical difference between a bruise produced immediately before death, and one produced immediately after, as effusion of blood from ruptured vessels of the skin may occur for a short time after death—that is, whilst the blood is fluid and warm. Absence of cardiac pulsation prevents the occurrence of extravasation of blood to any great extent after death; but in subcutaneous ecchymoses the difference in amount is too insignificant to enable a decided opinion to be expressed as to their ante- or post-mortem origin. The appearance of a bruise inflicted during life cannot, however, be produced on a dead body after the lapse of a short interval after death. If an individual has survived the infliction of injuries for a day or two, the usual colour changes at the margins of bruises will be visible.

Incised wounds made after death differ from those inflicted during life, in respect to absence of gaping and of much hæmorrhage; a short survival adds another indication—tumefaction of the edges of the wound; still longer survival leads to changes, due to reparative processes, which remove all doubt as to whether the wound was produced before death. Gaping being due to contractility of the skin, areolar tissue and muscles, is not an absolute sign of infliction during life; the edges of an incised wound made *immediately* after death will retract and cause the wound to gape; the extent of retraction is less than during life, but, since it occurs at all, a certain reserve must be maintained in the expression of an opinion. Within a very short time after death the contractility of the tissues is lost; an incised wound produced at or after this period presents the appearance of a slit, the edges of which lie closely approximated without any trace of eversion. On separating the edges, little or no blood will be found effused, unless a large vein has been divided; that which is present may be either fluid or more or less coagulated; any infiltration into the areolar tissue is slight as compared with that which takes plac in a wound inflicted during life. If, in the course of an incised wound inflicted during life, an artery of moderate size is included amongst the structures divided, a considerable amount of hæmorrhage takes place; if the wound is made after death, the bleeding will be relatively insignificant, being limited to the veins, therefore the amount of blood found on the body and clothing, and on the surface on which the body lies, may afford a valuable indication. Spirting of blood to a distance from a divided artery is a sign that the wound was inflicted during life, but it only occurs with small arteries; with large arteries the blood-pressure is lost at a short distance from the cut end, and the blood is not projected far. The appearance presented by blood spirted from a small artery on to a wall or piece of furniture is that of a succession of small spots forming a line, or possibly a confused mass with isolated spots around it; if a larger artery spouts on to an object close at hand, there may be a splash of blood which, as long as it remains sufficiently fluid, trickles down the surface and forms a vertical and more or less linear mark.

Punctured wounds made before or after death present appearances respectively analogous to incised wounds. A punctured wound made after death may (from perforation of a large vein) cause a considerable quantity of blood to be poured out into one of the cavities of the body.

Lacerated wounds made *immediately* after death may present appearances like those seen in wounds inflicted during life; if produced a short time after, the possibly ecchymosed margins will not be swollen.

When making a post-mortem examination of a body on which there is a wound, the first thing to do is to minutely examine the part without disturbing anything and to write down at the time all the points observed. The external appearance of the wound, its size and position, the amount of blood poured out, and, if the body is seen where it was originally found, the presence of blood-stains from spirting on neighbouring objects all claim special attention. If there is blood, observe if it is coagulated, and if so, whether firmly or not. The condition as to cadaveric rigidity and post-mortem stains is always to be investigated in medico-legal cases. The interior of the wound is to be examined, first, as to the presence of clots, blood, and staining of the connective tissue; and then, its direction must be ascertained. In the case of a stab-wound a blunt bougie may be cautiously passed in, but the operator must be prepared to answer a question that he may be subsequently asked as to whether by doing so he did not extend the wound; with due care there is no risk. The deeper part of the wound is to be reached by dissection in the direction taken by the bougie, if possible without interfering with the external opening. This is especially important if the weapon that is supposed to have caused the wound is not yet forthcoming; it may subsequently be found, in which case a comparison of it with the outer wound is very desirable. The depth of the wound and the structures through which it passes are to be noted. The possible presence of foreign substances must not be overlooked. If a bone is injured, it may be well to remove it (or the injured portion of it), as corroborative evidence.

## CHAPTER XXIII.

### SPECIAL WOUNDS AND INJURIES.

#### INJURIES OF THE HEAD AND SPINE.

The scalp is one of the regions where wounds resembling those caused by a sharp cutting instrument may be produced by blows from rounded or obtusely angled objects; in this way a flap may be detached leaving a portion of the skull bare. In the absence of unhealthy inflammation uncomplicated scalp wounds are not dangerous to life; any difficulty in prognosis is usually caused by the possible presence of complications in the form of injury to the skull or the brain.

Injuries to the skull are dangerous to life either remotely or immediately. The former is the case when a blow on the head is followed by inflammation of the diploë, producing septicæmia two or three weeks after the receipt of the injury; in the meantime the patient appears to be doing well. Immediate results follow extravasation of blood within the cranium, either between it and the dura, in the arachnoid or the pia mater, or in the brain substance itself; the symptoms are those of cerebral compression:—slow, laboured breathing and pulse, total insensibility with absence of reaction of the pupils, which may be either dilated, contracted, or unequal. When such an extravasation is the direct result of a blow on the head the skull is usually fractured. Occasionally a case occurs in which a man who is not suffering from marked degenerative changes of the vessels is knocked down and without the skull being fractured, shortly after develops the fatal symptoms just enumerated; in such cases medical opinion is required as to a possible causal relation between the blow and death. The transverse sinus most frequently suffers, more rarely hæmorrhage from traumatic violence without fracture takes place in the pia and arachnoid. This mode of death not unfrequently happens to habitual drunkards and to persons advanced in life, in both the vessels are liable to spontaneous rupture, which may occur at the time the injury was received. In one case of this kind the deceased was in a paroxysm of passion at the time, and was about to resort to extreme violence when his adversary struck him a blow which caused him to stagger and fall, afterwards, insensibility came on, which ended in death; on examination cerebral hæmorrhage from a degenerated vessel was found, but no signs of injury to the skull. In such cases allowance must be made for the condition of the deceased at the time, and without expressing a positive opinion it is to be admitted that in elderly people and habitual drunkards cerebral hæmorrhage may be determined by excessive mental excitement. Post-mortem signs of injury to the head, though without fracture, would point to local violence as the cause of the hæmorrhage. It is obvious that a mixed causation exists in many cases, a vessel is predisposed to rupture, and does rupture from a degree of violence that would not injure one in a normal condition. In such cases the medical witness must explain the condition of the parts and content himself with so doing, unless he has good reason for thinking that the rupture did or did not result from the blow.

The question is sometimes further complicated by apparent recovery from the effects of the blow or fall followed, after an hour or more, by relapse into unconsciousness which terminates in death. The defence naturally is that death was due to an independent cause, the interval of recovery showing that the blow could not have caused rupture of a vessel, else there would have been no return to consciousness and power of walking. This inference however is contrary to fact. In many instances cerebral hæmorrhage from both traumatic and idiopathic causes has commenced, producing a certain degree of unconsciousness, the bleeding has temporarily ceased, the brain has recovered from the pressure, and the patient has regained consciousness. Renewed bleeding from the same source has then ended fatally within a few hours.

Concussion of the brain is another way in which external violence may cause death without the skull being fractured. As generally understood, concussion of the brain does not cause disorganisation, therefore, no indications as to the cause of death are revealed at the necropsy. In fatal cases the injured individual is suddenly rendered unconscious, respiration is irregular and fitful for a short time and then ceases altogether; the pulse is probably imperceptible from the first, the surface is cold and there is entire absence of reaction. Less severe cases usually end in recovery.

Contusion of the brain is either circumscribed or diffused. In the former variety one or more centres of disorganisation, or of extravasation of blood occur; in the latter, the extravasations are distributed throughout the substance of the brain and, possibly, also on its surface. The mischief may be limited to the site of the blow, or it may be situated at an entirely different part, owing to the so-called *contre coup*; the base and the middle lobes most frequently suffer on account of the irregular conformation of the base of the skull. The symptoms are those of cerebral irritation; there is usually unconsciousness with great restlessness and, possibly, tonic or clonic spasms. In a slighter form the primary symptoms may pass away and the patient may recover; but there is risk of inflammatory changes occurring, which may spread to the meninges and ultimately cause death. In other instances the patient recovers with partial loss of memory or with some degree of paralysis.

Fractures of the skull may be divided into those produced by blows with weapons presenting a small striking-surface, which may be either pointed, rounded, or flat, and those caused by violent contact with surfaces of larger area. Fractures caused by blows with a heavy weapon of limited striking-surface, such as a narrow-headed hammer, very frequently display the shape of that part of the weapon which came in contact with the bone. If the striking-surface has a rectangular outline, and it strikes the bone in the vertical line with considerable momentum, the resulting fracture will also have a more or less rectangular shape, the portion of the bone on which the striking-surface falls being driven forward by the violence of the impact; the detached portion almost entirely absorbs the momentum with which the implement is endowed, so that comparatively little tension is put on the surrounding bone which consequently escapes injury more or less completely. If the same implement reaches the skull with a lesser momentum it may cause an irregularly depressed fracture with fissures traversing the surrounding bone. If the fracture, viewed from the outside of the skull, has a sharply-defined characteristic outline, the inner table will be found irregularly splintered off all round the aperture which is consequently much larger on its inner than on its outer aspect. Fractures equally characteristic of the causal weapon may be produced by sharp blows with the spherical knob of the poker or the head of a life-preserver; the resulting injury takes the form of a circular concave depression when viewed from the outside, and appears as an irregularly formed fissured projection on the inner surface. Penetrating injuries of the skull, made with sharp-pointed instruments having thin blades, like a dagger or a knife, take the form of the blade or else that of a depressed fracture, such as may result from a blow with any weapon having a very limited striking-surface.

The direction of fractures of the base and of the vault of the skull caused by blows or by sudden pressure with objects of large contact-area is determined by certain physical laws. Wahl[1] and Messerer[2] were the first to demonstrate the part played by the elasticity of the skull in the production of fractures of this kind and their deductions, which are of the highest importance to the medical jurist, have been corroborated by numerous clinical observations.

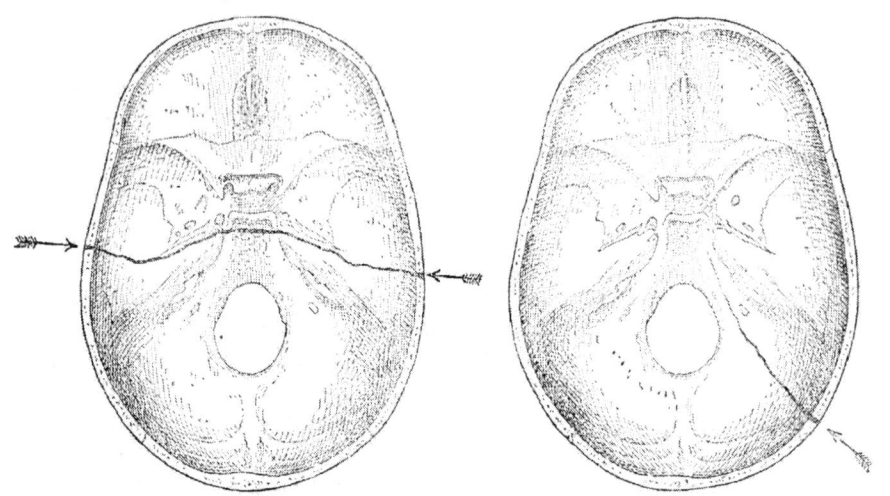

Fig. 19.—Fracture from bi-lateral compression.

Fig. 20.—Fracture from one-sided compression.

Fractures of this kind are divided by Körber[3] into two groups:—
(a) Those produced by bi-lateral compression of the skull; and (b) those which result from violence applied to one side only, the head as a whole being free to recede from the impact of the blow. In both groups the line of fracture runs parallel with the axis of compression.

(a) Fractures in the first group are produced not only by interposition of the skull between two opposing forces, both of which are in motion, but also if the skull is simply prevented from receding when the blow is delivered, as happens when a blow falls from above on the head of a prostrate person, the head resting on the ground, or when a person who is standing with his back against a wall receives a blow on the forehead. In these cases the skull is compressed

[1] Volkmann's *Klin. Vorträge.* (Chirurgie No. 73), 1883.
[2] *Exper. Untersuch. über Schädelbrüche,* 1884.
[3] *Deutche Zeitschr. f. Chirurgie,* 1889.

between two points or poles, the compression being greatest at the equatorial line, where the fracture begins and tends to spread towards each pole, in other words, it begins at the base or the vertex (more frequently the former), and spreads outwards in the direction of the two points where compression is applied, the fissure being widest at its starting point. Korber records, with drawings, a number of cases of fracture of the skull variously produced. In one instance, a woman was killed by being struck with a wooden mallet near the left ear while asleep with the head on a pillow, the line of fracture which resulted ran across the base from ear to ear. In another case a man lying asleep on the right side received a blow from a hatchet near the left eye; after death the skull was found to be fractured diagonally through the base, from the left orbit to the right parietal protuberance

Among this group are those fractures which result from blows on the vertex (the individual being in the erect posture) the counter pressure being derived from the resistance offered by the vertebral column

(b) When the compression is one-sided, as when a man in the upright posture is struck with a blunt instrument on the side of the head, the head being free to recede under the momentum imparted by the blow, the fracture begins at or near the point of impact and travels in a direction parallel with the axis of compression, it rarely goes beyond the middle line, and tends to narrow in width the further it advances For example, a man was struck on the left temporal region with a large stone and dropped down dead; a comminuted fracture was found where the stone struck the head, and a compression fracture running transversely across the left middle fossa, narrowing as it reached the sella Turcica, where it terminated.

A fracture of the skull in which a portion of the bone is driven in by a blow from a weapon having a limited striking-area may be accompanied by a compression-fracture, the impulse being sufficient to compress the skull as well as to force a fragment of it inwards. The compression-fracture may be situated at some distance from the spot where the blow fell, but it will run in a direction parallel with that of the blow

In some instances the bones of the cranium are exceptionally thin, being no thicker at parts than stout paper, a slight blow is then sufficient to cause a fracture The thickness of the skull should always be noted when examining the bodies of those who have sustained fracture of its component bones, excessive tenuity being frequently pleaded in criminal cases.

If a man standing in the erect posture is knocked down by a

blow on the head and dies in consequence, the skull being found to be fractured, the question may be asked is it not possible for the skull to be fractured by a fall on level ground? It is possible, provided that the ground is hard and unyielding

Severe fracture of the skull with depression or other injury to the brain is not invariably followed by insensibility, and many cases have occurred where great damage has been done to the skull without depriving the sufferer of power of movement. Agnew[1] relates two striking examples. A man was run over by a tramway-car, he got up immediately after the accident, walked a short distance to his house, opened the door with a latch-key, went up stairs to his bedroom on the second story and got into bed, where on the following morning he was found insensible with portions of the parietal and temporal bones deeply driven into the brain. In the second case, a man had half of the frontal bone with a considerable portion of the pre-frontal lobes carried away by the bursting of a fly-wheel, he was dazed for a few moments only, and eventually made a good recovery. Such instances show the necessity for expressing a guarded opinion as to loss of consciousness and power of locomotion in cases where a dead body is found with severe injury to the brain.

Injuries of the Spine.—The regions most liable to injury are the upper cervical, the lower cervical, and the upper lumbar. The extent of the injury sustained varies from a slight sprain up to fracture and separation of the bodies of one or more vertebræ. Slight sprains are often exceedingly difficult of detection, the symptoms being purely subjective, if the cord suffers, symptoms either immediate or remote supervene. Hæmorrhage into the meninges—*hæmatorrhachis*—usually produces sudden loss of power, violent pain at the seat of the hæmorrhage, which will probably radiate along the nerves given off from the affected segment, with clonic and tonic spasms, and subsequently more or less paralysis. The bleeding takes place either outside the membranes, within the arachnoid or, more rarely, beneath it. Concussion of the spine may be followed by delayed development of symptoms, several weeks elapsing before anything manifests itself more definite than the sensation of having undergone a severe shake. Then various paræsthesiæ develop, with difficulty of walking and especially of stooping, urination may be enfeebled from loss of expulsive power, and there may be partial paralysis of the legs. Along with these symptoms there are usually disturbances of the special senses, especially of sight and hearing, the mental condition deteriorates—evinced by loss of memory, inability to concentrate the ideas, and

[1] *Medical News*, 1887.

general irritability. These symptoms not unfrequently follow the shake produced by a railway collision, and it is no easy matter to determine how far they result from diffuse injury sustained by the cord and the effects of shock to the nervous system generally, and how far they may be simply of a subjective nature, due to the influence of "suggestion." An accurate mapping out of the anæsthesic and hyperæsthesic areas with subsequent comparison with the known origin of the sensory nerves of the parts will probably show whether the sensory disturbances are really due to changes in the cord or are only of psychical derivation. The subject is too wide to be discussed in a text-book on forensic medicine; special works must be consulted. Much valuable information on the distribution of the sensory spinal nerves is contained in Thorburn's *Surgery of the Spinal Cord.*

Fractures of the spine, with or without displacement, may be caused by direct or by indirect violence. The former results from the injured part being struck by, or striking against, some hard substance, as, for example, a blow with a bar of iron or a fall from a scaffold on to a projecting piece of timber. Fracture from indirect violence may result from forcible bending of the body forwards or backwards, it usually occurs in the cervical or dorsal regions. Forcible bending of the spine may be caused by external violence, as when a sack of flour falls from a height on the head of a man who is slightly stooping forwards and doubles him up, or by a sudden powerful voluntary muscular contraction, such as was made by an insane female patient in an asylum, who, to avoid the spoon by which she was being fed, violently jerked her head back and thus fractured the cervical spine.

The duration of life after fracture of the spine may be roughly stated to be in direct proportion to the distance between the injured part of the cord and the medulla. Much depends on the amount of displacement of the bones, if the cord is not compressed and has not been crushed, there is less immediate danger to life than when the converse is the case. A slight laceration of one of the intervertebral substances with displacement, so as to cause pressure on the cord without fracture of a vertebra is of more moment than a simple fracture without displacement. The cord is more likely to be damaged by an injury to the spine resulting from indirect than from direct violence. Fractures in the lumbar or dorso-lumbar regions, although accompanied by displacement, are not necessarily fatal, recoveries have taken place after fracture with displacement, even in the cervical region, though, as a rule, such injuries are speedily fatal. From the medico-legal standpoint it is of some importance to remember that fracture with dislocation of the upper cervical vertebræ is not necessarily *immediately* fatal. It is usually assumed that, on account of implication of the phrenics, injury to the cord at or above the level of the third cervical vertebra is suddenly fatal. Eve[1] records a case of fracture of the odontoid process with forward displacement of the atlas which compressed the cord, and yet the patient lived two hours and a half. Gurling[2] had a case in which death did not ensue for twenty-eight hours after fracture of the first three cervical vertebræ, although the cord was injured at the level of the third.

**Injuries of the Face**—Incised wounds of the face bleed freely, but, except when an artery such as the maxillary or lingual is divided, the hæmorrhage is not dangerous in a healthy individual. Blows with blunt weapons may fracture the nasal and malar bones, and cause "grievous bodily harm," so far as permanent disfigurement is concerned, but they are not dangerous to life, the possible occurrence of erysipelatous inflammation, however, is to be taken into account in giving an opinion as to the risk to life. Blows on the face may cause hæmorrhage into, or detachment of, the retina, in some cases atrophy of the optic nerve has followed a blow in the region of the eye, in both these conditions permanent blindness of the affected eye may result. The eyeball may be directly injured by the penetration of foreign bodies and opacity of the lens or capsule produced.

**Injuries of the Ear.**—Hæmatoma auris or, as it is also called, the insane or asylum ear, consists of an effusion of blood into the auricle caused by violence. As indicated by the latter designations it is frequently met with in insane people, especially in asylums, and is probably caused by blows on the ear delivered by impatient attendants, the left ear generally suffers, being the one convenient to a right-handed person. In the early stage the auricle is swollen and tense with the appearance of a collection of blood under the skin, this may subsequently become organised, and distort and shrivel the ear. Hæmatoma auris is not limited to the insane, it may result from various acts of local violence, such as occur in football scrimmages, in wrestling and pugilistic matches.

The tympanum may be ruptured in a variety of ways, of which one only, as occasionally giving rise to legal proceedings, need be particularised, it is when the injury is alleged to have been caused by a box on the ear. As a rule, it is the left tympanum that is ruptured, there will be no external bleeding, unless other injuries have been inflicted.

[1] *St. Barth Hosp Rep.*, 1887   [2] *Lond Hosp Rep*, vol. 1

## INJURIES OF THE NECK AND CHEST

**Injuries of the Neck.**—From the medico-legal stand-point injuries in this region may almost be paraphrased into "cut-throat," the greater number being of suicidal origin. When the close relation and superficial position of the numerous structures in the throat upon the integrity of which life depends is considered, and, further, the fact that most of the wounds in this region are self-inflicted with the object of causing death, it is strange how often that object is defeated by the more immediately vital structures escaping injury. A large proportion of suicidal wounds of the throat stop short just before the important vessels are reached, the structures actually divided being of secondary importance as regards the maintenance of life; it is to this fact that so many cases of cut-throat are seen in the wards of hospitals; if the large vessels are divided, death is almost certain to take place before surgical aid can be obtained.

Wounds in the neck are usually incised wounds or stabs, the former being most common. On account of the looseness of the skin, especially in old people, it is not unusual for more than one incision to result from a single stroke of the knife. Incised wounds of the throat vary to the fullest possible extent, from mere nicks through the skin to gashes that well nigh sever the head from the trunk. Punctured wounds of the neck are very dangerous from the risk of perforation of one or more of the large vessels. At the back of the neck a thin bladed knife may be passed between two of the vertebræ and produce death from injury to the cord with very little external mark.

**Injuries of the Chest.**—Sharp severe blows on the chest near the cardiac region, inflicted by objects of large area, may cause sudden death without leaving any trace of injury; blows with instruments of lesser dimensions are likely to cause fracture of one or more of the ribs. A common way of accidentally fracturing the ribs is by a fall against a projecting object, as the corner of a table; compression of the chest between two opposing forces is also a frequent cause. Very exceptionally, ribs are fractured by coughing, sneezing, and by sudden movement of the arms in endeavouring to preserve the equilibrium of the body when the feet slip whilst walking. **Stabs of the chest**, which do not penetrate the thoracic cavity, as a rule, are not dangerous, although there may be considerable bleeding from the mammary and thoracic arteries. Penetrating wounds are dangerous, but not necessarily fatal, unless a vital part has been injured. If the lungs are injured, emphysema, pneumo- or hæmo-thorax may ensue, as well as secondary results—pleurisy or pneumonia. The danger lies in the liability to profuse hæmorrhage, which may be speedily fatal, although severe penetrating wounds of the chest, followed by copious hæmorrhage, may be survived. A case came under the care of Hulke[1] in which the patient fell off some "high steps" whilst she had a picture covered with glass in her hands; the glass was shattered by the fall, and when the woman was lifted up a large fragment of it was found sticking in her back, the withdrawal of which was followed by much bleeding. The wound on the back, at the level of the tenth rib, and 3 inches to the right of the spine, was 3 inches long; the tenth rib was divided. The fragment of glass had transfixed the thorax, for in front there was another wound three-quarters of an inch long opposite the posterior wound, but higher, being in the seventh intercostal space. The woman recovered.

Laceration of the lungs, followed by hæmorrhage, may be produced by external violence without fracture of the ribs. A boy was run over by a cab, and died the following day; the ribs were uninjured, but the lung was extensively lacerated, and the pleural cavity was full of blood.

Penetrating wounds of the heart are usually fatal, but not necessarily immediately so; when death is not immediate, the duration of life varies from an hour up to many months, and, in exceptional cases, even years. West[2] records the case of a man who was stabbed with a knife, profuse hæmorrhage and great collapse following; he recovered and survived four years. After death, a linear cicatrix was found in the wall of the right ventricle; probably the cavity of the ventricle was not reached. The ventricles, especially the right, are more frequently wounded than the auricles, the left auricle being rarely penetrated. It might be supposed that immediately fatal hæmorrhage would more frequently follow penetrating wounds of the auricles than of the ventricles, on account of the thinner walls of the former. Statistics[3] however do not support this supposition. Coats[4] reports the case of a girl, aged ten years, who fell on to an iron railing, one of the spikes of which penetrated the right side of the chest where the fourth rib joins its cartilage; the patient survived nine days. Examination after death revealed an elongated wound in the pericardium three-quarters of an inch long and one-quarter of an inch broad, opposite to which was a wound through the wall of the right auricle. Slight superficial wounds of the heart may prove speedily fatal. In a case recorded by Thompson,[5] a man died within a few hours from the insertion of an ordinary pin, one and a-half inches long, through the space between the fifth and

---

[1] *The Lancet*, 1888.   [2] *St Thomas's Hosp. Rep*, vol. 1, N S
[3] See tables in Holmes & Hulke's *System of Surgery*, third edition, vol. 1.
[4] *Glasgow Med Journ*, 1891.
[5] *Trans. of the Royal Acad Med., Ireland*, 1888.

sixth ribs in the area of the cardiac impulse, the anterior wall of the left ventricle was wounded, but its cavity was not penetrated, the pericardium contained seventeen and a half ounces of blood.

It is important to remember that those who have sustained wounds of the heart may perform certain actions, although the injuries are speedily fatal; the following are instances selected from a number of cases of wounds of the heart collected by Fischer[1]—One individual, after being thus wounded, ran 450 paces; another mounted several steps; a third walked a mile and a-half, and a fourth (in whom the right ventricle, coronary artery, lung, diaphragm, liver, stomach, spleen, and colon were wounded with a sabre) made ten steps before he fell.

Blows on, or contusion of, the chest may be followed by myocarditis, which, by softening of the cardiac musculature, may lead to rupture many days or weeks after the receipt of the injury; in such cases, there will probably be no external signs of injury after death. In relation to immediate rupture of the heart or of the commencement of the aorta after a blow delivered by the fist on the chest, it is to be remembered that atheromatous ulceration, or the presence of a diminutive aneurismal dilatation, may predispose to spontaneous rupture. A man[2] was admitted under my care in the Salford Royal Hospital in 1892, who, whilst stooping, suddenly felt faint, and subsequently was profoundly collapsed. He rallied, and three days after, whilst in bed, he was again attacked in the same way; he rallied once more, but six days after the second attack he was found dead in bed. At the necropsy the pericardium was seen to contain a large amount of fresh blood, and there were signs of recent pericarditis with much organised fibrin. A small rupture had taken place at the commencement of the aorta, through the base of an ulcer; microscopical examination showed a gradual thinning of the coats down to the aperture, probably due to necrosis-ulceration from thrombosis. The weak spot gave way at the moment the patient was first attacked; temporary occlusion, with subsequent renewal of the hæmorrhage, occurred on two occasions, the last being speedily fatal. The patient was a vigorous healthy-looking man, and had followed a laborious employment up to the moment he was first attacked; had the rupture taken place after a push or slight blow of the fist, it might have been misinterpreted as proof of extreme violence. Rouse[3] records a somewhat similar case of a man, aged fifty-two, who, whilst playing football, suddenly fell down in a sort of faint; he recovered and continued to play, but after the game was over he again became faint and collapsed. He revived and lived for a week, when he had another attack and died in less than

[1] Langenbeck's *Archiv*, ix.   [2] *Trans Path. Soc, Manchester*, 1892
[3] *The Lancet*, 1892.

five minutes. At the necropsy a rupture was found in the left ventricle, half an inch in diameter, the pericardium containing twelve ounces of blood; fatty degeneration of the heart and of most of the other organs was present.

## INJURIES OF THE ABDOMEN

Death may suddenly result from a blow delivered by a blunt weapon on the pit of the stomach; in such cases it is probable that reflex paralysis of the heart is the cause of death. Maschka[1] records two such cases—in one, a boy was struck with the fist over the stomach; in the other, a strong man was struck over the same region with the flat part of a shovel, both died at once, and the result of the necropsy in each case was negative. Beach[2] records the case of an intoxicated man who was arrested in the street by the police; he resisted so violently that one of the officers struck him a blow with his "club" in the epigastric region, when he suddenly became quiet and powerless, and on arrival at their destination he was found to be dead; not the least trace of injury could be discovered, neither externally nor internally.

Rupture of the abdominal viscera may result from violence without any external sign of injury. The stomach is rarely ruptured; if it is the pyloric end and greater curvature generally suffer. The intestines are not unfrequently ruptured by external violence; according to Weil, the commencement of the jejunum and then the ileum most frequently suffer. Such accidents, probably, are invariably fatal, although the dangerous symptoms may not develop for some time. Even when the blow is inflicted with a formidable object, such as a horse's hoof, there may be no external marks. Hunter[3] saw a boy who had been fatally kicked in the abdomen by a horse; there were no ecchymoses nor signs of injury externally, but the jejunum was bruised and ruptured. After sustaining rupture of the bowel the injured person may walk a considerable distance.

The liver is frequently ruptured by heavy pressure, such as a wheel transmits from a loaded vehicle; the rotating movement of the wheel favours the absence of signs of external injury, and the liver may thus undergo extensive rupture without the skin of the abdomen being ruffled or discoloured; rupture from a blow or kick may occur without external bruising. Death usually results, and it may do so speedily, from hæmorrhage into the abdomen, but in spite of copious internal hæmor-

---

[1] *Vierteljahrsschr. f. ger. Med.*, xxx. *Wiener allg. med. Zeitung*, 1864.
[2] *Medical News*, 1882.
[3] *The Lancet*, 1885.

rhage, the patient sometimes lives several days; after slight ruptures recovery may take place. A ruptured liver does not necessarily prevent movements being made by the patient after receipt of the injury.

Rupture of the diaphragm is not common apart from other and severe injuries to the abdominal viscera. In itself it is not likely to be followed by immediate death, but will probably lead to serious results from protrusion of the stomach or bowels into the thoracic cavity. Laceration of the diaphragm usually occurs in consequence of falls from a height or from compression of the trunk by a cart wheel passing over it; it is generally met with on the left side.

Rupture of the spleen is usually fatal. What has been said about the liver applies equally to the spleen.

Extensive rupture of the kidneys is always fatal; slighter rupture may be recovered from. Much bruising of the organs without rupture is likely to be followed by suppuration, which may cause death at a more or less remote period from the receipt of the injury.

Rupture of the bladder is a subject of special importance to the medical jurist, because, unlike some of the previously described injuries, it may be caused by a blow of the fist or a kick that would be inadequate to reach less accessible organs. It is an accident likely to occur to a drunken man, who, on account of the amount of liquor drank and its benumbing effect on the nerve-centres, often goes about with a full bladder; in this condition a fall down stairs may be sufficient to cause rupture. The injury is almost invariably fatal when the intra-peritoneal portion of the bladder is ruptured, and but few recoveries take place when the extravasation of urine is outside the peritoneum. Bartels[1] states that 93 out of 94 cases of intra-peritoneal rupture died, and 26 out of 63 in which the mischief was extra-peritoneal. Extensive rupture of the bladder is not necessarily prohibitive of locomotion, the severity of the injury being in some instances concealed for a time. Bartsch[2] relates a case in which a drunken man fell through a window twelve feet on to hard ground. He was found lying on his side and began to joke, making no complaints of being hurt; he was placed in an out-house, where he lay for an hour, when he got up, went into the house and walked upstairs to bed. He arose the following morning, after having slept well, and took a walk of nearly a mile; he then had a rigor and returned to bed, after which he gradually became worse and died sixty-three hours after the fall. On section no external injury was seen, but the peritoneum contained about 52 ounces of urine, and there was a tear in the superior and posterior wall of the bladder, $2\frac{1}{3}$ inches in length, which went cleanly through the peritoneal coat. Eight hours elapsed

[1] Langenbeck's *Archiv.*, Bd. 22.  [2] *Vierteljahrsschr f. ger. Med.*, 1889.

before indications of the severity of the lesion manifested themselves, if, in the meantime, this man had quarrelled with anyone, and had in consequence received a blow, his antagonist might easily have been made responsible for his death.

A defence likely to be made in cases of rupture of the bladder from alleged criminal violence is that the organ ruptured spontaneously. Spontaneous rupture of the bladder is of exceptional occurrence, even in those cases where a diseased condition of the viscus or of the urethra exists as a causal factor, which is capable of being recognised as such after death, the conditions alluded to are ulceration of the bladder-wall and organic stricture of the urethra. Paralysis of the bladder might also lead to spontaneous rupture; in such a case, the previous history of the patient would help to explain its occurrence. Much is usually made by the defence as to absence of signs of external injury which, it is urged, proves that the organ ruptured from natural causes. This is fallacious, a full bladder—and the organ is always in this condition when ruptured by a blow which does not fracture the pelvis—is, of all the abdominal organs, the most likely to be ruptured from external violence without there being any outward signs of it.

Exceptional as is spontaneous rupture induced by previous pathological changes a still rarer event has been recorded—spontaneous rupture without any explainable cause. M'Ewen[1] relates the case of a young man, aged nineteen, habituated to excessive indulgence in alcohol, who on one occasion, whilst nearly insensible from this cause, was taken to a common lodging-house and put to bed. He remained in bed all the next day; on the evening of the following day he was drowsy and stupid and complained of pains in the abdomen; he died on the third day. After death the abdomen, free from external marks of violence, was found to contain a large quantity of straw-coloured fluid, of which the bladder also contained a small amount. At the junction of the upper and middle thirds posteriorly an aperture existed in the bladder which would admit the tip of the little finger. There were no indications of disease nor of ulceration nor gangrene, nor was there any peritonitis, the urethra was healthy and free from stricture or obstruction—a No 10 sound found its way into the bladder by its own weight. Brown[2] records another case of spontaneous rupture of the bladder without the presence of a stricture, the urethra allowing a No 10 catheter to pass. After death, the posterior part of the bladder was found coated with soft lymph, and about an inch below the reflection of the peritoneum, slightly to the right, was an aperture which admitted the forefinger

[1] *The Lancet*, 1873.  [2] *The Lancet*, 1886.

with difficulty; the margins were rough from the presence of recent inflammatory lymph; there was no evidence of ulceration nor of pre-existing disease. Such cases are of extreme rarity, only one or two being recorded. It is very difficult to understand the mode of their occurrence; the two alternative conditions usually assumed are paralysis of the bladder of functional origin and persistent spasmodic stricture of the urethra.

Incised and lacerated wounds of the abdomen are not in themselves dangerous when the peritoneum and viscera escape injury; the possible occurrence of peritonitis or of suppuration among the muscles and fasciæ must be taken into account when forming a prognosis. Punctured wounds are necessarily dangerous if they penetrate the abdominal cavity, both from the chance of protrusion of the viscera through the wound, and, to a still greater extent, from the possibility of the viscera themselves being wounded. Small punctures of the intestines are not necessarily fatal, the danger being proportional to the risk of their contents escaping into the peritoneal cavity; wounds of the small intestines are more dangerous than those affecting the large intestines. Incised or punctured wounds of the solid viscera are dangerous in proportion to the hæmorrhage they occasion.

Injuries of the External Genitals.—Injuries to the male organs are not usually dangerous to life, although the bleeding is sometimes considerable. Rupture of the urethra in the perineum leads to extravasation of urine into the connective tissue of the pelvis, which may be fatal unless surgical aid is promptly afforded.

Injuries to the Female Organs.—Incised or lacerated wounds of the vulva and vagina often give rise to dangerous hæmorrhage; apart from parturition, they usually result from accident. Birkett[1] relates two such cases. A lady going into a dark room to micturate sat down on a water-ewer, the handle of which was broken off leaving a sharp and jagged portion projecting about an inch; this produced a lacerated wound of the vagina, in the course of which the internal pudic artery was divided; death from hæmorrhage took place in about an hour after the infliction of the injury. In another case, a woman was knocked down by a man and died in a short time from hæmorrhage; the blood came from the vagina, in the wall of which was a wound extending towards the internal pudic artery. At first it was thought that the woman had been stabbed with a knife, but it turned out that she had fallen on and broken a spittoon, a sharp-pointed fragment of which caused the injury. In cases of criminal assault foreign bodies, such as pieces of stone or wood, are not unfrequently passed into the vagina, which may cause serious

[1] Holmes & Hulk, *A System of Surgery.*

bruising and rents of the vaginal walls. Violent sexual intercourse with young girls and sometimes with adult women may rupture the vagina, and occasion profuse and even fatal bleeding.

The unimpregnated uterus is not frequently injured unless it shares in a general injury inflicted on the pelvic organs; the **gravid** organ from its prominent position is much more frequently wounded. Penetrating wounds of the gravid uterus, whether caused by stabs through the abdominal walls, or by punctures inflicted by passing pointed instruments up the vagina in the attempt to procure abortion, are dangerous from the possible supervention of haemorrhage, peritonitis, and septicaemia. Kicks delivered against the abdomen of a woman advanced in pregnancy may produce miscarriage or, by separation of the placenta, may give rise to serious haemorrhage; violence of this kind may be followed by localised suppuration in the uterine wall or by the formation of clots in the sinuses, which may cause death from embolism of the pulmonary artery. The walls of the gravid uterus may be ruptured by blows, by pressure of the abdomen against hard projections, and by falls, and the foetus may escape through the rent into the abdominal cavity. Such accidents are usually fatal, though in some cases operative interference, and in others natural processes, have relieved the woman of the displaced foetus, her life being spared. Rupture of the uterus or vagina may take place during parturition, either in the course of natural labour, or during the performance of version or of extraction with the forceps. The medico-legal questions that arise relate to the reasonable amount of skill brought to bear in the treatment of the case.—On the one hand, was artificial delivery performed with a reasonable amount of care and skill, and on the other—the uterus rupturing in the course of natural labour—ought artificial assistance to have been resorted to? Such questions are usually referred to obstetrical experts.

## FRACTURES OF BONES.

Simple fractures are not dangerous to life except in certain regions, as the skull and spinal column; from the medico-legal standpoint, the question is rather one of "grievous bodily injury." The defence usually urged in criminal cases is either that the fracture resulted from accident or, if acknowledged to have been directly caused, that the injured bone was predisposed to fracture in consequence of disease or of some inherent abnormal condition.

Apart from diseases affecting the bones which, from their nature, are sufficiently obvious, such as cancerous and sarcomatous growths, rickets, and mollities ossium, there are other general diseases and conditions which tend to render the bones more fragile than ordinary. It is well known that trophic changes occur in the course of certain diseases of the nervous system, amongst the structures liable to participate in these changes are the bones. Chemical analysis shows that the proportion of organic to inorganic matter is inverted as compared with healthy bone, the inorganic matter from diminution of the phosphates, is reduced to less than half, and the organic matter, in consequence of a large excess of fat, is doubled. When these alterations in the composition of the bones are far advanced, spontaneous fracture of the long bones is not uncommon, when not so far advanced, a much less violent blow will fracture a limb than would do so in health. The diseases of the central nervous system, with which these trophic changes in the bones are chiefly associated, are locomotor ataxy and some forms of mental disease, especially general paralysis.

In some cases trophic changes in the bones appear to take place without the presence of any recognisable disease. Greenwood[1] states that a policeman taking part in a contest of throwing a cricket ball at some sports felt his arm snap in the act of throwing, on examination complete fracture of the humerus was found to have taken place at the lower third. The bones become brittle in old age from excess of inorganic constituents, and in young children they are liable to "green-stick" fracture from the converse condition. Ribs are occasionally fractured by coughing or sneezing. A curious case of apparently delayed completion of a fracture of the rib is related by Skyrme[2]. A man in getting out of an omnibus swung round and struck his right side against a projection, he felt some pain and tenderness, but went about as usual. Six days after, whilst sneezing, he felt something snap in his side, which was followed by severe pain, greatly increased by deep respiration, the tenth rib was found to be fractured at the junction of the bony and cartilaginous portions.

The medical witness may be called upon to state his opinion as to whether certain injuries to bones were the result of direct violence or not. A drunken man after quarrelling with another man is found to have sustained fracture of several ribs and dies from pneumonia; his adversary is accused of having caused the injuries by blows, but denies that he struck the deceased, stating that he simply pushed him away, and that in his drunken condition he fell helplessly to the ground. Such a question is to be decided on general grounds, the amount and character of external bruising, the position of the fracture, the number of ribs broken, whether fracture has occurred on both sides of the chest, together with other indications of violence more

[1] *Brit Med Journ*, 1880.  [2] *Ibid*, 1891.

than can be accounted for by the simple act of pushing a man away. A similar question arises from time to time in regard to asylums and prisons; an attendant or a warder is accused of having caused the death of an inmate or a prisoner by violence. The defence usually is that the injuries (often fracture of the ribs) were caused by a fall, or, in the case of a prisoner recently taken into custody, that they existed at the time of his arrest. With regard to the latter point it is possible for a man to go about with fractured rib or ribs without knowing that he has received any such injury. In the case of the insane the possibility of trophic changes in the bones must be borne in mind.

The length of time the fracture has existed may be of importance as regards determining the question of criminal violence or of accident; if it is clear that the fracture existed before the alleged violence was inflicted, the fact is, of course, greatly in favour of the accused. The processes which occur in the repair of fractured bones are well known, but their time-values are not capable of exact estimation. Apart from physiological variations, the age and the state of health of the injured person materially influence the rate of repair; the degree of injury sustained by the fractured ends and the closeness or otherwise of their apposition have also to be taken into consideration. Within the first week after the occurrence of the fracture there will probably be nothing to be seen on post-mortem examination beyond effused blood, with more or less tearing or bruising of the contiguous soft structures; shortly after, indications of repair begin to manifest themselves. In simple fractures in which the ends of the bone have been kept in apposition from the first, but little, if any, "provisional callus" is thrown out; it is mostly found in fractures of the ribs or of the clavicle—that is, in bones in which absolute rest cannot be attained. After fourteen or sixteen days, the blood at first extravasated will have disappeared or nearly so; the periosteum at the fractured ends will be very vascular, and beneath it and between the ends of the bone will be a number of cells proliferated from the osteoblasts amongst which calcification will be in progress. Under the most favourable conditions complete ossification does not take place, as a rule, in less than two months.

Evidence of previous fracture is usually not difficult to obtain when the examination is made after death. If on external examination the bone does not yield sufficiently clear indications, a longitudinal section of it will clear up all doubts. In the living an old fracture may easily escape detection. If immediately after receipt of the injury perfect approximation of the broken ends of the bone was secured and maintained until complete ossification took place, especially if the part is deeply surrounded with soft structures, it will be quite impossible to recognise a remote fracture; if the fracture is recent it will be easier of recognition. In exposed situations, such as the front of the tibia, the difficulty is lessened.

The distinction between fractures produced in the living and in the dead subject is well-marked, unless the fracture is produced immediately after death; if it takes place six or eight hours after death, there will be no blood effused round the ends of the bone, unless a large vein has been divided, and, even then, the appearance will be distinct from that caused by extravasation from a number of vessels during life. A fracture caused immediately after death—within a few minutes—may present an appearance indistinguishable from one inflicted during life.

## WOUNDS PRODUCED BY FIREARMS.

Wounds produced by firearms differ in appearance in accordance with the size and kind of projectile, the velocity with which it is endowed at the moment it impinges, the distance of the firearm from the body, and the angle at which it is presented.

Large bullets, other conditions being equal, produce more extensive wounds than those of lesser size. The old-fashioned spherical bullet is more apt to be deflected in its course than the modern cylindrical bullet with conical front; the wedge-like properties and higher velocity of the latter missile enable it to make its way through obstacles which would turn a spherical bullet to one side. A conoidal bullet endowed with high velocity causes infinitely greater damage than a spherical bullet, not only because it can penetrate a mass of tissues from side to side that would arrest a spherical bullet half way, but also because its crushing action on the soft tissues and its power of splintering the bones are vastly greater.

When a small conoidal bullet endowed with high velocity passes through some of the soft structures of the body without striking any bone, the difference presented by entrance and exit wounds is not great; under ordinary circumstances, however, the difference is considerable. A larger bullet traversing the body with less velocity produces a much more extensive aperture of exit than of entrance. If the weapon is fired point-blank the entrance-wound will be about the size of the bullet, and will have a more or less circular outline with torn edges which may form angular flaps; the margins will be slightly inverted and ecchymosed, except in parts where there is much subcutaneous fat, when they will probably be everted. If death is immediate, the surrounding skin may be pallid. The exit-wound will be less regular in outline and larger, with everted edges showing the subcutaneous fat. If the weapon is presented at an oblique angle to the body the entrance-wound will not present a circular outline, it will be more elliptical, the skin being ploughed up to one side. A bullet projected from a distance, if not too far spent to penetrate, will cause a larger and more lacerated entrance-wound than if it arrived with greater velocity. Only a limited value can be assigned to this as an indication of the distance from the body at which the weapon was fired; much depends on the kind of weapon, and on the amount and the kinetic energy of the explosive used. When a firearm is discharged into the body at a distance of a few inches only, the entrance-wound, in addition to the appearances already described, will be blackened and, possibly, scorched. The wound is diffusely blackened from the smoke of the explosion, and it is also tattooed by undeflagrated grains of powder being driven into it. The flame from the mouth of the firearm may not only scorch the skin, it may also set fire to the clothing in proximity of the wound. If the muzzle of the firearm is in actual contact with the surface of the body, the entrance-wound will be freely lacerated and ecchymosed in addition to being burnt.

If a gun loaded with small shot is fired into the body when close to it, a somewhat circular aperture, larger than a bullet wound and rather more irregular and contused at the edges, will be produced. There is nothing definite about the exit-wound, because the whole of the original charge scarcely ever leaves the body; if it does, the exit-wound will be larger and still more lacerated than that caused by a bullet, and will, of course, be proportionally larger than its own entrance-wound. Usually the pellets are severally deflected within the body and do not traverse it en masse, the consequence being that the exit-wound may be less than the entrance-wound; very often there is no exit-wound at all. If a gun loaded with shot is fired at the body from a short distance, the surface will be more or less peppered by the pellets, with possibly the production of an irregular wound caused by some which have not spread so widely; at a greater distance, there will be isolated pellet wounds only. It is impossible to assign with accuracy the respective distances at which these various results are produced. Some guns carry much closer than others; the quality of the powder also exercises a considerable influence, and probably the manner of loading.

When both entrance- and exit-wounds are present, a line drawn between them and prolonged on the side of the entrance-wound will enable some idea to be formed as to the situation of the weapon when fired. The information thus obtained is less reliable if the wound has been produced by a spherical bullet than with a conoidal projectile, because of the greater liability of the former to deflection. When the position of the deceased at the moment the weapon was fired is known, or can be inferred, the spot from whence it was fired may be approximately ascertained. A man has been shot dead when writing at a table on to which the upper part of the body fell forwards; in such a case it is not difficult to allot the position from whence the weapon was fired. If the projectile has traversed the body the entrance- and exit-wounds must be differentiated. When there is but one wound, the course taken by the projectile within the body may afford a clue as to the relative position of the firearm and the deceased, possible deflection of the bullet being taken into account.

Serious wounds may be produced by firearms charged with powder only, especially if the substance used as wadding is of a dense nature. If the wadding penetrates the skin it proves that the weapon was discharged within a few feet of the body.

When the bullet remains within the body it is not to be assumed that it was fired from a distance, its momentum being partly spent. A rifle bullet under ordinary conditions would traverse any part of the body if discharged into it at short range; but it is not so with all revolvers. A long-barrelled rifled-revolver would probably send a bullet through the body if fired at short range, but small pocket revolvers for the most part leave the projectile within the body; when such a weapon is fired at the head, in close proximity to it, the bullet remains within the cranium or is embedded in some part of the skull.

In estimating the risk to life from wounds produced by firearms it is to be remembered that after the immediate results of the injury are recovered from, secondary hæmorrhage and a variety of inflammatory processes of a kind dangerous to life may set in.

Is has been asserted that recognition of an assailant in the dark by the light given off from a firearm discharged near to the person assaulted is not possible. Much depends on the relative position of the parties; if the assailant is well within the field of vision of the person at whom he fires, recognition is quite possible; if at the extreme limit, it is doubtful.

## WOUNDS IN THEIR CAUSAL RELATION.

The duty of the medical witness does not end when he has arrived at a conclusion as to the mode of death. In many cases when a dead body is found without any history—death being due to wounding—

the question is asked, were the wounds caused by accidental, homicidal, or suicidal violence?

This important and, in some instances, formidable question—formidable on account of the obscurity of the indications from which an answer is to be obtained—involves the methodical consideration of a number of criteria which universal experience has formulated as aids to diagnosis, and, what is of no less moment, a keen observation of the smallest details which are special to each case. A wound has to be considered in relation to its position, its nature — whether incised, contused, &c.—its direction, and its extent. If the body is examined in the position, and at the place in which it was found, circumstances of external relation are to be taken into account—as footmarks, blood-stains, indications of a struggle having taken place, the presence of a weapon in the hand or near the body of the deceased, a change in the position of the body after death, with other matters that present themselves to an observant eye. A minute investigation embracing every perceptible detail should be made—note-book in hand—before anything is disturbed; if this precaution is not taken, the unravelling of some important particular may be enhanced in difficulty or even rendered altogether impossible.

## THE POSITION OF THE WOUND

Almost any part of the body may be wounded by a second person; certain parts are inaccessible to the suicide, and certain others are preferentially selected by him. These axioms, for the most part hold good, but they are not without exceptions. The front and more exposed parts of the body are usually selected by the suicide; the throat and chest for incised wounds and stabs; and the temples, mouth, and cardiac region, when firearms are resorted to. The position of suicidal wounds varies in relative frequency in different countries; in Great Britain, one of the commonest modes of committing suicide is by an incised wound of the throat; on the continent, cut-throats in comparison with other suicidal wounds, are not nearly so numerous. Stabs in the throat are suspicious of homicide, but instances are not wanting in which suicides have inflicted upon themselves wounds of this description. Incised wounds of the throat, apart from any other injuries, point to either suicide or homicide, and away from accident. Stabs in the back are more likely to be homicidal than suicidal, but, with the exception of the area covered by the scapulæ and the space between them, a man might stab himself in the back were he so disposed. The ordinary suicide selects an ordinary position on which he inflicts wounds for the purpose of putting an end to his life, with lunatics the case is different; they are just as likely to put an end to themselves in some unheard of way, as they are to adopt one of the more usual methods. Little[1] reports the case of a woman, aged thirty-six, recently discharged from an asylum, who, with a blunt table knife, made a wound in the back of her neck which half severed the head from the trunk; all the tissues were divided as far as the spinal canal, which was opened, the cord just escaping injury; she died on the sixth day after inflicting the wound. In another case,[2] a man was found standing with a large gash in his abdomen, from which he was pulling out his intestines; a coil of the ileum, almost severed, was outside the abdomen; he lived a few hours. It is interesting to note that a well-marked intussusception of the ileum of several days' standing was present.

Contused wounds on the head, when not due to accident, are indicative of homicide, but an insane person may inflict such wounds on himself. Smith[3] relates the case of a man who placed himself before a looking-glass, and struck repeated blows on the top of his head with a hammer weighing nearly 3 pounds. An area 3 inches in diameter was divested of scalp, and a fracture of the skull 2 inches in diameter, depressed ⅞ inch, was produced, the bones being splintered around. Staples[4] gives an extraordinary instance of self-inflicted injuries to the head which came under his notice, and supplements it with thirteen others by various observers. A man drove into his head two stone-chisels, each 8¼ inches long, and ⅜ inch in diameter, using for the purpose a wooden mallet weighing 2¾ pounds. One of the chisels was driven through the head from right to left, entering in the right temporal region, and emerging on the left nearly in a direct line, the point projecting 1½ inch, the head of the chisel being close down to the scalp. The other chisel was driven into the centre of the forehead, penetrating at least ½ inch into the frontal lobe. After inflicting the injuries, the man, with the chisels in his head, approached a glazed door, through which he was seen by two persons; he stooped and tried to unlock the door, but did not succeed in doing so. When the door was broken open, he walked a distance of 40 feet with but little aid, and was able to talk. The chisels were withdrawn with considerable difficulty, and he died about five hours afterwards. There is much to be learnt from these cases as regards the immediate effects of severe injuries to the head. In both, repeated blows were struck without producing unconsciousness, and in the second case the patient was not only conscious, but he could talk and walk in spite of the desperate nature of the injuries inflicted

[1] *The Lancet*, 1889.
[2] *London Med. Recorder*, 1890.
[3] *Med. Times and Gaz.*, 1878.
[4] *Journ. Am. Med. Assoc.*, 1887.

on the brain. Such instances are to be remembered by the medical witness when asked as to the possibility of similar wounds being self-inflicted, and also as to the possibility of individuals retaining consciousness and power of locomotion and speech after the receipt of severe injuries to the head, whether self-inflicted or not.

**Suicidal** wounds from blows on the head are usually inflicted within a limited area and have more or less the same direction. They are generally on the top or front of the head, being the parts most accessible. The presence of other wounds on the body may be significant—Are they all compatible with suicidal causation, or do they rather resemble homicidal wounds? Indications of resistance, especially on the hands and arms, should be looked for. **Homicidal** head-wounds are often on or towards the occiput, the victim being attacked from behind. If the victim is not rendered insensible by the first blow, he will involuntarily put up his hands to protect his head, and, consequently, the backs of the fingers will probably be bruised. **Accidental** wounds on the head are usually on the vertex when produced by falling head downwards, and partake of the nature of an injury caused by a single blow, which, however, if the body falls from a great height, may be of sufficient force as to smash the vault of the cranium into fragments. Accidental wounds resulting from stones and like objects being projected through the air and striking the head may, of course, be found on any part of it.

Wounds of the **male genital organs**, if not accidental, are for the most part suicidal. Ablation of the penis or of the testicles, or even of both, scrotum included, is not an uncommon act on the part of men labouring under sexual monomania, or under some form of insanity which is dominated by the idea that the sexual organs or functions are the cause of their misery. Occasionally, wounds of the male genital organs are criminally inflicted out of revenge. Wounds of the **female external genitals** are chiefly accidental, or are due to criminal violence.

Incised or punctured wounds of the limbs may result from criminal violence or from accident; in the former case, they are not unfrequently brought about by attempts at self-protection. Occasionally, suicides make incisions into the arms and legs, with the object of dividing blood vessels so as to cause death from hæmorrhage.

## THE NATURE OF THE WOUND.

**Contused** wounds are usually either accidental or homicidal; they are rarely of suicidal origin. **Incised** and **punctured** wounds may be homicidal, suicidal, or accidental, the probability in each case being governed by their position and extent. So far as position goes, the same may be said of wounds produced by firearms.

Unusual methods of causing death sometimes betray their homicidal or suicidal origin, and at others, in the absence of circumstantial evidence, or of that of an eye witness, they leave the matter in doubt. Of the former class are those exceptional cases in which a man prepares an elaborate apparatus for self-destruction. For example, a man constructed a guillotine in such a way, that a suspended axe-blade was liberated after a certain amount of water had run out of a can, in the bottom of which was a hole—the loss of weight caused by the water flowing from the can eventually released a detent by which the axe-blade was held up. An open cavity was prepared, in which a large quantity of ether was exposed immediately under the nose of the suicide. The axe fell in due time and decapitated the constructor of the machine, probably after he had been narcotised, or, possibly, was dead from inhalation of the ether vapour.[1] In a case reported by Leadman,[2] a man committed suicide by placing a dynamite cartridge in his mouth, lighting the fuse and then waiting the explosion. The soft palate and tongue were torn and mutilated, the teeth broken off, the superior maxillary bones separated and fractured, and the inferior maxilla was broken into about twenty pieces. Notwithstanding all this, the skin of the lips and cheeks was intact; the man lived two hours. Other similar cases have occurred. Such a mode of death could only result from suicide or accident, and much more probably the former.

As an instance of death caused in an unusual way, which would give rise to suspicion of homicide in the absence of eye-witnesses, the following, recorded by Stephens,[3] is a striking example:—A man suffering from melancholia (who not long before had been discharged from an asylum), whilst at work forging nails, was seen with a red-hot iron rod, about two feet in length, the cool end of which was against the wall, and the heated end against his belly. One of his fellow workmen gave him a push and made him drop the iron; he said that he should be all right if he was allowed to go on with his work, and he was permitted to do so. Not long after he made the iron white-hot, and succeeded in thrusting it four or five inches into the abdomen; he died on the following day.

## THE DIRECTION AND EXTENT OF THE WOUND.

Most men and women are right-handed, and, consequently, incised and punctured wounds suicidally inflicted, usually take more or less a

---
[1] *Boston Med. and Surg. Journ.*, 1880.  [2] *Brit. Med. Journ.*, 1881.
[3] *Bristol Med. Chir. Journ.*, 1888.

definite direction, due to the weapon being wielded with the right hand. Apart from exceptions which obviously occur in the case of left-handed persons the indications afforded by the direction of a wound are not to be regarded as absolutely distinctive. It is quite true that the direction of a wound often enables a correct opinion to be formed as to its suicidal or homicidal origin, but should the direction not agree with that which is held to be characteristic of suicidal wounds, suicide is not, therefore, to be excluded from consideration, unless the position and direction are such as to make it impossible for the wound to have been self-inflicted. Experience teaches the necessity of great caution in applying general rules to special cases; in all doubtful cases allowance must be made for exceptional occurrences.

Incised wounds of the throat self-inflicted by right-handed persons usually run from left to right in an oblique direction, the beginning of the cut being at a higher level than its termination. In producing them the blade of the razor or knife is applied to the left side of the throat above the thyroid cartilage and is drawn obliquely downwards across to the right. Such is the rule, but it has its exceptions. In a case recorded by Mackenzie,[1] a man cut his throat with a razor; the wound was on the right side of the throat, and extended from about the angle of the jaw to nearly the middle line of the neck on a level with the hyoid bone, the direction being from right to left. At its commencement the incision was clean, at its termination it was hacked and irregular. The patient was right-handed, and afterwards explained that he held the razor (which was blunt) in the right hand, and cut from behind forwards.

Suicidal cut-throat wounds are sometimes made below the thyroid cartilage; such wounds are usually short in length and horizontal in direction, occupying the middle of the throat, between the sterno-mastoids, which frequently escape injury. At other times a clean sweep is made through the whole of the soft structures of the anterior segment of the neck. In suicidal cut-throat wounds the skin is usually the last structure divided—the wound gradually becoming shallower as it reaches its termination. In homicidal wounds of the throat the end of the wound is often under cut—the skin not being divided as far as the underlying tissues are. Two statements are frequently accepted in relation to extensive wounds of the throat. One is, that after the carotid artery or jugular vein is wounded the person so injured is at once deprived of the power of movement and dies immediately; the other is, that in the case of suicides the incision is never deep enough to implicate the bodies of the vertebræ.

[1] *Brit Med Journ*, 1887.

Both these statements are shown to be incorrect by a case which happened in the Salford Royal Hospital in 1883. A man was admitted for fractured femur and was placed in the hoist for the purpose of being transferred to the ward. A nurse in an upper story, who happened to look down into the hoist as it ascended, saw the man take a pocket-knife out of his pocket and apply the blade to his throat. She gave the alarm, the hoist was stopped and a house-surgeon and a porter seized the man to prevent him doing himself further mischief. He had made a large wound, and, notwithstanding all efforts to restrain him, he succeeded in getting his fingers into it and tearing it further open, he died in a few minutes. I examined the body immediately after death, and found the right carotid artery and jugular vein divided and the body of one of the vertebræ distinctly notched by the blade of the knife. The fractured femur for which the patient was admitted was due to a fall from a height, which, at the time, was supposed to be accidental, it really resulted from an attempt at suicide, and having failed the man took the earliest opportunity of effecting his purpose in another way. It is not unlikely that the cries of the nurse increased his desperation and thus caused him to use unwonted force; hence the injury to the vertebra.

The extent of the injuries that a suicide may inflict on his throat is exemplified by another case which was admitted into the Salford Royal Hospital, reported by Lord[1]. A man, fifty-eight years old, was brought to the accident room with a large open wound in the throat; he died five minutes after admission, having survived the injury rather more than an hour. Shortly after, his son appeared with something in his hand which he said his father had cut out of his own throat; this turned out to be the entire larynx—the thyroid and cricoid cartilages, together with the first and part of the second ring of the trachea. The whole had been cleanly excised without injuring the large vessels of the neck. Harrison[2] relates a similar case of a woman, aged forty-one, who excised her own larynx, cricoid cartilage, and five rings of the trachea without wounding the carotids; death quickly followed. An instance of survival for a time from numerous and severe self-inflicted injuries to the neck and chest is afforded by a case admitted into Middlesex Hospital under Hulke[3]. A man committed suicide by attempting to cut off his head from behind with a shoemaker's knife; as this failed he stabbed himself repeatedly in the chest and finally cut his throat. Crossing the nape of the neck were three deep, jagged, incised wounds. A jagged incised wound crossed the front of the throat from the posterior border of the left

[1] *Trans Path. Soc. Manchester*, 1892.  [2] *Brit. Med. Journ.*, 1883.
[3] *The Lancet*, 1880.

sterno-mastoid to the middle of the right sterno-mastoid, severing the depressors of the hyoid bone and cutting out a portion of the thyroid cartilage. On the front of the left side of the chest were four stabs, two of which penetrated the pleural sacs. The man survived a week.

Homicidal incised wounds of the throat, when inflicted by a right-handed man facing his victim, are from right to left, and are usually more horizontal than suicidal throat wounds. If the assailant stands behind the victim the wound may closely resemble one of suicidal origin, the position and movement of the hand and arm being very like that of a person who inflicts a wound on his own throat. In such a case the incision will be from left to right, and will probably sever the whole of the soft structures down to the vertebræ, one of which may be nicked. Very deep and extensive division of the soft structures in front of the throat, especially when associated with nicking of a vertebra, is regarded as indicative of homicide. The indication, for the most part, holds good; but, as already stated, a like condition may exceptionally be met with in suicidal cut-throats.

Suicidal stabs of the chest are usually on the left side in the case of right-handed men, and they take a downward and inward direction. If there is more than one such wound, all will generally be found within a circumscribed area. Multiple stab wounds of the chest of homicidal causation are usually distributed over a wider area, and are more horizontal in direction. They may be from below upwards, which is rarely the case in suicidal stabs. The occurrence of several stab-wounds on the front of the chest, more than one of which may be sufficient to cause speedy death, does not necessarily contra-indicate suicide. An instructive case of this kind is related by Newnham.[1] A man was found dead with the right hand clenched tightly and a small knife lying in front of him on the floor. On the front of the chest, one inch to the inner side of, and three-quarters of an inch above, the left nipple, were five small wounds transverse in direction, each about three-quarters of an inch long by a quarter of an inch wide. Just to the inner side of the nipple was another wound half an inch in length; about one inch below the nipple was a small wound about half an inch in length. The direction of the six wounds first named was downwards and slightly inwards; all corresponded externally to the third intercostal space, and they penetrated the thoracic wall in the fourth interspace. On the left side of the pericardium was a transverse wound one inch in length. The left ventricle was penetrated by two transverse wounds each three-quarters of an inch long, and the heart was wounded in three other places. All the wounds were of suicidal origin. The multiplicity of wounds in this case might be regarded as

[1] *Brit. Med. Journ.*, 1888.

indicative of homicide, but against this view is the extremely limited area they occupied, more than one plunge of the blade, which produced a separate external wound, coincided so closely in direction as to make but one large opening in the pericardium, and the two penetrating wounds of the ventricle were only separated by a narrow tongue of the ventricular wall. It would be extremely improbable that a number of wounds homicidally inflicted could be planted so closely together; the struggles of the victim to escape would present a fresh part of the chest wall to the knife each time it fell. The fact that the right hand was tightly clenched, the knife being found on the floor, might, in a doubtful case, have given rise to suspicion. When the weapon that has caused the wounds is found *tightly* grasped in the hand which corresponds with the position and direction of the wounds, the presumption of suicide is strongly corroborated; if it lies loosely in the hand so that it can be lifted away without difficulty, no reliable inference can be drawn; the case may either have been one of suicide, or a second person after inflicting the wounds may have placed the weapon where it was found in order to simulate suicide.

Penetrating wounds of the back are very suggestive of homicide; in exceptional instances they may be due to accident, as when a man falls backwards on a pointed object.

As a means of determining between suicide and homicide when death has resulted from wounds inflicted by cutting instruments, considerable importance is attached to the presence of cuts on the hands and fingers; they are regarded as indications of resistance to homicidal violence, but, exceptionally, they may be met with in suicides. In a case reported by Alexander,[1] an officer was found with two deep incised wounds on the front of the abdomen, and one on the back near the spine. There were twenty-six wounds about the left breast, some penetrating the thorax. Both hands were dreadfully mutilated. A sword covered with blood and bent to an angle of 45° was lying beside the patient, who survived several hours, and explained that he had tried to transfix himself by placing the hilt of the sword against the wall and then pressing forward on the point of the blade. On failing he tried a second time, when the blade penetrated the abdomen and impinged on the spine; he withdrew it with great difficulty, his hands being cut in the act of pulling it out. He subsequently attempted to penetrate the heart. A somewhat similar case was admitted into University College Hospital under Beck.[2] A man placed the point of a sword-stick against the chest, just below and to the outer side of the left nipple, and drove it in by running against a wall. The blade penetrated eleven and a half inches backwards,

[1] *The Lancet*, 1885.      [2] *The Lancet*, 1882.

slightly downwards and to the right, it was firmly fixed, and was removed with difficulty, having probably pierced one of the vertebræ, at the point of entry one of the ribs was fractured. The man was living when admitted into hospital.

Maschka[1] relates a case which furnishes an extreme example of the excess of violence not unfrequently resorted to by lunatics in the suicidal act. A man, aged fifty one, after being in asylum for two months, had so far recovered as to be entrusted with a knife for the purpose of cutting an apple. He was afterwards found bleeding profusely from no less than 285 punctured wounds, of which 200 were on the left half of the chest, 50 on the inner side of the left forearm, and 28 on the inner side of the right forearm. The left radial and ulnar arteries were divided. Six of the chest-wounds penetrated the thorax, the left lung being compressed by blood collected in the pleural sac. The man survived nearly twenty-four hours, eventually dying from hæmorrhage.

## GENERAL CAUSAL INDICATIONS.

Amongst the indications by which an opinion may be formed, or strengthened, as to whether death was due to accident, homicide, or suicide, are —the position of the body when found, the presence on it of bruises or blood-stains, the state of the clothing and surroundings, the presence of a weapon, its position in relation to the body and, in the case of a weapon other than a firearm, marks of blood on it.

The position of the body itself may afford a clue to the way in which the wound was caused, especially when considered in relation to the surroundings. When called upon to investigate a suspicious case, careful scrutiny should be made for foot-marks on the floor of the room in which the body is found, and also in the adjoining corridors; any passing to and fro should not be permitted until a thorough investigation has been made. If blood has flowed on to the floor, it is probable, in the case of homicide, that the murderer will have trod in it and will have produced marks indicative of his subsequent movements. To avoid error the soles of the feet of the deceased should be examined, as a person after fatally wounding himself and soiling the floor with blood might tread in it and then walk about and thus make suspicious footprints. If he has done so, signs of the original hæmorrhage will probably accompany the footprints, as blood will continue to flow from the wounded parts whilst the individual perambulates the chamber. When a murderous outrage has been conducted with great deliberation, the murderer or murderers have

[1] *Prag med Wochenschr*, 1888.

been known to remain in the house a considerable time after the death of the victim, and to leave distinct imprints in masses of coagulated blood; these along with other foot-marks should be measured, and, if possible, sketched or traced. Marks produced by blood-stained fingers on clothing, furniture, or walls are to be minutely examined. If the impression left by a finger is sufficiently clear as to show the course of the papillary ridges, the substance on which it exists should be carefully detached and preserved for comparison and reference. In this relation Galton's[1] method may be of service as an aid to identification.—The same finger of a suspected person should be pressed and slightly rolled on a slab freshly covered with a thin layer of printer's ink, and afterwards on white paper. Galton states that the papillary ridges on the inner surface of the hands afford twenty-five to thirty distinct points of reference, every one, with the rarest exceptions, being absolutely permanent and persisting throughout life.

Marks on the dead body or clothing caused by blood-stained fingers, should be examined with reference to position: a mark on the right side of the body, produced by the fingers and thumb of the left hand, would be a suspicious indication. Finger-stains may exist on parts of the body where they could scarcely be self-produced, as, for instance, between the shoulders. The appearance of blood-spurts on clothing or on furniture has been previously described.

Bruises on the body of the deceased may be of great significance; they should be especially sought for on the throat, chest, and arms. Notice should be taken of the presence of marks or indents produced by the finger nails; they may be so well imprinted as to suggest that the assailant had exceptionally long nails and this may serve as a clue. Too much should not be made of slight ill-defined bruises which may have existed sometime before the fatal injury was inflicted.

A disordered state of the clothing is suspicious of homicide, but it may be due to frantic movements on the part of a suicide. If the body is in bed, clad in night attire, disarrangement of the clothing is very easily produced, and would only be of significance if sufficiently marked as to suggest that a struggle had taken place. On the other hand, if the bedclothes are exceptionally straight, they may have been re-adjusted by the murderer to obliterate previous disorder; in this case, the straightening will probably be overdone. Lunatics, before committing suicide, have been known to throw all the furniture in the room into disorder, giving rise to the appearance of a struggle having taken place; the fury of the insane person may be so maniacal as to cause him to completely wreck the contents of the room, before

[1] *Proc. of the Royal Society*, 1891.

putting an end to his life. Excess of damage to furniture, with probably the presence of a single fatal wound on the victim, would be sufficient to clear up the case; a lesser degree of disorder would be more suspicious, but when a madman begins he usually makes a full end.

Stabs or other similar wounds inflicted through the clothing should be carefully inspected, and the wounds on the body compared with the cuts through the clothing before the latter is taken off. This is especially necessary when the body is fully clothed.

A tightly gripped knife in the hand of the deceased has already been pointed out as an indication of suicide; more frequently it is found lying near the body. When an investigation takes place on the spot, the position of a weapon in relation to the body should be noted before anything is disturbed. In exceptional cases of suicide the knife or razor with the blade closed has been found by the side of the body; in one instance the razor was found in the pocket of the deceased. Such an unusual disposal of the weapon probably resulted from persistence of an habitual action which customarily follows the use of a pocket-knife—the folding blade of the razor suggesting the act. When death has been caused by stabs or incised wounds, the absence of a knife or other likely weapon is suggestive of homicide. Sometimes wounds are homicidally inflicted with one weapon and another is left near the body in order to suggest suicide. The implement left is almost always one belonging to the deceased, and it has happened that the only available one was much too small to have produced the injuries found on the body; for instance a clean sweep of all the soft structures of the neck down to the vertebræ, such as might be made with a carving-knife, could not well be made with a small-bladed penknife.

The amount of blood found on the weapon varies; it may be slight, even when no attempt has been made to remove all trace by wiping or washing it. A long-bladed knife rapidly plunged in and withdrawn may show slight indications of blood, although a large vessel may have been divided. This is partly due to quick withdrawal before the bleeding begins, and partly to the blade being clasped by the skin and thus wiped as it emerges; it is still more likely to be free from blood if the wound is inflicted through the clothing. In such cases the blade presents the appearance of having received a thin coating of red lacquer, the actual tint produced being yellow rather than red. A short-bladed knife will probably show more blood near to, and on the handle. Directions have been previously given for examining blood-stained instruments. All that it is necessary to say in addition is that before dissolving off the stain, the blade of the instrument should be scrupulously examined for hairs, &c, with the low power of a microscope

## THE CAUSAL RELATION OF WOUNDS PRODUCED BY FIREARMS

With regard to wounds inflicted with firearms there are certain special indications which aid in determining whether death resulted from accident, homicide, or suicide. The chief of these is the presence of particles of powder in the wound, and of general blackening in its vicinity, or of one hand. Blackening of the wound merely shows that the weapon was fired close to the body; blackening of the hand tends to prove that the wound was self-inflicted, either accidentally or suicidally. The character and size of the wound also yields evidence as to whether the weapon was fired close to or at some distance from the body. The bullet, if found, may give a clue as to the kind and bore of the firearm. The wadding used in charging a shot-gun has been found in the wound, and, being composed of a piece of paper, has been traced by the printing or writing on it to its original owner. At the present day the employment of breach-loading firearms, which necessitates the use of cartridges, lessens the chance of discovery in this way of the person who has discharged the weapon. In all cases any projectile or other substance found in the wound should be preserved.

Blackening of the wound being evidence of close proximity of the muzzle of the firearm to the body at the moment of discharge, is absence of blackening proof of the contrary? When a firearm is discharged at the body within one or two feet, some amount of blackening is almost invariably produced, but exceptional cases are recorded where no blackening of the wound was present, although the firearm was held in the hand of the victim. A case is recorded by Casper-Liman (l c), in which the dead body of a man was found shot through the heart. There was no blackening, neither round the wound, nor on the neck, nor face; the case, however, was undoubtedly suicidal. Hubbard[1] relates a very interesting case of this kind, with some experiments made in relation to it.—A man was seen flourishing a revolver; he then sat down under some bushes; a few minutes after a shot was heard, and his body was found with a bullet-hole in the centre of the forehead. The wound was not in the least powder-marked, but all the evidence, except want of blackening, pointed exclusively to suicide. The four remaining charges in the revolver were fired at targets covered with white chamois-leather at distances of 3, 8, 18,

[1] *New York Med. Journ.*, 1887.

and 30 inches respectively, and in every case the target was blackened. It appears from these cases that suicidal death from firearms is not invariably accompanied by blackening of the skin in the neighbourhood of the wound, and, therefore, that in suspected homicide by firearms absence of blackening is not inconsistent with the weapon having been fired close to the body—at a distance equal to that from which a man might fire a revolver at himself. The experiments with the targets seem to contradict this, as it would be impossible for any one to fire a revolver at his own forehead at a greater distance than 30 inches; the teaching of actual cases, however, must be accepted.

Blackening of the hand is not a necessary result of firing a revolver, and, therefore, it may be absent in cases of suicide by means of such a weapon.

Revolver-wounds of the head or of the heart are by no means invariably fatal at the moment. It would be natural to infer that a man who had projected a bullet through his heart would be quite unable to fire a second shot through his brain, or, having lodged a bullet in the brain, to shoot himself through the heart. Both of these events, however, have happened, not in one solitary instance only, but in a considerable number of cases. Want of knowledge as to the possibility of such occurrences has led medical witnesses to regard the occurrence of two such wounds, *ipso facto*, as proof of homicide. In a case recorded by Hubbard,[1] a man was found dead in his own barn, his revolver, which contained five chambers (three of which had been discharged), lay within reach of his right hand. There were three bullet-wounds on the body, two of them in the cardiac region—the scorched and powder-burnt clothing indicating very short range; the third was in the right temple, and penetrated the brain at least four inches; this wound was also powder-burnt and was evidently inflicted last. One of the bullets fired at the heart missed it; the other entered the cavity of the right ventricle. This was an undoubted case of suicide. In an important paper on this subject Agnew[2] quotes a number of cases of a similar nature. A student shot himself in the head, walked along a passage to his bedroom, and then shot himself in the heart. A policeman, in the presence of witnesses, shot himself through the head, and then fired a second shot into his chest. The first ball entered the right temple, and was found within the cranial vault on the opposite side; the second ball entered the right side of the heart, death from internal hæmorrhage occurring in about five minutes. A boy aged nineteen inflicted four wounds on his own person with a revolver. The first bullet entered the forehead,

[1] *New York Med Journ*, 1887.  [2] *Medical News*, 1887.

and after taking a circuitous route, lodged about the middle of the left temporal lobe; the second bullet passed through the sternum and cut through the left ventricle of the heart, on a level with the mitral valve; a third shot entered the abdomen, and the fourth penetrated the neck; death ensued from hæmorrhage into the pericardium.

Wounds from firearms on the back of the body are suspicious of homicide; it is not impossible, however, for them to be self inflicted either accidentally or, under special circumstances, suicidally. A wound in the back has been accidentally caused by a sportsman dragging a loaded gun after him through a hedge with the muzzle pointing towards him. A gun insecurely reared up against some object may be accidentally disturbed and discharged into the back of a bystander as it is falling. A man at the moment of pointing a revolver at his heart may be discovered and in the attempt to wrest the weapon from him it may be accidentally directed towards his own back, and fired whilst still grasped in his hand. There is obviously a limit to the angle at which a revolver can be presented to the back whilst in the hand of the suicide, but it is to be borne in mind that, during a desperate struggle, a direction of the barrel quite unattainable by voluntary effort may be accomplished with the unpremeditated assistance of a second person. In such cases, the position of the entrance-wound is of less importance than the direction taken by the bullet, allowance being made for deflection caused by its striking a mass of bone, such as the body of a vertebra. If the entrance-wound of an injury suicidally inflicted is situated towards the middle of the back, and the course taken by the bullet is nearly in the postero-anterior line, the muzzle of the revolver must have been close to the body, and there would consequently be blackening, bruising, and, probably, scorching of the surrounding surface.

In some cases of suicide with a revolver the weapon is found after death tightly gripped in the hand; this affords as conclusive proof of suicide as any evidence short of that of an eye-witness. More frequently the weapon will be found lying on the ground close to the body. If the revolver lies loosely in the hand the case may be one of suicide or of homicide; in the latter case, the weapon has been placed in the hand of the deceased in order to divert suspicion from the murderer. When a man accidentally shoots himself fatally whilst examining a revolver the weapon falls from his hand, as it is but loosely held at the moment it is discharged; the grip with which a revolver is retained in the hand after death is a prolongation of that—due to powerful emotion—with which it was held during life; this is wanting in accidental shooting. Sometimes the weapon cannot be found, although this is suspicious it is by no means conclusive of homicide. A suicide, after shooting himself, occasionally throws the weapon away; if this takes place in the open air the revolver may escape discovery, or a passer-by may pick it up without having any suspicion that its dead owner is lying a few feet away.

When more than one wound is found on a dead body it may be of importance to determine which was last inflicted. There is no great difficulty if only one of the wounds is of such a nature as to be speedily followed by death. In some instances there may be two wounds, each of which would be likely to cause immediate death, as, for example, bullet wounds of the heart and brain. The illustrations already given of double wounding of this description show that sometimes the heart and sometimes the head is first wounded. The course taken by the bullets and the amount of damage they have inflicted on the respective organs may possibly admit of the formation of an opinion, but, unless the indications are well marked, it is advisable not to make a definite statement. The opinion which has been often expressed that immediate insensibility of necessity follows bullet wounds of the brain is not in accordance with facts; it is quite true that immediate loss of consciousness usually follows the passage of a bullet through the brain, but exceptions are sufficiently numerous to forbid an unqualified assertion that this necessarily took place in the case of a dead body found thus wounded. In the greater number of the cases above cited the head was wounded before the heart, but this is not to be accepted as a precedent.

## THE CAUSES OF DEATH FROM WOUNDS

When death results from wounding, medical evidence will be required to prove the **cause of death,** and the relation between it and the injuries found on the body. In a great number of cases, the cause of death and its relation to the injuries is patent; in some, the cause of death is obscure; in others it is obvious, but its relation to the injuries is difficult to trace. The causes of death may be divided into those which are (*a*) immediate, and those which are (*b*) remote.

### (*a*) IMMEDIATE CAUSES OF DEATH

The immediate causes of death from wounds comprise —Hæmorrhage, shock, and injury of a vital organ.

Hæmorrhage is a frequent cause of death from wounding. It may occur either rapidly from a wound in a large vessel, or slowly and continuously from division of a number of small vessels. The rate of flow influences the result produced by the loss of a given quantity of blood. An amount of blood, which, in a few seconds, flows from a wound in a large artery and causes immediate death from syncope, may be sustained with impunity if spread over a longer time. The extremes of age, or the presence of debilitating disease, diminish the power of resistance to hæmorrhage, whilst certain diseases and constitutional conditions, as purpura hæmorrhagica and hæmophilia, strongly predispose to it. Internal hæmorrhage is frequently a cause of death in perforating wounds of the cavities of the body. In some situations, extravasation of a small quantity of blood is sufficient to cause death from mechanical disturbance, as, for example, in the brain or the pericardium; or from asphyxia, when the trachea is wounded and blood is drawn in through the wound.

Shock may cause death either as the result of a **single injury**, or from the **sum of a number of injuries**, no single one of which would be fatal. Illustrative of the first mode of production are those cases in which death immediately follows a fall from a height, a violent blow on the head, chest, or abdomen, without profound hæmorrhage occurring either externally or internally. Violent blows on the abdomen, by paralysing the splanchnics, and producing extreme dilatation of the vascular area supplied by them, may deprive the nervous centres of their proper supply of blood, and thus cause death from syncope. In other cases, blows on the chest or belly may cause reflex paralysis of the heart. (See section on injuries of chest and abdomen.)

Illustrative of the second mode in which fatal shock may be produced, are cases of severe flogging; examination of the body after death may reveal signs of multiple bruising, but not of any wound or other manifestation of a fatal kind. In a vigorous, healthy person done to death in this way, a very considerable amount of bruising may be reasonably expected to be visible, but in weakly children the post-mortem appearances of injury may be very slight. Such cases occasion the medical witness much anxiety, as the cause of death is purely inferential; there is no physical condition to which it can be attributed, and therefore it is clear that a positive assertion as to the cause of death is out of place; the witness will have to content himself with stating that, in the absence of other causes, death is referable to shock. He must be prepared for a searching cross-examination, and it is better candidly to avow from the first the impossibility of determining the cause of death with certainty, than to have that statement dragged out of him after an apparent attempt to conceal it. All the organs and tissues of the body should be carefully examined for pathological changes, the defence always being that death resulted from some latent disease.

Severe injury to organs necessary for the continuance of life is a sufficiently evident cause of death as to require no comment. The extensive injuries to the brain or the thoracic viscera which follow explosions, falls from high buildings, railway accidents, and the like, serve to illustrate this mode of death.

Occasionally, examination after death which has immediately followed some act of violence reveals the presence of a pathological condition to which death is due. Hæmorrhage due to advanced degeneration of the cerebral vessels, to the presence in them of a small aneurism, or to rupture of a thoracic or abdominal aneurism, may occur immediately after the infliction of an injury. Pre-existing cerebral disease may be found after death alleged to be due to violence. A boy was taken ill the day after receiving a slight blow on the head, and died in a few days. The person who had struck the blow was arrested and charged with having caused the boy's death. At the necropsy, old standing disease of the middle ear was discovered, with an abscess in the cerebellum, also of some standing; the accusation, of course, fell to the ground.

In cases in which death is due to a pathological condition which existed at the time the violence was inflicted, the question may be asked—Was death accelerated by the violence? For example, a man, with aortic regurgitation, immediately after a tussle with some one drops down dead; there are no signs of violence, nor is there any doubt that disease of the heart was the cause of death. It is well known that both physical exertion and mental excitement are likely to be suddenly fatal in such cases, and usually the accused is exonerated. It is not, however, necessary that external wounding should take place in order to establish a charge of manslaughter; much depends on the nature of the encounter. In the absence of malice or of intention to terrify, the accused would probably receive the full benefit of his inculpableness; but a man who frightened a boy to death by "personating" a ghost was held to be guilty of manslaughter. Death from pure psychical shock without predisposing lesion is very rare; Maschka relates one such case. Two women were in the midst of a furious verbal encounter, when one of them seized a besom and made as though she would strike the other; before any blow was delivered, the woman who was menaced fell down dead. At the necropsy not the least sign of mechanical injury was found, neither externally nor internally; nothing but hyperæmia of the lungs, and a full right heart, no other abnormal condition. Death was probably due to heart-paralysis caused by excessive mental perturbation. Templeman[1] records the case of a man, aged forty-three,

[1] *Edin. Med. Journ.*, 1898.

who died immediately after becoming extremely excited, and without being subjected to any physical violence. At the necropsy, sixteen hours after death, both sides of the heart, especially the right, contained a quantity of fluid blood. The heart-substance, the valves, and the coronary arteries were free from disease, and no pathological lesion was found to account for death.

### (b) REMOTE CAUSES OF DEATH

According to the common law of England, a person who inflicts an injury on any one shall not be held answerable if death is not caused until after the lapse of a year and a day; within this period, if death results from the injury, the assailant may be tried and punished. It is an exceptional occurrence for death due to an injury to be so long delayed; in the ordinary course of events it takes place within a few weeks or months.

The remote causes of death from wounds comprise **inflammation, septic processes, and exhaustion**. At a period still further removed, death may result from a traumatic lesion, which for a prolonged interval is either unattended by symptoms, or symptoms may be present during the whole time. An example of the first type of injury is found in rupture of the diaphragm, from the immediate effects of which the patient recovers. After an interval of several months, during which there may be entire absence of symptoms, some of the abdominal viscera pass through the opening and the patient dies of diaphragmatic hernia. The second type is illustrated by injury to the lumbar spinal-cord, the patient being paraplegic from the time he sustained the injury, death taking place at a remote interval from bed-sores and general exhaustion.

Wounds of a certain kind, or affecting certain organs or tissues, are specially liable to be followed by secondary pathological processes. Severe crushes, or violent stretching of the limbs, may cause rupture of the main artery without any external wound, gangrene being the result. Wounds of the scalp are frequently followed by erysipelas, such wounds are often sustained by intoxicated individuals in brawls, and, in the event of death taking place, the defence usually is that the erysipelas was due to drink. Even should this be the case, it does not exculpate the aggressor, but it may be the means of diminishing the punishment allotted to him. Wounds of the brain are sometimes followed by hyperæmia, or inflammation of one or of both lungs, which occasionally is of a peculiarly isolated kind; perhaps one lobe is gorged with blood, and the rest of the organ contains the normal or even less than the normal amount, but it may be œdematous, the appearance being very like that of one type of vagus-pneumonia. It is supposed that the condition arises partly from laboured respiration caused by disturbance of the vagus-nucleus, and partly from dilatation of the pulmonary vessels due to paralysis of the vaso-motor nerves following the injury to the brain. Another factor may be present—paralysis of the laryngeal muscles with consequent non-closure of the glottis during swallowing; this leads to the introduction of saliva and particles of food into the air-passages and, as the reflex irritability of the larynx is lessened or abolished, no adequate attempt is made to get rid of the foreign elements by coughing; the result is the occurrence of broncho-pneumonia.

**Septic processes** may cause death within a short time after receipt of an injury, or they may partake of a more chronic character and gradually exhaust the strength by the formation of multiple depôts of pus. A patient who has been the subject of homicidal wounding may be received into the ward of a hospital in which an outbreak of septicæmia or erysipelas occurs, and may succumb to one or other of these diseases. The original wound may not have been of a kind dangerous to life, and it will be consequently urged in defence that the accused ought not to be held responsible for a result which in the ordinary course of events would not have happened. The principle laid down by the law is that when a man criminally wounds any person he must abide by the full consequences of the act. It may be true that the said person would not have died had he not been exposed to an infective disease whilst in the hospital, but his presence there was due to the criminal violence to which he was subjected, and therefore, the accused is answerable for his death.

**Tetanus** is another disease of an infective nature which may entirely alter the prognosis of a case. A slight wound may be followed by tetanus, just as a compound fracture may. If death results from tetanus after a wound of a limb it may be stated in defence that had the limb been amputated the injured person would have recovered. Apart from the uncertainty of the benefit which might have resulted from the operation—the benefit being solely hypothetical—it is sufficient if the patient declined to have it performed, the refusal does not lessen the responsibility of the accused. Tetanus may occur at any period after the infliction of a wound; in the tropics it has been known to develop in a few hours, but in temperate climes it does not usually supervene until from the fourth to the tenth day. The incubation stage is not unfrequently discussed in medico-legal cases, in relation to which of two injuries caused death from tetanus. For example, a boy had his right foot injured by a horse; in a week he returned to school, and two days after he complained of stiffness in the neck, which he attributed to a thrashing he had received the day before from the schoolmaster; he died from tetanus in seventeen days. At the inquest, medical evidence was given to show that the beating was probably not the cause of the tetanus, on account of the shortness of the period which intervened—the disease showed itself within twenty-four hours after the administration of the correction; whereas the injury to the foot, both from its nature and from the interval that elapsed before tetanus developed—ten days—was an exceedingly probable cause.[1] The incubation-period of tetanus may be so far prolonged that doubts may arise as to whether an attack is, or is not, due to a particular injury inflicted some time before. It is exceptional for tetanus to set in after the third week from the occurrence of the injury; if it does, recovery is more likely to take place than when the disease develops earlier. Huntly[2] records the case of a boy, aged thirteen, who sustained a lacerated wound of the right foot followed by tetanus, which developed on the twenty-third day after the accident, recovery taking place. Of 367 cases of tetanus which occurred during the American war,[3] in seven the disease developed from the twenty-sixth to the thirtieth day; and in twenty-three, not until the thirtieth day. In one instance, it is stated that the disease did not make its appearance until seven months after the injury was sustained.

**Idiopathic** tetanus is of very exceptional occurrence in this country. Its existence is denied by some who hold that traumatic infection is a necessary factor in the causation of tetanus, and that in cases of so-called idiopathic tetanus some slight causal injury has been overlooked.

## MEDICAL RESPONSIBILITY.

The position of a medical man in charge of a case of criminal wounding likely to prove fatal is one of great responsibility; if the wounded person dies, the treatment he has adopted may be severely criticised. The object of the counsel for the defence is to transfer the blame as far as possible from his client to some other person, and the medical attendant is usually made the scapegoat; hence the necessity of treating such a case throughout with the full knowledge of what is likely to occur. Operative interference must only be resorted to when absolutely necessary, with the *sole object of saving life*. Before any operation is performed a consultation with one or more additional

[1] *Brit. Med. Journ.*, 1892.   [2] *The Lancet*, 1885.
[3] *The Med. and Surg. History of the War.* Part iii., Surg., 1883.

surgeons should be held. The same precaution should be taken if there appears to be any ground for considering an operation needful, since at the trial a medical man may be blamed, on the one hand, for having performed an operation which caused the death of the wounded person, or, on the other, for neglecting to have recourse to an operation, which would probably have saved his life. If the medical man brings to bear a reasonable amount of care and skill, the culpability of the accused is not affected whatever the issue of the treatment may be. Even if, through mistaken diagnosis, an operation is performed after due consideration and with a full conviction on the part of the surgeon of its absolute necessity for the purpose of saving life, and on examination after death it is found that the operation was unnecessary, and hastened or even caused death, still the person who inflicted the original wound is criminally responsible. The exonerating conditions so far as medical men are concerned, are,—that the original wound is likely to prove fatal, that the operation in the opinion of the surgeon is absolutely necessary to save life, and that a reasonable degree of skill and care were brought to bear in the performance of the operation.

If a wound is not originally of a fatal character, and death of the wounded person is caused by unskilful or negligent treatment, the accused is relieved of responsibility. If, for example, a popliteal aneurism resulted from an act of criminal violence, and it was mistaken for an abscess and laid open with the knife, death resulting from hæmorrhage, the person who inflicted the original injury would not be held responsible for the death. The law in requiring that a reasonable degree of skill should be exhibited in the treatment of these cases, means such skill as is supposed to be possessed by every duly qualified practitioner. In remote country places it is not to be expected that the services of operating surgeons of great experience are to be obtained as in large towns, nor does the law demand such a high standard of efficiency. A practitioner residing in a large town, who has charge of a critical case of criminal wounding for his own sake should avail himself of the assistance of a hospital surgeon of experience in order to meet the almost inevitable criticism to which the treatment of the case will be subjected in the event of a fatal issue; a practitioner in the country must bring his utmost skill to bear, he has then done all that the law requires.

Death caused by an anæsthetic administered for the purpose of performing an operation, would be judged by the same rules as if it was due to the operation itself.—Was the anæsthetic necessary, and was it administered with reasonable care and skill?

20

## MALAPRAXIS.

By malapraxis is meant want of reasonable skill or care on the part of a medical practitioner whether qualified or not, on account of which the person under treatment sustains damage to health, life, or limb. The all-important question in relation to this subject is—What degree of skill or of care is necessary to exonerate a practitioner from the charge of malapraxis? The question only permits of a relative answer; there is no arbitrary standard by means of which a sufficiency of skill can be estimated, and the same may be said of the amount of care bestowed. The qualifying expression, "reasonable,' admits of considerable latitude of interpretation. A greater degree of skill would be expected from a town physician or surgeon of high standing than from a country practitioner. The opportunity for calling the higher skill into action, however, may not occur; the treatment of a simple fracture of the arm can be carried out by a country practitioner equally well as by a hospital surgeon. In such a case, any flagrant error in treatment would be blamable in one as much as in the other. In order that criminal responsibility should accrue, the medical man accused of malapraxis must be proved to have been guilty either of gross negligence, or of gross ignorance of his profession. Any medical practitioner may make a mistake in diagnosis or in treatment, but that is not sufficient to establish a charge of malapraxis; it must also be proved that he did not bring a reasonable amount of skill and attention to bear.

It will be observed that criminal responsibility may be due to one or both of two causes—want of reasonable skill, and want of reasonable attention and care. A surgeon may perform an operation with the requisite skill, but if, for its success, great care and attention are afterwards necessary, and these are not bestowed, he lays himself open to an action for damages. The alleged subsequent neglect may be capable of such an explanation as to make it a debatable point, or it may be of such a nature as to leave no doubt of its existence. In a severe case of epistaxis, for example, a surgeon may skilfully plug the nares, and then leave the plug until it becomes putrid, and septic infection results. If accused of negligence, he might say that the bleeding was so profuse that he did not think himself justified in removing the plug at an earlier period. This is a feasible explanation, and the most that could be made of the case would be, that there had been an error of judgment; but such a mistake would scarcely be held sufficient for damages. On the other hand, a degree of negligence may be exhibited by a medical practitioner in omitting to relieve urgent symptoms, which an average knowledge of his profession would inform him ought to be relieved, that renders him liable to legal proceedings. At the Central Criminal Court 1882, a case was tried, in which an unqualified practitioner was found guilty of manslaughter, because he allowed a patient with a full bladder to remain unrelieved so long, that although an operation was at length performed by a hospital surgeon, the patient died from extravasation of urine. In this case, the practitioner had allowed himself to be regarded as a legally qualified medical practitioner, and he was adjudged accordingly. It has frequently been remarked that quacks escape the result of their unskilful treatment, when duly qualified medical men would be held criminally responsible. To a certain extent, this is so as a consequence of the rule already stated.—That the degree of skill regarded by the law as reasonable, is held to vary with the circumstances of each case. Gross want of knowledge may render even a quack responsible, but if the ignorance displayed is of a qualified nature, it may be held that less knowledge and skill are to be expected from a man who has not received a medical training than from one who has, and, therefore, that the culpability incurred is proportionally less.

Apart from absence of reasonable skill and care, a medical man may render himself liable to an action for damages if he adopts some entirely new mode of treatment which partakes more or less of the nature of an experiment, the result being unfavourable. It is seldom that this can occur, since improvements in treatment are of gradual development, and, although a new method may be quite different to what was formerly adopted, still it will either have sufficient relation to the older treatment as to deprive it of the nature of a pure experiment, or it will be based on physiological or pathological facts by appeal to which the new departure can be justified. It would be unreasonable that medical science should be restricted in its advances as regards treatment; this is so generally appreciated at the present time that new methods of treatment are welcomed and willingly submitted to by the public, although they are perfectly cognisant of their tentative nature. Wherever, in a particular case, a medical practitioner contemplates the adoption of a method of treatment that differs to a material degree from the methods which are recognised by the profession at large, he should take his patient into his confidence, explain the nature and object of the treatment and, before putting it in force, should obtain his freely given consent. If the patient, by reason of tender years or from any other cause, is incapable of appreciating the difficulty, the consent of the nearest relative should be obtained after all the facts of the case have been laid before him.

From time to time actions are brought against surgeons for having unskilfully treated a fracture of the arm or leg, the patient further emphasising his view of the matter by declining to pay the bill. In such cases, a curious compromise is occasionally effected by the court. Although there may be no evidence of want of reasonable skill or care, if the limb displays an altered appearance, a reduction is made in the amount payable to the surgeon, notwithstanding the fact that the judgment on the main issue is in his favour.

## SELF-INFLICTED WOUNDS FEIGNING HOMICIDAL VIOLENCE.

Such wounds are inflicted with the following motives:—revenge, or a desire to injure the reputation of some one who is accused by the wounded person of having inflicted the wounds; to avert suspicion, as when a man who has charge of money or valuables appropriates them and pretends that he has been robbed with violence; to obtain sympathy or notoriety, the subjects usually being hysterical girls or women; or, after committing murder, to make it appear that the wounds were inflicted by a third person who was guilty of the murder, or (it may be alleged) by the murdered person himself, who having attacked and wounded the survivor, was killed by him in self-defence.

Self-inflicted wounds of this type are almost invariably either stabs or incised wounds, and are limited to parts of the body accessible to the individual himself. They are frequently numerous, and, if so, are spread widely apart; they rarely penetrate below the cutis, and if they do, they are not on those parts of the body where wounds are popularly supposed to be mortal; in the two last-named characteristics they differ from suicidal wounds. The hands are seldom wounded, whereas in genuine homicidal violence this frequently happens from attempts at self-defence. A further and most important indication is afforded by a careful comparison between the wounds on the body and the cuts through the clothing by which it was covered, or alleged to have been covered, at the time the wounds were inflicted. In all cases a *direct comparison is essential*: the clothes must be placed on the body as they were worn at the time. It frequently happens that some of the wounds have been made whilst the surface was uncovered, the designedly corresponding cuts through the clothing having been made separately. In this case discrepancy is inevitable: there will be cuts through the clothing without corresponding wounds on the body, and, what is more significant, there will be wounds on the body covered by clothing which is intact. In one case of this kind there was an incised wound of the arm, but the cut in the sleeve of the coat, which was supposed to correspond, did not divide the lining, it only went through the outer cloth. Besides discrepancy between the cuts through the clothing and the wounds on the body, various portions of clothing may themselves yield contradictory results. Stabs inflicted through the ordinary clothing must pierce more than one layer of it, often several before the skin is reached. It is almost impossible so to arrange the various folds of clothing, such as are presented by the coat, waistcoat, shirt, and under-vest, when off the body, that the cuts through them will coincide when they are on it.

The medical witness should further carefully examine and compare each article of clothing at the parts perforated, with regard to blood-stains. If the suspected person possesses an ordinary degree of cunning he will not fail to smear the edges of the cuts with blood, this he will probably do to each garment separately. The result will be that in some instances two contiguous layers of cloth will be found unequally stained, the outer layer, possibly, being more freely stained than the one that underlies it.

It is said that individuals who have attempted suicide and have failed to kill themselves, out of a feeling of shame have accused some unknown person of homicidal wounding. Such a case would form a remarkable exception to the rule which obtains in cases of self-inflicted wounds with fraudulent intent, inasmuch as the intention to deceive being formed after the wound (probably only one) or wounds were made, they would not possess the characteristics which have been described. In such a case the wound would most likely be in a dangerous situation, and it may have been produced by a firearm.

## CHAPTER XXIII

### STARVATION

Starvation may be caused either by absolute deprivation of food or by insufficient amount or defective quality. Cases which come under the notice of the medical jurist are usually those of young children or of adults of feeble intellect, who have been isolated in a cellar or some other unfrequented part of the house, and entirely neglected both as regards nourishment and bodily attention. This treatment is adopted by those who put it in force with the design of ridding themselves of the presence of the victim without daring to kill him in a more direct manner. From parsimonious motives, servant girls have been deprived by their employers of sufficient food to support life. If the person undergoing starvation is rescued alive, medical evidence will be required to substantiate the charge of criminal neglect from the appearances present in the living subject.

The degree of emaciation after deprivation of food for a given period depends to a great extent upon the bodily condition at the time the starvation was commenced. For this reason, in cases of fatal chronic starvation in which the minimum amount of food to sustain life has been given for a prolonged period, followed by an interval of total deprivation, the degree of emaciation is much greater than when a well-nourished healthy individual is suddenly cut off from food until he dies.

Symptoms.—The natural feeling of hunger which indicates to a healthy person that the organism is in want of food, disappears after the first thirty-six or forty-eight hours of fasting. There may be pain and discomfort in the region of the stomach, but it is not associated with a desire for food. Intense thirst is always present, and want of fluids greatly increases the sufferings. Muscular weakness gradually occurs, and is quickly attended by emaciation, which is progressive until the end. The skin is wrinkled and is usually pale, dry, and of a parchmenty appearance; purpuric spots have been noticed, and, more frequently, brownish stains resembling ingrained dirt. The features and eyes are sunken, and the malar bones stand prominently out. The mouth and tongue are dry, and the breath has a disagreeable odour, which in some stages of starvation is of an ether-like nature; at a later stage the whole body gives off a peculiar putrescent odour, but unlike that of ordinary putrefaction. The abdominal wall is concave, so that the bodies of the vertebræ may easily be felt through it. To use the popular phrase, the limbs are little more than skin and bone. The mind may remain clear or may be enfeebled to imbecility; hallucinations are not uncommon. The pulse is feeble but does not present any constant numerical characteristic; it is often slower, and sometimes quicker, than in the normal condition. Two distinct statements are made with regard to the temperature: one is, that it does not fall until shortly before death, when it quickly diminishes; and the other is, that the temperature is subnormal throughout. Some of this discrepancy may be due to a blending of observations made on man and animals. Falck,[1] from experiments on animals, states that the temperature remained constant for fifty-three days, and then rapidly went down till death took place. Paton and Stockman,[2] when investigating

[1] *Beiträge z. Physiol.*, 1875.  [2] *Proc. of Roy. Soc. Ed.*, vol. xvi.

the case of a man who fasted thirty days, found that the temperature ranged from 96°F. to 93°·4. The amount of oxygen consumed by starving animals is not greatly below the normal, and, therefore, the temperature may be maintained at, or a little under, the normal point.

The loss of weight varies with the state of nutrition which exists at the commencement of starvation. A stout well-nourished man, cut off from food, will lose very much more weight during the earlier days than a spare man; after three or four days fasting their ratios become more equal. Paton and Stockman found that a man in a thirty days' fast lost 10,316 grms., or ·166 kilo. per kilo. of original weight ; in all, about one-sixth of original weight. The daily loss averaged ·34 kilo. Falck[1] states that warm-blooded animals lose about 40 per cent. of their original weight before they die from total deprivation from food and drink.

The daily amount of urine is lessened and, when no fluids are taken, the diminution is progressive, the colour and specific gravity being higher than normal. The daily excretion of urea during starvation has been estimated by countless observers. When food is cut off the excretion of nitrogen (urea) suddenly drops and then remains fairly constant for several days with a slight tendency to further diminution. When all the fat is used up, there may even be a little increase, which, in any case, is only temporary, and gives place to a progressive fall until death takes place. Luciani,[2] in his observations on Succi during one of his fasts, found that on the last day of taking food the N in the urine amounted to 16·29 grms. During the first twelve days of fasting it sank from 13·8 grms. to 7·29 grms. and progressively diminished to 3·2 grms. on the twenty-second day. Water was taken in small amount all the time ; the daily amount of urine varied from 600 to 250 cc. Paton and Stockman give the following daily average amounts of N for six consecutive periods (each consisting of five days) during a fast of thirty days. (1) 11·9 grms., (2) 5·4 grms., (3) 5·1 grms., (4) 4·2 grms., (5) 4·2 grms., (6) 3·1 grms. After the sixteenth day water was taken *ad lib.* Of the other constituents of urine—uric acid, sulphuric acid (in all its combinations), and phosphoric acid progressively diminish during starvation. The excretion of chlorine is not so constant ; in some cases it has been observed to progressively diminish ; and in others, at the end of prolonged deprivation from food, to very nearly equal in daily amount that given off at the commencement. Kreatinin is another irregular constituent ; it diminishes during the earlier period and may subsequently increase ; Baldi[3] found it present in very small amount during fasting.

[1] Maschka's *Handbuch.*   [2] *Fisiologia del digiuno*, 1889.
[3] *Lo sperimentale.*, 1890.

The daily excretion of $CO_2$ is diminished, but not so rapidly as the excretion of urea. In the earlier stages, especially if the animal subjected to starvation carries much fat, a considerable diminution in body-weight takes place before the out-put of $CO_2$ is much lessened; afterwards, it progressively diminishes.

The secretion of **gastric juice** during starvation varies. By passing a tube into the stomach Pick[1] sometimes obtained only a few drops and at others 28 cc. or more. The juice thus obtained often contained no HCl. If to the juice devoid of HCl a little of the acid was added it behaved as to power of digestion like normal gastric juice. Schreiber[2] states that the gastric juice continues to be secreted during fasting, and that, for the most part, it contains HCl. Other observers have found HCl frequently absent. The daily amount of **bile** diminishes as starvation progresses, but the gall-bladder is usually found distended after death. The fæces are at once diminished, and very soon are entirely absent.

Groll[3] found that the hæmoglobin is less quickly used up than the other solid constituents of the blood. Raum[4] found the blood-colouring matter in dogs increased during hunger.

**Post-mortem Appearances.**—Cadaveric rigidity may be present, as after other modes of death. The skin is dry, with scurfy surface, or it may be horny, and on account of absorption of the fat, is with difficulty separated from the underlying muscles; in chronic starvation fat is almost entirely absent throughout the body. The muscles are atrophied and soft. The brain and cord show no appreciable changes. The lungs are paler and contain less blood than usual. The heart is small and may contain blood in all its chambers. The whole of the intestinal tract is atrophied. The stomach is contracted, so as often to appear like part of the large intestine, it may contain a little bile-stained fluid, the mucous membrane is usually corrugated and pale, it may be slightly reddened. The small intestine is contracted, and is empty or contains a small quantity of bile. The large intestine may contain a trace of hard fæcal matter, the rectum may be hyperæmic. The walls of the intestines, especially of the duodenum, jejunum, and ileum are much atrophied, and in consequence are almost transparent, sometimes so much so as to render any substance within them easily visible. The liver is reduced in size, its surface being smooth and its colour dark. The gall-bladder is almost invariably distended with bile. The pancreas is atrophied, often to disappearance. The urinary bladder is contracted, and is usually empty or nearly so. The blood contains less than the normal amount of water.

[1] *Prager med. Wochenschr*, 1889.  [2] *Arch. f. exper. Pathol.*, 1888.
[3] *Pflüger's Arch.*, 1888.  [4] *Arch. f. Pathol.*, 1890.

The appearances which are most characteristic of death from starvation are—disappearance of the body-fat, and general atrophy of the soft structures. The disuse of the digestive tract results in well-marked and distinctive atrophy of its walls, and absence of stimulation to the flow of bile causes it to accumulate in the gall-bladder. The order in which the tissues waste are—first, the fat; then, the glandular organs; and afterwards, the skeletal muscles.

It will be observed that the signs of death from starvation are not such as to enable a positive opinion to be expressed as to its occurrence; similar indications are met with in death from various wasting diseases of organic origin, and also in some neuroses which leave no post-mortem evidence of their occurrence—a most important fact and one to be remembered by the medical witness. Before giving a definite opinion that death resulted from starvation, not only must all the characteristic signs which accompany that mode of death be present, but there must also be an entire absence of all indications of disease. The pathological conditions to be specially borne in mind are:—**Constriction of the œsophagus**, either from simple stricture, from malignant disease, or from external pressure, such as may be caused by an aneurism. **Malignant disease** in any part of the body. **Tubercle**, miliary and otherwise; in relation to which the condition of the pia mater, peritoneum, glands, and joints should be specially examined. **Addison's disease** is not always accompanied by emaciation, but the adrenals should always be examined. The possible occurrence of **diabetes** necessitates the examination of the urine for sugar. **Chronic diarrhœa** or dysentery are other causes of emaciation which require consideration at the time the necropsy is made. In addition to these more or less obvious causes of general atrophy, neuroses, such as hysteria, hypochondriasis or insanity, are to be taken into consideration when an accusation is brought against a person, or persons, for having caused the death of any one under their care by withholding food.

The case of *Reg.* v. *Staunton* and *Rhodes* (Cent. Crim. Court, 1877) affords a good illustration of the circumspection demanded of the medical witness when called upon to determine the cause of death in a case of alleged criminal starvation. Harriet Staunton, aged thirty-five, the wife of the first-named prisoner, was stated to have been starved to death by her husband and his paramour and co-prisoner, Alice Rhodes. Shortly before her death, Harriet Staunton was removed to Penge and was there seen by a medical man; she died directly after. A certificate of death from natural causes was given, but suspicion being subsequently aroused as to the real cause of death a necropsy was made, and the case was tried as above stated. The examination revealed great emaciation and a generally filthy, neglected condition of the body, which measured 5 feet 5½ inches and weighed 74 pounds; two and a half years previously the woman weighed 119 pounds. The brain was healthy, but there were a few miliary tubercles deposited in the pia mater. The heart was small. The lungs were healthy, except for a small patch of tubercular deposit at the apex of the left lung. The gall-bladder was full of bile. The coats of the stomach were thinned. The intestines were shrivelled and empty. The rectum was hyperæmic for about four inches, the rest of the intestines being pale in colour. There was a total absence of fat with general atrophy of all the organs. The bladder contained about three ounces of urine. Positive medical evidence was given at the trial that death was due to starvation, and the prisoners, who included Staunton's brother and his wife, were convicted and sentenced to death. The medical evidence was subsequently freely criticised, emphatic opinions being expressed that there was no medical proof of death from starvation. The line of objection taken was that no proper search had been made for other possible causes of death. The œsophagus was not examined, the urine in the bladder was not tested for sugar, and the adrenals were not examined although there was discoloration of the skin on the face. The absence of thinning of the intestines and the presence of tubercle both in the membranes of the brain and in the lungs was held, on the one hand, to negative death from deprivation of the food, and, on the other, to show the possibility of death from disease. The result was that Rhodes was pardoned and the capital sentences passed on the other three prisoners were commuted.

The lesson to be learnt from this case is valuable, and is applicable to all medico-legal investigations. —A medical practitioner should never approach a case with a pre-formed opinion as to its nature; he should never neglect making a searching examination of all the organs; and he should never ignore pathological indications that do not happen to agree with an opinion that has been formed, but should rather ponder as to their import.

The time required for death to result from deprivation of food varies according to certain conditions. Age exercises a considerable influence; very young children quickly succumb, adults resist better and old people best of all. The better the health and the nutrition of the body at the commencement of the fast, the greater the power of endurance. *Drinking water tends to prolong life considerably.* Conservation of the body-heat is another favourable factor; a person well clothed, especially if so placed that the surrounding air is still, and of a moderate temperature, will live longer without food than one who is exposed to the action of cold. Colletta[1] states that a girl, aged

[1] *Storia del Reame di Napoli.*

sixteen, was buried under the ruins caused by an earthquake. She remained underground without food or drink eleven days, holding in her arms an infant that died on the fourth day. When extricated, the corpse of the infant was undergoing decomposition, but, being hemmed in, the girl, who was alive when rescued, was unable to rid herself of it. Life has been prolonged fourteen days, and it is stated twenty days, without food or water. In the absence of food, but with access to water, a man has lived sixty-four days.

# PART II.—INSANITY.

## CHAPTER XXIV

### GENERAL INSANITY.

Disorders affecting the mind chiefly come under the observation of the medical jurist in relation to diagnosis, and to the fulfilment of those obligations which the law imposes on medical men who sign certificates for the purpose of placing persons of unsound mind under restraint. With prognosis and treatment he is less concerned

The various types of insanity have given rise to differential classifications, which have fostered the idea that each class represents a distinct disorder. Whilst recognising the special characteristics of the several types of mental disorders, it must be remembered that any differentiations or groupings, according to prominent symptoms or bodily causes are arbitrary, and are only to be accepted as designations which indicate the salient features of the insane condition. For the study and recognition of mental diseases some classification is necessary, but the present state of knowledge does not admit of the formulation of one that is free from defects. It is not necessary here to discuss the relative advantages of the various classifications devised by experts in morbid psychology, for forensic purposes, insanity may be studied from a stand-point such as that afforded by a slight modification of the classification drawn up by the International Congress of Alienists in 1867.

### CLASSIFICATION OF FORMS OF INSANITY

Simple insanity
- Mania
- Melancholia.
- Recurrent insanity
- Moral insanity.
- Delusional insanity
- Impulsive insanity

- Epileptic insanity
- General paralysis
- Toxic insanity.
- Insanity in relation to child-birth.
- Idiocy and Imbecility
- Senile dementia.
- Sequential dementia
- Dementia due to coarse brain-lesion.

**Indications of Simple Insanity.**—Insanity does not develop in a moment, there is a period of ingravescence during which the individual affected gradually deviates from his ordinary mental condition. Although the symptoms evinced during the various stages of insanity are irregular and do not follow any definite order, certain of them are of common occurrence, some of which are present in every case; a knowledge of these symptoms is essential to an early recognition of mental disease.

The onset of insanity may be so insidious that long before any distinctive indications are manifest an <u>alteration in temperament</u> is noticeable; the individual is different to what he was formerly, he has lost his equanimity. When insanity begins in this insidious way the emotions are affected long before the mind is impaired. The patient is subject to unaccountable waves of depression, which may alternate with periods of excitement; he becomes unwontedly irritable and is unable to control his temper under the petty annoyances of every-day life, this <u>instability of temper</u> may be the condition that first rouses suspicion in the minds of his friends that insanity is the cause of the change in disposition. A man who has been moody and reserved in his manner for some time is credited with being overtaxed with business, and is thought to be a little out of sorts, but nothing more; at some trifling contradiction or annoyance he suddenly blazes up into a frenzy of passion, and behaves for the moment so like a madman, that the bystanders are at once impressed with the idea that the balance of his mind is impaired.

A <u>change in the emotions</u> is also commonly shown by transformation of like into dislike, of love into hate. A man shows unwonted impatience at the remarks addressed to him by his wife whose opinion he previously valued, and then manifests an absolute antipathy to her, a sentiment totally at variance with their former relations. Loss of interest in objects and pursuits which formerly occupied his attention, desire for solitude, perhaps at first shown by avoidance of social intercourse in a general way, and then in a more special manner, by seclusion from the family circle, are further evidences of perverted sentiments. At this period, the person affected is often quite capable of brightening up in the presence of strangers, or of friends for whom he has a special liking; he will even remark that he feels better in company—meaning in the society of those with whom he is not necessarily brought into relation.

So far the intellect is unimpaired. The capacity to fulfil the duties which devolve upon a merchant or professional man may be equal to the requirements, but the work is done in a perfunctory way without the display of any interest. The morbid state of the emotions, however, soon reacts on the mind in such a way that the reasoning processes are interfered with, and the judgment is no longer that of a sane person: emotional [depression gives place to morbid apprehensions, and an indefinite feeling of melancholy to dread of impending ruin in this world or in the future state. At this stage, **delusions** occur. Amongst the commoner delusions in the early stages of insanity are:—the conviction that some one—generally a member of the patient's family—has commissioned the police, or a private individual, to act as a spy on the person labouring under the delusion; that there is a conspiracy to ruin him, or to deprive him of his rights; that attempts are being made to poison him. The last-named delusion frequently causes those who are afflicted with it to arm themselves with a number of bottles of medicine, or parcels of food, and to seek the advice of a medical man, requesting him to analyse the samples brought for poison. It is rather curious that suspicion is not always directed against those who might be reasonably suspected of criminal motives—such as members of the family who would be benefited by the death of the deluded person; but druggists and other shopkeepers who are total strangers to him are often the alleged secret assassins; sometimes the allegation of conspiracy is made to account for this inconsistency.

Delusions originating in the special senses are also frequent in the early stages of insanity. A man labouring under such delusions will state that he hears voices making disparaging or defamatory remarks about him, or calling upon him to commit certain actions; he sees people deriding or menacing him in the streets; he states that a friend who has been dead for years, walked past his house and looked at him as he went by; that he can taste poison in his food; that an enemy is influencing him by means of electricity which causes him to feel strange sensations; or that an offensive odour emanates from his body.

Among the early symptoms of insanity is a general feeling of doubt. This is perhaps most frequent in woman. A patient thus affected without any reason will reproach herself for having conveyed a wrong impression to some one as to her intentions or capability to perform some duty; or she will groundlessly accuse herself of having received money for which she has not rendered an equivalent service. This want of confidence will lead her to repeatedly recur to the same doubt, propounded in almost identical words; it often precedes melancholia.

The presence of delusions is evidence of insanity. An erroneous perception or idea is accepted by the reasoning faculties as real and the judgment is consequently perverted. If an erroneous perception is rejected by the intellect, the integrity of the judgment is preserved; in such a case, the individual is said to have been subjected to an illusion or to an hallucination. When giving evidence in a lunacy case it is impossible to avoid the use of one or more of the following three terms —illusion, hallucination, delusion; it is therefore necessary for the medical witness to be able to define the meaning he attaches to them. Experts are not in accord as to their precise significance; if, however, a medical witness grasps the distinctions about to be given he will be able to make his meaning clear and need not trouble himself about abstract definitions.

An illusion is a false perception of an external impulse; it is objective and is limited to one or more of the senses. It affords no indication of insanity, inasmuch as it can be experienced without participation of the intellect. Sane persons may be the subjects of illusions; thus, a man who suddenly awakes from sleep sees what appears to be the outline of a human figure in his dimly-lighted bed-room, yet he knows that he is alone in the room and that the door is locked; a few moments' reflection, or a closer inspection of the thing seen, reveals that the impression produced has been caused by a dressing-gown suspended from a toilet stand or other similar object. This is an example of a visual illusion which is corrected by an appeal to the reasoning faculties, or to the evidence afforded by another sense. The causation was objective—the thing seen was wrongly perceived by the visual organs. No delusion resulted—the error was at once detected and the mind remained uninfluenced.

An hallucination is a perception without an external impulse; it is subjective in character and affects one or more of the senses. An hallucination is not necessarily indicative of insanity, inasmuch as it may be rejected by the reasoning faculties, but if of a pronounced nature it is usually accepted by them and in this case determines a delusion. A man who sees some one watching him through an open window when no one is visible, or hears voices speaking when there is absolute silence, is subject to an hallucination. Less significant hallucinations, such as flashes of light, sparks, or figures having a crenated outline not unfrequently occur in simple neuroses, such as megrim; they may, however, be precursors of mental disorder. Non-existent animals, such as rats or mice, seen and believed in by patients suffering from delirium tremens, are delusional hallucinations. In simple insanity hallucinations of hearing are the most common.

A delusion is a perversion of the judgment by an erroneous perception or conception; unlike the two preceding terms, a delusion necessarily implies disordered intellect. The delusions of the insane are of a personal nature; in an impersonal way people may labour under delusions without being insane. The perennial sequence of religious and spiritualistic frauds, for example, is the result of perversion of judgment in a certain type of mind, a type that eagerly embraces unorthodox ideas without question; such people are not necessarily insane, but they are liable to become so. In them the reasoning powers are defective without the perceptions being essentially involved; they see and hear as other people do, but they form erroneous conceptions with regard to what they see and hear, and from them deduce false conclusions. The delusions of an insane person are not grounded on abstract conceptions solely relating to matters outside his entity, they concern himself; if he has delusions about religion, he is convinced that his soul is irretrievably lost, or that he is the Deity incarnate; if about spiritualism, he imagines that he is irresistibly influenced by departed spirits, or is possessed by the Evil One himself. In this way an insane person may be subject to delusions without hallucinations.

Some writers use illusion and hallucination as convertible terms, and others use illusion in a different sense to that above defined. The word illusion is unnecessary to the medical witness and need rarely be used.

A brief description of some of the recognised forms of insanity is necessary before entering into the medico-legal relations involved.

## MANIA.

This condition is characterised by absence of self-control with more or less excitement displayed by words and actions. The acute form is divided into (a) acute delirious mania and (b) ordinary acute mania. There is also a chronic form of mania.

(a) **Acute delirious mania** may develop from ordinary acute mania, or it may begin quite suddenly without premonitory symptoms. It is most common in young persons, especially in those that are of excitable or hysterical temperament. It is sometimes preceded by a period of depression followed by loquaciousness which rapidly passes into a state of acute delirium; if delirious mania develops in this way, it is likely to last longer than when it suddenly bursts forth without antecedent mental disturbance. When the delirium is at its height the patient is violently excited, will attack those who seek to restrain him, will tear his clothes, displaying an utter absence of decency, and will shout and swear or sing until his utterances are absolutely incoherent. In this stage there is absence of sleep; the tongue, from the first foul, becomes more and more so, and then dry and brown; sordes are present on the teeth and lips, and the breath is very offensive. The appearance, during the periods of lessened excitement, resembles that produced by an attack of enterica, but there is little elevation of temperature. The attack may consist of periods of frenzied excitement with intervals of comparative quiet, and may be accompanied by hallucinations, it may be only of a few hours' or days' duration, or it may last two or three months. During the early stage, if at intervals the patient sleeps for a few hours, the attack may be of short duration, being terminated by a long and profound sleep. The absence of sleep in intractable cases is one of the most marked symptoms; a patient may not sleep for four or five consecutive days and nights.

Diagnosis.—It is distinguished from delirium tremens by absence of the half-frightened manner, the tremor, the hallucinations of rats or serpents on the bed, the furtive glances over the shoulders and under the pillows, the constant purposeless picking at the bedclothes, or grasping at imaginary objects—with the retention usually of sufficient intelligence to answer questions—all of which are indicative of that disease. The history of the case will help to distinguish delirious mania from the delirium of a fever or an acute febrile disease. In a fever, or like bodily complaint, there is a period of illness characterised by elevation of temperature, quickened pulse, and other physical disturbances before the delirium comes on. The intensity of the delirium is much less than in delirious mania, although in some diseases, as, for example, in the pneumonia of alcoholic subjects, the delirium is often very violent. From encephalitis the diagnosis cannot give rise to much difficulty, in this disease there is severe pain in the head, vomiting, rigors, and a tendency to somnolence, which soon passes into coma, the accompanying delirium is less continued and less violent than that of delirious mania. In delirious mania pain in the head is not a frequent symptom, and there is absence of vomiting, rigors, and any tendency to somnolence. Meningitis of the cerebral cortex may give rise to wild delirium, but it is less persistent than that of mania, and it alternates with a state of partial stupor. The pulse is high, 130°, and the temperature also—103° or more—which is not the case in delirious mania, except in very bad cases. The occurrence of pain in the head, vomiting, and rigors afford further signs of differentiation from acute delirious mania.

(b) **Ordinary Acute Mania.**—This condition, as contrasted with acute delirious mania, presents more the appearance of a purely mental disorder, there being little or no resemblance to the delirium of bodily disease. Acute mania, unlike delirious mania, is not commonly limited to the young. It may begin suddenly, but usually is preceded by a chain of symptoms leading up to it, such as exalted emotional or intellectual disturbance; more frequently the initial stage is one of depression. The patient suffers from what is supposed to be dyspepsia, he has a sinking sensation in the region of the stomach with an indefinite dread of something about to happen. He is sleepless and feels a sense of confusion in the head, is fidgety, restless, and irritable, and is unable to apply himself to regular occupation. His tongue is coated and his breath offensive. His appetite fails and he loses flesh; this stage may continue for weeks or months. Then comes a change; he suddenly feels that he has emerged from under a cloud, he becomes lively—boisterously so—and says that he is once more himself. He is effusive and loquacious, which his friends at first attribute to a natural feeling of joy at recovery from his previous condition, but the loquacity soon passes into incoherence and the elation into outrageous behaviour. He is subject to hallucinations and to delusions, usually of an exalted kind. Appetite and sleep are fitful, and the bowels are constipated. The mind at this stage is as unstable as a fallen leaf on a windy day; it passes from subject to subject with phenomenal rapidity, the succession being apparently devoid of coherence. Not unfrequently a certain sequential order may be recognised in the words or phrases uttered, which depends either on association of past experiences or of the words pronounced; usually it is of a mixed type, a word now calling up a past experience, and now suggesting another word of similar sound or meaning. He is abusive and uses foul language; he destroys all within his reach and tears his clothes to shreds without any regard for decency; he is exceedingly filthy as to his person and openly indulges in indecent actions without shame. This state may continue for three or four months with partial remissions at intervals. Sleep is irregular; a maniac will pass several consecutive sleepless days and nights, will then sleep for several hours, and recommence his previous behaviour on awakening. The tongue loses some of its coating and the appetite often becomes voracious, notwithstanding which the patient grows thinner. Power of endurance is the most extraordinary feature in cases of mania; the continuous violent movements, shouting and singing that are kept up night and day surpass anything of the kind that can be accomplished by a sane person.

Acute mania may end in recovery; or it may pass into the chronic form, from which recovery rarely takes place, although there may be periods of remission. Chronic mania is more or less associated with dementia into which state the patient may lapse, or he may do so directly from the acute stage. In other cases, mania is succeeded by melancholia.

## MELANCHOLIA

This morbid state is characterised by mental depression associated with delusions, with special tendencies or with agitation. Melancholia may constitute a disordered mental condition in its entirety, or it may be one phase of a morbid state, which presents several aspects.

**Simple Melancholia.**—Few people, however healthy, pass through life without experiencing at some time or other unaccountable waves of depression which temporarily darken the out-look, and the oft repeated question involuntarily presents itself—is life worth living? Such a phase may be produced by an adequate cause—a great loss or disappointment, but it may also creep over the mind without any external impulse, the usually offered explanation being that the person so troubled is "bilious," or that he is over-worked. Allowing due weight to these possible causations, there are cases in which the most careful investigation fails to afford any clue to the source of the depression. Some individuals are more prone than others to this feeling, and, if subjected to severe mental strain, are apt to fall into a condition of true melancholia. The melancholic temperament is strongly hereditary; whole families frequently present marked indications of it. There is a condition of aggravated hypochondriasis which is very difficult to differentiate from actual insanity, and which passes almost imperceptibly into melancholia. The distinction is one of degree only, the hypochondriac frequently has a number of maladies or troubles which he dreads, but he shows more anxiety to submit to treatment than the melancholic who takes a gloomier view of his more limited ailments.

The **symptoms** of simple melancholia are depression of spirits, dread of some unknown evil, sleeplessness, and loss of appetite which eventually leads to the patient refusing to take food. As the disease advances the complaints about his health, which the sufferer at first reserved for the ears of an interlocutor, are uttered without regard to the presence of any one—he moans and repeats a set phrase with ceaseless reiteration, or, on the other hand, he sits absorbed in his misery sighing unutterable woe. Hallucinations and delusions are common; one patient declares that he has a reptile in his inside, another that his brain is fermenting and giving off gas, a third that his abdominal viscera are putrefying and passing away in the dejections, in proof of which he will instance their alleged cadaveric odour.

In some cases **delusions** are among the earliest manifestations of melancholia, and they play a special part throughout the entire course of the disorder. Such delusions are usually of the fixed type—the same morbid idea prevailing from first to last. To this class belong those cases of alleged persecution or ill-treatment which, at first, are looked upon as due to an absurd infatuation, the outcome of prejudice; the individual possessed with such ideas (before they have become sufficiently pronounced as to proclaim his insanity) will write defamatory letters or post-cards complaining of the actions of certain persons. Medical men are occasionally the recipients of communications of this kind, accusing them of having ruined the health of the writer by improper treatment, he asserts, for example, that he has been salivated, and that his body is so saturated with mercury that the metal exudes through the skin, or that medicines have been administered that have destroyed his sexual powers and caused wasting of the organs concerned. If legal proceedings are instituted against the writer, his friends readily seek to shelter him behind the plea of irresponsibility, an excuse that previously they would have indignantly repudiated, although his mental condition at that time was not one whit different. This unwillingness on the part of the friends of a person mentally afflicted to acknowledge his condition, except to absolve him from responsibility, places another difficulty in the way of medical men. When a delusion occurs at an early period of melancholia, the general disorder of the mind is either overlooked by the friends of the patient or is regarded as a result and not the cause of the delusion, they think that there is probably some ground for the delusion, and consequently they do not attach sufficient importance to the general condition. If at this stage of what may be really insanity the patient is certified to be insane and taken charge of accordingly, there will be no lack of evidence to testify to his sanity should he subsequently enter an action against the medical men who signed the certificates.

The delusions of melancholic patients often centre on religious matters. They select some of the denunciatory texts in the Bible and apply them to their own case—they have committed the sin unto death, they have grieved the Holy Ghost, the sentence of everlasting punishment has already and irrevocably been pronounced against them, and so forth. In times of religious revivals people with morbidly emotional minds rapidly develop delusional melancholia with this tendency, it has received the name of **religious melancholia** and is supposed to be a very unfavourable type.

A **suicidal tendency** is often prominent in melancholia. The depressed and hopeless state of the patient leads him to commit suicide as a means of escape, this is to be distinguished from true suicidal impulse, which may exist without melancholia. It is to be observed that melancholics sometimes make futile attempts at suicide which are suspicious of a desire on their part to deepen the interest of those around them in their cases. A **homicidal tendency** is much less frequent in melancholia than the tendency to suicide.

**Melancholia with agitation** is characterised by incessant movement, which results from an agonised terror-stricken condition of the mind; the patient moans and sobs aloud, wringing his hands, tearing his hair, and showing all the signs of the acutest mental anguish. Some patients thus afflicted hurry to and fro in the search of escape from their misery, others sit huddled-up in a corner rocking the body with ceaseless agitation to the accompaniment of heart-rending moans and utterances. Melancholics of this class are exceedingly prone to suicide.

**Melancholia with Stupor.**—In this condition the patient remains for hours in the same attitude without speaking, taking no notice of anything, and apparently overwhelmed with a sense of woe. Some patients thus affected are passive in the hands of their attendants, they allow themselves to be dressed and fed, and will walk if conducted, but show an entire absence of appreciation of external impressions. Others doggedly oppose any interference, they will not walk if the attempt is made to lead them nor will they take food. Although the state is one of absolute apathy, the tendency to suicide is very pronounced; such patients should never be left to themselves as the impulse to self-destruction may assert itself at any moment.

Attacks of melancholia and mania may alternate in the same individual. A degree of periodicity may be observed in most cases of chronic insanity, though in the greater number, the mental state merely undergoes fluctuations without reversal of character; when the amplitude of fluctuation is great, the state of depression is converted into one of exaltation, which in its turn is succeeded by renewed depression. In some cases the alternation is broken by the intercalation of a period of sanity, either between the stage of depression and that of exaltation, or *vice versâ*, for example, mania is succeeded by melancholia, and then comes a lucid interval, the sequence being periodically repeated; in the inverse order it will be melancholia, mania, lucid interval. The term 'circular insanity" has been applied to these alternations; it is of exceptional occurrence, and is most frequent in women.

## ACUTE DEMENTIA.

Acute dementia may be sequential to melancholia, or it may be a primary disorder. The state of mental abstraction evinced in melancholy with stupor is replaced by absolute apathy; the patient stares at vacancy by the hour, his expression being one of entire absence of intelligence, not that of an intelligence overwhelmed with misery. He does not resist the efforts of his attendant to clothe or care for him, but he requires feeding, and attention to all his bodily wants. The physical condition is one of extreme languor; the circulation is feeble and the extremities are consequently cold and livid. Sleep is not wanting, though it may be irregular.

## RECURRENT INSANITY.

Attacks of insanity may succeed each other at more or less prolonged intervals, the patient being free from mental disorder meanwhile, the periods of remission are designated by lawyers as "lucid intervals." In many instances, perhaps in the greater number, the patient is not absolutely free from a tinge of insanity; he might pass in a crowd, but if carefully examined, some eccentricity, or peculiarity of intellect, or instability of temper would be discovered. A patient may have as many as eight or ten or more attacks, with lucid intervals between, varying in duration from a few weeks up to as many years. There is a tendency for the patient at each succeeding insane outbreak, to commit deeds of violence of the same nature as homicide, suicide, rape, or destruction of goods. The attacks often commence very suddenly in an outbreak of excitement, during which the patient is liable to perpetrate some act of criminal violence; the condition may closely resemble epileptic mania, and in some instances probably is of that nature.

## DELUSIONAL INSANITY.

Delusional insanity is frequently called **monomania**, and by lawyers **partial insanity**. The term **Paranoia** is also used to indicate chronic delusional insanity, which is almost invariably of a primary nature. In its typical form delusional insanity is characterised by a fixed delusion of a limited kind, the patient being more or less rational on other subjects; when the delusion is of an innocent and very restricted nature, the behaviour of the patient resembles that of a harmless eccentric individual. Clouston[1] mentions such a case in which the patient was intellectually acute, and morally irreproachable, but he believed that twice two were not four, but four and a quarter. He spent his whole time not devoted to keeping the asylum accounts—which he did accurately on "the old system" in deference to prevailing prejudices—to making elaborate calculations by his own system as to the distance of the stars, and in formulating new tables of logarithms; his manuscripts filled two large chests which he solemnly left by will to the University of Oxford.

In another class the delusions are of an exalted type, the patient

[1] *Clinical Lectures on Mental Diseases.*

fancying himself some great historic personage, and comporting himself with a corresponding degree of hauteur, whatever the delusion may be, the position taken is defended in many cases with logical consistency. Such patients are absolutely impervious to demonstration or argument directed against their dominant ideas, and often exhibit an unmitigated contempt for the mental capacity of those who presume to differ with them. The ideas of such patients are inconsistent with the actual state of things, but the deductions drawn from these ideas are often quite rational grant them their premiss and the rest falls in, in orderly sequence. A woman fancies that she is the Princess of Wales, she conducts herself with what she believes to be a befitting degree of dignity, decks herself with fictitious jewellery and adornments, and exacts a deferential behaviour from those who come in contact with her. A man believes that he is endowed with the power of healing by the laying on of hands; he makes his power known by inflated addresses written and oral, calling upon all who have charge of sick folk to bring them to him to be made whole.

Delusions associated with depression, and ideas of persecution, are very common in delusional insanity. Patients so afflicted often fancy themselves the victims of some occult agency directed against them by certain people, who are often not specified, but vaguely spoken of as "the villains" or "those mesmerists." One man believes that if he allows people to touch him, or even to come near him, they can read his thoughts consequently he keeps everybody at a distance as far as he can. Another believes that there is an attempt on the part of some malicious agency to inflate him with gas, so that he will sail away like a balloon, and be lost; in consequence he will not sit down for months but walks about, or leans against objects, ready to start away should an attempt be made. In another class of cases suspicion is directed against individuals, a man suspects the chastity of his wife and believes that, with the aid of her alleged paramour, she is in some secret way depriving him of his mental and virile power.

Those who are subject to delusional insanity may be able to conceal their delusions under the influence of a strong incentive to do so, even without any effort to disguise their ideas, if their interlocutor does not happen to touch upon the subject of the delusion, they may be able to maintain a rational conversation for a considerable time without betraying themselves. Maudsley[1] quotes the case of a Commissioner who was sent to an asylum to liberate those whom he judged to have recovered. He examined an old man, who gave no indication of incoherence nor insanity in any way and an order was

[1] *Responsibility in Mental Diseases.*

prepared for his release to which he had to put his signature, he took the pen and wrote "Christ."

Hallucinations of hearing are common in delusional insanity; the patients constantly complain of voices proceeding out of the cellar and through the walls. Hallucinations of taste and smell are also frequent and give rise to notions of being poisoned or suffocated with noxious gases. Delusions which have for their foundation some nerve irritation arising in the genital organs are met with mostly in young women, in consequence of which they accuse men of having made improper advances to them, or worse, such ideas are sometimes very fixed, and a woman subject to them will persistently write compromising letters to the man whom she imagines has wronged her, and even to other people, making known his alleged misdoings.

### EPILEPTIC INSANITY

Apart from the tendency to progressive deterioration of the intellect in epileptics, the disease may produce psychical disturbances of an acute kind, which bear a certain relation to the periodic attacks. According to Hughlings-Jackson[1] epilepsy is "a sudden, rapid, excessive, occasional, and local discharge of the cerebral cortex." In the ordinary epileptic seizure, the first indication of the discharge is manifested by a sensory disturbance—the so-called aura, further recognition of development in this direction is checked by immediate loss of consciousness; the discharge then expends itself in the motor tracts. Inasmuch as the discharge may take place at any part of the cortex, the relation between the psychical and motor effects is not constant. In the ordinary epileptic seizure the psychical disturbance is limited to the aura which precedes and the lethargic sleep which succeeds it. In the cases which are of interest to the medical jurist the motor effects are negligible, and they may be entirely absent, his attention is concentrated on the disorder of the higher centres by which the mental attitude and the actions of the individual are effected. The psychical disturbances occur either before or after the motor discharge, and, what is of the greatest importance from the forensic standpoint, even in its absence. During a variable period before an epileptic seizure the individual often displays a restless, irritable, morose disposition, with delusions, in which suspicion of the motives of those about him plays a prominent part, less frequently there is elation. This mental change is easily recognisable by those who are in daily contact with the patient, and from it they infer that an attack is imminent. After a fully developed seizure the patient usually sleeps profoundly for a

[1] *West Riding Asylum Rep*, vol. iii.

variable period, and on awakening is in his former condition, except that he feels sore and fatigued; in some cases, automatic movements are made before consciousness returns. A man may have a fit in the street and, after it is over, may get up and walk a considerable distance without any perception of his surroundings; when he comes to himself he finds that he is in a neighbourhood quite unknown to him. Whilst in this condition he may perform a variety of actions of a purposive nature which demand complicated movements for their execution. The actions performed are determined by the influence of past co-ordinations on the motor centres acting in the absence of the restraint imposed under normal conditions by the highest controlling centres, the latter being in a state of passivity from exhaustion. Many of these actions present all the appearance of volitional movements, and yet the individual, both at the time and afterwards, is quite unconscious of having performed them; although described as automatic they are probably initiated by a slight peripheral stimulation, or by one of internal origin. There is a tendency to resume an action interrupted by the seizure, hence a person who is walking at the moment the attack comes on, may recommence doing so as soon as the motor exhaustion is recovered from, but before the psychical centres have regained their activity.

After an ordinary epileptic seizure has occurred and the subsequent comatose sleep has passed off, the patient, instead of regaining his previous mental state, may be furiously maniacal; this condition may come on at any time within twenty-four hours or more after a fit; it may immediately succeed the coma, but more frequently some hours elapse. It may follow a single fit, but is more likely to occur after several have taken place in rapid succession. In the absence of the higher control, the lower centres are let loose and give rise to a display of blind ungovernable frenzy which is in the highest degree dangerous to the patient and to those around; whilst under its influence the patient, without cognisance of the act, may commit deeds of brutal violence. It is important to remember that a dislike, or suspicion, aroused during the stage of irritability that precedes an attack, may determine the action after it; an animus thus conceived against any one may lead to his being assaulted after the fit is over, whilst the patient is still unconscious of his actions. Occasionally the mental disturbance after an ordinary epileptic seizure takes another form, the patient being simply excitable—talking, gesticulating, and behaving extravagantly—but without violence.

The condition of "automaticity" may occur during a slight epileptic seizure without motor symptoms—the so-called *petit mal*. During an attack of this description there may be no perceptible movement of the body nor limbs, the face will become pale for a moment or two and subsequently flushed, and that is all that usually is to be seen. The patient himself may, or may not, perceive a momentary loss of consciousness, if he is talking at the time the attack comes on, he stops and hesitates for an instant, and then resumes the conversation; if he is writing, the pen probably drops out of his hand, but the whole affair appears so insignificant that it might easily be mistaken for an accidental slip of the fingers. If he is doing something at the time the seizure occurs, he either continues the action on the same lines, or he does something absurd or incongruous which has a certain relation to the original purpose. For example, a woman who was toasting bread had an attack of *petit mal*, she thrust the toasting-fork with the slice of bread on it between the bars and vigorously stirred the fire. This association of ideas has an important medico-legal bearing, during or after a seizure that does not produce motor disturbance there seems to be a tendency to perform some action. If, at the time, the person is not manually occupied, he may do something that has a strong resemblance to a purposive unlawful act, without volition or cognition, the mere sight of an object may be sufficient to suggest picking it up and putting it in the pocket. This may be done in such a way as to resemble secret theft, but the action is not unfrequently committed without attempt at concealment. Colman[1] gives an instance in which a man had an attack of *petit mal* whilst in an ironmonger's shop, he placed a large coal-scuttle on each arm and deliberately walked out of the shop.

A patient under the influence of an attack of *petit mal* sometimes displays another tendency which may bring him within the sphere of the law, he is seized with a desire to micturate, and regardless of the surroundings, unfastens his clothes and deliberately performs the act in public, with the result that he is taken in charge for indecently exposing his person. Colman relates the case of a woman who whilst at a public entertainment had an attack of *petit mal*, in the course of which she lifted her clothes and there and then urinated; her friends had much difficulty in convincing the police that the act was not one of wanton indecency. Occasionally the patient commences undressing in public, Gowers accounts for this on the supposition that a feeling of illness experienced after the attack "suggests" the propriety of going to bed.

The cortical discharge, which under ordinary conditions determines an attack of epilepsy with clonic spasms, may be apparently entirely expended on the mental centres, producing a state of maniacal excitement like that already described as occurring after an ordinary seizure,

[1] *The Lancet*, 1890

but without the usual fit. Individuals thus affected will commit the most brutal acts of violence, being at the time perfectly oblivious both to the injuries they inflict on others and to the damage they themselves may sustain. For two reasons, no insane condition is more dangerous than this.—First, the immediately antecedent state of the individual who is subjected to its influence may be one of perfect sanity, and therefore he may be at liberty to attack the first person with whom he comes in contact without let or hindrance; second, his ungovernable fury knows no bounds and he "goes for" his victim regardless of consequences. This condition is sometimes called masked epilepsy, a term which is also applied to a state of unconsciousness accompanied by automatic actions without violence.

## GENERAL PARALYSIS OF THE INSANE

This disease is much more frequent in men than in women; the subjects of it are usually strong, vigorous, and in the prime of life—from 35 to 45 years of age. Persons of a sanguine temperament are more liable to be attacked than those of a melancholic type; it is probably more common in the lower than in the higher ranks of society. Among the predisposing causes are:—syphilis, abuse of the sexual function, and excessive indulgence in alcohol. Among the exciting causes are—prolonged mental strain, especially when followed by disappointment; shock to the nervous system, such as is caused by the sudden occurrence of a domestic or business trouble; less frequently brain-disturbances of a physical kind due to mechanical injury, or to sun-stroke.

The symptoms are divisible into psychical and physical, both kinds being highly characteristic when the disease is present in a typical form.

As in other forms of insanity, there is an incipient period which in this disease presents special features of a distinctive nature. A vigorous, healthy man, of sanguine temperament, who is fond of what is called "company"—i.e., good eating and drinking—becomes more than usually jovial and loquacious. His friends probably think that he is indulging too freely in alcohol, and, indeed, the condition very closely resembles that produced by slight excess of this kind. The patient is obtrusively familiar with people with whom he has but a slight acquaintance; he will call upon them at their houses and harangue them at great length about his private affairs; he will talk by the hour about himself, his family, or his possessions in an inflated style, describing everything as the superlative of excellence. He is prone to do outré things, the outcome of extreme self-complacency; he will "drop in" uninvited to dine with a family with a member of which he is merely on speaking terms. He becomes very forgetful, neglects appointments, and is irregular in his daily habits. An early indication, which is often the first to rouse the suspicions of the patient's friends as to his sanity, is <u>extravagance</u> in purchasing useless articles. If he sees a watch that pleases him, he will buy half a dozen, he will give orders to trades people for all sorts of goods, many times in excess of his requirements and income. Acquisitiveness may also be displayed by stupid thefts committed without attempt at concealment, the articles appropriated being often, though not invariably, useless.

The sexual proclivities usually assert themselves in a manner that demonstrates the loss of moral control, a man in the early stage of general paralysis will commit an indecent assault on a woman in a most casual way, without any of the cunning displayed in other forms of insanity. He does not appear to be driven to the act by sensual impulse, but, the opportunity being present, he avails himself of it out of mere caprice without considering the consequences, just as he senselessly commits a theft. In a less objectionable way he may show his inclination towards the fair sex by proposing marriage to several women on the same day. A good deal of this folly seems to depend on impairment of the memory as well as on exaltation of the sexual feelings, though there is an undoubted vein of lubricity present, which is evinced by a tendency to libidinous conversation.

The memory and the power of concentrating the attention is always seriously impaired, even in an early stage of the disease, the mind, butterfly-like, flits from object to object, and the one on which it last settles excludes, for the moment, its predecessors. A good way of testing the memory is to get the patient to write a letter, if the disease is at all advanced the writer will omit words, especially short words, such as articles and prepositions.

So far, although his conduct has been characterised by a variety of reprehensible actions, chiefly remarkable for their silliness, he may not have shown any decided indications of downright insanity. About this stage of the disease the <u>physical symptoms</u> are usually first observable; they may appear earlier, before the mental condition is so far advanced, or they may be delayed. The first indication is afforded by the speech, a man in the early stage of general paralysis blurs his words, or some of them, just as a person does who is slightly under the influence of drink. There is more of a hesitancy than a stammer, as though the muscles concerned in articulation co-ordinated badly, in the act of talking the lips quiver, imparting an appearance aptly compared by Bucknill to that of a person about to burst into weeping. If the tongue is protruded, fibrillar tremors of its muscles will probably be visible. The pupils are frequently unequal in size, or they may be extremely contracted or considerably dilated.

As the disease progresses the mental symptoms increase in intensity; bombastic utterances are supplemented by delusions which have a like tendency. The patient fancies himself wiser, stronger, or richer than other men; his wealth amounts to millions of pounds; he has country residences in every county of England, he can outstrip the fastest horse on foot. Delusions chase one another through his mind; he recurs to the same idea, but modifies or alters its expression, and, after a time, he takes up other grandiloquent notions. If taxed with the absurdity of his statements, he makes little attempt to defend or justify them, but maunders on regardless of controversion; he thus differs from melancholic and other insane patients who hold to their delusions and insist on the truth of their utterances. By this time the memory is so impaired that the patient is incapable of comparing ideas, he cannot perceive the least incongruity in his statements; they represent what to him actually exists. His face glows with transport as he recounts his heroic deeds and enumerates his vast possessions; in repose it presents the exactly opposite look of a half demented person—stolid and fatuous. The speech is now distinctly impaired, and subsequently becomes mumbling and difficult to understand.

Before this stage—sometimes quite early—the patient will have suffered from epileptiform seizures, varying in degree from a mere "faint" (*petit mal*) up to well-marked convulsions, and even true epileptic attacks. The ribs are sometimes fractured without the patient being aware of it, due partly to trophic changes in the bones producing unnatural fragility, and partly to insensitiveness, which blunts the perception of pain.

The last stage is one of paralysis and dementia; the patient may be able when supported to totter about for a little longer with a well-marked ataxic gait, and then he is confined to his bed, and lies with the knees drawn up against the abdomen, with body and mind paralysed until death occurs. The duration of the disease varies from a few months to three or, possibly, five years.

Exceptional Forms of General Paralysis.—In the early stage, and very rarely subsequently, the condition is melancholic instead of exalted. In the ordinary type of the disease the patient's life may be cut short soon after the psychical symptoms are first developed. Sankey[1] describes the symptoms in these cases as resembling those of acute meningitis.

In a limited number of cases remissions occur, and, for a time, the

[1] *Lectures on Mental Disease*, 1884.

patient is supposed by his friends to have recovered. Blandford[1] states that he has seen a wonderful disappearance both of bodily and mental symptoms, the improvement lasting for some time, and that amongst these cases he has seen some which certainly would not have been pronounced insane by a jury, they had either lost their delusions or were competent to deny and conceal them. If such cases remain free from mental work, they may slowly decline without return of the acute symptoms, if they attempt to occupy themselves with their former avocations, the acute symptoms return and the relapse is progressively and quickly fatal.

## TOXIC INSANITY.

### ALCOHOLIC INSANITY.

Mental disorder due to alcohol is either **acute** or **chronic**. Acute alcoholism is divisible into two types—**Delirium ebriosum**, and **Delirium tremens**.

**Delirium ebriosum**, or acute alcoholic delirium, is a condition of maniacal excitement, directly due to excess of alcohol, usually it immediately follows the bout of drinking. Excess of alcohol does not necessarily imply a large amount, for various reasons, such as hereditary idiosyncrasy, previous heat-stroke or traumatic injury to the head, a greater susceptibility to the exciting effects of alcohol exists in some people than in others, therefore, the amount which is to be regarded as excessive is a variable quantity. Where there is strong predisposition to become deliriously excited under the influence of alcohol, the amount taken may be relatively small, and there may be an interval of a day or more between the bout of drinking and the delirium. As a rule, the acute delirium immediately follows or, rather, is a continuation and exaggeration of the wild excitement that drink not unfrequently produces in some men at the time that it is taken. The condition is one of excitation of an aggressive type, with delusions of persecution or suspicion, the patient is usually clamorous, and vows that someone is trying to injure him, that his wife is unfaithful to him, and that he will kill those who have done him wrong. He is usually so violent as to need restraint. He has not the same kind of hallucinations as those which occur in delirium tremens—of rats and insects, but hears voices accusing him of crimes or defaming his character, or else he has sensations of a visceral type, which he says are caused by those who are persecuting him. The tongue is foul and the temperature may be elevated a degree or two

[1] *Insanity and its Treatment*, 1884.

The mental state resembles mania more than delirium tremens. Unless there is a strong predisposition to insanity the excitement passes off in a few days, though there may be hallucinations for a short time longer.

Delirium tremens.—This may come on in the course of a drinking bout, or some days after its cessation. The patient cannot sleep, or, if he does, he dreams horrible dreams that haunt him when awake. At first, he is tremulously anxious to follow his usual occupation, but cannot concentrate his attention on it; he then becomes more restless and excited, muttering and moving to and fro in a busy, purposeless manner. If spoken to he lends a momentary ear and answers a question, but immediately rambles off to something irrelevant, probably in the direction of his work. He stops in the midst of a muttered monologue to listen to an imagined voice, and will reply to it. he is extremely suspicious and looks and listens at all points of the compass. He constantly picks at the bedclothes, and tosses them to and fro. He sees rats, mice, or creeping things on his bed and running up the walls, which he tries to chase away or to catch with his hands. He will fix his eye on a distant spot and follow the movements of some hallucinatory creature till it reaches his bed, when he springs out, and, in a state of tremulous agitation, rushes away to escape from it. He is constantly lifting up the bedclothes, or pulling the curtains on one side to look for lurking foes. Associated with a blustering defiant demeanour, he displays a cowardly disposition that usually renders him amenable to firm moral treatment on the part of strangers, but he is utterly intractable to attempts to quieten him made by his wife, or those of his household. There is a tendency to suicide, which is often manifested by patients who have not displayed any marked degree of delirium; in the more excitable kinds of delirium tremens, homicide may be committed. In the usual course the disease lasts two or three days, and terminates in several hours sleep.

Chronic alcoholic insanity comes on after long continued excess of alcoholic beverages; it is accompanied by sensory and motor affections, due to peripheral neuritis, which impart a special character to this form of insanity. The mental condition is one of progressive enfeeblement, the memory fails, and the power of concentrating the attention diminishes until the patient becomes stupid and indifferent to all around him; he is negligent as regards his personal appearance, and goes about with dirty, ill adjusted clothing. He then develops delusions founded on hallucinations, mostly aural; he hears people speaking evil of him and conspiring to do him bodily harm, or voices ceaselessly repeating abominable suggestions. Visual hallucinations, so characteristic of delirium tremens, are much less frequent in chronic alcoholic insanity. The hepatic and gastric troubles caused by prolonged excess of alcohol give rise to delusions that living animals are inside the stomach, or that poison is being secretly administered. The paræsthesiæ due to peripheral neuritis are similarly misinterpreted—the patient declaring that he is being tormented by electricity administered by those who are plotting against him. It is characteristic of the change in direction taken by public thought during the latter half of the present century, that the delusions of the insane which are founded on tactual and other sensations are almost invariably referred by the sufferers to electricity—delusions which formerly would have been attributed to demoniacal influence. Patients suffering from chronic alcoholic insanity are prone to delusions relating to the sexual organs, they believe that they are being subjected to treatment intended to harm them and destroy their sexual powers, either by means of poison administered in their food or by some occult application of electricity. Another frequent delusion in this relation is that the patient groundlessly believes his wife is unfaithful to him, and is plotting with some one to get him out of the way.

More rarely the delusions in chronic alcoholic insanity are of an exalted type, and strongly resemble those of general paralysis. They are often equally lofty in sentiment—the patient thinking that he is possessed of boundless wealth or that he is one of the persons of the Trinity—but they are not accompanied by the fatuous self-complacency which is characteristic of general paralysis, there is always an undercurrent of distrust as to the motives of some person or persons.

The **physical** symptoms consist of **sensory** or **motor** disturbances, due to peripheral neuritis. The relation between the psychical and physical symptoms caused by alcoholic excess is not constant; an advanced stage of paralysis may exist, with but slight mental degeneration. The sensory disturbances take the form of extreme tenderness of the muscles of the legs chiefly, the least pressure causing acute pain, the nerve-trunks may be swollen and tender on pressure; there may also be paræsthesiæ of various kinds, a burning sensation in the feet being especially troublesome. In the early stage, cramps in the calves of the legs are common. The **motor** symptoms first show themselves by difficulty in walking, the legs feeling weak, the gait, though ataxic in appearance, is really paralytic. When the patient is in bed the ankles and toes are flexed, the heels being drawn up, later on the wrists drop also. As the paralysis progresses more muscles are implicated, including those necessary for the carrying on of respiration, and death results.

The drinking of alcohol in excess is not only a cause of insanity, but it may also be the result. the term dipsomania has been used to signify a morbid tendency to take drink. The habit of drinking to excess is but too easily acquired by those who have no special proclivity to it, but there are undoubtedly cases in which it is directly due to hereditary transmission; it may also be the result of the emotional state and enfeeblement of moral control which marks the onset of many forms of mental disease. In addition to the immediate effects of alcohol on the mind, a further and debasing change is produced in the moral character; the individual loses both self-control and all regard for truthfulness; he will resort to any subterfuge to gratify his cravings, and will lie in a most bare-faced manner to extricate himself when in a difficulty. Such people are pests to their families and to society at large.

The habitual use of morphine produces a still more debasing effect on the moral character. A dipsomaniac may pull himself together for a short time and abjure drink, but rarely does an opium *habitué* voluntarily cease taking the drug, his craving for it is such that nothing short of physical hindrance will restrain him. Under the sway of this habit, men, and even women of refined character, will resort to the meanest artifices to gratify it. If the habit is of long continuance the memory becomes impaired; this at first seems to be the result of inattention; the patient is absent-minded and does not give himself the trouble of focusing his thoughts upon the subject under consideration. At this period, if sufficient mental stimulus is brought to bear, he is capable of concealing his weakness by increased mental effort; subsequently, there is an actual loss of memory which cannot be overcome. In this stage, hallucinations are common and may give rise to delusions like those of chronic alcoholic insanity. The physical indications are loss of flesh, tremulousness when not under the influence of the drug, anorexia or capricious appetite and diminution in muscular power. A very significant symptom consists in recurrent visceral neuralgia, which may resemble the agony caused by the passage of a gall-stone; gastric crises (mistaken for "bilious attacks") are common. The habit is exceedingly difficult to eradicate, but if eradicated recovery is more complete than in the analogous condition produced by chronic alcoholism, because of the absence of vascular and other degenerative changes which accompany the latter, and which, of course, are permanent. It is not unfrequent for those who have been cured of the opium habit to take to drinking. Discussing the subject from the medico-legal aspect, Regnier [1] distinguishes between morphinism and morphine-mania. He believes that the former does not produce such a degree of mental enfeeblement as to

[1] *L'intoxication chronique par la morphine*, 1890

render its victims irresponsible for their actions, they are not liable to irresistible impulses; those subject to morphine-mania may be. If mental enfeeblement through opium-eating is pleaded as a bar to criminal responsibility, it is to be regarded much in the same light as the plea of chronic alcoholism.

Chronic lead-poisoning may give rise to certain psychoses. The symptoms produced do not appear to be always the same. Savage[1] observed acute mania in one case, and in another symptoms closely resembling those of general paralysis. In a case that I saw there were delusions with depression. The man informed me that his wife was unfaithful to him and wanted him out of the way, but his sister as well as his wife assured me that there was not the slightest ground for this statement. He had no hallucinations, but at times he was exceedingly depressed; there was some hesitancy of speech, but no tremor of the tongue.

## INSANITY IN RELATION TO CHILD-BEARING

There are three epochs during the child-bearing period in which insanity may be developed. During **pregnancy**, during the **puerperal** state, and during **lactation**.

**Insanity of Pregnancy.**—Emotional disturbance is a well-recognised accompaniment of the period of gestation; it is manifested by strongly-marked likes and dislikes in relation to food, and not unfrequently by alteration in the general mental state. Some women are morose or irritable, others are unusually complaisant during the period of gestation. If there is any neurotic taint, or even in the absence of discoverable hereditary proclivity, such emotional disturbance may exceed the limit recognised as compatible with self-control and may develop into actual insanity. Insanity during gestation is exceptional; when it occurs, it is usually after the third month. The condition is one of depression, accompanied with suspicion and dislike of husband and (should the patient be a multipara) of children, which may alternate with states of maniacal excitement, or the entire disorder may be of the exalted type. Mental disorder is most liable to occur in first pregnancies. There is always a strong tendency to suicide, and there may be to homicide. The patient sleeps little, and is subject to hallucinations and delusions.

**Puerperal Insanity**, when it occurs, usually comes on within a fortnight after parturition. The patient is sleepless for a night or two, and then is excitable and talks more than usual. She is capricious and without any reason, takes a dislike to those about her; she gives the

[1] *Insanity and Allied Neuroses*, 1884.

nurse all the trouble she can by demanding a number of trifling services and then complains of her inefficiency. She displays the greatest antipathy towards her husband and her child, and declines to speak to the doctor, or roundly abuses him to his face and calls him by some opprobrious epithet. Food is obstinately refused, necessitating forcible feeding. The delirium, accompanied by hallucinations and delusions, is very acute and is often characterised by obscenity of language and gestures. The mental state may be one of depression in place of exaltation, the patient being profoundly melancholic. In this state she takes no notice of anything, perhaps not even speaking for days together. In both forms the suicidal tendency is strongly developed, and as the patient is impelled to the act by overpowering impulse, originated by vivid delusions, there is always the probability of a sudden outburst, even during a period of temporary quiescence. The same observation applies to the homicidal tendency, which is also common in puerperal insanity, and is chiefly directed against the child or children of the patient; the temptation to take her child's life is so strong, that, although the woman's instinct rebels against it, she feels herself incapable of resisting, and will therefore sometimes ask that the child may be kept away from her.

**Insanity of lactation** may occur from the third to the sixth or eighth month after parturition, or even later. It is essentially due to enervation with, probably, some substratum of neurotic strain; if there is any predisposition to mental derangement, the sequence of gestation, parturition, and lactation causes it to develop. The insanity of lactation usually commences by loss of sleep, depression of spirits, delusional hallucinations, restlessness, and fretfulness. These symptoms may deepen into melancholia with or without outbursts of excitement, or a maniacal condition may predominate. Bevan Lewis[1] states that the more acute forms of excitement prevail within the first three months following parturition, and delusions of persecution, with the associated gloom and despondency of melancholia, when the mental symptoms first betray themselves six or more months after. The impulse to suicide and homicide is very great.

## WEAK-MINDEDNESS

Mental weakness may be developmental, or sequential. Idiocy, imbecility, and senile dementia belong to the first group, and dementia as a terminal stage of any of the forms of simple insanity, or when caused by coarse brain-lesions, to the second.

[1] *A Text-Book of Mental Diseases*, 1889.

## IDIOCY

Idiocy implies a condition in which there is either congenital deficiency of mind, or a deficiency caused by processes which take place after birth, but before the period when the mental faculties begin to develop. Imbecility is the same condition in a lesser degree. Lawyers include both forms under the term *dementia naturalis*. Idiots may be roughly divided into micro-cephalic and megalo-cephalic.

The micro-cephalic, or small-headed, idiot is of the congenital type. Ireland[1] states that the size of the head affords no evidence of the comparative intelligence of the idiotic child, but that if the head is less than 17 inches in circumference the intellectual power will be feeble. The megalo-cephalic, or large-headed, idiot belongs, for the most part, to the group which results from pathological changes after birth. Rickets (?), syphilis, and hydrocephalus are the diseases chiefly credited with the causation of this form of idiocy. Hypertrophy of the brain, and more especially hydrocephalus, may be congenital. Bury[2] shows that syphilis may lead to hindrance of brain-growth from thickening of the cranial bones caused by osteitis in early life, from thickening of the membranes and the coats of the arteries, and from sclerosis of the cortex, all of which usually come into play after birth; congenital deficiency of mind from inherited syphilis is comparatively rare. Idiocy may be initiated by convulsions, which often occur at the time of teething. Traumatic injury, such as the head sometimes sustains during difficult parturition, may give rise to imbecility or idiocy in combination with spastic paraplegia; this is due to meningeal hæmorrhage causing compression of parts of the cortex, which become flattened and atrophied. Idiocy may be accompanied by epilepsy. In the ordinary idiot the palate is narrow and highly vaulted, there are rarely more than twenty-eight teeth. Pronounced bodily deformity—cretinism and myxœdema—is sometimes associated with mental deficiency—the former with idiocy, and the latter more frequently with imbecility.

Idiocy comprises all grades of mental deficiency, from a state of mere automatic existence, with considerably less intelligence than that displayed by domestic animals, upwards, through the lesser degrees of imbecility, to the confines of normal mental development. The mental condition of many persons classed amongst the sane is scarcely, if at all, distinguishable from the milder forms of imbecility.

Idiots of the lowest type are absolutely devoid of any intelligence; they are incapable of attending to their natural requirements, and pass their time in rocking themselves to and fro, or moving their limbs

---

[1] *Idiocy and Imbecility.*    [2] *Brain*, 1883.

about in a purposeless manner. If slightly less debased, they display a marked tendency to cruelty—they will torture insects and small animals in a diabolical manner. They are mischievous, dirty and utterly without sense of shame, some are irritable and dangerous to those whom they have power to harm. Imbeciles of a less pronounced type often give rise to an infinity of trouble by running away from home and associating with the criminal classes. As they grow up, they show depraved tastes, they drink, gamble, are riotous and are addicted to the company of prostitutes and thieves, along with this shameless depravity, there is a considerable amount of low cunning and of knowledge of a certain type. Individuals of this class, or a little above it, who display a degree of sanity, often come under the notice of the medical jurist in relation to their fitness to manage their own property and affairs. A totally different type of imbecility is characterised by a gentle tranquility of conduct, the mental defect showing itself in a purely negative manner.

## SENILE DEMENTIA

Senile dementia is not an invariable accompaniment of advanced age, and therefore no limit can be assigned at which the mind begins to give way from physiological decay. Some men retain their mental vigour in a high degree until far advanced in life, they display a wonderful power of abstract reasoning, and of memory for words of highly specialised meaning, such as proper names, which being least organised, soonest undergo dissolution. A man of less mental vigour shows signs of decay and loses coherence of ideas ten or twenty years sooner. If signs of dementia occur before the age of sixty years, there has probably been some cause other than age which has interfered with the nutrition of the brain; defective memory frequently betrays itself at a much earlier period, but the reasoning powers remain active. A certain dulness of intelligence, as compared with that which formerly existed, is frequently the precursor of dementia. In this stage, a man of considerable attainments will be unable to solve at the moment a question involving abstract thought which would formerly have given him little trouble; if the question is written down, and he is so minded, he will arrive at a correct answer when left to himself for a time; the power of abstract reasoning is dulled, but not destroyed. This applies, though not so directly, to minds of lesser culture, and should be remembered when examining cases which are supposed to display great mental weakness.

When dementia follows a progressive course, the mental boundaries may slowly contract without other change than gradual intellectual dissolution. In some cases, phases of excitement or of depression occur at intervals; there is always more or less loss of self-control, and, frequently, excessive irritability of temper. Hallucinations and delusions are not uncommon, and there may be a tendency to suicide. Erotic impulses may be present, which are not unfrequently the cause of unchaste behaviour on the part of old men to young girls.

Dementia may be the final stage of any of the forms of ordinary insanity, such as mania or melancholia, this is known as **secondary dementia.** The condition is that of mental enfeeblement, advancing to one of complete abolition of intelligence. There may be occasional waves indicative of the causal psychosis, the patient being excited or depressed at intervals. The animal propensities, uncontrolled by reason, may display themselves, or the patient may be impassively tranquil unless annoyed, when he blazes up into a momentary fit of passion.

Dementia due to coarse brain-lesions is usually characterised by pronounced emotional instability. The lesions thus designated comprise those which give rise to ordinary hemiplegias—embolic or hæmorrhagic, tumours, and necrotic softening. The emotional weakness is chiefly displayed by bursts of weeping without any cause whatever; whilst answering a casual enquiry after his health, a hemiplegic thus affected will burst into tears, quickly brighten up again and continue the conversation. This is but an automatic representation of emotion, the patient at the time is incapable of true emotional feeling.

## MORAL INSANITY.

In many of the forms of mental disease described in the preceding pages, the moral aspect of the patient undergoes certain changes before the intellect becomes involved, although the subsequent insane condition is due to intellectual disorder. Moral insanity is said to exist when, without disturbance of the intellect, perversion of the moral sense occurs to a degree inconsistent with due control of the actions. It is denied by some that absence of the moral sense in itself constitutes insanity. Blandford[1] considers that those who have most strongly upheld the doctrine of moral insanity and morbid perversion of the moral sentiments have often underrated, or neglected, the intellectual defect or alteration observable in the patient. Hack Tuke[2] regards the term "moral insanity" as unfortunate, so far as it induces the belief that the moral feelings are themselves necessarily affected by disease, the other mental functions being sound; he looks upon the condition as one that

[1] *Insanity and its Treatment.*  [2] *The Journal of Mental Science,* 1891.

oftentimes is caused by weakening of the higher centres involving paralysis of the voluntary power, and thus transfers the seat of mischief from the feelings themselves to the volitional or inhibitory power.

In moral insanity the higher levels of cerebral development are either imperfectly evolved from birth, or after evolution become diseased and more or less functionless, the result being that, although the intellectual capacity is not seriously affected, the emotional and automatic functions have more than normal play. Such constitutes the mental condition which pervades the criminal classes, and here comes the difficulty, viz., to distinguish between moral depravity and moral insanity, for the former merges into the latter without any absolute line of demarcation. The question has been discussed from extreme standpoints:—one is, that the mere commission of a flagrant crime without remorse demonstrates moral insanity; the other is, that unless the reasoning faculties are so far weakened that the person who commits the crime cannot distinguish between right and wrong, he is responsible for the act; in other words, he is not insane. To countenance the first view is to place a premium on depravity. That individuals whose moral control is so far weakened as to place them in the ranks of the insane commit crimes of the vilest nature without remorse is perfectly true; but to accept the crime as a proof of insanity is another matter. The second opinion, which is held by lawyers, will be discussed presently.

Without entering into a discussion as to how far the emotions may determine the actions without implication of the reasoning powers, experience necessitates the conclusion that, for all practical purposes, the moral perceptions may be so far perverted as to render the individual irresponsible for his actions without signs of mental disease being present, either in the form of delusions or of intellectual enfeeblement. By this it is not meant that the intellect is absolutely intact, but that it is not weakened so far as to betray its condition, except by being unable to control the moral sense. Absence of the inhibitory influence of the higher levels by which moral control is effected may be the result of bad training, as well as of developmental defect or of morbid processes. In order that bad training should paralyse the influence of the higher levels within a single lifetime, it is probably necessary that a certain pre-disposition to succumb should be present; among the criminal classes, taken as a whole, this pre-disposition exists —in them the higher levels are innately reduced. Defective moral control may exist in various degrees, so that at one extreme the effect is displayed by vicious conduct and at the other by insane acts. That a certain disposedness is necessary seems probable from the existence of retained moral control on the part of some who have been brought up amidst the most unfavourable surroundings, and that others who have lost moral control may regain it when transplanted to favourable soil—that is to say, that their higher levels are unstable and disintegrate or reintegrate in accordance with the external influences brought to bear.

The instances of moral insanity which most forcibly demonstrate its existence are those occurring in early life in spite of the most favourable external relations. A short time ago I was consulted with regard to a young lady of only fourteen years of age, who had been "withdrawn" from boarding-school for repeated thefts from her fellow pupils, although she was abundantly supplied with pocket-money. She had not the least regard for truth, and took a malicious pleasure in fabricating statements which brought trouble upon innocent persons. When at home she behaved indecently with her own brother, and made improper overtures to her father's groom. Intellectually she was bright and clever, her schoolmistress reported that she was able to keep pace in classes with other girls of her age, but was fickle and lacked application. The evil strain came from her mother, who took to drinking after she was married, and eventually eloped with a man of low social position; the girl was born about a year after the mother gave way to intemperance. This is an instance of defective evolution of the higher mental levels, the finer traits of character were entirely absent, but there was no lack of a certain cleverness, which conveyed the impression that if the girl only had application and perseverance she could acquire as much knowledge as any of her compeers; moral lapses apart, her friends regarded her as sane enough.

Hack Tuke[1] relates a very typical case of moral insanity, of which the following is a condensed abstract:—A man, who in his youth was sullen, uncommunicative, idle, sly, and treacherous, at an early age evinced a disposition to torture domestic animals and to cruelly treat younger members of the family. On one occasion he took a younger brother into the fields, undressed him, beat him with long lithe willows, and bit and scratched him about the arms and upper part of the body, threatening to kill him with a table-knife if he cried out. Shortly after he was apprehended for cutting the throat of a horse, belonging to a neighbour, and confessed that he had maimed several other animals, and had twisted the necks of fowls and then concealed them in wood piles; he was sentenced to twelve months imprisonment. On his discharge from prison he attempted to suffocate a little child by piling clothing, &c., on the top of it; he then stole some money from his father's desk, for which act he was sentenced to

[1] *Journal of Mental Science*, 1886.

seven years in a penitentiary. After his liberation, being again at home, he saw his father accidentally cut his hand so that it bled profusely; this seemed to excite him, and he went to a neighbouring farm-yard and cut the throat of a horse, killing it. He escaped, and, whilst hiding in a wood, saw a young girl, seized her and committed a criminal assault on her. After being about ten years in prison for this offence, he was set free, and on his way home from prison he caught a horse, tied it to a telegraph-pole and mutilated it in a shocking manner, cutting a terrible gash in the neck, another in the abdomen, and taking a piece off the end of its tongue. For this he was tried and acquitted on the ground of insanity, and was transferred to an Asylum. After being there for five years he made his escape, and was only absent from the asylum about an hour, when he overtook and attempted to outrage a young girl almost in sight of the pursuing attendants. Beside all this he was guilty of innumerable acts of cruelty to fellow-patients in the asylum, and also to dogs, cats, fowls, &c.; he was a great coward and was never known to attack any person that would be likely to offer resistance. The sight of blood had a strange effect on this man; his face grew pallid; he became nervous and restless, and, unless watched, lost control over himself and indulged in the proclivities for which he was notorious. If so situated that he could not indulge his evil propensities he was a quiet and useful man; he had had a fair education and enjoyed reading the newspapers and letters sent to him.

## IMPULSIVE INSANITY

Impulsive insanity may lead to the commission of homicide, suicide, theft, acts of destructiveness, and other criminal actions.

A distinction is to be drawn between insanity with an impulse and impulsive insanity. Mania, melancholia and delusional insanity are all prone to be associated with impulse, but by impulsive insanity is meant a condition of loss of inhibitory control which allows of abnormal energising of the higher, but not the highest levels, by which a strong or ungovernable impulse to do some irrational act is developed, without delusion or loss of general self-control. An erroneous idea exists that such impulses are necessarily of momentary growth—an idea probably derived from a totally different cause of irrational impulse, such as is exemplified by a man in a paroxysm of anger, who, especially if subjected to renewed excitation, may suddenly develop an impulse to kill his opponent. His anger, which for a time is furious enough, is expended in words and gesticulations, suddenly he loses self-control and is seized with an impulse, to which he immediately yields, and the deed is done. The condition depicted partakes of the nature of a temporary mania which culminates in an explosive act, the result of loss of general control. The condition usually understood by the term impulsive insanity is not of this high-tension type. An individual may be sensible of an impulse and yet retain sufficient self-control as not to yield to it; at any rate for a time, he may either seek the help of external control, or, after struggling for a time, the impulse may overcome him, when he obeys its dictates whatever they may be. Indicative of the ebb and flow of self-control in such cases is the revulsion of feeling which not unfrequently occurs to the insane person in the midst of carrying the impulse into effect.

Homicidal Impulse.—A woman develops an impulse to kill all her children, and resists it for a time, possibly thinking about the matter for days, that is to say, the thought keeps continually recurring. At last she acts, but, after killing one of her children, control is re-established, she throws away the knife and bursts into tears. Such a case was tried before Lord Blackburn,[1] the woman, after cutting the throat of one of her children, was checked in her homicidal career by the child next in turn to be sacrificed throwing her arms round her mother's neck and speaking to her in a caressing manner. The woman subsequently explained that she was going to kill the child, but that, after the caress, she "had not the heart to do it." Although she evidently knew right from wrong and also the character of the act, the judge told the jury that there were exceptional cases, on the strength of which ruling a verdict of not guilty, on the ground of insanity, was returned. Maudsley[2] relates a very instructive example of homicidal impulse. Dr Pownall, a medical practitioner, was admitted to an asylum on certificates which stated that he had made a murderous attack on his mother-in-law, whom he usually respected and loved. He had an attack of mental disorder when he was twenty-two years of age, a second after an interval of fourteen years, and a third (the one for which he was now placed under restraint) after a further interval of four years and a half. Between the attacks he successfully conducted a large medical practice, and was so much respected by his fellow-townsmen as to be elected to the office of mayor. During his second attack of derangement he shot a gentleman with whom he was out shooting, and, although the coroner's inquest resulted in a verdict of accidental death, there were some who thought differently. He remained in the asylum for four months; during the whole of that time he betrayed no symptom of mental disease and, consequently, was discharged as recovered. Twenty days after leaving the asylum he killed a female servant by cutting her

[1] Cited by Orange, *Journ. of Ment. Science*, 1884.
[2] *Responsibility in Mental Disease.*

throat with a razor, having shown no indication of insanity up to within a few hours of the act. Acquitted at his trial on the ground of insanity he was sent to Bethlehem Hospital as a criminal lunatic, and the medical officer, after an observation of several months, said that he could not attach any particular symptom of insanity to him, and that supposing he was a private patient, and the Commissioners in Lunacy asked why he was detained, he could give no definite reason for it.

In another class of cases, the homicidal impulse exists along with, or rather in consequence of, pronounced delusions. A man falsely believes that a certain person has done him some great wrong, and, in consequence of this delusion, he murders him. Such cases are a common result of delusional insanity, and are usually easy of recognition, as the insane person makes no secret of his delusion. Occasionally, however, an extraordinary capacity is displayed to conceal delusions, which are yet sufficiently powerful as eventually to lead to a homicidal outbreak. Maudsley thinks it probable that Dr. Pownall was able successfully to conceal his delusions when he had a strong motive to do so.

**Suicidal Impulse.**—According to the popular notion, the suicidal act in itself constitutes evidence of insanity. This is fostered by the stereotyped addendum to the verdict of the coroner's jury of "temporary insanity," devised probably as a means of escape from the verdict of *felo-de-se*, which formerly carried with it certain penalties. The suicidal act is not necessarily indicative of insanity; it may be the result of a rational resolve. If a man of high social position, and by repute of great wealth, is discovered to have embezzled money or forged monetary documents, and is stared in the face by the inevitable consequences, he may prefer immediate death to penal servitude. The misery—mental and physical—he seeks to avoid is real and tangible; the question is one of balance of evil; the remedy is a desperate one it is true, but so is his condition, and the outcome is, that he determines to avail himself of the only means of escape at his command, and puts an end to his life.

Like homicidal impulse, insane suicidal impulse may exist either with or without delusions or other disorder of the mind; the impulse may be controlled for a time, or the patient may ask to be protected against himself. Suicide from impulse differs from that with delusions inasmuch as the patient appears to be sane on all but the one point. The tendency may be recurrent, the patient being free from mental disorder meanwhile. Instances have occurred in which an unsuccessful attempt to carry out the intention has been sufficient to restore control, and free the patient from the impulse. A case is related of a man going towards a river with the set purpose of drowning himself, he was attacked by thieves and defended himself lustily, and, having got away, he returned home cured of his suicidal impulse. The impulse may take a certain definite direction to the exclusion of all others; a man will neglect knives and razors or other means at hand, to go a considerable distance and place himself on a line of rails and allow a train to pass over him. The impulse once fully developed may recur, even after a long interval of apparent perfect sanity. A case is recorded in the Commissioners' Blue Book (quoted by Newington[1]) of a man who had been fourteen years under supervision; for the first part of that time he had been absolutely suicidal, but he improved, and used to go out and enjoy himself. At the end of fourteen years his mother sent him an old writing-desk; in it was a secret drawer, from which he took a bottle containing poison that he had placed there fourteen years before. He did not swallow the poison at once, but walked off into a wood, and there took it and died. Before the arrival of the desk, he had plenty of opportunities of procuring poison had he been so disposed.

When the impulse to suicide is the outcome of melancholia or other mental disorder, there is, usually, a definite delusion: the patient hears a constantly recurring command bidding him to kill himself, or accusations of horrible crimes are ceaselessly made by voices from the sound of which he seeks, in death, to escape. The delusion of persecution is a common cause of impulse to suicide. Heredity exercises a powerful influence in predisposing to suicide, the tendency often asserting itself about the same time of life in the child as in the parent. Ill-health reduces the higher inhibitive powers, and if there is a latent proneness to suicide, it is then likely to assert itself; the same remarks apply to business worries, loss of money and disappointments of all kinds. In the latter instances the impulse is of a mixed origin, and approaches in character that which determines the suicidal act in a sane person. If a man labours under the delusion that he is the victim of a secret society, whose agents are persecuting him and rendering his life unbearable, and in consequence of this delusion he puts an end to his life, the act is that of an obviously insane person, because he believes a delusion and acts upon it, as though it was a real occurrence. If a man has lost a great deal of money and is consequently obliged to retrench his household expenses, he may take such an exaggerated view of his difficulties as to develop an impulse to suicide; although a delusion determines the impulse it is one that is founded on an actual occurrence, and would not have come into play under more favourable external relations. The man with

[1] *Journ. of Mental Science*, 1886.

hallucinatory delusions is liable to develop the suicidal impulse in spite of his surroundings, the other, only in consequence of them.

The approach of the wave of depression which allows the impulse to develop may be felt by the patient, in some instances he requests that he may be taken care of until the depression is passed. Further evidence of consciousness of loss of self-control is afforded by the fact, that, in some instances, the patient himself will lock up knives and other instruments, which from propinquity might tempt him; this teaches an important lesson on the subject of irresponsibility. Suggestion may exercise a powerful influence on a pre-disposed mind; hearing of the suicide of an intimate friend, or even of that of an individual personally unknown to the patient, may be sufficient to incite him to the same act. The impulse may be controllable at one time and not at another, which further complicates the question of responsibility. Threats to commit suicide made by a person suffering from some distressing bodily ailment are not unlikely to be put into execution. Manning[1] relates the case of a perfectly sane man who was admitted into hospital for liver disease and dropsy. He told his wife that, if he ascertained from the doctor that his disease was incurable, he would commit suicide, and that he had at first thought of shooting himself with a pistol, but, considering that it would be a cruel shock to his fellow-patients in the ward, he had resolved to adopt another method. One day after this conversation, he learnt on enquiry from one of the resident medical officers that his case was hopeless; he watched his opportunity, went on to a balcony outside the ward, and deliberately flung himself over and broke his neck.

**Medico-legal Relations of Suicide.**—The law regards the suicidal act as felonious unless the individual is held to be irresponsible on the ground of insanity. A person who aids and abets another person to commit suicide is guilty of murder; the crime is not lessened if two persons mutually agree to commit suicide at the same time and in the presence of each other. If one dies and the other survives, the survivor is guilty of murder; the fact of his making a simultaneous attempt on his own life does not affect the crime committed against the deceased. If a person, in the attempt to commit suicide, occasions the death of another person (he himself recovering) he is guilty of manslaughter. A man jumped into a canal with the intention of committing suicide, but was rescued by a passer-by, who unfortunately was drowned in the act of rescue. The intended suicide was found guilty of manslaughter in spite of an attempt to prove him insane (*Reg v. Gathercole*).

**Kleptomania**, or impulse to steal, is of dubious existence apart from

[1] *Journ. of Mental Science*, 1886.

an insane condition due to general mental disease. That an insane person may have a raven-like propensity to steal is well-known, but that, because a person steals without a transparently obvious motive for doing so, he is therefore to be regarded as insane is simply to encourage vice. If the propensity to steal is really due to an insane state, there will be other evidences of mental disease apart from the act of theft; a person will not be absolutely sane in every respect save the desire to appropriate articles that do not belong to him. Acts of theft, we have seen, are not uncommon in the early stage of general paralysis, or after an attack of minor epilepsy, and they are usually traceable to their causation. Moral insanity with impulse, which is usually alleged in defence of the culprit when kleptomania is brought in question, is to be regarded with great suspicion. It is, of course, quite possible that a person who is the subject of moral insanity may pilfer, as well as do other acts contrary to the moral code, but it is improbable that loss of the highest control will solely exhibit itself in such a narrow channel—there will be other evidences of its existence. When kleptomania is pleaded in defence, it is usually manifest that no evidence worthy of the name is advanced to prove any antecedent disorder of the mind; the most that is urged is that the accused was quite capable of paying for the stolen articles, and therefore that the act was due to an insane impulse.

## MEDICO-LEGAL RELATIONS OF INSANITY.

The medical terms by which the various forms of insanity are designated are not recognised in law. The legal terms are:—**Dementia naturalis**, which is equivalent to idiocy and imbecility, and **Dementia adventitia** or acquired insanity; both of these are included in the term **Lunacy**. A further designation, **non compos mentis**, or unsoundness of mind, is used to indicate an indefinite condition of a lesser degree of insanity than the two preceding.

The subject of insanity comes under the notice of the medical jurist in relation to (a) **criminal responsibility**, (b) **lunacy certificates**, (c) **commissions of enquiry**, (d) **testamentary capacity**, (e) **feigned insanity**.

### (a) CRIMINAL RESPONSIBILITY.

The commission of a criminal act involves punishment, but if the person who commits a criminal act is proved to be insane at the time he committed it, he is held to be irresponsible to the law for what he has done. The questions that arise out of this statement are:—What constitutes insanity, and to what extent must the accused be under its influence in order that he should be held irresponsible?

No definition of insanity has ever been formulated that can be applied as a touch-stone to the individual, and his sanity or insanity thereby determined. In order to meet the difficulty, certain features assumed to indicate insanity, have been selected by the administrators of the law and converted into a test, to be applied to each individual case. This "legal test," after having undergone certain modifications in the course of time, now stands as follows:—

"To establish a defence on the ground of insanity, it must be clearly proved that at the time of committing the act the party accused was labouring under such a defect of reason from disease of the mind as not to know the nature and quality of the act he was doing, or, if he did know it, that he did not know he was doing what was wrong."

The first points that present themselves in relation to this test are:—That mental oblivion as regards certain external relations is assumed to be the necessary accompaniment of an exculpatory degree of insanity of all kinds and that its occurrence alone affords evidence of irresponsibility.

A slight acquaintance with the various forms of insanity is sufficient to show the inadequacy of the terms laid down to determine irresponsibility. A man may be so dominated by an impulse to homicide as to carry it into effect in spite of the knowledge that he is doing wrong and, therefore, is liable to punishment. At the Shropshire Winter Assizes in 1885, a man called Ware, who had been a patient in an Asylum, and had killed another patient with an iron bar, was indicted for murder. It was proved by the depositions that the prisoner was perfectly aware of the nature of the act he had committed at the time he committed it. he acknowledged that he had killed some one, and demanded a promise from the attendant that he should not be punished if he gave up the iron bar. The case did not come before the jury as the man was previously removed to the criminal lunatic asylum at Broadmoor, but Mr Justice Hawkins made some remarks which are very pertinent to the question at issue:—"It would be impossible to say that Ware did not know that he had killed a man, because he said himself that he had, and it would be impossible for anybody to urge that he did not know it was wrong, for he wanted a promise that he should not be punished, but unless one put a totally different construction on the law, *that* would have to be proved, although no man in his senses would suppose that any jury would find Ware responsible for what he had done."

It is well known to medical men that a man may be under the influence of a delusion or of an insane impulse which urges him to commit an act that he knows is punishable by law, if the delusion or impulse is sufficiently powerful to overcome his self-control he commits the act—that is to say, he is unable to restrain himself. Loss of self-control from mental disease is equally causative of irresponsibility as is want of knowledge between right and wrong, therefore any one subject to such loss of control ought not to be held answerable for his actions. The legal test as interpreted by almost all the judges will not admit of this. In *Reg* v *Cole* (C C C, 1883), for murder of a child, Denman, J, allowed "that it was established in evidence that the prisoner had been suffering from delusions [that there were men under the floor, and in a cupboard, who sought to injure him], but that he knew that he was doing wrong, and he knew that he acted contrary to the law of this country."

In his *History of the Criminal Law of England*, 1883, Sir James F Stephen puts a much more liberal interpretation on the legal definition of insanity as a plea for criminal irresponsibility.—In his opinion the law allows that a man, who by reason of mental disease is prevented from controlling his conduct, is not responsible for what he does, and that the existence of any delusion, impulse, or other state which is commonly produced by madness, is a fact relevant to the question whether or not he can control his conduct. The late Lord Chief-Justice Cockburn did not view the law in this light, but he expressed himself to a select committee of the House of Commons to the following effect.—"I have always been strongly of opinion that, as the pathology of insanity abundantly establishes, there are forms of mental disease in which, though the patient is quite aware that he is about to do wrong, the will becomes overpowered by the force of irresistible impulse, the power of self-control when destroyed or suspended by mental disease becomes, I think, an essential element of [ir-] responsibility." If the law thus stood, as one judge maintains it does, and another states that it ought to do, the sentences of the higher criminal courts would not subsequently be annulled as they often are by the influence of public opinion.

The **medical view** is, that a man who is the victim of mental disease may know that a certain act is wrong, and is punishable by law, but that an insane impulse, whether arising from a delusion or not, may overcome his self-control and he may commit the act, not because he does not know that he is thereby doing wrong, but because he cannot prevent himself from doing it.

In many instances the plea of insanity is abused, the mode of procedure being partly in fault. If a man who commits murder is arrested, he is taken before the magistrates, and no matter how insane he may be he is committed for trial at the assizes. If the mental disorder is of such a decided nature as to render it unadvisable that he should remain in jail, he may, by order of the Secretary of State, be removed to an asylum; such cases of course could give rise to no difference of opinion at the trial. The cases which admit of difference of opinion are not sufficiently pronounced as to be removed, and the prisoner probably remains until the trial without anything being said, or any steps taken, in relation to his mental condition. It is to be noted, however, that if after committal insanity is alleged, the public prosecutor if informed will direct an investigation as to the state of the prisoner's mind to be made by two medical men of experience, with whom an official referee may be associated. It does not follow that at the trial these gentlemen will be retained on behalf of the Crown, although the Home Office orders and pays for the investigation; in some instances, one or more of the examiners have been subpœnaed for the defence, their evidence being favourable to it.

At the trial, even if the prisoner has been examined under the authority of the public prosecutor as to his mental condition, some judges will only allow the medical witness to state what he saw and heard during his interview with the prisoner; they will not admit any expert evidence, ruling that the jury alone are competent to express an opinion as to his sanity or insanity. Other judges accept expert evidence. If the prisoner is so obviously insane as to be unable to plead on arraignment, he is sent to a criminal lunatic asylum until he recovers, when he is again brought before the Court, or if he does not recover he remains in the asylum. A less obvious degree of insanity, however, is not regarded as a bar to pleading, but it forms part of the defence, and is not unfrequently urged for the first time after the prisoner is condemned.

The absence of systematised procedure is productive of evils in a variety of ways. The prisoner is rarely examined by an expert until a considerable time after the commission of the act for which he was arrested; the law demands proof of insanity at the time the act was committed, therefore the nearer to it an examination into the state of the prisoner's mind is made, the more likely is it to remove doubts. Again, evidence as to sanity, or insanity, may be given by any medical man who happens to have formed an opinion on the subject; this fosters a dangerous tendency to push expertism too far, and with the aid of the prisoner's counsel, to strive to carry the point at all costs. Much stress is usually laid on real or assumed heredity, the importance of which may be over-estimated; the question is forcibly put by Bucknill [1] when discussing the plea of insanity in the case of Guiteau, the assassin of General Garfield, President of the United States.

[1] *Brain*, 1883.

"The argument in favour of insanity founded upon the supposed transmission of an hereditary tendency to mental disease has of late been used in most absurd and unjustifiable excess, and I do not know that the interests of justice would be damaged if it were to be excluded altogether in judicial inquiries, for if it could be clearly shown that both a man's parents, and all four of his grand parents, and all his uncles and aunts had been unquestionably insane, it would afford no proof whatever that the man himself had been insane Such evidence would at the most strengthen the presumption that he had been so under circumstances which would otherwise be more doubtful"

Recurrent insanity may be pleaded as a bar to criminal responsibility, and if the plea is sustained, the death penalty is not inflicted even when murder is committed in what lawyers term a **lucid interval.** If the accused is proved to have been actually insane at some previous period of his life, it is allowed that the mind might be so far diseased at the time the deed was done, as to render him irresponsible for his actions This statement does not mean that the prisoner is never found guilty and sentenced, he may be, but if so the convict's mental condition is subsequently investigated, with the result that he is probably detained in a criminal lunatic asylum "during Her Majesty's pleasure," instead of undergoing the capital sentence If the prisoner is proved to have been insane shortly before committing the deed, although at the trial he might present all the appearances of sanity, he would probably be acquitted on the ground of irresponsibility

**Moral insanity** is invariably a stumbling-block to lawyers, who usually regard it as the medical definition of unmitigated depravity. From what has already been said on the subject, it is to be admitted that there is some excuse for this view, inasmuch as the two conditions are not capable of precise distinction There exists what Maudsley terms "a borderland between crime and insanity, near one boundary of which we meet with something of madness, but more of sin, and near the other boundary of which something of sin but more of madness"

It was asserted in an early section of this subject that delusions are indicative of insanity, it is none the less true that insanity may exist without delusions This is a hard thing for lawyers to accept, and many of them decline to accept it To establish the plea in cases of simple moral insanity, the past family and personal history of the accused must be relied on to a great extent, and in those cases in which the absence of moral perception is due to the onset of a progressive mental disease—as in general paralysis—the concomitant symptoms must be sought for

The case of *Reg v Edmunds* (C C C, 1872) is a good example of moral insanity leading to the perpetration of criminal acts, by which the lives of innocent people are sacrificed without scruple or remorse in order to avert suspicion from the criminal, and to direct it against those who have done no wrong. Christina Edmunds, aged forty-three, was charged with the wilful murder of a little boy named Barker. The boy ate some chocolate-creams, which were bought at a respectable confectioner's shop; half an hour after he died with symptoms of poisoning by strychnine, the presence of the alkaloid being subsequently detected in the contents of the stomach. It was proved that the prisoner had obtained a considerable amount of strychnine under false pretences, had got possession of the druggist's poison-book, and had torn out leaves which recorded the purchase. It appeared that she incorporated part of the poison with some chocolate-creams, and then asked a small boy to purchase some more creams for her; when he brought them she said they were too large, and sent them back to be changed. Unknown to the boy she substituted poisoned creams which, when returned to the confectioner, were placed with his ordinary stock to be sold in due course. One or more of these poisoned sweets caused the death of the boy Barker, who was totally unknown to the prisoner; she also distributed poisoned sweets to many children who became ill. At the inquest which was held on the body of the deceased (before being suspected of the crime) she volunteered evidence in order to implicate the confectioner who had sold the sweets; she also wrote anonymous letters to the father of the deceased, inciting him to take legal proceedings against the confectioner. This was not done through malice towards the man, but to divert suspicion from herself. She had previously been accused of endeavouring to poison a lady, for whose husband she had conceived a regard, and the whole of this elaborately carried out public-poisoning was apparently the result of a scheme to make it evident that the lady's indisposition was also due to poisoned sweets owing to carelessness of the confectioner. It was proved in evidence that the prisoner's father on two occasions had been under restraint, and that he died in an asylum; that one brother had epilepsy and died in Earlswood Asylum; that a sister was hysterical, and had tried to throw herself out of a window, and that other members of the family had suffered from various psychoses. Expert physicians were called to prove that the prisoner was morally insane: she was without intellectual defect and was free from delusions, but she was indifferent to her position and to the enormity of her crimes. She was found guilty and was sentenced to death, but the sentence was subsequently changed to detention in Broadmoor Asylum.

This is a typical case of moral insanity, all the more so because of its marked resemblance to unbridled depravity. One of the medical witnesses spoke of her being on the border-land between disease and vice; there can be little doubt that mental disease, in the form of imperfectly evolved higher centres, deprived her of the self-control of a sane person, and was the true cause of her criminal conduct.

Impulsive insanity fares little better as a plea unless associated with some other manifestation of mental disease; in relation to this form of insanity it is to be noted that the insane person may be able to govern the impulse at one time and not at another, and thus a further difficulty is introduced. The bench is disposed to assume that if a man, alleged to be insane, can control himself at one time under certain conditions, he ought to be able to do so at another under like conditions; and further, that if he can control himself at all he ought to be able to do so always. An illustration of the way in which recurrent insanity with homicidal impulse is dealt with in courts of law is afforded by the case of *Reg* v *Cooper* (Norwich Assizes, 1887). The prisoner was a curate who, without any reason whatever, murdered his vicar, who was paralysed, by cutting his throat whilst in bed. Nine years before the prisoner had been under restraint and had developed homicidal mania. Whilst in the asylum he was very violent and attempted without provocation to cut the throat of another patient; he also attempted to throttle a second patient. Between his committal and trial the prisoner was examined by two experts employed by the Crown, and they certified to the Home Secretary that he was insane. The experts had an interview with the prisoner on the morning of the trial, but having previously had opportunities of satisfying themselves as to his insanity, they did not then specially test him for delusions. At the trial the judge would not allow any expression of opinion on the part of the experts but restricted their evidence to what had occurred at the interview held that same morning, and insisted that the jury should hear word for word the questions put by the witnesses and the answers made by the prisoner. The result was distorted evidence at variance with the real state of things, the prisoner was represented as taking part in a rational conversation and displaying no delusions, the witnesses not being allowed to refer to previously obtained ample evidence of their existence.

Delusional insanity appeals more cogently to the legal mind than the varieties just discussed; but even when delusions are present, it is demanded that they shall be of such a nature as to take away the power of distinguishing between right and wrong. Lawyers attach much importance to the presence of delusions as a sign of insanity, and admit that they may be so dominant as to disturb the judgment to a degree inconsistent with sane conduct. Martin, B., when summing up in the case of *Reg* v. *Townley* (Derby Winter Assizes, 1863), said that "what the law meant by an insane man was a man who acted under a delusion, and supposed a state of things to exist which did not exist, and acted thereupon." Thus mere delusions, whatever proof of mental disease they may afford to medical men, afford no proof in the eyes of the law unless the individual is thereby rendered unconscious of the nature and quality of the act of which he has been guilty. Delusions of a lesser type are called partial delusions by lawyers, and are not regarded as doing away with the responsibility of a criminal act.

Delusions which frequently bring the subjects of them within the grasp of the law are those of persecution, or of a sense of wrong or injury inflicted that imperatively demands justice. It is to a case of this kind that we owe the legal test of insanity which at present determines the ruling of the judges. In the year 1843 a man named M'Naughton shot Mr. Drummond, whom he believed to be conspiring with others against his life and character. M'Naughton was acquitted on the ground of insanity, and as there was a general outcry at the supposed failure of justice, the House of Lords propounded certain questions to the judges in order to elicit an authoritative ruling with regard to the plea of insanity. The answers to these questions constitute the law on the subject, as explained in the preceding pages.

Illustrative of the loss of self-control caused by a delusion is the case of *Reg* v. *Dodwell* (C.C.C., 1878). The prisoner was a clergyman who became involved in legal proceedings, and, after quarrelling with his legal adviser, conducted his own case in such an irregular manner that he did not obtain what he desired. On the strength of this he conceived that he had a grievance against the Master of the Rolls. One morning he awaited the arrival of his Lordship and fired a pistol at him; no injury was inflicted, as the pistol was only loaded with powder and wadding, the prisoner declaring that his sole object was to direct public attention to his wrongs. At the trial the Master of the Rolls stated that the prisoner was incoherent and irritable, and that he appeared to be under a delusion; no medical evidence was called on either side, and the jury returned a verdict of "not guilty on the ground of insanity." In this case there was no legal evidence of insanity, the prisoner's action might have been due to irascibility and culpable neglect to curb a violent temper, all the evidence went to prove that he knew perfectly well the quality of the act and that he was doing wrong. Possibly the heinousness of the offence—firing at a high legal functionary—was regarded as sufficient in itself to constitute proof of insanity. Dodwell's subsequent history is not without interest in relation to the recurrence of insane impulses, for, although he did not come up to the legal test of insanity, he was none the less a victim of delusional insanity judged from the medical standpoint. After the trial he was transferred to Broadmoor, and in 1882 he committed a murderous assault on the chief physician of the asylum by dealing him a heavy blow on the crown of the head with a stone slung in a handkerchief. The motive which instigated him was identical with that which prompted him to fire the pistol at the Master of the Rolls: he stated that as the previous act had not proved sufficient to redress his wrongs, he made up his mind to commit some still more serious act, and had come to the conclusion that nothing less than murder would be sufficient to deliver him from the conspiracy of which he imagined himself the victim.

In relation to the duties of medical men when called upon to pronounce as to the sanity or otherwise of a prisoner, it is to be observed that in many cases it is impossible to arrive at a reliable conclusion without having the individual under observation for some time. Usually several interviews are allowed, for which, and for obtaining the family and personal history of the case, every facility is afforded. In some cases more than this is required but is not obtainable. It should be possible to have such cases placed under skilled care not only of expert physicians, but of attendants also, who are accustomed to the insane; by close and continuous observation a trustworthy opinion might be formed as to the real nature of the case. No medical man is justified in going into the witness-box, and (if allowed) delivering himself of dogmatic statements as to the insanity of a prisoner after only a casual interview, unless indeed the mental state is so obvious as not to admit of doubt.

In every respect it would be advantageous if the plea of insanity was disposed of before the trial. The present state of the law is a stumbling-block to this proposal: as interpreted by the judges it will not allow what the Secretary of State is subsequently obliged to concede to public opinion. This leads to those unseemly discussions in the daily papers which so frequently follow a death-sentence. In one class of cases the outcry is the result of a genuine conviction that a judicial blunder has been made; in such cases the end doubtless justifies the means; the result is, that if there is reasonable ground for doubting the convict's sanity he is sent to Broadmoor instead of being hung. Encouraged by such cases philanthropists, and pseudo-philanthropists rush into print in season and out of season whenever a capital conviction takes place. No matter how utterly incongruous the pretence of insanity may be, the plea is promptly urged in not too moderate language, and it is echoed by those who on abstract grounds are opposed to capital punishment. Petitions are signed amid much display of sentiment, and frequently unfair pressure is brought to bear upon those in power. That sentiment, or prejudice, rather than equity, is the stimulant which determines such a display of ill-directed energy, is shown by the fact that if murder is associated with rape, the murderer is invariably left to his fate, he is too unclean to become sentimental over, or even to be mad.

An able address on Insanity, in relation to offences against the Criminal law, delivered by Orange at the annual meeting of the Medico-psychological Association, with the discussion thereon, is contained in the *Journal of Mental Science* for 1884.

## Drunkenness in Relation to Criminal Responsibility.

The law lays down no definite rules with regard to the plea of drunkenness as a bar to, or in mitigation of, punishment for crime committed under its influence. The principles which usually guide the judges when dealing with crimes of magnitude are—that simple intoxication affords no excuse for the commission of crime, but if by prolonged drinking the mind is impaired, the condition is regarded as being on a par with ordinary insanity, and may be pleaded as a defence against criminal responsibility. The view taken is—that simple intoxication cannot be held to excuse an offence committed whilst under its influence, because the loss of control was produced by the drunken man's own default. In the case of *Reg* v *Williams* (Old Bailey, 1886), Denman, J., ruled as follows:—that a crime committed during drunkenness was as much a crime as if it were committed during sobriety, and that the jury had nothing to do with the fact that the man was drunk. The prisoner was supposed to know the effect of drink, and if he took away his senses by means of drink, it was no excuse at all. Quite recently Sir Henry James[1] expresses the opinion that the man who chooses to drink to excess, and when drunk from time to time commits acts of brutal violence, must be taught that he is answerable both for being under the influence of alcohol, and for the acts such influence induces.

The fact that drink does not always affect people to a like degree constitutes a great difficulty. A man either from natural or acquired susceptibility may become maniacal under the influence of an amount of drink that would but slightly affect an ordinary man; such a man, under the influence of drink, is much nearer the condition of true insanity than that of outrageous drunkenness. The reply obviously is—that a man so constituted should not take drink, and that if he does, it is at his peril. Morally the question is hard of solution; but the administrators of the law act in accordance with the view just

[1] *The Times* Newspaper, Jan. 4, 1892.

enunciated, and punish the drunkard for committing a crime when he is partly drunk and partly insane, as though he was wholly the former. They are justified in doing so by the evil which would result if those who drink to excess were encouraged to believe that crimes committed under its influence would be lightly dealt with.

When mental aberration is due to the remote effects of alcohol, as in delirium tremens, judges usually allow that the condition is one of insanity, and it is dealt with accordingly; but even then the legal test for insanity may be applied, and the prisoner's criminal responsibility estimated by it. Great stress is laid by many judges on the permanency of the mental disorder which accompanies delirium tremens, but the exact meaning they attach to the term "permanent" is doubtful. Presumably, it refers rather to a continuance of the symptoms for a definite time after the individual has ceased to indulge in alcohol, than to an absolutely permanent insane condition. In *Reg* v *M'Gowan* (Manchester Assizes, 1878), Manisty, J., ruled that "a state of disease brought about by a person's own act—as delirium tremens, caused by excessive drinking—was no excuse for committing a crime unless the disease so produced was permanent." Recently a much less restrictive ruling has been given in the case of *Reg* v *Baines* (Lancaster Assizes, 1886), by Day, J., who said "that the question was whether there was insanity or not; that it was immaterial whether it was caused by the person himself or by the vices of his ancestors; and that it was immaterial whether the insanity was permanent or temporary." Mr. Justice Day further ruled—"that if a man were in such a state of intoxication that he did not know the nature of his act, or that his act was wrongful, his act would be excusable." This ruling is in marked contrast with that previously given by Denman, J., and also with that given by Bramwell, B., in *Reg* v. *Burns* (Liverpool Assizes, 1865), "that drunkenness was no excuse, and that a prisoner cannot by drinking qualify himself for the perpetration of crime; but if through drink his mind had become substantially impaired, a ground of acquittal would then fairly arise." The term "substantially" in this ruling replaces the term "permanent" in the ruling given in *Reg* v. *M'Gowan*, above quoted, and seems to point to an impaired mental condition, which, although caused by drinking alcohol to excess, is not due to the immediate presence of alcohol in the system, but to more lasting changes produced in the higher levels of the brain, by which the power of self-control is lowered or entirely lost, and the individual is thereby rendered subject to delusions, and is deprived of the knowledge of the nature and quality of his actions.

## (b) LUNACY CERTIFICATES.

Before a person of unsound mind can be legally placed under restraint, certain conditions specified by Act of Parliament must be fulfilled. The law jealously safeguards the liberty of the subject, and imposes a number of stringent regulations upon those to whom power is given of placing and receiving insane persons in institutions, or private houses, for the purpose of treatment and of preventing them doing injury to themselves and to others. Two recent Acts[1] have considerably modified and altered the mode of procedure previously in force. The subject, being of the highest importance to medical practitioners, demands careful and detailed consideration.

Lunatics may be placed under restraint by the following modes of procedure, which are varied to suit the exigencies of each individual case :—

>Reception Orders on Petition.
>Urgency Orders.
>Orders after Inquisition.
>Summary Reception Orders.
>Orders for lunatics wandering at large, and for pauper lunatics.
>Reception Orders by two Commissioners.

Reception Orders on Petition.—This is the usual mode of procedure in the case of private patients.

The Order for the reception of the patient is to be obtained by private application from a "Judicial Authority:" that is to say, either a specially appointed justice of the peace, judge of county courts, or magistrate; lists of judicial authorities are published. A petition for the order must be presented to the Judicial Authority, if possible by the husband or wife, or by a relative of the alleged lunatic; if by another person the reason for this departure must be explained. No person may present a petition unless he is at least twenty-one years of age, and within fourteen days before its presentation has seen the alleged lunatic. The petition must be accompanied by a statement of particulars, and by two medical certificates. Printed forms for all these documents are to be obtained.

The Judicial Authority if satisfied may make the order forthwith without seeing the patient, or he may appoint a time not more than seven days after the presentation of the petition for enquiries and consideration; he may also visit the alleged lunatic. At the time appointed for the consideration of the petition, he may either make an order or may adjourn the same for any period not exceeding four-

[1] The Lunacy Act, 1890 (53 Vict., ch. 5) and the Lunacy Act, 1891 (54 and 55 Vict., ch. 65).

teen days, and if he thinks fit he may summon further witnesses. If the Judicial Authority dismisses the petition, he must give the petitioner a statement in writing containing his reasons for doing so. A reception order ceases to be valid after the expiration of seven clear days from its date, except when suspended by a medical certificate of unfitness of lunatic for removal, in which case the lunatic may be received within three days after the date of a medical certificate to the effect that he is fit to be removed.

**Urgency Orders.**—In cases of urgency where it is expedient that the alleged lunatic (not a pauper) shall forthwith be placed under care and treatment, he may be temporarily received without the intervention of a Judicial Authority, upon an urgency order, accompanied by a statement of particulars, and one medical certificate. If possible the urgency order should be made by the husband or wife, or by a relative of the alleged lunatic, it may be signed either before or after the medical certificate. If the urgency order is not signed by one of the persons named, it must contain a statement of the reasons why it is not so signed, and of the connection of the person signing it with the alleged lunatic. No person may sign an urgency order unless he is at least twenty-one years of age and within two days before the date of the order has seen the alleged lunatic. An urgency order remains in force for seven days from its date, or, if a petition for a reception order is pending, until the petition is finally disposed of. The medical certificate must contain a statement that it is expedient for the alleged lunatic to be forthwith placed under care, with the reasons for such statement.

**Orders after Inquisition.**—A lunatic found so by inquisition (the procedure will be explained subsequently), may be received upon an order signed by the committee of the person of the lunatic, or upon an order signed by a Master in Lunacy.

**Summary Reception Orders.**—Every constable, relieving officer, and overseer of a parish, who has knowledge that any person within his district or parish, who is not a pauper and not wandering at large, is deemed to be a lunatic, and is not under proper care and control, or is cruelly treated or neglected by those in charge of him, shall within three days give information on oath to a justice being a Judicial Authority under the Act. Such justice may visit the alleged lunatic, but whether he does so or not he shall direct two medical practitioners to examine and certify as to his mental state, and shall then proceed as if a petition for a reception order had been presented to him. A lunatic as to whom a summary reception order has been made, may be taken care of by a relation, or friend, with the consent of the Justice who makes the order, or of the visitors of the asylum in which the lunatic is, or is intended to be, placed.

5. **Orders for Lunatics Wandering at Large.**—Every constable and relieving officer and every overseer of a parish who has knowledge that any person (whether a pauper or not) wandering at large within his district or parish, and deemed to be a lunatic, shall immediately apprehend and take the alleged lunatic before a justice, or the justice, if information on oath is tendered to him, may require such constable, relieving officer, or overseer to apprehend and bring the alleged lunatic before him. The justice shall then call in a medical practitioner, and if he signs a certificate and the justice is satisfied that the alleged lunatic is a lunatic, and is a proper person to be detained, he may issue an order to that effect. If the medical practitioner certifies in writing that the lunatic is not in a fit state to be removed, the removal order shall be suspended until his fitness is certified to. If a constable, relieving officer, or overseer is satisfied that it is necessary for the public safety, or the welfare of the alleged lunatic that he should be placed under control before the above-mentioned proceedings can be taken, he may be removed to the workhouse of the union in which he is, and detained not longer than three days; before the expiration of that time the proceedings required by the Lunacy Act shall be taken.

6. **Reception Orders by two Commissioners.**—Any two or more Commissioners in Lunacy may visit a pauper lunatic or alleged lunatic not in an institution for lunatics or workhouse; they may call in a medical practitioner, and if he certifies with regard to the lunatic, and they are satisfied that the pauper is a lunatic, they may order his removal to an institution for lunatics.

With the exception of the two last named these regulations do not apply to pauper lunatics or alleged lunatics. The usual proceeding in the case of **pauper lunatics** is for the medical officer of the union to give notice in writing to the relieving officer, or if there be none, to the overseer of the parish where the pauper resides, that a pauper resident within the district is a lunatic and a proper person to be sent to an asylum; this he is bound to do within three days after obtaining knowledge of such pauper lunatic. Every relieving officer, or if there be none, overseer of the parish in which the lunatic resides, who has knowledge either by notice of the medical officer, or otherwise, that a pauper resident within the district or parish is deemed to be a lunatic, shall within three days give notice to a justice having jurisdiction in the place where the pauper resides. The justice then orders the pauper to be brought before him and calls in a medical practitioner to examine him; and if the medical practitioner signs a certificate and the justice is satisfied that the alleged lunatic is a lunatic and a proper person to be detained, he orders his removal to an institution for lunatics. Thus it will be seen that in the case of pauper lunatics only one medical certificate is required.

If any lunatic who is detained, escapes, he may be re-taken at any time within fourteen days without a fresh order. A reception order remains in force for periods of one, two, and three years, for successive periods of five years. At the end of each period respectively, it may be continued by the Commissioners in Lunacy, on certification by the medical officer of the institution, or by the medical attendant of a single patient, that the patient is still of unsound mind and is a proper person to be detained under care and treatment. A patient may be discharged on the direction of the petitioner for the reception order, or, if dead or incapable, by the nearest of kin, or by a Commissioner, unless the medical man in charge certifies that the patient is dangerous and unfit to be at large. Two Commissioners may order the discharge of any patient.

The principle which governs the provisions of this Act is that no person can be legally placed under restraint as a lunatic without an order obtained from a Judicial Authority. Exceptions to this principle are constituted by cases which are dealt with by inquisition, and by two Commissioners. Urgency orders are made without the intervention of a Judicial Authority, but they are only temporary and provisional, being intended to prevent harm happening to or by the lunatic until the necessary formalities have been observed to permanently place him under restraint; so that although an alleged lunatic has been admitted into an institution for lunatics on an Urgency order, the entire procedure relating to obtaining a reception order on petition has to be gone through just as though the alleged lunatic had not been previously dealt with.

### Medical Certificates in Lunacy.

Apart from lunatics found so by inquisition, lunatics wandering at large, pauper lunatics, and lunatics who are temporarily taken care of on an Urgency Order, two medical certificates are required before any person can be placed under restraint as a lunatic.

Every medical certificate must state the facts on which the certifier has formed his opinion that the person to whom the certificate refers is insane; he must distinguish facts observed by himself from facts communicated by others, and it is important to note that a reception order will not be made upon a certificate founded only on 'facts communicated by others. In respect to orders on petition each medical practitioner who signs a certificate must have personally examined the alleged lunatic within seven clear days before the date of the presentation of the petition, and in all other cases within seven clear days before the date of the order. Where two medical certificates are required, each medical practitioner must examine the alleged lunatic separately from the other. In the case of urgency orders the practitioner must have examined the alleged lunatic not more than two clear days before his reception. A medical certificate may not be signed by the petitioner for an order, nor by the person signing the urgency order, nor by any near relative, partner, or assistant of the petitioner or person. One of the medical certificates accompanying a petition for a reception order should be under the hand of the usual medical attendant of the alleged lunatic; if this is not practicable the reason must be stated in writing by the petitioner to the Judicial Authority to whom the petition is presented. No certificates shall be signed by persons interested in the institution or house to which the lunatic is going, nor by any near relations of such persons, nor by two medical men related to or in partnership with each other, or standing in the relation of principal and assistant.

A medical practitioner who has signed a certificate upon which a reception order has been made shall not be the regular professional attendant of the patient while detained under the order. A person for whom a reception order on petition has been obtained may be placed in a "single-patient house," that is, a house in which one lunatic only is detained on payment, exactly as in an asylum, or in a licensed house—i.e., private asylum. Under special circumstances the Commissioners may allow more than one patient to reside in the same house under the same conditions as if each of them were a single patient. If the usual medical attendant of the lunatic desires to continue in attendance during the detention of the lunatic in a single-patient house, he must not only *not sign either of the certificates*, but neither he, his partner, nor any of his near relatives must derive any profit from the charge of the patient. The Commissioners may direct how often a single patient is to be visited by a medical practitioner; until such direction is given the patient must be visited once at least every two weeks. Any two Commissioners may direct that the medical attendant of a single patient shall cease to act in that capacity, and that some other person shall be employed in his place. The Commissioners may at any time require from the medical attendant of a single patient a report in writing as to the patient, with such particulars as the Commissioners may direct; this is in addition to any periodical reports required by law to be sent to the Commissioners.

The Commissioners may require a report of the mental and bodily condition of a lunatic, or alleged lunatic, who, without order and certificates, is detained or treated as a lunatic by any person receiving no pay for the charge, or who is in any charitable, religious, or other establishment, not being an institution for lunatics; the report is to be furnished by a medical practitioner, and repeated periodically if required. The Commissioners may also visit such patient, and may exercise all the powers (except that of discharge) given to them as to patients in an asylum or as to single patients. If they think fit they may inform the Lord Chancellor, who may make an order for the discharge of such patient, or for his removal to an institute for lunatics. This is a departure from the former custom, which was that the Commissioners had no control over patients treated in private houses where no one derived any pecuniary benefit from their detention.

**Examination of Alleged Lunatics in Relation to Lunacy Certificates.**—The objects of the examination are:—to determine whether the individual is or is not insane, and if insane whether he is a fit and proper person to be placed under restraint. The distinction is important as a person may be undoubtedly insane, and yet neither his language nor his actions may justify a medical practitioner in certifying that he ought to be sent to an asylum. The printed forms of certificates have marginal- or foot-notes explanatory of the mode in which they are required to be filled up; a reference to the appended form will at once show what is meant. Any practitioner who is not accustomed to fill up these forms should carefully read over the directions, and be sure he fully understands them before commencing to write. It is to be remembered that the law requires absolutely literal accuracy, the least omission is sufficient to invalidate the whole document.

When examining an alleged lunatic—which is best done in the character of a medical man, although in exceptional cases it may be advisable to personate a casual caller or some one other than a doctor —if his words or actions do not at once reveal insanity the examiner will soonest obtain an opportunity of judging as to his mental state by directing the conversation to personal matters. Should the case be one of delusional insanity some information previously obtained as to the nature of the delusion, or delusions, will materially help the investigation. Delusions may be of two kinds: they may carry their own refutation, or they may present no abstract inconsistency. If, in a certificate, it is stated that the patient says he is the Holy Ghost, comment is superfluous; but if it is stated that he says he is starving for want of money, no delusion is evident unless information is added, such as the further statement that he is really a wealthy individual with an income of a thousand a year. The officials into whose hands the certificates come know nothing, beyond what is contained in them,

## LUNACY ACT, 1890

### CERTIFICATE OF MEDICAL PRACTITIONER

IN THE MATTER OF *A B* of[1] . . . in the County[2] ... .
[3] . . an alleged lunatic
I, THE UNDERSIGNED, *C D*, do hereby certify as follows

1 I am a person registered under the Medical Act, 1858, and I am in the actual practice of the medical profession

2 On the        day of         189  , at [4]...
in the county[5]   . of        [separately from any other practitioner],[6] I personally examined the said *A B*, and came to the conclusion that he is a [lunatic, an idiot, or a person of unsound mind,] and a proper person to be taken charge of and detained under care and treatment

3 I formed this conclusion on the following grounds, viz —

(*a*) Facts indicating insanity observed by myself at the time of examination, viz —[7]

(*b*) Facts communicated by others, viz —[8]

[*If an urgency certificate is required it must be added here*]

4 The said *A B* appeared to me to be [or not to be], in a fit condition of bodily health to be removed to an asylum, hospital, or licensed house[9]

5 I give this certificate having first read the section of the Act of Parliament printed below.

                                Signed
                                  of[10]
Dated,

*Extract from Section 317 of the Lunacy Act, 1890*

Any person who makes a wilful misstatement of any material facts in any medical or other certificate, or in any statement or report of bodily or mental condition under this Act, shall be guilty of a misdemeanour

---

[1] Insert the residence of Patient

[2] City or Borough, as the case may be

[3] Insert profession or occupation, if any

[4] Insert the place of examination, giving the name of the street, with number or name of the house, or should there be no number, the Christian and surname of occupier

[5] City or Borough, as the case may be

[6] Omit this where only one certificate is required.

[7] If the same or other facts were observed previous to the time of the examination, the certifier is at liberty to subjoin them in a separate paragraph

[8] The names and Christian names (if known) of informants to be given, with their addresses and descriptions

[9] Strike out this clause in case of a private patient whose removal is not proposed.

[10] Insert full postal address

about the medical features of the case; the matter therefore should be made perfectly clear and understandable. When the alleged lunatic is not subject to delusions there may be considerable difficulty in obtaining anything definite to enter in the certificate, as facts observed by the certifier; in such cases more than one visit, possibly several, may be necessary before sufficient evidence of insanity is forthcoming as to warrant certification.

In relation to facts it may be well to direct attention to what might be supposed to be a very obvious difference, absence of appreciation of which, however, has often led to rejection of certificates; it is the distinction between facts indicative of insanity, observed by the certifier at the time of his visit, and communicated facts. For example, the fact was communicated to a certifier that the alleged lunatic was intemperate; on the strength of this, and seeing him drink a glass of beer, the statement that the man's habits were intemperate was incorrectly incorporated in a certificate under the head of facts observed by the certifier. It is by no means easy in all cases to obtain facts that afford conclusive proof of insanity; before entering facts of doubtful significance, their value should be well weighed by the practitioner. He should ask himself whether they afford reasonable proof of mental disease, and how far he could depend upon them to support his opinion if challenged in a court of law. In many cases of undoubted insanity it is absolutely impossible to obtain any one fact conclusive of the condition, and consequently dependence has to be placed on accumulative evidence. In such instances special care must be taken to reject matter that will not bear the test of legitimate cross-questioning. Clouston gives some ludicrous examples of "facts":—"He is incoherent in his appearance." "Eyes restless and wandering, but following the usual occupation of breaking stones." "Reads his Bible, and is anxious about the salvation of his soul." It is to be remembered that even though the Commissioners accept a certificate, legal proceedings may subsequently be taken by the alleged insane person, and the certifier may be placed in the witness-box and cross-examined on the statement he has made.

Mere defect of intelligence, which may exist without delusions, is another condition in which it is difficult to obtain evidence of sufficient value, as to be suitable for a certificate of lunacy. Tests of mental capacity in such cases should be restricted to those which are compatible with the station in life of the person under examination; a want of intelligence that would be abnormal in a man possessing all the advantages of a good education, would be much less significant in the case of an agricultural labourer. A degree of mental weakness that may be sufficient to justify a man being deprived of the management of his monetary affairs, may be insufficient to justify his being deprived of liberty of action in other respects, to warrant this something more is needed than absence of a certain degree of intelligence. On more than one occasion, when giving evidence on the subject of criminal responsibility, psychological experts have stated in the witness-box that although, on the ground of mental disease, they held the prisoner to be irresponsible for the crime he had committed, they would not have seen their way to certify him as a fit and proper person to be placed under restraint.

Actions and utterances also must be considered in relation to the social position and previous habits of the individual. It is deplorable for a costermonger to use bad language to his wife, or to assault her and destroy the furniture in his house, but such proceedings are of much less weight as indications of insanity than when the person implicated is, or rather has been, a sedate clergyman. General expressions as "excited and wild-looking," should, as far as possible, be avoided, and something more precise substituted. In recording utterances the actual words used by the alleged lunatic should be given.

A medical man is supposed by the law to exercise his own judgment when deciding as to the sanity or insanity of a patient: he must be on his guard not to be unduly influenced for or against by the statements of the wife, husband, or other members of the household. In some instances it is to the interest of the relatives to further the impression of the patient's sanity, and they will consequently seek to minimise the significance of his actions, attributing any out-of-the-way conduct to mere eccentricity, or to family worries; if the object is the converse, every action is unfavourably interpreted, and the truth by no means strictly adhered to.

**The Legal Responsibility of Medical Practitioners in Relation to Certificates of Lunacy.**—No medical practitioner is bound to certify, but if he undertakes to do so he is responsible for any breach of duty. A medical man who makes a wilful misstatement of any material fact in a medical certificate is guilty of a misdemeanour. Up to the time of the Lunacy Act of 1889, medical men who signed certificates of lunacy were liable to be the victims of harassing legal proceedings, although they acted in perfect good faith. Nothing can exceed the vindictiveness of some persons who, having been insane, have recovered sufficiently as to be released from restraint; they acquire a fixed idea that they have been the victims of a vile conspiracy and display a most objectionable pertinacity in attacking (through the law courts) each and every person concerned in the case. The medical practitioners who certified are invariably selected, and as a rule they fare badly, especially if they have committed any technical error. The last act has a clause (section 330, re-enacting section 12 of the Act of 1889) which provides for vexatious proceedings directed against those who have been engaged in carrying out the Act, and medical practitioners come in for a share of the protection thus conferred. The gist of the section is that such proceedings may, "upon summary application to the High Court, or a judge thereof, be stayed upon such terms as to costs and otherwise as the Court or judge may think fit, if the Court or judge is satisfied that there is no reasonable ground for alleging want of good faith and reasonable care."

This section renders it incumbent on the medical practitioner who is proceeded against to satisfy the Court that there is no reasonable ground for alleging want of good faith or reasonable care. "Good faith" is to be interpreted in its common sense meaning—that is, if the transaction was honestly carried out and there was no attempt to abuse the power conferred by law it was done in good faith. "Reasonable care" is held to have the same significance that it has in ordinary cases of malapraxis—the employment of such an amount of care and skill as a medical practitioner may reasonably be expected to possess.

The first case tried under this section was that of *Toogood* v. *Wilkes* (Queen's Bench Division, 1889). The plaintiff brought the action against a medical practitioner, to recover damages "for injury to the plaintiff from the defendant's negligence as a medical man, and for damages for injury to the plaintiff by reason of the defendant having negligently and wrongfully signed a certificate of the plaintiff's insanity whereby he was detained in a lunatic asylum." The judge, Field, J., ruled that the onus lay with the defendant to satisfy him that there was no reasonable ground for alleging want of good faith or reasonable care, and, after hearing the arguments, held that the defendant had made out that there was no want of good faith or reasonable care on his part in signing the certificate, the action was therefore stayed. This is a step in advance when compared with the former state of things, although it seems strange that the defendant was not allowed costs, the judge declining to give them unless the plaintiff appealed, which he omitted to do. Another case of a similar kind, *Mason* v. *Marshall, Shaw and Gauchard* (Bristol Spring Ass., 1888), in which the contention was that the medical men who had signed the certificates had not exercised sufficient care and that the certificates were criminally weak, was tried before the Act containing the relief section previously quoted was passed. The judge left the following questions to the jury:—(1) Did the doctors sign the certificates negligently and without due care? (2) Were the conduct, behaviour, and appearance of the plaintiff such as to induce the defendants to believe that she was a person of unsound mind and a proper person to be taken care of and detained under treatment, and were the acts complained of done by the defendants honestly acting upon such belief? (3) Was the plaintiff at the times in question of unsound mind and a proper person to be taken care of and detained under treatment? The jury answered all the questions in favour of the defendants

These cases illustrate the importance attached by the judges to the exercise of such an amount of skill and care as a medical practitioner might be reasonably expected to bring to bear in a case of the kind it is, further, of equal importance that the spirit as well as the letter of the law should be fulfilled; any shortcoming in this respect is liable to be severely dealt with In the case of *Weldon v Winslow* (Nisi prius, 1884), the defendant's conduct was held to be irregular and not to conform with the mind of the law The defendant, a medical man, was asked by the plaintiff's husband to see and give an opinion as to his wife's sanity, he did so, and reported that she was insane, advising removal to an asylum, and it was arranged that the lady should go to the defendant's own private asylum This was an undoubted mistake and a violation of the spirit if not of the letter of the law, which provides that persons who are interested in the institution to which a patient is going shall not sign either of the certificates Although the defendant did not actually sign a certificate he sent two other medical men (after having himself determined the question), and in this way violated the spirit of the law A further irregularity was committed by the two medical men who went to examine the patient instead of visiting her separately as required by law, they went together, one waiting outside the room whilst the other conducted his examination In commenting on these proceedings the judge, Mr Justice Manisty, said that the defendant "had it all in his mind that the plaintiff should be taken to his asylum, he ought to have told Mr Weldon at once, 'I can take no part in these proceedings I can take no part in obtaining certificates or getting the order You must get some one else to act in the matter'" The judge also asked whether the way in which the examination was carried out satisfied the law that the medical men should be absolutely independent, and should each exercise an independent judgment

### (c) JUDICIAL INQUISITION AS TO LUNACY

The Judge in Lunacy may upon application by order direct an inquisition whether a person is of unsound mind and incapable of managing himself and his affairs The inquisition may take place before a jury if the alleged lunatic demands one, unless the Judge in Lunacy, after personal examination of the alleged lunatic, is satisfied that he is of mentally competent to form and express a wish to that effect. (53 Vict., ch. 5, sec. 90.)

The object of an **inquisition** (*de lunatico inquirendo*) or **commission of inquiry** is to ascertain whether a certain person is, or is not, fit to retain charge of his affairs, and whether he ought, or ought not, to be placed under restraint. It is to be clearly understood that the two propositions are separate and distinct; the first does not necessarily include the second, although in this case the second includes the first. A man may be found incapable of managing his property by reason of deficiency of intellect, but it does not of necessity follow that he is a fit and proper person to be placed under restraint; if the commission of inquiry find that he ought to be detained under care and treatment, then the deprivation of civil rights—the management of his own affairs —follows. Lunatics who are taken charge of after inquisition, whether under restraint or not, are called "**Chancery Lunatics**," because the Lord Chancellor is at the head of the administration of the Lunacy Laws, and such lunatics are under his care.

It is to be observed that deprivation of civil rights is not a necessary result of placing a patient under restraint in the ordinary way by order on petition; if competent, such a person can make a will, and if liberated from the asylum, can at once resume the management of his affairs.

To obtain a Commission of Inquiry an application must be made to a Judge in Lunacy by one or more persons interested in the alleged lunatic, supported by affidavits taken by medical practitioners as to his mental condition; if the Judge in Lunacy is satisfied that there is ground for the inquisition, the cause is duly tried. The medical men who have signed certificates, or taken affidavits, with probably others also, representing both sides, are examined and cross-examined on oath as at an ordinary trial. If found to be of unsound mind, and a fit and proper person to be placed under restraint, the lunatic is treated as though found so on petition, and, further, his property is vested in the hands of a "committee of estate," which acts as his trustee and manages his affairs. The Lunacy Act limits the inquiry to things said and done by the alleged lunatic within a period of two years previous to the inquisition. As previously mentioned, he may be found mentally incompetent to manage his estate, and yet not incapable of managing himself; in this case his affairs are placed in the hands of a "committee," but he is not deprived of freedom of action in other respects; he can remain in his own house and go about as he pleases.

Commissions of inquiry are usually held in the case of men who, by acts of absurd extravagance, are ruining their estates; the object being to put an end to this, even though the owner of the estate may not be sufficiently insane as to warrant his being detained under restraint. Inquisition is an expensive way of determining the mental condition of a person alleged to be of unsound mind, not so much so, however, as before the passing of the recent Acts.

### (d) TESTAMENTARY CAPACITY.

By this is meant competency of mind to make a will disposing of personal or real property. In order that a will shall be valid, the law requires a "disposing mind" on the part of the testator. The interpretation placed on this term is somewhat elastic, and often depends upon the nature of the will itself rather than on the mental condition of the testator at the time he made it. The law is very jealous of any interference with documents of this kind, and even when the testator can be proved to have been of unsound mind, if the will is rational and of such a nature as to be consistent and free from unreasonable prejudice, or from indications of undue influence exercised by others, it is usually upheld. A patient labouring under a delusion is not necessarily thereby incapacitated from making a will. If the delusion is on a subject apart from the provisions of the will, the document itself need not be affected by it; it is quite possible for a man to have delusions of such a nature as not in the least to interfere with his capacity to make a rational will having the same disposing qualities with respect to his relatives as though he was free from any such delusion. A delusion bearing on the provisions of the will is a different matter, and might be held to invalidate the document.

Wills good in law have been made by patients in asylums. In the case of *Banks* v. *Goodfellow* (Queen's Bench, 1870), an attempt was made to upset the will of the testator, John Banks, who had been in an asylum, and who was subject to delusions. He believed himself to be persecuted by devils, which he stated were visibly present, and he also believed that a man who had been dead for a long time, and to whom he had a great aversion, was still alive, and that he pursued and molested him. Notwithstanding the existence of these delusions, the will, which was made in favour of a niece who had lived with the testator, was upheld by the ruling of four judges sitting in Banco, one of whom, Chief-Justice Cockburn, in delivering judgment, said:— "that the existence of a delusion compatible with the retention of the powers and faculties of the mind will not be sufficient to overthrow the will, unless it were such as was calculated to influence the testator in making it."

Wills are not unfrequently disputed, on account of alleged undue influence, exercised by some one who has access to a weak-minded person during the latter portion of his life. Unlimited influence can be brought to bear by a designing person on people who are naturally of feeble intellect or who have been rendered so by bodily disease. In this way perfect strangers succeed in obtaining utterly disproportionate legacies, or even the bulk of an estate, to the exclusion of those who have a rightful claim. Few medical men who have seen much practice have not had opportunities of observing the assiduity with which a distant relation or a friend of an elderly invalid, who lives alone and is possessed of money but is devoid of sons or daughters, watches and hovers round with ceaseless attention, brings and prepares all sorts of delicacies, and gradually insinuates himself, or more frequently herself, into the very existence of the sick person, until his volition is paralysed, and he yields an unquestioning assent to all suggestions made by the beneficiary *in posse*. In such a case, the will, if made in favour of the attentive person, is very likely to be contested, and it behoves the medical attendant of an invalid thus cajoled to keep his ears and eyes open as he is sure to be subpœnaed on one side or other when the case comes before the Probate Court.

The conditions which may render testamentary capacity doubtful, are those due to disease, to feebleness of mind apart from disease, and to the presence of delusions or other indications of unsoundness of mind. A frequent cause of doubt as to testamentary capacity is the occurrence of the stage of lethargy with partial loss of coherence of thought which is the precursor of death. A few questions put to the sick person will probably determine whether the mind is sufficiently clear or not; if he can recapitulate the provisions of the will he is desirous of making, after having once announced them, it is enough to establish his testamentary capacity. The necessary questions may be asked of the dying person in the presence of those who surround his bed—in such a case, witnesses are an advantage rather than otherwise. It is different, however, in cases of simple feebleness of intellect occurring in people who are not about to die; the medical practitioner, whose opinion as regards testamentary capacity is sought, should always insist upon speaking to such persons alone. The mere presence in the room of any one who has acquired an influence over their minds, without the utterance of a word, will render the investigation futile. In addition to questions which are intended to test the mental capacity of feeble-minded testators, others should be put with the view of ascertaining whether any undue influence is being exercised over their minds. If delusions are present, their influence on the "disposing mind" of the testator should be estimated as far as possible; he should be asked to state the principal provisions of the will, and if any clause appears contrary to what might be reasonably expected, to explain the motives that influence him in so willing.

The occurrence of aphasia may interfere with testamentary capacity; no rule can be formulated for the various forms and degrees of this defect, each case must be judged on its own merits. The primary consideration is:—Can any form of aphasia exist without such impairment of the mental powers as to invalidate a will or other legal document executed by a person labouring under this defect? Uncomplicated **motor aphasia** does not necessarily incapacitate a patient from executing such a document; it is obvious that a primal insane condition is excluded, such as dementia with aphasia. In pure motor aphasia the patient can signify by gesture his assent to, or dissent from, any proposition—he is quite competent to make his desires known. Pure motor aphasia is not inconsistent with the accomplishment of mental processes which demand differentiation and combination of ideas. **Sensory aphasia** cannot be disposed of so readily; the very nature of the condition gives rise to doubt as to whether the sufferer comprehends what is said to him, although the mental powers are not necessarily lost. In relation to this question Ross[1] observes that "when a lesion is situated in or near to the sensory inlets, a disorder of language results which is out of all proportion to the general impairment of the reasoning faculties." The difficulty consists in the absence of a channel of communication to the mind of the patient. If this is absolute the individual is incompetent to execute a legal document; but if the absence is only partial—either the visual or the auditory paths being intact—it would be possible to secure the necessary cognition. Mills,[2] who discusses the medico-legal relations of aphasia at some length, holds that it ought not to be necessary for competency that the person should be responsive by every channel of communication.

In no case should a medical man allow himself to be influenced by sympathy with the survivors, and countenance the signing of a will, the provisions of which may be just and equitable, by a person who from any cause is incompetent to do so. Attempts are not unfrequently made to complete a will, by the almost unconscious assent of a dying person, the document having been drawn up according to his directions at an earlier stage of the illness when his mind was clear. The practitioner's duty is clearly defined; it is limited to ascertaining the fitness or otherwise of the testator to understand the provisions of the document at the time that he signs it. It is to be remembered that the will may be disputed, and the state of the testator's mind may have to be described on oath under cross-examination.

[1] *Med. Chron.*, 1887.     [2] *Review of Insanity and Nervous Disease*, 1891.

## (e) FEIGNED INSANITY

Insanity is not unfrequently feigned in order to escape punishment for a criminal act. Usually some form is selected that corresponds with the popular idea of insanity, the symptoms imitated being those which demonstrate mental disorder to the most casual observer. Mania, delusional insanity, melancholia, and dementia are generally the types to which the sham lunatic devotes his attention. The cases which come under the notice of the medical jurist are almost invariably those of criminals who are already in the hands of the police. Unless there is a history of previous attacks, the occurrence of symptoms of insanity in a prisoner are naturally suspicious, all the more so if they are of a pronounced character. Pure moral insanity is ill adapted for imitation on the part of a criminal, as will readily be perceived from what has been said in relation to this mental disorder—it is too nearly allied to vice to be chosen by a culprit to exculpate him from the consequences of a criminal act. When mania is imitated there is a tendency to take the more excited type, which renders detection much easier than if a lower kind of exaltation was aimed at. The popular idea of mania is limited to what is described as raving madness, and the shammer consequently believes that the more furious his demeanour the more genuine does the attack appear. Fortunately for those who are called upon to decide the question, nature places a limit on the powers of endurance of a sane individual; no man who is not really insane can keep up for long together the constant action and vociferation characteristic of the true acute maniac. Exhaustion of the physical powers, which the real maniac seems to be able to defy, asserts itself, and the imposter falls asleep, and, as a rule, sleeps soundly, which is in direct contrast with the fitful sleep of acute mania. A true maniac will often pass several consecutive nights and days without sleep; an impostor is utterly unable to do so. If the suspected person manages to do without sleep for a long time, probably a hypodermic injection of morphine, which would produce no effect on a genuine case of mania, will procure sleep, and clear up doubts.

Melancholia is not often feigned. In a suspected case the patient must be watched without his knowledge to see if there is any change in demeanour when alone. If he sleeps soundly it is improbable that he is the subject of profound melancholia. The state of the tongue may afford evidence; it is often coated in genuine insanity. If suspicion is strongly aroused, and the individual refuses to speak or take any notice, a strong faradic current applied to various sensitive parts of the skin, by means of a stiff wire-brush, may promote recovery.

Delusional insanity is usually over-acted by the malingerer, though he may succeed in giving rise to considerable doubt in the mind of the observer as to the real nature of the case. Robertson[1] relates a case of feigned delusional insanity in a man who was awaiting trial for housebreaking. The prisoner first drew attention to his assumed mental state by a feigned attempt at suicide by hanging. He then refused to work, would not speak when addressed, and took very little food. Now and then he lay on the floor staring at the ceiling as though he saw some one there. He professed entire ignorance of any circumstances relating to the crime of which he was accused, but declared that he was to be tried for murder, and stated that it was quite true that he had murdered a woman by pushing her into a canal where she was drowned; he also said that the woman came into his cell at night and offered him a razor. He shed tears when telling the story of his avowed crime, and insisted that it was true, although when assured that the woman was alive and well, he expressed his thanks; subsequently, however, he recurred to the feigned delusion. Beside this fixed delusion, he said that thousands of rats came into his cell at nights, and made other absurd statements. At one interview he declared he had committed murder, that there was no hope for him, and that he was eternally lost; at the next, he said that he possessed £100, expected to inherit £4000, and owned the island of St Helena. This discrepancy was significant, the character of the exaltation was inconsistent with almost simultaneous depression. The attempt was kept up to the commencement of, and during the trial; but after conviction he confessed that the whole affair was an imposition. Dementia may be feigned with relative ease, but it is a condition that is rarely primary, and any history would probably clear up the case; the same remark, as to history, applies to feigned idiocy and imbecility.

The chief points of distinction are that a lunatic, as a rule, insists that he is sane; whereas a malingerer obviously tries to produce the impression that he is insane. If he is incoherent, his incoherency exceeds that of any lunatic, except, perhaps, that of the delirious maniac. If he has delusions he will show considerable perspicacity in relation to the delusions; but will, at the same time, exhibit the mental state of an imbecile as regards other matters, especially relating to himself and his doings. Delusional insanity is characterised by fixity of the delusions, but the shammer will invent new ones every day, and, as illustrated in the case above related, not of a congruous type. It has been said that although the sham lunatic may be dirty as far as his surroundings go, he will spare his person. This may be so as a rule, but it is not invariably the case; some will smear their

[1] *Journal of Mental Science*, 1888.

persons with excrement and other filth, having probably seen these actions done by a genuine lunatic.

## PLACING HABITUAL DRUNKARDS UNDER RESTRAINT.

An habitual drunkard may be guilty of actions which are quite as indicative of inability to manage himself or his estate, and they may be fully as obnoxious to the well-being of his family as those committed by a person, who by reason of disease of the mind is a fit and proper person to be placed under restraint, and yet, in such a case (unless the individual is actually insane apart from inebriety), the law does not admit of the procedure applicable to lunatics being put in force. In recognition of this difficulty an Act was passed in 1879 (42 and 43 Vict., ch. 19) to facilitate the control and cure of Habitual Drunkards, the duration of this Act was limited to a period of ten years after its coming in force. In 1888, the "Inebriates Act" (51 and 52 Vict. ch. 19) was passed, which had for its object the prolongation of the Act of 1879 (with some slight modifications) for another period of ten years.

By these Acts "Retreats" are licensed for habitual drunkards with provision for medical attendance. If the person holding the license is a duly registered medical practitioner, he may himself act as medical attendant to the Retreat. No such license is given to any person who is licensed to keep a house for the reception of lunatics.

Any habitual drunkard desirous of being admitted into a retreat may make an application in writing to the licensee of a retreat for admission, the application being couched in the terms dictated by a printed form drawn up in accordance with the schedule appended to the Act of 1879. The time the applicant undertakes to remain in such retreat must be specified in the application, which must be accompanied by a declaration made before two justices of the peace, who before attesting must satisfy themselves that the applicant is an habitual drunkard within the meaning of the Act, and must explain to him the effect of his application, and state in writing that he understood such explanation. The applicant after admission into a retreat will not be allowed to leave it till the expiration of the time mentioned in the application, provided that it shall not exceed a period of twelve calendar months. At any time after the reception of an habitual drunkard into a retreat he may, upon the request in writing of the licensee of the retreat, be discharged by order of a justice, if the request is deemed by him to be reasonable and proper.

At the request of the licensee the habitual drunkard at any time after his admission may, by permission of a justice, be allowed to live with any trustworthy person who is willing to take charge of him for a definite time, not exceeding two months; the leave may be prolonged every two months for a like interval until the whole period of detention is expired. Any time thus spent away from the retreat is deemed part of the time of detention, except where the leave of absence is forfeited or revoked.

If an habitual drunkard while detained in a retreat wilfully refuses to conform to the rules, he is liable on summary conviction to a penalty not exceeding five pounds, or, at the discretion of the Court, to be imprisoned for a period not exceeding seven days, and then returned to the retreat, the period of imprisonment being excluded from the original time he agreed to place himself under restraint. If he escapes he may be apprehended and remitted to the retreat.

These Acts apply, with certain provisions as to technical procedure, to Scotland and Ireland, as well as to England.

So far as restraint goes, the distinction between a lunatic and an habitual drunkard consists in the fact that the lunatic may be placed under restraint against his will, the habitual drunkard can only be detained with his own consent and for a limited time. It is necessary that an habitual drunkard should be sober at the time he makes the application before the justices.

Delirium tremens being legally regarded as a diseased condition of the mind may render the subject of it a fit and proper person to be placed under restraint. As a rule, the attack is too brief to necessitate the patient being sent under urgency order and certificate to an asylum, it is generally sufficient if he is restrained in his own house. In either case the position of the medical practitioner is uncertain as regards the steps that possibly may be taken by the patient after recovery. Actions for damages have been brought against medical practitioners for having improperly deprived the plaintiff of his liberty and for ill treatment whilst thus detained. In one such case, *Scot v. Wakem* (Guildford Ass., 1862), the plaintiff, who undoubtedly had been dangerous to others during his attack, and in consequence was taken charge of by a man placed in the house by order of the doctor, brought an action of this kind. The judge, Bramwell, B., ruled that if the plaintiff at the time was a dangerous lunatic and likely to do mischief to any one, the defendant would be justified in putting restraint upon him until there was reasonable ground for believing that the danger was over. Or, if the wife of the plaintiff had called in the defendant to cure her husband from delirium tremens, and that he did so, and left him when he believed he had recovered, he would be justified in what he had done provided he had done nothing that was not necessary nor reasonably proper under the circumstances. Notwithstanding this summing up a verdict was given against the defendant with, it is true, only a farthing damages, but the expense and annoyance of such a trial is no slight infliction. In another case, *Symm* v. *Fraser and Andrews* (Queen's Bench 1863), a similar action was brought a year after the alleged ill-treatment and restraint was put in force. In this case the verdict was for the defendants. Cockburn, C.J., before whom the case was tried, said, that even if attendants or nurses are not originally appointed by a medical man, yet if he assumes authority and command over them in reference to the management of the patient, he would be responsible for the personal restraint under which the patient was placed.

From this it will be seen that the position of the medical practitioner in charge of a case of delirium tremens is by no means secure, if he neglects to take proper precautions, and harm ensues, he is blameworthy, and if he takes these precautions he is liable to be proceeded against. If the medical attendant in a case of delirium tremens performs his duty to his patient in a proper manner he need not fear an adverse verdict should an action for damages be brought against him; he cannot, however, avoid the possibility of such an action being brought. If he is dealing with people who are strangers to him, or he sees any probability of subsequent trouble, it is well to have an authorisation in writing from the husband, wife, or other near relation, to do what is necessary as to restraint. Such an authorisation will not guarantee the medical attendant against an action, but it will be of material value in defending it. In the case of *Scot* v. *Wakem*, already quoted, the wife denied having authorised the defendant to interfere, although when he was called in he found the plaintiff with loaded pistols in his hands threatening to shoot her. In this case the facts contradicted the wife's statement, but it might happen otherwise.

If a patient with delirium tremens was duly certified, and in consequence was placed under restraint, an action entered against the medical practitioner who gave the certificate would probably be stayed upon summary application to the High Court, or a judge thereof, as provided in the Lunacy Act, 1890; but the medical practitioner would have to satisfy the Court that there was no reasonable ground for alleging want of good faith or reasonable care.

# PART III.—TOXICOLOGY.

### CHAPTER XXV

#### POISONS IN THEIR GENERAL ASPECT.

TOXICOLOGY is that branch of science which relates to poisons. It is generally understood to include a description of the symptoms and treatment of poisoning, as well as of the nature, chemical constitution, and methods used in the isolation and detection of poisons. An accurate and, at the same time, terse definition of the word poison is not readily attained. In the broad sense, a poison is a substance which, on being absorbed into the living organism, or by its chemical action on the tissues, injures the health, or destroys life. Such a definition would include pathological ferments, which, though regarded as poisons from the medical standpoint, do not come within the range of toxicology. Again, many substances when absorbed into the organism in large quantity are deleterious to health; and yet they can hardly be regarded as poisons, since the amount in which they solely become injurious is so excessive that they may be taken with impunity in much larger doses than is the case with a substance which is recognised as a poison. Any substance that is not absolutely inert would produce injurious effects if administered in excess, so that noxious activity has to be taken into account. A substance which produces no ill effects when given in a single small dose, may do so if similar doses are repeatedly administered. This is a question of practical moment to the toxicologist in relation to the frequent reception by the organism of minute quantities of poisons, such as arsenic, lead, and mercury; the amount introduced on any one occasion may be insufficient to produce an injurious result, but if taken day after day the repeated small doses would eventually be harmful. Some substances, such as the mineral acids, when swallowed destroy tissues without being absorbed, and in this way may cause death by "poison."

In cases of criminal poisoning it is no longer necessary to determine whether the substance administered comes under the definition of a poison, the law in relation to this subject (24 and 25 Vict, ch. 100, section 11) runs thus —

"Whosoever shall administer, or cause to be administered or taken by any person, any poison or other destructive thing, with intent to commit murder, shall be guilty of felony."

Two points are to be observed in relation to this quotation: that the intent to commit murder determines the culpability of the act, and that the comprehensive words, "or other destructive thing," makes it immaterial whether the substance given comes under the usual definition of a poison or not. The question of amount has to be considered. Lord Chief-Justice Cockburn ruled in *Reg* v *Hennah* (Cornwall Ass, 1877), that unless the thing administered was in sufficient amount to be noxious, it does not come under the legal definition of a noxious thing, and, further, that a distinction is to be drawn between a thing that is only noxious when given in excess, and one that is recognised as a poison and known to be noxious and pernicious in its effect. This ruling throws great responsibility on the medical witness, for, although he may not be called upon to define a poison in the abstract, he will be required to express an opinion as to whether the substance given was a noxious substance and whether it was given in excess. The law is very comprehensive in dealing with the culpability of an intentional poisoner, thus 24 and 25 Vict, ch. 100, s 23, states —

"Whosoever shall unlawfully and maliciously administer to, or cause to be administered to or taken by any other person, any poison or other destructive or noxious thing, so as thereby to endanger the life of such person, or so as thereby to inflict upon such person any grievous bodily harm shall be guilty of felony."

The amount of damage sustained that would constitute "grievous bodily harm" is capable of being variously estimated, and the medical witness may have great difficulty in conveying his opinion to the jury through the media of examination and cross-examination only, as to whether the substance, in the dose in which it was given, could or could not cause such harm. In respect to the administration of many substances a variety of conditions determine the intensity of the noxious effects which may ensue. When the prosecutor has not received any harm from the alleged "noxious thing," the medical witness may be asked questions with regard to hypothetical cases, of which a full description of the conditions and surroundings is not afforded; opinions given under such circumstances are liable to mislead the jury.

The law provides that the administration of any poison, or other destructive, or noxious thing, with the *intent* to injure, aggrieve, or annoy, constitutes a misdemeanour, and, further, that if a prisoner is charged with felony for having administered a poison or other noxious thing, and the jury are not satisfied that he is guilty of felony, but are satisfied that he is guilty of a misdemeanour as above, they may find him guilty of the lesser crime.

Medical evidence in cases of poisoning, therefore, is not limited to the bare statement that the substance administered is possessed of poisons or noxious properties; it must go further and establish the dose at which the substance becomes poisonous or noxious. Several conditions require to be considered in determining the toxic effects of poisons, among which are *age, idiosyncrasy, habit*, and *state of health*.

**Age.**—Young children succumb more easily to the effects of poison than adults; this is especially the case with morphine. On the other hand, children tolerate a poison like belladonna better than adults. Young adults tolerate the action of irritants, such as tartar emetic, better than old people.

**Idiosyncrasy.**—Some persons are naturally tolerant, and others intolerant, of various substances which have poisonous properties. In some cases an ordinary full medicinal dose of arsenic acts as a poisonous dose, and causes gastro-intestinal irritation. Medicinal doses of strychnine occasionally produce muscular twitchings, and even slight general spasm. Small doses of mercury salivate some people, whereas others can take it for a prolonged period without any apparent effect being produced. In some persons certain articles of food invariably produce symptoms of poisoning—nausea, vomiting, and diarrhœa—whilst in others the disagreeable effects are limited to an attack of nettle-rash, the majority of people being able to eat such food without any ill effects whatever.

**Habit.**—The regular and prolonged use of some poisons in small doses tends to develop tolerance on the part of the system to their action. Morphine, arsenic, tobacco, alcohol, chloral hydrate are examples of poisons towards which tolerance may be thus acquired. Persons who in this way are habituated to the use of such substances can with impunity take what would be a poisonous dose to a novice.

**The State of Health.**—In a broad sense, healthy individuals are less likely to succumb to the effect of poison than those who are weakened by disease; there are certain notable exceptions, however. Patients suffering from acute mania, delirium tremens, tetanus, or dysentery can take an amount of opium that would be sufficient to cause the death of a non-habituated healthy person. On the other hand, opium is exceedingly dangerous in granular kidney, apoplexy, and hyperæmic diseases of the lungs. Digitalis, tobacco and tartar emetic are badly tolerated in cases of fatty or weak heart. Any irritant would aggravate the symptoms of gastro-intestinal catarrh. Gouty subjects, especially if suffering from granular kidney, are intolerant of repeated small doses of lead.

The **physical condition** of the poison, and the **mode of its introduction** into the system exercise a considerable influence on the rapidity and the intensity of its action. Poisons that are capable of assuming the gaseous form act much more immediately and energetically when thus administered than when given as liquids or solids. Arsenic, if inhaled in the gaseous form, as arsenetted hydrogen, acts more rapidly than when arsenious acid dissolved in water is swallowed; solid arsenious acid is still less active. The mode of administration largely influences the effects produced by a given dose of the poison, its physical condition remaining the same. A solution containing a poison acts most promptly if injected directly into the blood current, less rapidly if brought in contact with the serous membranes, cellular tissue, mucous membranes, and the skin; the rapidity of absorption diminishes in the order of the tissues named, absorption from the intact skin being the slowest of all.

Two points have to be considered in relation to the effect produced by a given dose of a poison; the rapidity of absorption and the rapidity of elimination. If a poison is eliminated as rapidly as it is absorbed, and the rate of absorption is too slow to immediately bring the system under its lethal influence, no permanently deleterious effects are produced. For this reason some poisons can be received into the mouth, and even swallowed with impunity, in amounts that would be lethal if introduced under the skin. Curare, some kinds of arrow-poison, and the venom ejected from the fangs of poisonous serpents are examples of poisons of this type. The wound inflicted by a poisoned arrow may have a sufficient amount of the poison deposited in it as to cause the death of the wounded person if left to his fate; but if a second person immediately and vigorously sucks the wound, no mischief results to either of them. The same immunity follows if the wounded individual himself is able to suck his wound, and does so at once. The poison sucked out of the wound is at once spat out, and thus only comes in contact with the mucous membrane of the mouth, the absorptive capacity of which is too limited to allow, during the period of contact, of the introduction of an amount of poison into the system sufficient to cause mischief. The poison extracted by the suction might probably be swallowed with impunity, as it would be eliminated by the kidneys as quickly as the gastric mucous membrane took it up.

The law makes no distinction in relation to the mode in which a poison is introduced into, or acts upon, the system. Hypodermic, or endermic administration of a poison, or the injection of it into the bowel, with intent to commit murder, are regarded precisely as though the poison had been given by the mouth

The **chemical combination** in which certain poisonous substances exist, and the degree of **concentration** in others, exercise a powerful influence on their lethal potency. Silver nitrate and hydrochloric acid are both energetic poisons when taken separately, but when combined the resulting salt—silver chloride—is inert, or thereabouts, because of its insolubility. In some instances the action of the poison is entirely altered by chemical combination, another effect being substituted for that which is characteristic of it in the uncombined state. Strychnine alters the rate of transmission of stimuli from cell to cell in the spinal cord, or possibly increases the excitability of the cells, the result being the occurrence of clonic muscular spasm. If strychnine is so treated as to become a methyl derivative, it no longer acts on the cord, but it paralyses the motor nerve-endings, like curare. In the case of poisons, such as the mineral acids, which act directly on the tissues with which they come in contact, the degree of concentration is an important factor. An amount of concentrated acid that would be sufficient to cause death, might be swallowed with impunity if largely diluted with water.

When poisons are taken by the mouth, the state of the stomach as regards **presence or absence of food**, considerably modifies the rate of absorption and the intensity of local action. A person has been known to swallow more than a lethal dose of undissolved white arsenic with impunity, because the stomach was well filled with oatmeal porridge. When a poison is received into a full stomach the usual symptoms are delayed much beyond the customary time of onset, and if the poison is one that is quickly eliminated by the kidneys an average fatal dose may be survived although the whole of it is eventually absorbed. On the other hand an empty stomach and bowel quickly absorb any poison received, and the onset of the symptoms is accelerated.

**Classification of Poisons.**—A comprehensive classification is scarcely feasible without involving great complexity and, when accomplished, is of little use. The division of poisons into **inorganic**, and **organic**, with the sub-division of the first into *corrosives* and *irritants*, and of the second into *irritants* and *neurotics*, affords a basis sufficiently broad for practical purposes. Both organic and inorganic groups comprise poisons which act by disintegrating, or by interfering with the function of the red corpuscles of the blood.

## THE DIAGNOSIS OF POISONING

The effects severally produced on the living organism by various poisons differ within limits in accordance with the kind of poison taken. Common to almost all forms of poisoning, however, are a number of symptoms, or effects, some of which are intrinsic, affecting the individual, others are accidental and do not personally implicate him.

In the first group is **sudden occurrence of** acute symptoms in a person previously in his usual health. In relation to this indication it is to be remembered that the initial symptoms produced by many poisons bear a certain **resemblance to** those due **to disease.**—Arsenic causes symptoms which have been mistaken for those of cholera or of gastro-intestinal catarrh, strychnine for those of tetanus, morphine for those of apoplexy, belladonna for those of acute delirious mania. Errors of the opposite kind have been fallen into: the rapid onset of an **acute disease** in a person who appeared to be in good health up to the time when the symptoms showed themselves has been **mistaken for the effect of poison.** Among diseases of this nature are—an acute gastric ulcer which ruptures, perforation of the bowel, rupture of an abdominal aneurism, the formation of a peri-uterine hæmatocele, acute intestinal obstruction with persistent vomiting, choleraic diarrhœa, hæmorrhage into the pons. Some of these conditions could only give rise to momentary doubt, others may cause prolonged anxiety to the medical attendant.

The occurrence of symptoms of an anomalous nature **shortly after eating** or drinking, or taking medicine is a suspicious indication, which for its interpretation requires considerable discrimination. Violent vomiting and purging may be due to some change undergone by the food itself before cooking. The food may be in its normal condition, but the state of the recipient's stomach may be at fault: a person who has fasted long beyond his usual meal time, if he hurriedly eats some food difficult of digestion, may forthwith be attacked by vomiting and pain which closely resemble the effects of an irritant poison. An unsuspected gastric ulcer may give way under like conditions. Poison may be intentionally added to medicine which is being taken by a sick person, and the ill results which follow every dose may be attributed by him to its legitimate therapeutic action. When attending a case in which anomalous symptoms repeatedly recur, the medical practitioner should be silently observant, unless the indications of foul play are conclusive, or the state of the patient is becoming critical, in either of these events it is his duty at once to take such measures as are necessary to prevent further mischief. The position is an extremely delicate one. It is a very serious matter for a practitioner to make an unfounded charge against an innocent person, but to allow a patient to be poisoned under his eyes is infinitely worse. If the medical attendant's suspicions are aroused, he should especially distrust the ministrations of any one who is studiously attentive to the invalid, who prepares all his food and insists on giving it to him with his or her own hand, and who displays an exaggerated interest in the treatment of the patient, and in the visits of the doctor. Such a person will stand by the invalid as he takes his food and will throw away what is left, under the pretext that everything partaken of should be freshly prepared. All this is not inconsistent with innocence and a genuine desire for the welfare of the patient, but when incongruous symptoms arise which are at variance with the natural course of disease, such a person is to be regarded with suspicion and carefully watched. The patient should be cautiously, but not mysteriously interrogated as to the food or fluids that he has partaken of, and the times when he felt any accession of the suspicious symptoms. The most practical safeguard in cases of suspected foul play is the engagement of a couple of trained nurses for night and day duty respectively. They should be instructed not to leave the patient when on duty, and to prepare and give all food and medicine with their own hands. In giving strict injunctions to this effect it is not necessary that the nurses should be taken into the confidence of the doctor, unless the condition of matters is critical, or for some other reason he deems it advisable. A twenty-four hours' supply of the patient's urine should be obtained and submitted to chemical examination for the suspected poison; this may be done without giving rise to suspicion, as doctors frequently require specimens of urine for examination in the course of ordinary diseases. To take away food or beverage prepared for the patient would of course be to reveal suspicion, and should only be resorted to when the conviction of foul play is very strong and concealment is no longer possible. If the urine, or other substance is sent to an analyst, it should be accompanied by a statement of the kind of poison it is suspected to contain.

The state of the medical attendant's mind when he believes that an attempt is being made to poison his patient may be described as having two stages—first one of suspicion, and then one of conviction supposing that his suspicions are well founded. These states of mind have different obligations. When from symptoms irreconcilable with the ordinary course of the disease, or on account of some suspicious circumstance or chain of events, the idea dawns upon the medical attendant that his patient is the victim of a secret poisoner, he is not therefore justified in immediately proclaiming his suspicion. It is quite possible that he may be wrong, and as a statement to the effect that he believes some one is attempting to commit murder, cannot be made without implicating people who may be innocent, such a statement is not rashly to be made. The practitioner would also render himself liable to legal proceedings on the part of those whom he had directly, or by implication, accused of the crime. Errors of interpretation, or of judgment, are easily fallen into, and, under circumstances such as are being discussed, it would be unwarrantable, on the first feeling of mistrust, to act as though the matter was beyond all doubt. The steps to be taken when suspicion is aroused, but no evidence has been obtained, are to protect the patient in the way previously described, and to keep a sharp look out for renewed attempts.

If the matter has gone further, and the medical attendant is fully convinced that poison is being administered, what is he to do? There are three courses open—to tell some member of the family, other than the suspected person, to tell the patient himself, or to inform the police. A fourth plan has been recommended, it is to tell the person believed to be the culprit, that proof of the administration of poison has been obtained (without accusing him of being the administrator), and that, in the event of any further attempts being made, it will be necessary to inform the police. This would probably put an end to the matter, but it comes too near compounding a felony to be justifiable. Strictly speaking, it would be the duty of the medical attendant to inform the police as soon as he is fully convinced that a criminal attempt is being made on the life of his patient. Circumstances may make it advisable for him to take a member of the family whom he can trust into his confidence before doing so. Just as precipitancy was deprecated in the stage of mere suspicion, so is promptness necessary when that suspicion is converted into certainty. The medical attendant's duty is clearly defined, and he is bound to fulfil it without fear or favour.

**Indications of poisoning** may be shown by circumstances **apart from** the symptoms which affect the individual. A number of healthy persons may be simultaneously attacked with analogous symptoms after a common meal; this may be due to intentional or accidental admixture of poison with the food, or to abnormal constitution of one or more of the food-stuffs partaken of. Another way in which suspicion may be aroused, apart from any symptoms manifested by the patient, is by the discovery of an unusual appearance or odour possessed by the food or medicine which has been prepared for his use.

When a medical man is in attendance on a case in which he suspects poisoning, he should note down all he observes immediately after each visit; such notes may be of the utmost value should the case end fatally

If the conviction of foul play is believed to be well-founded, medicine-bottles, specimens of foods and drinks provided for the patient should be taken possession of, and guarded until handed over to the police or to the analyst. Vomited matter, and sheets or other fabrics stained therewith, should also be impounded.

## THE GENERAL TREATMENT OF POISONING.

The conditions to be fulfilled are:—to empty the stomach of any poison it may contain, or to neutralise it; to combat the effects of that which has been absorbed, and to promote its elimination; to keep the patient alive until the effects of the poison have passed off; to alleviate general symptoms.

There are two ways of forcibly emptying the stomach—by means of an *emetic*, and by means of the *stomach-pump*.

**Emetics.**—Half drachm doses of zinc sulphate dissolved in warm water, repeated if necessary, act quickly without causing depression; if not at hand, a dessert spoonful of mustard may be given in a tumbler of warm water. For children, a teaspoonful of ipecacuanha wine is a good emetic. In any case the patient should drink copiously of warm water, which materially aids emesis and washes out the stomach. Tartar emetic and copper sulphate are to be avoided; the former is a depressant, and both would tend to add to the difficulty of a subsequent chemical analysis, should it be necessary. An exception is to be made with regard to phosphorus poisoning in which copper sulphate may be given. Instead of giving an emetic by the mouth, a hypodermic injection of a solution of apomorphine hydrochlorate may be administered; the B.P. solution for hypodermic injection contains two grains in one hundred minims, of which five minims—one-tenth of a grain—is a proper dose to inject in a case of poisoning. This method of procuring emesis is convenient, especially in cases of narcotic poisoning where there is great difficulty in making the patient swallow. In the absence of an emetic, the fauces may be tickled with a feather, or even the finger, and copious draughts of warm water given.

The **stomach-pump**, or tube, is an efficacious mode of emptying the stomach independently of physiological function, and is therefore entirely under the control of the operator. If the mouth of the patient can be kept open, there is little difficulty in passing the tube of the instrument down the œsophagus, keeping it well against the posterior wall. It may be necessary to forcibly open the jaws, and to keep them open with a gag. Before withdrawing any of the contents of the stomach, a pint or so of warm water should be injected; the same amount is then withdrawn, and a further supply injected, which is also withdrawn. The object of this is to wash the stomach out, and to make sure that it is not entirely emptied, which might lead to injury of its coats. If the stomach-pump is not to hand, five or six feet of india-rubber tubing, such as is used for small gas supplies, fitted with a funnel at one end, may be substituted. The free end is then passed down the patient's throat and, when in the stomach, a pint or more of warm water is poured into the funnel, which is held as high as the length of tubing will allow. When the funnel is almost empty the tube close to it is pinched between the finger and thumb, and the funnel depressed until it is lower than the stomach; on removing the finger and thumb the tube acts as a syphon, and evacuates the stomach. The process is to be repeated as with the stomach-pump until nothing but clear, non-odorous water comes away. When the stomach contains much solid matter of a lumpy consistence, it may be advisable to give an emetic before using the pump or tube, in order to avoid clogging. *Neither the stomach-pump nor emetics are to be used in cases of corrosive poisoning;* the proper treatment in such cases is to neutralise the poison. The passage of the tube is exceedingly risky in any case where the walls of the œsophagus and stomach are softened and corroded; for this reason, the stomach-pump requires using with great caution in the case of certain irritants, especially if the patient is not seen for some time after the poison is swallowed. In cases where the proper treatment is to empty the stomach, and the introduction of the stomach-pump, or tube, would be risky, an emetic is to be given. The stomach-pump is especially useful in cases of poisoning by opium, alcohol, chloral hydrate, chloroform in the liquid state, the vegetable, and most of the mineral irritants, phosphorus (if the case is seen shortly after the poison is swallowed), and the alkaloids. In strychnine-poisoning it will probably be necessary to place the patient under chloroform before the tube can be passed. In the absence of the stomach-pump, or tube, an emetic may be administered in appropriate cases; but where time is of importance the mechanical method is preferable.

Antidotes are remedies which counteract the effects of poisons. They act either *mechanically, chemically,* or *physiologically.*

Flour and water, or chalk mixture, act as mechanical antidotes, when given in poisoning by phosphorus or cantharides. Magnesia and chalk are chemical antidotes to the mineral acids; as are the alkaline sulphates to the salts of lead and barium. Physiological antidotes will be discussed separately, under the heading of "antagonism of poisons."

The elimination of the poison that has been absorbed is to be assisted by purges (when not contra-indicated) diuretics, and special remedies in the case of certain poisons

The patient, if possible, is to be *kept alive* until the effect of the poison has passed off—by artificial respiration and cold douche (hydrocyanic acid), by being kept awake (opium), by external warmth (chloral hydrate and carbolic acid) and by stimulants

**General symptoms**, as excessive pain, exhaustion, useless vomiting and purging, are to be combated by appropriate remedies

## ANTAGONISM OF POISONS

This term is applied to the power certain poisons are supposed to possess of counteracting the effects of other poisons, either by the direct exercise of an opposing influence—if a poison paralyses a certain tissue, its antagonist stimulates it—or, as suggested by Ringer,[1] by chemical displacement. The latter hypothesis supposes that a poison which acts as an antagonist to another poison, has a stronger affinity for the tissue attacked, and that it displaces the poison towards which it is an antagonist, substituting its own action for that of the poison

In its full meaning the term "antagonism" includes more than mere reversal of some of the effects produced by a poison; it comprises counteraction of the influence of the poison step by step in the tissues originally attacked. This is altogether different from setting up at a distance an opposing force or obstacle, which only changes or reverses outward indications, leaving the tissues originally attacked still under the influence of the primary poison—merely blocking the way to external manifestations. For example, morphine slows the action of the heart and atropine quickens it; therefore, so far as outward appearances go, atropine in this respect acts antagonistically to morphine. But morphine slows the heart by excitation of the vagus at its origin in the brain—as shown by the fact that if the vagi are divided before morphine is given, no retardation occurs. Atropine quickens the heart's action by paralysing the terminations of the vagi, and also the inhibitory ganglia in the heart—as shown by absence of slowing on irritation of the vagi in animals under the influence of atropine. Under these circumstances it is clear that the influence exerted by morphine, in the direction of slowing the heart, is not removed by atropine; it is simply arrested at a point distant from the seat of action

Again, a true antagonist would counteract in every direction the influence of the poison to which it is opposed; it is not enough for it

[1] *Handbook of Therapeutics*.

to combat some effects, and to leave others unopposed. It is probable that atropine is truly antagonistic to morphine as regards the respiratory function : atropine stimulates the respiratory centre and morphine depresses it. Unverricht,[1] however, denies that atropine is a stimulant for the normal respiratory apparatus, and cites some experiments by Orlowski[2] in support of his views. Atropine also at first stimulates but subsequently depresses the vasomotor centre; opium in large doses depresses it from the first. In regard to other functions the action of the two poisons, though apparently antagonistic, is not really so; and in others again there is not only absence of antagonism, real or apparent, but similar results are produced, though not in the same manner. As is well known opium contracts the pupil and atropine dilates it. In this relation it is probable that opium acts centrally and atropine peripherally, paralysing the terminals of the oculo-motor nerves. Both poisons cause dryness of the mouth—opium by lowering reflex excitability, and atropine by paralysing the secretory fibres of the chorda tympani. Opium causes sweating by stimulating the central nerve-apparatus concerned; atropine arrests it by paralysing the nerve terminals in the sweat glands. Opium, after causing an initial increase in the intestinal movements, arrests them probably by lowering the reflex excitability. Atropine is believed ultimately to deprive the intestines of movement by paralysing their motor nerves and, finally, the muscular elements themselves. The terminals of the inhibitory fibres of the splanchnics are also paralysed by atropine.

Thus, although in respect to one or two prominent symptoms, atropine and morphine are opposed in their action, they are not true antagonists. Their modes of action are different; broadly speaking, *atropine acts peripherally, morphine centrally.* Morphine, in poisonous doses, depresses the excitability of the ganglionic cells of the cerebrum, and probably of the cord also, and lessens reflex function. This is disputed by some; Unverricht[3] states that opium does not lower, and may increase, the irritability of the cortex. Atropine stimulates the central nervous system, and in this way increases the reflex function; but it also paralyses many of the peripheral nerves, and thus cuts off the organs supplied by them from their centres. The ultimate effect of both poisons is to paralyse the motor and the sensory nerves. Morphine, when used as an antagonist to atropine, is much feebler in its effects than atropine is when used to antagonise morphine.

Notwithstanding the absence of proof of antagonism, many cases are

[1] *Centralbl. f. klin. Med.*, 1891 and 1892.
[2] *Einwirkung des Atropins auf die Resp.*, 1891.
[3] *Centralbl. f. klin. Med.*, 1891.

recorded in which life is believed to have been saved by the administration of atropine to patients suffering from poisonous doses of opium. When active treatment is successful, there is a tendency to attribute the good results to some specific cause, and the remedy, or the means used, that is apparently the most active, is the one selected for this purpose. A careful study of the recorded cases of treatment of opium-poisoning with atropine occasions great doubt as to the correctness of the inference drawn by those who advocate the treatment. It is quite excusable for a medical man, after administering atropine, to be greatly impressed by the recovery of a patient from an apparently moribund condition, the result of a poisonous dose of opium. It is not customary, however, in such cases to trust to one remedy solely, no matter how much importance is attached to it; other treatment is actively carried out during the critical period, and the effects of such treatment are often ignored, or underrated. There are grave reasons for believing that too active treatment of opium poisoning with atropine has sometimes been the means of hastening, rather than preventing, the fatal issue. Lenhartz[1] states that out of 132 cases of opium poisoning, of which 59 were treated with atropine, and 72 without, 38 per cent. of the former died, and only 15 per cent. of the latter. In three cases that came under his own observation, subcutaneous injection of atropine produced no effect beyond dilating the pupils and increasing the rapidity of the heart beats, the unfavourable symptoms persisted. Recovery ultimately took place in two; the third died, and the cumulative effect of the atropine was regarded as not being beyond suspicion of having exercised a deleterious influence.

Without going so far as to deny the possibility of benefit from the use of atropine in the treatment of opium poisoning, the exercise of great caution is strongly urged, as the repeated heroic doses that have been given are altogether unjustifiable in the face of the known ultimately mutual effects of the two poisons. It is to be remembered that whatever antagonistic effect small doses of atropine may exercise, its ultimate effect is to paralyse the heart.

Perhaps the best illustration of antagonism between poisons is afforded by atropine and physostigmine. Frazer's[2] experiments have demonstrated that physostigmine increases the excitability of the vagi, while atropine diminishes and suspends it; physostigmine lowers arterial tension, atropine augments it; physostigmine increases glandular secretion, atropine diminishes, or arrests it; physostigmine contracts the pupils, atropine dilates them. In the greater number of these instances, the antagonism is real, being effected in the same structures and in the same order.

[1] *Archiv. f. exp. Path. u. Pharm.*, 1887.
[2] *Transactions of the Royal Soc. Edin.*, vols. xxiv., xxvi.

Limited antagonism between poisons may be advantageously utilised for antidotal purposes. The effects produced by strychnine on the respiratory centres and on the reflex mechanism of the cord are, within limits, capable of being antagonised by chloral hydrate. Reciprocally chloral poisoning may be beneficially treated by the administration of strychnine; atropine is also a limited antagonist to chloral hydrate. Muscarine antagonises atropine by stimulating the endings of the oculo-motor nerves, the endings of the secretory fibres of the chorda tympani, and the inhibitory cardiac ganglia, at the same time paralysing the cardiac muscles. It also depresses the activity of the respiratory centres. Muscarine ultimately paralyses the inhibitory action of the vagi, and is thus finally in accord with, instead of antagonistic to, atropine.

Other poisons are accredited with a limited degree of mutual antagonism, such as atropine to aconite, digitalis to aconite, chloral hydrate to picrotoxine, atropine to pilocarpine, aconite to strychnine, morphine to hyoscyamine, strychnine to nicotine. Theine and its congeners, caffeine and guaranine, to some extent antagonise morphine.

## GENERAL SYMPTOMS OF CORROSIVE AND OF IRRITANT POISONING

Before considering the evidences of poisoning that are available in the dead body, it will conduce to their due appreciation if a general description is first given of the symptoms which occur during life. The poisons which give rise to the most characteristic post-mortem appearances are corrosives and irritants.

A corrosive, as the name indicates, is a substance which destroys tissue by direct chemical action; a corrosive also acts as an irritant, and, if administered in a dilute form, it may do so exclusively, without producing any corrosive effects. When a poison which acts as a corrosive is swallowed, an *immediate* and violent sensation of pain is produced, which extends from the mouth, along the œsophagus to the stomach, and then radiates over the abdomen. Uncontrollable retching and vomiting comes on within a few minutes, the appearance of the vomited matter being determined within certain limits by the nature of the corrosive; shreds of mucous membrane, coagulated mucus, and blood are always present, the colour of the blood being sometimes altered by the chemical action of the poison. During this first stage the patient is frequently partially or wholly convulsed, a reflex symptom caused by the excruciating pain. There is intense thirst, with difficulty or impossibility of swallowing, each attempt to do so causing increased vomiting. The patient is in a condition of extreme collapse—the surface is pale, cold and bedewed with clammy sweat, the features are pinched, the eyes, sunk into their sockets, have a wild, terrified look. The voice is hoarse, or there may be complete aphonia, in the latter case it is probable that some of the corrosive has reached the larynx. The mouth is filled with ropy mucus; the salivary glands secrete profusely; the lips are swollen, and, along with the corners of the mouth, may show signs of the local action of the corrosive. The mucous membrane of the mouth is detached and the underlying tissues are corroded, the colour of the surface varying with the nature of the corrosive. The abdomen is usually distended. The breathing is laboured and noisy; attempts to clear the air-passage give rise to a distressing cough, which has a peculiarly hoarse, laryngeal sound. The pulse, thread-like, and of low tension, is scarcely perceptible at the wrist. The bowels are confined, the urine is diminished in amount, or entirely suppressed, and attempts to relieve the bladder are painful and futile. The mind usually remains clear to the end, death taking place from extreme collapse; in some cases death is preceded by convulsions. In an acute case, as above described, death takes place within twenty-four or thirty-six hours.

An **irritant** poison is one which by its specific action sets up inflammation in the intestinal tract. A pure irritant does not produce corrosion, although some substances classed as irritants may act as corrosives. When a substance that acts solely as an irritant is swallowed, the symptoms do *not* come on in the act of swallowing *nor immediately after*, as is the case with corrosives; an interval elapses of from half an hour to an hour or more. In the case of metallic irritants (the symptoms they produce being taken as a type of irritant poisoning) there may, or may not, be an astringent or metallic taste perceived at the time the poison is swallowed. The presence or absence of this symptom depends partly upon the nature of the poison itself, and partly upon the medium in which it is administered. The first symptoms are those of gastro-intestinal irritation—violent and persistent vomiting and purging, with severe gastric and abdominal pain. The vomited matter probably at first consists of food, then it becomes bilious, and finally may be blood-stained. There is intense thirst, and attempts to allay it provoke further vomiting. A hot burning sensation along with a feeling of constriction is felt in the throat. The purging is accompanied by violent tenesmus, and the dejections may be blood-stained; they are sometimes colourless, of the rice-water type. The symptoms of collapse appear—the surface is cold and clammy, and the pulse feeble and intermittent; occasionally the skin is hot and dry, probably due to an attempt at reaction. There is great restlessness and anxiety, the mind often remaining clear to the last. The patient may be troubled with violent cramps in the legs, or he may have general convulsions. In fatal cases, death from exhaustion takes place in from one to four days.

## EVIDENCE OF POISONING FROM THE DEAD BODY.

As the symptoms of poisoning during life vary according to the nature of the poison that has been taken, so do the post-mortem appearances differ when the result has been fatal. The two classes of poisons which yield the *most characteristic* post-mortem appearances are corrosives and irritants. All corrosives and all irritants do not produce the same after death appearances, but certain characteristic indications are usually met with in each class respectively.

In making a post-mortem examination on a case of suspected poisoning, it is important to distinguish between the effects of poison, and those due to disease on the one hand and to incipient putrefaction on the other. The post-mortem indications afforded by corrosive and irritant poisons are to be sought for along the digestive tract. They comprise *hyperæmia, softening*, and *ulceration* of the mucous membrane, with *perforation* of the wall of a viscus either due to ulceration or, more frequently, to the direct action of a corrosive.

The ordinary effect of an irritant poison is to cause hyperæmia of the mucous membrane of the œsophagus and stomach, and possibly of that of the small intestine. The hyperæmia may either be diffuse, or isolated in patches; it is usually most marked about the cardiac end of the stomach; more rarely is the pyloric end affected. With some irritants there is a tendency to the formation of small hæmorrhagic points, or striæ, or there may be large dark patches, which stand out in contrast with the neighbouring and less deeply coloured mucous membrane. The hyperæmia may be most intense along the summits of the rugæ of the gastric or intestinal mucous membrane, or the entire mucous coat of the stomach may be hyperæmic and thickened, presenting a velvety appearance—frequently seen in acute arsenical poisoning. The mucous surface may be covered with viscid secretion, which may be blood-stained.

Softening of the mucous membrane of the stomach when due to poison is usually caused by corrosives; indications of the same condition are to be found in the œsophagus and possibly in the mouth as well. It is not a common result of poisoning; when it occurs it is chiefly due to the direct chemical action of the poison. All corrosives do not cause softening; carbolic acid corrugates and hardens the mucous surfaces with which it comes in contact, and some other corrosives occasionally do the same. Softening is an almost invariable result of poisoning by the alkalies.

**Ulceration** of the mucous membrane of the stomach is occasionally seen as a result of irritant poisoning; it appears to be chiefly due to the local action of a portion of the poison on a limited surface of the membrane. In this way phosphorus may set up ulceration as a primary result, apart from its secondary effects. Sometimes ulceration is due to infarcts, the result of inflammatory processes causing blood stasis. Removal of patches of mucous membrane by the direct action of corrosives is to be distinguished from ulceration—the former is due to chemical destruction of tissue, the latter to pathological processes.

**Perforation**, as a result of poisoning, is usually due to the direct chemical action of a corrosive on the coats of the stomach or more rarely of the small intestine. The appearance of a perforation thus caused is characteristic; there is no indication of limitation by inflammatory processes, the margins instead of being thickened, are partially disintegrated, a condition that extends some distance from the aperture, which is usually large and is irregular in outline; the edges of the opening and the contiguous parts (when the perforation is due to sulphuric acid) are blackened and charred. Ulceration due to irritant poisoning may be followed by perforation, but such an event is of exceptional occurrence; the appearances would more nearly resemble those met with when an idiopathic gastric ulcer has given way. The poison which most frequently causes perforation is strong sulphuric acid.

## THE LOCAL EFFECTS OF POISON CONTRASTED WITH THOSE OF DISEASE AND THOSE PRODUCED BY POST-MORTEM CHANGES

Some of the above described appearances cannot be distinguished from similar appearances which are due to disease, others are only met with as the result of poisoning. Acute idiopathic inflammation of the mucous membrane of the stomach is exceedingly rare, so that the inflammatory appearances described when distinctly present, are always suspicious of irritant poisoning; on the other hand, such appearances may be absent, or feebly marked, after death from an irritant poison. The colour of the gastric mucous membrane should always be noted at the time the stomach is opened, as it becomes redder on exposure to air. *The colour alone is not to be relied on* as an indication of inflammation, it may result from food or medicine which contain pigmentary matter. Some fruits, such as black cherries and elderberries, will colour the gastric mucous membrane, which is also reddened during digestion of food, and it is said, by copious draughts of ice-cold water. Post-mortem staining produces redness, but it is limited to the posterior part of the stomach—the body being on its back, the mucous membrane is not thickened, there is no glairy mucus on its surface, and the general appearance is unlike that due to inflammation. Incipient **putrefactive changes** produce softening of the mucous membrane of the stomach along with colour changes. These changes commence at the posterior part, at the seat of post-mortem staining, the softening affecting the entire thickness of the coats of the stomach. When softening is the result of poisoning it is either limited to the mucous membrane, or, if it extends to the muscular coat, the mucous membrane will probably be detached in patches over the parts that are softened. In post-mortem softening the mucous membrane is rarely detached—the several coats of which the stomach is composed soften together usually without separating from each other.

**Ulcer** of the stomach is much more frequently due to pathological conditions than to poisoning. The idiopathic gastric-ulcer is small, sharply defined, and very frequently is situated along or near the lesser curvature. The floor of the ulcer is formed by the muscular coat or, if this is perforated, by the peritoneum, which, at the spot, may or may not be adherent to the liver or pancreas. The opening in the mucous membrane is circular and cleanly "punched out," and is larger than that through the muscular coat. In the early stage of the formation of a gastric-ulcer the edges are not raised, subsequently they may become so, the mucous, muscular, and serous coats are firmly adherent for some distance from the ulcer. If the ulcer gives way a small opening usually forms through the floor, so that, in vertical section, the ulcer is V-shaped—the aperture being at the apex. All this points to gradual formation. An ulcer caused by an irritant poison is usually more quickly produced, and presents the appearance of an erosion with surrounding signs of recent inflammation, which are generally absent in the idiopathic ulcer. There is less tendency to thickening round the margin, which is more irregular and not so cleanly "punched out." When perforation is due to the immediate action of a corrosive, the comparatively large size of the aperture, the irregular and ill-defined margin, the surrounding softening and friability of all the coats, and the discoloration of the structures make the diagnosis easy.

**Perforation** of the stomach wall may take place from the action of the gastric juice **after death**. This could not be mistaken for the effect of a corrosive poison, as there is entire absence of an indications of inflammation, and the edges of the aperture, though irregular, are free from the colour changes which characterise the action of corrosives. The surrounding mucous membrane is often swollen and gelatinous.

The appearance presented by the mucous membrane of the stomach in cases of suspected poisoning is to be *interpreted with caution*, especially in relation to colour-changes. Mere redness of the surface is too often assumed to indicate the occurrence of inflammation, which is at once attributed to the effects of poisoning; as previously stated, something beyond this is required to warrant such an interpretation.

The post-mortem appearances after death from narcotics, convulsives, and deliriants are mostly limited to hyperæmic conditions of the nervous centres and their membranes, and are relatively of little diagnostic value.

## EVIDENCE OF POISONING FROM CHEMICAL ANALYSIS OF THE VISCERA AND THEIR CONTENTS

The substances obtained at the post mortem examination of a case of suspected poisoning are sent to the analyst in bottles or jars, duly secured and sealed, as directed when the method of making post-mortems in medico-legal cases was described. Before opening the jars an inventory of them should be taken, and the covers and seals should be carefully scrutinised, in order to ascertain whether they have been tampered with; once in the possession of the analyst the jars and their contents must be kept under lock and key.

After each jar is opened its contents are to be measured, or weighed, in accordance as to whether they are fluid or solid. A careful examination of the physical appearance of the various substances should then be made, a lens or microscope being used if necessary. All food-stuffs present should be noted, and the odour of the contents of each jar ascertained; should any crystals or particles of inorganic matter be present, a few should be picked out and submitted to a preliminary examination; any seeds or fragments of leaves of plants that may be observed should be removed and investigated as to their nature and source.

When the symptoms observed during life are either obscure or are not indicative of a special poison, or in cases where no history is forthcoming, it may be necessary in the absence of post-mortem indications to make a systematic analysis of the viscera and their contents. Usually some clue is obtainable as to the nature of the poison suspected to have been administered, and in such cases the chemical investigation is chiefly directed to such poison. The amount of material at the disposal of the analyst being limited, it is very important that he should be made acquainted, as far as possible, with the nature of the poison, as indicated by the symptoms during life and the appearances after death. It does not follow that the chemical enquiry is to be restricted to the discovery of a suspected poison; the possible presence of other poisons is not to be ignored. Usually, however, only one poison is present, and, if the analysis is from the first directed towards its discovery, the probability of success is much greater than if the investigation has to include the whole series of poisons. This is of special importance as regards quantitative analysis, and in criminal trials much importance is not unfrequently attached to the amount of the poison obtained from the dead body. Only a portion of the organs and substances at the disposal of the analyst should be used in making the analysis, unless the amount is too small half should be reserved for a corroborative investigation by another expert.

In making a systematic analysis attention is first to be directed to the possible presence of volatile poisons. The chief volatile poisons are—hydrocyanic acid, oil of bitter almonds, nicotine, conine, phosphorus, alcohol, chloroform, benzene, and its derivatives nitro-benzene, anilin, and phenol. If the odour of any of these bodies is present in the substance under investigation, the clue thus afforded is to be followed up; in any case their presence or absence must be determined.

The next step is to ascertain whether any alkaloids are present; for this purpose, one of the many modifications of Stas' process for the separation of alkaloids from organic matter may be resorted to. The principles on which this process is founded are—that the salts of the alkaloids are soluble in water and in ethyl alcohol, but not in ether and some other solvents, as amyl alcohol, benzene, acetic ether, and chloroform. On the other hand, the uncombined alkaloids (or most of them) are nearly insoluble in water, but are more or less soluble in ether and in the other solvents named. This property of the alkaloids is made use of to extract them from organic admixture in the following way:—The alkaloid present is dissolved with the aid of slightly acidulated alcohol, with which it is digested for several hours at a moderate temperature. The liquid is then filtered off and evaporated down to a syrup at a gentle heat. When cold, the syrupy mass is treated with absolute alcohol, the object being to precipitate as much of the foreign matter as possible, and to retain the alkaloid in solution. The process of evaporation and subsequent treatment with absolute alcohol may have to be repeated several times before the bulk of the extraneous matter is got rid of. Finally, the last alcoholic extract is evaporated down to a syrup, which is then dissolved in a small quantity of water, with the result that any alkaloid in the original substance will be held as a salt in aqueous solution. As long as this solution remains acid it may (except in the case of certain alkaloids and active principles) be shaken with ether without parting with the alkaloid, and by repeated shaking-out with ether, more of the remaining organic impurities, chiefly fatty matter may be removed. When this is accomplished, the aqueous solution is made alkaline, and is once more shaken out with ether. The addition of the alkali displaces the acid of the alkaloid, and, being insoluble in water but soluble in ether, the free alkaloid is taken up by the ether, which is then separated and evaporated to dryness, leaving the alkaloid in a sufficiently pure state for testing.

So much for the principles on which Stas' process is founded; in putting them into practice several important details require attention, and on the skill with which they are carried out success depends. Stevenson's[1] great experience has enabled him to develop and to refine Stas' process as follows:—The substance under examination is digested with twice its weight, or, if fluid, twice its volume, of rectified spirit, at a temperature of 35°, after several hours the fluid is poured off (the solid matter being subjected to pressure), and is replaced with fresh spirit, which is allowed to digest as before. After decantation of the second extract the process is repeated several times more with spirit acidulated with acetic acid. The extracts obtained with the acidulated spirit are mixed together, but are kept apart from those obtained without the acid, which are also mixed together. The extracts separately are quickly raised to a temperature of 70°, allowed to cool, filtered, and the residue on the filter washed with spirit. The extracts are then evaporated to a syrup at a temperature not exceeding 35°, excess of acid being neutralised with soda. The syrupy liquid is drenched with 30 cc of absolute alcohol, and well stirred in a mortar, the alcohol is poured off, and the process is repeated with successive quantities of 15 cc of alcohol until it comes away colourless. These extracts are filtered and evaporated to a syrup, as before. The syrupy extracts from the acid and from the non-acid digestions are each diluted with a small quantity of water, filtered, and then mixed together. The united extracts, whilst still acid, are shaken with twice their volume of ether, the operation being repeated until the ether, on evaporation of a few drops, leaves no residue. The ethereal solutions are washed by vigorous shaking with 5 cc of water, to which a few drops of $H_2SO_4$ have been added. The acid aqueous solution which was washed with the ether, and the water which was used to wash the ether after separation, are mixed and alkalised with sodium carbonate. They are then exhausted, first with a mixture of one volume of chloroform and three volumes of ether (which previously has been well washed with water), and subsequently twice or thrice more with washed ether alone. The ethereal extracts are washed with 5 cc of water, then with 10 cc of water acidulated with $H_2SO_4$, and again

[1] Watts' *Dictionary of Chemistry*, 1890.

with 5 cc of water alone. The acid liquid and the final wash-water are washed once or twice with a little ether, re-alkalised with sodium carbonate, and well extracted with washed chloroform and ether, and afterwards with ether alone. These ethereal extracts are washed with water barely alkalised with sodium carbonate, filtered through a dry filter, and evaporated in an oven under 35° in tared glass basins. When evaporation is complete, the basins may be dried at a temperature of 100°, then cooled over sulphuric acid and weighed. To extract morphine Stevenson uses a well-washed mixture of equal volumes of acetic and ethylic ether.

The object of these repeated washings and transferring of the alkaloid from water to ether, and from ether to water, is to get rid of fatty and other matters which seriously interfere with the colour-tests, and also to enable a correct estimation to be made of the amount of alkaloid present in the substance under examination. When an alkaloid is sufficiently freed from organic matter the usual tests are applied to establish its identity.

When extracting an aqueous fluid containing an alkaloid with a fluid that is insoluble in water, care must be taken not to agitate the two fluids to such an extent as to cause them to emulsify. Some fluids which retain small quantities of organic matter in solution very readily form emulsions with the solvent used for extraction, especially after alkalisation. Various methods have been devised to promote separation of the fluids after emulsification, such as the addition of more of the solvent, the immersion of the containing tube for a few minutes in a freezing mixture, or in hot water, imparting a rotary motion to the tube, or a series of slight shocks by repeatedly tapping it with the finger nail—any of which may or may not be successful. The best plan is to avoid emulsification by first cautiously inverting the tube two or three consecutive times, and observing the rate at which the fluids separate; if they show a disposition to blend, the process of extraction must be conducted with great deliberation, time being allowed for separation after every two or three inversions of the tube.

The process of extraction may be conducted in a stoppered tube, like a large test-tube, or in a small tubular-separator, furnished with a stop-cock, through which the lower stratum of fluid may be withdrawn. The separator is most convenient when the solvent is heavier than water; when a tube is used the solvent has to be pipetted off. The amount of solvent in toxicological work is usually small, and may be conveniently dealt with by means of a pipette furnished with an india-rubber ball attached to its upper end by a short piece of rubber tube, on which is placed a spring pinch-cock, as shown in Fig. 21. Before using the pipette the pinch-cock is opened, and the ball compressed so as to empty it of air; the pinch-cock is then released. The pipette is passed down to the lowest stratum of the fluid to be removed, and the pinch-cock gently pressed open when the ball expands and draws up the fluid into the pipette. When the whole of the fluid, or as much as the pipette will contain, is removed, the pinch-cock is again allowed to clip the tube, the pipette is withdrawn, and its contents expelled by compressing the ball and opening the pinch-cock. The advantage of this little device is that separation can readily be effected at the level of the eye, and arrested at the desired moment with the greatest nicety. The lower end of the pipette is turned sidewise, so as not to draw up the fluid beneath.

To separate alkaloids in aqueous solution, when more than one is present, Dragendorff devised the method of using various solvents in sequence. The principle on which the method is founded is that some solvents take up certain alkaloids to the exclusion of others. The preference displayed by solvents for certain alkaloids, however, is not completely exclusive; most alkaloids are soluble in more than one solvent, though possibly to a greater degree in one than in others. The process consists in shaking out the acid aqueous solution containing the mixed alkaloids, successively with petroleum ether, benzene, and chloroform, and after alkalising it, repeating the operation with the same solvents. Many of the substances capable of being obtained by this process are of no interest to the toxicologist; the following are the most important.

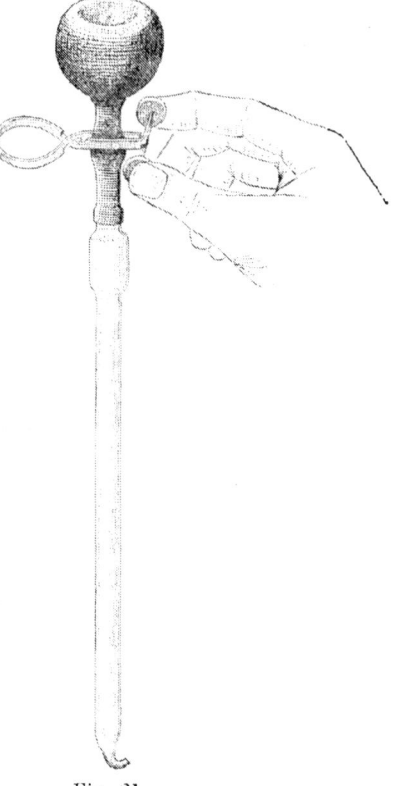

Fig. 21.

From the *acid* solution **benzene** removes caffeine, colchicine, digitalin, cantharidin. **Chloroform** removes papaverine, colchicine, narceine.

From the *alkaline* solution **petroleum ether** removes strychnine, brucine, aconitine, veratrine, conine, nicotine, lobeline. **Benzene** removes atropine, hyoscyamine, physostigmine, narcotine, codeine, strychnine, brucine, veratrine. **Chloroform** removes strychnine, brucine, morphine, narceine. **Amyl alcohol** removes morphine, solanine, narceine.

Inorganic poisons remain to be dealt with. Mineral poisons maintain their integrity when submitted to processes that destroy alkaloids, therefore they can be treated in a different manner. If inorganic poisons were simply mixed with organic matter it would be sufficient directly to convert them into insoluble salts, and to wash away the impurities; the association between the two, however, is usually much more intimate, and then they can only be separated by destruction of the organic matter. Some have to be separated from organic matter in special ways, as they are liable to be dissipated by methods which do not effect most inorganic poisons; of these, arsenic is a notable example.

Various processes are used to destroy the organic matter, of which three only need here be described; they are known amongst chemists as the moist, and the dry methods. The moist method is accomplished as follows:—The substance which is suspected to contain the poison, if solid, is reduced to a pulp, is mixed with sufficient water as to be of the consistence of thin gruel, and is then placed in a large flask along with some crystals of potassium chlorate. Each pound weight of the organic mixture will require about half an ounce of the chlorate. Pure hydrochloric acid to about the same weight as the original substance is then added, and the flask is placed on a water-bath and heated. Chlorine, or rather a mixture of chlorine and of chlorine peroxide, is evolved, which attacks the organic matter, breaks it up, and liberates any mineral poison that may be present. If necessary, additional crystals of potassium chlorate are added until the fluid becomes limpid, and of a light yellow colour, or, if there is much organic matter, until it assumes the appearance and colour of thin oatmeal gruel. On account of more gradual evolution of chlorine, the chlorate that is present before the flask is heated acts much more energetically, weight for weight, than fragments that are added after the liquid is hot, as a great deal of the gas then escapes without rendering any service. To minimise the waste of chlorine, and also the risk of frothing over (an accident very liable to occur) only moderate heat should be applied; substances containing sugar, starch, or alcohol are very troublesome in the latter respect. After the last addition of chlorate, the liquid is transferred to an evaporating basin, and is allowed to remain on a water-bath until the smell of chlorine has disappeared;

it is then filtered hot. When cold, a stream of sulphurous acid gas is passed through the liquid to reduce any metals present to a lower state of oxidation, and so to prepare them for subsequent treatment. The whole of the organic matter is not destroyed by this process, fatty substances especially being resistant, but if the original matter is reduced to small fragments, any mineral poison present will be liberated.

The objections to this process are that some important poisons, as arsenic and antimony, especially the former, are liable in part to escape in the form of vapour as chlorides, and that others such as lead and silver, may remain as insoluble chlorides on the filter. The first difficulty may be avoided by furnishing the flask with a condenser and receiver, and the last—so far as lead is concerned—by taking care that the solution is filtered hot. If only a limited amount of lead is present it will remain in solution as chloride so long as the liquid is hot, and will consequently pass through the filter; a considerable quantity is kept in solution in the cold, as it forms a combination with potassium chloride, which is more soluble than lead chloride alone. If a large amount is present it will not all be found in the filtrate; the substance left on the filter, therefore, should always be tested for lead. In toxicological work, however, the amount of lead present is not as a rule, more than will remain dissolved in the cold. Silver chloride, being insoluble either in hot or cold water, will not pass through the filter, consequently the salts of silver require dealing with in a special manner. Arsenic is also best dealt with in the way described in the section devoted to that metal.

Destruction of organic matter by the **dry method** is effected by heating it to redness so that it is either carbonised or completely incinerated. When cold, the residue is drenched with nitric acid, and sufficient heat is afterwards applied to drive off the free acid; the nitrate of the metal is then dissolved in water, filtered, and dealt with according to the kind of metal present.

The dry method is unsuitable in the case of the more volatile metals as arsenic, antimony, mercury, and, in a lesser degree, lead, tin, and zinc; further, it is exceedingly difficult and troublesome to carry out with large masses of organic matter; it is convenient with small amounts, and, in the absence of the more volatile metals, yields good results.

Another mode of destruction of organic matter is to heat it with an equal weight of $HNO_3$ until the whole assumes the consistence of soup; then to add $KOH$ to neutralisation and to evaporate to dryness. The dried residue is deflagrated piece by piece in a porcelain capsule, additional saltpetre being added, if necessary, so as thoroughly to oxidise any metals present. The residue after deflagration is extracted with boiling water, the oxides of most of the metals that are insoluble in water will be rendered soluble by being treated with nitric acid. This method is convenient when operating on large masses of organic matter.

The purity of the chemical agents respectively used in these processes should be ascertained.

Special methods of separation will be described under the headings of the poisons concerned.

# INORGANIC POISONS.

## CORROSIVES

## CHAPTER XXVI

### SULPHURIC ACID

Sulphuric Acid [$H_2SO_4$], or oil of vitriol is a typical and most powerful corrosive. On coming in contact with organic matter, it combines with the water that may be present and chars the solids; if much water is present in the tissues, and the amount of acid is limited, they may be converted into a slimy mass of a brownish colour. Albumen is at once coagulated and subsequently dissolved. Muscle at first swells and becomes gelatinous and then liquefies, the colour being brownish-red. Hæmoglobin is immediately converted into acid hæmatin. Sulphuric acid enters into chemical combination with albumen, and if no excess of acid is present, on digesting the albuminous compound with water, and applying the usual tests to the solution, no trace of free acid can be obtained. With progressive dilution of the acid the above-named effects diminish in degree until they cease to be produced.

**Symptoms.**—When the concentrated acid is swallowed intense pain is immediately experienced in the mouth, throat, and down to the stomach, from whence it rapidly spreads over the whole abdomen. The pain may be so violent as to cause tetanic spasms or general convulsions. Within a few minutes gaseous eructations, retching, and vomiting occur, the ejected matter consisting of coffee-coloured or blackish fluid (altered blood) with shreds and masses of mucous membrane and coagulated mucus. There is intense thirst with difficulty or impossibility of swallowing, each attempt being followed by renewed retching and vomiting. Respiration is laboured and noisy from tumefaction of the larynx. The voice is hoarse, or, probably, there is complete aphonia, and the mouth is filled with sticky mucus and shreds of membrane. The general condition is one of profound collapse—the skin is pale, cold, and clammy; that of the face may be cyanosed from imperfect respiration, or, in some instances, it is suffused and of a dusky red. The eyes are sunk and have a wild look, the pupils often being dilated The pulse, of low tension, is quick and thready, frequently almost imperceptible The bowels are almost invariably confined , in rare instances diarrhœa has occurred, the dejections containing altered blood and shreds of membrane The urine is suppressed or nearly so , albumen, blood discs, hæmatin, and casts have been found in it, but their appearance is not constant , any sulphuric acid that has been absorbed is eliminated in combination, chiefly with calcium and as ether-sulphates

The mucous membrane of the mouth is swollen, corroded or excoriated, the exposed parts being raw , sometimes the membrane is white, due to cloudy swelling of the epithelium The lips are usually swollen and excoriated, and there may be further evidence of the action of the acid in the shape of brown streaks extending from the mucous lining to the skin on the lower jaw, especially at the angles of the mouth In the case of young children the front part of the mouth may be free from corrosion on account of the acid having been administered in a spoon passed well back towards the throat.

Death may take place in the stage of collapse within a few hours after the poison is swallowed , if from the primary effects it is not likely to be delayed beyond twenty-four hours Death is often sudden , either from asphyxia due to tumefaction of the glottis or, probably, from pulmonary thrombosis or embolism caused by the action of the acid on the blood, or from perforation of the stomach. When death occurs *very* shortly after the poison is taken it may be due to shock

If the patient survives the early stage, reaction sets in, the temperature rises and the pulse becomes fuller The parts acted on by the acid slough and undergo the usual processes of separation, leaving a raw surface after they are detached Several weeks after contact with the acid, a portion of the mucous membrane of the œsophagus may exfoliate and come away as a tube Death from exhaustion may occur during the stage of reparation, towards the end of the first week being a fatal period During the second or third week, pain along the distribution of the intercostal and abdominal nerves has been observed in some cases, and in others diffuse hyperæsthesia, due probably to peripheral neuritis

Should the strength of the patient hold out, cicatrisation of the abraded parts begins and the raw surfaces gradually close in This involves the usual result of the extensive formation of internal cicatrices—loss of a corresponding area of mucous membrane, and contraction of the newly formed tissue, which leads to the stricture when a canal or an aperture is the part affected The lower end of the œsophagus and the pylorus are the usual seats of stricture, less frequently the œsophagus is affected higher up Sometimes a stricture does not develop until the patient appears to have entirely recovered. The loss of gastric glands gives rise to apepsia, and the patient emaciates from insufficient nutrition due to this cause, or to the presence of an œsophageal stricture, death may take place from inanition several months after the injuries were sustained

**Fatal Dose**—Half a teaspoonful of the strong acid killed a child a year old One fluid drachm may be regarded as the smallest lethal dose for an adult, death at the end of a week having been thus caused in the case of a young man Death has occurred within an hour, usually it takes place within thirty hours, but may be indefinitely delayed when due to secondary causes Recovery has taken place after an ounce of the strong acid was swallowed

Sulphuric acid has caused death by being accidentally administered as an enema, and also by being injected into the vagina in order to procure abortion

The prognosis of sulphuric acid poisoning is unfavourable, from 60 to 70 per cent of the cases prove fatal.

**Treatment.**—Prompt neutralisation of the acid is the first step. For this purpose calcined magnesia is the best, the alkaline carbonates are not so good, but, since saving of time is all important, any alkaline substance at hand should be utilised Egg-shells, chalk, or plaster chipped off a cornice or the ceiling, may be powdered and administered suspended in water, white of egg, or soap and water are also handy remedies If nothing else can be obtained administer water freely The stomach-pump must not be used The next step is to mitigate pain by hypodermic injections of morphine If the immediate effects are survived, nutrition will probably have to be maintained by nutrient enemata, preferably peptonised Tracheotomy may be necessary

**Post-mortem Appearances.**—The conditions found after death vary with the length of time the patient survived If death takes place within twenty-four hours the lips will probably be corroded and stained brown, similar stains from spilling of the acid may be present on other parts of the surface The clothing should be examined for indications of the action of the acid produced either in the act of administering or taking it, or by the early vomited matter, stained portions of fabric should be cut out and preserved for chemical examination The buccal mucous membrane will be greyish, yellowish-white, or dark brown in colour, it will be softened and disorganised so as to be easily detached from the underlying structures, in parts it will probably be absent, the raw surface being covered with dark-coloured blood. A like condition extends to the pharynx and down the œsophagus which appears contracted and thrown into longitudinal folds. The stomach is also contracted, and on being opened shows evidence of profound disorganisation, any contents will probably consist of a viscid, dark-coloured substance (not necessarily having an acid reaction), which is blood partially changed into hæmatin, mixed with serum and mucus. The gastric mucous membrane may be converted into a slimy coating, absent in parts, or it may be corrugated and hardened, in patches or strips, it is dark coloured, even to being absolutely black, the areas which surround the parts chemically corroded by the acid show signs of intense inflammation. The entire coats of the stomach may be so far disorganised as to be easily torn, and there may be actual perforation, which occurs more frequently with sulphuric acid than with any other corrosive. The aperture is irregular, has blackened margins, and the coats of the stomach which form them are soft and friable. When the contents of the stomach escape through the perforation (which is not invariably the case) one or more of the neighbouring viscera may be corroded and even perforated from the outside—the colon has been thus perforated, and the surfaces of the liver and spleen have been rendered hard and friable. The corrosive action of the acid may extend beyond the stomach to the duodenum, in one case it could be traced to the ileum. Fatty changes have been found in the liver and kidneys, the latter may yield indications of parenchymatous inflammation. The bladder is generally contracted and empty. Clots have been found in the blood-vessels, and the intravascular blood has been observed to be dark and tarry. During life the blood has never been found to yield an acid reaction, after death it may do so.

If the victim of sulphuric acid poisoning has survived a week or more, the post-mortem appearances will be modified accordingly. After a still longer interval, cicatrices will replace the corrosions, and the usual effects of stricture (if present) will be observed, if the lower end of the œsophagus is the seat of stricture, the part immediately above will be dilated, and the stomach probably contracted. In such cases the post-mortem appearances usually met with in cases of death from inanition will be more or less obvious.

**Chemical Analysis.**—In the examination of organic admixtures for sulphuric acid, it is first necessary to ascertain the presence of a free acid. This may be done by adding a few drops of the suspected fluid to a weak aqueous solution of tropæolin OO (diphenylamine-orange) which changes in the presence of free acids from light yellow to ruby or lake colour. This reagent reacts to an acid solution containing one drop of one of the mineral acids in 100 cc. of water; it is not affected by acid salts. Another way is to dissolve a fragment of the potassio-tartrate of iron of the Pharmacopœia in a little water so that it is tinged yellow, and to add a drop or two of a solution of potassium sulphocyanide; the addition of a liquid containing a free acid changes the colour to red.

If qualitative analysis only is aimed at, it will be sufficient if the suspected substance, after having been reduced by evaporation if necessary, is digested with alcohol and then filtered; the free acid is soluble, whilst the sulphates that may be present are insoluble in alcohol. The filtrate is neutralised with soda or potash, evaporated to dryness, and the residue dissolved in water acidulated with hydrochloric acid.

Tests.—A solution of barium chloride produces a precipitate of barium sulphate which is insoluble in hydrochloric acid. If some of the precipitate is mixed with an equal bulk of sodium carbonate and made into a paste with a few drops of water, and is then fused on charcoal with the aid of the blow-pipe, it is converted into a sulphide, and, when cold, may be submitted to the usual tests; a small fragment placed on a clean silver coin and moistened with water, produces a brown stain of silver sulphide. If a drop of a liquid which contains free sulphuric acid is allowed to fall on a piece of filter-paper and dried before the fire, the paper, where covered by the drop, becomes charred.

Although alcohol, by rejecting any combined sulphuric acid that may be present in the form of sulphates, prevents error as to the source of the sulphide eventually formed, it is open to the objection that a certain amount of the acid may enter into chemical combination with it, in which case the acid given up falls short of that which was originally dissolved.

When an *exact estimation* of the amount of free acid present in an organic mixture is required, advantage may be taken of the solubility of quinine sulphate in alcohol. Sufficient freshly precipitated quinine is added to the mixture so as to take up the whole of the acid; the liquid is then evaporated to a paste and extracted with alcohol, which dissolves the quinine sulphate, but not any other sulphates that may be present. The alcoholic solution is filtered and evaporated to dryness, the residue being taken up by hot water; when cold, the quinine is precipitated as hydrate by the addition of ammonia water. The solution of ammonium sulphate thus formed is acidulated with hydrochloric acid and raised to 100°; barium chloride is then added until the whole of the sulphuric acid is carried down as barium sulphate, the liquid being kept hot. The precipitate may be separated by filtration through a close filter (or if preferred by decantation), washed, and dried. Its weight multiplied by ·411 equals the amount of concentrated sulphuric acid present. Barium sulphate will pass through almost any filter paper when precipitated in the cold, but by boiling it becomes granular, and can then be kept back by a close-textured paper.

The presence of free sulphuric acid cannot always be demonstrated in the tissues of those who have succumbed to it. In the case of *Reg v. Berry* (Liverpool Assizes, 1887), the prisoner was convicted of having poisoned her daughter, a young child—as Harris[1] and other medical men strongly suspected—with sulphuric acid. The usual indications of corrosive action in the lips, mouth, and œsophagus were present, and the stomach and small intestines were inflamed, but not corroded. No trace of the acid was found in the body. Cases have occurred in which the presence of sulphuric acid was readily demonstrated in the early vomit which fell on the clothing or floor, but after the death of the victim none could be found in the body. In one case, within an hour or two after half an ounce of oil of vitriol was swallowed, the mucous fluid that welled up into the mouth would not redden litmus paper. This disappearance of free acid is due to the combinations which it forms with basic substances contained in the organism.

## NITRIC ACID

Nitric Acid [$HNO_3$], or aqua fortis, is a powerful corrosive which produces symptoms resembling those caused by sulphuric acid. The chief points of difference are due to the fumes which are given off by the concentrated acid, to the colour of the stains produced by it, to the absence of charring of the tissues, and consequently to diminished liability to perforation of the stomach.

The symptoms come on immediately after swallowing the concentrated acid. They comprise intense pain, gaseous eructations, retching, vomiting, and collapse. On account of the formation of a larger amount of gas, the abdomen is usually more distended, and, if possible, is more exquisitely tender than in sulphuric acid poisoning. The lips, tongue, and mucous membrane of the mouth are softened and swollen, and of a yellow hue, resulting from the formation of xanthoproteic acid. The teeth are sometimes attacked; the acid may dissolve the enamel and colour them yellow. The air-passages are more liable to be attacked than is the case with sulphuric acid, pneumonia being a very possible complication from inhalation of the fumes of the acid. The remaining symptoms do not materially differ from those met with in sulphuric acid poisoning.

[1] *Med. Chron.*, 1887.

**Fatal Dose.**—The smallest recorded fatal dose is two drachms. Recovery has taken place after half an ounce. Death has occurred in less than two hours, but this is unusual; from twelve to twenty-four hours or more is the average duration of life in fatal cases.

**Treatment.**—As in sulphuric acid poisoning.

**Post-mortem Appearances.**—In acute cases, allowing for the difference in colour of the parts acted on and a somewhat less intense corrosive action, the appearances resemble those produced by sulphuric acid. The mouth, teeth, and œsophagus present a tint varying from yellow to brown. The yellow stains due to nitric acid may be distinguished from those due to iodine by touching them with ammonia water; the colour remains or is deepened; in the case of iodine it disappears. The mucous membrane acted on is softened and easily detached; if the acid has reached the stomach its mucous coat is stained yellow in parts; there may also be patches of a blackish-brown, resulting from alteration of effused blood. The stomach may be perforated, but not so commonly as with sulphuric acid; if not perforated, the entire thickness of its wall may in parts be softened and friable. The duodenum may be affected in the same way, or both it and the stomach may be simply inflamed. When life has been prolonged for weeks or months, cicatrices and stricture may be present.

**Chemical Analysis.—Tests.**—When mixed with organic matter (after proving the presence of a free acid) simple qualitative analysis may be made by neutralising the mixture with potassium carbonate; filter paper dipped in the solution and dried forms touch-paper, which deflagrates on ignition. On evaporating a little of the solution to dryness and adding a few drops of strong sulphuric acid to the residue, and then stirring in a crystal of brucine, a bright-red colour is produced. This test is very delicate, the reaction being sufficiently distinctive as to yield decisive results notwithstanding the presence of a considerable amount of foreign colouring matter. If a crystal of ferrous sulphate is substituted for the brucine it becomes surrounded by a brownish ring; this test is valueless unless the solution to be tested is free from colour. If a fragment of gold leaf is boiled in a test-tube, with a little strong hydrochloric acid and a few drops of a solution containing nitric acid are added the gold leaf is partially or wholly dissolved. The solution of gold chloride thus obtained should be proved to be such by the addition of a little stannous chloride, which produces the colour known as the purple of Cassius. If to an aqueous solution of diphenylamine a few drops of a liquid containing nitric acid or a nitrate are added, and subsequently a little concentrated sulphuric acid is gently poured down the side of the inclined test-tube so as to form a layer at the bottom, a blue ring develops above it. Before using this test a control experiment should be made by adding sulphuric acid in the manner above described to the solution of diphenylamine, without any of the suspected fluid, as some specimens of sulphuric acid are contaminated with nitric acid and give the reaction alone. The test is so delicate that it reacts to a cubic centimetre of water which contains one drop of nitric acid in 100 cc.

For quantitative estimation when in organic admixture, the acid may be taken up by freshly precipitated quinine, the solution evaporated to a paste, and the paste extracted with alcohol. The alcoholic solution is then filtered and evaporated to dryness; the residue is dissolved in water and the quinine is precipitated with sodium hydrate. The solution of sodium nitrate thus obtained is evaporated to a syrup, and is treated in a close vessel for some time with powdered aluminium, or with nascent hydrogen evolved by a voltaic couple. It is then distilled into a receiver containing strong hydrochloric acid; excess of platinic chloride is added to the distillate, and the whole is evaporated to dryness. After being washed with small quantities of alcohol, and dried, the residue—ammonio-platinic chloride—is weighed: 100 parts equal 28·3 parts of nitric acid. This method is founded on the power possessed by nascent hydrogen of converting the nitrogen of nitric acid into ammonia which is estimated as the double chloride of ammonium and platinum.

Nitric Acid fumes have occasioned death in several instances. One of the masters and the janitor of the Edinburgh Institution were carrying a jar of nitric acid when it fell and broke, and, in endeavouring to save some of the spilt acid, they were exposed to the fumes. The master went home unconscious that anything was wrong with him; in an hour or two difficulty in breathing set in, and he died ten hours after the accident; the janitor died the following day.[1] Stickler[2] records an instance in which a bottle of nitric acid was broken in the hold of a vessel; several men went below to remedy the mischief, and felt no immediate trouble, but within a few hours they began to complain of illness and in a short time died. A similar accident happened to two firemen whilst helping to extinguish a fire in a chemical store; they inhaled the fumes of nitric acid, and died the same day.[3]

It is noteworthy that in cases of poisoning by the fumes of nitric acid the sufferer feels nothing wrong at the time; the dangerous symptoms begin, however, within two or three hours after, and, as a rule, death rapidly ensues. Death has resulted after symptoms resembling those of pneumonia, or of capillary bronchitis, and the air-passages have been found blocked by softened membrane and mucus tinged

[1] *The Lancet*, 1863.  [2] *New York Med. Rec.*, 1886.
[3] *Pharm. Journ.*, 1890-91.

with blood. In addition to the action of the acid vapour on the mucous lining of the bronchi and the air-vesicles, it appears that the pulmonary terminals of the vagi are rendered functionless, and the reflex of the respiratory centre is thus cut off; probably the pulmonary vaso-motor nerves from the sympathetic are also paralysed. The result is rapid excessive secretion of mucus into the bronchi and alveoli, with lessened capacity for its expulsion, and consequent speedy death from asphyxia. The formation of nitro-compounds with hæmoglobin has been assumed, but their existence is doubtful. Conversion of part of the hæmoglobin into methæmoglobin has also been postulated. Schmeiden[1] examined the blood in a case of fatal poisoning by nitrous fumes, both before and after death, without discovering any abnormality in the spectrum.

When a large quantity of nitric acid is accidentally spilt, chalk should be thrown on it, and ventilation promoted, the individuals concerned keeping to the windward, and, as far as possible, holding their breath when near the acid.

## HYDROCHLORIC ACID.

**Hydrochloric Acid** [HCl], or spirits of salt, is a corrosive of less activity than the two preceding acids, but on account of its volatility it is more apt to attack the air-passages than either of them. The symptoms resemble, but are not so severe as, those produced by sulphuric acid. On account of the comparatively feeble corrosive action of hydrochloric acid, stains are not caused by it falling on the skin; this forms a notable distinction from the other mineral acids.

**Fatal Dose.**—The smallest quantity that has proved fatal is one teaspoonful. In two instances, both young girls, this was sufficient to cause death, and in one[2] perforation of the stomach was produced. On the other hand, recovery has taken place after an ounce and a half of the commercial acid has been taken, calcined magnesia having been administered ten minutes after it was swallowed.[3] In another case, recovery took place after swallowing two ounces. Death has occurred in two hours, and has been delayed for several days; the usual period is from eighteen to thirty hours.

**Treatment.**—As for the other mineral acids.

**Post-mortem Appearances.**—The mucous surfaces acted on are usually of an ashy-grey colour, interspersed with erosions. The inner surface of the stomach may appear reddened from acute gastritis, or blackened at parts from extravasation of blood which has been acted on by the acid.

[1] *Centralb. f. die ges. Med.*, 1892.
[2] Von Beyerlein, *Friedreich's Blätter f. ger Med.*, 1880.
[3] Ross, *The Lancet*, 1886.

Perforation is exceptional, but, as shown by the case above-mentioned, may occur even with a minimum fatal dose. In other respects the post-mortem appearances resemble those seen in sulphuric acid poisoning, but they are less pronounced.

**Chemical Analysis.**—After ascertaining the presence of a free acid, as described when dealing with sulphuric acid, an organic admixture containing hydrochloric acid may be distilled, and the distillate tested qualitatively and quantitatively.

**Tests.**—When silver nitrate is added it produces a precipitate of silver chloride, which is insoluble in nitric acid, but is soluble in ammonia water. A fragment of gold leaf in boiling nitric acid is dissolved if a few drops of the solution containing hydrochloric acid are added. The amount of hydrochloric acid present may be estimated by precipitation, as silver chloride, which is dried, ignited, and weighed 100 parts equal 25.44 parts of hydrochloric acid. If preferred, the amount of acid present in the distillate may be estimated volumetrically.

## OXALIC ACID

Oxalic Acid [$H_2C_2O_4, 2H_2O$] in combination with soda, potash, and lime, occurs in many plants and vegetables, as sorrel, rhubarb, the common dock, and some lichens. The acid is used commercially in the manufacture of straw hats, for the cleansing of articles of brass, in dye- and print-works, and also for domestic cleansing purposes. It is soluble in about 10 parts of cold water, and in about 2½ parts of alcohol. It volatilises at a temperature of 150° without residue, and in this way may be distinguished from its combinations (excepting with ammonia), which leave residues. When heated with strong sulphuric acid, it is decomposed without blackening, into water, carbon dioxide and carbon monoxide. Oxalic acid crystallises in the form of slender prisms, and on this account has been mistaken for Epsom salts.

When swallowed in poisonous doses, oxalic acid produces local effects which resemble those produced by the mineral acids, but, unlike them, it exercises a special influence on the nervous system and upon the action of the heart.

**Symptoms.**—The symptoms vary not only with the amount of acid, but also with concentration of the solution in which it is taken. If half an ounce or more of the acid is dissolved in water so as to form a concentrated solution, the local effects resemble those produced by the mineral acids. Immediately, or soon after the solution is swallowed, pain is felt in the mouth and throat, which extends to the stomach and radiates over the abdomen; vomiting usually quickly follows and persists, the vomited matter chiefly consisting of altered blood. If the acid is swallowed in more dilute solution, the above-named symptoms are delayed and are less violent. General indications of collapse are manifest, the respiration is gasping, the pulse small and irregular, and the extremities, or even the entire surface, may be cyanosed. Clonic spasms are not unfrequent; they may alternate with tonic contractions of the muscles, especially of those of the lower jaw, producing trismus. Aphonia may occur, and may persist for some time during convalescence.

The effects produced by oxalic acid on the nervous system are exceedingly irregular, sometimes they constitute the chief symptom, and at others they do not exceed those which might be reasonably expected from the reflex of the parts with which the poison comes directly in contact. The nerve symptoms comprise paræsthesiæ and anæsthesia of the limbs or trunk, with aching and shooting pains in the loins, numbness of the tips of the fingers has been observed and tenderness of the muscles of the legs, convulsions are common, and sometimes resemble those due to strychnine. In other cases oxalic acid seems to act as a narcotic; I saw a case of this kind in which the sufferer lay unconscious, breathing stertorously, the surface being cold and clammy as in opium poisoning, without there being any vomiting or other signs of gastric irritation. When the nervous symptoms form the prominent feature of the case, the poison has often been taken well diluted, or the stomach has contained some amount of solid food, the indications of gastritis being slight or entirely absent; in these cases post-mortem signs of local irritation, although present, are not as well marked as is usual. Large crystals of calcium oxalate are frequently present in the urine.

**Fatal Dose.**—The smallest recorded fatal dose is 60 grains, which taken in the solid form caused the death of a boy aged sixteen. Recovery has occurred after an ounce and a quarter. Death has occurred in ten minutes; usually it takes place within two hours, but it may be delayed for several days—seven in one case, and twenty-one in another.

**Treatment.**—Chalk suspended in a small quantity of water or milk may be given, although the consequent liberation of carbonic acid is disadvantageous; saccharated solution of lime has been recommended by Husemann. Plaster chipped from the walls, or egg-shells, powdered, and suspended in a little water are good; calcined magnesia may be given. The alkalies or their carbonates should not be given, as the resulting compounds are both soluble and poisonous. All antidotes should be given in as little water as possible in order to limit diffusion of the poison, its action not being solely local. After the acid is

27

neutralised the bowels should be relieved by an enema or castor oil.

Post-mortem Appearances.—These vary in accordance with the amount of the poison and the concentration of the solution; if the poison is taken in concentrated solution, or in the solid form, the local effects will probably be well marked. There may be corrosion of the mucous membrane of the mouth, œsophagus, and stomach, or it may be white, softened and easily detached from its bed. The inner surface of the œsophagus may be longitudinally corrugated, displaying numerous small erosions. The degree of inflammation of both œsophagus and stomach varies from a slight redness to an almost gangrenous condition; the inflammation may reach the duodenum. In a specimen in the Museum of Owens College, the interior of the stomach is blackened, resembling the condition met with in poisoning by sulphuric acid. Perforation of the stomach is exceptional, although the walls are often considerably softened; the mucous membrane not unfrequently presents cloudy spots, which are due to deposition of calcium oxalate; they often occur near hæmorrhagic infarcts. The kidneys may show a whitish zone between the cortical and the medullary portions, due to the deposit of crystals of calcium oxalate chiefly in the convoluted, and to a lesser extent in the straight tubules; the glomeruli are free from deposit.[1] Examined microscopically the deposit is seen to consist of rhombic prisms, or of octahedral crystals.

Chemical Analysis—Tests.—Oxalic acid forms a precipitate of calcium-oxalate on the addition of a solution of calcium chloride or calcium sulphate. Calcium oxalate is insoluble in acetic acid, and is soluble in hydrochloric acid. Silver nitrate gives a white precipitate of silver oxalate, which is easily soluble in nitric acid, and also in ammonia. Lead acetate gives a white precipitate, which is soluble in nitric acid.

Organic admixtures may be evaporated down at a gentle heat and exhausted with hot alcohol, to which a little hydrochloric acid has been added; after filtration, the alcoholic solution is evaporated to dryness, and the residue dissolved in water.

Quantitative Estimation.—To a measured quantity of the aqueous solution calcium acetate is added in slight excess, and the deposit of calcium oxalate is separated, washed with acetic acid and then with water, and dried. By careful ignition at a moderate temperature the calcium oxalate is converted into carbonate: 100 parts equal 126 parts of crystallised oxalic acid.

Potassium Binoxalate [$KHC_2O_4 2H_2O$] or salt of sorrel, or, as it is also called, salts of lemon, is an acid salt soluble in 40 parts of cold and in 6 parts of boiling water. It is used in the household for

[1] Kobert and Küssner, Virchow's *Arch.*, Bd. 78.

removing iron stains from underclothing. It is nearly, if not equally, as poisonous as oxalic acid, like symptoms being produced. Half an ounce has proved fatal. The chemical tests are the same as for oxalic acid, from which it may be distinguished by its leaving a deposit of potassium carbonate when ignited on a slip of platinum foil.

## POTASSIUM

**Potassium Hydrate** [KOH] is met with as a poison in the impure condition in which it is used in the arts and manufactures. It has a strongly caustic action on the tissues, and on account of its affinity for water the effects produced by it tend to radiate to a considerable distance from the spot to which it is applied. It combines with fatty matters and decomposes the soft structures leaving a greasy mass which keeps soft and moist, the local damage thus differing from that produced by the mineral acids. In the form of a basic carbonate—as pearl ash—it acts much in the same way.

**Symptoms.**—When a strong solution of potash is swallowed an immediate burning sensation is experienced in the mouth and throat, which extends to the stomach, and radiates over the abdomen. Vomiting usually occurs, the vomited matter has a strong alkaline reaction, is slimy and may be coloured by blood which escapes from the inner surface of the stomach and œsophagus, shreds of mucous membrane are generally present in the vomit. Purging is not unfrequent. Collapse quickly occurs, the pulse is thin and feeble, and the surface is cold and clammy. The lips, tongue, and inside of the mouth are red and swollen. Convulsions may occur as in sulphuric acid poisoning. Stricture of the œsophagus is very liable to follow in cases in which the immediate symptoms are recovered from.

**Fatal Dose.**—The smallest recorded fatal dose is 10 grains, usually a much larger dose would be required, probably 3 or 4 drachms. Death has occurred within a few hours, more frequently it results after weeks or months from secondary symptoms.

**Treatment.**—Vegetable acids, as acetic (vinegar), or citric (lemon juice) in a dilute form, should be given, with olive oil, demulcents, and opium. The stomach tube must _not_ be used.

**Post-mortem Appearances.**—The lips and, possibly, the surrounding skin on the face may show traces of the caustic action of the poison. Within the mouth the mucous membrane will be softened and of a brown colour, in parts it will probably be detached. In recent cases the tongue will be swollen and inflamed, the mucous membrane of the pharynx and œsophagus presenting more or less the same appearance. The mucous coat of the stomach is inflamed and softened, the colour is not constant, sometimes it is bright red and at others dark it may be completely or merely superficially eroded in parts. If, as is frequently the case, the patient survives some weeks, stricture is usually found at the lower end of the œsophagus or at the pylorus

**Chemical Analysis.**—The organic substance containing potash may be evaporated to dryness and incinerated to burn off the organic matter. The residue is then dissolved in a small quantity of water, slightly acidulated with hydrochloric acid, and precipitated with platinic chloride, precipitation may be aided by the addition of alcohol. The precipitate is dried and then washed with alcohol in small quantities until it comes away colourless; and again dried and weighed 100 parts equal 19 272 parts of potash

**Tests.**—If there is much potash present in the original solution it may be directly precipitated as a double salt with platinic chloride. A saturated solution of tartaric acid also precipitates potash. Before the suspected substance is submitted to analysis, its alkaline reaction should be ascertained. The spectroscopic reaction of potash is too delicate to be of much use, it demonstrates the presence of the alkali in the tissues and in articles of food that may accidentally be present

## SODIUM.

**Sodium Hydrate** [$NaOH$] or caustic soda, is commonly met with as washing soda, which is a mixture of the hydrate and the basic carbonate

The symptoms, lethal dose, treatment, and post-mortem appearances are precisely the same as in poisoning with potash

**Chemical Analysis.**—For toxicological purposes there is no satisfactory chemical test for soda, it is best identified by exclusion. If there is a solid residuum after evaporation and incineration of the suspected substance, and both it and the original substance yield a marked alkaline reaction, and no precipitate is formed on the addition of platinic chloride to a concentrated solution of the incinerated product, the alkali which is proved to be present will be soda. Absence of the alkaline earths must be ascertained. The spectroscopic reaction of sodium is useless in toxicological investigations on account of the ubiquitous presence of its salts

## AMMONIA

**Ammonia Water** [$NH_4OH$], also known as spirits of hartshorn, consists of a solution of gaseous ammonia in water. When freshly prepared the gas is freely given off, and serious results have followed its inhalation when large bottles containing the solution have been broken. The gas attacks the structures of the larynx and the mucous lining of the lower air-passages, often producing alarming dyspnœa; it is to this characteristic that the special features of ammonia poisoning, as compared with the effects produced by the fixed alkalies, are due.

**Symptoms.**—Immediately after swallowing strong ammonia water a violent, burning sensation is experienced from the mouth down to the stomach, which is followed by vomiting; the ejected matter may contain blood. The epithelial layer of mucous membrane is at once stripped off and the mouth feels as though it was filled with "skins." Some of the vapour is sure to be drawn into the larynx, producing a sensation of suffocation, which is followed by a real difficulty of respiration from tumefaction of the glottis; the breathing is noisy and stridulous, and the greatest distress is manifested from fear of impending suffocation. The voice is at once rendered feeble and hoarse, or it may be entirely gone. The patient is continuously occupied in attempts to rid himself of the detached membrane and viscid mucus which accumulate in the mouth. He sits up in bed with an extremely anxious expression, pointing towards the throat and intimating an earnest desire for relief. He suffers from intense thirst, which his condition disables him from alleviating. The symptoms of collapse are present: small pulse, cold, clammy surface, sunken features, and usually great restlessness. If the case goes on to a fatal issue coma usually supervenes, the breathing becoming more and more difficult, partly from swelling of the mucous lining of the air-passages, and partly from excessive secretion of mucus. Even when the symptoms are at their worst and death appears imminent, recovery may take place so far as the immediate condition is concerned; the breathing improves, the patient becomes able to swallow and to dislodge the mucus, and in a comparatively short time is out of danger. In one case of this kind, which was under my care in the Salford Royal Hospital, the patient (a woman) who had swallowed more than an ounce of commercial ammonia water, became gradually more and more collapsed, dyspnœic, and cyanosed, until tracheotomy was contemplated. She recovered from the acute stage, but, later on, developed stricture of the œsophagus at its lower part. Pregnant women frequently abort in consequence of ammonia poisoning.

When recovery takes place from the acute stage, apepsia—from destruction of some of the gastric glands—and stricture of the œsophagus or of the pylorus are to be feared.

**Fatal Dose.**—This is difficult to estimate as the amount of gas present in a given quantity of the solution is subject to great variation. Two drachms have proved fatal, and recovery has taken place, as in the above-mentioned case, from more than an ounce. Death has taken place in a few minutes. The usual period for acute cases is twenty-four to forty-eight hours; when death is due to secondary effects, life may be prolonged for months.

Treatment is the same as in the case of the fixed alkalies, special attention being paid to the respiratory symptoms, such as placing the patient in a tent, the air of which is rendered moist with steam.

Post-mortem Appearances.—If death takes place in the **acute** stage the lips are swollen, the mucous membrane of the mouth is softened and more or less detached, a similar condition existing along the œsophagus and, possibly, in the stomach. Immediately after the poison is taken the mucous membrane presents a white appearance, but it quickly changes to an angry-looking red; the whole thickness or the epithelial layer only of the membrane may be detached. In severe cases the muscular coat of the œsophagus or of the stomach is also softened and completely disintegrated; actual perforation is of exceptional occurrence. The effects of the poison rarely pass beyond the stomach. The laryngeal mucous membrane is infiltrated and thickened; it has been observed to be eroded and, in some cases, to be covered with exudation, forming a kind of false membrane. The smaller bronchi have been found to contain tubular casts. The kidneys may be inflamed. The **chronic** cases show corresponding post-mortem indications to those met with under similar conditions in poisoning with the fixed alkalies.

Chemical Analysis.—Ammonia is recognised by its odour; it may be separated from organic admixture by distillation; if the solution containing the ammonia is not alkaline, it may be neutralised with calcined magnesia before distilling. The gas is received into water acidulated with hydrochloric acid, and the ammonia is afterwards precipitated with platinic chloride in excess, the precipitate being washed with alcohol to remove the excess, dried and weighed: 100 parts equal 15·68 parts of $NH_4OH$. The ammonia separated by distillation may be estimated volumetrically, if preferred. If decomposition of the tissues is in progress it is of little use to examine them for ammonia as a poison, since it is evolved from nitrogenous organic matter.

Tests.—Ammonia responds like potash to platinic chloride, and to tartaric acid; it gives a brown precipitate with Nessler's reagent, and white fumes in the presence of gaseous hydrochloric acid.

Ammonium Carbonate $[(NH_4)_2 CO_3]$ when swallowed in large doses produces symptoms and organic changes resembling those produced by uncombined ammonia.

# IRRITANTS.

## CHAPTER XXVII

### SALTS OF THE ALKALIES AND OF THE ALKALINE EARTHS

#### SALTS OF POTASSIUM

Potassium Nitrate [$KNO_3$], saltpetre, or sal prunella, when swallowed in doses of one ounce or more, produces violent pain in the stomach and abdomen, with vomiting and purging, the ejected matter sometimes containing blood. Collapse occurs and is evinced by cold surface bedewed with sweat, and small, rapid, irregular pulse, which may subsequently become slow. Occasionally laboured respiration, unconsciousness and convulsions, pains in the loins, cramps in the calves of the legs, muscular twitchings, paræsthesiæ, paralysis of the limbs and aphonia have been observed. Death is usually preceded by coma, it may take place suddenly from heart paralysis. Gastric derangement may persist for a considerable time after the acute symptoms have subsided.

Fatal Dose.—The smallest recorded fatal dose is two drachms, which caused the death of a man aged forty. Recovery has taken place after one ounce. Death has occurred in from five to sixty hours.

Treatment.—Empty and wash out the stomach, give ice and opium to allay the sickness and pain, and alcohol if necessary. Mustard may be applied over the region of the stomach. Warmth and the recumbent posture are to be maintained.

Chemical Analysis.—If fluid, the suspected substance is filtered; if pultaceous, it is extracted with water and then filtered. The filtrate is evaporated to a small volume and the salt allowed to crystallise out. The crystals are tested for nitric acid and for potash.

Potassium Chlorate [$KClO_3$] possesses peculiar toxic properties. When taken in large doses, the red blood corpuscles are broken up by it, and the hæmoglobin is converted into methæmoglobin. The mode in which the effects are produced is still *sub judice* some observers hold that the salt is not decomposed within the organism, and therefore that the toxic effects are due to its specific action; others have demonstrated by experiments that when mixed with certain organic substances, such as pus and fibrin, the salt gives off oxygen. Binz[1] states that after prolonged action of these substances on potassium chlorate, the presence of chloric acid cannot be demonstrated. If blood is mixed with potassium or sodium chlorate to the amount of four per cent., it becomes syrupy, and on spectroscopic examination shows the bands of methæmoglobin, either alone or in combination with those of oxyhæmoglobin. The stroma of the red corpuscles parts with the hæmoglobin, which is subsequently changed into methæmoglobin, and the debris of the corpuscles produces certain pathological conditions, which will be described among the post-mortem appearances.

Symptoms.—When large doses are taken the first symptoms are those of gastro-intestinal irritation: vomiting, pain in the stomach and bowels, with more or less collapse. Shortly after, pain is felt in the lumbar region, the urine, which may contain albumen, is diminished, or suppressed; hæmoglobin and hæmatin have been found in it, but not methæmoglobin. The skin becomes cyanosed, and subsequently it is frequently jaundiced. Landerer[2] considers the jaundice to be partly polycholic and partly hæmotogenous. The patient is delirious, or apathetic and somnolent. At this stage the blood is brownish in colour and somewhat viscid; examined microscopically, colourless erythrocytes (the stroma of the red corpuscles) are seen along with normal corpuscles, interspersed with granular particles of free hæmoglobin, or of methæmoglobin. The white corpuscles are increased in number. The combined spectra of hæmoglobin and methæmoglobin will be present. Recovery may take place even when the symptoms have arrived at a very critical stage; when death occurs, an interval of several days usually elapses after the reception of the poison.

Fatal Dose is uncertain; one ounce and a half has caused death. The fatal period ranges from six hours to as many days.

Treatment.—The stomach should be emptied and washed out. The after treatment will be symptomatic. Diuretics and vapour baths, with fomentations or dry-cupping of the lumbar region may be indicated.

Post-mortem Appearances.—The mucous membrane of the stomach has been found swollen, softened, and easily separated from its bed; it may exhibit small ecchymoses. The mucous membrane of the duodenum may present a similar swollen and softened appearance. The blood is chocolate-coloured. The kidneys are also chocolate-coloured, and on section show the most intense colour in the medullary

[1] Arch. f. exp. Pathol., 1879.   [2] Deut. Arch. f. klin. Med., 1891.

portion, the glomeruli are visible as points to the unaided eye. Examined microscopically, the straight and convoluted tubules are filled with reddish-brown deposit formed of the debris of the red blood corpuscles, the epithelium is swollen and cloudy. The spleen has been found enlarged and of a peculiar reddish-brown colour, besides normal red corpuscles the pulp may contain colourless erythrocytes.

**Chemical Analysis—Tests.**—The presence of potassium chlorate may be ascertained by adding a few drops of sulphuric acid to a solution containing the salt, and sufficient indigo sulphate as to produce a moderately deep blue colour, two or three drops of sulphurous acid added to the mixture cause the colour to disappear. If in organic admixture, some of the potassium chlorate may be separated by dialysis and examined as above.

Several other salts of potassium and sodium—as the chlorides, sulphates, and carbonates—act as irritants when swallowed in large doses.

## BARIUM

**Barium Chloride** [$BaCl_2, 2H_2O$] has been taken in mistake for Epsom salts and other saline purgatives. It has been taken for suicidal purposes in the form of rat poison, into the composition of some varieties of which it enters.

**Symptoms.**—In poisonous doses it acts locally as an irritant, and centrally as a nerve poison. In from a few minutes up to an hour or more after the poison is swallowed, violent pain is felt in the stomach and abdomen, accompanied by extreme nausea, which is followed by severe vomiting and purging. The action of the heart is depressed, and pain may be experienced in the cardiac region. The implication of the nervous system is shown by ringing in the ears and diplopia; pains in the limbs, convulsions, and, in some instances, paralysis.

Barium is eliminated by the kidneys and bowels, some of the amount taken is deposited in the bones.

**Fatal Dose.**—One teaspoonful of the powder has caused death. The fatal period has been as short as one hour, and has extended to seven days.

**Treatment.**—The stomach-pump should be used, or an emetic given, unless vomiting has spontaneously occurred. Sodium sulphate, or magnesium sulphate, should be given in large doses—half an ounce to an ounce or more. Hypodermic injections of morphine and external warmth are useful.

**Post-mortem Appearances.**—The mucous membrane of the stomach and of the duodenum may be swollen and diffusely injected, or spotted with ecchymoses, in one instance the stomach was perforated. Particles of the poison have been found in the stomach in a case in which it was taken in the form of barium carbonate.

Chemical Analysis—Tests.—The presence of a salt of barium in organic admixture can be readily ascertained by rolling up the end of a piece of thin platinum wire into a small ball, dipping it into the mixture, and transferring it to a Bunsen flame; a minute quantity of barium reveals itself by colouring the flame green; the experiment is best conducted in a darkened room. If the green flame is examined with the spectroscope, the flame-spectrum of barium will be seen. After taking up and drying some of the suspected fluid on the ball, the reaction will be rendered more distinct by dipping the wire in strong HCl.

A solution of barium in organic admixture may be evaporated to dryness and incinerated; the product is drenched with $HNO_3$, and the excess of acid volatilised. The nitrate, dissolved in water, may then be tested by adding dilute $H_2SO_4$, or an alkaline sulphate, either of which produces a white precipitate insoluble in $HNO_3$; it is also precipitated by a solution of KOH. If the barium is present as phosphate, or sulphate, it must be boiled with a concentrated solution of potassium carbonate for some time, and filtered; the filtrate is precipitated with dilute $H_2SO_4$, and the insoluble substance on the filter is dissolved in HCl, diluted with water, and also precipitated with $H_2SO_4$. The combined precipitates, after washing and ignition, are weighed; this gives the amount of barium present as sulphate. The absence of strontium and calcium should be ascertained by means of the spectroscope.

Other salts of barium—the carbonate, nitrate, and acetate—have acted as poisons.

Strontium salts cannot be regarded as poisonous; the bromide, lactate, and nitrate have recently been administered medicinally in large doses, as much as 200 grains of the nitrate have been given in one day.

## MAGNESIUM

Magnesium Sulphate [$MgSO_4 7H_2O$], or Epsom salts, is usually regarded as a harmless purgative, but in large doses it has caused death. In experiments on animals it has been found to paralyse the respiratory movements, and also those of the heart. The former of these effects is well illustrated by the following case reported by Sang[1]:—A woman, aged thirty-five, dissolved four ounces of Epsom salts in some warm water and drank the solution. When seen shortly after she complained of a burning pain in the stomach and bowels, and a choking feeling, with

[1] *The Lancet*, 1891.

a sensation as though she was losing power of her legs and arms there was neither vomiting nor purging, the pulse was 96 per minute. An emetic of zinc sulphate was administered, but did not act, and before the stomach-pump could be obtained profound collapse occurred. The pupils were dilated, the muscles of the face twitched, and there was complete paralysis, she then became comatose, and died in one hour and twenty minutes after swallowing the salts. The radial pulse was felt two or three minutes after the respirations had ceased.

Christison relates the case of a boy, aged ten, who after swallowing two ounces of Epsom salts was observed to stagger and appear very ill. Half an hour after, the pulse was scarcely perceptible, and the respirations were slow and laboured, in ten minutes more he died without vomiting having taken place.

## METALS.

### ARSENIC

**Metallic Arsenic** is probably not poisonous, but, as it easily undergoes oxidation in the digestive tract, it may produce the usual symptoms of arsenical poisoning. A preparation known as fly-powder, which consists chiefly of finely-divided metallic arsenic, probably along with some arsenious acid, is strongly poisonous.

**Arsenious Acid** [$As_2O_3$], or white arsenic, is the form in which arsenic is chiefly used as a poison. When fresh, it is a glassy-looking substance, with smooth vitreous fracture, after being kept some time it becomes white and opaque, resembling porcelain. In the form of powder it looks like flour, for which on several occasions it has been mistaken with fatal results. It has little taste, and having no colour, is easily administered for homicidal purposes, it has one compensating property—that of slight solubility in water. The solubility of arsenious acid varies according to its molecular state which is not constant, its density slightly diminishing with age, consequently, not only do the transparent and opaque varieties vary in respective solubility, but each individual specimen tends to differ from the rest. When the opaque variety is boiled with water for some time, 11.5 parts are dissolved per 100 parts of water, on cooling, from 2.5 to 3 parts of arsenious acid per 100 of water are retained in solution, crystalline arsenious acid is slightly less soluble. Cold water dissolves about ⅓ grain to 1 grain of arsenious acid per ounce. The solution slightly reddens litmus paper. In acids and in alkaline solutions arsenic is much more soluble. The law requires that when arsenic is sold in quantities of less than 10 lbs., it shall be mixed either with soot or with indigo, at the rate of 1½ ounces respectively to the pound of arsenic

When powdered arsenious acid is added to water, or to liquid food, some of the finer particles float on the surface, forming a kind of white scum which cannot be got rid of by stirring, the appearance produced is very significant, and should be remembered when examining fluids which are suspected to have had arsenic added to them

When combined with potash or soda, arsenious acid is relatively much more soluble, and in this form it is used for domestic and other purposes, as well as in medicine. Some kinds of "fly-papers" are saturated with sodium or potassium arsenite, and much stronger solutions of arsenic can be obtained by soaking such papers in small quantities of water than by dissolving arsenious acid itself; this fact has been utilised for criminal purposes

**Arsenic Acid** [$As_2O_5$] is used in the manufacture of aniline colours, and, in combination with sodium, as a fly poison. It is slightly less poisonous than arsenious acid.

**Arsenious Sulphide** [$As_2S_3$], or orpiment, is almost insoluble in water, and when pure is said not to be poisonous, the commercial variety usually contains uncombined arsenious acid

**Copper Arsenite** [$CuAsO_3$], or Scheele's green, and a mixture of copper arsenite and copper acetate, known as Schweinfurt green, though insoluble in water, are partially dissolved by the gastric juice. These pigments have produced toxic effects by their presence in the atmosphere in a state of minute division, the particles being derived from wall-paper or fabrics coloured with them

**Arsenetted Hydrogen** [$AsH_3$] is extremely toxic, it has produced poisonous effects in workmen who have been subjected to its influence when using hydrochloric acid contaminated with arsenic, to prepare iron for "galvanising," and also in the separation of silver from zinc. Serious results have followed its accidental inhalation in the laboratory.

Eczematous eruptions on the legs have been caused by wearing stockings coloured with aniline dyes prepared with arsenic

## Acute Arsenical Poisoning.

**Symptoms.**—The interval between the reception of the poison and the first appearance of the symptoms is determined by several conditions. In a state of solution the same dose acts more quickly than when administered in the solid form, the presence of food in the stomach tends to retard, and the absence of it to accelerate, the onset of the symptoms. The interval ranges from ten minutes, or even less, when a strong solution is swallowed on an empty stomach, to twelve or eighteen hours under converse conditions. If a poisonous dose of undissolved arsenious acid is taken into a full stomach, and the recipient immediately after retires to bed and sleeps, an unusually long period of quiescence may follow. The usual period is from half an hour to an hour. In a typical case a sensation of heat, rapidly developing into a violent burning pain, is felt in the throat and stomach; then follows nausea, with uncontrollable vomiting and sensation of constriction in the gullet. The vomited matters at first consist of food that may be present in the stomach; and, if the poison has been administered as powdered arsenious acid only partially dissolved, opaque white masses of mucus may be mixed with it. After the contents of the stomach have been ejected, the vomit may consist of slimy mucus, or of fluid resembling rice water, which may contain blood, or it may be bile-stained. If commercial arsenic mixed with soot or indigo-blue has been taken, the early vomit will probably be tinged accordingly. Soon after the commencement of the vomiting, purging sets in, accompanied by distressing tenesmus, and, frequently, by a burning sensation in the rectum; after the evacuation of any fæces contained by the bowels, the dejections tend to take on the rice-water appearance, and they may contain blood. The pain in the stomach is usually, but not always, increased on pressure. The patient suffers from intense thirst, attempts to relieve it being immediately followed by rejection of the swallowed fluid.

The feeling of sinking, or depression, which precedes the primary vomiting develops into one of extreme prostration and collapse. The face presents an appearance of great anxiety, the features are sunken, the surface is cold, moist, and cyanosed—especially the limbs—the pulse is small and thready, respiration is laboured, and the voice is hoarse. As a rule, the tongue is at first thickly coated with a white fur; subsequently it often becomes red at the tip and round the edges; sometimes it is unnaturally red over its entire surface. Owing to the profuse vomiting and purging the urine is scanty, and it may contain albumen or blood; attempts to urinate are painful. Cramps, especially in the calves, torment the sufferer, who tosses about to obtain relief. Death may be preceded by coma which is not unfrequently accompanied by clonic or tonic spasms, or consciousness may be maintained to the end.

It will be observed that in many respects the symptoms strongly resemble those of cholera; when that disease is epidemic, errors in diagnosis may easily be made. If doubts arise in the medical attendant's mind, he should examine the excretions for arsenic.

The above description of the symptoms of acute arsenical poisoning embraces the principal features of a typical case; it is not to be inferred, however, that all these symptoms invariably occur in every case, nor that their progress is precisely the same

In exceptional instances the poison seems to spend its force on the nerve centres, the gastro-enteric symptoms being less pronounced, or they may be entirely absent In such cases from the very first extreme collapse occurs with superficial and deep anæsthesia of the limbs, faintness, extremely small, feeble pulse, and coma, which quickly comes on, and terminates in death within six or eight up to twenty-four hours Complete general paralysis may be present some hours before death

It is not unusual in cases of criminal poisoning for **repeated doses** of the poison to be given With arsenic, as with other poisons, such a mode of administration considerably modifies the course of the symptoms The early doses produce gastro-enteric disturbance shown by vomiting, purging, pain in the stomach, foul tongue, loss of appetite, and a feeling of depression and languor, as the symptoms are passing off, but probably before they have quite subsided, another dose of the poison is given and the acute symptoms are renewed In these cases, some of the symptoms of chronic arsenical poisoning are also present, there may be itching and smarting of the eyeballs and the margins of the lids, the conjunctivæ being reddened and granular, a similar hyperæmic condition of the mucous membrane of the fauces and throat causes constant hawking apart from actual vomiting, the patient having a sensation as though a hair was in his throat The tongue and mouth are dry, the former being either thickly coated or red and irritable-looking The skin has an unhealthy, half jaundiced hue, and may display erythematous or eczematous eruptions. More pronounced symptoms of **neuritis** than occur in the acute form of poisoning are present —creeping and tingling, especially in the fingers, numbness of the hands and feet, severe cramps, not limited to the calves, dropping of the ankles when the patient is lying on his back in bed, and extreme tenderness of the muscles on pressure The patient is very restless, and cannot sleep. The temperature at first will probably be slightly elevated

The acute and chronic symptoms may be combined in variable proportion not necessarily corresponding to the length of time the patient has been under the influence of the poison. In some cases in which life has been prolonged for several days after the first inception of the poison, there may be almost entire absence of the chronic features, while in others several may appear within the first twelve hours Diarrhœa, instead of coming on at once, may be delayed for one or more days, the abdomen being either tender or free from tenderness in the interval In the case of *Reg. v Maybrick* (Liverpool Ass., 1889), in which the accused was found guilty of having caused the death of her husband by the administration of arsenic, purging did not occur until the third or fourth day, the abdominal pain being less violent than is usually the case; there was also absence of cramps in the calves, which, however, is a less constant symptom than diarrhœa. In the case of the Duc de Praslin,[1] the abdomen was painful and distended during the first four days after taking a fatal dose of arsenic, but there was only one evacuation of the bowels.

The combinations of arsenic with copper produce the usual symptoms of arsenical poisoning. In one case related by Seidel,[2] a girl aged 19 swallowed a tablespoonful of mixed paint, the basis of which was Schweinfurt green; she died in sixteen hours. Indications of the presence of the pigment were visible in various parts of the digestive tract. Huber[3] relates the case of a man who took about 4 grammes of Schweinfurt green; he recovered from the immediate effects, but suffered severely from arsenical paralysis.

Death has resulted from the application of arsenical paste to destroy morbid growths, and in infants from the use of nursery-powder adulterated with powdered arsenious acid. Arsenic has been used as a cosmetic; in the case of female poisoners with arsenic, any of the substance traced to their possession is generally accounted for on this ground. Applied as a solution for a limited time to the unbroken skin of an adult, it would not be absorbed to any dangerous extent, if at all. Very exceptionally arsenic has been surreptitiously introduced into the vagina and has caused death; this mode of administration is of ancient origin. A tract printed in 1598 gives an account of the trial and condemnation of one Henry Robson, a fisherman of Rye, for thus poisoning his wife, who died five days afterwards. Chabanat[4] records a case of fatal poisoning by arsenic from the application to the breast of an ointment composed of arsenious sulphide and butter; arsenic was found in the internal organs. If the orpiment was pure, the case proves that, although insoluble, it is not so inactive as is generally supposed.

**Fatal Dose.**—Two grains of arsenious acid have proved fatal. Recovery has taken place after much larger doses. When a fatal dose is taken the symptoms usually persist continuously until death takes place, which occurs in from twelve to forty-eight hours. Life is not unfrequently prolonged beyond the limit here stated; in such cases there are usually remissions in the course of the symptoms. The Duc de Praslin lived until the sixth day, Maybrick lived until the eighth day, and in exceptional cases death has not occurred until the fourteenth or even

[1] Annales d'Hygiène, 1847.
[2] Maschka's Handbuch, Bd. 2.
[3] Zeitsch. f. klin. Med., 1888.
[4] Annales d'Hygiène, 1890.

the sixteenth day  In one case, after a large dose, death took place in twenty minutes; it has not unfrequently occurred in two and three hours

**Treatment**—Evacuate the stomach with tube, or emetic, and then give freshly-precipitated ferric oxide  This can be prepared by adding ammonia water, or a solution of potassium carbonate, to the tincture of iron perchloride; the precipitate is strained off and administered suspended in water  Calcined magnesia may be substituted if ferric oxide cannot be obtained  Demulcents and subsequently morphine should be given  External warmth will be required

**Post-mortem Appearances**—Externally the body may present a somewhat shrunken appearance, the eyeballs being sunk, and the surface may be slightly cyanosed; these appearances are by no means invariable  Rigor-mortis sometimes lasts unusually long  The important internal signs are afforded by the stomach and intestines. On opening the stomach indications of intense inflammation present themselves, the whole of the mucous membrane may have a reddened velvety look, or the appearance may be limited to the greater curvature and the posterior part, or it may exist in two or more separate spots, the colour may be dark red or bright vermilion  Usually small dots or streaks of a darker colour are more or less numerously distributed over the inner surface of the stomach, which is frequently corrugated; this appearance is not invariable, it has been found absent in cases in which arsenic in a soluble form was administered  In some parts larger-sized submucous hæmorrhages may be seen  The surface of the mucous membrane is occasionally eroded, and particles of undissolved arsenious acid are not unfrequently found embedded at or near the spots so attacked  Very rarely, the inflammatory condition has gone on to gangrene, or to perforation; softening of the mucous membrane, so that it can be easily separated from its bed, is less rare  The wall of the stomach is sometimes thinned  The more profound lesions of the stomach wall are caused by the local action of the poison present in the solid form, in addition to the changes which are due to absorption  When a fatal dose of arsenic has entered the system by some other channel than the mouth, the post-mortem evidence of gastritis is nevertheless present; like some other poisons arsenic is partially eliminated through the stomach, irrespective of the mode of its administration  The **duodenum** generally participates in the appearance presented by the stomach, the signs of inflammation may be limited to a few inches below the pylorus, or they may extend the whole length of the duodenum  The **jejunum** has also been found inflamed, and the rectum frequently so  Along with signs of diffuse inflammation in the intestines, small submucous hæmorrhages may sometimes be seen, the solitary glands and Peyer's patches are often swollen. The œsophagus, as a rule, is not inflamed. The liver and kidneys may yield microscopic evidence of granular or fatty degeneration, but such a condition is not usually distinguishable in rapidly fatal cases. None of the other organs show any characteristic changes.

In those exceptional cases in which paralysis of the nerve centres is substituted for the usual gastro-enteritis, the appearance presented by the stomach may be relatively trivial. Milford[1] describes the post-mortem appearance of the stomach in a case of this kind in which no vomiting had occurred, although after death the stomach contained not less than 200 grains of arsenic. Only about a quarter of the surface of the mucous membrane near the pylorus presented a bright scarlet colour, the remainder was normal; the duodenum presented a similar, but less marked discoloration; the rest of the digestive tract was unchanged.

## Chronic Arsenical Poisoning

Arsenic may be received into the system in small quantities for a prolonged period, and thus produce symptoms differing from the acute form of poisoning. The sources from which the poison is derived comprise wall-papers, fabrics, artificial flowers, toys, and fancy papers which have been used to envelope confectionery. Trade risks constitute another source. Copper arsenite, either alone or in admixture with copper acetate, is the usual form in which the poison is used for colouring purposes. In the case of wall-papers and fabrics the pigment is usually so loosely attached that particles are freely given off, and, floating in the atmosphere, are inhaled and swallowed. Some years ago many cases of arsenical poisoning were thus caused, and public attention being drawn to the subject, manufacturers ceased to employ the dangerous pigment. The evil, however, is not altogether a thing of the past. Harding[2] records an example which occurred quite recently in an asylum. A number of cases of chronic arsenical poisoning took place one after the other among the nurses; the symptoms were eventually traced to the use of some green baize curtains, which were found to contain a large amount of arsenic.

**Symptoms.**—The early indications consist of gastric disorders, loss of appetite, headache, general feeling of malaise, and constipation or diarrhœa, then follow colicky pains, irritation of the eyelids, cachectic hue of the skin, and eczematous eruptions, especially in the folds of the axilla, or between the scrotum and thighs. Sooner or later pronounced indications of peripheral neuritis develop, the characteristic

[1] *Australasian Med Gaz.*, 1890   [2] *The Lancet*, 1892.

features of which are sensory disturbances, motor paralysis, and ataxia, the effects of arsenic on the nerves resemble those of alcohol, and differ from those produced by lead, in the prominence of the sensory disorders. The symptoms come on at variable intervals, from a week to three or four weeks, after the initial effects of the poison have manifested themselves; the affected muscles rapidly atrophy, the knee-jerk is usually lost, and the reactions of degeneration are present, in the arms the paralysis has the same distribution as in lead paralysis. The sensory disturbances usually commence with tingling, numbness, formication, and, in some cases, cutaneous anæsthesia. After death Erlicki and Rybalkin[1] found pigmentary changes in the ganglion cells of the anterior cornua in the cervical and lumbar enlargements, as well as degeneration in the peripheral nerves.

When the action of the poison is continued the cachexia becomes more pronounced: anæmia, falling off of the hair, defective nutrition of the finger nails causing their detachment, pigmentation (bronzing) of the skin, and other trophic disturbances develop.

In relation to the chronic ingestion of arsenic, mention must be made of the tolerance to the poison that may be acquired by its habitual use. The peasants in Styria, by progressively augmenting the dose, acquire the capacity of swallowing with impunity four or five grains of arsenious acid at a time. The object is to enable the "arsenic-eater" to endure greater fatigue in mountain-climbing than he otherwise could do. It is said that arsenic is sometimes given to horses in order to improve their coats and general appearance.

The elimination of arsenic takes place by the kidneys, the bowels, and, to some extent, by the skin. It commences very rapidly after ingestion; the poison can readily be detected in the urine half an hour after a single dose of five drops of liquor arsenicalis—equal to about $\frac{1}{7}$ grain of arsenious acid—has been taken. After a like dose it may be detected in the fæces. Arsenic is not accumulative, although a certain amount may remain in the organism for some time; it has been detected in the urine forty days after its administration ceased. That which has been absorbed is found after death in largest amount in the liver, as much as one to two grains may be present; the kidneys and the other soft organs contain lesser amounts. Arsenic has been found in the bones and in the hair. In prolonged poisoning the spongy bones, as the cranium and bodies of the vertebræ, and in rapid poisoning the compact bones, as the femur, are the most likely to contain it. Arsenic is not a physiological component of the body, therefore, if detected, its presence has to be accounted for. When arsenic is found in disinterred bodies

[1] *Neurologisches Centralbl.*, 1892.

it has been suggested that its presence may be due to transudation of the poison from the soil which surrounded the coffin. Arsenic has been found in the soil of certain graveyards, usually, however, in combination with iron and in an insoluble form. It is therefore in the highest degree improbable that a body free from arsenic when buried, should become contaminated from the soil of a cemetery or churchyard; but to avoid possibility of error in this respect, a sample of the soil which surrounds the coffin should be collected and examined.

The body of a person who has died from arsenical poisoning is accredited with the power of resisting putrefaction. If at the time of death the tissues contain much arsenic, it will exercise a preservative influence, but it is not to be assumed that decomposition is retarded in every case of arsenical poisoning. Much of the poison would not be present in the body after a minimum lethal dose, and in such a case putrefaction would follow the ordinary course. Instances of delayed putrefaction in the bodies of those who have died from arsenic have frequently been observed. In the case of *Reg.* v. *Cross* (Munster, Ass. 1887), for the murder of his wife by poisoning her with arsenic, Pearson[1] states that when the body was exhumed, seven weeks after death, all the organs were in an excellent state of preservation, the stomach and the intestines appearing as fresh as though the deceased had died but twenty-four hours previously. In this case the fatal illness lasted about three weeks, during which time repeated doses of arsenic had probably been given; chemical analysis showed that the body contained a large amount. Brouardel and Pouchet[2] examined the body of a woman who died from arsenical poisoning in May. The body was exhumed on the thirtieth of October following, and was found to be in a remarkable state of preservation, not a trace of the gases of putrefaction being present. The woman suffered from the effects of arsenic for six weeks before her death, and a considerable amount of the poison was found in the body.

**Chemical Analysis.**—If arsenious acid has been administered in the solid form, it is probable that undissolved particles may be found lying on, or embedded in, the mucous membrane of the stomach. If any such particles are found, they should be picked out or scraped off, dried, and tested. Attention should be paid to the presence of any particles of colouring matter—as soot or indigo—with which the arsenic may have been mixed. If the body has been interred, it is possible that the particles of arsenic may be changed into the sulphide.

**Tests.**—In the first instance Reinsch's method of testing for arsenic may be adopted. Urine should be evaporated down to one-fourth or one-sixth its volume before being tested. Solid sub-

[1] *Dublin Journ. Med. Science*, 1888.   [2] *Annales d'Hygiène*, 1889.

stances should be pulpified and mixed with sufficient water as to render them fluid. Previous to testing the suspected substance, the reagents themselves should invariably be tested for arsenic; pure copper is easily obtained, but hydrochloric acid absolutely free from arsenic is the exception. To some water in a flask, one-sixth its volume of strong hydrochloric acid is added, together with two or three small pieces of copper foil; the flask is placed on a support covered with wire gauze over a Bunsen flame, and the acidulated water is allowed to boil gently for a quarter of an hour. The copper is then examined: if it retains its primitive brightness and colour, absence of arsenic in the reagents may be assumed. The acidulated water is now replaced by some of the suspected substance, to which one-sixth its volume of strong hydrochloric acid is added from the same bottle as that from which the previous supply was taken, one or more of the same pieces of copper being dropped into the flask. After gently boiling for four or five minutes, the foil is again examined: if the amount of arsenic in the fluid was very small, the foil will only exhibit a purple tint; if a little more arsenic was present, the foil will present a steel-grey appearance; if a large amount was present, it may be covered with a black amorphous coat which is easily detached. The presence of sulphur-yielding bodies in organic mixtures may cause the copper to be stained. The foil is washed in distilled water, carefully dried on filter paper, and then introduced into a small dry reduction-tube; the form shown in the illustration is convenient for subsequent microscopical examination, the flattened walls producing less distortion than those of a cylindrical tube.

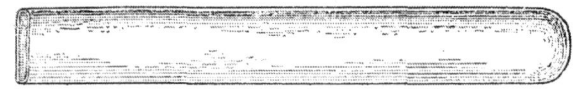

Fig. 22.—Reduction tube.

The closed end of the tube, on which the foil rests, is brought into the margin of a Bunsen flame and there retained until the film of arsenic is volatilised. When the arsenic leaves the copper, it combines with some of the oxygen of the air, and is deposited, as a ring—a centimetre or more up the tube, in accordance with the heat brought to bear—of octahedral or tetrahedral crystals of arsenious acid. On microscopical examination the largest crystals will be found nearest the foil, where (unless the amount of arsenic is very small) the ring is sharply defined; the crystals, unlike those deposited from aqueous solutions, are always separate and distinct. A crystalline deposit, obtained as described, is very characteristic of arsenic. Having shaken the pieces of copper out of the tube, a couple of drops of water are introduced and, with the aid of heat, the crystals are dissolved; this takes a few minutes to accomplish on account of the feeble solubility of arsenic, especially when in the crystalline form. When all the deposit is dissolved, the solution is shaken out on to a colour-slab, so as to form two separate drops; to one a drop of a solution of silver nitrate is added, and to the other a drop of a not too strong solution of copper sulphate. A glass rod that has been dipped in ammonia water is then held horizontally over the drops, close to (so as to allow the gaseous ammonia to act upon them), but without touching them. The one to which silver nitrate was added turns yellow, and the other becomes first blue and subsequently green; the salts formed are respectively silver arsenite and copper arsenite or Scheele's green. Reinsch's test is inapplicable in the presence of chlorates and nitrates.

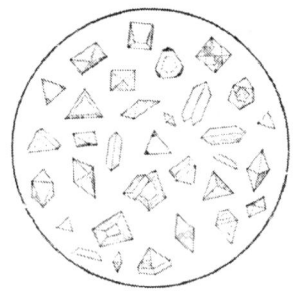

Fig. 23.—Crystals $As_2O_3$.

In addition to arsenic—antimony, mercury, silver, bismuth, platinum, palladium, tin, and gold are deposited on copper when boiled with it in acid solution; of these only three—arsenic, antimony, and mercury—yield sublimates in the reduction tube.

Marsh's test is founded on the power possessed by nascent hydrogen of reducing arsenious and arsenic acids, and of combining with the metallic arsenic they set free, forming arsenetted hydrogen, from which the arsenic can afterwards be disassociated by heat, and by chemical reagents. The necessary apparatus consists of a bottle or flask, through the stopper of which a long thistle-funnel and an exit-tube pass; between the flask and the free end of the exit-tube a chloride of calcium tube is interposed to dry the gas as it escapes. The accompanying figure is taken from a convenient model which I had constructed entirely of glass, in order to avoid the possibility of contamination from the accidental introduction of arsenic by the use of rubber stoppers [1].

Metallic zinc free from arsenic is placed in the flask, and some dilute sulphuric acid, also free from arsenic, is added. The purer the zinc, the less freely is it attacked by the acid; with some specimens it is necessary to promote action by the addition of a single drop of a solution of platinic chloride to the contents of the flask; rapid evolution of hydrogen, however, is disadvantageous; it is therefore best to allow the acid to act unaided if it will do so. When sufficient hydrogen has been evolved as to render it probable that all the air is expelled from the flask, a sample of the gas should be taken in an inverted test-tube

[1] May be obtained from Messrs. Jackson & Co., Half Moon St., Manchester.

and tested by applying a light to the open end. A sharp shrill report reveals the presence of an explosive mixture of gases; a slight pop indicates that the hydrogen is sufficiently pure to allow of ignition without danger of explosion. As soon as this is the case a lighted Bunsen burner is placed under the exit-tube and allowed to remain; the tube being supported on both sides of, and near to, the flame.

The flame is allowed to play on the tube for thirty minutes before any of the suspected substance is introduced into the flask; this is necessary in order to prove the absence of arsenic in the acid and the zinc. If the tube remains free from deposit, the purity of the reagents is established. The gas which escapes from the exit-tube may be ignited and allowed to play on a surface of cold porcelain, such as a

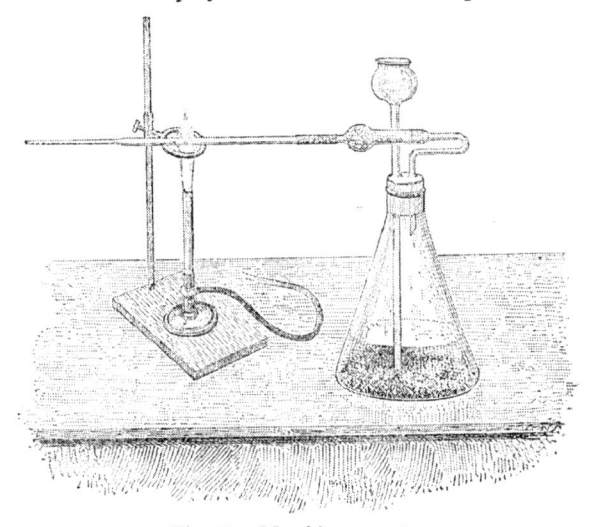

Fig. 24.—Marsh's apparatus.

crucible lid; the porcelain also remains unstained if the materials used are pure. Having determined the absence of arsenic in the gas that is escaping, some of the suspected fluid is poured down the thistle-funnel. If arsenic is present, a deposit of gradually increasing density makes its appearance in the tube an inch or more away from the Bunsen flame in the direction of the free end of the tube. The hydrogen flame burning at the end of the exit-tube, from being almost invisible, becomes of a whitish-lilac colour, and if a large amount of arsenic is present it gives off fumes of arsenious acid. On the approach of a cold porcelain surface to the flame a deposit is obtained which varies in density with the amount of arsenic present, and the length of exposure. Unless a long length of tube is heated by a row of Bunsen's burners a considerable portion of arsenetted hydrogen escapes disassociation during its passage through the heated portion, especially if the hydrogen is rapidly generated.

Instead of burning the gas as it escapes, the exit-tube may be turned downwards into a small vessel containing a solution of silver nitrate, so that the gas bubbles up through it; in doing so it causes the silver nitrate solution to turn brown or black. Arsenetted hydrogen has a disagreeable garlic-like odour when it escapes into the air.

Marsh's test may be used with organic matter containing arsenic, but with many organic fluids it is extremely difficult to avoid the formation of froth on the surface of the liquid, which is liable to mount up to the exit-tube and spoil the results. Marsh's test is not applicable to fluids containing nitrates, nitrites, chlorides, or free chlorine.

Examination of the Deposits.—The colour of the deposits on the porcelain varies from light-brown to black; the heaviest deposits show a brown tinge at their margins, although the bulk of the deposit is black. A drop of a solution of bleaching powder allowed to fall on one of the deposits immediately dissolves the portion on which it falls, leaving a white circle of porcelain visible. Ammonium sulphide applied in the same way merely detaches the film from the porcelain, and breaks it up; it dissolves but a limited amount. If a deposit is treated with a few drops of nitric acid and heated, it is dissolved and converted into arsenic acid. The free nitric acid being evaporated, a drop of a solution of silver nitrate added gives the brick-red colour of silver arseniate. It will be remembered that silver arsenite is yellow.

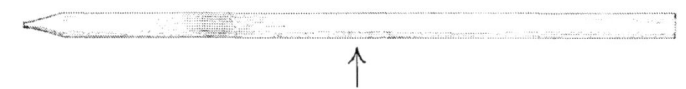

Fig. 25.—Deposit of arsenic on exit-tube of Marsh's apparatus.

The deposit in the **exit-tube** also has a brown hue, especially at the less dense parts; when very dense it is black. If heat is applied to the tube after it is detached from the flask, the film is volatilised, and combining with oxygen is deposited away from the source of heat as crystals of arsenious acid. If, whilst the heat is being applied, a current of dried hydrogen is passed through the tube, the deposit will be volatilised, and re-deposited as metallic arsenic. When dealing with minute amounts of arsenic, it is well to have the end of the exit-tube drawn out for a couple of inches into capillary dimensions, and after a deposit is obtained in the wider part to drive it by the aid of heat into the capillary portion whilst hydrogen is still passing through it, before detaching the tube from the apparatus. If, when filled with hydrogen, the tube, or the stained portion of it, is hermetically sealed at both ends, it can be preserved as *corpus delicti*.

The solution of silver nitrate through which the arsenetted hydrogen passed will be partially converted into a solution of arsenious acid with deposition of metallic silver from which it can be separated by filtration. If ammonia water is added to the filtrate, the arsenious acid combines with some of the remaining undecomposed silver nitrate and produces a precipitate of yellow silver arsenite.

Copper arsenite may be tested by dissolving a little in ammonia water: the colour changes from green to blue, which is evidence of the presence of copper. If to a drop or two of the ammoniacal solution placed on a colour-slab, a crystal of silver nitrate is added, yellow silver arsenite forms round the crystal. The other tests for arsenic and copper respectively may also be applied.

The best way of separating arsenic from organic admixture is to take advantage of the volatility of arsenious chloride [$AsCl_3$]; this method is especially convenient as regards the viscera. Before being submitted to it, the substance under examination should be finely divided, and thoroughly dried in a hot-water oven. When sufficiently dry, it should be powdered in a mortar and then placed in a flask connected with a condenser, the lower end of which dips into a receiver containing either water alone or a solution of potassium or sodium hydrate; both condenser and receiver should be kept cold with a stream of cold water. The powdered material is then well covered over with pure strong hydrochloric acid, and the heat of a water bath is applied to the flask until about three-fourths of the hydrochloric acid has passed over. The heat is temporarily withdrawn, and more hydrochloric acid is added to the flask, a fresh receiver being substituted for the one already used; distillation is then resumed. The whole of the arsenic usually comes over by the time the second distillation is complete; if not, the process must be repeated. The combined distillates are then dealt with as will presently be described.

In order to secure free volatility of the arsenic as chloride, it is essential that the liquid under distillation should be saturated with gaseous hydrochloric acid. If, therefore, the organic matter cannot be dried, or in the case of liquid organic substances containing arsenic, the plan recommended by Hufschmidt,[1] which is a modification of Sonnenschein's[2] method, excellently fulfils its purpose. After the hydrochloric acid is added to the organic matter in the flask, a stream of hydrochloric acid gas is passed into it to complete saturation; heat is then applied, and distillation carried on whilst a stream of hydro-

[1] *Berichte der deutsch. chem. Gesellsch.*, 1884.
[2] *Handbuch der gerichtlichen Chemie.*

chloric acid gas is being passed through the liquid undergoing distillation. The result of securing complete saturation of the acid is that the arsenic is rendered so volatile, that the whole of it readily passes over in the first distillate ; less heat is required, and, consequently, the product obtained is not so much contaminated with organic products. Care must be taken to have all the joints in the apparatus free from leakage, as the gaseous $AsCl_3$ is extremely volatile. Filter paper dipped in a solution of $AgNO_3$ blackens if held to a leaky joint.

When gaseous arsenious chloride is dissolved in water it is decomposed into arsenious and hydrochloric acids. If the amount of arsenic that comes over is small, it will all be dissolved by the water in the receiver as arsenious acid ; if it is in excess, the water will be rendered turbid by undissolved particles ; the addition of a little potassium or sodium hydrate to the water, before distillation, ensures the solution of the whole of the arsenic as potassium or sodium arsenite.

Quantitative estimation may be effected by passing sulphuretted hydrogen, to complete saturation, through the distillate obtained from the arsenious chloride. When all the arsenic is precipitated as sulphide, removal of the excess of $H_2S$ can be accomplished by passing a stream of $CO_2$ through the liquid. The precipitate is then thrown on to a tared filter, washed, dried at 100°, and then weighed : 100 parts equal 60·98 of metallic arsenic. If, as is probable, some sulphur has fallen, it may be removed by dissolving the arsenious sulphide in ammonia, with the aid of gentle heat ; separating from any deposit, and reprecipitating as sulphide by the addition of hydrochloric acid.

After weighing, the sulphide may be reduced to the metallic state by mixing it with potassium cyanide and sodium carbonate, and placing the mixture in a piece of hard glass-tubing drawn narrow for a couple of inches at the end. Dry $CO_2$ is passed through the tube from the thick end, and gentle heat applied until the tube and its contents are free from moisture ; the heat is then increased so as to reduce the sulphide to metallic arsenic, which is deposited on the narrow part of the tube, which should be kept cool. The part of the tube containing the deposit may be sealed off from the rest, and preserved as proof of the presence of the poison.

When a portion only of an organ—the liver, for example—is used for quantitative estimation, in order to avoid the objection raised at the Maybrick trial, it is advisable to reduce the entire organ to a pulp, and to take a portion of the pulp for analysis. The objection raised was that the poison is not equally distributed throughout the organ, and therefore that a reliable estimation of the total amount of poison contained cannot be made from proportional calculations founded on the amount obtained from isolated fragments. Whatever value the objection may or may not have, it is important to meet it in the way indicated.

## ANTIMONY

The preparations of antimony, which are met with in toxicological enquiries, are antimony and potassium tartrate, and antimony chloride, chiefly the former.

**Antimony and Potassium Tartrate** [$KSbC_4H_4O_7, H_2O$], or **tartar emetic**, is a well-known medicinal preparation, which contains about 35 per cent of metallic antimony. It is very soluble in water.

**Symptoms of Acute Poisoning.**—When a poisonous dose is taken into the stomach an astringent metallic taste is usually experienced almost immediately, which is usually followed in a few minutes by violent pain from the mouth down to the stomach. The pain is hot and burning, and is accompanied by a sensation of constriction in the throat. Immediately after, profuse vomiting comes on, and a little later diarrhœa, blood may be present in the vomit, but is more usually absent. The depressing effects of the poison quickly show themselves in the form of a small, frequent pulse, diminished arterial tension, cold clammy surface, shivering, and profound collapse; in this stage the surface may be cyanosed, and the patient unconscious. Clonic spasms may precede death. Respiration is slow and laboured. The urine may be almost entirely suppressed.

Anomalous symptoms not unfrequently occur. Vomiting may be delayed as long as an hour after the poison is swallowed, and then it may either be slight or very violent. In some instances the symptoms resemble those produced by a narcotic. Dobie[1] records a case in which one drachm of tartar emetic was followed by a comatose condition, the patient dying on the sixth day. Respiration is not invariably affected; Carpenter[2] records a case in which, after 170 grains dissolved in water were swallowed, the respirations remained unaffected, recovery taking place.

**Fatal Dose.**—The smallest recorded is one grain and a half of tartar emetic, following a similar dose taken twenty-four hours previously. No effect was produced by the first dose, but the second caused violent vomiting and purging, death taking place in about thirty-six hours, the patient was a healthy woman of twenty-five years of age.[3] This is an exceptional case. Five to ten grains probably represent a minimum fatal dose for a healthy adult. Children have succumbed to less. On

---

[1] *The Lancet*, 1887.      [2] *New York Med. Rec.*, 1883.
[3] *Bulletin de Thérapeutique*, vol. li.

the other hand, recovery in adults has followed 170 grains (see above) and in one case even 200 grains. Death may occur in from a few hours to several days.

When large doses are quickly rejected, the local effects of the poison are often speedily recovered from, the danger to a great extent appears to be in its depressing effects, including those due to violent vomiting and purging.

**Sub-acute or Chronic Poisoning.**—When death results from homicidal poisoning with tartar emetic it is usually due to repeated doses, which progressively depress the systemic powers, prevent the retention of food, cause persistent vomiting and purging, and thus eventually lead to a fatal issue. In the case of *Reg v. Pritchard* (High Court of Justiciary, Edin., 1865), the prisoner was accused of having poisoned his mother-in-law and his wife by the administration of tartar emetic. The latter was in her usual health up to the end of October, 1864, when she began to suffer from frequent attacks of vomiting; on leaving home she gradually regained her usual health, but after her return she again began vomiting and was attacked with severe cramps. The vomiting occurred within an hour or two after meals, which were always sent to her by her husband; not only food but also beverages, such as camomile tea, egg-flip, and port-wine, were rejected. Death took place on March 18th, 1865. During the illness of the deceased cramps constituted a prominent symptom; the wrists were turned in and the thumbs powerfully flexed. Retching, vomiting and diarrhœa were persistent, the tongue was foul, and there was constant thirst with profound depression. A considerable amount of antimony was found in the viscera after death, especially in the liver and in the contents of the intestines, in which it was present in a soluble form; it is probable that the last dose of the poison was administered a short time before death. The prisoner was condemned, and, before his execution, confessed having poisoned the deceased.

Tartar emetic is not unfrequently administered in dangerous doses to drunkards during a debauch, not with the object of poisoning them, but to produce such vomiting and nausea as to render them incapable of further excess for the time being. In a case of this kind recently seen by me the patient vomited, and was purged excessively; the tongue was foul and the surface was cold, but the pulse and respiration were not much affected. Cramps of the muscles of the limbs were severe and continuous; they lasted more than forty-eight hours, and persisted in the hands after the other parts originally attacked were free. Antimony was found in the urine. The patient recovered from what in all probability was a single dose, with a celerity that strongly contrasted with the severity of the symptoms.

**Antimony Chloride** [$SbCl_3$], or butter of antimony, is used in an impure state for certain trade purposes, and, exceptionally, has been administered as a poison. In addition to the toxic effects of antimony, this salt has a powerfully corrosive action on the tissues with which it comes in contact, and produces symptoms and post-mortem signs accordingly.

**Treatment of Acute Antimonial Poisoning.**—The poison usually promotes its own evacuation; if it has not done so, the stomach must be emptied either with the stomach-pump or an emetic, or probably tickling the throat will be sufficient to excite copious vomiting. When antimony chloride has been taken the stomach-pump should be used with great caution, if used at all. Then tannin, or some substance containing it, should be given so as to form an insoluble combination with any of the poison that remains in the stomach. After the poison is evacuated useless vomiting should be checked by ice and opium. External warmth should be applied, and stimulants given if needed. It is characteristic of antimony poisoning that after a large dose, either a speedily fatal issue may be expected from exhaustion, or an almost equally speedy recovery; in this respect it differs from arsenic. Antimony is eliminated by the kidneys and the bowels.

**Post-mortem Appearances.**—After acute poisoning by tartar emetic the mucous membrane of the stomach is usually strongly injected and swollen, and in parts may show indications of loss of superficial portions; it is covered with a slimy mucus, and is frequently ecchymosed. A similar appearance, less intense, will be found in the duodenum. In some instances the mucous membrane of the stomach has been found ulcerated, and detached down to the muscular coat, the mucous membrane of the œsophagus being also ulcerated; in others there is no appearance of ulceration of the stomach, the mucous membrane being also free from signs of inflammation. In the case of Bravo, who was poisoned with tartar emetic in 1876, both stomach and duodenum were pale and yellowish on their inner surfaces; there were ulcers in the cæcum, and the large intestines were blood-stained. The liver and kidneys may show fatty changes, usually only when death has been caused by several doses, with intervals between them. The post-mortem appearances of poisoning by antimony are neither so characteristic nor so constant as in arsenical poisoning.

**Antimony Chloride** produces post-mortem appearances like those of a corrosive, such as hydrochloric acid; exceptionally, corrosive effect may be absent. Cooke[1] records the case of a woman, aged forty, who swallowed the contents of a four-ounce bottle of butter of antimony immediately after a meal; vomiting without blood occurred, and profound

[1] *The Lancet*, 1883.

collapse. Death took place in less than two hours. On post mortem examination no corrosion of tongue, mouth, fauces, nor œsophagus was found; the mucous membrane of the stomach was intensely congested, almost black.

**Chemical Analysis--Tests.**—Organic fluids, or solids, when pulpified and mixed with water to a fluid consistency, may be tentatively examined by Reinsch's method, as described in the preceding section. The amount of antimony present and the length of time the solution is boiled with the copper-foil, and, to some extent, the acidity of the solution determines the appearance presented by the deposit. If it is but slight, the foil merely acquires a purple tint; if thicker, it resembles tarnished sheet zinc; and if very copious, it is covered with an amorphous black coat. When the foil is heated in a reduction tube, the deposit is volatilised, and condenses on a cooler part of the tube as a white amorphous cloud of antimonous oxide, which, when only minute traces of antimony are present, is scarcely visible. Under the microscope no trace of crystalline formation can be seen. Sometimes there is an appearance that at first sight might be taken for a crystalline deposit, but careful examination corrects the impression.

After shaking out the copper foil the deposit of antimonous oxide may be dissolved with gentle heat in a couple of drops of a solution of tartaric acid, and tested with $H_2S$, which gives the orange-coloured sulphide. If preferred, the deposit of antimony on the copper foil may be dissolved off in a weak solution of potassium hydrate, to which a little potassium permanganate has been added. Heat is applied until the deposit is dissolved, and then the fluid is separated by filtration from the precipitate of manganese that forms, is acidulated with HCl, and treated with $H_2S$.

The suspected fluid may be further tested by **Marsh's process**, as described in the last section. Antimonetted hydrogen is without odour and burns with a greenish-white flame.

**Examination of the Deposits.**—In thin films the deposit on porcelain obtained from the flame is of a neutral tint, without trace of brown; where the deposit is heavy, it is amorphous and black—like a smoked surface. The deposit is insoluble in a solution of bleaching-powder, but is freely soluble in ammonium sulphide, leaving, when dry, an orange-coloured residue of antimonous sulphide. When a deposit is dissolved in $HNO_3$ with heat, evaporated, and treated with a solution of silver nitrate, no colour change is produced; the deposit of arsenic similarly treated yields a brick-red colour.

In the exit-tube of the Marsh apparatus the deposit of antimony in the first instance appears immediately over the flame; it then separates into two portions, the larger one being towards the free end of the tube, that to the flask-side of the flame being lighter, and sometimes scarcely visible. The two deposits are most widely separated at the under part of the tube where it is hottest; they curve over towards each other at the upper and cooler part. When the deposit has taken up its final position, it is much nearer the flame than is the case with arsenic; all this is due to antimony having a higher volatilising point than arsenic. The deposit of antimony has a bright metallic lustre, like that of mercury; at the part where it fades away —furthest from the flame—it is smoky, but without trace of brown, as is the case with arsenic. If the deposit is very slight, it may be devoid of metallic lustre, being smoky, or greyish if moisture is present. On applying heat to the tube, the film of antimony is volatilised with difficulty; it comes down again, if oxygen is present, as a white amorphous deposit of antimonous oxide.

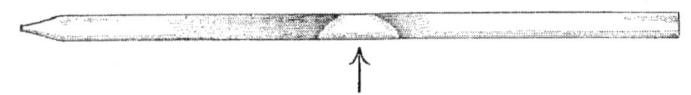

Fig. 26.—Deposit of antimony on exit-tube of Marsh's apparatus.

Antimony may be obtained from organic admixture by acidulating the organic fluid with HCl, and placing it in a platinum capsule, in which a small piece of pure tin or zinc is laid; where the metals touch each other a black deposit of metallic antimony is formed in a few minutes, or in an hour or two, according to the amount present. After removal of the fluid and of the tin or zinc, the deposit should be washed, and then treated with strong $HNO_3$, with the aid of heat, and the free acid driven off; the residue may be dissolved in strong HCl. If the solution thus obtained is largely diluted with water, the oxychloride is precipitated as a white insoluble salt, which may be dissolved in a solution of tartaric acid, and precipitated with $H_2S$ as antimonous sulphide, recognised by its orange colour. In some instances antimony may be directly precipitated from organic admixture by passing $H_2S$ through it to saturation, previously adding a little tartaric acid, and boiling to ensure the metal being in solution.

When dealing with the tissues it will be necessary to break them up by the moist process, taking the precaution to adapt a condenser to the flask in which the chlorine is evolved, in order to prevent possible loss from volatilisation of antimonous chloride. There is not much risk, however, as antimonous chloride is not nearly so volatile as arsenious chloride.

**Quantitative Estimation.**—Through a given proportion of the filtrate obtained after breaking up the organic matter, sulphuretted hydrogen is passed to complete saturation, so as to precipitate the antimony as sulphide. As antimony sulphide cannot be thoroughly dried at 100°, it is necessary to conduct the drying in an atmosphere of $CO_2$, otherwise at the requisite temperature it would lose sulphur. There will probably be also some free sulphur to get rid of that has fallen from the $H_2S$. The precipitate, after drying in the ordinary way at 100°, should be powdered in an agate mortar, and put into a porcelain boat, which is placed in a hard glass tube through which dried $CO_2$ is passing. Heat is applied until all moisture and free sulphur are expelled; the residue is pure $Sb_2S_3$. 100 parts equal 71.77 of antimony. If free from uncombined sulphur, the sulphide dissolves in strong HCl without leaving any residue.

## MERCURY

Metallic mercury in bulk has only very exceptionally produced symptoms of poisoning. In a finely-divided state, as in blue pill or blue ointment, or in a state of vapour, the toxic effects of the metal are readily produced. The principal poisonous salt is mercuric chloride; much less toxic, and much less frequently encountered in forensic investigations are mercurous chloride, mercuric oxide or red precipitate, and mercurammonium chloride or white precipitate. Mercuric nitrate resembles mercuric chloride in its effects. When pure, mercuric sulphide, or cinnabar, excepting in the form of vapour, is inert. The combinations of mercury with the organic radicles methyl and ethyl, are virulent poisons.

### Acute Mercurial Poisoning

Mercuric Chloride [$HgCl_2$] or corrosive sublimate, dissolves in 16 parts of cold water and 3 parts of boiling water. It readily combines with albumen, a property upon which its corrosive action depends.

**Symptoms.**—Immediately after a poisonous dose of mercuric chloride in solution is swallowed an acid metallic taste is perceived, which is accompanied by a sensation of constriction in the throat. A hot, burning sensation quickly develops, which spreads from the mouth, along the œsophagus down to the stomach. Vomiting of white slimy masses, which are frequently mixed with blood, rapidly follows. The pain radiates to the abdomen, there it assumes a colicky character, and is succeeded by copious diarrhœa accompanied by severe tenesmus; the stools are watery, often blood-stained, and they, as well as the vomited matters, contain shreds of mucous membrane. Blood is more constantly present in the vomited matters and in the motions than with poisoning by either arsenic or antimony. The mucous membrane of the mouth and pharynx is white and swollen, that of the larynx frequently being also swollen, making the voice hoarse, and the breathing difficult and noisy. The urine is often completely suppressed for twenty-four hours or more; any that may be passed will probably contain albumen, and it may be tinged with blood. Symptoms of profound collapse are present; the surface is cold, moist, and cyanosed, the pulse being small and irregular. There may be severe hiccough, or convulsions. If the victim survives the early symptoms, salivation is likely to appear twenty-four or more hours after the inception of the poison; this is not always the case, even when a large dose has been taken and recovery takes place. Other symptoms of stomatitis may be present.

The external use of corrosive sublimate has produced fatal poisoning from applications of a strong solution to ulcered surfaces. Absorption may take place through the unbroken skin. The extensive use of corrosive sublimate as an antiseptic has occasionally been the cause of accidents. Legrand[1] records the case of a woman who received two uterine injections of a solution of corrosive sublimate, 1 in 2000, and in consequence died in three days. In a case related by Huber[2] a woman accidentally had 150 cc. of a 0·5 per cent. solution of corrosive sublimate, diluted with an equal volume of water, administered as an enema; violent vomiting and purging set in, with subsequent collapse, which ended in death on the fifth day.

Fatal Dose.—Three grains of mercuric chloride taken by the mouth have caused death in a child. From 3 to 5 grains would probably prove fatal in an adult. Recovery has followed 90 grains in one case, in which salivation occurred; and 100 grains in another, in which there was no salivation. Death usually occurs within three or four days; it may take place in a few hours, or be postponed for seven or eight days.

Red Precipitate [HgO] when taken in large doses produces the usual symptoms of irritant poisoning. Ord[3] relates a case in which one tea-spoonful was taken; vomiting, diarrhœa (without blood) and tenderness of the abdomen were present; recovery took place without salivation. In another case recovery followed two drachms.

White Precipitate [$NH_2HgCl$].—About 35 grains, sold in mistake as one of the ingredients of a seidlitz powder, caused the death of an adult. Forty grains taken by a man, aged fifty-two, caused death in five hours. Twenty grains produced violent vomiting and purging, with blood in the stools, in a woman of forty-eight, followed by salivation and stomatitis; recovery took place. In other cases it has been taken in

[1] *Ann. de Gynécologie*, 1890.  [2] *Zeitschr. f. klin. Med.*, Bd. 14.
[3] *The Lancet*, 1888.

much larger doses—as much as two drachms—without fatal result. This salt has been regarded as non-poisonous; on one occasion a woman indicted for administering it to her husband was acquitted on this ground !

Mercuric Nitrate [$Hg(NO_3)_2H_2O$] on several occasions, when administered as a poison, has been in admixture with free nitric acid, in which condition it is used for veterinary purposes; it is a powerful corrosive. Half an ounce of the solution in nitric acid caused the death of an adult in twenty-five minutes. Death has also resulted from its use externally as an escharotic.

Metallic mercury in a finely-divided state is absorbed as such, but is probably partially oxidised, and combined with albumen before being taken up by the blood. Mercuric salts, as before stated, at once combine with albumen, and probably exist in this combination in the systemic fluids, being held in solution by excess of albumen. Mercurous salts are taken up with difficulty on account of their insolubility, a large proportion being rejected either by vomiting, or by the bowels. The relative insolubility of mercurous salts does not deprive them of toxic properties, however, as is shown by many instances of fatal poisoning with them. Runeberg[1] relates the case of a woman who received three subcutaneous injections of calomel—1½ grain in each—within one month. Ulcerative stomatitis, with profuse salivation and diarrhœa set in, followed by collapse and death, which took place in a few days.

Mercury is eliminated by the urine, fæces, saliva, and skin. When abundantly present in the body it may be found in the serum of blisters, in the milk, and in any other normal or abnormal secretion.

Treatment.—In acute poisoning, if emesis has not already occurred, the stomach should be emptied by an emetic followed by plentiful administration of raw white of egg; the albuminate thus formed though insoluble in water, is soluble in excess of albumen, therefore it should be removed as quickly as possible by producing further vomiting. Magnesium carbonate is useful to reduce the mercuric salt to a less active form. Afterwards demulcents and opium will be required.

Post-mortem Appearances of Acute Mercurial Poisoning. Taking the appearances of mercuric chloride as a type, the lips and the mucous membrame of the mouth, including that of the tongue is usually swollen, softened, and of an ash-grey or white colour; this appearance may persist along the œsophagus, the affected membrane being sometimes corrugated, and sometimes eroded. The mucous lining of the stomach is swollen and softened; it has been found deeply injected—of a bright scarlet colour—with ecchymoses; in other cases the indica-

[1] *Arch. f. Dermatologie u. Syph.*, 1889.

tions of inflammation are not nearly so obvious. Eschars have been found in the vicinity of the pylorus. The small intestines are usually much less affected than the cæcum, colon, and rectum, which are generally deeply injected, the lining membrane being probably ulcerated in parts, with indications of hæmorrhage. If death was very rapid, the intestines may present no abnormal appearance. Evidence of interstitial nephritis will probably show itself, unless the case was so very acute as not to allow time for its production. Deposits of lime salts have been found in the tubules of the cortex of the kidneys; when this is the case, a corresponding diminution of lime salts has been observed in the bones. A case was investigated by Kaufmann,[1] in which a woman of twenty years died in nineteen days after swallowing a solution containing from 8 to 12 grms. (124 to 186 grains) of mercuric chloride. On the fourth day anuria occurred, which lasted two days; on the three following days the urine was plentiful. On section the kidneys were found to be deeply injected and to contain a number of calcareous deposits in the cortices. Microscopical examination showed that the appearances presented by the kidneys did not depend on parenchymatous inflammation, but on a non-inflammatory necrosis of the epithelium, due to coagulation- or anæmic-necrosis. The calcareous deposit existed in the epithelial cells and not in the lumen of the tubules. The epithelial layer of the mucous membrane of the stomach also contained numerous minute calcareous deposits. A number of thromboses due to alteration of the blood, which is regarded by Kaufmann as the essential nature of corrosive sublimate poisoning, were found in the capillaries of the lungs and elsewhere. Whether the blood stasis in the capillaries is caused by changes in the red corpuscles themselves, or to liberation of fibrin-ferment is not certain, possibly to both.

## Chronic Mercurial Poisoning.

When mercury is taken into the system in repeated small doses, the effects produced are of a special character, differing in their salient features from those met with in acute poisoning. Chronic mercurial poisoning occurs almost exclusively among workers in the metal, or among those who handle substances which contain its salts: looking-glass makers, thermometer and barometer makers, workers in quicksilver mines and in manufactories in which the preparations of quicksilver are produced, represent the first division; furriers, bronzers, and others the second.

The order varies in which the symptoms of chronic mercurial poison-

[1] Virchow's *Arch.*, 1889.

ing occur The first indications usually are symptoms of dyspepsia, anorexia, colicky pains, loss of flesh and of strength Increase in the secretion of saliva is observed, accompanied by fœtor of the breath, tenderness of the gums, and the general symptoms of stomatis The sufferer looks anæmic, he is subject to attacks of nausea, vomiting, and diarrhœa The skin shows erythematous, eczematous, or pustular eruptions

Sooner or later the occurrence of special symptoms indicate that the nervous system is implicated, in some instances the nerve symptoms are the first to show themselves The earliest and most characteristic is a fine tremor of the muscles of the tongue and face, at first only manifest under excitement the tremor tends to spread to the arms, and later to the legs Although at first called up by exertion only, its fineness—resembling paralysis agitans—distinguishes it from that of disseminated sclerosis Subsequently the tremors are continuous, although still accentuated on voluntary movement, rendering co-ordinated muscular action difficult, during sleep they may be absent, or simply lessened, in accordance with their intensity when the patient is awake As is the case in all tremors that affect the muscles of articulation, the patient stammers and hesitates when speaking The tremors may exist without appreciable loss of muscular power, but, as a rule, more or less paralysis occurs Letulle[1] found this to be the case with a number of workers in the Almaden Mercury Mines, the diminution in muscular power as tested by the dynamometer, was proportional to the duration of the mercurial influence Muscular weakness may occur without tremors, but complete paralysis is invariably preceded by tremors Sensory disturbances, such as imperfect tactile sensibility, hyperæsthesia, and painful sensations, are, as a rule, localised and not profound Psychical disturbances are frequent, and take the form of mental irritability, loss of power of concentration, with headache and palpitation The condition called mercurial erythism may be present, the patient being subject to hallucinations, and to attacks of acute mania In the majority of cases observed by Letulle, the digestive organs were healthy The teeth may be blackened, and appear as though corroded by an acid; the condition, however, differs from ordinary caries

**Chemical Analysis** —The presence of mercury in organic admixture, in not too small an amount may be demonstrated by Reinsch's test The film of mercury on the copper foil is very characteristic, presenting the appearance of polished silver, if the foil after being dried is put into a reduction tube and heated until the mercury is driven off, minute globules of the metal are deposited

[1] *Arch de Phys Norm et Pathol* 1887

on the cooler part of the tube. Under the microscope by transmitted light they appear like black balls; by reflected light they show a metallic lustre round their margins. When the tube is cool (the copper being shaken out), the vapour given off from a scale of iodine introduced into it, soon colours the mercurial deposit yellow, which gradually deepens into scarlet mercuric iodide. The presence of mercury in organic fluids may also be ascertained by immersing in the fluid after acidulation with hydrochloric acid, a slip of gold foil in contact with a piece of tin wire; a white stain (metallic mercury), appears on the foil where it is touched by the tin. On account of the volatility of the metal the moist method should be used in order to separate mercury from organic matter. If the amount of mercury is not very small, the liquid obtained after treatment of the organic matter with potassium chlorate and hydrochloric acid may be saturated with $H_2S$, and allowed to stand until a black precipitate of mercurous sulphide falls, which, after separation, must be thoroughly washed free from all trace of chlorides. Any silver, lead, or copper sulphides present may be separated by treatment with nitric acid in which they are soluble; mercurous sulphide is insoluble in nitric acid. After the precipitate is washed and dried, it may be weighed and the amount of mercury calculated—100 parts equal 86·2 mercury. The sulphide is then treated with nitro-hydrochloric acid, evaporated to dryness, and dissolved in water. The solution thus obtained may be tested in various ways for mercury.

Tests.—With mercuric salts potassium iodide gives a scarlet precipitate soluble in excess. Potassium hydrate gives a yellow precipitate. Stannous chloride gives a white precipitate of mercurous chloride which changes to grey—metallic mercury. With soluble mercurous salts potassium hydrate gives a black precipitate; potassium iodide a green precipitate; stannous chloride a white precipitate changing to grey; potassium chromate a brick-dust coloured precipitate.

A number of methods have been devised for separating mercury present in very small amount along with organic matter. Some modification of the moist method is usually adopted to destroy the organic matter, and much ingenuity has been expended on the subsequent separation of the metal. Hofmeister's method as adopted by Winternitz[1] dispenses with destruction of the organic matter when urine is the fluid to be examined. The urine is acidulated with 10 per cent. of HCl, and is left for two days to deposit uric acid; after filtration it is slowly passed through a system of glass tubes containing rolls of copper gauze. The mercury present is deposited in the metallic

[1] *Arch. f. exp. Pathol. u. Pharmak.*, 1889.

state on the gauze, and after washing and drying, is driven off by heat, and is deposited on a cool part of the combustion tube in which the volatilisation is performed, and weighed. Bohm[1] modifies this process by destroying the organic matter in the moist way, and after freeing the liquid from chlorine, allows it to pass over copper gauze as above described. Ludwig and Zillner[2] after destroying organic matter with hydrochloric acid and potassium chlorate, precipitate the mercury with zinc dust, from which it is volatilised by heat. The tube containing the deposit is weighed, and again after the mercury is driven off by heat.

These recent methods, which for the most part are modifications of older processes, present certain advantages, and enable approximately exact results to be obtained, but after some experience in their use, I prefer the electrolytic method as being easier of application, and of equal accuracy. The organic fluid after treatment with potassium chlorate and hydrochloric acid, is submitted to electrolysis, as described in the following section, a small slip of gold-foil being substituted for platinum as the cathode. After the mercury is deposited, the gold-foil is washed, first with water, then with absolute alcohol, and lastly with ether, and carefully dried and weighed. It is then introduced into a piece of hard glass tubing through which a current of dry air is passed and sufficient heat is applied to drive off the mercury from the foil on to the tube. The foil is re-weighed, and, for control purposes, the tube is weighed with the deposit, and again after it has been driven off by heat.

## LEAD

The salts of lead chiefly encountered as toxic agents are the neutral acetate (sugar of lead), the basic acetate (Goulard's lotion), the carbonate (white lead), the tetroxide (red lead), and the chromate (yellow chrome); other salts of lead, as the chloride and nitrate, are poisonous but are not so accessible to the public. Fine particles of metallic lead are poisonous when repeatedly taken into the system.

The salts of lead act as mild irritants, some being more powerful poisons than others. The chromate, for example, although insoluble in water, acts more energetically than the acetate, which is soluble.

Lead poisoning may be **acute** or **chronic**, an intermediate **subacute** form is not unfrequently encountered.

[1] Zeitschr. f. phys. Chemie, 1891.   [2] Wiener Klin. Wochenschr., 1889.

### Acute Lead Poisoning.

**Lead Acetate** [$Pb(C_2H_3O)_2 3H_2O$], the salt of lead most frequently used, has a sweetish taste. It only produces acute poisoning when taken in large doses.

**Symptoms.**—If an ounce or more is swallowed, a strong astringent metallic taste is at once perceived, followed by a feeling of constriction in the œsophagus, and a hot sensation, which spreads to the stomach. Within half an hour after, vomiting comes on, the vomited matter consisting of white opaque masses, which may be tinged with blood. There is great thirst, and violent colicky pains in the abdomen, which come on in paroxysms; the abdominal muscles are tense, and the patient eases the pain by bending himself forward and compressing the abdomen. The bowels are usually constipated, but exceptionally diarrhœa has occurred; the motions are dark, almost black, from the presence of lead sulphide. The urine may be partially suppressed. Great prostration, vertigo, and pains in the head and limbs are experienced, with general numbness, or paræsthesiæ, cramps in the calves, and occasionally paralysis of the limbs. Drowsiness is not unfrequent; the tongue is coated, and the breath is offensive; the pulse is small and frequent. In acute lead poisoning, from a single dose the gums do not exhibit the blue line which is characteristic of chronic lead poisoning. The greater number of cases of acute lead poisoning recover. The subacute form occurs after taking repeated doses of a soluble salt of lead, which, though small, are not minute. The patient is troubled with intense thirst and a metallic taste. Colic, with retraction of the abdominal muscles is a prominent symptom; the bowels are obstinately confined. The urine is lessened in quantity. The blue line round the margin of the gums is usually present; the pulse is weak, and slow; the tongue is coated and the breath is offensive. There may be some of the more acute symptoms present, as prostration, numbness, and vertigo. Death rarely occurs, the symptoms passing off in a week or two, after the poison ceases to be administered. Gastric disorder and colic are the symptoms which first indicate the occurrence of the subacute form of lead poisoning, which occasionally happens in consequence of active medicinal treatment by means of lead acetate. Usually lead acetate may be administered in medicinal doses for a considerable time without producing poisonous symptoms, as, for example, when given to check the obstinate diarrhœa which accompanies tubercular ulceration of the bowels; on rare occasions poisonous symptoms follow a single dose.

**Fatal Dose.**—The exact amount of lead acetate which will cause death is not known. Recovery has followed an ounce

**Treatment of Acute Poisoning.**—The stomach should be emptied either by the tube or emetics unless there has been free, spontaneous vomiting. Sodium and magnesium sulphates should be given in half ounce doses, dissolved in half pints of water; dilute sulphuric acid may be substituted. The lead sulphate thus formed should be got rid of by purgatives, as, although an insoluble salt, it is not entirely harmless. Demulcent drinks, as barley water, milk, or white of egg are beneficial. Opium may be necessary for the colic and to restrain useless vomiting.

**Post-mortem Appearances.**—On account of the comparative rarity of fatal cases, the post-mortem signs are not well known. In addition to the usual indications of acute gastro-enteritis, the mucous membrane of the stomach has been found to be covered with a whitish-grey deposit. Erosions of the mucous membrane of the stomach and of the bowels have been observed, apparently due to the lead salt remaining in contact with it in parts. The mucous membrane of the stomach, in addition to being inflamed may be thickened and softened, a condition which sometimes extends to the duodenum. The other organs yield no reliable indications.

## Chronic Lead Poisoning

The sources from which the lead is derived in chronic poisoning are almost illimitable. They may be divided into those due to occupation-risks, and those due to the accidental presence of lead in fluids and comestibles, and in substances which are repeatedly brought in contact with the surface of the body; in the latter case it is probable that the poison is accidentally transferred to the mouth by the finger, in handling food for example.

Among the first division are those employed in the manufacture of, and workers in, white and red lead—painters, fitters, plumbers and others; workers with metallic lead, as smelters, file cutters (who use a thick plate of lead on which to bed the files while they are being cut), compositors, those who melt down old lead, shot manufacturers, and lead pipe makers, together with workers in lead glaze for earthenware, and makers of lead glass. Among the accidental causes are :— drinking-water which has been stored in lead cisterns, has passed through lead pipes, or is derived from contaminated sources, food cooked in so-called tinned vessels, the coating in the cheaper kinds sometimes containing lead, or in earthenware vessels lined with lead glaze, or food preserved in "tins," the solder of which contains a percentage of lead. Wine bottles that have been cleaned by shaking lead shot within them, confectionery coloured with lead chromate tea, and snuff packed in lead foil; hair dyes and cosmetics containing lead, and soda-water syphons fitted with pewter or lead valves, have all from time to time given rise to chronic lead poisoning.

It is doubtful whether metallic lead can be taken into the system through the intact skin, the usual portals are the mouth and nostrils. Workers in metallic lead do not suffer unless they are frequently in the presence of large quantities of the molten metals, or inhale fine particles of solid lead or of its oxide from manipulating old metal. Ordinary plumbers, who handle unoxidised metallic lead all day long, comparatively rarely suffer from lead poisoning unless from the use of white or red lead in fitting. Lead, although not usually classed amongst the volatile metals, is capable of volatilisation at a high temperature, and in the form of vapour may be taken into the system through the respiratory tract and also into the stomach. One of the worst cases of chronic lead poisoning I ever saw was that of a man who bought the sheet-lead linings of old tea chests, and melted them down into pig-lead. He did the work in a small room without any contrivance for ventilation, and attended to the whole process himself. File cutters abrade small particles of lead by constant hammering, and in this way the metal gets into the mouth and air-passages. In other trades in which lead is used, the salts of the metal are introduced into the system by want of cleanliness, a workman is content to wipe his hands on his apron, or other cloth already contaminated with lead, and then to handle food in the act of taking his meals. He will also hold between his teeth brushes or other articles soiled with lead paint.

Idiosyncrasy has much to do with chronic lead poisoning, of half a dozen persons subjected to the same risks, perhaps one only develops symptoms. The use of alcohol increases the tendency to chronic lead poisoning, Oliver[1] regards it as a most potent factor. Gouty subjects easily succumb to the influence of lead, and in its turn, the metal tends to develop gout. Oliver states that women succumb to the influence of lead more quickly than men and at an earlier age—18 to 23, in the case of men the usual age is from 41 to 48. Cases have been observed in which symptoms of chronic poisoning appeared years after the individual had ceased to be exposed to the action of the metal. In pregnant women abortion frequently results from chronic lead poisoning.

**Symptoms**—The early symptoms are usually referred to indigestion, the patient has pains in the stomach or abdomen, which may or may not be evoked, or increased by taking food; the appetite is diminished and the bowels are constipated. A disagreeable, sweetish, astringent taste is experienced in the mouth, and the breath is offensive. The skin acquires an unhealthy colour, at first it is yellowish, subsequently

[1] *Lead poisoning in its acute and chronic forms*, 1892.

it is anæmic. Round the free margins of the gums a blue line is seen most strongly marked in the upper jaw, where teeth are absent the blue line is also absent. The lead is due to deposition of lead sulphide in the substance of the gums, small quantities of food containing sulphur cling to the teeth, and in consequence of decomposition slowly give off $H_2S$ which combines with the lead present in the gums. Nutrition is interfered with and the patient consequently emaciates. The pulse is usually slow, and of high tension.

Patients in this condition often go on for a long time without much change, although they may continue to be under the influence of the poison, usually, however, one or other of the more pronounced symptoms of chronic lead poisoning is developed. They comprise — colic, arthralgia (pain in the neighbourhood of the joints), paralysis, and encephalopathy (psychical disturbances).

Colic is usually the first to appear, although cases of typical lead paralysis occur in which the patients deny ever having had colic, as a rule one or more attacks of colic precede the other symptoms. Colic is usually ushered in by recurrent abdominal pains as mentioned in the general symptomatology, an attack may suddenly occur, however, without any antecedent pain. In most cases the pain radiates round the umbilicus, and is accompanied by tenesmus and retraction of the abdominal muscles, whether the muscles are retracted or not, they are tense and resistant, and the pain is relieved on pressure. Except in rare cases, when there is diarrhœa, the bowels do not act in spite of the tenesmus. During the attacks of colic the pulse becomes still slower, and is full and hard. There is no rise of temperature of any significance.

Arthralgia.—The pains to which this name is given probably originate in the sensory nerves of the muscles in the neighbourhood of the joints, they may be preceded by shooting or flying pains, or they may come on suddenly without warning. They occur most frequently about the knees, less frequently about the elbows and shoulders. The sensation is that of a boring, tearing pain, which seems to affect the bone itself. The flexors suffer most frequently, as a rule, the small joints are not attacked. The pain may extend to the muscles of the trunk, especially to the lumbar muscles. Contraction and twitchings of the muscles have been observed.

Paralysis.—The muscles most frequently attacked are the extensors of the hand and fingers. The order in which they succumb is usually—the extensor communis, the extensores digiti minimi, pollicis longus, carpi ulnaris, radialis, pollicis brevis, and (after a longer interval) the ossis metacarpi pollicis. The supinator longus usually escapes, and shows up in contrast to the wasted muscles. The result of the muscular paralysis is that when the arms are held out horizontally, with the palms of the hands downwards, the hands drop, and cannot be raised, the condition being known as "wrist-drop." Exceptionally, the paralysis begins in the muscles of the upper arm, the deltoid, biceps, and coraco-brachialis being affected, and in this—the upper arm type—the supinator longus is attacked. Both arms usually suffer, though one may be more affected, or further advanced than the other. The interosseous muscles of the hands and those of the ball of the thumb are sometimes specially attacked, producing the "claw-shaped" hand. The legs may be attacked, but usually not until arms have suffered for some time; the anterior muscles—the extensors of the foot—are the first to suffer, the tibialis anticus, like the supinator longus, usually escapes. The muscles of the trunk are rarely affected.

The characteristics of lead paralysis are:—little if any disturbance of the sensory fibres—probably limited to the early period if present—with profound trophic changes; the affected muscles undergo extreme atrophy, and yield the reaction of degeneration. Lead paralysis is usually regarded as peripheral, but it does not correspond with the distribution of the peripheral nerve supply; in the arm, for example, all the muscles supplied by the musculo-spiral are not affected. Changes have been found both in the nerves and in the ganglion cells of the anterior cornua of the cord.

**Encephalopathy.**—Psychical disturbances usually commence by headache, dizziness, and sleeplessness; there may also be amaurosis: further development may lead to a condition of drowsiness, or to one of excitability, which may be accompanied by hallucinations or wild delirium. Eclampsia is common, especially in women, and involves an unfavourable prognosis; the convulsions may be repeated at intervals for days, the patient remaining unconscious for some time after each attack.

Lead possesses selective properties in relation to the nervous system, which is attacked by it both centrally and peripherally; it is capable of entering into combination with nerve-substance and thus of directly interfering with its function. Blyth[1] chemically examined the brain of a man who had succumbed to the influence of lead, and found an amount of the metal in it equal to 117 1 milligramme of lead sulphate.

**Treatment of Chronic Lead Poisoning.**—Removal of the patient from the influence of the poison is essential; when dyspeptic symptoms, especially if accompanied by pains in the abdomen, are complained of, the margins of the gums should always be examined. Various remedies, of which the favourite is potassium iodide, have been used to promote elimination of the metal. From the results of some investi-

[1] Abstract of *Proc. Chem. Soc.* 1887-88.

gations recently made,[1] I have arrived at the conclusion that potassium iodide does not influence the rate of elimination of lead. In two cases of chronic plumbism, it was given in 15 and 10 grain doses respectively three times a day for a week or ten days, and then stopped for a like period, and again resumed; during the whole period of the experiments the fæces and urine voided in the preceding twenty-four hours were analysed three times a week. The results showed that slow elimination, chiefly through the bowels, was going on the whole time, and that it was not increased when potassium iodide was being taken in conjunction with which magnesium sulphate was sometimes given. Several other accredited eliminants were also tried with negative results. The only treatment that to a slight degree seemed to increase the amount of lead in the excretions was a combination of hot baths and general massage, with occasional purges. Fresh air, good diet, as much exercise as can be judiciously taken, with hot baths and general massage, are the means chiefly to be relied on to promote cure in cases of chronic lead poisoning.

The **special symptoms** require appropriate treatment. Colic will require opium; arthralgia, hot fomentations and probably opium; paralysis, local massage and electricity.

The elimination of lead from the system takes place chiefly by the bowels, to a much lesser extent by the kidneys. It has been asserted that lead is eliminated by the skin, but I have never succeeded in obtaining any evidence of this; the instances of blackening of the skin by baths containing potassium sulphide, which are cited in proof, were probably due to the presence of the metal, derived from external sources, in the pores of the skin.

When a medicinal dose of a soluble salt of lead is administered, about half or two-thirds of it passes in in insoluble form directly through the bowels without being absorbed; what remains is gradually eliminated in the fæces and urine, a small percentage being probably retained in the tissues for an indefinite period. Two grains of lead acetate were given to a patient three times a-day for five consecutive days; on the last day of administration the fæces (227 gms.) yielded 0·1762 gm. of lead, equal to about 3 grains of lead acetate; on the second day after the administration ceased, 290 gms. yielded 0·1411 gm. (about 4 grains) of the acetate; on the fourth day the amount fell to 0·0053 gm., and on the sixth to 0·0006 gm., after which there was little more than a trace. The largest amount obtained from the urine in any one day was equal to a little over one milligramme of lead; this rapidly fell to less than one half. In a few days after there was a mere trace. In each instance the fæces and urine analysed were

[1] British Med. Journ. 1892.

respectively the excretions of twenty-four hours. It is evident that only a small percentage of lead is absorbed when given medicinally, the instances therefore, in which symptoms of lead poisoning are produced by medicinal doses, demonstrate that it is not essential for much of the poison to be stored up in the tissues, but that what is stored up exists in a very stable form and probably in intimate combination with them

The elimination in cases of chronic poisoning was investigated in a similar way, the fæces and urine passed in twenty-four hours were analysed every second or third day, the weight of the fæces and the volume of the urine being noted on each occasion. The results showed that the daily elimination in the fæces was from five to ten times greater than that in the urine the amount in the fæces varied from 3 milligrammes of metallic lead down to a mere trace, the largest amount obtained from the urine in any one day was 0.9 milligramme

**Chemical Analysis** —Any lead that comes away with the excretions, or is contained in the tissues after death, exists in combination with organic matter from which it requires disassociating before it will respond to reagents. If the amount of organic matter with which the lead is combined is small, it may be evaporated to dryness if a fluid, or simply dried if a solid, and then incinerated at as low a temperature as will effect the purpose. The residue is drenched with nitric acid, the acid driven off with a gentle heat and the nitrate thus formed is dissolved in a little water and tested

**Tests** —Sulphuretted hydrogen produces a brown or black precipitate in accordance with the amount of lead present. Potassium iodide gives a yellow discoloration, or precipitate, the former when the lead is in very small amount. The precipitate is soluble in boiling water from which it crystallises on cooling in gold-coloured scales. In making use of this test with minute quantities of lead that have been treated with nitric acid, it is essential that all the free acid should be driven off, otherwise the reagent is decomposed and a yellow colour is produced by the liberated iodine. There are grounds for believing that some of the extraordinary results which have been obtained with potassium iodide, in testing urine for lead, were due to this fallacy. Potassium chromate gives a yellow precipitate. Sulphuric acid gives a white precipitate, hastened, when in very dilute solution, by the addition of alcohol, the precipitate is soluble in ammonium acetate. A lead salt mixed with sodium bicarbonate, and heated on charcoal in the reducing flame of the blowpipe, yields beads of metallic lead incrusted with its yellow oxide

When minute quantities of lead are present in combination with large amounts of organic matter, the dry process is tedious, difficult to

carry out, and uncertain in its results. The plan adopted in the investigations on the elimination of lead above-mentioned was as follows —
The urine was evaporated down to the consistence of gruel, and the fæces were mixed with distilled water to a like consistence, they were then severally treated with potassium chlorate and hydrochloric acid, as described on p. 404. The filtrate after cooling was placed in a glass cell, the bottom of which consisted of a sheet of vegetable parchment. The cell was immersed to such a depth in an outer cell containing distilled water acidulated with a few drops of sulphuric acid, that the liquids in the inner and outer cells stood at the same level. A piece of platinum foil exposing a surface of about 50 cm square was submerged in the liquid contained in the inner cell, and connected with the cathode of four Grove's elements, a similar piece of platinum foil connected with the anode being immersed in the outer cell; the pieces of foil were so placed as to be opposite each other separated by the parchment diaphragm. The circuit was closed from six to eight hours, after which the foil was removed from the inner cell, gently washed and dried. The metallic lead was dissolved off the foil with dilute nitric acid aided with heat, and after driving off most of the free acid, the solution was decomposed with dilute sulphuric acid, and an equal volume of alcohol added; it was then set aside for twenty-four hours. The precipitate of lead sulphate was washed with water containing 12 per cent of alcohol, until all the free acid was removed; it was then separated by decantation, ignited, and weighed. The amount of lead was calculated from the weight of the sulphate. 100 parts of sulphate equal 68.319 parts of metallic lead.

Whether the moist or the dry process is used, the residue after the primary filtration should be tested for lead which may exist as sulphate, and remain undissolved. If the original substance contains lead, as sulphate, the salt should be dissolved with heat in an aqueous solution of ammonium tartrate, to which a little free ammonia has been added, and precipitated with sulphuretted hydrogen. 100 parts of lead sulphide equal 86.61 parts of metallic lead. It is better, however, to convert the sulphide into sulphate, by treating it with nitric, and subsequently with sulphuric, acids. It may be then ignited, weighed, and calculated by the factor for lead sulphate.

In place of the electrolytic method, the solution obtained after destruction of the organic matter in the moist way may be precipitated with sulphuretted hydrogen, and the precipitate dealt with as above described. When the amount of lead is very small, the electrolytic method is much preferable.

## COPPER

The salts of copper having a distinctive colour and a strongly astringent taste are ill adapted for criminal purposes, still cases have occurred in which the sulphate and the acetate have been administered with homicidal intent, acute copper poisoning, however, is usually due to accident or to attempted suicide. Metallic copper is slightly if at all poisonous, many cases have happened of accidental swallowing of copper coins, which in some instances have remained within the digestive tract for a considerable time, but with one exception, no toxic effects are recorded. When a soluble salt of copper is swallowed, it is probably transformed into an albuminate, and, if in small amounts, produces but slight local changes; if in greater quantity, it not only combines with any free albuminoid substances in the stomach, but it also attacks the mucous membrane and erodes it.

### Acute Copper Poisoning

The salts that are usually answerable for acute poisoning are the sulphate $[CuSO_4(H_2O)_7]$ or blue vitriol, and the basic acetate $[Cu(C_2H_3O_2)_2 2CuO]$ or verdigris.

**Symptoms.**—When a poisonous dose of either of these salts is taken, the usual effects of an irritant poison are produced within five or ten minutes. There is violent vomiting and purging, pain in the stomach and abdomen, a metallic taste, thirst, and the symptoms of collapse. The vomited matter at first is green or blue, the lips also and the inside of the mouth may be thus coloured. The vomit may be distinguished from bile by the addition of ammonia water, which strikes a deep blue with the copper salt, the colour of bile remaining unchanged. Pain in the head is frequent, and sometimes convulsions occur. The urine is diminished in amount, and may contain blood. Jaundice has been observed. In children the nervous system from the first may be seriously disturbed, producing profound depression, irregular respiration, tonic, or clonic spasms of the muscles of the limbs, or complete paralysis, the condition rapidly passing into coma, and death.

**Fatal Dose.**—Is not known exactly. One ounce of the sulphate, and the same quantity of the acetate, have each proved fatal. Death may occur in a few hours, it is more usually delayed for several days.

**Treatment.**—If vomiting is taking place it may be aided by draughts of warm water, in which the white of egg is beaten up. If necessary, the stomach-pump must be used. Demulcents, such as barley water, arrowroot water, and milk should be given. Morphine may be necessary to relieve pain and subdue useless vomiting.

**Post-mortem Appearances.**—Indications of the effects of an irritant will be present probably from the mouth down to the stomach and bowels; the mucous membrane will be tumefied and softened, and in the stomach it may be eroded: the whole tract will show signs of inflammation. There may be distinctive indications of the poison, especially with the acetate, in the form of green coloured particles adhering to the gastric, or intestinal mucous membrane; with the sulphate (if the discoloration exists) the appearance will be that of a bluish stain; the staining may be distinguished from that due to bile by the addition of ammonia water. The liver may show fatty changes.

### Chronic Copper Poisoning

Chronic poisoning with copper is not nearly so frequent as the corresponding form of lead poisoning; whether this is due to feebler toxic action, or to non-accumulation of the poison in the system, is a disputed point. Roger[1] maintains that copper salts are barely toxic when taken into the stomach, owing to their reduction by glucose and their removal from the circulation by the liver; but when injected directly into the blood-current they are distinctly toxic. As proof of the innocuousness of copper in small doses, it has been asserted that workers in the metal never suffer from its effects; it is probable, however, that the continuous introduction of small amounts of copper into the system produces symptoms which, though longer delayed, closely resemble those due to lead. In brass workers Suckling[2] observed wrist drop and other symptoms attributable to peripheral neuritis. A green line was present on the margins of the gums, and the lower parts of the teeth were stained green. In other cases metallic taste, dyspepsia, attacks of vomiting, and diarrhœa with colic, have been observed. It is stated that the colic differs from lead colic in not being accompanied by retraction of the abdominal muscles; the tendency to diarrhœa is also a distinguishing feature from chronic lead poisoning. Some observers who have noticed the line on the margin of the gums describe it as being of a reddish-purple; others as indistinguishable from the blue line of lead; others again as in the cases instanced above.

Copper may find its way into the system along with food, with which it has been accidentally, or purposely, mixed. Accidental admixture occurs from the use of brass cooking utensils, the risk being increased by want of cleanliness. Certain foods, or condiments, are more liable to act on metallic utensils than others: fats easily decom-

[1] *Revue de Méd.*, 1887.     [2] *Brit. Med. Journ.*, 1888.

pose, and then acids, and also the vegetable acids contained in some fruits quickly attack copper. In large establishments it is sometimes customary to substitute copper hot-water pipes for those of lead, as being ultimately more economical; if water conveyed by these pipes is examined, copper in small amount may be detected. The copper boiler and hot-water cylinder, in use in many households, may be a source of contamination, especially when supplied with some kinds of water.

Copper is purposely added to certain articles of diet in order to improve their appearance; this is frequently done in the case of preserved green peas, and some kinds of pickles, as gherkins. The chlorophyll, to which the bright green colour of the vegetables is due, is partially decomposed with corresponding loss of colour during the process of conservation, and a soluble copper salt (usually the sulphate) is added in order to restore the colour and make them attractive to the eye. The amount of copper varies in different specimens from one grain per pound of peas upwards. In one case[1] the enormous amount of copper, equal to twenty-six grains of crystallised copper sulphate per pound of peas, was detected. The possible toxic effects that may accrue from the consumption of vegetables thus adulterated is repeatedly discussed before the law courts, with varying results—a certain percentage of copper is pronounced injurious on one occasion, and not on another. Except in the case of those, who from idiosyncrasy are unusually susceptible to the influence of copper, it is very unlikely that poisonous symptoms would manifest themselves after a single meal, of which preserved peas containing a small amount of copper formed a part. Hence it is difficult to do other than admit that the occasional use of vegetables thus adulterated would not be attended by symptoms of poisoning. At the same time it is to be regretted that the door is left open for the introduction of a substance which might be productive of harm. Any mischief that resulted would be due to the copper absorbed, and to its local action on the gastric mucous membrane, the vegetables themselves do not appear to be affected so far as their digestibility is concerned. Experiments by Ogier[2] and by Charteris and Snodgrass[3] on the artificial digestion of greened vegetables show that the presence in small amount of a salt of copper exercises no adverse influence in this respect. In greened vegetables copper probably exists as an insoluble leguminate from which the metal is liberated and rendered soluble by the action of the gastric and pancreatic digestion.

In France where the system of greening vegetables is largely carried

[1] *Sanitary Record*, 1877.     [2] *Laboratoire de Toxicologie*, 1891.
[3] *The Lancet*, 1892.

out, the law which formerly prohibited the use of copper salts for this purpose has been repealed. The New York Board of Health allow canned peas to be sold that contain not more than three-quarters of a grain of metallic copper—equal to three grains of the crystallised sulphate—per pound, provided that the label on each tin contains a statement to that effect.

In relation to this subject the question of the natural occurrence of copper in certain vegetables has to be considered; minute quantities have been found in wheat, coffee, and a number of other articles of every day consumption. This, to a certain extent, accounts for the fact that copper is almost invariably present in the human body, of which it has been erroneously assumed to be a physiological constituent. It is probable that copper is being continuously introduced into the system from the source just mentioned or from the use of copper or brass cooking utensils, and hot-water apparatus.

When making the investigations on the elimination of lead mentioned in the preceding section, although the patients were not taking any substance known to contain copper, I rarely failed to obtain evidence of its presence in the faeces. The amount varied; it was sometimes considerable, as much as two milligrammes of metallic copper being eliminated in the twenty-four hours. Copper was not detected in the urine in these cases. The faeces from a number of individuals were subsequently examined for copper, with the result that traces at least, and often much more, were invariably obtained. These analyses show that copper is almost constantly present in the system, and they also prove that the metal is chiefly eliminated by the bowels; corroborative of the latter statement is the fact that when a soluble salt of copper is therapeutically administered, so that one or more grains are taken daily, although minute quantities may be found in the urine, the bulk is eliminated in the faeces. It is probable that, like lead, copper is partially retained in the system, but the accumulation takes place more slowly.

**Chemical Analysis.**—Organic matter may be got rid of either by the dry or the moist way. If the former is adopted the residue, after evaporation of the nitric acid, will betray the presence of copper by a greenish or bluish tinge.

**Tests.**—The clear solution may be tested with potassium ferrocyanide which gives a chocolate-brown precipitate; by ammonia water, which gives an azure blue; by potassium sulphocyanide, which, in dilute solution, gives an emerald green, and in stronger solution an olive green, in either case, on the addition of ammonia water, the ordinary blue reaction of that reagent with copper is obtained. If a drop of a solution of a copper salt, having a slightly acid reaction, is allowed to remain for a minute or two on the bright blade of a knife it leaves a deposit of metallic copper. Another method is to place in the liquid a bright steel needle, or piece of iron wire; the resulting film of copper may be dissolved in a few drops of ammonia water, to which it imparts a blue tint; this test may be used in the presence of organic matter—tinned peas, for example.

Quantitative estimation may be made by precipitating the copper as sulphide, and then dissolving it in strong nitric acid; the acid is evaporated and the residue gradually heated to a full red heat until all the combined nitric acid is driven off. The result is cupric oxide: 100 parts equal 79·85 parts of metallic copper. If the quantity of copper is very small in proportion to the organic matter present, the latter may be destroyed by the moist method, and the resulting fluid dealt with by electrolysis, as described in the last section. The deposit of copper is dissolved off the platinum with dilute nitric acid, aided by heat, and, if the amount is very small, estimated volumetrically; if larger, it may be treated with $H_2S$, converted into oxide and directly weighed.

## SILVER.

Acute poisoning by a salt of silver is exceptionally rare, and usually results from the accidental swallowing of a piece of "lunar caustic" which is being used to cauterise the throat.

**Symptoms of Acute Poisoning by Silver Nitrate [$AgNO_3$].**—When swallowed in the solid it acts as a violent irritant and corrosive on the mucous membrane of the stomach. Pain is felt in the stomach and abdomen, followed almost immediately by vomiting and probably purging; the early vomited matter consists of cheesy masses of coagulated mucus, which darken on exposure to light; blood may be present both in the vomit and in the dejections. Collapse, cardiac depression, and cramps may occur. Silver is eliminated to some extent by the kidneys, but most of that which is received into the system is deposited in the metallic state in the tissues.

**Fatal Dose.**—Not determined. Scattergood [1] reports a case occurring in an infant, in which a piece of lunar caustic, three-quarters of an inch long, accidentally slipped down the throat; although antidotal treatment was at once resorted to, the child died in six hours. A similar and fatal case happened some years ago to an adult in Manchester.

**Treatment.**—Common salt and water, followed by an emetic or the stomach-pump; afterwards, white of egg and ice. If the solid lunar caustic has been swallowed, an emetic is preferable to the stomach-pump.

[1] *Brit. Med. Journ.*, 1871.

## Chronic Poisoning by Silver.

This usually results from the prolonged internal use of a silver salt medicinally. Instances have occurred in which absorption, resulting in chronic poisoning, has taken place from long-continued application of the nitrate to granulations; workers in metallic silver have also suffered from local symptoms affecting the skin. A common result of chronic poisoning by silver is discoloration of the skin—argyria—due to deposition of particles of the reduced metal in the papillary layer of the corium, not in the rete mucosum, as is the case in physiological skin-pigmentation; on account of the nature of the pigment and its position, the discoloration is very permanent. A dark line is also formed on the margins of the gums; the mesentery, kidneys, and other glandular organs have been found stained. In animals staining does not take place, but disturbances of nutrition, paralysis and fatty degeneration of the liver and kidneys occur. Gowers[1] relates the case of a man who, after taking silver medicinally for years, suffered from paralysis of the long extensor of the fingers, and of the extensors of the phalanges of the thumb, on both sides; on the right, the radial extensors of the wrist were also paralysed; argyria and the black line on the gums were present.

Post-mortem Appearances.—In acute poisoning indications of the caustic effect of the poison may be present as streaks or patches of a greyish white colour on the parts with which it came in contact. When solid lunar caustic is swallowed, the stomach suffers most severely at the lower part where the caustic lay. In addition there will be inflammation of the stomach, and probably of the duodenum. In chronic poisoning the tissues will be found stained as above described.

Chemical Analysis.—Destruction of organic matter by the moist method is not feasible as the silver chloride which would be formed is insoluble. Incineration may be adopted, in the course of which if the poison is present in not too small amount, a coating of metallic silver will be deposited on the bottom and sides of the capsule due to the reducing action of the organic matter.

Tests.—On adding dilute hydrochloric acid a white curdy precipitate is produced, which is insoluble in nitric acid, but is soluble in ammonia water. A solution of caustic potash gives a brownish precipitate insoluble in excess, but soluble in ammonia and in nitric acid. Potassium iodide gives a yellow precipitate, and potassium chromate a red precipitate. The quantity of silver may be estimated by precipitating it

[1] *Diseases of the Nervous System*

from a solution of the nitrate by means of sodium chloride, filtering on a tared filter, drying and weighing the precipitate. 100 parts of silver chloride equal 75.28 parts of metallic silver. The operation should be conducted by gas light.

## ZINC.

Acute poisoning by zinc is limited to two of its salts—the sulphate, and the chloride. The action of the two salts is different—the sulphate when taken in poisonous doses is simply an irritant, the chloride is a corrosive.

### Acute Poisoning by Zinc

Zinc Sulphate [$ZnSO_4 7H_2O$], or white vitriol, very closely resembles Epsom salts in naked-eye appearance, for which it has been accidentally administered.

The **symptoms** produced by a poisonous dose are violent vomiting, pain in the stomach and abdomen, metallic, astringent taste, which quickly follow the act of swallowing the poison, to these purging usually succeeds. The immediate emesis, together with the comparatively feeble toxic action of zinc sulphate render a fatal issue exceptional, when death takes place it is in consequence of exhaustion.

**Fatal Dose.**—Not known. Recovery has followed one ounce.

Zinc Chloride [$ZnCl_2 H_2O$], known in commerce in the form of Burnett's fluid, and also as soldering fluid, is a violent corrosive.

**Symptoms.**—Severe burning sensation in mouth, throat, stomach, and abdomen, followed by immediate vomiting and diarrhœa, with severe tenesmus, and distension of the abdomen, the ejected matters contain traces of mucous membrane and of blood. Profound collapse is shown by cold surface, clammy sweat, thin pulse, great prostration, and, in immediately fatal cases, coma, with irregular breathing. It is not uncommon for the acute symptoms to mitigate for a time, and then to recur after an interval of days, or even weeks, which is due to progressive disorganisation of the tissues of the digestive tract. Ward[1] records an instance where several men on board ship were attacked with symptoms resembling those of cholera, caused by drinking water in which zinc plates were placed, to prevent corrosion of the boiler, from whence it was obtained. Death has resulted from the application of chloride of zinc paste as an escharotic. The elimination of zinc takes place by the bowels and to a lesser extent by the kidneys.

**Fatal Dose.**—Six grains have proved fatal, but recovery has followed 3 or 4 drachms of the solid salt.

**Treatment.**—Poisoning by the **sulphate** will probably require little

[1] *The Lancet*, 1886.

more than attention to the symptoms, usually the stomach spontaneously relieves itself of the poison, if not the tube should be used, then warmth should be applied, and stimulants and opium given if required. In poisoning by the chloride, potassium or sodium carbonate, tannic acid, white of egg, milk, and demulcents should be administered, followed by opium if necessary.

**Post-mortem Appearances.**—The sulphate only gives rise to the appearances usually observed in acute gastro-enteritis, as previously stated the poison is purely an irritant and therefore causes no destruction of tissue. With the chloride the case is different. If the patient dies shortly after swallowing the poison, the digestive tract, from the mouth down to the stomach, possibly as far as the duodenum, will show more or less indications of corrosion. There will be patches of softened membrane having a white appearance, which in parts may be detached, together with the usual signs of acute inflammation. If the patient survives the reception of the poison for some weeks, the gastric mucous membrane will probably be completely disorganised and in parts replaced by cicatricial tissue. Jalland[1] records the case of a man who committed suicide by swallowing an unknown quantity of a saturated solution of zinc chloride, he died on the seventy-ninth day. At the necropsy the stomach was found to be completely destroyed, the remains consisted of a sausage like mass of inflammatory adhesions without any trace of mucous membrane, the cavity—four inches long and three-quarters of an inch in diameter—resembled that of a chronic abscess.

**Chronic poisoning** by zinc has been observed, chiefly in smelters of the metal. The symptoms to some extent resemble those produced by lead, derangement of the digestive organs, colic with constipation, or, more frequently, diarrhœa, indications of peripheral neuritis have been observed. Gastric symptoms have resulted from drinking water or milk stored in zinc-lined vessels. The zinc used for "galvanising" iron vessels is impure, and fluids containing chlorides will act on it.

**Chemical Analysis.**—In neutral or alkaline solution zinc may be precipitated from organic admixture by sulphuretted hydrogen. The precipitated sulphide will probably carry down with it some organic matter, and therefore, if weighed, would indicate an amount in excess of that which was really present. For this reason it is better to convert the sulphide into nitrate or sulphate, and then to precipitate it as carbonate by boiling with sodium carbonate in excess. After being well washed with hot water, the precipitate is strongly ignited so as to convert it into oxide, and is weighed. 100 parts of zinc oxide equal 80.26 of metallic zinc.

[1] Brit. Med. Journ. 1887.

**Tests.**—A white sulphide is formed in neutral or alkaline solutions in the addition of ammonium sulphide, or of sulphuretted hydrogen, the precipitate is insoluble in a solution of potassium hydrate. A solution of potassium hydrate added to a solution of a salt of zinc produces an opalescent, gelatinous precipitate, which has a tendency to adhere to the sides of the test-tube; it is soluble in excess. The same result is produced by ammonia water, unless free acid or ammonium salts are present, when no precipitate is formed. Potassium ferrocyanide gives a pale gelatinous precipitate, and potassium ferricyanide a fawn-coloured precipitate. Ammonium carbonate gives a white precipitate soluble in excess. If zinc oxide is strongly heated it turns yellow, becoming white again on cooling; when moistened with cobalt nitrate and heated with the blowpipe flame, zinc oxide forms a green pigment—Rinman's green.

The salts of **Cadmium** when swallowed act much the same way as zinc, but more powerfully.

### TIN

Poisoning by the salts of tin is exceptionally rare, and has only resulted from accident, for the most part from the use of tinned meat and fruit. In Belgium and France it has been found that some confectioners put stannous chloride into gingerbread in order to obtain with inferior materials an appearance like that legitimately due to fine flour. In some instances as much as 5 kilogrammes per 200 kilos of bread were present. After making a series of experiments, Pouchet and Riche[1] have recommended legal prohibition of the practice on the ground of its being injurious to health. No fatal case of poisoning by tin has yet been recorded. A case[2] that has more than once been cited as one of fatal poisoning by the chloride, was really one of hydrochloric acid poisoning, and is so stated by the original reporter. Half a tea-cupful of hydrochloric acid, having some tin in solution, was swallowed, and ultimately caused death.

**Symptoms.**—Metallic taste, vomiting and diarrhoea, with pain in the stomach; pain in the head has also been observed. In some cases the poison has depressed the action of the heart; Luff[3] records the cases of four adults who suffered from severe symptoms of poisoning after having eaten some tinned cherries, in all four the pulse was feeble, rapid, and irregular, and the surface was cyanotic. Luff found 1.9 grain of stannic oxide, derived from solder used in the construction of the tins, per ounce of the cherry juice. The doses of tin

[1] *Annales d Hygiène*, 1892.   [2] *Med Times*, 1841.
[3] *Brit. Med. Journ.*, 1890.

malate respectively received by the sufferers were calculated to range from four to ten grains. All the cases recovered. Sedgwick[1] relates how nine persons, after eating pears which had been stewed in a newly tinned pan, were simultaneously attacked with diarrhœa, vomiting, and abdominal pains. The juice of the fruit was found laden with tin salts. Tin is eliminated by the kidneys and bowels.

**Treatment.**—Empty the stomach, and then give demulcents, white of egg, milk, and ice, with opium if necessary.

**Chemical Analysis.**—Organic matter may be destroyed by the moist method and the resulting solution precipitated with $H_2S$. The sulphide may then be ignited and converted into stannic oxide, 100 parts of which equal 78.38 parts of metallic tin.

**Tests.**—With mercuric chloride and a little hydrochloric acid, stannous chloride gives a white precipitate of mercurous chloride, which turns grey and subsequently black (hastened by boiling) from the formation of finely-divided metallic mercury. With gold chloride it gives a purple precipitate. If a little brucine is dissolved in a few drops of strong nitric acid and then diluted with about fifty times its volume of water, boiled, and allowed to cool, a reddish fluid is obtained. A few drops of this added to a solution of a tin salt produces a lilac colour. Stannic salts give a yellow precipitate with $H_2S$, stannous salts a dark brown.

## BISMUTH

Exceptional cases of poisoning by the subnitrate [$BiONO_3, H_2O$] have occurred both from internal and external use.

**Symptoms.**—Salivation, metallic taste, pain in stomach, vomiting and purging, the dejections having a greyish-black colour, and collapse. The gums may be inflamed and even gangrenous; the breath is very foul. A disagreeable garlic-like odour has been observed from prolonged medicinal use of bismuth, which it is stated is due to impurities, in the form of tellurium or arsenic. In toxic doses the usual symptoms of gastro-enteritis occur. Bismuth is eliminated in the fæces, urine, and saliva; like lead much passes directly through the bowels without being absorbed.

**Fatal Dose.**—In one case two drachms caused death in nine days.

**Treatment.**—Evacuate the poison, and then give ice and opium if necessary.

**Post-mortem Appearances.**—Those due to acute gastritis.

**Chemical Analysis.**—Organic matter may be destroyed by the moist method, the bismuth precipitated as sulphide, and afterwards dissolved

---
[1] *The Lancet*, 1888.

in concentrated nitric acid ; the solution of the nitrate thus obtained is evaporated to dryness and the residue is dissolved in water with the aid of a little nitric acid.

**Tests**—Potassium hydrate produces a white precipitate, insoluble in excess, which becomes yellow on boiling. Dilution with water produces a precipitate, which may be distinguished from the precipitate similarly produced with antimony by its insolubility in solution of tartaric acid. Potassium chromate produces a yellow precipitate which is soluble in nitric acid and insoluble in potassium hydrate.

Quantitative analysis may be conducted by diluting the solution of the nitrate and then adding ammonium carbonate and boiling for some time. The precipitate, after ignition, is weighed. 100 parts of the oxide equal 89.65 of metallic bismuth.

### IRON

The salts of iron which come under the observation of the toxicologist are the **sulphate** [$FeSO_4, 7H_2O$], copperas, or green vitriol, and the **chloride** [$Fe_2Cl_6, 6H_2O$] in alcoholic solution known as tincture of iron.

**Symptoms**—Large doses of the sulphate give rise to a metallic taste, pain in the stomach, vomiting, and purging, the dejected matters being black from the formation of ferrous sulphide. The chloride is a more active irritant; in large doses it has been found to act somewhat like hydrochloric acid. Both these salts, but especially the chloride, are not unfrequently administered in poisonous doses for the purpose of procuring abortion; the inefficacy of the proceeding has been already discussed in the section on criminal abortion. Iron is eliminated by the bowels and kidneys.

**Fatal Dose.**—That of the sulphate is unknown. An ounce and a half of the tincture of the chloride has caused death in about five weeks.

**Treatment**—Evacuate the poison, then give demulcents, ice, and, if necessary, opium.

**Post-mortem Appearances**—If death takes place in the early stage there will be the usual signs of gastritis, with probably some special discoloration of the membrane due to the action of the metal. In the fatal case from the chloride above-mentioned, Christison found a thickened, inflamed condition of the stomach towards the pyloric end.

**Chemical Analysis**—Examination of the vomited matter or of the contents of the stomach only is required; on account of the physiological presence of iron, the tissues yield no satisfactory evidence.

Tests.—Potassium sulphocyanide produces a bright red with a ferric salt, no change with ferrous salts. Potassium ferricyanide gives a brown coloration with ferric salts, and a blue precipitate with ferrous salts. Potassium ferrocyanide with ferrous salts produces a whitish precipitate which becomes blue on exposure, with ferric salts a deep blue precipitate of Prussian blue. Potash gives a red brown precipitate with ferric salts, and a whitish precipitate with ferrous salts.

The amount of iron present in vomited matter may be estimated by converting the metal into a ferric salt, if it is not originally in that form, and then precipitating the oxide with ammonia, igniting and weighing. 100 parts of ferric oxide equal 70 parts metallic iron.

## CHROMIUM

The compounds of chromium which are of interest to the toxicologist are chromic acid, potassium dichromate, and lead chromate.

**Chromic Acid [$CrO_3$].**—A case of poisoning from swallowing about ten ounces of a solution of chromic acid, such as is used for charging zinc-carbon batteries, is recorded by Limbeck[1]. The poison was taken for suicidal purposes, and the patient when seen two and a half hours after had violent pain in the abdomen, accompanied by vomiting and purging, which commenced a quarter of an hour after the solution was swallowed; indications of severe collapse were present—cold surface, small frequent pulse, quickened respiration, slight cyanosis visible on the lips and mental depression. The stomach was well washed out with 18 litres of warm water, and yet half an hour after, about a litre of a dark brown viscid mass was vomited which contained much chromic acid; this had evidently passed the pylorus and was regurgitated. The mucous membrane of the mouth was not corroded, but in parts was coloured yellow; the abdomen was distended and tender. The urine was dark brown-red and contained 5 per cent albumen; the dejections from the bowels for the first twenty-four hours were of a peculiar grey-green colour. Chromic acid was found in the vomit, fæces, and urine; in the vomit it was free, and could be separated by simple filtration, but it could not be detected in the fæces and urine until the organic matter was destroyed. The patient recovered in six days.

White[2] records a fatal case from the external use of chromic acid. A young woman suffering from a mass of papillary growths on the external genitals, was treated by a single application to it of about half an ounce of a solution of chromic acid, 100 grains to the ounce; the vagina and the anus were protected by tampons of cotton wool soaked in carbolised oil. Shortly after the patient experienced pain

[1] *Prager med. Wochenschr.*, 1887.   [2] *University Med. Mag.*, 1889.

and thirst, and vomited; in twenty-four hours she was collapsed; the surface was pale, the pulse rapid, and the extremities were cold; she died twenty-seven hours after the application. Post-mortem examination revealed nothing of moment; the kidneys were passively congested, the capsules peeling easily; the stomach showed some fine ecchymoses. Chemical analysis of the kidneys and liver demonstrated the presence of a salt of chromium. Fowler[1] relates how one or two drops of a saturated solution of chromic acid accidentally swallowed during an application to the throat produced violent pain in the epigastrium half an hour after, followed by severe vomiting of a green ropy fluid; the patient was collapsed, the face being pale and anxious. Recovery gradually took place.

**Potassium Dichromate** [$K_2Cr_2O_7$] is used for a variety of trade purposes, such as staining wood, and for dyeing, and in this way is very accessible as a poison.

**Symptoms**.—A bitter acrid taste, followed by burning pain in the stomach, vomiting, purging, intense thirst, and prostration are usually present; the vomited matters and the motions may contain blood; there is a tendency for the respiration to be affected. Stewart[2] records a fatal case in which a woman became unconscious five minutes after swallowing one ounce of potassium dichromate dissolved in water; there was severe vomiting and purging, collapse, small, thin, irregular pulse, slow, irregular, gasping respiration, with intervals amounting to fifteen seconds between the breaths; the heart continued to beat fully one minute and three-quarters after respiration had ceased. In another case recorded by Turnbull,[3] in which recovery took place, the respirations were at one time forty-eight to the minute. In all cases the symptoms of collapse and of acute gastritis are very pronounced. Pander[4] found experimentally that chromium salts produce disturbance of the respiration and of the central nervous system, the heart's action not being directly affected. Parenchymatous nephritis and blood changes occur in chronic cases. Chromium is eliminated chiefly by the bowels; to a lesser extent by the kidneys.

In the manufacture of potassium dichromate the workmen are liable to suffer from sores on the body, which have an indurated, cup-like border, and strongly resemble hard chancres. Destruction of the cartilage of the nose is not uncommon, the septum being perforated at the lower part.

**Fatal Dose**.—Two drachms have caused death in four hours. Recovery ensued after a dose estimated at 273 grains.

**Treatment**.—Stomach-pump, or emetic, followed by magnesium

[1] *Brit Med Journ*, 1889.     [2] *Brit Med Journ*, 1888.
[3] *The Lancet*, 1892.     [4] *Beitrage zur Chromwirkung*, 1887.

carbonate or chalk, suspended in water or milk. Opium and the usual treatment for excessive vomiting and collapse will probably be required.

Post-mortem Appearances.—When death quickly follows the reception of the poison the mucous membrane of the stomach has been found superficially eroded in parts, and presenting the usual appearances of acute inflammation. In addition, it has been observed to be stained a deep olive-green, due to the presence of oxide of chromium; greenstained mucus has been found in the stomach. Externally, yellow stains may be present on the lips and the corners of the mouth. Ruttan and Lafleur[1] found the blood chocolate-coloured, and obtained from it the spectrum of methæmogoblin.

**Lead Chromate** [$PbCrO_4$] is used as a pigment under the name of chrome yellow.

The symptoms produced by this poison are a complex of those due to chromic acid and those due to lead. Although the salt is insoluble in water, when swallowed in large quantities it may produce symptoms like those of potassium dichromate. It is not nearly so actively poisonous as the dichromate, but it gives rise to after-effects due to the lead, which render it a very dangerous preparation. Most of the recorded cases resulted from the use in confectionery of lead chromate as a pigment, or from inhalation of the salt in the process of its manufacture. Stewart[2] gives a clinical analysis of 64 cases of poisoning by chrome yellow, which had been used to colour cakes; the doses were small, but were repeated; the symptoms were those due to lead. In larger doses death has resulted after a period of drowsiness and apathy.

Chemical Analysis.—After being liberated from organic matter by the moist method, the solution of chloride, with the addition of a little sulphuric acid, is boiled for some time with alcohol until it turns a green colour. The alcohol is then driven off, and ammonia is added in excess; the liquid is again boiled for some time, after which the precipitate of chromic oxide is filtered off, dried, and ignited—100 parts equal 68.62 of chromium.

Tests.—The soluble salts of chromic acid in acid solution are changed to green by sulphuretted hydrogen. Barium chloride gives a yellow precipitate soluble in hydrochloric acid. Silver nitrate gives a crimson precipitate soluble both in ammonia and nitric acid. Lead acetate gives a yellow precipitate soluble in potassium hydrate, and with difficulty in nitric acid. Lead chromate digested with dilute sulphuric acid yields a precipitate of lead sulphate, chromic acid remaining in solution. If the solution is filtered, and to the filtrate a little hydro-

[1] *Montreal Med. Journ.*, 1888.     [2] *Medical News*, 1887.

chloric acid is added, and then sulphuretted hydrogen is passed through it, the colour after a time changes from red to green; the precipitate of lead sulphate may be reduced with the blow-pipe to the metallic state and subsequently tested.

## CHAPTER XXVIII.

### NON-METALLIC ELEMENTS.

#### PHOSPHORUS.

THE toxic properties of phosphorus are chiefly utilised as a means of committing suicide, to this end some kind of vermin-killer or rat-paste containing phosphorus is swallowed. These pastes consist of fatty matter, amongst which finely-divided phosphorus is distributed to the extent of about 3 or 4 per cent. mixed with flour, sugar, and usually some pigment; a small-sized pot will contain 4 to 6 grains of phosphorus. In default of the paste, the heads of a number of matches are sometimes detached, mixed with water, and swallowed; children are occasionally accidentally poisoned by sucking off and swallowing the heads of matches. Only the matches made with yellow phosphorus are poisonous; "safety-matches" which solely ignite on surfaces of red amorphous phosphorus are inert. Phosphorus poisoning is much more common in women than in men.

When phosphorus is swallowed, especially when the poison is in a finely-divided state (in which it invariably exists in the combinations used for suicidal purposes), it is capable of being taken into the system as such, without previously undergoing oxidation.

#### Acute Phosphorus Poisoning.

**Symptoms.**—After a poisonous dose of phosphorus is swallowed, pain in the stomach, followed by vomiting, comes on in from a few minutes to twelve or twenty-four hours. In exceptional cases the symptoms have first appeared at a still more remote period, not even until the second or third day; usually they occur in from two to five hours. In a dark place the matters first vomited and the patient's breath often appear luminous. A phosphorus- or garlic-like odour may be perceived in the breath both by the bystanders and by the patient himself, after the stomach has been well emptied, the subsequent vomited matter will not be phosphorescent although the odour may for a time persist. Intense thirst, eructations, and a burning sensation in the throat and stomach are experienced. Diarrhœa is more frequently absent than present; it occurs in about 25 or 30 per cent of cases. In *rapidly fatal cases* the collapse which accompanies these symptoms increases; the vomiting continues, the rejected matter probably contains blood, the abdomen is distended and is exceedingly tender, the patient is anxious, restless, and exhausted, and death takes place in eight or ten hours. Delirium and convulsions may precede death.

Such, however, *is not the usual course* of acute phosphorus poisoning; *in most cases the primary symptoms diminish* in intensity, sometimes so much so as to convey an impression to the inexperienced observer that the danger is past. This stage of partial passivity may last for two or three days or even longer, the patient appearing to have little the matter with him; or he may continue to have occasional attacks of vomiting, a distended, tender abdomen, and a quick feeble pulse. The diarrhœa, if present in the initial stage, ceases and gives place to pronounced constipation. The tongue is coated and the thirst continues. In exceptional instances two, or even three weeks have elapsed before the appearance of the secondary symptoms. West[1] records a case in which after a piece of phosphorus-paste the size of a walnut was swallowed there were no symptoms for six weeks; the patient then commenced to be ill and died in six days.

The commencement of the **secondary symptoms** is often indicated by yellow discoloration of the sclera, the skin usually participating in the icteric hue which may spread over the whole body; pain is felt in the epigastric region, and on examination the liver is generally found enlarged, sometimes the spleen is also enlarged. The abdomen becomes greatly distended and tympanitic, vomiting returns, and the bowels are more or less relaxed, both the vomit and the motions containing much blood. A general hæmorrhagic tendency is evinced by bleeding from the nose, and in women from the vagina, and by the formation of purpuric spots and ecchymoses under the skin and mucous surfaces. The urine becomes high coloured and scanty; it has a strong acid reaction, and frequently contains bile-pigments, albumen, and blood-colouring matter. The pulse is quickened—80 to 100 per minute—the temperature varies, but usually is not much above the normal. Pain in the head, restlessness, and sleeplessness occur, together with affections of the special senses—as singing in the ears, deafness, and impaired vision. In some instances formication and

[1] *The Lancet*, 1893.

cramps have been observed. Bollinger [1] relates a case in which a girl died in four and a half days after swallowing the heads of some lucifer matches; paresis of the extremities occurred on the third day, and on the fourth the feet were completely paralysed. On section the spinal meninges, especially at the nerve-roots in the dorsal and lumbar regions, were infiltrated with blood. In fatal cases the condition of the patient rapidly becomes worse: the pulse is irregular, and a state of stupor or coma supervenes, which is soon followed by death. The mind may remain clear until nearly the last, or there may be acute delirium, with or without convulsions. The temperature sometimes sinks considerably towards the end; in other cases it rises, and has been known to continue to rise for a short time after death. Exceptionally a diminution in the size of the liver has been noticed during the last days of life. In a few cases recovery has taken place after the occurrence of enlargement of the liver and jaundice; the liver gradually acquiring its normal size, and the skin its colour.

Fatal Dose.—The smallest fatal dose was probably 1½ grains. Recovery has taken place after 4 to 6 grains, swallowed in the form of rat-paste. Death has occurred in twelve hours, and even earlier; more frequently it is delayed until the second to the fourth day; in the greater number of cases it takes place within a week, although life has been prolonged for over twice that period.

Treatment.—Evacuate the contents of the stomach with the stomach pump, or give doses of two or three grains of copper sulphate dissolved in water. The copper salt acts as an emetic; it is also reduced by the particles of phosphorus, upon which the metallic copper is precipitated, and thus tends to render them inert. Half drachm doses of old, unrectified turpentine, especially the French variety, is recommended as an antidote, but it is difficult to obtain. If, as is supposed by some, the efficacy of the turpentine depends on its containing oxygen in the form of ozone, it is probable that "Sanitas," which consists of artificially oxidised turpentine, containing hydrogen peroxide, might be equally or even more efficacious. It has been recently recommended, in cases of acute phosphorus poisoning, to wash out the stomach with a 0·1 per cent. aqueous solution of potassium permanganate. Purgatives should afterwards be given, and then ice, demulcents, and morphine. The fæces voided a week or longer after the poison was taken have been observed to be luminous, showing that it was present in an active form; repeated evacuation of the bowels, therefore, should be procured, but not with castor oil. No oily, nor fatty matter should be given, as such substances are solvents of phosphorus, and would promote absorption.

[1] *Deutsch. Arch. f. klin. Med.*, 1869.

**Post-mortem Appearances.**—The cavities of the body, when opened, may yield the odour of phosphorus, and in some cases phosphorescence has been observed. The œsophagus is not usually inflamed. The mucous membrane of the stomach is yellowish or greyish-white, it it is infiltrated, and the epithelium is cloudy and swollen, limited erosions and ecchymoses may be present. The epithelial cells of the gastric glands show more or less advanced fatty degeneration; they are at first filled with fine granular matter, later on fat globules appear. Similar changes may be found in the duodenum, which, as well as the stomach, may contain blood-stained fluid. The intestines frequently show no changes other than small ecchymoses, in some instances they have been found inflamed. The heart and the kidneys show signs of fatty degeneration. The spleen is usually enlarged. Elkins and Middlemass[1] found fatty changes in the nerve cells of the cerebral cortex.

The most marked appearance is that presented by the liver, in the greater number of cases the organ is considerably enlarged, but it may be unaltered in size, and has been found contracted. It is of a doughy consistence, easily torn, varying in colour from a bright to a dirty pale-yellow; the entire surface may be uniformly tinged, or it may present a marbled appearance—the normal hue of the liver being preserved in parts; this is more especially observable on making a section of the organ. Small hæmorrhagic spots are often present on the surface, and in the substance of the liver. Microscopical examination shows that the abnormal appearance is due to the presence of a large amount of fat. It was formerly disputed as to whether the fat resulted from degeneration of the liver cells, or simply from infiltration; recent investigations have shown that it is the result of metamorphosis of the tissues it replaces. Nathanson[2] extracted the fat out of the hardened pieces of liver by boiling them in ether. In the normal liver no change was produced; in fatty infiltration the fat was removed, leaving the liver cells intact; in phosphorus-liver the tissue was dissolved out by the ether, and consequently the liver structure was obliterated. Endeavours have been made to trace the steps of fat formation by ascertaining the amount of lecithin in the phosphorus-liver, and comparing it with that present in the normal liver. Stolnikow[3] found that phosphorus causes an increase in nuclein, which leads to excess of lecithin, from which the phosphorus is split and the fat formed. Leo[4] found no increase. Hefter[5] found a distinct diminution in lecithin, averaging nearly 50 per cent., the greater the amount

[1] *Brit. Med. Journ.*, 1891.   [2] *Dissert*, 1890.
[3] *Arch. f. Anat. u. Phys.*, 1887.   [4] *Zeitschr. f. physiol. Chemie*, 1885.
[5] *Arch. f. exper. Pathol.*, 1891.

of fat in the liver, the less the amount of lecithin. He believes it unlikely that phosphorus causes fatty degeneration of albuminoid substances, with the formation of lecithin as an intermediate product; more probably the store of lecithin already formed in the liver cells undergoes chemical change. The processes by which the liver changes are produced are still undetermined; by some they are referred to the direct action of the phosphorus on the cells, and by others to morbid processes set up in the parenchyma. The jaundice probably results from blocking of the primary gall ducts by tumefied epithelium.

The resemblance between acute phosphorus poisoning and acute yellow atrophy of the liver has long been observed. Recent pathological investigations tend to support the view that the relation is an intimate one, if the two diseases are not actually one and the same. Against this view is the usually found hypertrophic condition of the phosphorus-liver with well-marked acini; in acute yellow atrophy the liver is small, and all indications of acini have disappeared. It has been asserted that the morbid anatomy of the acute atrophic liver is characterised by inflammation of the intralobular connective tissue, with molecular degeneration of the liver-cells; that of the phosphorus-liver by simple fatty infiltration of the liver-cells. The difference seems to be one of degree. Wyss[1] treated some sections of phosphorus-liver with turpentine, to remove the fat, and found in some parts that the liver-cells were sharply defined, while in others they had entirely disappeared. In acute atrophy the morbid processes in the liver appear to progress more quickly than in phosphorus poisoning; when the phosphorus-liver has had time to undergo advanced changes, it cannot be distinguished from the acute atrophic liver. Heffter states that in chemical composition the two livers are identical. In exceptional instances Reiss found proliferation of cells of the interstitial tissue as in acute atrophy. Hessler[2] states that out of sixty-four cases of phosphorus poisoning, in thirteen the liver was small, as in acute atrophy. The question is not yet determined; but the analogies between acute atrophy and phosphorus poisoning render it probable that the underlying pathological conditions are the same.

The investigations of Silbermann,[3] Badt,[4] and others show that in cases of acute phosphorus poisoning the blood corpuscles acquire a tendency to agglutinate together, and thus to give rise to numerous thromboses of the capillary vessels. Jaksch[5] states that the alkalescence of the blood is diminished, and the number of red corpuscles increased. The localised hæmorrhages, so universal in phosphorus

[1] Virchow's *Arch.*, 1865.  [2] *Vierteljahrsschr. f. ger. Med.*, Bd. 36.
[3] Virchow's *Arch.*, 1889.  [4] *Stoffwechsel bei Phosphorvergiftung* (Diss.), 1891.
[5] *Deutsch. med. Wochenschr.*, 1893.

poisoning, are probably due to fatty degeneration of the vascular walls, together with the formation of thrombi within the lumena of the smaller vessels.

Acute phosphorus poisoning gives rise to certain well-marked alterations in metabolism, the characteristic features of which are—diminished oxidation of tissues and consequent alteration in the chemical constitution of the excretory products, together with increased splitting-up of the albuminoids attributable to diminished supply of oxygen to the tissues. In many cases of acute phosphorus poisoning the daily excretion of urea has been found to be below the normal, some of the nitrogen thus wanting being represented by an increased percentage in the form of intermediate products, especially ammonia, tyrosin, leucin, albumen, peptones, and some nitrogenous aromatic acids may also be present. The total amount of nitrogen excreted daily in many instances has been found not to be much below the normal until shortly before death; some observers state that the total nitrogen is diminished. Ammonia has been found in the urine in excess proportional to the absence of urea. Engelen[1] in experiments on animals found only a slight increase. Starling and Hopkins[2] found a large increase in a fatal case of acute phosphorus poisoning, the N represented by the ammonia in the urine being to that represented by urea as 1 to 7, the normal proportion being 1 to 70. Badt in one case found double the normal amount, in a second case 25.8 per cent.—more than one-fourth of the total N present in the urine. Munzer[3] found that the urea-N was diminished from 70 to 80 per cent., the ammonia-N being increased from 10 to 18 per cent.; he attributes the increase of NH in the urine to its combination with acid products, such as sarcolactic acid, developed in excess by imperfect metabolism. Tyrosin has only occasionally been met with, and leucin still more rarely. Poore[4] investigated a case in which a large quantity of phosphorus (8 to 10 grains) in the form of rat-paste was taken, jaundice set in on the third day and the patient died on the fifth day. In some urine obtained during the last hours of life a small amount of tyrosin, but no leucin, was found. Riess[5] found tyrosin in six out of thirty-six cases. A few other observers have recorded instances in which tyrosin was present. Leucin has been found by Ossikowski,[6] Blenderman,[7] Rothammer[8] (along with tyrosin), and three or four others. It is to be noted that in several of these cases, the urine in which tyrosin and leucin were found, was voided immediately before death. Albumen

[1] *Dissert*, 1888
[2] *Guy's Hosp. Reps.*, 1890.
[3] *Centralbl. f. klin. Med.*, 1892
[4] *The Lancet*, 1888
[5] *Real Encyclopaedie*, 1888
[6] *Wiener med. Wochenschr.*, 1881
[7] *Zeitsch. f. physiol. Chemie*, 1882
[8] *Dissert*, 1890

is commonly present but not in large amount. Peptones, or substances giving the same reaction, and aromatic acids, such as oxymandelic acid have been found in the urine by one or two observers. Free fat has also been met with.

Defective metabolism is further shown by the presence of non-nitrogenous abnormal bodies in the urine. Sarcolactic acid has been frequently found. Riess found it in twenty-six out of twenty-seven cases. Poore found it in the case previously mentioned. Under normal conditions sarcolactic acid is excreted as carbon dioxide and water, its presence in the urine therefore is very significant of imperfect oxidation. Sugar has been found in the urine in a few cases, in the one recorded by Poore it was present. In Bollinger's case a small quantity was present. Grose[1] found it on the third and fourth day in a child three and a half years old who was fatally poisoned with rat-paste.

In experiments on animals Bauu[2] found that the intake of oxygen and the output of carbon dioxide are both considerably diminished, this, taken in conjunction with the increased splitting up of the albuminoids, to a great extent accounts for the accumulation of fat in the various tissues—the non-nitrogenous bodies, such as fats, which result from splitting up of the albumen, are retained in the system instead of being burnt up into $CO_2$ and $H_2O$. The mode in which phosphorus produces these pronounced alterations in tissue metamorphosis is not known. Typical effects have followed such small doses that it is impossible to refer them to chemical processes directly due to the reducing properties of phosphorus. Whether its presence in the organism determines the change in tissue metamorphosis somewhat after the mode in which a ferment acts, or in some other way damages the physiological properties of cell protoplasm remains an open question.

Large doses of phosphorus, of which some has undoubtedly been absorbed, do not invariably produce the chain of symptoms described. Stevenson[3] records the case of a woman aged twenty-two who swallowed nearly half an ounce of rat-paste. The vomited matters and the breath were luminous, and gave off the odour of phosphorus; the abdomen was distended and tender; severe collapse occurred, but there was no jaundice; the woman completely recovered in five or six days. I recently saw a case under the care of my colleague, Dr. Edge, in which more than half an ounce of rat-paste was swallowed by a woman, who subsequently vomited large quantities of blood, the abdomen was very tympanitic and tender, and remained so for weeks, with recurrent hæmatemesis. The urine first passed after the poison was taken smelt strongly of phosphorus, and showed its presence by

---

[1] *The Lancet*, 1889.   [2] *Zeitsch. f. Biologie*, vii u xiv.
[3] *The Lancet*, 1880.

Mitscherlich's test, demonstrating that some of the phosphorus had been absorbed. There was never the least sign of jaundice, nor of any of the symptoms due to changes in metabolism.

## Chronic Phosphorus Poisoning

Ordinary yellow phosphorus is largely used in the preparation of lucifer matches, the manufacture of which formerly gave rise to numerous cases of chronic poisoning. The partial employment of red phosphorus has done something to abolish the evils which existed in the older match-manufactories, but improved hygienic surroundings and greater precautions have done much more to render the occurrence of chronic phosphorus poisoning less frequent.

Chronic phosphorus poisoning is caused by frequent inhalation of the fumes of phosphorus, the special pathological condition produced being necrosis of the bones of the upper and lower jaw, especially of the latter. Phosphorus vapour acts locally on bone tissue wherever the periosteum is exposed; as long as it is covered with mucous membrane it possesses complete immunity. The usual path by which the vapour finds its way to the bone is that afforded by a decayed tooth, or in an interspace where a tooth is absent. The surrounding gum inflames, swells, and separates from the alveolar process, the teeth loosen, and either fall out or have to be removed on account of the pain. The bone is first attacked with periostitis; this leads to necrosis, which in severe cases spreads far beyond the spot originally attacked. The general health suffers, partly from the action of the phosphorus on the system at large, and partly from disordered digestion resulting from imperfect mastication, and from swallowing pus derived from the diseased jaw. Bronchial catarrh and constipation have been observed to precede the bone necrosis.

The treatment of the bone disease is surgical. As preventives, free ventilation and the employment only of workmen with sound teeth, together with periodic examination of their mouths, are necessary.

**Chemical Analysis.**—Vomited matters, and the contents of the stomach obtained post mortem, should be examined in the dark for luminous particles; if much phosphorus is present the whole mass will give off phosphorescent vapour. By daylight the substance should be searched for particles of Prussian blue, or other pigments with which the phosphorus may have been mixed. The odour of phosphorus is perceptible when present in small amount only, provided it is not overpowered by the odour of other volatile bodies.

**Tests.**—The most delicate test for phosphorus when in organic admixture is afforded by distillation in the dark; this method, known as Mitscherlich's test, is carried out as follows:—The suspected substance if alkaline is acidulated with a few drops of sulphuric acid, and if necessary mixed with sufficient water as to be of a fluid consistence; it is then put into a flask furnished with a condenser, the free end of which dips into a receiver containing some solution of silver nitrate; the condenser is enclosed in a box, the interior of which is painted dead black, and two eye-holes are provided so that the tube may be observed in perfect darkness. Heat is applied to the flask, and if phosphorus is present, even only in minute quantity, the inner tube of the condenser becomes partially or wholly luminous. Certain substances, of which those most likely to be encountered are turpentine (given as an antidote), alcohol, ammonia, ether, and sulphuretted hydrogen prevent the development of luminosity. A small amount of phenol diminishes the delicacy of the test. The solution of silver nitrate is blackened by reduction of the silver to the metallic state, and it contains phosphoric acid. Another test is that known as **Dussart-Blondlot's**:—Hydrogen is passed through a flask containing the suspected substance, when, if phosphorus is present, some of it combines with the hydrogen, forming phosphuretted hydrogen, which burns with a characteristic flame. The apparatus specially constructed for the purpose enables two flames to be placed side by side for comparative observation—one derived from ignition of the hydrogen before it has passed through the flask containing the suspected substance, and the other after it has done so; both jets must be of platinum, as those made of glass tubing (on account of the soda that is present) do not yield sufficiently non-luminous flames. The flame of phosphuretted hydrogen has a green tint in the centre, most marked when it plays on a cool surface. Examined with the spectroscope it gives three lines in the green—one at the E line, another between E and F, and the third between D and E; there are other lines present when the flame is viewed under the most favourable circumstances, but those enumerated are sufficiently distinctive. Hypophosphites give the same results. A third test, known as **Scherer's**, is founded on the reducing power of phosphorus, by which filter paper moistened with a solution of silver nitrate is blackened if exposed to the action of phosphorus, or of phosphorous oxide vapour. One way of making the experiment is to place some of the suspected substance in a flask along with some powdered lead acetate in order to combine with and fix any sulphuretted hydrogen that may be present; a little ether is added, and the whole is well shaken up, after which a slip of paper moistened with silver nitrate solution is suspended above the ether by attaching it to the cork with which the flask is secured, and the flask is then placed in a dark place to avoid the actinic effects of light. In from a few minutes to an hour the paper will be blackened, and will acquire a lustre from deposition of metallic silver.

Although in the dead body it is advisable to make the examination for phosphorus as early as possible, positive results may be obtained at long intervals after death. In a case that had been poisoned with phosphorus, Hofmann[1] found the head of a match in the intestines five months after death, and, with Mitscherlich's test, obtained satisfactory evidence from it of the presence of phosphorus. Pelletan,[2] by both Mitscherlich's and Dussart-Blondlot's methods demonstrated the presence of phosphorus in an exhumed body twelve months after death, and in another case thirteen months after death. When dealing with exhumed bodies an objection may be raised that sufficient phosphorus might be yielded by the putrefying tissues to afford indications of its presence with the above described tests; from experiments that have been made this has been found to be impossible, and therefore when the reactions are obtained they must be due to phosphorus derived from an extraneous source.

## IODINE

The colour and smell of iodine prevent its being used for criminal poisoning, and its exceptional presence in the household in any but small quantities—usually in the form of tincture—accounts for the rarity with which it is resorted to as a means of committing suicide. It is strongly irritant, and if swallowed in the solid form may produce corrosion.

**Symptoms** produced by swallowing large doses of the tincture.— Burning pain in the mouth and throat, and shortly after in the stomach, followed by salivation, vomiting, and diarrhœa. The vomited matters afford evidence of the presence of iodine; if the stomach contained starchy food at the time the poison was swallowed, the vomit will be blue; if not, or if the iodine is in excess, the colour will be yellowish or brown. Blood has been found in both the vomit and the motions. The lips and possibly the corners of the mouth and the chin, may be stained yellow, the mucous membrane of the tongue and mouth being whitish; the pulse is small, the surface cold, and the usual symptoms of collapse are present.

Injection of strong solutions of iodine into the cavities of the body for therapeutic purposes has produced the more essential of the above-named symptoms—vomiting, with the presence of iodine in the rejected matter, thin pulse, cold, pallid surface, salivation, and dyspnœa from tumefaction of the mucous membrane of the larynx. All the mucous

[1] *Lehrbuch der ger. Med.*, 1887.  [2] *Gyógyászat*, Budapest, 1889.

surfaces and the eyelids are swollen, and the skin is not unfrequently covered with an eruption. There is a tendency to heart-paralysis, which sometimes occurs a day or more after the acute symptoms have subsided. Formerly many deaths occurred from the treatment of ovarian tumours, chronic abscesses, and empyæma by the injection of solutions of iodine; the proceeding is not without considerable risk when the iodine is exposed to a large absorptive surface.

Iodine is freely eliminated by the kidneys. Huber[1] found 0 278 gramme of iodine in 300 cc. of urine, obtained from a woman who swallowed about four grammes of the tincture. It is also eliminated in the saliva, milk, and in the secretions of mucous membranes.

**Fatal Dose**—Not precisely known, as the tincture which has usually been taken is of no definite strength. One drachm of the tincture has caused death, and recovery has taken place after one ounce, calculated to contain half a drachm of solid iodine. Only eight or nine fatal cases are recorded. Death has occurred in twenty-four hours.

**Iodoform**—The use of iodoform in dressing wounds, and its injection in solution into chronic abscesses, have caused death; grave symptoms followed by recovery not unfrequently occur. A variety of symptoms have been observed—as elevation of temperature, rapid pulse, gastro-intestinal irritation, skin-eruptions, cerebral disturbance, with delirium or coma. Iodoform is most likely to produce dangerous effects when injected in the form of ethereal solution. Gaillard[2] records a case in which the injection into an abscess of about eighty grains, dissolved in ether, produced cessation of breathing and apparent death; artificial respiration was resorted to, and the patient recovered. Barois[3] records a case in which the patient died in a comatose condition on the ninth day after injection of an ethereal solution containing forty-five grains of iodoform. Death has resulted from the free use of iodoform to dress open wounds, such as those produced by amputation of the breast or of the leg. Czerny[4] relates the case of a woman, aged fifty-eight, in whom the wound produced by removal of a breast and the axillary glands was dressed with a drachm and a half of iodoform; three days later symptoms resembling those of meningitis set in, decubitus followed, and death occurred on the twenty-third day.

**Potassium Iodide**, when administered medicinally, occasionally produces a number of toxic symptoms, which are of therapeutical rather than toxicological interest; iodism, with its accompanying skin eruptions and glandular affections, is a well recognised condition, but as it results from medicinal treatment, and is rarely fatal, medico-legal

[1] *Zeitschr. f. klin. Med.*, 1888.
[2] *Bull. de Chirurg.*, 1889.   [3] *Arch. de Med. et de Pharm. Milit.*, 1890.
[4] *Wiener med. Wochenschr.*, 1882.

investigation is not required. Death is stated to have occurred in one or two instances from the use of potassium iodide. Wolf[1] records the case of a woman who took four six-grain doses, at intervals of four hours, which produced swelling of the face and a pemphygoid eruption, involving the mucous membrane of the nose, mouth, throat, and larynx; on the fourth day diarrhœa with blood-stained stools occurred, the woman dying on the eighth day.

Treatment.—Acute poisoning by free iodine demands evacuation of the stomach with tube, or emetic, followed by farinaceous mixtures as starch, arrowroot, flour, and the like, which have been cooked so as to rupture the starch-granules. Morphine and stimulants may be required.

Post-mortem Appearances.—Not well known. Yellow staining and softening of the mucous membrane of the mouth, œsophagus, and stomach have been observed; a kind of exudation product, resembling false membrane, has been found in the larynx. Gastritis may be present, and the inflammation may advance as far as the duodenum.

Chemical Analysis—Tests.—If free iodine is present with organic matter, some of it may be extracted by shaking with carbon bisulphide, which acquires a rose, or violet red colour, in accordance with the amount of iodine taken up. If the iodine is in simple combination, it may be liberated by nitric acid, and then extracted as above. If in combination in organic admixture, potassium hydrate should be added, and, after desiccation, the organic matter should be destroyed by heat; when cold the iodide is dissolved out in alcohol, evaporated to dryness, and treated with sulphuric acid, so as to set free the iodine, which is recognised by its reaction with starch.

## BROMINE.

Only three fatal cases of poisoning by bromine in the liquid state are recorded. In one reported by Snell,[2] a man swallowed one ounce of bromine on an empty stomach; half an hour after he was found suffering from intense burning pain and eructations; there was neither vomiting, purging, nor thirst, but the patient experienced a frequent desire to evacuate the bowels. In two and a half hours symptoms of collapse occurred, and death took place seven and a half hours after the poison was swallowed. On section, the mucous membrane of the œsophagus was inflamed, the external surface of the stomach was much injected, and displayed several ecchymosed spots; internally its surface appeared like tanned leather, hard, and black in colour, and

[1] *Berliner Klin. Wochenschr.*, 1886.   [2] *New York Journ. of Med.*, 1850.

could easily be peeled off, the duodenum presented the same appearance, the mucous membrane between the valvulæ conniventes was softened, the peritoneum and omentum were stained a reddish-yellow. In a case reported by Schmalfuss,[1] the dead body of a man was found, the lips and tongue being dry, hard, and dark-brown in colour. On opening the abdomen the odour of bromine was perceived; the posterior wall of the stomach was altogether wanting, a portion of its anterior wall, which was grey-green in colour, being all that remained, the appearance was as though it had been burnt, a similar condition existing in the duodenum. About fifty grammes of a yellowish substance were found free in the abdominal cavity. The intestines, liver, and spleen were softened; some of the contents of the cæcum yielded bromine by simple distillation. The quantity swallowed was about ninety grammes. A third case is recorded by Herwig.[2] A girl, aged ten, was given by a quack a mixture containing potassium bromide, to be taken with chlorine-water. In four hours after the third dose collapse set in, followed by death in twelve hours; at the necropsy hæmorrhagic inflammation of the stomach was found. It was afterwards ascertained that each dose of the mixture, on the addition of chlorine, yielded 0.44 gramme of free bromine.

When inhaled the dense fumes given off by bromine are very irritating to the respiratory mucous membrane. Duffield[3] relates the case of a laboratory assistant who accidentally inhaled the fumes from about three pounds of bromine, which produced spasm of the glottis and impending death from asphyxia; by the use of steam to the throat the spasm was relaxed, and the man recovered. Kornfeld[4] relates a case in which a child, aged one year and three quarters, inhaled bromine vapour, and died from respiratory and gastric disturbances on the sixth day; after death the skin of the face and neck, where the vapour came in contact with it, was parchment-like; bromine was detected in the skin and the clothing.

**Potassium Bromide.**—The evil effects of prolonged treatment with potassium bromide are not unfrequently seen, but death resulting from its use is rare. Eigner[5] records the case of a woman who suffered from epilepsy, for which she took potassium bromide in increasing doses until they amounted to two teaspoonfuls daily, which was continued for several weeks. She became salivated, with fœtor of the breath, and inflammation of the gums; delirium supervened, and she died in five days.

**Treatment.**—In the exceptional cases in which bromine is swallowed,

[1] *Vierteljahrsschr. f. ger. Med.* (Supplement), 1889.
[2] *Zeitschr. f. Medicinalbeamte*, 1889.  [3] *American Journ. Pharm.*, 1867.
[4] *Friedreich's Blätter f. ger. Med.*, 1883.  [5] *Wiener med. Presse*, 1883.

treatment would probably be of little avail; after evacuation of the contents of the stomach, albumen or starch might be given. Poisoning with the vapour is best treated with steam inhalations.

**Chemical Analysis.**—Uncombined bromine may be separated from organic admixture by distillation; if it is in combination, it may be set free by saturating the solution with potassium dichromate, and acidulating with dilute sulphuric acid before distilling. Solid masses of organic matter may be pulpified, mixed with a saturated solution of potassium hydrate, evaporated to dryness, and the organic matter burnt off: the residue is treated with potassium dichromate and sulphuric acid, and distilled.

**Tests.**—Bromine may be recognised by its smell, by colouring starch-paste yellow, and by giving a yellowish-white precipitate with silver nitrate. A solution of bromine in water, added to a solution of phenol, gives a white precipitate of tri-bromophenol.

## CHLORINE

Fatal poisoning by chlorine is rare, the opportunities for its occurrence being limited to chemical works and bleach-works. In the latter a form of chronic poisoning is met with, in which the patient acquires an anæmic or chlorotic look, loses flesh, and suffers from dyspeptic troubles associated with gastric catarrh; the sense of smell is blunted, and the bronchial mucous membrane may be affected.

The following fatal case of acute chlorine poisoning is recorded by Sury-Bienz[1]. A man, aged forty-eight, who worked in a chemical manufactory, accidentally took one or two breaths of pure chlorine: he at once experienced irritating cough, dyspnœa, and stabbing pain in the breast. On the following day the cough persisted and the dyspnœa was urgent, but there was very little expectoration; the respirations were accelerated to 48, and the pulse retarded to 48 per minute. There was no albumen in the urine. The breathing became worse, the expirations being very short, and the patient died in less than forty-eight hours. On section the lungs were found to be emphysematous and œdematous: they were not consolidated, but the air-passages contained a reddish, frothy fluid; the epiglottis was pale and free from tumefaction, as was also the mucous membrane of the larynx; that of the trachea and bronchi was diffusely reddened; no fatty changes were observable in the heart and other organs. Death appeared to be due to heart-paralysis, which is in accord with the results of physiological experiments. Cameron[2] relates the case of a man who was

[1] *Vierteljahrsschr. f. ger. Med.*, 1888.
[2] *Dublin Quarterly Journ. of Med. Sc.*, 1870.

found dead in the forecastle of a vessel in which chlorine had accumulated from some casks containing chlorinated lime, the appearances were those of death from asphyxia, the odour of chlorine was perceived in the ventricles of the brain

**Bleaching Fluid**, which consists of a solution of potassium, or sodium hypochlorite, with free chlorine, has been used for suicidal and homicidal purposes. The symptoms and post-mortem appearances are more marked in the digestive tract than is the case in poisoning with gaseous chlorine, gastro-enteritis is produced along with the respiratory symptoms just described. Between three and four drachms caused the death of an infant, recovery has followed twenty ounces.

**Treatment.**—The dyspnœa caused by the inhalation of chlorine is best relieved by steam inhalations. Dilute sulphuretted hydrogen has been recommended on the ground that chlorine combines with the hydrogen causing separation of the sulphur, but it is of doubtful value, the only benefit that could accrue would be the removal of any free chlorine in the air-passages—which is accomplished by fresh air, sulphuretted hydrogen could not undo the damage sustained by the mucous membrane, though it might increase it. Poisoning with bleaching fluid should be treated by evacuation of the stomach, by demulcents, and morphine.

## BORON

**Boracic Acid** [$B(OH)_3$], or boric acid, is used surgically as an antiseptic, and commercially as a preservative of milk and other articles of food, it has very little taste, hence its use as a food preservative. When experimentally administered to animals, boracic acid produces prostration, feebleness of the pulse, and diminution of the respiratory activity, parenchymatous nephritis, cloudy swelling with fatty degeneration of the epithelium, and hæmorrhages under the capsule of the kidney have been observed.

Fatal poisoning has followed the injection of solutions of boracic acid into natural and into abscess-cavities of the body. Molodenkow[1] relates two such cases. In one a 5 per cent solution was injected into the pleural sac on account of an empyæma, vomiting occurred and the pulse was small and weak, the following day erythema appeared on the face and spread over the body, on the third day the patient died. The second case was that of a boy who half an hour after having an abscess-cavity washed out with a boracic solution began to vomit and to be collapsed, erythema and hiccup occurred on the second day when he died. The necropsy yielded negative results, except that there were a few ecchymoses on the inner surface of the pericardium, death was due to

[1] *Petersburg med Wochenschr.*, 1881.

heart-paralysis. Three fatal cases from washing out the stomach with a solution of boric acid are recorded by Hogner.[1] The symptoms produced were:—General depression, erysipelatous eruption on face and purpuric spots on the body, elevated temperature, vomiting, diarrhœa, frequent desire to urinate, blood in the urine, stupor, and death, in one case on the third day. Welch[2] records a case of poisoning from the use of a vaginal tampon of boric acid.—Formication of hands and feet, swelling of the skin of the face, hands, and feet, with pronounced depression of the nervous system, dysuria, prostration, and collapse ensued. Recovery took place, the skin undergoing general desquamation. The affection of the skin is one of the most constant of the signs of boric poisoning. Lemoine[3] reports four non-fatal cases from surgical practice.—Erythema and urticaria were present in all; among the other symptoms were vomiting, delirium, hallucinations, and in one case diplopia.

As a food preservative boric acid is usually employed in combination, in the form of borax. Although it may be difficult to trace any ill-effects to the swallowing of small doses of borax, there are good grounds for assuming its noxiousness, especially when added to milk which constitutes the chief food of young children; in the law-courts it has been held to be injurious, convictions having been obtained against those who had thus adulterated milk.

**Chemical Analysis.**—Organic fluids containing boric acid or borax, may be evaporated down, treated with sulphuric acid, and extracted with alcohol. **Tests.**—The alcoholic extract of boric acid burns with a green-coloured flame. Boric acid partially reddens blue litmus-paper and browns turmeric paper; the reaction with turmeric is distinguished from that due to alkalies by not disappearing under the influence of acids.

## CHAPTER XXIX

### GASEOUS COMPOUNDS

#### SULPHURETTED HYDROGEN.

POISONING with pure sulphuretted hydrogen [$H_2S$] excepting in chemical works, is rare; in those cases in which mischief results from

[1] *Eira*, 1884.     [2] *New York Med. Rec.*, 1888.
[3] *Gaz. de Paris*, 1890.

its inhalation, the mixed gas known as sewer gas is the combination in which it usually exists. Sewer gas is composed of a variable mixture of sulphuretted hydrogen with free hydrogen, carburetted hydrogen, ammonia, carbon dioxide, and atmospheric air deprived of part of its oxygen. Although several of these gases are poisonous, the toxic effects of sewer gas are chiefly due to the sulphuretted hydrogen it contains; one description of the symptoms and post-mortem appearances, therefore, will serve for both sulphuretted hydrogen and for sewer gas.

**Symptoms.**—When a small dose only of the gas is received into the system the respirations are rendered difficult, the pulse becomes small, there is a feeling of oppression in the head, accompanied by sickness, dizziness, and probably diarrhœa, at the same time great muscular prostration is experienced. If the dose is larger, urgent symptoms of asphyxia and heart failure, with profound collapse, cyanosis, dilated pupils, unconsciousness, delirium, and convulsions may occur.

Secondary effects are very rare. Wiglesworth[1] records the case of a man employed in a chemical works who became maniacal, and continued so for two or three weeks, after having accidentally inhaled sulphuretted hydrogen. He began to improve at the end of a month, but did not recover his mental vigour for five months after his admission into the asylum, which took place about a week after the onset of the symptoms.

Asphyxia, due to the action of the gas on the hæmoglobin, and probably also on the tissues, by which they are respectively rendered incapable of yielding up and of receiving oxygen, is believed by some to be the cause of death; others attribute death to certain disturbances of the nervous system by which the pulmonary and the cardiac innervation is deranged. Kaufmann and Rosenthal[2] demonstrated experimentally that inhalation of sulphuretted hydrogen lowers the blood-pressure, and lessens cardiac action by stimulation of the vagus-centre. Brouardel and Loye[3] found that in animals which are made to respire sulphuretted hydrogen the pupils are dilated, the heart-beats slowed, and the respirations are gradually diminished in amplitude; in some cases the heart continued beating for two minutes after respiration had ceased. Pohl[4] believes that the presence of sulphuretted hydrogen in the blood determines the formation of sodium sulphide which causes paralysis of the central nervous system. Lehmann[5] thinks that in animals death is not solely due to changes in the blood and to paralysis of the central nervous system, but also to œdema of the lungs. Uschinsky[6] infers from experiments on animals that the toxic action of $H_2S$ cannot

[1] *Brit. Med. Journ.*, 1892.
[2] *Arch. f. Anat. u. Physiol.*, 1865.
[3] *La France Médicale*, 1885.
[4] *Arch. f. exper. Path.*, 1887.
[5] *Arch. f. Hygiene*, 1892.
[6] *Zeitschr. f. physiol. Chemie*, 1892.

depend on the formation of sulphur-methæmoglobin since large quantities of blood charged with the gas can be injected into the circulation without causing the least harm, although sulphur-methæmoglobin can readily be distinguished in blood subsequently withdrawn from the animal, and further that in animals which have been poisoned with $H_2S$ sulphur-methæmoglobin cannot always be detected. He considers death to be solely due to paralysis of the central nervous system.

It has always been taught that $H_2S$ is freely eliminated by the lungs, but recent investigations are against this view. Laborde[1] found that a residuum of the gas remained in the blood after it had passed through the lungs; Uschinsky states that $H_2S$ is only feebly eliminated by the lungs.

**Treatment.**—In order to combat the tendency to death, and at the same time promote elimination, artificial respiration should be vigorously carried out. Cold effusion has been recommended, but if the surface is already cold it would be worse than useless; the application of external warmth would rather be indicated. Cautious inhalation of chlorine diluted with air has been suggested on the ground that it combines with the hydrogen of the $H_2S$ and precipitates the sulphur; it might be very carefully tried along with artificial respiration.

**Post-mortem Appearances.**—Putrefactive changes quickly follow death. In some cases cadaveric rigidity is reported to have been well marked, which is contrary to what might be expected, as after poisoning by sulphuretted hydrogen the molecular vitality of the muscles disappears with the occurrence of somatic death. The blood is fluid and dark in colour, and in consequence the organs which are rich in blood—as the liver, lungs, and spleen—are also darker than usual. The brain has been found of a peculiar dirty greyish-green owing to the colour of the blood; the muscles are dark, including those of the heart; they sometimes present a bluish tint. The remaining appearances are common to other forms of death from asphyxia.

The blood of human beings poisoned by $H_2S$ has been examined spectroscopically by many observers with negative results. Laborde, Uschinsky, and others, in experimental poisoning of animals with sulphuretted hydrogen, obtained the characteristic spectrum of methæmoglobin in combination with sulphur.

**Chemical Analysis—Tests.**—The odour is sufficiently distinctive to indicate the presence of even minute amounts of sulphuretted hydrogen. A piece of white filtering paper dipped in a solution of lead acetate, is rapidly discoloured when suspended near tissues or other substances impregnated with the gas.

[1] *Comptes rendus de la Societe de Biologie*, 1886.

## CARBON DIOXIDE

Poisoning with carbon dioxide [$CO_2$] occurs in coal-mines (from the gas generated by explosions, to which the name "choke damp" is applied), in deep wells and excavations, in brewer's vats, and in the neighbourhood of lime-kilns and brick-kilns, which are in operation. The percentage of carbon dioxide in atmospheric air that will cause fatal results to human beings who respire it, is not accurately known; under ordinary conditions probably 20 per cent and even much less, would soon prove fatal. Human beings can breathe air mixed with 20 per cent of *pure* $CO_2$ for some time without life being endangered, but a much lower percentage of the gas as it is exhaled from the lungs is lethal. Within limits both men and animals may acquire a certain tolerance for the gas, and breathe air contaminated with it that would be noxious to the untrained organism. The test usually used to ascertain whether air charged with $CO_2$ is respirable or not, is to lower a lighted candle into the mixed gases; if it goes out the atmosphere is poisonous. To this extent the test is trustworthy, but the converse is not to be assumed, namely, that if the candle burns the air is harmless: a candle will burn in a percentage of $CO_2$ that is dangerous to life.

Symptoms.—When a poisonous but not concentrated mixture of carbon dioxide and air is respired, heaviness in the head with giddiness, noises in the ears, a sensation of tightness across the chest, and an inclination to sleep are experienced; shortly after, the muscles lose power, so that if the individual is standing at the time, he falls to the ground. The subsequent symptoms are those of asphyxia: coma, stertorous breathing, cyanosis, and possibly convulsions; sometimes delirium occurs. When an individual is plunged into a concentrated atmosphere of carbon dioxide, as occasionally occurs to workmen who are lowered by a rope into a well or vat which is filled with the gas, immediate loss of consciousness and of muscular power takes place, death rapidly ensuing unless the victim is at once rescued.

When carbon dioxide diluted with air is respired, it acts both as a poison and also—when the partial pressure of the gas in the atmosphere is greater than that in lungs—as a preventive to excretion of the physiologically-formed $CO_2$. The ultimate effects on the organism, allowing for the degree of concentration in which $CO_2$ is respired, are the same as those of asphyxia resulting from the cutting off of oxygen and the consequent accumulation of carbon dioxide in the tissues, but the respiratory movements more quickly cease than when the respired air is simply deficient in oxygen; in the latter case the excretion of $CO_2$ is but little affected.

The **treatment** is that for asphyxia—artificial respiration, external warmth, and stimulants

**Post-mortem Appearances**— They are simply those of death from asphyxia—dark-coloured, fluid blood, fulness of the right heart and veins, with usually hyperæmia of the lungs, and frothy mucus in the air-passages

**Chemical Analysis**—The analysis that may be required is that of the atmosphere in which the poisoning took place. A sample may be obtained by displacing the air in a dry flask or bottle of five or more litres capacity when immersed in the suspected atmosphere; this may be done with a pair of bellows; or if the gas is contained in a well or other excavation the flask may be filled with fine dry sand, attached to a cord and let down to the required depth, by means of a second cord fastened to the lower part of the flask it is inverted, so that the sand flows out and is replaced by gas; the flask is withdrawn mouth upwards and immediately stoppered. The amount of $CO_2$ in the flask is ascertained by adding 20 to 30 c.c. of a titrated solution of barium hydrate, replacing the stopper and shaking well for some minutes. The loss of hydrate by conversion into carbonate, which falls as a white precipitate, is estimated by titrating the solution with oxalic acid

## CARBON MONOXIDE

The chief combinations in which carbon monoxide [CO] is met with in medico-legal practice are—emanations from slow combustion stoves or fire-places to which a restricted amount of air is admitted, and mixtures of atmospheric air with coal-gas or water-gas; death has resulted from sleeping in a closed room, in the open fire place of which coke instead of coal was burnt. Poisoning by CO not unfrequently causes the death of those who are unable to escape from a building which is on fire

In all these instances other gases besides CO and air are present, but the toxic effects are chiefly, if not entirely, due to the CO. It is impossible to determine the minimum percentage of CO in air that will cause death to human beings; one per cent is usually accepted as a fatal admixture. Coal-gas contains a variable amount, from 4 to 7 or 8 per cent of CO along with varying amounts of hydrogen, carburetted hydrogens, watery vapour, nitrogen, and carbon dioxide. Water-gas, which is sometimes used as a substitute for coal-gas contains as much as 40 per cent of CO, its dangerous properties being accentuated by the absence of any characteristic odour, by which its presence might be revealed. In some gas-works coal gas is adulterated with water-gas, the consumers being thus supplied with an unnecessarily dangerous illuminant, and at the same time cheated out of the candle-power they have a right to expect. The absence of odour, together with the lethal potency of water-gas, has led to its prohibition in some countries, the former difficulty has been met, but not very successfully, by causing the gas to pass through some volatile substance, in order to impart an odour to it.

The use of gas burners on the Bunsen-principle to heat large bodies of cold water, as is done in some bath-rooms, is attended with considerable risk. The flame is rapidly cooled by contact with the surface of the water reservoir, and combustion is consequently rendered imperfect, the oxides of carbon, with acetylene being given off; when water is heated in this way, provision for abundant ventilation should be made. Gasoline stoves, if used in small rooms, are not free from danger. M'Cormick[1] relates a case in which a man and his wife were found dead in a bedroom heated by a gasoline stove, the gas given off being principally carbon monoxide.

Carbon monoxide poisoning occurs in two forms—acute and chronic.

## Acute Poisoning by Carbon Monoxide.

**Symptoms.**—There may be a preliminary period of excitation, which is quickly followed by a sensation of heaviness in the head, dizziness, noise in the ears, accelerated cardiac and respiratory movements, oppression on the chest, and occasionally nausea and vomiting. Along with these symptoms muscular weakness occurs, with drowsiness, loss of sensation and of the reflexes, to which coma succeeds; in fatal cases convulsions frequently precede death. The pulse is small and becomes more so as the gravity of the case increases, so that not unfrequently, when the patient is first discovered, the radial pulse is imperceptible. In the state of coma the conjunctivæ are strongly hyperæmic, the eyes having a staring appearance, with partially dilated and insensible pupils. The whole of the skeletal muscles, including the sphincters, are relaxed, the surface is cold and cyanotic, and the lips are often covered with froth.

It has been frequently stated that sugar is almost invariably present in the urine of those suffering from poisoning by carbon monoxide; its occurrence, however, is only occasional. Maschka[2] in two out of twelve cases found a trace only of sugar in the urine. Hoppe-Seyler[3] constantly found a substance present in the urine which reduced copper salts, but never any glucose. Garofalo[4] examined the urine

[1] *Med. News Phil.*, 1891.   [2] *Prager med. Wochenschr.*, 1880.
[3] *Physiolog. Chemie*, 1881.   [4] *Glicosuria per Ossido di Carbonio*, 1891.

from a number of dogs poisoned with carbon monoxide, and failed to find a trace of sugar

In medico-legal practice the symptoms observed in poisoning by carbon monoxide are not always exactly the same, this arises from the admixture of other gases. Poisoning by pure CO can only be procured experimentally, but the salient features of CO poisoning are present in all cases in which that gas is the principal toxic component

The powerful toxic action of carbon monoxide is due to its affinity for hæmoglobin. When CO is inhaled it displaces the oxygen of the hæmoglobin, with which it combines, forming carbon monoxide hæmoglobin—a much more stable compound than oxyhæmoglobin. The combination is sufficiently intimate to resist the action of reducing agents, but it gradually yields to the action of oxygen; if air or oxygen is passed for a long time through a solution of COHb the CO is gradually separated from the hæmoglobin, O taking its place. In the living body carbon monoxide hæmoglobin neither takes up nor gives off oxygen, and therefore is incapable of acting as an oxygen carrier to the tissues, death usually occurring before the whole of the hæmoglobin is saturated with CO; upon the degree of saturation depends the possibility of recovery. If such an amount of hæmoglobin remains free as to enable internal respiration to be carried on so as to maintain life until the combined CO is gradually got rid of, recovery is possible; if not, death takes place from asphyxia. Dreser,[1] when experimenting with rabbits, found that death occurs when the capacity of the blood to take up O is reduced 30 per cent. below the normal. In carbon monoxide poisoning the blood presents a very different appearance to that which is met with when death from asphyxia results in the usual way. In ordinary asphyxia the blood is dark, in CO poisoning it is bright-red. This is due to COHb being irreducible; it retains its colour under circumstances that would deprive O₂Hb of its oxygen and cause it to assume the dark appearance of reduced hæmoglobin

It is stated that carbon monoxide possesses an intrinsic toxic action in addition to its power of depriving the tissues of oxygen, from experiments Linossier[2] deduces that CO does possess such an action, but that it is very feeble. Heineke[3] states that coal-gas, along with other poisons, produces ferment-intoxication in the blood, and in consequence the white corpuscles develop a tendency to adhere to each other and to form thrombi

**Treatment.**—Artificial respiration should be perseveringly kept up,

[1] *Arch. f. exp. Pathol.*, 1891  [2] *Lyon Medical*, 1889
[3] *Deutsches Arch. f. klin. Med.*, 1887-8.

and warmth applied externally. Oxygen may be administered by inhalation from time to time. Stimulants are useful, if the patient cannot swallow they may be administered by the rectum, or ether may be injected under the skin. Two cases are recorded in which subcutaneous injections of nitro-glycerine were followed by recovery, in one, the pulse improved, and the respirations deepened forthwith. Venesection with transfusion has been tried out of twenty-three cases in eight only was the treatment attended with success. Stocker[1] records a very encouraging case in which transfusion was used. A man slept in a room heated by a stove, and was found next morning insensible and apparently dying. Ether injections, artificial respiration, and electrical stimulation of the phrenics were tried for forty-eight hours without effect, at last 800 grms of blood were withdrawn from the median vein, and replaced by 110 grms of defibrinated human blood, in two hours gradual improvement set in, but the pulse, respiration, and temperature did not become normal until the third day, the ultimate recovery was prolonged over many weeks. When transfusion is resorted to, it should be preceded by withdrawal of blood, and the transfused fluid should be human blood—in other words, an appropriate oxygen-carrier—saline solutions are useless. The views of Heincke are opposed to transfusion, as defibrinated blood, injected into the circulation, would tend by the introduction of a certain amount of fibrin ferment to increase the evil.

**Post-mortem Appearances.**—The external appearance is very characteristic, on account of the bright pink colour of the post-mortem stains, cadaveric rigidity is usually well marked, and passes off slowly. Internally, the colour of the tissues is equally striking.—The blood is cherry-red in colour, and is for the most part fluid, the blood-vessels are dilated, and, being filled with the bright-red blood, impart a very characteristic appearance to many of the viscera, microscopically examined, the red corpuscles show no change. The brain and membranes may be hyperæmic, but they often contain no excess of blood, serous effusion is not unfrequently found in the cerebral ventricles. The lungs may be hyperæmic, they have been found œdematous. The mucous membrane of the trachea and bronchi often presents a normal appearance, but it may be coated with froth. Another characteristic feature has been frequently observed to follow death from poisoning by carbon monoxide—the organs and the blood strongly resist putrefactive changes. Stevenson[2] states that portions of the liver from a case of poisoning by water-gas showed an unchanged aspect, and retained the odour of the fresh organ two months after they were removed from the

---

[1] *Correspondenz-Blatt f. schweizer Aerzte*, 1888.
[2] Guy's Hosp. Repts., 1890.

body although no preservative was used; the stomach and duodenum in parts were also unchanged in appearance.

**Spectroscopic Examination of the Blood.**—When blood is fully saturated with CO (all the hæmoglobin being converted into COHb), the absorption spectrum yielded by it consists of two bands resembling those of $O_2$Hb, but they are slightly nearer the violet end of the spectrum; the change of position, however, is only appreciable by direct comparison of the two spectra side by side. If this constituted all the difference, it would be insufficient to afford convincing evidence for medico-legal purposes; but a further and more decided difference is manifested on the addition of a reducing agent, such as ammonium sulphide—the bands of COHb are unaltered, which is in marked contrast with the change that takes place in $O_2$Hb when similarly treated. As previously stated, death usually occurs before the whole of the Hb has been converted into COHb; when this is the case, a mixture of COHb and $O_2$Hb is present in the blood, and consequently the addition of a reducing reagent does not affect the Hb which is in combination with CO, but it reduces that which is in combination with O. Thus the spectrum yielded by the blood of a person who has died from CO poisoning does not necessarily remain unchanged on the addition of a reducing agent: the Hb which is combined with O is reduced, and shows the broad band of reduced Hb, on which are superimposed the two persistent bands of that portion of the Hb which is combined with CO [*vide* Diagram of Blood-Spectra].

Hoppe-Seyler's test of adding a solution of sodium hydrate to CO blood yields a cinnabar red; normal blood is converted into a dirty brownish-green mass. Salkowski[1] has modified this test by diluting the blood with distilled water to twenty times its volume, placing the solution in a test-tube, and adding an equal volume of a solution of sodium hydrate (S.G. 1·34): the solution containing carbon monoxide blood, after a momentary turbidity, becomes bright, and light-red in colour; that containing ordinary blood changes to dirty brown.

**Quantitative Estimation.**—A convenient method of ascertaining the quantity of CO contained in the blood is that adopted by Gréhant.[2] The blood to be examined is placed in a flask connected with an apparatus for the extraction of gases, some glacial acetic acid is added, and the flask is placed in boiling water; the result is that the hæmoglobin is converted into hæmatin, with liberation of the carbon monoxide. The carbon dioxide that is given off is absorbed by potassium hydrate, and the oxygen by pyrogallol, the remainder consists of a

[1] *Zeitschr. f. physiol. Chemie*, 1888.
[2] *Comptes rendus de la Société de Biologie*, 1892.

mixture of nitrogen and carbon monoxide. The relative proportion of the two gases is arrived at by introducing a small quantity of a solution of copper chloride in hydrochloric acid, which completely absorbs the carbon monoxide.

Dreser[1] makes use of Hufner's spectrophotometer to determine the percentage of COHb in blood. This method is founded on the relative constancy of the absorption of light at two selected parts of the spectrum, by blood from the same animal species; this applies both to O₂Hb and to COHb. The extinction coefficients of each are calculated in wave lengths, and from certain known data previously determined by experiments, the relative proportion of oxyhæmoglobin and of carbon monoxide hæmoglobin is deduced.

### Chronic Poisoning by Carbon Monoxide.

It is probable that some of the less toxic effects of carbon monoxide are of more common occurrence than is generally suspected. Chronic CO poisoning occurs in those who work for long hours in small or imperfectly ventilated rooms heated by slow combustion stoves, or gas stoves which give off CO in too small quantity to produce immediate effects; furnacemen and stokers are subject to the risk of repeatedly inhaling it in small doses. Employees in works where water gas is made, or used, incur the risk both of acute and chronic carbon monoxide poisoning.

**Symptoms.**—The earlier symptoms are headache, neuralgic pains, indications of defective nutrition, as anæmia, and loss of flesh, with a sensation of want of breathing-power—breathlessness being developed by incommensurate exertion. The more advanced symptoms are those associated with peripheral neuritis, and psychical disturbances. Ross[2] relates the case of a healthy, well-fed, and temperate man employed in making gas, whose business it was to attend to the retorts. After working at this employment for six months he was pale and anæmic, and was much troubled with shortness of breath; he then began to feel shooting pains in the legs and shoulders; his hands and feet were numb, and he suffered severely from cramp in the calves of the legs. The fingers were often spastically contracted on the palms, and his gait was 'high-stepping.' He improved under treatment.

### GASES PRODUCED BY EXPLOSIVES

In mines in which explosives are used toxic effects have been caused by inhalation of the gases thus generated; the composition of the

[1] *Arch. f. exp. Pathol.*, 1891.
[2] *Peripheral Neuritis*, Ross & Bury, 1893.

mixed gases varies with the composition of the explosive. With all explosives the bulk of the gas generated consists of carbon dioxide and nitrogen. **Gunpowder** in addition yields carbon monoxide in considerable amount, and sulphuretted hydrogen. **Nitroglycerine** and **dynamite** also yield a large percentage of carbon monoxide. **Guncotton** yields much the same. **Tonite**, which is composed of a mixture of equal parts of guncotton and barium nitrate, produces very little if any carbon monoxide. **Roburite**, which consists of chloro-dinitrobenzene and ammonium nitrate, when detonated experimentally gives off no CO. The introduction of the last-named explosive has been the occasion of a number of investigations as to its alleged injurious effects. Chemical analyses of the gases in the coal mines after the detonation of roburite were separately made by Professor Dixon of Owens College, and Professor Bedson of Durham College, the results clearly showed that much less CO (which constitutes the dangerous gas) was given off by roburite than by gunpowder. It will be observed that although experimental detonation of roburite produces no CO, in actual use a small quantity was present. This is partly given off by the fuse when burning and, as suggested by Professor Dixon, is probably also produced by hot CO$_2$ passing over the coal; in any case the amount is small and the gas is dissipated in a short time. Still, as a very small percentage of CO is deleterious if the air which contains it is long respired, it is important to minimise all risk of contamination. To this end experts recommend the use of electricity for the purpose of detonating roburite, thus obviating the necessity for a fuse, together with the allowance of sufficient time for dissipation of the products given off by the explosive before the miners resume their work. No evidence was obtained of injurious effects from nitrobenzene present in the air after explosion of roburite. The toxic effects of roburite, as such, are dealt with in the chapter on benzene and its derivatives.

## CYANOGEN COMPOUNDS

**Hydrocyanic Acid** [HCN], or prussic acid, in its commercial form contains from 2 to 5 per cent of the anhydrous acid. It has a penetrating odour, but when smelt at in very dilute solution it produces a bitter taste at the back of the tongue, rather than an olfactory sensation. It is feebly acid, slightly reddening litmus-paper. Unless hermetically sealed up and kept in the dark, it loses strength more rapidly than is generally supposed even when preserved in well-stoppered bottles.

**Oil of bitter almonds**, used as a flavouring adjunct, contains a varying percentage of anhydrous hydrocyanic acid, in the crude oil amounting to from 5 to 15 per cent. **Cherry-laurel water** contains about 0·1 per cent.

**Potassium Cyanide** [KCN], largely used in photography and in electro-plating, is a salt which has a strong alkaline reaction. Hydrocyanic acid is displaced from KCN by carbon dioxide, therefore the percentage of acid diminishes by keeping; the "cyanide" of commerce usually contains some potassium carbonate, and from absorption of oxygen tends to be converted into cyanate. Potassium cyanide yields the odour of hydrocyanic acid without the addition of a displacing acid. Several other cyanides are poisons but are rarely used as such.

Many of the natural order *Rosaceæ*, especially the sub-orders *Pruneæ* and *Pomeæ*, contain a crystalline substance—**Amygdalin**—which is capable of yielding hydrocyanic acid. Amygdalin itself is not poisonous, but when it is subjected to the action of a natural ferment —emulsin—which is found along with it in the fruit or leaves of the above-named sub-orders, it is decomposed into oil of bitter almonds, glucose, and hydrocyanic acid; the same result is produced when amygdalin is boiled with dilute acid. In cases of criminal poisoning with hydrocyanic acid endeavours have been made to utilise the occurrence of hydrocyanic acid-forming substances in edible fruit to account for its presence in the human body in amount sufficient to cause death. Bitter almonds excepted, it is very improbable that a sufficient quantity of such fruit could be eaten as to introduce a fatal dose of hydrocyanic acid.

**Symptoms.**—When a fatal dose of hydrocyanic acid is swallowed the symptoms usually appear within a few seconds; they may be delayed for thirty or forty seconds, and exceptionally for a little over a minute; when thus delayed, the victim may be able in the interval to walk and speak. When animals are poisoned with hydrocyanic acid they almost invariably give utterance to a spasmodic cry; this symptom is frequently absent in human beings. After a few gasps the patient becomes insensible, and if in the upright posture when the poison is swallowed, he falls to the ground. The surface is cold, the face usually pallid, the eyes are open and staring, and the pupils are dilated and insensible to light. The breathing is laboured, irregular, and gasping, the breaths being drawn at longer and longer intervals; after apparently final cessation, convulsive efforts at respiration may occur with prolonged intervals between. Tetanic spasms affecting the muscles of the jaws and limbs usually occur in the early stage, followed by complete relaxation of all the muscles. The pulse is almost or quite imperceptible at the wrist; if it can be felt it is found to be exceedingly rapid —120 or more in the minute—small and irregular; if death does not take place immediately the pulse may become slower towards the end. The lips are frequently covered with froth, vomiting, involuntary micturition and movement of the bowels are not infrequent. Death usually takes place within five or ten minutes, it may occur almost immediately after the poison is swallowed, or, when a minimum lethal dose is taken, the fatal issue may be delayed for an hour and even longer. Stevenson[1] records a case in which death did not take place for an hour and a quarter. If life is prolonged over half an hour there is considerable chance of recovery.

The mode in which hydrocyanic acid causes death has been the subject of much discussion. The earlier opinion, founded on the exceeding rapidity of its action, was that it paralysed the central nervous system (Preyer[2]), the present view is that death is produced by arrest of internal respiration. It has been found experimentally by Gaethgens[3] that in poisoning by hydrocyanic acid less carbon dioxide is excreted, and less oxygen taken up than in the normal. In many cases of hydrocyanic acid poisoning the blood has been observed to be light coloured, especially when viewed in thin layers though in some instances it is dark, the rapidity with which death occurs exercises a modifying influence. Geppert[4] explains the arrest of internal respiration on the hypothesis that hydrocyanic acid deprives the tissues of their power to take up oxygen. According to this view the oxygen of the blood is neglected by the tissues and it therefore accumulates until the whole of the blood—venous as well as arterial—assumes a bright red colour, asphyxia thus takes place in the presence of excess of oxygen. Another explanation attributes the arrest of internal respiration to the condition of the blood. Kobert[5] states that HCN forms a definite compound with methæmoglobin, if a few drops of the dilute acid are added to a 2 per cent solution of methæmoglobin, its brown hue is changed to bright red, and its spectrum to one resembling that of reduced hæmoglobin. Cyanmethæmoglobin possesses considerable stability and resists the reducing influence of the tissues so as to be capable of recognition eight days after death in the blood of an individual poisoned with hydrocyanic acid; ammonium sulphide also produces no effect, and a current of air may be passed through it without disassociating the HCN. According to Kobert's views hydrocyanic acid, when taken into the living organism kills the protoplasm of the red corpuscles, rendering them functionless as oxygen carriers and by combination with methæmoglobin causes the blood to assume a bright red which determines the peculiar tint of the post-mortem stains and also that of the mucous membrane of the stomach.

[1] Guy's Hosp. Repts., 1869.   [2] De Blausaure, 1868-70.
[3] Hoppe Seyler, Med. chem. Untersuch.   [4] Zeitschr. f. Klin. Med., 1889.
[5] Ueber Cyanmethæmoglobin und den Nachweis der Blausäure, 1891.

**Fatal Dose.**—The smallest recorded fatal dose was half a drachm of the B P acid—equal to 0 6 grain of anhydrous acid—which caused death in one hour and twenty minutes, Garstang[1] who records the case states that hydrocyanic acid was inadvertently substituted for hydrochloric acid in dispensing a prescription, therefore the amount taken could be accurately ascertained  The largest dose followed by recovery was half an ounce of medicinal acid, equal to 4 8 grains of anhydrous acid, the case is described by Shiveley [2]—A student of pharmacy was found insensible, the pupils being widely dilated, the right more so than the left, respiration was laboured and there was extreme dyspnœa, with coldness of the surface, but without lividity or cyanosis, the face having a rosy tint  The pulse was 86 per minute, but rapidly went up to 112, and was thready and irregular, the temperature in the rectum was 97° 5 F  Trismus and rigidity of the limbs were present for a short time  The stomach-tube was used, and alcohol, camphorated ether, and atropine sulphate were administered, the two latter subcutaneously, the alcohol by mouth and rectum, faradisation of the phrenics was also resorted to  The urine contained albumen, crystals of calcium oxalate, and gave a precipitate with ferric and ferrous salts  On recovery the patient explained that the first sensation he experienced after swallowing the poison was numbness of the lips, which was quickly followed by shortness of breath and loss of consciousness  In another case[3] recovery took place after two drachms—about 2 5 grains of anhydrous acid  A woman swallowed the dose by mistake, after which she rushed upstairs to her master who was a medical man, told him what she had done and then fell down insensible  The stomach-pump was used immediately, and apomorphine was given, followed by electricity and artificial respiration, the treatment being attended with success  This case is remarkable not only for recovery after a dose more than double that which is usually fatal, but also for the actions performed by the patient in the interval that elapsed between swallowing the poison and the occurrence of insensibility; the power of moving and speaking after swallowing fatal doses has been observed in many cases, but not often, if ever, to such a degree.

In cases of fatal poisoning by very small doses, and of recovery after very large ones, a doubt exists as to the percentage of anhydrous acid present in the solution swallowed  Examination of specimens of dilute acid obtained from several sources showed that some were above and some below the standard strength. It may be accepted that an amount of dilute acid which contains one grain of anhydrous acid constitutes a fatal dose.

[1] *The Lancet*, 1888.  [2] *Internat. Journ Med Sciences*, 1880
[3] *Brit Med Journ*, 1890

**Treatment.**—Immediate evacuation of the stomach with stomach-pump, or emetics. Zinc sulphate or mustard may be given by the mouth, or apomorphine subcutaneously. Then artificial respiration, faradisation of the phrenics and the diaphragm, external warmth and friction, subcutaneous injections of ether, brandy by the mouth or rectum, and if the surface is not cold, effusion with cold water. If effusion is resorted to it should be intermittent, either vigorous friction or hot applications being used in the intervals. Subcutaneous injections of atropine have been recommended on theoretical grounds—stimulation of the respiratory centre; the advantage is doubtful. Chemical antidotes are useless: first, because all the poison should be evacuated, and not left for chemical neutralisation; and second, because the action of the poison is far too rapid to permit of the effective administration of an antidote that requires special ingredients, and time to prepare it.

**Post mortem Appearances—External.**—The eyes, with dilated pupils, may be prominent and bright, the fingers and the jaws clenched, the lips may be covered with froth, and the post-mortem stains are frequently pink or light red. **Internal.**—On opening the abdomen the odour of HCN may be perceived; if not it may sometimes be recognised on removing the calvarium. The blood is often bright arterial-red in colour, but it may be dark: it is always fluid. The mucous membrane of the stomach may be brilliant red, due to the colour of the blood; when this is the case all the mucous surfaces and even the muscles show more or less a like tendency.

**Potassium Cyanide** produces symptoms like those of HCN with the addition of more or less local action on the mucous membrane of the mouth and stomach. The lips and mouth may be eroded or the mucous membrane softened, and capable of being easily detached. The mucous membrane of the stomach has been found partially or wholly of a bright red, deeply injected, thickened, softened, and even eroded; its surface may be covered with blood stained mucus. The stomach contents will be alkaline in reaction until all the poison is evacuated.

**Fatal Dose.**—Death has resulted from five grains, and recovery after about forty grains were taken in the solid form.

**Oil of Bitter Almonds.**—In one case[1] a teaspoonful of the crude oil, which was afterwards found to contain 3·4 per cent. HCN, caused the death of a girl in an hour and three-quarters; the dose taken contained about two grains of anhydrous HCN. The contents of the stomach yielded HCN fourteen days after death. It has been frequently noticed that the odour of HCN in the dead body lasts longer when received into the system in the form of oil of bitter almonds than as a solution of pure hydrocyanic acid.

[1] Reg. v. Timins (Maidstone Ass., 1883).

Baker[1] records the case of a man who ate two handfuls of bitter almonds Sometime after he became insensible with all the symptoms of poisoning by hydrocyanic acid, prompt use of the stomach-pump and active treatment led to recovery. The contents of the stomach yielded the reactions of HCN.

Chemical Analysis—Tests.—If a drop of a solution of silver nitrate is placed on the concave surface of a watch-glass, and is inverted immediately over a substance which contains free hydrocyanic acid, the drop becomes milky from the formation of silver cyanide If the amount of HCN is small, the milky appearance first manifests itself as a white line around the margin, which gradually spreads over the whole of the drop, when slowly formed the deposit, examined under the microscope, is seen to consist of delicate acicular or prismatic crystals, if rapidly formed a crystalline mass is produced without distinctive appearance Silver cyanide is soluble in hot, concentrated nitric acid A drop of a solution of potassium hydrate substituted for the silver solution, and exposed as before to the vapour of HCN, undergoes no visible change on being allowed to remain for a few minutes A drop of a solution of ferrous sulphate subsequently added to the potash produces a greenish-grey precipitate, which becomes blue (Prussian blue) on the addition of dilute hydrochloric acid A drop of ammonium sulphide on a watch-glass, inverted as before, allowed to remain two or three minutes, and then evaporated to dryness at a gentle heat, yields a blood red (ferric sulphocyanide) on being touched with a glass rod dipped in a solution of ferric chloride; the colour disappears on the addition of a drop or two of a solution of mercuric chloride

In performing all three tests, if the temperature is low, it may be necessary to slightly warm the substance tested In order to liberate HCN from potassium cyanide, the addition of tartaric acid is necessary, in sufficient amount to produce an acid reaction

Kobert directs attention to the property possessed by HCN of preventing and of abolishing the reaction of iodine with starch, and suggests that it constitutes an exceedingly delicate test, which may be performed in two ways —If a little very dilute cold solution of starch (prepared by boiling) with potassium iodide, is divided between two test-tubes, to one only of which a minute quantity of HCN is added, on dropping into each tube some aqueous solution of peroxide of hydrogen the contents of that to which HCN was added remain unchanged, those of the other become blue The second way is to tinge a little dilute solution of starch with iodine, on the addition of a minute amount of HCN the colour is discharged A few drops of a distillate

[1] *Brit Med Journ*, 1881.

obtained from the blood of an individual poisoned with HCN may be thus tested. The same reaction, however, is produced by H₂S and some other substances.

**Quantitative Estimation.**—The organic admixture if necessary should be rendered acid with tartaric acid, and distilled over a water-bath. It is difficult, if not impossible, to get all the HCN over, as some of it will probably be decomposed. The amount of cyanogen present in the distillate is best estimated by titration with a standard solution of silver nitrate. If preferred the distillate may be acidulated with nitric acid, and precipitated with silver nitrate, the precipitate is washed, dried, and weighed—100 parts equal 20.15 of anhydrous hydrocyanic acid.

## CHAPTER XXX

### ALCOHOL

Acute poisoning with alcohol [$C_2H_6O$] is the only form that it will be necessary to describe, the chief medico-legal interest being centred in the diagnosis. As a rule the lesser degrees of alcoholic intoxication are easily recognised; the difficulty arises when a profound comatose stage is reached, and no history is forthcoming to aid diagnosis—as, for example, when a medical practitioner is called upon by the police to determine the condition of a man found in a state of insensibility in the street or other public place; in order to arrive at a reliable conclusion in such instances, method is necessary.

The first consideration is—What toxic and pathological conditions may be mistaken for profound alcoholic intoxication? Among these are **Cerebral lesion**, as hæmorrhage into the pons, internal capsule, or cortex, **poisoning by opium**, chloral hydrate or other narcotics, **mechanical injury**, as a blow or fall on the head, **diabetic**, or **uræmic coma**, **post-epileptic coma**, and some forms of **hysterical or non-organic neuroses**.

An initial difficulty presents itself: two of these conditions may be combined. A drunken man may have received a violent blow on the head, or he may be the victim of cerebral hæmorrhage from the giving way of a vessel, without external violence. First, as to the pupils: if dilated, they suggest alcohol; if contracted, opium, or hæmorrhage into the pons. In hæmorrhage into the pons the temperature is frequently elevated (103°.5) from the first; in the stage of opium poisoning that corresponds, the temperature is subnormal. If one pupil is dilated and the other contracted, or normal, some intracranial lesion is probable. Conjugate deviation of the eyes suggests hemiplegia. Note if there is flapping of one cheek, and if the arm and leg are equally limp on both sides; lift up alternately the arm and the leg on one side and let them fall, and then repeat the process on the other side, comparing the results; in hemiplegia, unless there is initial rigidity, the limbs on the paralysed side will fall more like inanimate objects than those on the unaffected side. Pinching the skin will sometimes evoke movements that reveal the presence or absence of hemiplegia; the plantar reflexes may be tried with the same object. Bilateral inequality of any of the reflexes is suspicious of organic trouble. If by shouting into his ear the patient can be sufficiently roused to give his name, occupation, and address, the stupor is not likely to be due to organic lesion; it may result from opium in the early stage or from alcohol. The odour of alcohol in the breath is of little significance, since brandy is often given as a remedy to patients found insensible; its absence, however, eliminates alcoholic poisoning from the possible causes of insensibility. If opium as such, or in the form of tincture, is the cause of insensibility, its odour may possibly be perceived in the patient's breath. Examine the head for indications of bruising, or cuts of the scalp, or of fracture of the skull; look for signs of hæmorrhage from the nostrils or ears. It is to be remembered that comparatively slight blows, or falls on the head, may produce effusion of blood into the arachnoid, which often does not cause any obvious symptoms for some time after the injury has been inflicted, this is especially the case when the condition is masked by alcoholic intoxication.

In alcoholic coma the face may either be flushed or pale, the pupils either contracted or dilated—frequently contracted at first and afterwards dilated. The stertor is not usually so marked as in apoplexy, unless a fatal issue is imminent. If on using the stomach-pump a large quantity of strongly alcoholic fluid is removed, the diagnosis of alcoholic poisoning is strengthened. The severest form of acute alcoholic poisoning occurs when the patient has obtained access to an unlimited amount of spirit (as by boring a hole in a whisky-cask), and has swallowed enormous doses of it undiluted. The symptoms quickly develop into those of coma of a profound type, which, in the absence of any evidence of a focal lesion, cannot be distinguished from that due to apoplexy. The presence of alcohol in the urine of those who have partaken freely of it may be ascertained by the potassium dichromate test subsequently described.

In uræmia the pupils will be contracted, and there will be recurrent convulsions, the temperature will be subnormal. The presence of albumen in the urine is not of much diagnostic value, as it is frequently found in apoplexy. **Post-epileptic coma** is chiefly met with in young people; it resembles profound sleep rather than true coma; the tongue should be examined for injuries inflicted by the teeth. **Diabetic coma** has often been mistaken for drunkenness, not only in the comatose stage but also in the preceding stage of excitement, which strongly resembles that due to alcohol. The diagnostic signs are a peculiar odour of the breath—like that of American apples—and sugar in the urine; the respirations are slow and sighing, and the temperature is considerably below the normal. Unconsciousness, due to **hysteria**, may resemble that due to meningitis. The diagnostic signs are the age and sex, the absence of indications of cerebral lesion, with probably normal temperature, pulse, and condition of the skin.

**Treatment.**—The stomach-pump is to be resorted to, or in its absence an emetic. Faradisation, or flicking the patient with a wet towel, compelling him to attempt to walk with the aid of a man on either side of him; cold douche, with alternate friction, and the administration of hot coffee are the means to be used for promoting return to consciousness. If there is doubt as to the cause of the coma, treat the case as possibly due to cerebral lesion, and keep the patient under observation until the diagnosis is established.

Alcohol is eliminated by the kidneys and the lungs.

**Post-mortem Appearances.**—The most characteristic appearances of acute alcoholic poisoning are found in those who have died shortly after swallowing large doses of alcohol. Cadaveric rigidity is usually well marked, and sometimes lasts for several days; putrefactive changes advance slowly. Unless the stomach was well washed out before death, the odour of the spirit partaken of is perceived on opening it; the abdominal, thoracic, and cranial cavities yield similar evidence. The mucous membrane of the stomach is sometimes injected and bright red in colour, at others it is pale, with or without isolated reddened spots. The right heart and the veins are usually filled with dark fluid blood, and the lungs are hyperæmic, either throughout or at the posterior part of the lower lobes. The bladder generally contains a large quantity of urine. The cerebral vessels as a rule are well filled with blood, and there may be extravasations in the membranes or in the substance of the brain.

If the deceased was an habitual drunkard, the ordinary pathological changes due to chronic alcoholism will be present in addition to the appearances above described.

**Chemical Analysis.**—Alcohol may be separated from organic admixture by distillation at a gentle heat. If the substance to be distilled is strongly acid, sodium carbonate should first be added until the reaction is neutral, redistillation may be necessary, along with rectification by lime or potassium carbonate.

**Tests.**—The distillate may be tested by heating some in a test-tube with a few drops of a solution of potassium dichromate and a little sulphuric acid. The colour changes from yellow to green, and the odour of aldehyde is given off. The odour of acetic ether may be produced by heating some of the distillate with an equal volume of sulphuric acid and an acetate. A little of the distillate, heated with an aqueous solution of iodine decolourised with potassium hydrate, yields a crystalline deposit of iodoform, recognised by its odour, and, if slowly formed, by the rosette-like, or hexagonal, appearance of the crystals under the microscope. It is to be remembered that other substances than alcohol—as aldehyde and acetone—give the iodoform reaction.

Quantitative estimation, as a rule, is not feasible, or at least would not convey any idea of the amount of alcohol swallowed.

**Paraldehyde** [$(C_2H_4O)_3$], when taken in excess, has, in a few instances, produced toxic symptoms, but no fatal case is recorded. Mackenzie[1] relates a case in which three and a half ounces were swallowed, and produced a condition resembling chloroform narcosis; strychnine was administered hypodermically, and the patient recovered.

**Ether** [$C_4H_{10}O$] is of little interest as a poison, when swallowed in the liquid form it causes symptoms resembling those due to alcohol. In parts of Ireland it is habitually used for intoxicating purposes, Hart[2] gives an exhaustive account of the subject, showing that the habit is wide-spread. Two to four drachms is the usual intoxicating dose, but those used to drinking it can take an ounce or more.

**Amyl Alcohol** [$C_5H_{12}O$], or fusel oil, is formed in the manufacture of ethyl alcohol from grain, potatoes, must of grapes, and other sources. Crude fusel oil is an admixture of ethyl, propyl, and butyl alcohols and their ethers, the principal component being amyl alcohol; fusel oil prepared from potatoes consists of about equal parts of ethyl and amyl alcohols, with traces of some of the other alcohols.

Amyl alcohol is of lighter specific gravity than water, in which it is but slightly miscible. It is an oily, colourless liquid, having an acrid taste, and a peculiar odour; its vapour is very irritating to the respiratory organs, producing a sense of suffocation, accompanied by coughing, and if inhaled for a short time it causes headache.

In a case recorded by Ord,[3] the **symptoms** of acute poisoning by fusel oil were as follows:—A man, aged sixty-four, drank about half a pint of fusel oil, which was afterwards found to consist of equal parts of amyl and ethyl alcohols; he felt no ill effects for four and a half hours, when he became unconscious. The muscles were slightly rigid;

[1] *Brit. Med. Journ.*, 1891.   [2] *Ibid.*, 1890.   [3] *The Lancet*, 1889.

the teeth were tightly clenched; the face was flushed, but the surface was cold; the respirations were shallow and slow; the pulse was only just detectable at the wrist; the pupils were small, and acted feebly to light. The breath had an odour resembling amyl nitrite, or essence of pears; later on the breathing ceased, necessitating artificial respiration several times, the pulse continuing in the meanwhile. The urine contained both amyl and ethyl alcohols. Recovery took place.

Swain[1] records a fatal case of poisoning by "faints," a refuse after distillation of spirit from potatoes, consisting of a mixture of amyl, propyl, and other alcohols. The mucous membrane of the stomach was soft and thick and the organ contained a grumous fluid tinged with blood. The odour of amyl nitrite, but sweeter, was perceived on opening the body; there was fluid in the ventricles of the brain which also was odorous. No cirrhotic changes were found in the liver nor kidneys, although the patient had frequently indulged in raw amyl alcohol.

Test.—By distillation with potassium acetate and sulphuric acid, amyl acetate is produced, which is known commercially as essence of jargonelle pears; it may be recognised by its odour.

**Amyl Nitrite** [$C_5H_{11}NO_2$].—A case, interesting in more than one respect, is recorded by Rosen[2]. A student, aged twenty-two, who was subject to epileptic seizures, had some amyl nitrite given to him for treatment by inhalation. On one occasion, feeling an attack imminent, he got the bottle of amyl nitrite in order to inhale some; he had a fit, and on recovering consciousness, experienced sensations which convinced him that he had drunk some of the fluid during a state of epileptic automatism. Eructations and vomiting occurred. When seen the face was pale, the lips were bloodless, the respirations quiet and the pulse 110 per minute; he had pain in the head, was much depressed, felt a burning sensation in the throat, and oppression in the region of the stomach. The mucous membrane, touched by the poison, was slightly eroded; gastric catarrh followed, with ultimate recovery. The amount swallowed was from twelve to fifteen grammes.

## NITROGLYCERINE

**Nitroglycerine** [$C_3H_5(NO_3)_3O_3$] is an oily liquid which detonates violently on percussion; it is slightly soluble in water, and freely soluble in alcohol and ether. It produces the physiological effects of a nitrite in a powerful degree.—The arteries relax, causing a sensation of fulness and throbbing in the head, frequently accompanied by violent pain; the action of the heart is quickened and the blood tension lowered; paralysis, both motor and sensory, occurs, and death from

[1] *Brit Med Journ*, 1891.   [2] *Centralb' f klin Med* 1888

respiratory paralysis. Nitroglycerine lessens the capacity of hæmoglobin to take up oxygen; the blood is sometimes chocolate-coloured, and yields the spectrum of methæmoglobin.

**Symptoms.**—A burning sensation in the throat, nausea, vomiting, giddiness, excessively violent pain in the head, flushing of the face, tumultuous action of the heart, pulsation felt all over the body, prostration, unconsciousness, muscular twitchings, perspiration, stertorous, dyspnœal breathing, and cyanosis, with complete paralysis, have been observed.

The **fatal dose** is not known. About one ounce caused death in four hours. A man recovered, after extremely violent and dangerous symptoms, who swallowed a tablespoonful of dynamite (a mixture of nitroglycerine with about one-third of its weight of silicious earthy matter), to which a few extra drops of nitroglycerine were added. A man committed suicide by eating two "bobbins" of dynamite four inches long by three-quarters of an inch thick.

## CHLOROFORM.

**Chloroform** [$CHCl_3$].—Poisoning with liquid chloroform is not common and is almost invariably the result of accident or of attempts at suicide; its pungent taste and powerful odour render it unfitted for homicidal purposes, although in one case at least it was strongly suspected to have been administered by the mouth with homicidal intent.

**Symptoms.**—The effects produced by chloroform swallowed in the liquid form resemble those caused by its inhalation plus the local action of the liquid on the mucous membrane of the stomach and bowels, on which it acts as an irritant, producing symptoms of gastro-enteritis. After a poisonous dose is swallowed, vomiting usually occurs, the vomited matters not always yielding the odour of chloroform; in a short time the patient becomes unconscious and presents the appearance of a person deeply under the influence of chloroform administered by inhalation:—The face is pale and cyanotic; the features are sunken; the pupils are insensitive to light, and are frequently dilated but they may be normal; and the entire surface is cold and bedewed with sweat. Unless the tongue is drawn forward the breathing is stertorous and gradually becomes feebler and slower; the pulse is small and slow, the blood-pressure falling considerably. Death may result from paralysis of the respiratory centres or from heart-paralysis.

If the patient recovers consciousness, he complains of a hot, burning pain in the stomach and bowels; he may have diarrhœa, and the motions may be tinged with blood. The liver may be enlarged and tender, and the skin icteric. Death has occurred from heart-paralysis after the patient has recovered consciousness. A case is recorded by Brasch[1] of a man who drank seventy grammes (a fluid ounce and a half) of chloroform which produced profound unconsciousness lasting for ten hours. He then came to himself and complained of pain in the region of the liver, which was enlarged; sixty-seven hours after the poison was taken he died of heart-failure.

**Fatal Dose.**—The smallest recorded fatal dose swallowed by an adult was about seven fluid drachms; one third the amount caused the death of a boy four years old. Recovery has taken place after two ounces in one case, and after three in another, in which the odour of chloroform was present in the breath for two days; in both cases profound narcosis was produced. Death has taken place in three hours; more commonly in twelve or more.

**Treatment.**—Evacuate the stomach with the tube and wash it well out; follow up with artificial respiration and faradisation of the phrenics; if the breathing fails, administer inhalations of amyl nitrite at frequent intervals; keep the patient in the horizontal posture and apply external warmth. To diminish the risk of heart-failure the patient should be kept in bed for several hours after recovery of consciousness. Chloroform is principally eliminated by the lungs.

**Post-mortem Appearances.**—Unless the presence of chloroform in the body can be ascertained, there is no characteristic indication of the cause of death. The mucous membrane of the stomach and bowels may be injected, softened, and even eroded; incipient fatty changes in the liver, kidneys, and heart have been observed; the blood is frequently fluid, and dark in colour.

**Chemical Analysis—Tests.**—The most delicate test is that afforded by splitting up chloroform vapour into chlorine and hydrochloric acid. The substance containing chloroform is placed in a flask furnished with a piece of hard glass tubing, bent at a right angle just above the stopper of the flask, and again, twelve or fourteen inches away from the flask, at a right angle, downwards; at a point midway between the two bends a Bunsen flame is allowed to play until the tube is red hot. A second tube, through which air is gently forced, perforates the stopper and dips below the level of the contents of the flask, which are heated so as to volatilise the chloroform. When the vapour arrives at the incandescent spot it is split up into chlorine and hydrochloric acid; the former may be recognised by holding to the end of the tube a piece of starch-paper moistened with a solution of potassium iodide, which becomes blue from the action of the liberated iodine on the starch;

[1] *Deutsche med. Zeitung*, 1890

the latter by substituting a piece of moist blue litmus-paper which is reddened, showing the presence of an acid. If the end of the tube is plunged into a solution of silver nitrate, silver chloride is formed, which may be recognised by being insoluble in nitric acid, and soluble in ammonia. This test is so delicate that by finely mincing the lungs, adding sodium carbonate to slight alkalinity, and treating as above described, chloroform has been detected several weeks after death from its inhalation. Chloroform may be separated by distillation from organic admixture, such as the contents of the stomach, if present in sufficient amount to be recognised by its odour, otherwise it is better to adopt the process just described.

After separation chloroform may be tested thus:—A little alcoholic solution of potassium hydrate is put into a test-tube along with ten or twelve drops of aniline, and a little of the chloroform-containing fluid, and is well shaken up. On gently warming the mixture for a short time, the suffocating and disagreeable odour of phenyl-isocyanide or isonitril is developed. The reaction is thus expressed—

$$CHCl_3 + 3KOH + \underbrace{C_6H_5NH_2}_{\text{Aniline}} = \underbrace{C_6H_5NC}_{\text{Phenyl-isocyanide}} + 3KCl + 3H_2O$$

Another test is to dissolve a little β-naphthol in an aqueous solution of potassium hydrate, to which a few drops of the suspected fluid is added, and the solution gently warmed; if chloroform is present the liquid turns blue. Chloroform reduces Fehling's solution.

Quantitative estimation may be made by introducing the organic admixture into a flask as before described and passing the vapour through an incandescent combustion-tube containing small fragments of pure caustic lime, with which the chlorine combines. The lime is afterwards dissolved in dilute nitric acid and the chlorine precipitated with silver nitrate—100 parts of silver chloride equal 27.758 parts of chloroform.

## CHLORAL HYDRATE

**Chloral Hydrate** [$C_2H_3Cl_3O_2$] in poisonous doses produces profound coma and abolishes the reflex irritability of the spinal cord. It lowers the blood-pressure partly by paralysing the vasomotor centre and partly by its action on the cardiac ganglia.

**Symptoms.**—Shortly after the reception of a poisonous dose of chloral hydrate the patient becomes drowsy and gradually passes into a state of coma, from which he cannot be roused. Respiration is slow and laboured, long intervals sometimes occurring between the breaths; the pulse is thready, and in the later stage slow. The pupils are generally contracted; the face is sunken and cyanotic, or it is pallid and ghastly, the surface of the whole body, but especially of the limbs, is remarkably cold and is bedewed with perspiration. The reflexes are abolished, and there is absence of sensibility. In fatal cases the temperature is further lowered, and death takes place from <u>heart-paralysis</u>. It is characteristic of poisoning by chloral hydrate for the toxic symptoms to come on very suddenly, sometimes directly after the poison is swallowed; in these cases the rapidity with which the fatal symptoms appear points to immediate paralysis of the heart, which causes death before the usual effects of the poison have time to manifest themselves.

In cases of impeded circulation through the lungs, or of fatty heart, small doses produce toxic effects. In the case of *Reg* v *Parton* (Manchester Ass., 1889) the prisoner was convicted of having caused the death of an elderly man by the administration of chloral hydrate in beer with the object of robbing him whilst insensible; the man was found in a cab in a state of unconsciousness, and he died shortly after. Post-mortem examination revealed nothing characteristic; the heart was covered and infiltrated with fat, and death probably resulted from heart-paralysis. In the course of the day the deceased had drunk alcohol freely, but there were no indications of death from acute alcoholism. Traces of chloral hydrate were found in the contents of the stomach; the dose taken was probably small, but it was sufficient to paralyse a feeble heart.

**Fatal Dose.**—The toxic action of chloral hydrate is extremely irregular. Twenty grains caused the death of a patient (who took it for neuralgia) in half an hour; in another case thirty grains were fatal. Kane[1] states that ten grains rendered a woman of thirty-four profoundly comatose, with contracted pupils; she recovered. An old lady of seventy died in nine and a half hours after taking ten grains. Three grains caused the death of a child one year old. On the other hand, recoveries are numerous after enormous doses of several hundred grains; in one case recovery took place after four hundred and twenty grains taken in one dose. Death has occurred in fifteen minutes; it may be delayed for six or more hours.

Chloral hydrate to a great extent is decomposed in the organism, one product—urochloral acid—is found in the urine, in which also small amounts of unchanged chloral hydrate may sometimes be detected.

**Treatment.**—The stomach should be emptied by the tube or by an emetic. Warmth is of the utmost importance; it should be maintained by hot bottles, and the body should be surrounded by blankets, underneath which friction may be applied. Persistent attempts at rousing the patient should be made by means of the faradic current and other

[1] *New York Med. Rec.*, 1880.

usual methods. If the breathing fails, artificial respiration should be performed. Hypodermic injections of strychnine ($\frac{1}{15}$ grain) have been recommended, but strychnine is not so good an antidote to chloral hydrate as chloral hydrate is to strychnine. Stimulants will probably be required — ether hypodermically, or alcohol by mouth or rectum. Hot coffee is useful.

**Post-mortem Appearances.**—There is no characteristic appearance. The heart and lungs have been found to correspond with the usual conditions of these organs when death has resulted from cardiac or respiratory failure. In a few instances, the mucous membrane of the stomach has been found softened, reddened, and easily detached. The blood is usually fluid, but not invariably so. It has been stated that putrefactive changes are retarded in chloral poisoning, but this effect is not constant.

**Chemical Analysis.**—The contents of the stomach should be digested for twenty-four hours with about three times their volume of absolute alcohol acidulated with a few drops of sulphuric acid, the mixture being repeatedly agitated ; the alcoholic extract is then separated, and the alcohol evaporated. The residue is first extracted with petroleum ether, to remove fats, &c. (chloral hydrate is insoluble in petroleum ether), and is then shaken out with ethylic ether, which dissolves the chloral hydrate and deposits it on evaporation. On account of chloral hydrate being decomposed in the living organism, it may escape detection on analysis of the viscera and their contents after death. Urine also may be first treated with petroleum ether and then with ethylic ether in order to extract chloral hydrate.

**Tests.**—The most delicate test for chloral hydrate, as such, is ammonium sulphide. A drop or two added to a weak solution of chloral hydrate produces no immediate change, but in a short time the mixture becomes opalescent and gradually acquires a yellowish or reddish milky appearance, very suggestive of urine overloaded with urates and charged with pigment. Unless chloral hydrate is present in very small amount its presence may be demonstrated by adding a few drops of a solution of potassium hydrate, which decomposes the chloral into chloroform and potassium formate :—

$$C_2H_3Cl_3O_2 + KOH = KCHO_2 + H_2O + CHCl_3,$$

the chloroform is recognised by its odour, and subsequently by the production of phenyl-isocyanide (see under Chloroform), and the potassium formate by boiling it in solution with silver nitrate, which it reduces to the metallic state. Trichloracetic acid also yields chloroform when treated with alkalies. The $\beta$-naphthol test (see under Chloroform) may also be used for chloral hydrate from which chloroform is liberated by the potassium hydrate used to dissolve the naphthol. When chloral hydrate is present in very small amount, the best plan is to place the organic admixture in a flask, render it alkaline with sodium hydrate, and then carry out the method described in the chemical analysis of mixtures containing chloroform. Wynter Blyth[1] recommends the addition of tartaric or phosphoric acid in the first instance; any chloroform obtained by distillation of the acid fluid must have existed as such in the organic matter. If the fluid in the flask is then alkalised and distillation resumed, all the chloroform vapour that subsequently comes over is derived from chloral hydrate.

Urochloral acid may be obtained from the urine by evaporating it down, acidulating with hydrochloric acid, and shaking out with ether. On evaporation of the ether, needle-shaped crystals arranged in stars are deposited; an aqueous solution of these crystals reduces Fehling's solution, and turns the polarised ray to the left.

## SULPHONAL

**Disulphonethyl-dimethylmethane**, or sulphonal, is used to procure sleep. It is a crystalline substance, produced by oxidation of a mixture of ethyl-mercaptan and dimethylketone (acetone). It is sparingly soluble in water and ether, and is more freely so in alcohol. As is the case with all hypnotics, sulphonal is used by the public on their own responsibility, and in this way has given rise to serious results.

In a fatal case recorded by Knaggs,[2] a man took rather more than an ounce of sulphonal. He became comatose, with slow respiration, slow pulse, sometimes increasing to 90 beats per minute and elevated temperature—ranging from 100° to 103° F; the pupils were of normal size and reacted to light. There was profuse perspiration, and total suppression of urine. He remained in the same condition for three days, when the breathing became short and jerky, and finally ceased. In a case recorded by Reinfuss,[3] a woman, aged forty-seven, took sulphonal in doses of fifteen to twenty-two grains almost daily until the total amount reached between two and three ounces. She began to vomit and complained of pain in the stomach and abdomen. She then lost power over the legs, and had two attacks of clonic spasms; the pupils were contracted and equal, and reacted to light. Thirst, diminution in temperature, profuse perspiration, and during the last twenty-four hours muscular tremors and unconsciousness ended in death on the thirteenth day after the commencement of the vomiting. A

[1] *Poisons*, 1884.   [2] *Brit. Med. Journ.*, 1890.
[3] *Wiener med. Blatter*, 1892.

peculiar appearance was observed in the urine, which from the first was dark, and reddish-brown in colour, due to the presence of hæmatoporphyrin, albumen and renal epithelium were present. Kober[1] relates the case of a man, aged fifty, who for four or five weeks took doses of from 7 to 22 grains of sulphonal. As in the last case, the urine varied in colour from burgundy-red to reddish-black, it contained albumen and casts, but no red corpuscles, later on suppression of urine occurred, and the patient died. In addition to hæmatoporphyrin and albumen, Jolles[2] found unchanged sulphonal, and increase of the combined sulphuric acid in the urine. In the case of a man, aged thirty-four, who took sulphonal in very large doses—a teaspoonful at once—Ullmann[3] observed reeling gait, stammering speech, and erratic gesticulations, which lasted four or five days. In another case there were ataxic symptoms, which prevented locomotion and impeded speech.

On the other hand, enormous doses have been taken without any permanent ill effects. Neisser[4] records a case in which a youth, aged fifteen, for the purpose of committing suicide, took 50 grammes of powdered sulphonal, and shortly after another 50 grammes, amounting together to more than 3 ounces. In three-quarters of an hour he became unconscious, and was found about six hours after, when he was taken to the hospital, emetics were administered, and the stomach was washed out. He slept until the sixth day, and on the ninth day was perfectly well. The urine contained neither albumen nor sugar, but unchanged sulphonal was obtained from it. In another case a man, after taking over an ounce, slept for five days and then recovered.

Tests.—If a little dry sulphonal is heated in a test-tube with charcoal or iron in powder, the odour of mercaptan is given off, if iron is used, the subsequent addition of hydrochloric acid to the residue liberates sulphuretted hydrogen. If a little dry sulphonal is melted and the heat is continued until the clear liquid boils, the addition of pyrogallol produces a brown colour with evolution of mercaptan.

## CARBON BISULPHIDE.

Carbon Bisulphide [$CS_2$,] has only exceptionally caused acute poisoning, chronic poisoning, by its vapour, is more common in consequence of its wide-spread use in india-rubber and gutta-percha works.

**Symptoms of Acute Poisoning.**—In a case recorded by Davidson[5] a man swallowed about two ounces of carbon bisulphide. When seen

[1] *Centralbl f klin Med*, 1892.  [2] *Internat klin Rundschau*, 1891.
[3] *Corresp Blatt f schweiz Aerzte*, 1889.  [4] *Deutsche med Wochenschr*, 1891.
[5] *Med Times and Gaz*, 1878.

the patient was in a state of collapse, the muscles were relaxed and the pupils dilated and insensible to light, the pulse was quick and feeble, the breathing laboured, the odour of the poison being perceptible in the breath, the lips were blue, and the surface was cold, occasional convulsive tremors or shiverings occurred. The odour of carbon bisulphide could be perceived both in the urine and the fæces. Recovery took place, the patient being well on the fifth day. A fatal case is recorded by Foreman.[1] A man swallowed about half an ounce of carbon bisulphide and became comatose in half an hour. The respirations were slow and laboured, the pulse 150 to 160 in the minute, the surface was cold and clammy, the pupils were normal. Death occurred two and a quarter hours after the poison was swallowed. At the necropsy the odour of the poison was perceptible; the posterior wall of the stomach was congested for about the size of a crown-piece, hæmorrhagic points were visible in the gastric mucous membrane. The veins were gorged with black blood, the blood throughout being fluid. The urine yielded the odour of carbon bisulphide.

Treatment.—The stomach-pump should be used, and the drowsiness then combatted as is customary with other narcotics. Warmth should be applied to the body, and stimulants administered internally. In case of need, artificial respiration is to be resorted to. If there is no diarrhœa, purgatives should be given.

Carbon bisulphide is eliminated by the lungs, kidneys and bowels. Death is apparently due to paralysis of the respiratory centres, which is also the cause of death in animals experimentally poisoned with carbon bisulphide.

Chemical Analysis.—From organic admixture carbon bisulphide may be separated by distillation. It is recognised by its odour, and by giving a black precipitate of lead sulphide when heated with lead acetate and potash.

Chronic Poisoning.—Like many other volatile poisons carbon bisulphide, when long inhaled, produces peripheral neuritis in addition to disorders of the digestive tract. In the early stage of chronic poisoning as it occurs amongst workmen in certain departments in rubber factories, the appetite fails, and the patient is always conscious of the odour of the bisulphide, even when away from his work. Sometimes a state of mental exaltation or of depression occurs, with sleeplessness, headache, nausea, vomiting, and colicky pains. These symptoms are followed by those of neuritis. In some cases investigated by Ross[2] the earliest of the neural symptoms was a burning sensation in the hands, alternating with numbness; then followed tingling and numb-

[1] *The Lancet*, 1886.     [2] *Med Chron*, 1887.

ness in the feet, with weakness. In one case the immediate narcotic effects of the vapour were demonstrated by the patient's desire to return to his work, because when he inhaled the vapour he felt some relief from the symptoms. The extensor muscles of the forearm and those of the leg were atrophied and partially paralysed, producing wrist-drop and ankle-drop respectively. There were numbness and tingling in the toes and feet, and in the tips of the fingers. The field of vision was restricted for all colours. Another patient was disturbed by horrible dreams, fancying himself surrounded by animals, sometimes, when at his work, he found himself talking nonsense. When the vapour of carbon bisulphide is present in considerable amount, the workmen not unfrequently develop symptoms resembling those of delirium tremens.

### PETROLEUM AND PARAFFIN OIL

**Petroleum** is a natural oil, consisting of a mixture of the higher, but not the highest, paraffins or hydrocarbons of the series $C_n H_{2n+2}$, of which marsh-gas is a type. The commercial oil varies in S G from 7 to 825, and in boiling point from 150° to 300° C. If well refined, it is a transparent, slightly fluorescent liquid, free from colour, but it usually presents a slight yellowish tinge when examined in bulk; it has a peculiar penetrating odour. It is largely used as an illuminant. An early product of distillation of the crude oil is known as petroleum ether, which has a S G of 66 to 67, and a much lower boiling point [50° to 60° C] than the ordinary variety. Petroleum ether is used for extracting fats from organic fluids, and as a solvent.

**Paraffin Oil** is a mixture of paraffins obtained by distillation of shale; from the toxicological standpoint it does not differ from petroleum. In retail trade petroleum and paraffin oil are sold indifferently, the one for the other.

The toxic properties of petroleum depend greatly upon the kind of oil taken, but in any case it is not an active poison. Lewin,[1] basing his conclusions on a number of experiments on animals, and observations on the human subject, does not regard petroleum as a poison in the ordinary sense of the word, the dose necessary to produce toxic effects being so large. M'Culloch[2] saw a man, aged forty-three, one hour after he had swallowed nearly half a pint of paraffin oil; he was pale, and his breath had the odour of the oil; he complained of his throat being hot and dry, and he had a feeling of warmth in the epigastric region, but no pain; the pupils were normal; the pulse was full, but this probably resulted from excitement. After an emetic he

[1] Virchow's *Arch*, 1888.   [2] *The Lancet*, 1885.

vomited a little food and about eight ounces of paraffin oil. The oil was in his stomach an hour, along with very little food, but it did not cause the least indication of gastric irritation; the man was quite well the next morning. Vincent[1] saw a girl, aged fifteen and a half, who swallowed about half a pint of paraffin oil. Fifteen or twenty minutes after she vomited, and was cold, with pale anxious face, feeble pulse—132 in the minute—and sighing respiration. She had pain in the throat, epigastrium, and left hypochondrium. Recovery took place. Unusually severe symptoms occurred in the case of a woman, aged thirty-six, who was seen by Caruthers.[2] During a debauch she swallowed half a cupful of paraffin oil; in half an hour she had violent pain, and vomited, the vomit was stated to contain blood. When seen she complained of pain in the epigastrium, and afterwards of pain in the left lumbar region. The motions contained blood, and also paraffin oil. A considerable quantity of oil floated on the surface of the urine after it had stood a while; on distillation 6 cc of pure oil were obtained; subsequently the urine contained albumen and blood. The odour of the oil was present in the breath for twenty-four hours. The patient was not seen for three or four hours after she swallowed the oil, and although she vomited in the interval, a considerable quantity had remained in the stomach, as was shown by the matter subsequently vomited. She was well in a week. On more than one occasion a pint of petroleum has been swallowed without causing more than temporary disorder.

Some writers doubt the possibility of petroleum being present in bulk in the urine. Lewin in his experiments on animals found that it did not appear as such in the urine, and disputes its occurrence in the human subject. Several cases are recorded, however, besides the one just related, in which unaltered oil was found floating on the urine after the individual had swallowed it in large amount.

Biller[3] records a fatal case, in which an infant, eighteen months old, drank some 'gasoline.' It became unconscious, powerless, livid in the face, tympanitic in the abdomen, and cold on the surface; death occurred in thirty minutes.

**Vaseline**, which is a mixed intermediate product between the liquid and solid members of the paraffin series of hydrocarbons is usually regarded as a harmless substance. One instance is recorded by Robinson,[4] in which half a teaspoonful was respectively given to three children for sore throat, it produced vomiting, pains in the knees, and cramps in the legs, with partial collapse; all the children recovered

[1] *Brit. Med. Journ.*, 1886.  [2] *The Lancet*, 1890.
[3] *New York Med. Journ.*, 1889.  [4] *Brit. Med. Journ.*, 1886.

## CHAPTER XXXI.

### BENZENE AND ITS DERIVATIVES

Benzene [$C_6H_6$], or benzole, is one of the principal ingredients in coal-tar, from which it is obtained by fractional distillation; commercial benzene contains small quantities of some of the other light hydrocarbons. It is a colourless, volatile liquid, having an odour which recalls that of coal gas; it is exceedingly inflammable, and gives off a vapour which is explosive when mixed with air; it is insoluble in water, on which it floats. It is used in the manufacture of aniline, and also in cleaning gloves and wearing apparel.

Symptoms of acute poisoning much resemble those of alcohol—a stage of excitement, which is quickly followed by heaviness in the head, and a tendency to stupor or coma. Foulerton[1] records the case of a man who, in the pursuit of his avocation, entered a large and almost empty tank used to store benzene; when found, he was insensible, and could not stand; he could answer questions in an indistinct way, moaning and laughing hysterically. The face was flushed, and the surface of the body cold; there were muscular twitchings; the pupils were dilated, and reacted to light; the pulse was 88 full and soft; the respirations, reduced to 8 or 9 in the minute, were deep, stertorous, and irregular, as much as fifteen seconds sometimes intervening between the breaths. The patient vomited, the ejected matter smelling of benzene. Recovery took place. Averill[2] met with a case, in which a man accidentally swallowed three or four drachms of benzene. He became pale and unconscious, with small, weak, rapid pulse, and slow breathing; the pupils did not react to light. The stomach was evacuated, and the vomited matter contained oily-looking globules, which took fire on applying a light. Recovery occurred, the odour of benzene being perceptible in the breath sixty-two hours after the poison was swallowed. Falk[3] records a fatal case in a child two years old, death taking place ten minutes after a mouthful of benzene was swallowed; the postmortem appearances, beyond a faint odour of benzene on opening the abdomen, were negative.

A fatal case of poisoning by benzene-vapour is recorded by Sury-Bienz.[4] It occurred to a workman in a chemical manufactory, who had to attend to a process, in the course of which a great deal of benzene

---

[1] *The Lancet*, 1886.  [2] *Brit. Med. Journ.*, 1889.
[3] *Vierteljahrsschr. f. ger. Med.*, 1892.  [4] *Ibid.*, 1888.

was volatilised. He was heard to call out that he was on fire, he then reeled, fell to the ground, and died forthwith; a fellow-workman who ran to his help perceived a powerful odour of benzene, but there was no fire. At the necropsy the veins were found filled with fluid blood, and there was some œdema of the lungs, but nothing else of moment.

## NITRO DERIVATIVES OF BENZENE

**Nitrobenzene** [$C_6H_5NO_2$], or nitrobenzole, is the product yielded by the action of nitric acid on benzene. It is a light yellow liquid having an odour resembling that of oil of bitter almonds, and is known in commerce as **artificial oil of bitter almonds** or **oil of mirbane**; it is largely used in the preparation of aniline and also to scent toilet soaps.

**Dinitrobenzene** [$C_6H_4(NO_2)_2$].—The compound used commercially is the meta-dinitrobenzene which forms long rhombic prisms of a light yellow tint when pure; the commercial variety is yellowish brown. It is soluble in alcohol and ether, and when impure, to a slight extent in water. It is produced in aniline works and enters into the composition of the explosive "roburite" now largely used in coal mines for the purpose of blasting. Roburite consists of a mixture of dinitrobenzene, or chloro-dinitrobenzene and ammonium nitrate.

### Nitrobenzene

**Symptoms** of acute poisoning with nitrobenzene. The most characteristic symptom is the occurrence of a livid or cyanotic appearance of the face, the lips especially acquiring a dull lead colour; the fingers and toes, and even the whole body may be intensely blue. If the patient is able to walk, his gait is unsteady, and his muscular power feeble; vomiting may occur, the vomited matters probably having the odour of the poison which also pervades the breath; drowsiness develops and rapidly passes into stupor or coma. The pulse is usually feeble and quickened, and may be intermittent; the breathing is often shallow and irregular with quickened expiration; the temperature is reduced and the surface is clammy. The pupils have been observed to be contracted in some cases and dilated in others; dilatation is common in the comatose stage. Blood withdrawn during life has been found darker than usual.

Filehne[1] found that in dogs poisoned with nitrobenzene the blood was chocolate brown in colour; on spectroscopic examination it yielded a band in the red near the hæmatin band, which he regards as directly

[1] *Arch. f. exp. Pathol.* 1878.

due to the action of nitrobenzene. In no case did he find that the nitrobenzene was converted in the system into aniline. Filehne explains the dyspnœa as being due to incapacity of the hæmoglobin to carry oxygen to the tissues; animals poisoned with nitrobenzene exhale more $CO_2$ and take up less O than in the normal. Lewin[1] found the band in the red to be identical with that of hæmatin.

**Fatal Dose.**—Twenty drops have proved fatal. Recovery has occurred after very nearly an ounce, but the patient received prompt and efficient treatment. Dodd[2] records the case of a man, aged forty-seven, who swallowed two drachms of nitrobenzene and then eat his dinner, after which he walked three quarters of a mile. One hour and a half after the poison was swallowed extreme cyanosis developed, the skin was clammy, the pulse feeble, and the respirations were shallow, irregular, and sighing; among other symptoms was trismus. The breath had the odour of nitrobenzene. The stomach was well washed out, and the patient recovered. In fatal cases death takes place in from one to twenty-four hours.

**Treatment.**—Evacuate and thoroughly wash out the stomach; apply external warmth and friction, and if necessary use artificial respiration and faradism. Stimulants may be required; they should not, however, be given by the mouth unless the stomach has been thoroughly washed out, as alcohol is a solvent of nitrobenzene. In severe cases, transfusion of defibrinated human blood may be resorted to after removal of an equal amount of blood from the patient.

## Dinitrobenzene

Poisoning with dinitrobenzene usually occurs in manufactories where this substance is used; it is received into the system either in the form of vapour or of finely-divided particles floating in the air, or from handling it in bulk. It is customary in many works to provide the men with rubber gloves as otherwise their hands become contaminated with the poison which is thus transferred to food; it is probable that prolonged handling of dinitrobenzene may lead to its introduction through the skin.

The **symptoms of acute poisoning** resemble those produced by nitrobenzene.—Headache, giddiness, loss of power in the limbs, blue coloration of the lips, cold and livid surface, quickened feeble pulse, dyspnœa, shallow irregular respiration, with long intervals between the breaths, and coma. The cyanotic appearance may be limited to the face or it may spread to the limbs, usually the trunk is not much affected, the

[1] Virchow's Arch., 1879.   [2] Brit. Med. Journ., 1891.

blood is dark, and sometimes chocolate-coloured. Vomiting frequently occurs spontaneously.

Chronic poisoning with dinitrobenzene, which also occurs amongst those who prepare or purify it, produces a different class of symptoms. Schröder and Strassmann[1] investigated several cases and describe the chief symptoms as follows:—headache, pain in the stomach with irregular action of the bowels, loss of appetite, sleeplessness and general feeling of lassitude. The lips are blue and the skin acquires a dirty yellow tint, the sclera being yellow; in some cases the mucous membrane of the mouth especially of the uvula and pharynx looks as though it was covered with a yellow bloom which, however, can not be wiped off. The gastric and hepatic regions are very tender on pressure, the liver usually being enlarged. The urine is dark brown, but quite clear; dinitrobenzene was proved to be present in it. The symptoms present very much the appearance of those due to catarrhal jaundice, but the urine yields no trace of bile, the motions retain their colour, and the prostration and blue colour of the lips are different from anything observed in cases of jaundice. Rohl[2] describes certain effects produced on the nervous system by chronic dinitrobenzene poisoning resembling those of peripheral neuritis.—Numbness a sensation of cold in the feet, with various paræsthesiæ and cramps.

From experimental researches by Huber[3] it appears that dinitrobenzene combines with hæmoglobin which then yields a spectrum identical with that of acid hæmatin, but it does not respond like hæmatin to reducing agents. On the addition of ammonium sulphide the band in the red, between C and D, persists, but it is slightly displaced; the other two bands remain unchanged. The spectrum is probably the same as that described by Filehne in his investigations on nitrobenzene it is not always obtained with the blood of animals poisoned with dinitrobenzene, nor has it been observed in the human subject.

The urine as before stated contains dinitrobenzene, which exists as such, no derivatives have so far been detected. By means of treatment with zinc and hydrochloric acid, the dinitrobenzene present in the urine may be converted into phenylenediamine. If the urine is then alkalised with soda and shaken out with ether, and the residue after evaporation of the ether is treated with sodium nitrite and acetic acid, a brown colour—Bismarck-brown—is produced. If the urine is shaken out with ether, without being previously treated with zinc and HCl, no effect is produced on the ethereal residue by sodium nitrite, showing that the dinitrobenzene is not decomposed in the system into phenylenediamine nor into nitraniline.

[1] *Vierteljahrsschr. f. ger. Med.* (Supp.), 1891.
[2] *Ueber acute u. chron. Intox. durch Nitrokorp. d. Benz-lreihe*, 1890.
[3] *Virchow's Arch.*, 1891.

Roburite being largely composed of dinitrobenzene produces similar toxic symptoms. Spurgin[1] reports an interesting case of acute poisoning with this explosive.—A boy of sixteen slept in a room in which roburite had been sprinkled to poison cockroaches; he was found deeply cyanosed—the lips, tongue, and fingers being nearly black, the surface was cold, there was dyspnœa with laboured breathing, and the pulse, 135 in the minute, was very weak. Another lad who slept in the same room was only slightly cyanosed. Recovery took place in both cases.

Chronic poisoning with roburite is identical with that due to dinitrobenzene. Ross[2] investigated some cases and found well-marked symptoms of peripheral neuritis in addition to the gastro-hepatic symptoms.

It is to be observed that the symptoms produced by roburite are due to dinitrobenzene being introduced into the system as such, and not to the fumes produced by detonation of the explosive. See section on the gases given off by explosives.

Treatment.—In the acute form the treatment is like that for poisoning with mononitrobenzene, excepting that the stomach-pump will not be needed unless the poison has been swallowed in bulk. Chronic poisoning demands withdrawal from the influence of the poison and general treatment of the symptoms as they present themselves, unless the condition is far advanced, improvement, if not ultimate recovery, takes place.

Post-mortem Appearances.—When death occurs from acute poisoning with either mono- or dinitrobenzene, with the exception of the odour of the poison, the indications are far from being characteristic. The blood has been found dark, or chocolate-coloured, ecchymoses have been observed on the mucous membranes, and the internal organs have been found paler in colour than usual, the cyanotic hue of the skin and mucous membranes, is not always visible after death. Letheby,[3] who was one of the first to investigate poisoning with nitrobenzene, found the liver purple in colour, and the heart and veins as in death from asphyxia.

Chemical Analysis—Tests.—Nitrobenzene may be separated from organic admixture by distillation; it is distinguishable by its odour. If the distillate is treated with zinc and hydrochloric acid, the nascent hydrogen liberated converts the nitrobenzene into aniline, the product, diluted with water, filtered if necessary, and treated with bleaching powder added a little at a time, yields a purple colour which tends to black. If after conversion into aniline, potassium hydrate and a few drops of chloroform are added to the distillate, and it is heated, the

---

[1] *Brit. Med Journ.*, 1891  [2] *Med. Chron.*, 1889
[3] *Proc. Royal Society*, 1863

presence of phenyl-isocyanide may be recognised by its odour. (See tests for chloroform.) If dinitrobenzene was the poison, it may sometimes be detected in the blood by directly converting it into metaphenylenediamine (as described in the case of the urine) shaking out with ether, and after evaporation of the ether testing the residue with sodium nitrite.

Dinitrotoluene [$C_6H_3(NO_2)_2CH_3$] produces effects in every way similar to the nitrobenzene compounds with which it is closely allied. Maceroy[1] records the case of a child three years old, who swallowed a piece of dinitrotoluene the size of a pea. One hour after there was complete relaxation of the muscles and coma; the breathing was rapid and shallow, the pulse rapid, the surface cold and cyanotic, the pupils were equal and insensive to light; convulsions occurred. The cyanosis disappeared within twenty-four hours, the lips being the last to regain their natural colour, and the child was quite well the next day. The cyanotic hue was totally different to that seen in asphyxia.

## ANILINE

Aniline [$C_6H_5NH_2$], phenylamine, or amine oil which forms the basis of various aniline colours, is produced commercially by reducing nitrobenzene. When pure and freshly prepared, it is a colourless oily liquid, having a peculiar odour; after a time, especially with access of air, it turns brown; crude commercial aniline contains toluidine in admixture. It is very slightly soluble in water, but is freely so in alcohol and ether. Aniline can be absorbed by the unbroken skin as well as by the lungs and mucous membranes.

**Symptoms.**—When a poisonous dose of aniline is swallowed the symptoms appear in from five to ten minutes up to an hour or more. Nausea and vomiting usually occur, and the patient experiences a sensation of giddiness and drowsiness which deepens into coma; soon after the poison is taken the lips, face, the ends of the fingers and toes, the conjunctivæ, and the lobes of the ears become cyanotic. The respirations are laboured and frequently slowed; sometimes they are accelerated. The pulse is variable; it has been found small, frequent, and irregular; but in one fatal case it was regular, moderately full, of normal tension, and not more than 80 to 88 in the minute. The skin is cold and clammy to the touch; the breath may have the odour of aniline, the pupils are sometimes dilated and reactionless, at others they are contracted and slowly respond to alternations of light and darkness; the reflexes are sometimes present and at others absent.

[1] *The Lancet*, 1888.

The blood has been found chocolate-coloured, and, when examined with the spectroscope, yields a spectrum like that of methæmoglobin. Muller[1] records the case of a woman who swallowed about 25 cc (six drachms) of aniline, and became comatose and deeply cyanosed. A little of the blood taken from the finger gave the spectrum of methæmoglobin, and, on the addition of ammonium sulphide, that of reduced hæmoglobin thus differing from the spectrum obtained with dinitrobenzene, which does not materially change on the addition of a reducing agent. In fatal cases the cyanosis and subnormal temperature persist, and not unfrequently convulsions occur shortly before death. In mild cases the only pronounced symptom may be the blue discoloration of the lips and face, without dyspnœa; this leads to a consideration of the cause of the cyanosis.

It appears very probable that the blue colour so universally present in cases of poisoning with aniline and other benzene derivatives is not wholly due to asphyxia caused by functionless hæmoglobin, but that some of the poison undergoes such chemical changes in the system as to yield coloured products which are largely accountable for the "cyanosis." The reasons for this supposition are:—That the colour differs from that of ordinary cyanosis; that it has been observed without any indication of dyspnœa, and that in those cases in which the respiratory function is profoundly implicated and recovery takes place, the blue colour persists for a time after the breathing has returned to the normal condition. Many observers have stated that the colour was unlike anything they had ever seen in simple asphyxia, and also that it was much more pronounced. Reynolds,[2] in reporting a case of nitrobenzene poisoning, remarks that the intense blueness of the whole body was more marked than in any kind of cyanosis he had previously seen. Dehio[3] describes the colour of the skin in the case of a woman who drank ten grammes of aniline as not being at all like that of ordinary cyanosis—it was more of a lead tint. It did not produce the impression that it was due to overfilling of the veins (an explanation that has been suggested), for it remained when the blood was pressed out with the finger. The colour resembled that produced by a pigment which had transuded from the blood within the vessels into the skin. An interesting incident, illustrating the production of blue discoloration without dyspnœa, is related by Rayner[4]—A kind of epidemic in newly-born children broke out in a workhouse; in typical cases the lips, gums, and palate were as blue as a wimberry, and the entire surface of the body was dusky, although the children were quite lively; the breathing was natural, and the temperature

[1] *Deutsche med. Wochenschr.*, 1887.
[2] *Med. Chron.*, 1889.
[3] *Berliner klin. Wochenschr.*, 1888.
[4] *Brit. Med. Journ.*, 1886.

normal. It was discovered that napkins, name-marked with a large four and a half inch oval stamp charged with aniline chloride, were being used without being previously washed. The buttocks and vulva of the children were stained with the pigment, from whence it had been absorbed through the skin; when the napkins ceased to be used, the children gradually regained their natural colour. Persistence of discoloration, after disappearance of the conditions causative of cyanosis, is illustrated by three cases of antifebrin poisoning (*vide post*), in which methæmoglobin was found in the blood during the stage of cyanosis, but had completely disappeared some time before the skin resumed its natural colour. It has been denied that aniline undergoes any changes in the body which could lead to the formation of pigments, but there are strong reasons for assuming such changes to be possible. Dragendorff[1] investigated the case of a woman who became comatose after swallowing about three drachms of aniline, most of which was rejected by vomiting; eighteen hours after, the tips of the fingers, the feet, lips, and gums were cyanosed. The rejected contents of the stomach gave the reactions of aniline and of paratoluidine; the urine contained only a minute quantity of aniline, but much more paratoluidine; Dragendorff believes that some of the missing aniline was converted in the body into pigment. Exceptionally, aniline may cause destruction of the red corpuscles, and in consequence icterus, followed by hæmoglobinuria, has been observed.

**Fatal Dose.**—Six drachms have proved fatal. Probably much less might do so.

**Treatment.**—The same as in poisoning with nitrobenzene.

**Post-mortem Appearances** are not characteristic. In one case the veins were found distended with dark-coloured blood; the mucous membrane of the bronchi and of the stomach was in parts swollen and reddened.

**Chemical Analysis.**—Aniline may be separated from organic matter by alkalising and then distilling the mixture; if much aniline is present, it will be visible as oily-looking drops in the distillate. It may also be separated from organic matter by alkalising and shaking out with ether.

**Tests.**—An aqueous solution of aniline, treated with bleaching-powder cautiously added, yields a purple colour, tending to black. A drop of aniline on a colour-slab, treated with a drop of strong sulphuric acid, yields a dirty white solid; if this is mixed with a couple of drops of water, and then with a drop of a solution of potassium dichromate, a bronze-green colour is produced, which rapidly

[1] *Fortschritte d. Med.*, 1887.

changes to blue, and then to black. If a minute quantity of aniline is dissolved in an aqueous solution of phenol, and a solution of bleaching powder is dropped into the mixture, a yellowish streak, which shortly changes to blue, follows the course of each drop as it passes through the liquid. The previously described test with chloroform, resulting in the formation of phenyl-isocyanide may be utilised in the detection of aniline.

Methylacetanilide or Exalgin has several times given rise to dangerous symptoms of the aniline type. Bokenham and Jones[1] state that a woman, aged twenty-four, after taking exalgin in six grain doses three times a day for a week, became blue in the lips and cheeks, with a feeling of weight in the epigastrium; subsequently she became more deeply cyanosed, and was delirious; stimulants and strychnine were administered, and recovery took place. It was noticed that inhalation of amyl nitrite, by causing dilatation of the vessels, temporarily increased the blueness. Giltay[2] records a case in which seventeen and a half grains of exalgin were swallowed in mistake for sulphonal; unconsciousness, recurrent convulsions, profuse perspiration, foaming at the mouth, weak, rapid and intermittent pulse, and dilated pupils resulted; recovery took place. Beorchia-Nigris[3] found methæmoglobin in the blood thirty days after the administration of exalgin; he states that it diminishes the number of red corpuscles, the percentage of hæmoglobin, and the excretion of $CO_2$.

Acetanilide or Antifebrin has frequently produced toxic symptoms accompanied with cyanosis. Marenchaux[4] relates the case of an infant, five months old, to whom a little over three grains of antifebrin were accidentally given, which produced deep cyanosis, coldness of the surface, and insensibility; the breathing was excessively quick—72 respirations to the minute—the pulse being 160. Recovery took place. Muller distinguished the bands of methæmoglobin in the blood of three patients who were cyanosed after taking large doses of antifebrin; he noticed that the blood became normal before the cyanosis disappeared, and attributes the continuance of the cyanosis to overfilling of the veins. Neither antifebrin nor aniline could be found in the urine, but there was an increased amount of combined sulphuric acid.

Chemical Analysis.—Antifebrin may be extracted from acid aqueous solution by ether or chloroform.

Tests.—Sulpho-vanadic acid produces a brownish-red, which changes

[1] Brit Med Journ, 1890.  [2] Ibid, 1892.
[3] Annali di Chim e Farm, 1892.  [4] Deutsche med Wochenschr, 1889.

to dirty green. If a drop of a solution of potassium dichromate is mixed with a drop of strong sulphuric acid on a colour-slab, and a fragment of antifebrin added, a red colour which changes to brown and then to dirty green is produced. Boiled with an aqueous solution of potash, antifebrin is decomposed into aniline and potassium acetate, which may be respectively recognised by appropriate tests. Antifebrin may be distinguished from antipyrin by the absence of reaction on the addition of ferric chloride.

**Phenyldimethylpyrazolone** or **Antipyrin** has occasionally produced toxic symptoms. Rapin[1] reports the case of a woman, aged twenty-eight, who took four doses of fifteen grains each on five consecutive days without ill effect; on the sixth day she took a like dose, which produced collapse, the cheeks and lips being almost black from "cyanosis," a rash came out on the body. She was well on the following day.

**Chemical Analysis.**—Antipyrin may be extracted by chloroform from both acid and alkaline solution, but it is preferable to alkalise before shaking out.

**Tests.**—With ferric chloride a dark-red colour is produced, which is destroyed by mineral acids in excess. When antipyrin is heated with a solution of bleaching-powder a brick-red precipitate is formed. If a little potassium nitrite is dissolved in water, and excess of strong sulphuric acid is added, the nitrous acid set free produces a green colour with antipyrin; this test is common to all pyrazolones. The urine from patients taking antipyrin yields the ferric chloride reaction on simple addition of the reagent. Antipyrin is precipitated by most of the alkaloidal group reagents.

**Naphthalene** [$C_{10}H_8$] is a coal-tar derivative which forms colourless, crystalline plates, having a faint odour; it is insoluble in cold water, slightly soluble in hot, and freely soluble in alcohol and ether. It is used in medicine as an antiseptic, and when taken internally is supposed to act on the mucous membrane of the bowel without being absorbed, but even when quite pure it may produce toxic effects. Rossbach[2] relates a case in which toxic symptoms occurred after six grammes; the lips and cheeks were slightly cyanosed, and twitchings of the muscles occurred over the whole body; the urine was dark-brown, and became inky-black on standing. Cases have occurred in which naphthalene has produced hæmoglobinuria and strangury. Symptoms of poisoning have also followed its external use.

[1] *Revue Med. de la suisse Rom.*, 1888
[2] *Berliner klin. Wochenschr.*, 1884

Resorcin [$C_6H_6O_2$] in toxic doses produces symptoms analogous to those due to phenol. Murrel[1] records the case of a girl, aged nineteen, in which two drachms produced almost immediate giddiness, and a sensation of pins and needles all over the body; she became insensible, and perspired profusely; the temperature was low, the pulse imperceptible, the face pallid, the lips were blanched, the pupils normal, the conjunctivæ insensitive to the touch, and the chest-walls almost motionless. There was a state of general muscular relaxation; recovery took place. In another case epileptiform convulsions occurred.

Tests.—Ferric chloride produces a violet colour. Sulpho-vanadic acid blue and then violet. If a crystal of sodium nitrite is mixed with a drop or two of concentrated sulphuric acid and a little resorcin is added, a violet colour, which changes to blue and then brown, is produced.

Pyrogallol [$C_6H_6O_3$], or pyrogallic acid, when absorbed into the system in large amount, destroys the red blood corpuscles, causes dyspnœa, reduction of temperature, lessened sensibility, paralysis, and the presence of free hæmoglobin in the urine; methæmoglobin has been found in the blood. The dyspnœa, which may be excessive, is probably due to the formation of thrombi, which are the ultimate cause of death.

Four cases of fatal poisoning have occurred since the introduction of pyrogallol in the treatment of psoriasis in 1878. When extensively applied to the surface in the form of an ointment absorption takes place; the following is a *résumé* of the results which occurred in all four cases :—The toxic symptoms came on very suddenly; in one case after the first rubbing, in a second case on the third day, in a third case on the sixth day, and in a fourth on the fifteenth day; they comprised rigors, nausea, prostration, quick pulse, primary elevation, followed by rapid fall of temperature, acute anæmia, jaundice, vomiting, diarrhœa, hæmoglobinuria, hæmaturia with albumen, broncho-pneumonia, and great dyspnœa. On section the blood was found bluish and fluid; the kidneys black and intensely congested.

Absorption does not appear to be so rapid when pyrogallol is taken internally. Benerji[2] records a case in which a man and his wife each swallowed more than a drachm; vomiting was procured in half an hour, and only the man experienced any symptoms; they were limited to a sensation of drowsiness coming on at intervals, nausea, slight paroxysmal numbness about the limbs and face, palpitation, dryness of the throat, and a black tongue; the following day he was quite well. A case of mixed poisoning is related by Maillart and Andeoud,[3] in

[1] *Med. Times and Gaz.*, 1881.      [2] *The Lancet*, 1892.
[3] *Revue Med. de la suisse Rom.*, 1891.

which a man swallowed about four grains of pilocarpine, and, immediately after, two drachms of pyrogallol, in three or four minutes most of the poison was rejected by vomiting. The symptoms that ensued were due to the pilocarpine; profuse sweating occurred, and increased secretion from all the mucous surfaces and the glands, with pain and tenesmus in the abdomen, reduction of temperature to 96° F, and temporary abolition of sight, which was quickly restored by atropine; recovery took place. Both pilocarpine and pyrogallol were detected in the urine.

Treatment consists in evacuation of the stomach if necessary, the administration of stimulants, the inhalation of oxygen, and external warmth.

The post-mortem appearances are not characteristic.

Chemical Analysis.—Pyrogallol may be dissolved out of dried organic matter by digestion with alcohol. After filtration the alcohol is evaporated, the residue is extracted with water and shaken out with ether, which on evaporation leaves the pyrogallol behind.

Tests.—With lime-water a purple-red is produced, with basic lead acetate a reddish colour, and with ferrous sulphate a bluish-black. A solution of sodium molybdate added to a solution of pyrogallol produces a brownish-red colour.

Salicylic Acid [$C_7H_6O_3$] used in medicine for the most part in combination with sodium, has occasionally produced toxic effects. The symptoms vary; they comprise:—hæmorrhage from the gums and the kidneys, retinal hæmorrhage, epistaxis, hæmaturia, albuminuria, vomiting, irregularity of the pulse, urticaria, hallucinations and insensibility. Charteris and Maclennan[1] state that the toxic effects of sodium salicylate are due to impurities which exist in the artificially prepared salt, and that the natural salt is not toxic. In one of two cases recorded by Auld,[2] one hundred grains daily for six days caused great and stridulous dyspnœa, extreme slowness of the pulse, general paralysis, and some delirium; in another case the delirium was more marked. Recovery has occurred after very large doses. A patient was given an ounce and a half of sodium salicylate in mistake for sodium sulphate; the symptoms produced were:—Burning sensation in the throat and stomach, thirst, nausea, vomiting, profuse sweating, coldness of the limbs, defective vision without alteration of the pupils, slow action of the heart, noise in the ears with deafness, and a state of collapse, which with the deafness lasted several days. Albumen was present in the urine.[3]

[1] *Glasgow Med. Journ.*, 1889.   [2] *The Lancet*, 1890.
[3] *Deutsche med. Wochenschr.*, 1881.

**Chemical Analysis.**—From organic matter salicylic acid may be separated by acidulation and then shaking out with ether.

**Tests.**—Both salicylic acid and phenol strike a violet colour with ferric chloride; the addition of acetic acid destroys the colour produced by phenol, but leaves that produced by salicylic acid unaltered. In ammoniacal solution salicylic acid undergoes no change on the addition of bromine-water; under like conditions phenol turns blue. Salicylic acid is chiefly eliminated by the kidneys and may be detected in the urine by the addition of ferric chloride.

## PHENOL OR CARBOLIC ACID

Phenol [$C_6H_5OH$] when pure forms a crystalline mass without colour, which reddens if exposed to air. The change in colour is due to oxidation and not to the presence of bi-products, such as cresol and the like; chemically pure phenol becomes red if frequently melted with free exposure to air. It has a penetrating odour indicative of its presence in the smallest amount. Although commonly called **carbolic acid** it has no acid reaction, but it coagulates albumen, and destroys tissue; it is slightly heavier than water, in which it dissolves in the proportion of 1 part to 15; it is freely soluble in alcohol and ether. For sanitary purposes crude carbolic acid is used, which consists of from 15 to 60 per cent of phenol along with a varying admixture of other products of distillation from coal-tar; it is a dark-coloured liquid having the odour of phenol, modified by the impurities which are present.

When strong carbolic acid is applied to the skin it causes a white appearance; the epiderm is destroyed and easily peals off, the part subsequently becoming brown and parchment-like; absorption may take place through the unbroken skin to such a degree as to cause death.

The toxic action of carbolic acid is both local and remote; locally it acts as a corrosive, remotely it exercises a complex influence on the nervous system. In animals it first stimulates and then paralyses the centres in the brain and cord; in human beings poisonous doses seem to paralyse from the first. The vasomotor and respiratory centres are early affected; the pulse becomes small and of low tension, and the breathing irregular and laboured; almost at the same time the higher centres are attacked; giddiness, reeling gait, and tendency to delirium are quickly followed by profound coma. In some instances the rapidity with which the cortical centres are attacked is very striking, and puts the local symptoms quite into the shade. Death is due to respiratory and cardiac paralysis.

**Symptoms**—When the strong acid is swallowed, immediate burning pain is experienced from the mouth down to the stomach; a sensation of giddiness and impending loss of consciousness is felt, soon followed by coma with all the symptoms of collapse. The face is ghastly, the breathing is stertorous, the lips are livid, or stained and swollen from contact with the poison; the pupils are contracted, the pulse, small and scarcely perceptible, is usually rapid; the temperature is low, and the surface is bedewed with moisture, or it may be dry. Vomiting is not so constant as in poisoning by other corrosives; it may not only be absent, but may be difficult to procure. The urine is usually diminished or suppressed, that which is voided is often dark in colour, or becomes so on exposure to the air, probably due to an oxidation product of phenol—hydroquinone. Much of the phenol and hydroquinone that is eliminated in the urine is in combination with the sulphuric acid of the sulphates, hence when freshly voided the urine may be of normal colour, but subsequently becomes dark from liberation and further oxidation of these products. Albumen and casts and, exceptionally, blood may be present. The remote effects of phenol have been developed by its injection into the bowel; an instance occurred in which about 144 grains were diluted with water and administered to a boy of five, as an enema to kill worms; no pain was produced but immediate insensibility, which terminated in death in about fourteen hours.[1]

The external application of phenol has proved fatal. Warren[2] mentions a case in which it was applied to the back of an adult, producing coma, trembling of the muscles, and death in twenty minutes. Injection of phenol into abscess cavities has also caused death. Prolonged breathing of air impregnated with the vapour of phenol may produce symptoms of poisoning. Unthank[3] relates the case of a man who was exposed for three hours to the fumes of strong phenol; he was seized with giddiness, stupor, and convulsions. When seen shortly after he was comatose; the neck and face were livid, the surface was cold, and the pulse scarcely perceptible; recovery took place.

Poisoning by carbolic acid is almost invariably either suicidal or accidental; the facility with which it may be obtained accounts for the former, and carelessness for the latter. In poorer households it is frequently kept in an ordinary wine bottle, which leads to its being drunk in mistake for some potable fluid; or, being contained in a medicine bottle, it is thoughtlessly given instead of physic.

**Fatal Dose.**—One drachm has caused death in twelve hours. Sometimes death occurs very rapidly in less than half an hour; it has

[1] *The Lancet*, 1883.     [2] *Med. Press and Circ.*, 1882.
[3] *Brit. Med. Journ.*, 1872.

occurred in three minutes, and, on the other hand, it has been delayed for sixty hours, the usual period is from three to four hours. Recovery has followed enormous doses. Greenway[1] reports the case of a woman who swallowed more than an ounce of carbolic acid containing 90 per cent of phenol, there was profound collapse and total insensibility, but recovery took place. Davidson[2] records the recovery of a woman of forty, after she had swallowed four ounces of crude carbolic acid, the stomach-pump being used twenty minutes after the poison was taken. Hind[3] relates the case of a girl of seventeen who recovered after swallowing six ounces of crude carbolic acid; vomiting was provoked at once; the acid only contained about 14 per cent of phenol.

**Treatment.**—Empty the stomach with a soft tube; if nothing but the ordinary stiff stomach-pump-tube is to hand, great care should be exercised in its introduction, as the walls of the œsophagus are less resistant than in the normal condition. After emptying, the stomach should be well washed out with lukewarm water, in which some magnesium sulphate, or saccharated lime, may with advantage be dissolved, in order to afford an opportunity for the phenol to combine and form an innocuous ether-sulphate. White of eggs and milk may be given. Olive oil has been recommended, but with doubtful advantage. Several observers have noticed that apomorphine failed to produce emesis in phenol poisoning. External warmth, with stimulants such as ether administered hypodermically, or alcohol by the mouth or rectum, are of great value. If death from respiratory paralysis appears imminent, breathing should be promoted artificially.

**Post-mortem Appearances.**—Stains produced by the poison may be present at the angles of the mouth and on the chin, and its odour may be perceptible. The mucous membrane of the mouth may be softened, and either white or ash-grey in colour, that of the œsophagus being similarly affected in parts; on account of shorter period of contact, the changes in the mouth and œsophagus are not usually so well marked as those in the stomach. The peritoneal surface of the stomach may be injected, its mucous coat usually being corrugated, toughened, and of a brown colour; in parts it sometimes appears stiff and leathery as though it had been tanned; in other instances it is softened and easily detached. It has been observed to be of an ash-grey colour with small hæmorrhagic points; actual erosion is uncommon. Blood-stained mucus has been found in the stomach. The duodenum may present a similar appearance, the brown colour being sometimes limited to the summit of the valvulæ conniventes; in a preparation in the Museum of Owens College this is well shown in the form of a series of parallel brown lines running across the bowel for fully twelve inches.

[1] *The Lancet*, 1891.     [2] *Med. Times and Gaz.*, 1875.
[3] *The Lancet*, 1884.

**Chemical Analysis**—After the addition of a little sulphuric acid, separation from organic matter may readily be effected by distillation.

**Tests.**—The presence of phenol in the distillate may be recognised by its giving with bromine-water a precipitate of tri-bromo-phenol [$C_6H_2Br_3OH$], the precipitate is soluble in excess of phenol. If a little ammonia water and a small quantity of bleaching-powder, or bromine water, are added to an aqueous solution of phenol, on gently heating the mixture a blue colour is produced; acidulation after cooling changes the blue to red or yellow. The addition of a solution of ferric chloride to a solution of phenol produces a violet colour, and acid nitrate of mercury (Millon's reagent) a bright red. If a weak solution of furfural is added to a solution of phenol, and strong sulphuric acid is allowed to trickle down the side of the test tube, a red colour which changes to blue develops above the acid.

**Quantitative** estimation of the phenol present in the distillate may be made by precipitation with bromine-water, the precipitate being washed, dried, and weighed—100 parts of tri-bromo-phenol equal 28.39 parts of phenol. The phenol may be liberated from its combination with bromine by treatment with sodium amalgam, and then extracted with ether and the residue, after evaporation of the ether, tested as above described.

Combined phenol-sulphonic acid in urine may be decomposed and the phenol estimated as follows:—Evaporate the urine to a syrup, extract with absolute alcohol, filter, and precipitate the alcoholic solution with oxalic acid as long as any precipitate falls; then add potassium hydrate to feeble alkaline reaction and evaporate again to a syrup. Render the residue acid and distil the phenol thus set free from the potassium phenol sulphonate; the amount is estimated by conversion into tri-bromo-phenol.

## PICRIC ACID

**Picric Acid** [$C_6H_2(NO_2)_3OH$], or trinitrophenol, is formed by the action of nitric acid on phenol. It consists of yellow prismatic or laminar crystals which are sparingly soluble in cold water, more soluble in hot water, and freely so in alcohol; it is somewhat soluble in ether and chloroform, but much more so in amyl alcohol. It is odourless, has an intensely bitter taste, possesses strong acid properties, and forms salts which detonate on percussion. A solution of picric acid stains objects yellow, and it has been used for this purpose in confectionery; on account of its bitter taste it has been used to replace hops in beer. Very few cases of poisoning by picric acid are recorded and none with fatal results.

In experimenting on animals Erb[1] found that picrates cause the blood to become dirty brown in colour, with the formation of distinct nuclei in the red discs and free nuclei in the serum, the white blood corpuscles show a tendency to undue numerical increase. The cause of death is heart paralysis. Elimination takes place by the kidneys, bowels, and mucous membranes.

**Symptoms.**—The following case related by Adler[2] illustrates the effects of a toxic dose.—A girl, aged sixteen, endeavoured to commit suicide by swallowing about 300 grains of picric acid mixed with water. Violent pain in the stomach and repeated vomiting speedily occurred, and diarrhœa soon followed; the sclera and the skin were coloured an intensely dark yellow almost brown; the pupils were moderately dilated and reacted feebly to light; the fingers were spastically stretched and bent at the metacarpo-phalangeal articulations. The urine was ruby-red in colour; it contained neither albumen nor bile pigment; a slight sediment formed which partially consisted of brown-stained epithelium, the stools were fluid and ruby-red in colour. Both urine and fæces contained picric acid in considerable amount; six days after the reception of the poison traces of it were present in the urine. In a few days the discoloration of the skin diminished and the patient was quite well at the end of a week. Chéron[3] relates a case of poisoning from inhalation of picric acid dust which caused discoloration of the skin, pain in the epigastrium, depression, delirium, vomiting, diarrhœa, and red-coloured urine; recovery took place. In another case symptoms of poisoning occurred from the application of about six grains of powdered picric acid to the vagina; in one hour the skin was discoloured and erythematous, and the urine was red; pain in the stomach and the kidneys with somnolence were amongst the symptoms; recovery took place, but the skin was discoloured for a week, and the erythema persisted for eleven days. A teaspoonful of picric acid has been swallowed without other ill effect than violent vomiting and purging.

**Treatment.**—The stomach should be evacuated and well washed out, and elimination promoted by diuretics and, if necessary, aperients; morphine will probably be required to relieve pain and cramps.

**Chemical Analysis.**—Organic matter should be acidulated with hydrochloric acid and digested with alcohol over a water-bath; after filtration the alcoholic extract is evaporated to a syrup, taken up with boiling water, filtered, acidulated with sulphuric acid, and shaken out with ether, chloroform, or amyl alcohol. Dragendorff directs attention to the fact that if chloroform or benzene are used for extraction, the

[1] *Die Pikrinsäure*, 1865.  [2] *Wiener med. Wochenschr.*, 1880.
[3] *Journ. de Thérap.*, 1880.

solution though containing picric acid will be almost colourless, if ether or amyl alcohol are used they acquire a yellow tint. The extract is evaporated to dryness and the residue dissolved in water and tested.

Tests.—An aqueous solution of picric acid, gently warmed with a little potassium cyanide, changes to a deep blood-red colour. Ammonio-copper sulphate yields a green precipitate with picric acid. Basic lead acetate gives a yellow precipitate. A piece of white silk allowed to remain a short time in a solution of picric acid is dyed yellow; the colour is not discharged by subsequent washing in water.

## CREASOTE.

Creasote, which chiefly consists of cresol and guaiacol, is slightly soluble in water, and is freely soluble in alcohol and ether. It coagulates albumen and acts as an escharotic. When swallowed in poisonous doses it causes nausea, vomiting, abdominal pain, and diarrhœa. Fatal poisoning by creasote is rare. A case is reported by Marcard[1] of an infant which suddenly became ill and died in fourteen hours, the child's jacket was stained with yellowish spots, and there was a strong odour of creasote in the room. Examined seven hours after the commencement of the symptoms the mucous membrane of the lips, tongue, and mouth was partly red and partly grey, and showed signs of the action of a caustic, but no smell of creasote was perceptible, the child vomited and passed motions mixed with blood. At the necropsy the lips and the tip of the tongue were brown and hard, various sized erosions were found in the mucous membrane of the stomach, but no odour of creasote could be perceived, nor could any trace be obtained by chemical analysis of the viscera, the spots on the jacket, however, yielded evidence of the poison. As the result of a series of experiments on animals it was found that when a minimum lethal dose of creasote is given and the animal lives some hours, the odour of the poison may entirely disappear. In another case reported by Purckhauer,[2] a child ten days old was given from twenty-four to thirty drops of creasote, it became insensible, was convulsed, and died in sixteen hours. At the necropsy, inflammation and corrosion of the digestive tract, dark coloured blood, and the odour of creasote were present. An adult who was taking creasote medicinally gradually increased the dose until it reached one hundred drops. On one occasion she took a second hundred drops after the usual dose, Freudenthal,[3] who reports the case, saw her afterwards and found her insensible, breathing stertorously, with

[1] *Vierteljahrsschr. f. ger. Med.*, 1889
[2] *Friedreich's Blätter f. ger. Med.*, 1883
[3] *New York Med. Rec.*, 1892

clenched jaws, cyanotic lips, contracted insensitive pupils, and absence of the reflexes, recovery took place.

It is stated that creasote, unlike carbolic acid, does not cause the urine to become dark coloured, and only exceptionally does it produce nephritis. Creasote is eliminated by the kidneys, and after large doses its odour may be perceived in the urine.

The treatment of tuberculosis by creasote has led to the administration of enormous doses, apparently without injurious effects; the system is gradually trained to toleration by daily augmentation of the dose from a drop or two up to as many as one hundred or more drops. In the case just quoted, the patient after recovery from the effects described, still further increased the dose until it reached two drachms and three-quarters twice a day. In fatal cases death may take place in from seven to twenty hours.

The treatment is the same as in poisoning by phenol.

The post-mortem appearances resemble those produced by phenol.

**Chemical Analysis.**—Separation from organic admixture is to be effected as is directed for phenol.

**Tests.**—Creasote may be recognised by its odour. In alcoholic solution it may be distinguished from phenol by adding a few drops of a solution of ferric chloride; a green colour is produced, which disappears on dilution with water. Phenol similarly treated gives a lilac which does not disappear on the addition of water.

## CHAPTER XXXII

### ALKALOIDS AND VEGETABLE POISONS.

Alkaloids are basic bodies which may be considered as compound ammonias. Vegetable alkaloids are almost exclusively derivatives of pyridine; they contain carbon, hydrogen, nitrogen, and—with the exception of a few volatile alkaloids—oxygen. They are for the most part solid, crystalline, and colourless; a few, such as nicotine and conine, are liquid and volatile. Alkaloids combine with acids, the salts formed being much more soluble in water than the free alkaloid. Unless specially qualified, the term alkaloid is applied to substances derived from plants or trees; basic products of an analogous constitution obtained from animal tissues are known as "animal alkaloids." Alkaloids possess certain properties in common, amongst which is that of being precipitated from solutions by substances which thus serve as alkaloidal group reagents, some of which throw down most of the alkaloids, others only a limited number most of them also form precipitates with ammonia

Group Reagents — Phosphomolybdic acid, which may be extemporaneously prepared by dissolving sodium phosphomolybdate with the aid of heat in water freely acidulated with nitric acid, precipitates almost all alkaloids, whether vegetable or animal, together with ammonium salts, and derivatives of ammonia, such as phenylamine, methylamine, and the like; it also precipitates salts of lead, silver, and mercury, unless sufficient nitric acid is present to keep the metals in solution. Phosphotungstic acid is another delicate group-reagent, yielding much the same reactions as phosphomolybdic acid. Iodine dissolved in water with the aid of potassium iodide gives a brown precipitate with most of the alkaloids. Potassio-mercuric iodide—made by adding a solution of potassium iodide to a solution of mercuric chloride until the red precipitate first formed is just dissolved, leaving a colourless solution—produces a gelatinous precipitate with a great many of the alkaloids. There are other alkaloidal group-reagents—as platinic chloride, picric and tannic acids, bismuth-potassic iodide, &c.—but the above-mentioned are the best.

Special Reagents are described in the sections respectively devoted to the various alkaloids; for the most part they are best applied to the solid alkaloid, obtained by evaporating to dryness a few drops of a solution which contains it.

## STRYCHNINE

Strychnine [$C_{21}H_{22}N_2O_2$] occurs in several plants of the natural order *Loganiaceæ*, and is prepared from Nux Vomica, or from the Ignatius bean, in both of which it is associated with brucine. Strychnine forms colourless crystals, sparingly soluble in water and ether, rather more freely soluble in spirit, and much more freely so in chloroform. It has an exceedingly bitter taste, which is perceptible in a solution composed of 1 part in 70,000 parts of water; it is one of the most permanent of the alkaloids, and may be detected in the putrefied remains of animals that have been poisoned by it. Strychnine has powerful basic properties, and will neutralise the strongest acids; it may be exposed to the action of concentrated sulphuric acid for an indefinite time without undergoing decomposition. The salts of strychnine met with in commerce are the sulphate, the nitrate, and the acetate.

Strychnine is easily accessible to the public in the form of powders for killing rats, mice, and other vermin; those most commonly used are known as Battle's vermin-killer, sold in threepenny and sixpenny packets. Analyses made of these powders purchased at retail shops show that a threepenny packet weighs about 0·713 gramme (11 grains), and contains about 0·11 gramme (1·6 grain) of strychnine, the rest of the powder consists of flour mixed with Prussian blue; a sixpenny packet weighs 1·413 gramme (21·7 grains), and contains 0·182 gramme (2·7 grains) of strychnine. These powders are prepared in large quantities; they are roughly measured out, and the percentage of strychnine is not constant, but each may be regarded as containing a fatal dose for an adult human being. Butler's strychnine vermin-killer consists of flour and soot, with strychnine in much the same amount as in Battle's. In some of these powders ultramarine is used as colouring agent, and as the gastric juice is sufficiently acid to destroy the colour of this pigment, if such a powder is swallowed no coloured particles may be found in the stomach after death.

In poisonous doses strychnine causes general clonic spasms, which, from experiments on animals, are found to be due to increased excitability of the reflex centres in the spinal cord. It appears as though strychnine had the power of lessening the resistance of the cells in the anterior cornua, both to reflex stimuli and to the reception of impulses from contiguous cells; the result being that a stimulus which, under normal conditions, would produce a response limited to the muscles supplied by the cells actually stimulated, spreads from cell to cell, and sets up universal spasm; an impulse set up in the cord travels wave-like in all directions, the motor cells having lost their self-inhibitory power. The inhibitory influence of the higher centres is probably not interfered with; a striking illustration of this is occasionally seen in the human subject when under the influence of a toxic dose of strychnine:—The least external stimulus is sufficient to provoke the liberation of a torrent of motor nerve-impulses, which throws the whole of the skeletal muscles into the most violent movement; the slamming of a door, the touch of a hand, or even a current of air will produce an attack; yet the patient, in the lull after a seizure, will sometimes ask a bystander to rub his legs in order to ease the pain; and the action is unattended by reflex spasm. This points to a certain degree of inhibitory control, which the higher centres are capable of exercising over the spinal centres, notwithstanding their instability.

**Symptoms.**—In three or four minutes, up to a quarter of an hour or longer, after a poisonous dose of strychnine has been swallowed, muscular twitchings, accompanied by a feeling of anxiety and impending suffocation are experienced by the patient, and immediately after he is seized with a violent convulsion of a tetanic character. The arms and legs are stretched out, and the muscles of the trunk are hard and unyielding, then jerking movements occur, forcing the head and legs backwards and the trunk forwards, the feet being strongly flexed and the hands clenched. The clonic spasms increase in severity, and the extensor muscles are so forcibly contracted that the body is arched in the posture of opisthotonos—the back of the head and the heels forming the ends of a curve, of which the abdomen constitutes the most prominent part; exceptionally the body may be arched forward or sidewise. When this stage is reached the spasm for a time becomes tonic; the muscles of the chest and abdomen, including the diaphragm, are tense and rigid, and the whole frame remains arched and still; the pulse is very rapid and feeble, and respiration is much impeded or entirely arrested, producing marked cyanosis. The sufferer is fully conscious, and experiences the most acute physical pain, with mental anguish at the prospect of immediate death, which he feels to be imminent; when capable he cries out for something to be done to relieve his sufferings. The terror-struck face, the prominent eyeballs, dilated pupils, and cyanotic complexion, vividly portray the agony suffered. After a minute or more the muscles relax, the eyeballs cease to protrude, and the pupils regain their usual size; normal respiration recommences, the cyanosis disappears, and the pulse diminishes in rapidity. The patient lies exhausted, dreading a repetition of the spasm which sooner or later recurs, being provoked by the least external impulse. During the remission, which lasts from a few seconds up to five or ten minutes, the face, without losing its anxious appearance, looks less wildly agonised than during an attack. If the case is about to terminate fatally the spasms succeed each other in rapid sequence, and death usually occurs within two hours either from asphyxia produced by fixation of the respiratory muscles, or, during an interval from exhaustion, probably the result of the excessive expenditure of force, leading to paralysis of the nerve elements. When recovery is about to take place the attacks diminish in severity, and the intervening periods are more and more prolonged, until at last the patient, free from convulsions, is left feeble and exhausted, a condition from which he recovers in a few days; in some cases the recovery is more prolonged but actual complications are very exceptional.

Along with the other skeletal muscles, those of the lower jaw participate in the spasm; it may be to such a degree as to clench a spoon or feeding vessel firmly between the teeth. The difference between the trismus of strychnine poisoning and that which accompanies the tetanus of disease consists in the former being secondary to the spasms which affect the muscles of the limbs and trunk, whilst in tetanus it precedes the general spasms. In strychnine poisoning the muscles of the jaw are relaxed in the intervals between the attacks, in tetanus the trismus persists during any mitigation of the general spasm. In fatal cases of strychnine poisoning death usually occurs within two or three hours, the patient being in his customary health previous to the commencement of the attack; tetanus is never so rapidly fatal; for several hours soreness and stiffness of the muscles of the face and neck precede the tetanic convulsions, and death rarely occurs within twenty-four hours, being usually delayed for several days.

In exceptional cases a much longer interval than usual elapses between the reception of the poison into the stomach and the commencement of the symptoms; two hours and more have been known to intervene. When a narcotic has been simultaneously swallowed the interval may be still further prolonged. Macredy[1] reports a case in which a grain and a half of strychnine and two ounces of tincture of opium were taken; the symptoms of strychnine poisoning did not appear until eight hours after, the opium producing narcosis in the meantime. The opposite extreme is illustrated in a case reported by Fegan,[2] a man sucked an egg which, for the purpose of killing vermin, had been charged with from two to three grains of strychnine; symptoms commenced in from four to five minutes, and death took place in one hour and a half. Hunter[3] records a case in which the first convulsion occurred within five minutes; and Barker[4] one in which the symptoms began in from three minutes and a half to four minutes, after about six grains of strychnine were swallowed.

The period of survival, after the commencement of the symptoms, is also subject to variation. In Barker's case above quoted death took place within thirty minutes; in the case of Cook (*Reg* v *Palmer*, C C C, 1856), the interval was only twenty minutes; Christison records a case in which it did not exceed fifteen minutes. The shortest interval known was in Hunter's case, above cited; the patient, a woman of seventy, died five minutes after the symptoms first appeared. Death may be delayed beyond two hours, which was stated to be the usual limit of survival; in rare instances it has not occurred until three, five and a half, and even seven hours after the poison was swallowed. Under exceptional conditions, as when a narcotic has been taken with the strychnine, still longer intervals have been recorded.

**Fatal Dose.**—Half a grain of strychnine sulphate has caused death in twenty minutes; a little over a grain of strychnine has frequently proved fatal. Recovery has taken place after four, five, and even ten grains. Two cases are recorded in which twenty grains respectively

---
[1] *The Lancet*, 1882.    [2] *Ibid*, 1889.
[3] *Med. Times and Gaz.*, 1867.    [4] *Amer. Journ. of Med. Sc.*, 1864.

were swallowed immediately after a meal vomiting was at once procured, and in both instances the patients recovered. In a third case twenty-two grains of strychnine were in the stomach for two hours before vomiting occurred, yet recovery took place.

Idiosyncrasy plays an important rôle in determining the effect produced by minimum doses of strychnine; in some instances intolerance to the poison is due to exceptional irritability of the nervous structures towards the alkaloid; in others, retarded elimination may be the cause. Strychnine is eliminated in the urine, fæces, and saliva. Whilst making some investigations on this subject, the only cases in which I failed to detect it in the urine of those to whom it was being medicinally administered, were two in which incipient symptoms of toxic action were produced—a feeling of apprehensiveness, accompanied by muscular twitchings and involuntary jerking of the limbs. In neither of the cases was strychnine detected in the urine, although it was invariably found in other cases in which similar doses were being taken. The kidneys, for some reason, failing to eliminate any of the poison, it was eliminated by the liver, and possibly the stomach, and passed into the duodenum, where some of it would be re-absorbed, the rest being voided along with the fæces. This made the process of elimination slower, and the continued administration of the alkaloid led to its accumulation in the blood, until an incipient physiological effect was produced. Such cases are very exceptional, the rule being for speedy elimination by the kidneys to take place. Kratter[1] found strychnine in human urine half an hour after administration; in animals, Ipsen[2] found it in three to five minutes after reception. Elimination proceeds rapidly; Kratter failed to find strychnine in the urine forty-eight hours after its administration had ceased, a result with which my own experience agrees.

Treatment.—If possible introduce the stomach tube and wash out the stomach; the administration of chloroform may enable this to be done, otherwise an emetic should be given. Spontaneous vomiting does not usually occur. After emptying the stomach the patient may be kept under the influence of chloroform, or chloral hydrate may be given. A striking instance of the value of chloral hydrate as an antagonist to strychnine is afforded by a case related by Jones[3]. A man swallowed two threepenny packets of Battle's vermin-killer, which produced typical symptoms of strychnine poisoning; the patient did not vomit, nor was the stomach emptied. Twenty grains of chloral hydrate dissolved in water were injected subcutaneously, followed by a second dose of twenty grains, and subsequently by ten grains more; twenty

---

[1] *Wiener med. Wochenschr.*, 1882  [2] *Vierteljahrsschr. f ger. Med.*, 1892
[3] *The Lancet*, 1889.

grains were also given by the mouth as soon as the patient could swallow, recovery took place. If death from asphyxia appears imminent artificial respiration should be resorted to.

**Post-mortem Appearances.**—The statements as to cadaveric rigidity are contradictory. In the case of Cooke, who was poisoned with strychnine by Palmer, the body was found five days after death much stiffer than is usually the case—the hands were stiff and firmly closed and the muscles strongly contracted. In other cases the rigidity has been of the ordinary type and duration, the usual interval of muscular relaxation intervening immediately after death. In Hunter's case previously mentioned rigidity was not present fifteen minutes after death, nor yet three hours after; it was developed to a slight degree seven hours after death.

Internally there are no characteristic appearances. Hyperæmia of the cerebral and spinal meninges has been recorded, and also fluidity of the blood, probably due to death occurring from asphyxia.

**Chemical Analysis.**—The alkaloid is to be separated from organic matter by the process described in Chapter XXV, and weighed if in sufficient amount. Chloroform, or a mixture of chloroform and ether, are the best solvents for extracting strychnine from an aqueous solution; it is advisable to precipitate the free alkaloid in the presence of the solvent, and to shake out without delay; if allowed to become crystalline the alkaloid is much less soluble.

The quantity contained in the various organs is inconstant. I analysed some of the viscera and their contents in three cases of suicidal poisoning by strychnine with the following results:—In one, a grain and a half of strychnine (0.1 grm.) caused death in about three hours, the stomach-pump being used in the interval; the contents of the stomach yielded a trace only, the liver 0.013 grm., the urine (278 cc.) 0.005 grm., and one kidney a trace. The second case, poisoned with a similar dose, also died within three hours, but without evacuation of the stomach; only the stomach and its contents (90 cc.) were obtained; treated separately, both yielded evidence of the presence of strychnine, but not in weighable amount. The third case was poisoned with a sixpenny packet and died in about two hours without the stomach being evacuated; as in the last case only the stomach and its contents (155 cc.) were obtained, the stomach yielded sufficient strychnine for identification and no more, but from its contents 0.078 grm. (1.2 grain) was obtained.[1] The discrepancy between the last two cases is very striking: in neither was the stomach evacuated, yet in one the contents yielded a mere trace, and from the other more than half the amount probably taken was isolated, a double packet of the

[1] *Med. Chron.*, 1889.

vermin-killer having been swallowed. It is noteworthy that although the stomach contained such a large amount of the alkaloid after death, the viscus itself yielded a mere trace. The absorption-rate of the stomach is much slower than that of the small intestines.

After absorption, the blood and the liver contain the largest amount of strychnine, the firm organs—as the kidneys—yield much less. The theory that the liver acts as a magazine and stores up strychnine is probably incorrect; it is more likely that the relatively large amount usually found in it is dependent upon the vascularity of the organ.

As previously stated strychnine resists the influence of surrounding putrefaction to a very considerable degree. Wolff[1] communicates a case in which strychnine was detected in an exhumed corpse three hundred and twenty-two days after the reception of the poison. Prescott[2] quotes a case in which it was found in the stomach, liver, and intestines in a body exhumed one year and three days after death. In another case it was found six months after burial.

**Tests.**—If a minute drop of a fluid containing strychnine is conveyed by the tip of the finger to the tongue, a characteristic bitter taste will be perceived unless the alkaloid is in very small amount and its bitterness is masked by the presence of some substance possessing a strong, penetrating taste; this test should never be omitted when searching for alkaloids, and should precede chemical tests. A fragment of strychnine thoroughly mixed on a colour-slab with a couple of drops of strong sulphuric acid undergoes no change of colour; if a few granules of manganese dioxide are then stirred in with the point of a glass rod a blue colour which rapidly becomes purple and more gradually changes to orange-red is produced. Lead peroxide, potassium dichromate, potassium permanganate, and other oxidising agents give the same reaction. Manganese dioxide is to be preferred on account of its slower action and freedom from any embarrassing intrinsic colour. On this ground ceric oxide has been recommended, as when pure it has little colour of its own; it is usually contaminated with didymium however which imparts a brownish-red hue almost as pronounced as that of lead peroxide; ceric oxide is much slower in its action than any of the other reagents mentioned. A drop of a solution of ammonium vanadate in strong sulphuric acid (1 : 200) yields the same colour reactions as manganese dioxide. If a mixture of strychnine and sulphuric acid is placed on a piece of platinum foil connected with the anode of a voltaic couple, on touching the liquid with a platinum wire which forms the cathode the same colour reactions are produced as with manganese; by means of this, and the manganese test, the

---

[1] *Einige Fälle von Strychninvergiftung. Dissert.*, 1887.
[2] *Organic Analysis*, 1887.

merest trace of strychnine—.01 milligramme—may be identified. If strychnine is heated with dilute nitric acid, and a crystal of potassium chlorate is added, a scarlet colour is produced, which becomes brown on the addition of ammonia water.

The physiological test may also be tried by injecting a few drops of a suspected solution into the dorsal lymph-sac of a small frog, and then placing it under a glass shade; if the solution contains but a minute quantity of strychnine tetanic convulsions occur in a few minutes. After the convulsions have once occurred they may subsequently be provoked by rapping the shade, or the table on which the frog is placed.

## BRUCINE

Brucine [$C_{23}H_{26}N_2O_4$] is found associated with strychnine in nux vomica and in the Ignatius' bean. It is more soluble in water than strychnine; is soluble in alcohol and in chloroform, but not in ether. It has a bitter taste like that of strychnine, and produces similar toxic effects, the potency of which has been variously estimated; it has probably only about one twenty-fourth the physiological action of strychnine. Mays[1] states that with frogs the convulsions are later in coming on with brucine than with strychnine, and that even with a lethal dose they may be altogether wanting. Brucine, not being accessible to the public, is practically unknown as a poison.

**Symptoms and Treatment** as in strychnine poisoning.

**Tests.**—Nitric acid added to a fragment of brucine produces a bright blood-red colour which is destroyed by excess of stannous chloride. If, after adding the nitric acid, the product is mixed with a little water and solution boiled, and then allowed to cool, the red colour is changed to purple on the addition of stannous chloride or of sodium thiosulphate. Ammonium sulphide produces a similar but less characteristic reaction; if the reagent is in excess, free sulphur is precipitated. Sulphomolybdic acid or Frohde's reagent [prepared by dissolving a little sodium molybdate in strong sulphuric acid with the aid of gentle heat] gives with a fragment of brucine a purple-red colour which changes to greenish or blue. Sulphovanadic acid produces a yellow, changing to orange-red. A solution of ammonium selenate in strong sulphuric acid produces a pink changing to yellow.

## NUX VOMICA.

The seeds of the *Strychnos nux vomica* are exceedingly hard and tough, and are too large to be swallowed whole unless with considerable

[1] *Journ. of Physiol.*, 1887.

effort, the powder, the extract, and the tincture of the seeds have produced toxic effects resembling those of strychnine. The symptoms are usually longer in appearing than when strychnine is taken; in one case a man swallowed about five drachms of nux vomica and was not affected for two hours when he quickly died convulsed. Thirty grains of the powder and three grains of the extract have proved fatal. Stevenson[1] records the recovery of a boy of twelve after taking about eight grains of the extract; both strychnine and brucine were detected in the urine.

## COCCULUS INDICUS

Cocculus Indicus, or Levant nut, the fruit of the *Anamirta cocculus*, contains an active principle picrotoxin, along with other bases.

Picrotoxin [$C_{12}H_{14}O_6$] is a colourless, neutral, crystalline body which does not form salts; it is not very soluble in water, but is freely soluble in alcohol, ether, and chloroform; it has an intensely bitter taste and is odourless. Picrotoxin acts as a gastro-intestinal irritant, and is a stimulant to the motor centres of the brain and cord. In small toxic doses it produces a tendency to stumble and reel—as in alcoholic intoxication—followed by stupor; in large doses it produces clonic spasms like those due to strychnine. Picrotoxin is eliminated in the urine.

Fatal poisoning by cocculus indicus is exceptional, probably not more than a dozen instances are recorded. Sozinsky[2] relates the case of a man, aged thirty-nine, who drank by mistake several ounces of whisky in which cocculus indicus berries had been long steeping, the mixture being intended for killing vermin. When seen an hour after, he had vomited once; he was unconscious, and had powerful general convulsions every five minutes, each convulsion lasting about two minutes; between the attacks there was complete muscular relaxation. Each convulsion commenced by twitching of the left corner of the mouth and a cry like that of an epileptic; there was considerable opisthotonos; the pupils were contracted. The respirations were slow, the heart not being much affected; profuse perspiration and diarrhœa were present. Death took place in three hours from failure of respiration and from exhaustion. Shaw[3] records the case of a man who purchased, as he supposed, wild cherries, but which proved to be cocculus indicus berries; he put them into a bottle and filled it with brandy, and from time to time drank small doses without ill effect. One morning he drank a considerable quantity and felt dizzy and sick in consequence;

[1] Guy's Hosp. Reps., 1868.
[2] *Med. News, Phil.*, 1883.  
[3] *Ibid.*, 1891.

he produced vomiting by tickling his throat, but a few minutes after he fell on the floor in convulsions and became unconscious, the convulsions continued for thirty minutes when death took place. At the necropsy nothing abnormal was found except congestion in patches of the mucous membrane of the stomach.

Recovery has taken place even after very threatening symptoms. Dutzmann[1] records the case of a man, aged sixty, who crushed some of the berries and swallowed a handful, half an hour after he fell to the ground, vomited, perspired profusely, and was unconscious. The temperature was elevated, the pupils normal in size but reactionless, the pulse 80 and full, and the respirations laboured and quickened. He then had convulsions which were attended with foaming at the mouth and cyanosis, the pulse rose to 110. Recovery took place, but pain and oppression in the chest were felt for some days.

Death has taken place in consequence of the external application of the poison. Thompson[2] states that a child, aged six, who had porrigo of the scalp and was infected with vermin, was treated externally with an alcoholic solution prepared by infusing one pound of cocculus indicus berries in three gallons of alcohol. Half an hour after tetanic spasms came on, during which the pupils contracted to the smallest size, dilating in the intervals between the spasms, the spasms could be produced by touching the eyelid, they continued for six hours when the patient died. The necropsy yielded negative results. Another child to whom a similar application was made also had clonic spasms but she recovered. In all these cases the convulsive action of the poison completely eclipsed any gastro-enteric symptoms that might be present, in many ways the effects closely resembled those of strychnine, even to the reflex excitation of the spasms, they correspond to the action of picrotoxin experimentally produced on animals.

A minor degree of poisoning by cocculus indicus, called "hocussing," has occurred from its surreptitious administration in admixture with alcohol in order to produce a helpless condition of stupor favourable to the perpetration of robbery from the person. Formerly low-class publicans sometimes added small quantities of cocculus indicus to beer in order to increase the intoxicating effects of the beverage, and thus obtain for it a fictitious reputation for alcoholic potency.

**Treatment.**—Evacuate the stomach by the tube or an emetic. If clonic spasms are present chloral hydrate may be given, or chloroform administered as in strychnine-poisoning. Artificial respiration may be necessary. In the minor degree of poisoning evacuation of the stomach with symptomatic treatment will probably be sufficient.

**Chemical Analysis.**—Picrotoxin may be shaken out of *acid* solution by ether or chloroform.

[1] *Wiener med. Presse*, 1869. [2] *Med. Examiner, Phil.*, 1852.

**Tests**—Picrotoxin is not precipitated by phosphomolybdic acid, nor by a solution of iodine. It is dissolved by concentrated sulphuric acid, producing a yellow colour which changes to black on heating. If picrotoxin is mixed with three times its weight of potassium nitrate, and the mixture is moistened with a few drops of sulphuric acid and then excess of a strong solution of sodium hydrate is added a brick-red colour is produced. Picrotoxin reduces Fehling's solution.

## OPIUM AND ITS ALKALOIDS

**Opium**—The inspissated juice of the *papaver somniferum* contains a large number of alkaloids and alkaloidal substances, several of which possess powerful toxic properties. Morphine is the alkaloid to which opium owes its potency as a poison; next in importance come narcotine and codeine, which act as hypnotics but are much less powerful than morphine. Thebaine, another alkaloid, and apomorphine, a derivative of morphine, act in a totally different way: the first is a convulsive and the second an emetic. With the exception of morphine the alkaloids of opium rarely come under the notice of the toxicologist, but one other substance—Meconic acid—on account of its constant presence in opium and its characteristic reactions is frequently sought for.

Of the preparations containing opium, which most frequently cause death from accidental, suicidal, or homicidal administration, some are official and some not. The former class comprises:—Tincture of opium or **laudanum** which contains one grain of opium in fifteen minims. Compound tincture of camphor or **paregoric** which contains one grain of opium in half an ounce. Compound ipecacuanha powder or **Dover's powder** which contains one grain of opium in ten of the powder. Of the non-official preparations of opium which come under the observation of the medical jurist from time to time are:—**Napenthe**, which is of the same strength as laudanum; **Dalby's carminative**, which contains about two and a half minims of tincture of opium to the fluid ounce; **Atkinson's infant's preserver**, which contains three minims of tincture of opium to the fluid ounce; **Godfrey's cordial**, which contains from half a grain to a grain and a half of opium to the ounce. The three last named are frequently given to infants with fatal result, although usually without homicidal intention. So-called syrup of poppies not unfrequently contain laudanum. **Chlorodyne** contains about four grains of morphine hydrochlorate to the ounce.

Morphine [$C_{17}H_{19}NO_3$] is a colourless crystalline substance, slightly soluble in cold water, more soluble in hot water and in ethyl alcohol, and freely soluble in amyl alcohol, especially when hot; it is also very soluble in acetic ether; in ethylic ether and chloroform it is but feebly soluble. The salts of morphine are freely soluble in water and spirit. Morphine has a bitter taste, and an alkaline reaction.

### Acute Poisoning by Opium and Morphine.

Symptoms.—Excitation of the higher nerve-centres is the first result of the reception of a poisonous dose of opium or of morphine; with opium it occurs in from half an hour to an hour after the dose is swallowed; with a salt of morphine in solution the interval is less—from a few minutes to a quarter of an hour. The excitation may show itself by producing accelerated action of the heart, flushing of the face, and a feeling of increased mental activity accompanied by exhilaration of spirits, or it may simply cause physical restlessness; its duration is short, and it is succeeded by an opposite condition of depression of the nerve-centres. A sensation of lassitude, oppression in the head, giddiness, and a strong desire to sleep steal over the patient, who becomes more and more drowsy and less capable of responding to external stimuli; before this stage is reached the pupils are contracted; the stupor subsequently deepens into profound coma. In the earlier stages of insensibility the patient may be partially roused by being shaken and loudly spoken to; when the comatose condition is reached no external stimulus evokes any response. The muscles are relaxed, the surface is cold and moist, the features are shrunk and pallid, or cyanotic, the pupils are exceedingly contracted, the pulse is slow and compressible, and the breathing is laboured, irregular, and stertorous; although the patient now presents all the appearance of a dying person, recovery may take place. If the case goes on to a fatal issue, the breathing becomes more embarrassed and may assume the Cheyne-Stoke's type; mucous râles are heard, the pulse becomes more irregular and scarcely to be felt, the cyanosis deepens, and the face looks even more ghastly, the jaw drops, and but for the hard-drawn breaths, the appearance is that of a corpse. Twitching of groups of muscles is often observed, and at this final stage the pupils may be dilated—death is then imminent. The heart may continue to beat for a short time after respiration has ceased.

Certain other symptoms may be present. If opium or the tincture has been taken its odour may be perceived in the breath. Vomiting may occur, and very exceptionally relaxation of the bowels; almost invariably an opposite condition of constipation obtains. The urine and the saliva are suppressed in the later stages; sometimes the urine is simply retained from paralysis of the bladder; but the excessive perspiration leaves little for the kidneys to do so that in any case the quantity of urine is lessened, although from accumulation the bladder may be full. The only secretion which is not diminished is the sweat, and this is usually increased from first to last.

Amongst symptoms of an *exceptional* character are—dilatation of the pupils in the earlier stage, apart from that which may occur immediately before death, acceleration of the pulse, which has been known to alternate with, or to replace, the usual slow pulse, spasms or convulsions of a tetanic character, which are less unfrequent in the case of children than in adults. The action of opium on the cerebral cortex is to increase its motor irritability; this, so far as the evidence afforded by faradic stimulation goes, has been proved by Unverricht.[1] Direct stimulation of the cortex, which under normal conditions would determine the occurrence of simple motor impulses, liberates them so freely when it is under the influence of opium as to give rise to convulsive movements; the condition produced by opium is the opposite of that due to ether, chloroform, and chloral hydrate, by which the cortical irritability is lowered. In children the nerve-cells have not acquired their full self-inhibitory capacity, hence it is easily broken down during a state of increased irritability; in adults opium poisoning accompanied by trismus and general spasms of a clonic, strychnine-like character, is an extremely rare occurrence.

In *very* exceptional instances morphine produces profound coma within a few minutes after it is swallowed, followed by death in forty minutes or an hour; in other exceptional cases the advent of the symptoms is delayed for two or even three hours, and death may not take place for more than twenty-four hours. The interval between the reception of the poison and death *usually ranges from six to twelve hours*.

A noteworthy condition has been observed in severe cases of opium poisoning: partial recovery from the urgent symptoms has taken place to such a degree as to remove all apprehension, and then after several hours' interval, the patient has relapsed into coma and died. As suggested by von Boeck,[2] it is probable that renewed absorption of the poison takes place under the influence of increased blood pressure. In other instances patients who recover from the immediate symptoms succumb after a much longer interval, possibly of several days; in such cases cardiac disease probably has as much to do with the fatal issue as the poison. When recovery takes place it is, as a rule, complete, but in rare instances sequelae have been recorded. Albuminuria was present on the third day after the acute symptoms in a case recorded by Olivier,[3] and at about the same period in a case recorded by Huber.[4] A unique case is reported by Scheiber[5] in which acute poisoning produced by

[1] *Centralbl. f. klin. Med.*, 1891, 1892.    [2] *Ziemssen's Cyclop.*, Bd. 17.
[3] *Gaz. des Hôpitaux*, 1871.    [4] *Zeitsch. f. l'n. Med.*, 1889.    [5] *Ibid.*, 1888.

the subcutaneous injection of morphine was followed by psychical disturbance, aphasia, and by the formation of bed-sores.

Fatal Dose—Adults.—Four grains of opium in one case and two drachms of the tincture in another proved fatal. Recovery has taken place after three ounces of the tincture, equal to ninety-nine grains of opium (Burgess[1]), and as recorded by Bowstead,[2] even after eight ounces of laudanum were swallowed by a woman, aged thirty-eight, who was not discovered for fourteen hours after she took the poison. One grain of morphine hydrochlorate has caused death; recovery has taken place after thirty, thirty-six, and in one instance fifty-one grains, the greater part of which remained in the stomach thirteen hours (Morse). Disease of the kidneys, especially cirrhotic kidney, predisposes to a fatal issue from opium or morphine.

Infants.—It is well known that infants are susceptible to the influence of opium to an extraordinary degree; on more than one occasion a single drop of laudanum has been recorded as fatal. A dose of paregoric equal to the ninetieth of a grain of opium, and in another case a dose of Dalby's calminative equal to half a minim of laudanum, are stated to have caused death; as regards such very minute doses as the last two named, there is reasonable ground for doubt, since the preparations concerned are made from crude opium, containing an unknown percentage of morphine. Recovery in an infant three months old is recorded by Bramwell,[3] after a teaspoonful of laudanum (vomiting occurring soon after it was swallowed). Chamberlain[4] witnessed the recovery of an infant six days old, which had swallowed a powder containing a grain and a half of opium; two hours afterwards it was apparently dead, breathing having ceased; artificial respiration was kept up for three hours, and in twenty-four hours the child was quite well. Morgan[5] saw an infant, one month old, which was comatose after three drops of laudanum, and the breathing gradually ceased; artificial respiration was kept up almost continuously for three hours, and recovery took place after complete unconsciousness had lasted for forty-five hours.

Preparations of opium have caused death from external application, but probably not without the skin being broken. Morphine sprinkled on an open sore has proved fatal.

Treatment.—If the poison was swallowed the stomach-pump should be used, and the stomach well washed out; in default, an emetic may be administered by the mouth, or apomorphine may be injected subcutaneously. Persevering attempts are to be made to rouse the patient

---

[1] *Dublin Journ. of Med. Sc.*, 1892.   [2] *The Lancet*, 1873.
[3] *Boston Med. Journ.*, 1887.   [4] *The Lancet*, 1889.
[5] *Boston Journal*, 1858.

by external stimulation, the faradic current, applied to various parts of the body with a wire brush, is an efficacious stimulant; walking the patient to and fro between two assistants may be resorted to, but only in the less severe forms of poisoning. When the coma is profound, artificial respiration may be needed; this constitutes a most *valuable aid to recovery*, it may be supplemented by faradic stimulation of the phrenics. Ammonia may be applied to the nostrils in the form of smelling-salts; the vapour of ammonia-water should not be used, it is too irritating to the respiratory mucous membrane. Hot coffee may be given by the mouth if the patient can swallow; if not it may be administered by the stomach-pump or as an enema. One-twentieth of a grain of atropine sulphate, injected hypodermically, and repeated if necessary, is recommended for the purpose of stimulating the respiratory centres, but its utility is doubtful, notwithstanding the number of successful cases in which it has been used. (See section on Antagonism of Poisons.) Hypodermic injections of ether are efficacious. Strychnine is strongly advocated by some. Lucatello[1] had a case in which a patient swallowed about forty-five grains of opium and twenty-two grains of morphine sulphate on an empty stomach. Symptoms did not appear for an hour. Breathing having nearly ceased, artificial respiration, with faradisation of the phrenics, were resorted to, but without effect; under the influence of hypodermic injections of strychnine respiration was resumed.

In cases which are not very severe, the cold douche and perambulating the patient may be sufficient, but the former should never be used when the surface is cold, nor should the latter be carried to excess, so as to exhaust the strength. *In severe cases it is worse than useless to drag a comatose individual about.*

Post-mortem Appearances.—Apart from discovery of the poison in the body, the post-mortem indications are not characteristic. When opium itself has been swallowed, its odour may be perceptible in the stomach; if the organ has been well washed out with the tube, or cleared with emetics, or if morphine was the poison, this indication will be absent. Injection of the gastric mucous membrane has been described; it is by no means constant, and, when present, is probably due to the treatment more than the poison. Hyperæmia of the brain and its membranes is not unfrequent, and in addition there may be œdema into the subarachnoid space and the ventricles. The amount of blood present in the lungs varies; they may or may not present the appearance regarded as due to death from asphyxia. The blood has been found dark and fluid; it has also been found coagulated.

Chemical Analysis.—The difficulty which attends the isolation of

[1] *Rivista Italiana*, 1888.

morphine from the organs and tissues of those poisoned by it has led to the supposition that it undergoes decomposition in the living organism. A number of researches have been made with the object of ascertaining what becomes of the alkaloid after its administration. Some investigators state that it is eliminated as such in both urine and fæces; others have failed to find it in the urine, but have detected it in the fæces; others again have found oxidation products—as oxidimorphine—in the urine, and hold that morphine is entirely changed in passing through the body.

When the delicacy and the distinctiveness of some of the reactions of morphine are taken into consideration, the undoubted difficulties that surround its detection in the organs of those who have succumbed to its influence requires explanation. Neglecting for the moment the question of decomposition of morphine within the organism, there are one or two errors of procedure which may prevent its recognition. One is excess of acid, especially after concentration, in the fluid used to extract the alkaloid from organic admixture; another is the use of too high a temperature for the purpose of evaporating the solution obtained; when these two adverse conditions are combined, the probability is that small amounts of morphine which originally may be present will be decomposed and rendered incapable of recognition by the usual tests. Further, delay in shaking out after alkalisation, and the use of an inappropriate solvent, such as ether, impedes or prevents extraction; if the aqueous solution is over alkalised with sodium or potassium hydrate (which are sometimes used), morphine is redissolved, and, if present only in minute amount, can not be shaken out by any solvent.

The only solvents that can be depended upon to take up morphine from neutral or slightly alkaline aqueous solutions are:—amyl alcohol (preferably hot) and acetic ether. As a solvent the former is undoubtedly the best, but it is disagreeable to work with, its evaporation demands a relatively high temperature, and, as met with in commerce, it is liable to contain resinous substances which may vitiate the results. Udránszky [1] attributes the formation of coloured and resinous products in amyl alcohol to the presence of furfural, from which the alcohol can be purified, but the process is troublesome. The solvent action of amyl alcohol on urea and extractives constitutes a further objection. Wormley [2] found that although amyl alcohol is nearly insoluble in water, 100 volumes of it agitated with water measure 109 after the liquids have separated. He also found that amyl alcohol dissolves a certain amount of the *salts* of morphine from aqueous solution, but that the amount is diminished if the alcohol is previously

---

[1] *Zeitschr. f. physiol. Chemie.*, 1889.      [2] *The Chemical News*, 1890.

saturated with water; the acetate is taken up more freely than the sulphate or the hydrochlorate. As the result of a number of experiments, in which morphine was successfully extracted from urine with hot amyl alcohol, Wormley states that the presence of urea constitutes an almost insuperable difficulty as regards purification of the alkaloid. Acetic ether is not free from objections; it is soluble in water to a considerable extent (1 in 10), and dissolves extractives freely. The most convenient solvent consists of a mixture of equal parts of acetic and ethylic ethers, well washed by being shaken with water. Alkalisation with sodium bicarbonate (excess of which does not redissolve morphine) should be effected in the presence of the solvent, and extraction accomplished without delay; if time is allowed for the precipitated alkaloid to become crystalline, it is much more resistant to the action of all solvents.

Tests.—A drop of strong nitric acid added to a fragment of morphine produces an orange-red colour. If a little of the alkaloid is dissolved in concentrated sulphuric acid and allowed to stand for fifteen to eighteen hours, and then treated with nitric acid, a blue violet colour, which changes to blood-red, is produced (Husemann). Sulphomolybdic acid (see tests for Brucine) produces a reddish purple, which changes to blue; this and the previous test are the most delicate and conclusive for morphine; they will react to ·01 milligramme. It is important to note that the *initial* colour-change is the one that is distinctive; the subsequent changes are common to several alkaloids. If a fragment of morphine is mixed with a couple of drops of strong sulphuric acid no coloration, or but the faintest pink, is produced; the addition of a little ammonium selenate develops a pale yellow, which changes to light green, sap-green, and brown. A small crystal of potassium dichromate, added to morphine and sulphuric acid, yields a green colour. If a little iodic acid is dissolved in a cubic centimetre of water in a test-tube, and an equal volume of carbon bisulphide is added, agitation produces in it no change of colour; the addition of a drop or two of a solution containing morphine liberates iodine from the iodic acid, and on gentle agitation the carbon bisulphide becomes pink or rose-red. A drop or two of a solution of ferric chloride added to a solution of a salt of morphine produces a blue colour; if the reagent is in excess, the colour will be green; with morphine meconate this test produces a dark red—the reaction of meconic acid, which displaces the blue of the morphine.

**Meconic Acid** may be tested for when the presence of opium, in which it exists in combination with morphine, is suspected. As just stated, it gives a red colour with ferric chloride; the colour is not destroyed by mercuric chloride. With meconic acid lead acetate gives a white precipitate which is soluble in nitric acid.

Elimination of morphine to a great extent takes place by the bowels, to a lesser extent by the kidneys; some experiments made by Alt[1] at the instigation of Hitzig show, in a striking way, the part played by the stomach in the process of elimination. A subcutaneous injection of morphine was given to a dog; in about four minutes after, the animal vomited, and the vomited matter was found to contain morphine. Further experiments show that, soon after morphine is subcutaneously introduced into the system, its elimination is commenced by the gastric mucous membrane even when the stomach is empty, and is continued until at least half of the dose injected is thus removed from the circulation, and is eventually voided with the fæces; a portion of the alkaloid is said to be excreted in the bile. In some experiments of my own, conducted with the excretions from patients taking large medicinal doses of morphine, the alkaloid could always be detected in the fæces and occasionally in the urine; it is exceedingly difficult, however, to obtain morphine in the crystalline form, either from the tissues or the excretions of those who have been subjected to its influence. Rosenthal[2] finds that morphine is eliminated in the saliva, and also that it may to some extent accumulate in the system.

The question of the decomposition of morphine in the organism must be regarded as undetermined. It is not improbable that a portion of the quantity taken may be changed into oxidimorphine, or some other derivative or combination of the alkaloid. For a chronological account of investigations on the subject, see Tauber[3] "Ueber des Schicksal des Morphins im thierischen Organismus."

## Chronic Poisoning by Opium and Morphine

The habitual use of opium in gradually increasing doses produces an extraordinary degree of tolerance towards it, the practice of this habit is known as opium-eating or morphinism. It is frequently originated by the legitimate use of opium to relieve pain, and is afterwards continued on account of the agreeable sensations it produces, and to banish the feeling of depression which is experienced as soon as the effects of the drug pass off. A morphine *habitué* quickly loses his moral perception, and will descend to the lowest level of unblushing deceit in order to satisfy his cravings; when fully under the influence of the habit his moral fibre is disintegrated in all directions; ethically he is a coward, and avoids all methodic mental effort; if taxed with taking opium or morphine, he will deny the imputation with an earnestness and apparent sincerity that would

---

[1] *Berliner klin. Wochenschr.*, 1889.   [2] *Centralbl. f. klin. Med.*, 1893.
[3] *Arch. f. exp. Path. u. Pharm.*, 1890.

convince any one unacquainted with the facts. **Physical symptoms** develop after a time; visceral neuroses are evinced by the recurrence of violent pains in the region of the stomach and abdomen, which might be mistaken for those due to the passage of gall-stones; attacks of vomiting resembling gastric crises occur, and the bowels may be relaxed from time to time. The appetite is capricious and defective; considerable—sometimes excessive—emaciation takes place, and the patient looks shrunken and pallid in the face, like one suffering from malignant disease. Later, symptoms resembling those due to peripheral neuritis develop: as paræsthesiæ, neuralgias, trembling of the hands and ataxic gait, with numbness of the feet and tips of the fingers.

The introduction of the hypodermic syringe has placed a convenient mode of self-administration of morphine within the reach of those disposed to make use of it. When the rapidity with which the system is brought under the influence of morphine injected subcutaneously is taken into consideration, the enormous doses that can be tolerated without producing the usual toxic effects are very astonishing. Stuart[1] records a case in which forty grams of morphine acetate were injected daily for months; even this amount has been exceeded.

The best **treatment** is to cut off the supply at once. This demands either great resolution on the part of the patient, or the bringing to bear of very powerful moral control on the part of a second person (which is seldom available), or, lastly, physical restraint. Conditions may exist which render a gradual deprivation necessary, but the process is tedious and uncertain. When there appears to be danger of collapse from sudden total deprivation, Erlenmeyer[2] advocates rapid withdrawal of the drug in from six to twelve days. Unless there is some very cogent reason for doing so, it is better not to carry out "treatment" by substituting some other drug for morphine. During and after the cure the patient must be restrained from the abuse of alcohol, otherwise an interchange of habits may occur.

## BELLADONNA AND ATROPINE

**Atropa Belladonna** (natural order *Solanaceæ*) or the deadly nightshade contains the alkaloid atropine to which it owes its toxic effects. Poisoning by belladonna occurs either from the improper use of one of the medicinal preparations of the drug, or from eating the berries in the fresh state.

**Atropine** [$C_7H_{23}NO_3$] is a colourless crystalline substance with a

---
[1] *Brit. Med. Journ.*, 1889.
[2] *Die Morphiumsucht und ihre Behandlung*, 1887.

strong alkaline reaction It is odourless, sparingly soluble in water but more so than most alkaloids, it is much more soluble in ether, still more so in spirit, and most of all in chloroform. The mydriatic alkaloids atropine, daturine (datura stramonium), hyoscyamine, and hyoscine (hyoscyamus niger), duboisine (duboisia myoporoides) are all isomeric and probably convertible Atropine can be split up into tropic acid and tropine, the latter being capable of forming combinations with other acids

For the physiological action of atropine see p 391 Elimination rapidly takes place by the kidneys, Dragendorff states that atropine will probably only be found in the urine which is first excreted after the reception of the poison

**Symptoms** —The essential symptoms respectively produced by the plant, and the alkaloid are identical, but when portions of the plant —as the berries—are eaten nausea, vomiting, and other signs of gastric irritation may be superadded A hot, dry sensation, accompanied by a feeling of constriction, is experienced in the throat, accompanied by thirst; the saliva is inspissated, and the tongue dry; swallowing is difficult or impossible. The pupils are dilated, usually to the uttermost, leaving only a narrow ring of the iris visible; they are insensitive to light, the conjunctivæ are suffused The pulse, accelerated to 120 or 160 in the minute, is small and sometimes scarcely to be felt at the wrist The skin, often covered with a scarlatina-like rash, which may be followed by desquamation of the epiderm, is hot and dry in the earlier stage, but may become cold during the stage of collapse Alternate flushing and pallor of the face have been observed In the early stage the patient complains of dizziness, indistinctness of vision—sometimes of diplopia; later on there may be complete loss of vision, he is unable to walk, and reels or stumbles on attempting to do so. Active delirium comes on which often partakes of the imitative type, the patient will industriously perform a series of movements resembling those of a person employed in sewing with needle and thread, or he will tear off strips from an imaginary piece of cloth; in a case of poisoning by belladonna berries the patient imitated the acts of plucking fruit from a tree, conveying it to his mouth, and then swallowing it. These imitative acts are sometimes performed with such gravity and persistency as to excite the risibility even of anxious friends who witness them Hallucinations of sight are common, as may be gathered from the description of the mimic actions; sometimes the patient in the attempt to escape an imaginary danger will try to jump out of the window, or to rush through the door The voice is stammering and the utterances are incoherent, but the patient is often extremely loquacious, intermitting his loquacity with wild peals of laughter, or vociferous shouting. Twitching of the muscles of the face and limbs often occurs and may go on to tonic or clonic spasms affecting the entire body, which to some degree appear to be reflex in character; in a case recorded by Oliver[1] they were aggravated by the passage of the stomach tube and by the withdrawal of the contents of the stomach. Sensory disturbances such as numbness of the fingers may be present. The urinary bladder and the intestines are usually paralysed.

In severe cases total insensibility with cold surface may supervene and last for many hours; on awakening delirium has been known to recur. If the case is about to be fatal the insensibility increases; there may be recurrent convulsions or simply progressively deepening coma. Death from paralysis of the heart and lungs occurs in from six to twenty-four or more hours.

When recovery takes place it is slow; several days elapse before the whole of the symptoms subside. The pupils continue dilated and only very gradually return to their normal size; accommodation may be defective for some time, and the memory is often enfeebled for three or four days, an aphasic condition existing in the meanwhile.

**Fatal Dose.**—One drachm of belladonna liniment, which was swallowed, and the same amount of the extract have respectively proved fatal. Recovery has taken place after a tablespoonful of the liniment was swallowed, and in another case after half an ounce of the extract mixed with glycerine. Fourteen belladonna berries caused the death of an old man; recovery has taken place after fifty. Children are less susceptible to the toxic action of belladonna than adults; recovery has followed in children after thirteen berries and even after thirty. Belladonna applied externally as a plaster or in the form of extract has often produced toxic effects.

Two grains of atropine have been fatal; severe symptoms have been caused by a quarter of a grain. In one case recovery followed three and a half grains of atropine sulphate, and in another five and a half grains. A child two and a half years old recovered from one quarter of a grain of atropine. Alarming and typical symptoms of poisoning have not unfrequently occurred after the instillation of a solution of atropine into the eyes for the purpose of dilating the pupils. Death has been caused by the application of atropine ointment to a blistered surface.

Although atropine is not often used criminally, a few cases of homicidal poisoning have occurred; one took place near Manchester, and was the subject of judicial inquiry at the Assizes held there in 1872 (*Reg v. Steele*). The resident surgeon at a workhouse died from

[1] *The Lancet*, 1891.

atropine poisoning, the alkaloid being detected in his body. He became ill after breakfast with typical symptoms and died in about twelve hours; the poison had been added to some milk used at breakfast, which produced toxic symptoms in two other people who tasted it. A nurse, who it was alleged had a strong motive and the opportunity for committing the crime, was charged with the murder but was acquitted. A curious case of belladonna poisoning is recorded by Bachner.[1] A man became ill after eating some soup prepared by his wife. When seen by a doctor he was flushed in the face, the eyes were bright and slightly bloodshot, the pupils were dilated and insensitive to light, the tongue was dry and covered with sticky saliva, the speech was stammering, the fingers trembling, the hands swollen and the limbs cold. The patient complained of dizziness, singing in the ears, heaviness and heat in the head, indistinct vision, thirst, vomiting, and partial retention of urine. He recovered, and on judicial investigation it was found that he himself had added some belladonna seeds to the soup in order to accuse his wife of attempting to poison him.

**Treatment.**—When the poison has been swallowed the stomach-pump should be used and the stomach well washed out; if the apparatus is not at hand an emetic must be given, after which stimulants and hot coffee are useful. Strong, stewed tea, or an infusion of tannic acid, helps to precipitate and render innocuous any of the poison which may remain in the stomach. Douching of the burning, dry surface in the early stage, and artificial respiration in the stage of collapse are to be resorted to. Hypodermic injections of pilocarpine (one-third or half a grain of the nitrate or hydrochlorate) tend to slow the pulse, tranquillise the respirations, and relieve the spasms if they are present. In default of pilocarpine a hypodermic injection of morphine may be given. Binz[2] directs attention to the tolerance of morphine exhibited by cases of atropine poisoning, and instances this as being in favour of the antagonism of the two poisons.

**Post-mortem Appearances.**—In the absence of fragments of some parts of the plant there is no characteristic appearance in belladonna poisoning. If the berries have been eaten there may be signs of reddening of the mucous membrane of the stomach; the seeds should be carefully sought for in the stomach and intestines. The blood has sometimes been recorded as dark and fluid, with hyperæmia of the cerebral vessels, but such signs are of little value. The pupils usually remain dilated after death.

**Chemical Analysis.**—Any seeds or fragments of leaves found in the stomach should be examined under the microscope. The seeds are

[1] *Friedreich's Blatter f. ger. Med.*, 1887.
[2] *Centralbl. f. klin. Med.*, 1893.

small, ovoid or kidney-shaped, and are covered with small projections which, under a low power, present a honeycombed appearance. The fresh berries are blackish-purple in colour, and their juice stains a white surface purple; the mucous membrane of the stomach has sometimes been found thus stained. The addition of an alkali changes the purple to green, acids change it to red.

Atropine may be extracted from organic matter by the usual process, like morphine; it is soluble in excess of potassium and sodium hydrate; it is very prone to undergo hydrolysis, especially in the presence of free alkalies. The evaporation of a solution containing atropine should be conducted at a temperature not exceeding 35° C and excess of acid avoided. A mixture of three volumes of ether and one of chloroform is the best solvent for extracting the alkaloid from an aqueous solution.

**Tests.**—The chemical tests for atropine do not of themselves afford conclusive proof of the presence of the alkaloid; they give place to the physiological test, and are to be regarded only as corroborative of it. Alone among the ordinary fixed alkaloids free atropine reddens phenolphthalein, a minute fragment placed on phenolphthalein paper and moistened with a drop of water causes the paper to become red; if alcohol is dropped on to the stain, the colour disappears, but returns when the alcohol has evaporated; the reddening of phenolphthalein paper by alkalies is not affected by alcohol. With a little atropine mix two or three drops of strong nitric acid and evaporate to dryness over a water-bath; add to the yellow-coloured residue a few drops of alcoholic solution of potash—a reddish-violet or purple colour is produced. A fragment of atropine yields a yellow colour with sodium nitrite and strong sulphuric acid, which changes on the addition of alcoholic potash to reddish-violet, fading to pale rose.

**Physiological Test.**—After proving the presence of an alkaloid by means of one of the alkaloidal group reagents, a drop or two of a neutral aqueous solution prepared from the ether-chloroform extract should be instilled into the eye of a cat, or preferably a kitten; if atropine is present in only infinitesimal amount—·001 mgrm.—the pupil is dilated in from a few minutes to an hour, according to the amount present. The test may be repeated on the eye of a human being. Cocaine also dilates the pupils when dropped into the eye, but a much stronger solution is required, and anæsthesia is also produced. The above reactions, chemical and physiological, are yielded by all the tropines.

Dragendorff detected atropine after it had been mixed with organic matter, which was then allowed to remain in a warm room two and a half months, until it was quite putrid.

## HENBANE.

**Hyoscyamus Niger**, or henbane, contains two basic substances — hyoscyamine and hyoscine — which are isomeric with atropine. The fresh plant has a disagreeable odour, its juice, when dropped into the eye, dilates the pupils.

**Hyoscyamine** [$C_{17}H_{23}NO_3$], with which hyoscine is isomeric, is obtained from several atropaceous plants, it is convertible into atropine. Hyoscyamine is a colourless crystalline substance, without odour, moderately soluble in water, and freely soluble in spirit, ether, and chloroform. It has an alkaline reaction, and combines with acids to form salts.

**Symptoms.** —In many respects the symptoms produced by hyoscyamus are identical with those of belladonna, certain differences, however, have been observed. The face is flushed, the surface is hot and dry, the mouth and throat are parched, the pupils are enlarged and insensitive to light, vision is impaired, the pulse is quick and small, the respirations are of a sighing character, and in the early stage there is delirium. It has been noticed in cases of poisoning by hyoscine that the tendency to busy, wild delirium is not so great as with atropine. Trismus and clonic spasms of the muscles of the jaw and limbs have been observed. In the later stages the patient is comatose and collapsed; there is greater tendency to sleep and insensibility with hyoscyamine, and more especially with hyoscine, than with atropine. Recovery is slow, as is the case with belladonna poisoning.

The fatal dose of henbane is not known; recovery has taken place after six drachms of the tincture were swallowed. Death followed one-eighth of a grain of hyoscyamine swallowed along with the same quantity of morphine sulphate. A hypodermic injection of one-thirtieth of a grain of hyoscine in one case, and the swallowing of about one-fortieth of a grain in another, produced severe symptoms of poisoning, followed by recovery. Some non-fatal cases of poisoning recently occurred through the accidental admixture of henbane seeds with celery seeds, for which they were purchased.

**Treatment.** —As in poisoning with belladonna.

The **Post-mortem Appearances** are not characteristic.

**Chemical Analysis.** —The alkaloid may be isolated by the usual process, and submitted to the same tests as those described for atropine.

## STRAMONIUM.

**Datura Stramonium**, or thorn-apple, is another solanaceous plant which yields an alkaloid or alkaloids, that act in much the same way as those of belladonna and henbane. All parts of the plant are poisonous. The seeds are dark-coloured and kidney shaped; they are about one-eighth of an inch in length, and have a rough surface.

**Daturine** is an isomer of atropine. According to Ladenburg the kind known as "light daturine" consists principally of hyoscyamine.

**Symptoms.**—The following case related by Steiner [1] illustrates the toxic action of stramonium. A man aged forty-five drank a decoction prepared by boiling the leaves and fruit of the datura stramonium, to relieve pain in his chest. About three-quarters of an hour afterwards he sprang out of bed and ran about the room, looking into all the corners like a person bereft of reason; he was put to bed by force and held there as he made violent efforts to escape, being all the while unconscious. The face was red, the pupils were widely dilated and did not react to light; the limbs moved spasmodically; the pulse, which intermitted, was 130 in the minute; the respirations were deep and quickened; the skin was dry, and the temperature 96°.5 F. Swallowing was difficult, cutaneous sensibility was abolished, the abdomen was distended but not painful on pressure. The patient subsequently lay quiet and became comatose, the redness of the face changing to pallor, the respirations became quieter and slower, and the pulse sank to 120. The patient appeared to be dying, but shortly after began to improve and gradually recovered, weakness and trembling of the limbs persisting for a week. A man swallowed a teaspoonful of Himrod's asthma-specific which is intended for inhalation. Many of the symptoms of stramonium poisoning occurred, but the pulse was very slow, only twenty-five to the minute. Recovery took place. The remedy contains stramonium with probably lobelia and potassium nitrate.

**The fatal dose** is not known. About one hundred seeds, and seventeen or eighteen grains of the extract, have caused death. Death has occurred in seven, and in twenty-four hours.

**Treatment.**—As in poisoning with belladonna.

The **Post-mortem Appearances** are not characteristic.

**Chemical Analysis.**—After isolation and proof of the presence of an alkaloid, its physiological effect should be tested as with atropine; the same chemical tests may also be used.

The tropines, respectively derived from belladonna, henbane, and stramonium being isomeric, and possessing the same chemical properties, indentification of the group, one of which was the poison administered, is all that can be accomplished in a toxicological investigation; there is no reliable test by which one of these alkaloids, in minute quantity, can be distinguished from another.

[1] *Berliner klin. Wochenschr.*, 1887.

Duboisine, obtained from the leaves of the *duboisia myoporoides*, is another isomer of atropine. It is considered by some to be identical with hyoscyamine, Ladenburg believes it to be identical with hyoscine. It is a powerful mydriatic, and produces symptoms like those of atropine.

A case is recorded by Chadwick[1] in which one-hundredth of a grain of duboisine sulphate, dropped into the eyes of an old man, produced dizziness, weakness, and loss of control of the legs, dryness, with bitter taste in the mouth, huskiness and indistinctness of speech, visual hallucinations—the patient grasping at imaginary objects in the air, and glancing suspiciously under the bed clothes and behind his back—slow pulse, and a copious flow of words without relevancy. Kollock[2] relates an almost parallel case caused by the instillation of two drops of a solution of duboisine sulphate (one grain to two drachms) into the eyes. The face was flushed, the pupils dilated, the patient was dizzy and moved himself from side to side, though apparently rational he made remarks devoid of meaning and relevancy, and was unconscious of all that had occurred whilst in this condition.

The treatment is the same as for atropine.

## INDIAN HEMP

Cannabis Indica, or Indian hemp, is a delirant and hypnotic, and has been used in the form of *haschish* to procure sensuous hallucinations

Cannabin, an active principle prepared from it is a brown syrupy liquid which has the odour of Indian hemp. Cannabinon is a dark-blown resin which has sedative properties

The symptoms of an overdose are thus described by a medical man who took forty drops of the tincture Giddiness and fulness in the head, heaviness and numbness of the feet and legs; complete loss of sensation as far as the knees, which rendered standing difficult and walking impossible. The same symptoms commenced in the tips of the fingers and reached to the elbows, but the anæsthesia was not so complete as in the legs Anxiety and dread of death were experienced, and the heart's action was tumultuous and irregular. The mental condition was emotional—laughing and crying alternating; no pleasurable excitement was experienced In a case recorded by Casiccia[3] two drachms of the alcoholic extract produced the following symptoms in half an hour —Mental exaltation with a tendency to physical movements, paræsthesiæ of hands and feet, heat in the epigastrium;

---

[1] *Brit. Med. Journ.*, 1887.   [2] *Med. News*, 1887.
[3] *Riv. di Chim. Med. e Farm.*, 1883.

dryness of the fauces; dilatation of the pupils which reacted to light, and full, slow pulse of fifty-eight to the minute. The patient talked incoherently without intermission, uttering cries or howls at intervals, recovery took place.

The fatal dose is not known. Seven and a half minims of the tincture have caused toxic symptoms. Death has occurred in twelve hours, it may be delayed for several days; in one case it did not occur until the nineteenth day. Untoward effects have also been observed after the medicinal use of Cannabinon.

The treatment is the same as for opium.

## GELSEMIUM.

**Gelsemium Sempervirens** or the yellow jasmine of North America owes its toxic properties to the presence of an alkaloid gelsemine, which when instilled into the eye is a powerful mydriatic, when administered internally in small doses it contracts the pupils, in poisonous doses it dilates them. It paralyses the spinal cord and the respiratory centres, and produces tetanus specially affecting the facial muscles and the muscles of articulation; it also gives rise to ataxic symptoms. It has little effect on the heart and brain. Gelsemine is eliminated by the kidneys.

**Symptoms**—A case in which a comparatively small quantity of the tincture produced toxic symptoms is related by Jepson[1]. A woman who had been previously taking the drug without obtaining any benefit took an increased dose of twenty minims of tincture of gelsemium every three hours for three or four doses. She lost power over her tongue, being unable either to articulate or to swallow except with great difficulty, the pupils were widely dilated and vision was indistinct. She had a sensation of uncertainty in the movements of her hands and arms, but retained consciousness, and recovered under treatment. Myrtle[2] prescribed some pills containing one-tenth of a grain of *gelsemin* (the powdered alcoholic extract of gelsemium root, the dose of which is from half a grain to two grains) for which the dispenser substituted hydrochlorate of the alkaloid *gelsemine*, the dose of which is from a sixtieth to a twentieth of a grain. The patient became giddy, was sick, and lost the power of speech, the tongue was drawn to one side, the muscles on the right side of the face quivered, and she could not guide her hand. Trismus, clonic spasms, exhaustion, and unconsciousness for two hours were amongst the symptoms, recovery took place. Three teaspoonfuls of the fluid extract of gelsemium caused the death of a woman in seven and a half hours.

[1] *Brit. Med. Journ.*, 1891.     [2] *Ibid.*, 1880.

**Treatment**—If taken by the mouth the poison should be evacuated either by the tube or an emetic, then stimulants should be administered, warmth applied, and artificial respiration resorted to if necessary. Atropine and strychnine have been recommended as antidotes in order to stimulate the respiratory centre.

**Chemical Analysis**—Separation from organic matter is effected as with the alkaloids in general; ether or benzene may be used to shake out from aqueous solution.

**Test.**—Gelsemine has a bitter taste. If a fragment on a colour-slab is dissolved in a little strong sulphuric acid, and a granule or two of manganese dioxide is stirred into the mixture, a deep crimson-red colour is produced which changes to green.

## COCAINE

Cocaine [$C_{17}H_{21}NO_4$], benzoyle methyl-ecgonine, one of several alkaloids yielded by the *erythroxylon coca*, is a colourless crystalline substance, it has a bitter taste, and leaves a sensation of numbness on the tongue. It is only slightly soluble in water, much more soluble in alcohol, and still more so in ether, benzene, and chloroform.

It is largely used as a local anæsthetic and acts in that capacity by paralysing the terminals of the sensory nerves, it blanches mucous membranes, and produces some dilatation of the pupils.

Taken internally cocaine first stimulates and then paralyses the nerve-centres of brain and cord. With poisonous doses the action of the heart, in animals, is slowed and the blood pressure reduced; the respiratory function after an initial increase is lowered and finally paralysed. The temperature is raised. Convulsions may occur. Cocaine probably undergoes decomposition in the body into ecgonine —free or combined—although it has been found in the urine.

**Symptoms**—The following case related by Haenel[1] illustrates the course of acute cocaine poisoning. A dentist injected into the gums of a girl of nineteen a solution equal to about one grain and a-third of a salt of cocaine, to lull the pain of tooth-extraction. The patient became pale, fell down, and was severely convulsed, clonic spasms of both trunk and limbs being present, she was unconscious; the pupils were widely dilated and reactionless to light. At first the pulse was too quick to count, subsequently it dropped to 176 in the minute, the temperature was 100° 8 F., and the respirations were 44 in the minute. The patient remained unconscious for seven hours, and on regaining consciousness experienced diminished sensibility of the hands, anæsthesia of the mucous membrane of the mouth and nostrils, with

[1] *Berliner klin. Wochenschr.*, 1888.

loss of taste and smell; during the first twenty-four hours there was retention of urine. The stimulating effects of the poison on the respiratory centres with paralysis of the vagi would account for the heart and lung disturbance. Montalti[1] records the case of a man who took twenty-two grains of cocaine hydrochlorate; fifteen minutes after delirium came on, he tried to vomit but did not succeed; rigors occurred, the face was pale, the pupils were dilated and the lips cyanotic. he became pulseless and unconscious and died forthwith. Zambianchi[2] states that a woman had about three and a half grains of cocaine injected into the breast preparatory to an operation; she immediately had epileptoid convulsions and died in twenty minutes.

**Fatal Dose.**—About two-thirds of a grain injected subcutaneously caused the death of a woman aged seventy-one in five hours. A man died almost immediately after taking twenty-two grains by the mouth. On the other hand a man habituated to the use of cocaine, injected under his skin twenty-three grains daily for some time. In another case recovery took place after forty-six grains were taken into the stomach. Death has occurred from the injection of a solution of cocaine into the tunica vaginalis. The injection of one drachm of a 20 per cent solution of cocaine hydrochlorate into the urethra caused immediate dilatation of the pupils, flushing, twitching of the face, and convulsions; death occurred twenty minutes after the first convulsion.

**Treatment.**—The danger usually arises in consequence of the hypodermic injection of a solution of cocaine, and the treatment is consequently limited to the administration of stimulants, with the inhalation of chloroform if necessary to relieve the spasms which interfere with respiration.

**Post-mortem Appearances.**—The principal changes—which are due to vaso-motor paralysis—are hyperæmia of the membranes of the brain and cord, and of the viscera generally.

Chronic poisoning by cocaine occurs in those who have acquired the habit of injecting the alkaloid hypodermically, in the same way in which morphine *habitués* use morphine. A number of ill-effects are produced on both the moral and the physical well-being of those who have become victims to the habit. Mental apathy and moral degeneration are accompanied by disturbances of the digestive organs, anomalous pains, and general emaciation.

**Chemical Analysis.**—Separation from organic matter is effected in the usual way, ether or chloroform being good solvents.

**Tests.**—Mezger[3] recommends the following tests.—To a solution of cocaine hydrochlorate in water add a few drops of a 5 per cent solution

[1] *Lo Sperimentale*, 1888.   [2] *Gazz. degli Ospedali*, 1888.
[3] *Chem. Centralblat*, 1890.

of chromic acid, as each drop of the chromic acid solution is added a precipitate is formed which immediately redissolves; if a small quantity of strong hydrochloric acid is now added a heavy yellow permanent precipitate is formed. Several alkaloids are precipitated from neutral solution by chromic acid—strychnine, brucine, veratrine, quinine, for example—but no alkaloid except cocaine requires the addition of hydrochloric acid after the chromic acid before permanent precipitation takes place. If a little cocaine is treated with a few drops of strong nitric acid, and the mixture is evaporated to dryness on a water bath, on adding a few drops of a strong alcoholic solution of soda or potash to the residue and stirring them well together, an agreeable, aromatic, ethereal odour is given off somewhat resembling that of the flower called the meadow-sweet.

The physiological action of cocaine can be tried on the tongue, or the lips.

## SOLANUM DULCAMARA.

Solanum Dulcamara, or bittersweet, contains two alkaloids—*solanine* and *dulcamarine*

Poisoning by substances containing solanine occurs from eating the berries of the bittersweet or other plants of the same species. Vomiting and diarrhœa, with more or less collapse, pain in the stomach, cramps in the legs, followed by clonic spasms, dilatation of the pupils, pallor, and coldness of the surface, hallucinations, and coma are amongst the symptoms which may be met with. The respiratory function is lowered, and in fatal cases the respiratory centres are paralysed, death taking place from asphyxia.

The **treatment** consists in furthering the evacuation of the stomach—vomiting almost invariably occurring spontaneously—the administration of stimulants, and possibly opium, with the application of warmth.

## MALE FERN.

Felix mas, or male fern, is extensively used as an anthelmintic in cases of tape-worm. It contains filicic acid, an amorphous, white, tasteless powder without smell, which is probably the active principle of the rhizome. Experiments on animals made by Poulsson[1] show that filicic acid produces tetanic convulsions, followed by paralysis, the convulsions resembling those produced by strychnine; heart paralysis occurs along with the general paralysis, although the heart may beat a few times after respiration has ceased.

**Symptoms.**—A man, thirty years old, was given a draught containing

[1] *Arch. f. exp. Path.*, 1891.

one ounce and a half instead of one drachm and a half of the extract of male fern, which he took in two doses. Soon after the first dose he felt unwell, and after the second, which was given some hours subsequently, he began to vomit, and was purged, then followed cramps, profuse sweating, delirium, and coma, which ended in death about twenty hours after the draught was taken. At the necropsy the omentum and the peritoneal covering of the small intestines were bright red, and in the submucous tissue of the stomach were ecchymoses with linear extravasations on the surface of the mucous membrane. An instructive case is related by Freyer,[1] in which a child, aged two and three-quarters, took eight capsules—each containing about fifteen grains of extract of male fern, along with the same quantity of castor oil—in five hours, she became somnolent, and as though paralysed, and died after the occurrence of some spasms. Section showed petechial ecchymoses in the mucous membrane of the stomach, pronounced injection of the mucous membrane of the intestines and venous filling of the various organs. The interesting point to note is that three weeks previously the child took double the quantity of the extract, *but without the castor oil.* A case is recorded by Hofmann,[2] in which a child, five and a half years old, had very nearly two drachms of the extract given to her in three draughts; death took place in six hours, with symptoms of trismus and general spasms. Much the same appearances were found as in the other cases.

The case recorded by Freyer has a practical bearing. The toxic properties of the extract of male fern are augmented by the presence of additional oil to that contained in the extract itself; the same child tolerated twice as much of the extract alone as that which proved fatal when given in combination with castor oil. It is advisable, therefore, not only to avoid giving a mixture of the extract with castor oil, but also to give some other laxative than oil, if one is subsequently needed. A case is recorded by Schlier,[3] in which an adult very nearly lost her life, probably owing to a tablespoonful of castor oil being given one hour after a draught which consisted of extract of male fern mixed with the powdered root.

Treatment.—If spontaneous vomiting does not occur, the stomach should be emptied either by the tube or an emetic, after which general treatment will be required, and probably the administration of stimulants.

[1] *Therapeutische Monatshefte*, 1889.   [2] *Wiener klin. Wochenschr.*, 1890.
[3] *Münchner med. Wochenschr.*, 1890.

## LOBELIA.

**Lobelia Inflata**, or Indian tobacco, contains a basic substance, *lobeline*, which is the active principle of the plant. Lobeline is an oily, yellowish-coloured fluid, with a burning taste; it is soluble in ether, and slightly so in water; it resembles nicotine in many of its properties.

When taken in large doses lobelia acts as a depressing emetic, like tobacco. Cases of poisoning by lobelia chiefly result from its free administration by quacks, especially by a class designated Coffinites, from Coffin, the appropriate name of the man whose therapeutic creed they adopt, one article of which is that lobelia is not a poison, and that it is important when administering it to avoid falling into the vulgar error of not giving enough! In a case recorded by Wharton and Stillé,[1] a woman was poisoned by one of these quacks giving her half a teacupful of infusion of lobelia, seeds and all; she died in half an hour, and on examination the stomach was found to contain a tablespoonful of lobelia seeds, its mucous membrane was softened and much inflamed; the intestines were also inflamed. In another case[2] one drachm of the powdered leaves was given by a quack, great pain was produced, with vomiting, small pulse, contracted pupils, insensibility, spasmodic twitchings of the face, collapse, and death in thirty-six hours. In this case also the mucous membrane of the stomach was found much inflamed.

The **treatment** consists in emptying the stomach in those exceptional cases in which vomiting has not occurred spontaneously, and then administering stimulants freely. Warm applications should be made to the surface, and the recumbent posture maintained until the heart has quite recovered itself.

**Chemical Analysis.**—The basic principle may be extracted with ether from an alkaline aqueous solution.

**Tests.**—On evaporation of the ether, the residue gives a violet coloration with sulphomolybdic acid; this is like the reaction of morphine, but the fluidity, odour, and colour of lobeline will prevent any confusion between the two; moreover lobeline turns red on the addition of strong sulphuric acid—a reagent which does not affect morphine.

## TOBACCO

**Nicotiana Tabacum**, or tobacco, contains an alkaloid nicotine—in combination with malic or citric acids—upon which its toxic properties depend.

[1] *A Treatise on Med. Jurisprudence.*  [2] *Pharmaceutical Times*, 1874.

Nicotine [$C_{10}H_{14}N_2$], liberated by the action of alkalies from tobacco, is closely allied to pyridine, it is a colourless, volatile, oily liquid, which turns brown and resinous on exposure to air. It has a marked alkaline reaction, and forms salts with acids, it is freely soluble in water, alcohol, and ether, and has an acrid taste, and a strong odour like that of the juice of an old well-used pipe.

After first stimulating the vagus both centrally and peripherally, thus slowing the heart-beats, nicotine paralyses the cardiac terminals and causes rapid, irregular action of the heart. The respiratory rate is first accelerated and then retarded. The peripheral blood-vessels are contracted by poisonous doses of nicotine, hence the pallor and coldness of the surface. Nicotine first stimulates and then paralyses the cerebral and spinal centres. With small doses the pupils may at first be contracted, but they are dilated when the toxic symptoms are fully developed. Nicotine is to some extent eliminated in the urine.

The symptoms of acute poisoning by swallowing tobacco juice or nicotine are:—A burning acrid sensation in the throat, a sudden feeling of depression, with giddiness, loss of power over the limbs, faintness, nausea, vomiting, tremors, coldness of the surface with clammy sweat, loss of consciousness with or without convulsions, contraction of the pupils, which in fatal cases are subsequently dilated, feeble irregular action of the heart, laboured sighing respirations, complete relaxation of the whole musculature, with possibly delirium and convulsions. Before the patient loses consciousness he may experience a feeling of oppression or of sinking in the cardiac region, accompanied by great anxiety, dimness of vision, and loss of power of speech. Occasionally the bowels and the bladder are involuntarily evacuated. In some instances the lethal action of the poison is exceedingly rapid; in one case death occurred in eighteen minutes; in another in three or four minutes. In the celebrated case of Count Bocarmé—who poisoned his wife's brother, Fougnies, with nicotine which he prepared for the purpose—death took place in five minutes.

The leaves of the tobacco plant applied to the unbroken skin have caused symptoms of poisoning; an infusion of them similarly applied in order to kill parasites, has on several occasions caused death. The infusion injected into the rectum as a vermifuge, has frequently proved fatal; on one occasion after only twelve drops, and on another after an infusion prepared from half a drachm of tobacco. Even smoking tobacco has caused acute fatal poisoning, although most of the nicotine present is converted into pyridine-bases during the combustion of the tobacco. A boy smoked a pennyworth of twist tobacco and afterwards became very sick and fell in the street, he went home to bed, and at four o'clock in the morning vomited again; three hours after he was found lying on the bed, dead and cold.[1] Two or three drops of nicotine taken into the stomach would probably be fatal in a few minutes. A drunken man was killed by his companions emptying the juice of their pipes into some spirit and giving it him to drink. Tobacco in the form of infusion or juice has caused death in from twenty minutes to seven or eight hours.

**Treatment.**—If the poison was swallowed the stomach-tube should be used, or an emetic given, followed by stimulants, external warmth, artificial respiration if necessary, and the maintenance of the recumbent posture. Hypodermic injections of strychnine (one twenty-fifth grain) have proved serviceable. Strong tea, or a solution of ten or twenty grains of tannin in water may be given.

**Post-mortem Appearances.**—The odour of tobacco is usually perceptible on opening the abdomen. When the poison has been swallowed the mucous membrane of the stomach may be injected or ecchymosed; the intestines have been found contracted and to contain blood-stained mucus.

**Chemical Analysis.**—Nicotine may be separated from organic admixture by the usual process for the isolation of alkaloids. Ether is the best solvent; after its evaporation the residue consists of oily looking drops.

**Tests.**—Nicotine is freely soluble in water. If a solution of mercuric chloride is added to an aqueous solution of nicotine a white precipitate is formed which subsequently becomes yellow and crystalline. Silver nitrate produces a white precipitate which subsequently becomes black. Chlorine-water added to an aqueous solution of nicotine produces no turbidity. A little ethereal solution of iodine added to an ethereal solution of nicotine produces an oily mass in which red crystals are formed which have a watch-spring lustre when viewed by reflected light. The odour of nicotine and its toxic effects on animals afford further means of identification.

Chronic nicotine poisoning results from excessive smoking, and also from the inhalation of tobacco-charged air in manufactories. The symptoms are dyspepsia, anæmia and nervous disorders, among which amaurosis, intermittent action of the heart, and a tendency to faintness and dizziness are the most prominent.

## SPOTTED HEMLOCK.

**Conium Maculatum** or spotted hemlock, so named from dark purple spots on the stem, is a plant belonging to the natural order *umbelliferæ*; its leaves resemble parsley sufficiently to cause them to have been mis-

[1] *The Lancet*, 1885.

taken and eaten for that plant. It has a peculiar, very characteristic "mousy" odour, which can be developed by pulpifying the leaves or other part of the plant in the presence of a little caustic soda or potash. The plant contains two alkaloids—conine and methyl-conine—along with other bases.

Conine [$C_8H_{17}N$] is a colourless oily liquid, which turns brown on exposure to air; it possesses the "mousy" odour of the plant in a high degree, and has an acrid bitter taste. It is strongly alkaline, and combines with acids to form salts; it is sparingly soluble in water, and is freely soluble in alcohol, ether, and chloroform.

Conine paralyses the motor nerve-terminals, and subsequently the motor centres of the brain and spinal cord, the paralysis spreading from the periphery to the centre. Death is due to respiratory paralysis, and is usually preceded by asphyxic convulsions. Conine is eliminated in the urine.

Methyl-conine [$C_9H_{19}N$] abolishes the reflex of the spinal cord.

Symptoms.—A burning sensation with a feeling of constriction in the throat is experienced, followed by nausea, vomiting, pain, oppression in the stomach and bowels, and diarrhœa. The nerve-symptoms are variable, probably on account of differences in the relative proportion of conine and methyl-conine present in the poison swallowed. Progressively increasing muscular weakness with dyspnœa, the respiratory movements becoming slower and slower, without disturbance of the higher centres, are the symptoms usually met with, but sometimes delirium, coma, and partial convulsions are prominent from the first. The pupils are dilated, and the surface of the body is cold. In the pure motor-paralysis type the patient first feels weakness in the legs which causes him to stumble when trying to walk; this deepens into complete paralysis which creeps up towards the trunk; the arms are not so rapidly affected. The paralysis eventually invades the muscles of respiration, the patient becomes cyanotic, and death takes place from dyspnœa.

In the pure paralytic type convulsions are not infrequent during the final stage, but they are due to asphyxia caused by the respiratory paralysis. The sensory nerves are relatively but slightly affected.

A peculiar case is recorded by Schulz[1] of a student who, after repeatedly smelling at some conine, experienced weakness of the limbs, inability to keep the eyes open, burning sensation of the conjunctivæ, pain in the head, affection of speech, general feeling of heat followed by profuse perspiration; he rambled and was unable to sleep. The headache continued for twenty-four hours, along with a tendency to perspire profusely on the least movement.

[1] *Deutsche med. Wochenschr.*, 1887.

**Treatment**—Evacuate the stomach and then give stimulants and apply warmth. Artificial respiration is sure to be required in severe cases and should be persistently kept up; life may be saved by this means when the condition appears almost hopeless.

**Post-mortem Appearances.**—In the absence of traces of the poison in the viscera, there is no characteristic appearance. The blood will probably be dark and fluid, with other indications of death from asphyxia.

A child, eight months old, had given to it one teaspoonful of a mixture containing one drachm of extract (prescribed in mistake for succus) of conium with one drachm of potassium bromide in an ounce and a half of chloroform water. When seen, the legs were paralysed, occasional twitchings of the arms and head occurred, but no decided convulsions, the pupils were dilated, the face was livid, and the respirations were diaphragmatic, death took place in seven hours. Pepper, who made the post-mortem examination, found the organs generally congested, along with an increased amount of serum in the cerebral ventricles and under the arachnoid, and an injected condition of the membranes of the spinal cord. The right heart was distended with blood, the bases of the lungs were hyperæmic, and punctiform extravasations were observed on the surface of the liver. The contents of the stomach yielded no odour of conium until they were treated with potassium hydrate and heated, the "mousy" odour was then apparent. An ethereal extract obtained from the contents of the stomach, when treated with hydrochloric acid, yielded crystals of conine hydrochlorate.[1]

**Chemical Analysis.**—Separation of conine from organic admixture may be accomplished as with nicotine. Considerable caution is necessary in the identification of conine, since substances somewhat resembling it may be obtained from cadavers that have undergone putrefactive changes. Any such products, however, do not yield the chemical reactions of conine, nor are they strongly toxic; they probably consist of or contain cadaverin—a ptomaine which has an odour somewhat resembling that of conine, but it is scarcely so "mousy."

**Tests.**—Conine is less soluble in hot water than in cold, therefore if a cold saturated aqueous solution is heated it becomes turbid, like albuminous urine similarly treated, but, unlike the urine, it clears up again on cooling. If conine is exposed to the vapour of hydrochloric acid crystals of conine hydrochlorate are formed. A few drops of a solution of mercuric chloride added to a solution of conine in water produce a white amorphous precipitate, which does not change to

[1] *The Lancet*, 1885.

yellow nor become crystalline, as is the case with the precipitate formed by nicotine when similarly treated. Silver nitrate produces a dark-brown precipitate, which turns black. Chlorine water added to an aqueous solution of conine produces turbidity. Treated with chromic acid, conine yields butyric acid, which may be recognised by its odour.

## ŒNANTHE CROCATA

Œnanthe crocata, or water dropwort, is another umbelliferous plant with toxic properties. The symptoms comprise convulsions, cyanosis, insensibility, laboured respirations, collapse, dilated pupils, delirium, small, feeble, slow pulse, with gastro-enteric disturbance. On one or two occasions the convulsions have been of a strychnine-like character. In some instances the symptoms have been almost entirely psychical, consisting of hallucinations, wild laughter, and actions like those seen in delirium tremens.

## FOXGLOVE

Digitalis Purpurea, or foxglove, is a plant belonging to the natural order *Scrophulariaceæ*, the leaves of which possess toxic properties due to the presence of three glucosides—digitalin, digitalein, and digitonin—with one other active principle. A variety of preparations are sold under the name of digitalin, which differ in chemical constitution and physiological effects, in accordance with the mode in which they are obtained. The most poisonous of the active principles is digitoxin, which is not a glucoside.

Digitalis is essentially a heart poison, and causes death from heart paralysis, the pulse usually ceasing before respiration; the respiratory rate is often slowed, especially when death is imminent. The active principles of digitalis probably undergo decomposition in the body, very exceptionally traces of them have been found in the urine.

**Symptoms**.—The digestive tract is primarily affected by a poisonous dose either of digitalis or of its active principles. Nausea, vomiting—which is often very obstinate and persistent—pain, with a sensation of oppression in the region of the stomach, thirst, and colicky pains in the abdomen, with or without diarrhœa, are common. After a varying interval the more specific effects of the poison manifest themselves—giddiness, with a feeling of faintness, headache, increased oppression in the epigastric region, moisture and coldness of the surface, especially of the limbs, prostration and various affections of the special senses, as dimness of vision, noise in the ears, are present, with which mental disturbances, in the form of hallucinations or delirium, may be associated. The action of the heart is profoundly affected; the pulse sinks hour by hour in rapidity and tension, and becomes very intermittent and fluttering. The respirations are slow and assume a sighing character. If the patient lifts his head when in the recumbent posture a tendency to syncope asserts itself, and if he stands upright actual syncope probably occurs, which may prove instantaneously fatal. An inclination to somnolence, which may deepen into coma, is not unfrequent; cyanosis, with or without asphyxic convulsions, may precede death.

It is to be noted that the special action of digitalis on the heart renders the patient liable to fatal syncope for several days after the immediate effects of the poison have passed off. In the acute stage, the pulse-rate may be lowered to under forty beats per minute, in the case of a woman who drank some infusion prepared from fresh digitalis leaves, the pulse sank to thirty-six, with periods of entire cessation of the heart's action at short intervals.

Fatal Dose.—Nine drachms of the tincture of digitalis have proved fatal, and recovery has taken place after more than three times as much. Thirty-eight grains of the powdered leaves have caused death, and recovery has followed one drachm. The fatal dose of digitalin is not known; Mawer[1] relates the case of a woman who swallowed fifty-six granules, each containing one milligramme of Homolle's digitalin, the total dose being equal to eighty-four grains of digitalis-leaf. The effects produced were giddiness, vomiting, pain in the stomach, duskiness of the face, dilatation of the pupils, coldness of the extremities, oppression in the præcordial region, slow respirations with prolonged inspiration, and slow, irregular, weak pulse, which sank to forty-four in the minute; recovery took place. Death has taken place in twenty hours, but it may be delayed to a much more remote period.

Treatment.—If necessary use the stomach-pump or give an emetic such as mustard or zinc sulphate with hot water. Stimulants should be freely given and external warmth applied, the patient being kept in the recumbent posture for several days. Hot applications, friction, or mustard leaves, to the epigastrium are useful. Hot coffee with brandy in it may be given. If the vomiting is prolonged, ice in small quantities will be useful.

The Post-mortem Appearances are not characteristic. There may be some signs of irritation, or of inflammation of the gastric mucous membrane.

Chemical Analysis.—Fragments of the leaf, should the poison have been taken in that form, may be detected in the stomach, in which case they should be examined microscopically.

[1] *The Lancet*, 1880.

The aqueous extract obtained in the usual way from organic matter is best shaken out with chloroform, in which all the active principles of digitalis are soluble; they are not all soluble in ether nor in benzene. it is to be remembered that digitalin in acid solution is taken up by chloroform

Tests.—If digitalin is dissolved in a little concentrated sulphuric acid, and some bromine-water is added to the mixture, a violet-red colour is produced. A little digitalin gently heated with a few drops of a mixture of equal parts of sulphuric acid and alcohol turns yellow-brown; on the addition of a drop of a dilute solution of ferric chloride a green or bluish-green colour is produced.

The physiological test may be resorted to as performed by Tardieu in the celebrated case of Pommerais, who was convicted of fatally poisoning a woman with digitalin. Three frogs were prepared so that their hearts were exposed—one frog was left unpoisoned, into the pleural sac of the second a solution of digitalin was injected, and into that of the third some of the suspected poison obtained from the body of the deceased; the heart-beats of the three frogs were respectively counted at stated intervals. The heart of the unpoisoned frog showed little change; that of the one to which digitalin was administered promptly and progressively slowed until it ceased to beat: the heart of the frog to which the suspected poison was administered behaved like number two, excepting that the effects were less rapidly produced.

## COLCHICUM

Colchicum Autumnale, or meadow saffron, is dependent for its toxic effects upon the presence of an active principle colchicine, with a small trace of veratrine, both of which are chiefly contained in the root and the seeds.

Colchicine [$C_{22}H_{25}NO_6$] is a yellowish crystalline powder when pure, but is often met with as an amorphous resinous-looking substance. It is soluble in water, and freely so in alcohol and chloroform; it is slightly, if at all, soluble in ether, and is insoluble in petroleum ether. Colchicine is decomposed by acids with the exception of tannic acid, with which it combines.

Colchicine in poisonous doses causes irritation of the nerve-endings in the intestines, along with gastro-enteritis. The motor centres in the cord and medulla are paralysed, and death is produced by paralysis of the respiratory centres; the sensory nerves are also paralysed. From experiments on animals Jacoby[1] concludes that colchicine may be converted into oxydicolchicine within the organism. Colchicine is partly eliminated by the kidneys and bowels, chiefly by the latter.

[1] *Arch f. exp Path u Pharm*, 1890

**Symptoms**—A burning pain in the throat which extends down the œsophagus to the stomach, where it assumes an aggravated form, is experienced shortly after the poison is swallowed, then follow copious vomiting and purging, the latter being accompanied by violent colicky pains in the abdomen. There is intense thirst; the face is shrunken and pallid, or cyanosed, the surface is cold and moist, the pulse is small, irregular and rapid, the breathing is slow and laboured—the whole symptoms in fact resemble those due to an attack of cholera. This resemblance is increased by the nature of the evacuations from the bowels, which, after the normal contents are discharged, chiefly consist of serous fluid, subsequently they become blood-stained. A sensation of oppression is felt in the region of the heart, the patient is profoundly depressed, and, being fully conscious suffers greatly. Muscular twitchings or spasms may occur, the whole body occasionally being convulsed, the pupils are sometimes dilated, sometimes contracted, stranguary may be present, with increased or diminished amount of urine. Towards the end the cyanosis often becomes more marked, the collapse then being very profound, the mind usually remains clear till towards the last, in exceptional cases stupor occurs earlier.

**Fatal Dose**—Three and a half drachms of colchicum wine have caused death. Recovery has taken place after ten drachms, which produced severe toxic symptoms. The lethal dose of colchicine is not known; a woman, aged forty-three, swallowed about six grains, which had been substituted for another drug, and died in thirty-one hours (Albertoni e Casali[1]). Death has taken place in seven hours, it usually occurs within thirty hours, but has been delayed for three, and even seven days.

**Treatment**—The stomach should be emptied by the tube, and well washed out with a solution of tannic acid; or an emetic may be given, followed by strong tea, then brandy, by the mouth, or if vomiting forbids, ether injections, external warmth and friction, with artificial respiration if required. Probably a subcutaneous injection of morphine will be advisable to relieve the intense colicky spasms of the bowels.

**Post-mortem Appearances**—They are not characteristic; there may be signs of inflammation in the mucous membrane of the stomach and bowels, possibly with spots of ecchymoses; but in some cases there has been an entire absence of such indications.

**Chemical Analysis**—Advantage may be taken of the insolubility of colchicine, in petroleum ether, to dissolve out fatty substances from an aqueous solution obtained from the organic matter. Colchicine is

[1] *Bollet. delle scienze med*, 1890.

dissolved out of acid solution by chloroform. The chloroform solution may either be evaporated to dryness, or after it has undergone some degree of concentration, petroleum ether may be added so as to cause the colchicine to crystallise out.

Tests.—A drop of nitric acid, S.G. 1.4, brought in contact with colchicine, produces a violet colour, which changes to brownish-yellow. One part of ammonium vanadate dissolved in two hundred parts of sulphuric acid produces a green coloration (sometimes very evanescent, and not distinct except with the pure alkaloid), which changes to a brownish-violet; the reagent should be freshly prepared. The physiological test does not afford decisive information; the conclusions arrived at by a committee of French experts, who were appealed to in a case of suspected colchicine poisoning, were —that experiments on animals do not afford the means of determining that poisoning by colchicine has taken place.

Ogier[1] was able to obtain the reactions of colchicine isolated by the usual process, from the exhumed bodies of dogs which he had poisoned with it five and a half months before. In the bodies of animals poisoned with it, Oblonski[2] detected colchicine four and a half months after death.

## VERATRUM

**Veratrum Album**, or white hellebore, and **Veratrum Viride**, or green hellebore, contain a number of alkaloids; Wright and Luff[3] found jervine, pseudo-jervine, rubi-jervine, cevadine, veratralbine, and veratrine. Commercial veratrine is an impure alkaloid obtained from sabadilla seeds.

Veratrine [$C_{27}H_{33}NO_{11}$] is a white, crystalline powder, having an acrid burning taste; when it comes in contact with the nasal mucous membrane it excites violent sneezing. It is insoluble in water, and is soluble in ether, chloroform, and spirit. It has an alkaline reaction.

Veratrine first stimulates the motor nerves, and then paralyses their endings. It alters the character of muscular contractility: contraction is prolonged, and relaxation takes place slowly—a condition resembling, but not identical with, tetanic spasm. The sensory nerves also undergo primary stimulation, followed by paralysis, which is more complete than is the case with the motor endings. The activity of the heart is reduced, the vaso-motor apparatus paralysed, and the blood pressure consequently lowered. Respiration is first quickened, then slowed, and finally arrested from paralysis of the respiratory centres, and probably also of the vagus endings in the lungs. The

[1] *Annales d'Hygiène*, 1886.   [2] *Vierteljahrsschr. f. ger. Med.*, 1888.
[3] *Journ. Chem. Soc.*, 1879.

result of all this is that the temperature is lowered. Veratrine is quickly eliminated by the kidneys

Symptoms.—An acrid, burning sensation, with constriction, is experienced in the throat, the burning sensation extends along the œsophagus down to the stomach, and is followed by vomiting and great thirst. Diarrhœa is not invariable, but may occur; if it does there is usually tenesmus. The pulse is feeble, and the respirations slowed and sighing in character; the pupils are sometimes dilated. Pallor and coldness of the surface, with rapid collapse, twitching of the muscles, and even convulsions, have been observed. Giddiness and paræsthesiæ, followed by superficial anæsthesia, may occur in the early stage; consciousness is usually maintained until the stage of collapse is reached, but occasionally, early on, there is a tendency to delirium and stupor.

Fatal Dose.—Not known. In one case death took place after about eighteen grains of the powdered root of V. album, recovery has occurred after more than twelve times that amount. Grenander[1] records the case of a woman who drank some liniment containing four and a half grains of veratrine. The pupils were dilated, the pulse was slow (50 per minute) and feeble, the respirations were slow and shallow, consciousness was not impaired. Salivation and profuse sweating occurred. Vomiting was frequent, great oppression was felt in the epigastric region, together with soreness of the throat, and profound prostration, there was no diarrhœa, recovery took place under prompt treatment. In another case reported by Blake[2] nearly three grains of veratrine were accidentally swallowed by an adult. The patient complained of giddiness, sickness, constriction of the throat, thirst, diarrhœa with tenesmus, and a tired, weak, faint feeling. The tongue was swollen and the mouth and throat were sore, the pupils were extremely contracted, the respirations hurried, and the pulse was quick and small, micturition was frequent. A continued tingling was felt over the entire body, with now and then intolerable fits of itching in different parts, there was no sneezing. Recovery took place under treatment, the irritation of the skin being the last symptom to subside.

Treatment.—After evacuation of the stomach with the tube or an emetic, stimulants and hot coffee should be administered. External warmth and friction may be required, with maintenance of the recumbent posture and artificial respiration. If excessive diarrhœa is present, morphine will be advisable.

Post-mortem Appearances are not characteristic; only few reports are extant and they afford no definite information.

Chemical Analysis.—Chloroform, or a mixture of chloroform and

[1] Hygeia, 1885.  [2] St. George's Hosp. Rep., 1870.

ether, is the best solvent to extract veratrine from aqueous solution. It can be shaken out of an *acid* solution, but more perfectly after alkalisation.

**Tests.**—Applied to the mucous membrane of the nostrils veratrine causes violent sneezing. A drop or two of strong sulphuric acid added to a little veratrine in a watch-glass and well mixed, develops a yellow colour, which quickly changes to orange and finally to cherry-red; if the mixture is warmed it becomes red immediately. Salicine treated with sulphuric acid turns red immediately without heating. Narcotine gives a similar reaction but takes hours to acquire the red colour. Hydrochloric acid with veratrine produces no change until the mixture is heated, when it becomes red. Sulphomolybdic acid added to a fragment of veratrine produces a brick-red, which becomes dirty brown, greenish, and finally blue. If a little veratrine is mixed with five or six times the amount of cane-sugar, and moistened with concentrated sulphuric acid, a yellow colour is first produced, which changes to green and finally to blue. With ammonium selenate and sulphuric acid veratrine yields a brownish-yellow which changes to rose-red.

## MONK'S-HOOD

Aconitum Napellus or monk's-hood, sometimes called wolf's-bane, is a common plant belonging to the natural order *Ranunculaceæ*; it is extremely poisonous in all its parts. The root has been eaten for horse-raddish although the difference between the two is so marked as to make it impossible for any observant person to mistake one for the other.—Aconite-root quickly tapers to a point whereas horse-raddish is cylindrical or thereabouts; aconite-root is brown, horse-raddish is a dirty white. On section, aconite-root is soft in texture, and white in colour, the cut surface quickly changing to pink on exposure to air; horse-raddish is tough and white, and retains its colour unchanged. The taste also of the two roots is different: aconite is acrid and imparts a tingling sensation, followed by numbness, to the tongue and lips, with a feeling of constriction in the throat; horse-raddish is simply pungent.

The aconite plants contain a number of alkaloids and derivatives, which have been investigated by Wright, Luff, and Menke,[1] several of them not being poisonous. Commercial aconitines consist of variable admixtures of some of these alkaloids, and therefore greatly differ in potency; English and French aconitines are the strongest, German aconitine is much less powerful. Recent investigations by Dunstan, Passmore, and Umney[2] indicate that aconitine is mono-benzoyl aconine.

[1] *Journ Chem. Soc.*, 1877, 1879.  [2] *Proc. of the Chem. Soc.*, 1892.

An exhaustive account of the aconite bases is contained in Allen's *Commercial Organic Analysis*, vol. iii, part ii, 1892.

Aconitine [$C_{33}H_{45}NO_{12}$] is one of the most active, if not the most active, poison known, it is crystallised with difficulty, and is usually met with in white amorphous masses, it has an alkaline reaction, and forms salts, of which the nitrate is preferred. English aconitine is but slightly soluble in water, and is not very freely soluble in alcohol and ether, whilst the German alkaloid is soluble in all three, and freely so in ether

German aconitine has a bitter, sharp, burning taste, the English alkaloid is not bitter, but is sharp and burning. All aconitines produce a peculiar tingling and numbness of the lips and tongue, which comes on shortly after a drop of a dilute solution is applied to them, the sensation lasts for some time and is very characteristic of the poison.

When introduced into the system in poisonous doses aconitine produces a general tingling all over the body, the parts liberally supplied with sensory nerves being most affected The poison first stimulates and then paralyses the sensory nerve-terminals, it produces the same effect on the motor nerves and centres of the medulla and cord. The higher cerebral centres are little affected The heart-beats, at first retarded, may consequently be quickened, the motor ganglia and the muscular substance of the heart are eventually paralysed Respiration becomes slow, and afterwards shallow, due to the action of the poison on the respiratory centre. Death is usually due to arrest of respiration, after cessation of which the heart may continue to beat for a short time The temperature sinks from the first Aconitine is eliminated in the urine and probably in the fæces, in experimenting with animals Dragendorff found it in both

**Symptoms**—Shortly after swallowing a poisonous dose of a preparation of aconite, tingling, followed by numbness of the lips, mouth, and throat, is experienced, due to the direct contact of the poison with the parts affected, then a feeling of nausea and pain in the stomach develops which is usually followed by vomiting and sometimes by purging A tingling, numb sensation—due to the poison which has been absorbed—is now felt over the whole body, with giddiness, imperfect vision, restlessness, anxiety, twitching of the muscles (sometimes with spastic contractions), darting pains in the legs, and muscular prostration The pulse is feeble and intermittent, the respirations are laboured and spasmodic, and the temperature sinks, the limbs especially being cold and moist to the touch The pupils may alternately dilate and contract, and there may be delirium, or a tendency to drowsiness and stupor, towards the end convulsions may occur, which are probably not altogether asphyxic. In an instance of multiple aconite poisoning related by Baker,[1] in which four boys, from fourteen to eighteen years of age, chewed pieces of aconite root, the symptoms developed in from a few minutes to half an hour. All the patients felt heavy and sleepy, and experienced most of the symptoms just described; in the worst case the pupils were widely dilated, the respirations were spasmodic, but the pulse though small was quiet and regular; all recovered.

**Fatal Dose.**—One drachm of aconite root, two grains of the pharmacopœal extract, and one drachm of the tincture have respectively proved fatal. The smallest recorded fatal dose was eighty minims of the pharmacopœal tincture taken in ten doses, spread over four days, the largest individual dose being ten minims; this is quite an exceptional case. Twenty-five minims of Fleming's tincture, equal to about two drachms of the official tincture, have proved fatal, and recovery has followed one ounce. A fatal case of poisoning by aconite liniment is recorded by M'Whannell.[2] A woman swallowed one ounce of the pharmacopœal liniment (equal to about five and one-third drachms of dried aconite root), and became collapsed, with small, irregular pulse, slow, laboured breathing, cold clammy limbs, and pallid lips. There were no convulsions, the pupils dilated immediately before death, which took place in sixty-five minutes after the poison was swallowed. Death has occurred in from three-quarters of an hour up to fifteen or even twenty hours after the poison was swallowed. The usual period of survival is from three to four hours.

As regards the fatal dose of aconitine, experience is more limited. An instructive case is recorded by Tresling.[3] A medical man, who had prescribed aconitine nitrate, was informed that the medicine produced strange symptoms, and, in order to demonstrate its harmlessness, took a dose himself equal to about one-fifteenth of a grain; in about an hour and a half after he began to feel ill. When seen four hours after he was pale, the surface was cold, the pupils were contracted, the pulse was small and irregular, but not rapid, the tongue was swollen, and the patient experienced a burning sensation in the throat, with pain down to the stomach, headache, weakness of the limbs, and shivering. The pupils suddenly dilated, and synchronously there was loss of vision, shortly after the pupils resumed their previous condition, vision returning. Vomiting occurred both spontaneously and in consequence of emetics. In four hours and forty minutes a convulsion occurred, followed by a succession of others, respiration became more laboured, and the pupils again dilated with accompanying loss of vision. Later, the vomiting became very violent, unconsciousness supervened, the pupils remained dilated and insensi-

---
[1] *Brit. Med. Journ.*, 1882.   [2] *Ibid.*, 1890.
[3] *Weekbl. van het Nederl. Tydschr. v. Genees.*, 1880.

tive to light, the respirations grow slower, and the heart ceased to beat, death occurring five hours after the aconitine was taken. At the necropsy pallor of the skin and of the muscles was observed, with hyperæmia of the stomach and first part of the intestines, the colon was pale and the rectum bloodless. The lungs were hyperæmic, and the heart contained fluid blood. The cerebral membranes were injected, the ventricles contained blood-stained serum, and blood was extravasated on the choroid plexus, the blood throughout was fluid and cherry-red in colour. Death was attributed to heart paralysis. In this case French aconitine (Petit's) was dispensed in place of a weak German preparation (Friedlander's), by experiments on animals, Plugge[1] afterwards found that the alkaloid dispensed was one hundred and seventy times more potent than that which was prescribed.

The *cause célèbre* of aconite poisoning was that of *Reg* v. *Lamson* (C C C, 1882), the prisoner being a medical practitioner who was accused of having poisoned his brother-in-law. He paid a visit to his victim, a boy of nineteen, who was a boarder in a school, and persuaded him to swallow a gelatine capsule, which he pretended to fill with sugar, but which, as the result showed, contained aconitine (Morson's). In about twenty minutes the boy complained of heartburn, and then vomited, he had great pain in the stomach, a sense of constriction in the throat, was restless, and tossed himself violently about whilst in bed, the breathing became slower, the heart's action feebler, and he died about four hours after swallowing the capsule. At the necropsy the membranes of the brain were slightly congested, but there was no fluid under them nor in the ventricles, the lips were pale, the pupils dilated, the lungs congested, especially at the lower part, the heart was empty, the liver, spleen, kidneys, and mucous membrane of the stomach and of the first part of the duodenum were congested; on the surface of the gastric mucous membrane were six or eight small, slightly raised patches. From a portion of the vomited matter, from the urine obtained after death, and from the viscera, Stevenson and Dupré obtained aconitine, which responded to the usual physiological tests. The prisoner was condemned and executed.

A fatal case of poisoning due to aconite and belladonna combined is recorded by Lipscomb[2]. A girl of seventeen swallowed two tablespoonsful of a liniment composed of equal parts of the aconite and belladonna liniments of the pharmacopœia. The face and neck were flushed, the neck, arms, and to a slighter degree the legs, were convulsed, the movements being aggravated by external stimuli. The pupils were dilated, the heart's action was quick, turbulent, and irregular—probably 300 per minute, the radial pulse could not be

[1] *Arch. der Pharm.*, 1882.  [2] *Brit. Med. Journ.*, 1888.

felt. In one hour and forty minutes the heart suddenly ceased to beat, respiration continuing for a few seconds longer

**Treatment.**—Evacuate the stomach with tube or emetic. Administer stimulants freely: brandy, by mouth or rectum; ether subcutaneously. External warmth, friction, artificial respiration, and the recumbent posture will be required.

**Post-mortem Appearances.**—Not characteristic; see the account already given. If the poison has been taken in the crude form, search should be made for fragments of the root or other parts of the plant. In a recent case in which six persons were poisoned, three fatally, by the accidental addition of aconitine to quinine-wine, the only special feature noticed at the necropsy was the presence, in all three, of sub-pleural ecchymoses.[1]

**Chemical Analysis.**—Separation from organic matter is accomplished by the usual process, in the course of which exceptional care is necessary to prevent decomposition of the alkaloid, which easily undergoes hydrolysis. The alcoholic extract is preferably made without the addition of an acid; in any case a mineral acid must not be used.

**Tests.**—After proving the presence of an alkaloid, the only reliable procedure is to make use of the physiological test. A tingling sensation, followed by numbness of the lips or tongue, produced by the application to them of a drop of a solution of the product obtained from the vomit, excreta, or tissues, is strongly indicative of aconitine; the subsequent administration of a known quantity of the solution to one of the smaller animals, the toxic effects being compared with those produced by aconitine on other animals of the same species and weight, will yield sufficient evidence of its presence.

Opposite opinions are given with regard to the permanency of aconitine in the presence of putrefying organic matter. Lewin maintains that it is not destroyed; Stevenson states that if allowed to remain some time along with decomposing animal matter which has become alkaline it cannot be detected.

## HELLEBORE

**Helleborus Niger**, or true hellebore, has a dark coloured root which is sometimes used as a vermifuge by herbalists and others; the leaves are also used for the same purpose. The toxic properties of hellebore depend upon the presence of two glucosidal active principles, **helleborin** and **helleborein**, both of which tend to produce muscular paralysis and to cause vomiting and diarrhœa. Helleborin acts on the brain and causes insensibility; it also produces local anæsthesia, and if applied

[1] *Annales d'Hygiène*, 1892.

to the nostrils occasions sneezing. Helleborein produces first slowing and then quickening of the heart, and also dyspnœa.

Symptoms.—A stinging, numb feeling of the tongue extending to the throat, with colicky pain in the stomach and abdomen, followed by violent vomiting and purging, are experienced, together with dizziness, heavy sensation in the head, drowsiness, prostration, collapse with cold, pallid, perspiring surface, feeble pulse, and laboured respiration; in event of a fatal issue, death may be preceded by convulsions. The pupils are frequently dilated. In a case recorded by Ilott,[1] a young man put about two teaspoonsful of powdered hellebore into some water and drank it off. He was seized with violent cramps, giddiness, dimness of vision, inability to stand, and violent vomiting; the pulse was only 40 in the minute; the pupils were dilated; a burning pain was felt in the epigastrium and a sensation of constriction in the throat; the fauces were red and swollen; recovery took place.

The fatal dose is not determined. Half a drachm of a watery extract is recorded as having been fatal. Death has occurred in from three to twelve hours.

Treatment consists in promoting evacuation of the stomach, followed by the administration of stimulants and morphine to allay excessive action of the bowels; external warmth should be promoted.

The Post-mortem Appearances are not characteristic; as with other vegetable irritants, signs of inflammation in the mucous membrane of the stomach have been observed.

Chemical Analysis.—Helleborin, but not helleborein, may be shaken out of *acid* aqueous solution with ether; it is still more soluble in chloroform. After evaporation of the solvent, the residue immediately yields a bright red colour on being touched with a glass rod which has been dipped in strong sulphuric acid.

### STAVESACRE

Delphinium Staphisagria, or stavesacre, a plant belonging to the natural order *Thalamiflora*, yields seeds which contain several active principles, among which are the two alkaloids dephinine and staphisagrine; in toxic action the former resembles aconitine and the latter curare.

Poisoning with stavesacre is exceptionally rare. A case is recorded in which a man by mistake swallowed two teaspoonsful of a powder, two-thirds of which consisted of powdered stavesacre-seeds. The heart was slowed to 35 or 40 beats per minute and was very feeble in its action; severe collapse came on, the surface being very cold; the

[1] *Brit. Med. Journ*, 1889.

breathing was laboured, the pupils were dilated, and the abdomen was distended and exceedingly painful; consciousness was undisturbed. Under treatment recovery took place in a few hours.[1]

## LABURNUM.

**Cytisus Laburnum**, or common laburnum, contains an alkaloid—cytisine [$C_{10}H_{17}N_2O$], which has basic properties and forms salts with acids. Cytisine is freely soluble in water, alcohol, acetic ether, and chloroform; it is insoluble in ether. It has a bitter taste and is powerfully toxic. Cytisine first stimulates and then paralyses the cord and motor nerves, the paralysis beginning in the peripheral endings; the respiratory centres also are first stimulated and then paralysed, death being due to respiratory paralysis. The heart-beats are accelerated. After slight excitation of the brain, cytisine produces somnolence and coma. Cytisine is eliminated in the urine and to some extent in the fæces; it has been found in the saliva.

The symptoms of fatal poisoning by laburnum flowers, seeds, bark, wood, or root supervene in from five minutes up to an hour or more. They comprise:—A hot feeling in the throat, thirst, vomiting, eructations, pain in the stomach, diarrhœa, collapse, cold moist surface, feeble, irregular pulse, gasping respiration, profound prostration and coma; in some cases delirium and convulsions have occurred. The pupils are usually dilated, but they have been observed to be contracted. Death is usually due to asphyxia and may be preceded by cyanosis.

Poisoning by laburnum is most frequent in children who are tempted to chew or eat parts of the tree on account of its sweetish taste; out of 155 cases collected by Falck 120 were in children. An instance of wholesale poisoning resulted from 58 boys chewing pieces of the root of a laburnum tree which had been recently cut across. In the worst cases vomiting occurred with slowing of the pulse, irregular dilatation of the pupils, unconsciousness, and convulsive movements of the legs, followed by profound sleep; in all the cases the pupils were dilated, and the symptoms were of a purely narcotic type; the patients all recovered.[2] A case is recorded by Johnson[3] of six children, from eight to ten years of age, who ate laburnum seeds; they perspired and then went cold and shivery, and vomited; the pulse was scarcely perceptible at the wrist, the pupils were dilated; giddiness, drowsiness, and collapse were observed. One child was purged once, and another repeatedly— in this case purging was the chief symptom; the rest were not purged;

[1] *Friedreich's Blätter f. ger. Med.*, 1868.
[2] *Brit. Med. Journ.*, 1875.
[3] *Ibid*, 1891.

they all recovered. Two children, respectively aged three and eight years, presumably ate some laburnum seeds or pods. Vomiting, diarrhœa, and prostration occurred in one, with death in fourteen hours. The younger child felt tired and sleepy, and then vomited and was convulsed until death occurred eight hours after the symptoms commenced. At the necropsy irritation of the gastro-intestinal mucous membrane was found; no fragments of the seeds were present in the stomach, but cytisine was detected in its contents.[1] Out of the 155 cases collected by Falck only four died. Of the fatal cases two had violent cramps and died within an hour; a third died in twelve hours, and the fourth not until the seventh day after taking the poison.

Treatment consists in thoroughly washing out the stomach, or in giving emetics followed by copious draughts of warm water. Warm applications and friction to the surface, artificial respiration, strong coffee, and stimulants may be necessary.

The Post-mortem Appearances are negative. The signs of inflammation of the gastric mucous membrane which the symptoms during life would indicate have not always been found after death.

Chemical Analysis.—Cytisine is best extracted from an aqueous solution by chloroform. Radziwillowicz[2] recommends amyl alcohol for this purpose, but Moer and Plugge[3] state that the pure alkaloid is much more soluble in chloroform than in amyl alcohol.

Tests.—Cytisine dissolves in concentrated sulphuric acid without undergoing change of colour; on warming, the mixture becomes yellow. If to a little cytisine dissolved in a few drops of concentrated sulphuric acid in the cold a drop of nitric acid is added a yellow colour is produced. If to a mixture of cytisine and sulphuric acid a fragment of potassium dichromate is added, a yellow colour is produced which changes to dirty-brown and finally to green. With a solution of a ferric salt cytisine yields a red colour, which disappears on the addition of a few drops of a solution of peroxide of hydrogen; on subsequent warming a blue colour is produced. This test is very delicate; according to Moer and Plugge it will indicate the presence of 0.5 mgrm. of the alkaloid.

## MEZEREON.

Daphne Mezereum, or mezereon, occasionally gives rise to accidental poisoning in children who pluck and eat the berries. The juice is strongly irritant, and tends to destroy mucous surfaces with which it comes in contact.

[1] *Brit. Med. Journ.*, 1882.    [2] *Ueber Nachw. u Wrk. des Cytisins. Diss.*, 1887.
[3] *Arch. der Pharm.*, 1892.

The **symptoms** are illustrated by the following cases Eagar[1] saw a child, four years old, after it had eaten at least twelve mezereon berries Convulsions occurred before any other symptoms, an emetic was given, and vomiting procured, three hours after, the lips and tongue were swollen, the tongue, twice its natural size, was raw, and protruded beyond the lips, there was difficulty in swallowing, the limbs were cold, and the pulse—130 in the minute—was very weak, recovery took place Dunne[2] saw a child of the same age which had also eaten some mezereon berries It was restless, and complained of pain in the mouth and throat, vomiting took place spontaneously before the child was seen, an emetic was afterwards given which brought away further portions of the berries The child was drowsy, prostrate, pale in the face, with dilated pupils, scarcely perceptible pulse, and cold limbs, the mucous membrane of the tongue and of the roof of the mouth was white from the action of the acrid juice of the berries, the child recovered

**Treatment**—Evacuate the stomach, and afterwards administer an aperient, with such further treatment as the symptoms require

## TURPENTINE OIL

**Symptoms**—A poisonous dose of turpentine oil causes a burning sensation in the mouth and stomach, followed by symptoms of gastro-enteritis Vomiting, thirst, diarrhoea, tympanites, and a condition like that of the early stage of alcoholic intoxication are present, the pulse and respiration vary, the surface is cold, and, in fatal cases, coma supervenes, there may be muscular spasms Strangury is a constant symptom, and the urine has an odour resembling that of violets, a similar odour being often observable in the breath, severe pain in the loins, with hæmaturia, may be present Turpentine is excreted by the lungs, kidneys, and skin The urine excreted after poisonous doses of turpentine has been found to reduce Fehling's solution

Prolonged inhalation of the vapour of turpentine produces toxic symptoms which are occasionally observed in those who have slept in newly painted rooms A case, illustrative of poisoning by the vapour of turpentine, is recorded by Reinhard[3] A man who was occupied in a room in filling small vessels out of a large vessel containing turpentine, began to feel dizzy on the first day, on the second day dryness of the mouth and depression came on, and on the third day increased heaviness and painful micturition. When seen, the patient

---
[1] *Brit. Med. Journ*, 1887.      [2] *Ibid*, 1890.
[3] *Deutsche med Wochenschr*, 1887.

was very drowsy, the bladder was distended to the umbilicus, and the urine contained blood and albumen; it had an odour of violets which it continued to yield for a week after the patient ceased to inhale the turpentine vapour

Fatal Dose.—A tablespoonful has caused the death of an infant five months old, whilst another infant recovered from four ounces. Six ounces were fatal to an adult

Treatment.—The stomach-pump, or an emetic, will be required, followed by demulcents, a purge should be given if diarrhœa has not occurred. Opium and other general treatment may be advisable

Post-mortem Appearances.—The blood has been observed to be dark coloured, and hæmorrhagic spots have been found in the stomach, sometimes with erosion of the mucous membrane

## SAVIN.

Juniperus Sabina, or savin, is a coniferous plant containing, as a toxic principle, an essential oil, odour of which is given off by the plant, it is peculiar, and is easily recognisable; both the leaves and the oil have an acrid burning taste. Savin is rarely taken for the purpose of committing suicide, but it is regarded as an ecbolic by the lower classes, and death has frequently resulted after its use for this purpose. Savin possesses no ecbolic properties; it is an irritant, and when abortion has ensued after its administration, the result has been due to general disturbance of the system, and not to any specific action of the poison on the womb

The symptoms comprise a burning sensation from the throat to the stomach, colicky pains in the abdomen, vomiting, purging, and strangury. Laboured respiration may occur, followed by unconsciousness, collapse, coma, and death; blood may be present in the motions It is very exceptional for abortion to take place without the woman paying the penalty with her life; on the other hand, death of the woman has frequently occurred without abortion being produced.

The Post-mortem Appearances are limited to signs of inflammation of the mucous membrane of the stomach and bowels, with the possible presence of fragments of the leaves. Sometimes no signs of inflammation have been visible; at others, punctiform ecchymoses in the gastric mucous membrane have been observed.

## YEW.

Taxus Baccata, or common yew, another *conifera*, owes its toxic action to the presence of an alkaloid—**taxine**—which is present in the leaves and in the seeds of the fruit; it is most abundant in the leaves. It is soluble in alcohol and ether, and feebly so in water.

Poisoning occurs from the use of the leaves as an emmenagogue, or as an ecbolic, or from accidental causes. As a uterine stimulant yew, like savin, is inert, nevertheless the lower orders make use of the leaves from time to time to determine menstruation, or to procure abortion.

**Symptoms.**—Giddiness, vomiting, muscular weakness, pain in the stomach and bowels, irregular action of the heart, laboured breathing, collapse, general spasms or convulsions, and delirium, have been observed. A girl, on four consecutive mornings, drank a tumblerful of a decoction of yew leaves to promote menstruation; vomiting occurred, and death, preceded by delirium, took place eight hours after the last dose; the post-mortem appearances were negative.[1] Taylor relates the case of a lunatic woman who, whilst preparing evergreen decorations, ate a few pieces of yew leaves; she became collapsed, and died in less than three hours after the symptoms first appeared; the fragments of leaves in the vomit and in the contents of the stomach after death amounted to less than a teaspoonful.

**Treatment.**—Evacuate the stomach, give stimulants, relieve the bowels, and apply external warmth, with general treatment of prominent symptoms.

**Post-mortem Appearances.**—Fragments of leaves or the seeds may be found in the stomach, with signs of inflammation of the gastric mucous membrane. In a case recorded by Carter,[2] a girl was found dead in bed with a history leading to the assumption that she had taken yew leaves as an abortifacient; no vomiting occurred, and death took place within nine hours. The stomach contained fragments of the leaves, and the mucous membrane was inflamed.

## PENNYROYAL

Hedeoma, or pennyroyal, much used as an emmenagogue, contains a volatile oil which may produce toxic effects. Wingate[3] states that a pregnant woman, aged twenty, took a teaspoonful of oil of pennyroyal as an ecbolic; she became unconscious; the limbs were cold, the pulse was small, and the pupils were slightly dilated; vomiting, delirium, and two attacks of opisthotonos occurred. Recovery, without abortion, took place.

[1] *L. Imparziale*, 1870
[2] *Brit. Med. Journ.*, 1884.
[3] *Boston Med. and Surg. Journ.*, 1889.

## TANSY.

Tanacetum Vulgare, or tansy, contains a volatile oil, which, along with the leaves of the herb itself, has a reputation as an ecbolic, emmenagogue, and also as an anthelmintic. It is poisonous, and has caused death after being taken for the above-named purposes. In a case recorded by Jewett[1] the symptoms were as follows:—A woman, aged twenty-nine, took fifteen drops of oil of tansy at eleven in the forenoon, three hours afterwards she took a teaspoonful, having had dinner between the two doses. Fifteen minutes after the second dose she threw herself on the sofa and then sprang up with a wild cry and was convulsed; respiration was for a time suspended and she became deeply cyanosed especially about the face, neck, and hands; the eyes were open, the pupils were widely dilated, and there was great restlessness. The surface was cold and moist; the pulse was 120, and the respirations 35 to the minute, the odour of the oil being perceptible in the breath and also in the matter which the patient vomited after taking an emetic; recovery took place. In a case communicated by Dalton a woman was found on the floor in violent convulsions; she was unconscious, the cheeks were flushed and of a bright red colour, the eyes were open and very brilliant, with widely dilated and fixed pupils; the respirations were hurried, laboured, and stertorous, the breath having the odour of tansy; the pulse (128) was full. Spasms occurred at intervals by which the head was thrown back, the arms were raised and rigid, and the fingers spastically contracted. The pulse gradually grew feeble and suddenly ceased three-quarters of an hour after the first appearance of the symptoms. At the necropsy no indications were discovered except the odour of tansy oil which pervaded the entire body, and was perceived as the cavities were respectively opened; globules of the oil were found in the stomach; a fœtus at about the fourth month was found in the uterus. There was reason to believe that about eleven drachms of oil of tansy were taken.

## OIL OF WINTERGREEN.

Oil of Wintergreen, or oil of gaultheria, consists for the most part of methyl salicylate; it has an agreeable odour and a sweetish taste.

The symptoms produced by poisonous doses may be gathered from the following cases:—Hamilton[2] saw a woman after she had swallowed half an ounce of the oil; she was dizzy, drowsy, and delirious. An emetic caused evacuation of the contents of the stomach which were coated with a film of the oil and contained shreds of mucous membrane.

[1] *Boston Med. and Surg. Journ.*, 1880.  [2] *New York Med. Journ.*, 1875.

The pupils were contracted, the respirations quick and laboured, and the limbs cold, hallucinations of audition and vision, pain in the head, and a strong disposition to sleep, verging towards coma, were present. Hemiparesis of the left side, with extreme irritability of the nervous system—starting at the least sound—and profuse salivation were prominent symptoms; recovery slowly took place. Pinkham[1] reports the case of a woman who swallowed one ounce of oil of gaultheria which caused profuse sweating, pain in the abdomen, frequent painful micturition and purging, followed by convulsions, loss of sight and hearing, flushed face, rapid respirations, feeble pulse, and death in fifteen hours. At the necropsy the blood was found black and fluid, and the mucous membrane of the stomach and duodenum intensely congested; the contents of the stomach yielded the odour of the oil.

## ERGOT

Ergot is a parasitic formation consisting of the mycelium of the *Claviceps purpurea* developed from the ovary of various gramineæ, especially rye; it occurs in wet seasons, and may be so widely diffused as to give rise to epidemics of ergotism in the districts where the diseased grain is grown.

Ergot contains more than one active principle; Kobert has found three —*ergotinic acid*, *sphacelinic acid*, and *cornutine*, the last is regarded as an alkaloid; the substance known as ergotin is an admixture of these principles. Although by means of experiments on animals, considerable information has been obtained as to their respective actions, the specific effects produced by them on the human subject have not yet been satisfactorily differentiated; from the toxicological standpoint therefore ergot and ergotin are to be regarded as complex bodies which possess certain definite toxic properties.

Ergot poisoning may be acute or chronic, the latter is frequently named ergotism.

**Symptoms of Acute Ergot Poisoning.**—When one or more poisonous doses of ergot, or of ergotin, are taken, giddiness, pain in the stomach, thirst, nausea, vomiting, great oppression in the cardiac region, numbness and tingling—beginning in the fingers and toes, and tending to spread along the limbs—cramp, dyspnœa, shivering, coldness, especially of the limbs, great anxiety, delirium, coma, and convulsions are among the symptoms which may be produced.

In a case recorded by Debierre[2] a woman recovered after swallowing one drachm and a half of Bonjean's ergotin. In a few hours intense dyspnœa, faintness, dryness of the mouth and throat, giddiness, noises

[1] *Boston Med. and Surg. Journ.*, 1888.   [2] *Ballet Gén. de Thérap.*, 1884.

in the ears, dimness of vision, tingling, and a sensation of coldness in the limbs were experienced. There was complete anæsthesia of the tongue and of the surface of the body, with severe pain in the epigastrium and the abdomen; the temperature was 96° 8 F, the pulse 50 per minute, and the respirations also 50 per minute, epileptiform convulsions occurred. In another and fatal case recorded by Davidson[1] a woman who was pregnant had been taking the liquid extract of ergot for several months, she then swallowed "two handfuls" of powdered ergot without infusing it. When seen the day after, the face and the upper part of the body were jaundiced; ecchymoses were present under the skin around the eyes, the lips and tongue were swollen and coated with dry black blood, there was intense thirst, the skin was pale, and the temperature 96° F. The pulse was peculiar—it could not be counted, but could be just perceived, and then disappeared before its character could be estimated, the heart-beats were of a rolling character—150 per minute, the respirations were 48 per minute. The patient had periods of stupor and apathy, she vomited red pultaceous matter and pure blood, the urine also contained blood. An attempt was made to effect instrumental delivery, but the woman died before it could be accomplished, the respirations increased to 56, and stupor with paroxysmal movements supervened immediately before death. At the *necropsy* much fluid blood, effused from small vessels, was found extravasated in the abdominal cavity, but no large vessel was ruptured. The liver, kidneys, and lungs were bloodless, the liver and kidneys presenting a pale yellow, waxy appearance, all the viscera, though bloodless, were ecchymosed, and ruptured vessels were found within the stomach and bowels. In the uterus, which contained no blood, a five months' fœtus was found. The bladder was empty.

The effect of ergot on the quiescent uterus is discussed in the section on criminal abortion.

**Treatment.**—Evacuate the stomach with tube or emetic, and clear out the bowels. Stimulants and external warmth will be needed. Inhalations of amyl nitrite, or, as recommended by Murrell, nitroglycerine, administered by the mouth, may be tried.

**Post-mortem Appearances** chiefly consist in presence of ecchymoses and extravasation of blood on and into the internal organs, as described in the above quoted case. The bodies of three pregnant women who died in consequence of taking ergot to procure abortion, all presented unusual post-mortem appearances; externally they were jaundiced to some extent, internally the usual ecchymoses were found, and in addition, the liver in all three, and the kidneys in two, showed fatty

[1] *The Lancet*, 1882.

changes, so pronounced as to give rise to suspicion of phosphorus poisoning. On chemical examination ergot was found in the intestines, but no trace of phosphorus. In two of these cases the uterus contained a four months' and a six weeks' fœtus respectively, in the third, a fœtus surrounded by its membranes was at the vaginal outlet [1]

**Symptoms of Chronic Ergot Poisoning**—Chronic ergot poisoning mostly occurs as a consequence of eating bread made from grain contaminated with the fungus, it has occurred epidemically for many centuries, and still appears from time to time in Germany, Russia, and other countries

The early symptoms indicate disturbance of the gastro-intestinal tract, they comprise pain and oppression in the gastric region, general depression, either loss or increase of appetite, nausea, occasional vomiting, sometimes diarrhœa and at others constipation, together with dizziness, sleeplessness, and a general feeling of weariness and absence of energy. Subsequently the symptoms may take one or both of two courses—**gangrenous** or **nervous** (spasmodic ergotism)

**Gangrenous Ergotism** is first indicated by the occurrence of patches of anæsthesia—the patient experiencing a sensation of cold in the parts affected—or by a burning sensation, accompanied by redness of the skin Gangrene, mostly of the dry type, which may or may not be preceded by the formation of serous blisters, then sets in, the peripheral parts of the limbs—the toes and fingers—being most frequently affected The gangrene, which seldom affects the trunk, may advance as far as the knees or elbows, when it has reached its limit, separation by slow ulceration takes place, unless the process is expedited by surgical operation In rare cases the skin only is attacked, the entire cutis undergoing necrosis, and separating from the underlying tissues

**Spasmodic Ergotism** is preceded by paræsthesiæ of various kinds, such as a creeping sensation beginning in the fingers and toes and spreading along the limbs, in some instances there is complete anæsthesia Motor disturbances follow first, twitching of the muscles occurs, then spastic contraction of groups of muscles, by which the fingers and toes are flexed and drawn together, the hands are flexed at the wrists, presenting the appearance of clenched fists with the thumbs drawn towards the palms, the ankles are extended, the heels being sometimes so powerfully drawn up that the feet and the legs form straight lines The spasm may extend along the muscles of the limbs to those of the spine, so as to produce opisthotonos, rarely, the muscles of the lower jaw are similarly affected. The spasms are exceedingly painful, and cause the patient to roll about in agony, the surface being covered with

[1] *Petersb med. Wochenschr*, 1884

a cold sweat, they last from a few minutes to many hours, when they pass off the patient is left exhausted and powerless. Sometimes the contractions are tetanoid in character, at others, clonic spasms resembling epilepsy occur; the breathing may be affected as though the diaphragm participated in the spasmodic seizure. Dysuria due to spastic contraction of the bladder may be present. Paralysis, with complete superficial anæsthesia, sometimes follows. Disturbances of the special senses have been recorded, as diplopia, alterations in the field of vision for colours, deafness, and aphasia. Exceptionally cataract has been observed.

Psychical disorders, as hallucinations, delirium, mania, mental enfeeblement, with stupor, and, exceptionally, indications of tabes—lightning pains, girdle sensation, staggering gait, and unsteadiness in the erect posture with the eyes closed—have occurred. Tuczek[1] found sclerosis of the posterior columns of the cord, implicating the root zones as in tabes.

Both the gangrenous and spasmodic types of ergotism are probably due to persistent contraction of the smaller arteries, which deprives the tissues respectively implicated of their normal supply of blood, as previously stated, the two varieties may co-exist a patient with spasmodic ergotism may lose the toes and fingers from gangrene.

From a report made by Griasnoff,[2] on seventeen cases of ergotism which were admitted into the Poltava hospital in Russia during the epidemic of 1881, the following statements are taken:—The ages of the patients varied from twelve to forty-five years, thirteen were males and four were females, four died—two males and two females. All suffered from agonising pains and numbness of the limbs, sleeplessness, exhaustion, diarrhœa, weak accelerated pulse, and, all but one, from loss of appetite. Five suffered from spasms, a few from headache, nausea, and vomiting. In all but one, gangrene—of the humid type in eight, and of the dry in seven—occurred, all of these patients had pyrexia (104° F. and more), with evening exacerbations. The quantity of ergot present in the rye-meal which had been eaten by the patients, was not more than one per cent, which is much lower than the percentage usually stated as liable to cause ergotism.

The **treatment** of ergotism is mostly prophylactic, with ordinary medical or surgical treatment of the symptoms as they arise.

**Chemical Analysis.**—Bread or flour suspected of containing ergot should be extracted with hot alcohol acidulated with sulphuric acid. The extract is red in colour, and, if examined with the spectroscope, yields two bands one in the green and another in the blue, the latter being the broadest and best defined. It is practically impossible to

[1] *Arch. f. Psychiat.*, 1882.  [2] *The London Med. Record*, 1883.

separate ergot from the tissues so as to identify it; in acute poisoning the contents of the stomach may be treated as above, and the ergot if present identified

## JABORANDI.

Jaborandi, the dried leaflets of the *pilocarpus pennatifolius*, owes its toxic properties to the presence of an alkaloid pilocarpine, with possibly two others

Pilocarpine [$C_{11}H_{16}N_2O_2$] is a colourless, syrupy-liquid, without odour; with acids it forms crystallisable salts, of which the hydrochlorate and the nitrate are most used. Pilocarpine powerfully stimulates almost all the secretions, especially the saliva and the sweat; it also stimulates the motor nerves of the involuntary muscles. In small doses it stimulates, and in large doses it paralyses the vagus-endings in the heart, and thus slows or accelerates the pulse. Respiration is impeded by excessive secretion of mucus into the bronchi; the temperature is lowered, the pupils are contracted, and increased peristalsis of the intestines occurs. Pilocarpine is eliminated in the urine

Symptoms —The following case by Fuhrmann[1] illustrates the effects produced by a large dose. A man aged thirty-one had 01 gm (about one-sixth of a gram) of pilocarpine injected subcutaneously; the face immediately grew red, then the neck, and shortly after the whole body, which began to perspire freely. In a few minutes the patient experienced sudden severe oppression of the heart and extreme difficulty of breathing, as though the chest was filled with fluid; the severe cardiac oppression subsided in ten minutes, but traces could be felt for two hours. Increased secretion of saliva, tears, and of mucus from the nostrils occurred. Cramps were experienced in the stomach, as though the organ "would turn round", nausea and vomiting followed, with movements of the intestines which produced a strong desire to evacuate the bowels. Great thirst, prostration and a tired feeling, especially in the legs, were experienced; the pupils were contracted and vision was impaired; the pulse was small and frequent, and the patient became collapsed. The amblyopia lasted two hours, the sweating two and a half hours, the salivation four and a half hours, during which time 500 grammes of saliva were expectorated; the patient recovered. A case is recorded by Sziklai[2] in which a patient by mistake had a Pravaz-syringeful of a 20 per cent. solution of pilocarpine injected under the skin. Immediately on withdrawing the canula salivation, copious sweating, and shortly after dizziness,

[1] *Wiener med. Wochenschr.*, 1890.  [2] *Ibid.*, 1881.

vomiting, diarrhœa, oppression, and a tearing-pain in the eyeballs with pronounced myopia occurred; the pupils were contracted to the uttermost. The patient micturated twice, the salivation and diaphoresis lasted two hours; after five hours the acute symptoms began to disappear, and the patient recovered. Jaborandi has also produced psychical disorder with hallucinations.

Treatment.—If necessary evacuate the stomach and then give stimulants. One-fiftieth of a grain of atropine sulphate should be injected subcutaneously, and repeated if necessary.

### CALABAR BEAN.

Calabar Bean, the seed of the *physostigma venenosum*, is kidney-shaped, having a groove with elevated borders along its convexity; it is blackish-brown in colour, and its surface has a texture like that of the fine morocco leather used for book-binding. The bean varies from an inch to an inch and a half in length; if split lengthwise it is seen to consist of a brown-coloured rind containing two white cotyledons which adhere to the shell. It contains two alkaloids—physostigmine and calabarine, its characteristic toxic effects being due to the former.

Physostigmine [$C_{15}H_{21}N_3O_2$] or eserine when pure, is a white crystalline body which rapidly changes colour on exposure to air and light; it is not very soluble in water, but is easily soluble in alcohol, ether, and chloroform. It has an alkaline reaction, and forms salts with acids, which are colourless and soluble in water; on exposure to air they deliquesce and acquire a red colour.

Physostigmine increases the irritability of both the voluntary and the involuntary muscles—shown by twitching of the skeletal muscles and peristalsis of those of the intestines. It eventually paralyses the respiratory centres in the medulla and causes death from arrest of respiration. It augments the irritability of the vagus, and thus tends to slow the heart; it increases the secretions, probably by direct action on the secreting elements themselves, and paralyses the motor centres in the brain and cord. When applied directly to the eye physostigmine contracts the pupils and causes spasm of accommodation, probably from stimulation of the third nerve. Physostigmine is eliminated in the urine, fæces, and saliva.

Calabarine resembles strychnine in its action and causes clonic spasms.

Symptoms.—After a poisonous dose of calabar bean giddiness and faintness are experienced, quickly followed by profound prostration; pain is felt in the stomach usually followed by vomiting, diarrhœa may occur but is not very frequent. The heart's action is enfeebled, the pulse being usually small and slow, and there may be dyspnœa. The surface is cold and moist, the pupils may be, but are by no means invariably contracted; salivation and thirst have occurred. The mental condition varies: in some instances it is undisturbed, in others drowsiness and even unconsciousness have been observed. Muscular spasms have been present in rare cases, probably due to calabarine. In the year 1864, forty-six children were poisoned in Liverpool through eating calabar beans which had been discharged from a ship; they all suffered from pain in the region of the stomach, thirty-eight were attacked with vomiting, and fifteen with diarrhœa; only one died.

A unique case of suicidal poisoning with physostigmine is recorded by Leibholz.[1] Two girls, aged twenty-four and eighteen respectively, obtained possession of a sealed tube containing 0.1 gm. of physostigmine sulphate, which they dissolved in water, and each girl drank half of the solution; for half an hour they pursued their household avocations without experiencing any effects, they then suddenly became unconscious. In each case the face was red and shining, the pupils, dilated to the maximum, were reactionless; the pulse, 60 to the minute, was full and of high tension; the respirations were shallow, rapid, and moaning; pain was experienced in the region of the stomach and abdomen; vomiting occurred early and persisted for some time after return to consciousness. Dilatation of the pupils, with feeble reaction to light, lasted for several days, perfect recovery ultimately taking place. The activity of the alkaloid was vouched for by Merck after chemically examining a companion sample. Tested physiologically three milligrammes injected under the skin of a rabbit weighing four pounds produced paralysis of the voluntary muscles, difficulty of respiration, violent diarrhœa and death in ten minutes; a solution dropped into the human eye caused marked contraction of the pupil. The dilatation of the pupils in the above recorded cases is remarkable; cases of calabar bean poisoning have occurred without contraction of the pupils, but none with dilatation. The absence of diarrhœa is in marked contrast to its universal occurrence in animals poisoned with physostigmine.

Eserine (physostigmine) has produced symptoms of poisoning after being dropped into the eyes for ophthalmic purposes. Dunlop[2] relates the case of a man, aged sixty, who had one drop of a solution of eserine (inadvertently prepared with one grain to the drachm instead of to the ounce) dropped into each eye; a quarter of an hour after, clonic spasms of the eyelids, stiffness of the lips, a feeling of tremor in the arms and

[1] *Vierteljahrsschr. f. ger. Med.*, 1892.    [2] *The Lancet*, 1887.

legs, together with mental confusion occurred, the symptoms passing off after a time.

Treatment.—If the poison has been swallowed, evacuate the stomach with tube or emetic, then give stimulants, and apply external warmth. Atropine sulphate injected subcutaneously in one-fiftieth of a grain doses, repeated until the pupils dilate and the pulse-rate is quickened, is recommended by Fraser. Strychnine is also regarded as an antidote. In any case, should respiration fail, it must be promoted artificially.

Post-mortem Appearances are negative.

Chemical Analysis.—The alkaloid may be extracted from organic matter in the usual way, special care being taken not to allow excess of acid, of heat, nor of light to come into play; ether is a good solvent.

Tests.—Bromine water, added to a solution of physostigmine, produces a red or orange coloured turbidity, which clears up on heating. Strong chlorine water added to the solid alkaloid produces a red colour.

The physiological test should be resorted to: a drop of an aqueous solution instilled into the eye of a rabbit produces contraction of the pupil; the test may be repeated on the human eye.

### NUTMEG

Nutmeg, the kernel of the seed of the *myristica fragrans*, though of every-day use as a food adjunct, is capable of causing poisonous symptoms when taken in excess. Bentliff[1] records the case of a man who swallowed the whole of a grated nutmeg as a remedy for boils. He afterwards went to bed and slept until six o'clock in the morning, when he felt giddy and could not stand; he had pain in the head, and could not distinguish objects; he was drowsy, but could be roused by shouting; thirst, numbness of the limbs, and somewhat contracted pupils were the other symptoms present; he recovered in a short time. Sawyer[2] relates the case of a boy, aged three, who ate portions of five nutmegs. He was dizzy, and then became unconscious, with relaxed muscles, and could not be roused; he slept for thirty consecutive hours; the pupils were dilated; there was no delirium. In contrast to this case is one related by Reading,[3] in which a lady, three months pregnant, in order to procure abortion, swallowed three powdered nutmegs; she vomited several times, and became delirious with hallucinations, accompanied by laughter; the pulse was strong and rapid. Notwithstanding treatment, the delirium recurred at intervals during the succeeding twenty-four hours, when she became rational, and recovered without abortion taking place.

[1] *Brit. Med. Journ.*, 1889.   [2] *New York Med. Journ.*, 1889.
[3] *Therap. Gaz.*, 1892.

## CAMPHOR.

In poisonous doses camphor acts as an irritant and produces the usual symptoms of collapse, it first stimulates and then paralyses the nerve centres, and tends to cause convulsions. East[1] records the case of a youth, aged nineteen, who swallowed a large lump of sugar saturated with essence of camphor, and an hour afterwards drank an equal quantity added to some water, the total amount being about two drachms. In two hours after the first dose he felt giddy, talked incoherently, and fell down in a "fit." The pulse was full, and the pupils were dilated; the patient vomited spontaneously, the rejected matter having the odour of camphor; recovery took place. Davis[2] saw a child, two and a half years old, after it had eaten a piece of solid camphor the size of a nut—about half a drachm; it was pale, and convulsed, the lips being blue, and the pulse very rapid; on evacuation of the stomach it recovered somewhat from the collapse, but died in eighteen hours after swallowing the poison. Honman[3] saw a girl of eighteen who had swallowed an unknown dose of camphor; she was unconscious, the pupils were dilated, the legs were cold, the pulse was thready, and the breath had the odour of camphor; convulsive movements occurred, followed by paralysis; the breathing became shallower and the patient died within thirty-six hours. At the necropsy camphor was found in the stomach.

## SANTONIN

Santonica, the dried flower-heads of the *artemisia maritima*, contains a crystalline active principle santonin, which is almost insoluble in water but is freely soluble in hot alcohol, and in chloroform. Cases of poisoning by santonin, or by substances containing it, occur almost exclusively among children, to whom it is given as a vermicide.

Symptoms.—The most constant symptom is one that occurs even with non-poisonous doses—disturbance of colour-vision; objects first assume a bluish tinge, and subsequently yellowish-green or yellow. The most probable explanation is that primary stimulation of the violet-seeing retinal elements takes place—causing violet or blue vision, with sequential paralysis and consequent absence of blue vision, the period of stimulation being very short may pass unobserved; the paralysis lasts much longer, and therefore the condition is usually described as "yellow vision." Singing sounds in the ears, dizziness, pain in the stomach, vomiting convulsions, and stupor, with a tendency to

---
[1] *Brit. Med. Journ.*, 1886.   [2] *Ibid.*, 1887.
[3] *Australian Med. Journ.*, 1888.

asphyxia, are among the remaining symptoms. The urine is coloured saffron-yellow. In a severe case observed by Demme[1] a boy aged three took about two-thirds of a grain of santonin six times a day. On the third day there was vomiting, dilatation of the pupils, coldness of the surface, cyanosis of the lips and cheeks, dyspnœa and convulsions, with deep stupor. Bleeding at the nose and hæmoglobinuria occurred; the urine had a dark saffron tint with a greenish shimmer. The temperature was 102°·5 F., cold effusion was used, and recovery took place, a scarlatina-like rash appearing on the chest.

Chronic Santonin poisoning is very unusual. Rey[2] records the case of a boy, aged eleven years, who, on account of pain in the abdomen, which was supposed by his mother to be due to worms, had santonin given to him for months. Clonic spasms then developed, to combat which the doses of santonin were increased. Paralysis, twitchings, dizziness, pain in the head, vomiting, yellow and violet vision, sparks before the eyes and finally loss of speech occurred and necessitated medical advice. Under treatment the patient was able to walk in six weeks, but it was nine weeks before he regained the power of speech.

Fatal Dose.—About two grains of santonin taken at twice proved fatal in twelve hours to a child five and a half years old; recovery in a child has followed ten grains. A man aged forty took one ounce in mistake for Epsom salts; giddiness, incessant vomiting, prostration, laboured breathing, and epileptiform convulsions ensued, but recovery eventually took place.[3]

Treatment.—Evacuate the poison and administer stimulants. Convulsions may be combatted by potassium bromide and chloral hydrate.

Post-mortem Appearances are not characteristic. In a case recorded by Kilner[4] the stomach and duodenum of a child aged four and a half, who died thirty-five minutes after taking six grains of santonin, displayed signs of inflammation.

Chemical Analysis.—Santonin may be extracted from *acid* aqueous solutions by shaking out with chloroform; it will not come away from alkaline solutions, as it plays the part of a weak acid, forming combinations with alkalies which are soluble in water.

Tests.—A solution of sodium hydrate produces a violet-red colour with santonin. Dragendorff has devised a modification of a former test which is thus peformed:—A little sulphuric acid diluted with half its volume of water is added to some santonin, and gently heated until a yellow colour is produced; when cold a few drops of a very dilute solution of ferric chloride are added, and on again warming a blue or reddish-violet colour is produced.

[1] *Klinische Mittheilungen*, 1891
[2] *Therap. Monatshefte*, 1889
[3] *Annali univ. di Med.*, 1882
[4] St. Thomas' Hosp. Reps., 1880.

The presence of santonin in the urine may usually be ascertained by the addition of a little sodium hydrate; if present a red colour is produced. Rhubarb present in the urine yields the same reaction; but if, after the addition of sodium hydrate, excess of milk of lime is added, and the urine afterwards filtered, the filtrate is colourless if the reddening is due to rhubarb, but retains its colour if it is due to santonin.

## COLOCYNTH

**Colocynth,** or bitter apple, the dried pulp of the *citrullus colocynthis,* contains an active principle **colocynthin,** which is soluble in water and alcohol but not in ether. Colocynthin is an active cathartic, and, in large doses, a gastro-intestinal irritant. A few fatal cases of poisoning by colocynth are recorded. In one a teaspoonful and a half proved fatal in twenty-four hours. In another recorded by Tidy[1] a woman took from one to two drachms of bitter apple as an emmenagogue; on the following day, vomiting and violent purging occurred, and the patient died in about forty hours after taking the poison; the result of the post-mortem examination was negative. In another case the intestines were found reddened, and the stomach ulcerated; the kidneys and bladder being inflamed.

## ELATERIUM.

**Elaterium,** the dried juice of the *ecballium elaterium,* contains an active principle **elaterin,** which is insoluble in water, but is soluble in hot alcohol and in chloroform. Elaterium is an exceedingly powerful cathartic, and in poisonous doses may produce, in addition to its drastic effects, nausea, eructation, vomiting, salivation, prostration, clonic spasms, insensibility, and dyspnœa. Two-fifths of a grain has proved fatal. One sixth of a grain caused the death of a woman aged seventy. Recovery has taken place after three-quarters of a grain of elaterin, severe symptoms of poisoning being produced.

## CROTON OIL

**Croton Oil** is a fixed oil expressed from the seeds of the *croton tiglium* which resemble, but are smaller than, castor oil seeds. Both seeds and oil are active gastro-intestinal irritants; by direct contact, the oil produces inflammation of the skin, as well as of mucous membranes.

**Symptoms.**—When taken in poisonous doses into the stomach, croton oil produces a hot, burning sensation in the mouth and throat, pain in

[1] *The Lancet,* 1868

the stomach and abdomen, violent vomiting and purging, with dizziness, great prostration, cold surface and collapse. The pulse and the respirations are slowed; in fatal cases, death takes place in a few hours. Half a drachm of the oil in one instance, and twenty drops in another, proved fatal. Recovery has taken place after a drachm, and even after half an ounce, but in the latter case the oil was not pure. The seeds have also proved fatal; in one case four caused death.

## CASTOR OIL SEEDS

Castor Oil seeds, the seeds of the *ricinus communis*, are smooth, oval-shaped and bean-like; in addition to the oil, which is a well-known harmless purgative, the seeds contain a poisonous albuminoid body, which Stillmark[1] regards as an unformed ferment. From experiments on animals it is found to be a gastro-intestinal irritant; it possesses no intrinsic purgative properties, hence in some cases of poisoning by castor oil seeds, purging has been conspicuous by its absence.

**Symptoms.**—They comprise nausea, pain in the stomach, with a burning sensation in the throat, persistent violent vomiting, colicky pains in the abdomen, pale, collapsed appearance of the face, cold surface, great prostration, small pulse, with retention of consciousness in some cases and insensibility in others. Purging may or may not occur.

In a case recorded by Langerfeldt,[2] a boy ate ten to fifteen seeds; he vomited—the rejected substance containing blood—had headache, and lay on his back groaning, with his legs drawn up, pale, cold, and cyanosed; the skin was clammy, the pulse (110) scarcely to be felt, the abdomen was retracted, and the tongue was dry and furred. He complained of a burning sensation in the throat and pain in the epigastrium; the bowels were obstinately constipated; on the sixth day he was quite well. In a case recorded by Bouchardat,[3] a girl, aged eighteen, ate about twenty seeds, which produced violent purging, vomiting and profound collapse; the stools consisted chiefly of blood-stained serous fluid; death occurred on the fifth day. The mucous membrane of the stomach was found softened and abraded in parts.

**Fatal Dose.**—Three seeds proved fatal in forty-six hours to an adult, aged thirty-two. Recovery, even in children, has followed larger doses; adults have recovered from seventeen and twenty seeds respectively. Park[4] records the recovery of a man who had eaten twenty-four seeds.

**Treatment in Poisoning by Cathartics.**—Promote evacuation of the

---

[1] *Dissert*, 1888.  [2] *Berliner klin. Wochenschr*, 1882.
[3] *Annales de Thérapeutique*, 1872.  [4] *Glasgow Med Journ*, 1880.

poison, and then administer morphine hypodermically, followed by stimulants and external warmth. As soon as the stomach will retain anything, demulcents with a little ice may be given. If purging is excessively violent, starch and opium enemata may be advisable; mustard leaves to the abdomen and epigastrium will be of service. If the collapse is very severe hypodermic injections of ether may be needed.

Post-mortem Appearances are usually limited to signs of inflammation of the gastro-intestinal mucous membrane, such as hyperæmia and softening, with possibly erosion in parts. Fragments of the seeds should be sought for.

## FUNGI.

Fungi have been classified as edible and poisonous; some are definitely known to be poisonous, but it by no means follows that all others may be eaten with impunity. It is obvious that those only which contain intrinsic toxic principles can be classified as poisonous; according to Husemann, these comprise—*amanita muscaria, amanita phalloides, russula integra, boletus luridus,* and their varieties. Such fungi are poisonous in the same sense as are any of the known poisonous vegetables; there are however many fungi which contain no essential toxic principle, and yet from time to time they act as poisons. In England the common mushroom (*agaricus campestris*) and the champignon (*agaricus oreades*) are the only fungi eaten; on the Continent a much more liberal selection is made.

The erratic way in which fungi, regarded as harmless, occasionally produce violent toxic effects, has been variously accounted for. Many edible fungi contain amanitin which, though itself inert, may be resolved by incipient decomposition into neurin—a closely allied, or, as some authorities hold, an identical substance—and may thus give rise to symptoms of poisoning. Some edible fungi contain more albumen and fatty matter than others, and are therefore more liable to undergo decomposition either before gathering, when past their prime, or after gathering and before cooking. The morel, according to Kohlrausch, contains 35 per cent. of albumen and 2.39 per cent. of fat, whereas the common mushroom contains only 17 per cent. albumen and 1.4 per cent. fat—hence poisoning from decomposition changes is less frequent by the latter than by the former. It has been supposed that fungi (especially the morel) when gathered in wet weather are likely to become poisonous; in some instances it is probable that specimens of a poisonous variety have been accidentally included among edible fungi. Idiosyncrasy may have something to do with the matter, but not much; the severity of the symptoms respectively produced in a number of people who have partaken of a poisonous dish of mushrooms, depends on the quantity each has eaten, and more especially on the amount of the juice or gravy consumed (as representing an extract of the fungi) rather than on idiosyncrasy. Many years ago I saw three fatal cases of mushroom poisoning in one family. The mother and three children partook of mushrooms to supper, and were taken ill the following morning, with symptoms of acute gastro-enteritis; the mother and two of the children died within forty-eight hours, the third just escaped. The symptoms were by far the most violent in the woman, and on enquiry it was found that after helping the children she took the dish to herself and soaked up the juice with bread, which she ate in addition to the mushrooms; the excess in number of mushrooms she ate in comparison with those eaten by the children, was insufficient alone to account for the relative violence of her symptoms. That the poison is easily dissolved out is shown by the fact that in some parts of the Continent the poisonous fly-fungus (*amanita muscaria*) is eaten with impunity after being well extracted with water. Mushrooms which have been dried and kept for some time may develop ptomaine-like poisons; mushrooms which have been cooked, should not be eaten after being put on one side and warmed up again.

Symptoms of Poisoning by Fungi are divisible into two groups—*gastro-enteric* and *neurotic*—both of which are usually represented in the same patient.

Gastro-enteric symptoms may not appear for six or ten hours after the fungi are eaten, and not unfrequently they are still further delayed. A feeling of uneasiness in the stomach gradually develops into pain, with a hard tender condition of the abdomen; nausea is experienced, and then vomiting, which is followed by diarrhœa. The vomiting and diarrhœa are not solely due to the immediate presence of the irritant, but to the condition set up by it in the gastro-intestinal mucous membrane; therefore they do not at once subside when all the fragments of fungi are discharged; the enteric derangement is further shown by the character of the evacuations, which are serous—ricewater-like—and contain flakes of lymph, and sometimes blood; notwithstanding treatment the diarrhœa and vomiting may persist for several days. Great thirst, prostration, shrinking of the tissues, livid countenance, cold surface, small pulse, and laboured respiration are the natural results of the excessive drain on the blood; exceptionally jaundice may occur. These symptoms may directly lead to death with or without the appearance of any special nerve complications, or they may subside, and recovery may take place.

**Neurotic symptoms** comprise muscular twitchings, general convulsions or tetanic spasms, delirium, disorders of the special senses, especially of vision, with dilatation of the pupils, and stupor or profound coma. In some instances the symptoms are solely neurotic, such cases present all the appearances of certain forms of alkaloidal poisoning.

Illustrative of the gastro-enteric symptoms is the following case reported by Boyce[1]:—A man, aged fifty-three, ate heartily of a dinner of which mushrooms formed a part; three and a half hours after he felt griping pain in the abdomen, followed by diarrhœa, and on the following morning by vomiting; constant pain and vomiting continued for two days when he sought medical assistance. His face was then dusky and bluish, the pupils were dilated, the breathing was short and rapid, the pulse weak and quick, and the surface cold; much pain was experienced in the stomach, and there was great prostration. In spite of treatment the vomiting and diarrhœa continued, the motions consisting of dirty water with flocculi of lymph; death took place on the fourth day after the mushrooms were eaten. The deceased's son who also partook of the mushrooms, was attacked in the same way but he recovered. The following case reported by Matthes[2] illustrates the neurotic type of mushroom poisoning. A woman and three children were taken ill, about four hours after eating mushrooms, with pain in the abdomen and delirium. In each case the face was cold and pale, the pulse slow, the lips were cyanosed, the respirations quick and shallow, and the pupils dilated and inactive. For two hours, violent clonic spasms, like those due to strychnine, occurred every eight or ten minutes, together with coma; all the patients recovered. Cases have been recorded in which the symptoms have been of a purely narcotic type.

Muscarine, the active principle of the fungus *amanita muscaria* or fly-fungus, has been isolated, and its properties have been investigated by Schmiedeberg and Koppe (who were the first to obtain it in a pure form) and subsequently by others. An infusion of the fresh fungus acts as a fly-exterminator—hence its name; the effect on flies however is not due to muscarine which is innocuous to them, but to some other and probably volatile substance, since the dried fungus no longer acts as a fly poison. The fly-fungus has been used by the poor in Siberia and Kamtschatka as an intoxicating medium; its active principles are eliminated by the kidneys, and this is so well known that those habituated to its use drink their own urine, or that of others who have partaken of the fungus, in order to produce intoxication.

Muscarine [$C_5H_{15}NO_3$] is a colourless, syrupy liquid, without taste or smell. It is alkaline in reaction; is soluble in water and alcohol,

[1] *Brit. Med. Journ.*, 1887.  [2] *Berliner Klin. Wochenschr.* 1888.

slightly so in chloroform, and is insoluble in ether; it forms salts with acids, of which the nitrate is most commonly met with.

According to Brunton muscarine produces uneasiness in the stomach, vomiting, purging, a feeling of constriction in the neck, want of breath, giddiness, faintness, prostration and stupor. It slows the heart by stimulating the intracardiac inhibitory apparatus, lowers the blood pressure, depresses the respiratory centres, causes contraction of the pupils, and of the muscular coat of the intestines, stimulates the secretion of sweat and saliva, and diminishes that of urine. Muscarine strongly resembles pilocarpine in its action, and is antagonistic to atropine. Muscarine and pilocarpine differ, however, in their action on the pupils, when applied locally pilocarpine contracts the pupils, muscarine dilates them; both contract the pupils when administered internally.

So much for the physiological action of muscarine. In the human subject poisoning by fly-fungus presents other symptoms.—There may be delirium, clonic spasms or convulsions, often dilated pupils, and quick pulse; this difference has led to the assumption that another active principle is present in the fungus, which is more or less antagonistic to muscarine.

From another poisonous fungus *amanita phalloides*, Kobert[1] obtained a toxalbumen which he calls phallin. This substance is a blood-poison which disintegrates the red corpuscles, liberates fibrin-ferment, and causes the formation of thrombi. Fatty changes—especially in the liver—and the formation of multiple ecchymoses ensue, the train of symptoms closely resembling those due to acute phosphorus poisoning. The mucous membrane of the intestinal canal is injected and the urine may contain hæmoglobin. In a case recorded by Handford[2] a man, aged thirty-two, ate about a quarter of a pound of cooked A. phalloides. In nine and a half hours he experienced a sense of weight and constriction in the chest, and pain in the bowels; he subsequently vomited and was purged; profuse sweating, dimness of vision, and headache occurred. When seen, about twenty-four hours after eating the fungi, the pulse was 92, small, scarcely to be felt at the wrist, and the respirations, of a sighing character, were 17 to the minute; the pupils were normal. The patient complained of pain in the abdomen; he was drowsy, passed very little urine, and became delirious; death took place on the third day. At the necropsy punctiform ecchymoses were found on the lungs and under the pericardium; the liver was in an advanced stage of fatty degeneration; the mucous membrane of the stomach was much congested and presented numerous points of capillary hæmorrhages and small superficial erosions; the whole of the intestines were slightly

[1] *Petersb. med. Wochenschr.*, 1891  [2] *The Lancet*, 1886

congested. A daughter of the deceased, who ate part of one of the fungi along with her father, vomited and was purged, but had no abdominal pain; she died in twenty-nine hours. At the necropsy no signs of gastro-enteritis were found.

**Treatment of Poisoning by Fungi.**—Evacuate the stomach with an emetic and the bowels with castor oil, and then treat the symptoms. Atropine is recommended as an antidote. In poisoning by muscarine, it acts as nearly like a true physiological antidote as any antagonist well can do; unfortunately, in poisoning by fungi even by the fly-fungus, its antagonism is less efficacious; still, it should be tried, especially if the symptoms partake of the muscarine type. Warmth and stimulants will probably be required, and morphine if the gastro-enteric symptoms prevail.

**Post-mortem Appearances.**—The necropsies of the cases already quoted illustrate the salient post-mortem indications.—Inflammation of the gastro intestinal mucous membrane, with hæmorrhagic spots and erosions, punctiform sub-pleural, and sub-pericardial hæmorrhages; and not unfrequently signs of fatty changes in the solid viscera, especially in the liver, comprise the most important indications. The fatty changes scarcely seem to have received sufficient attention; Maschka, Husemann, and Boudier[1] observed them many years ago both in animals and in the human subject, and since then numerous cases have occurred in which fatty liver has been recorded as one of the post-mortem signs of poisoning by fungi. It appears to be most common after poisoning by *amanita muscaria* and *amanita phalloides*. In Handford's case of poisoning by the last-named fungus, already quoted, the liver was in an advanced stage of fatty degeneration. Muller[2] examined the body of a woman who was found dead four days after having eaten part of a fly-fungus. The heart, kidneys, and liver, all showed fatty changes; the liver especially presented such a typical "phosphorus-liver" appearance as to give rise to doubts whether death had been caused by phosphorus or by the fungus.

[1] *Des Champignons*, 1868.   [2] *Veertelyaarsche f ger Med*, 1890.

# ANIMAL POISONS.

## CHAPTER XXXIII.

### CANTHARIDES.

Cantharides, or Spanish flies, contain an active principle or acid—*cantharidin*, partly free and partly combined with organic and inorganic bases. It is insoluble in water, slightly soluble in cold alcohol, and more freely so in hot alcohol, fixed oils, ether, and chloroform. When combined with bases, its solubility in these solvents, respectively, is the converse of that which obtains when it is in the free state. Cantharidin is eliminated in the urine and fæces.

Symptoms.—When taken internally in poisonous doses cantharides causes a burning pain in the throat, which quickly extends to the stomach, with difficulty in swallowing, intense thirst, salivation, swelling of the salivary glands, and vesication of those parts of the digestive tract with which it first comes in contact. Nausea and vomiting occur, the rejected matter containing shreds of membrane, and probably blood; diarrhœa, with tenesmus, may follow. Pain in the lumbar region, accompanied by strangury and irritation of the urethra, is almost invariable; the urine contains albumen, and occasionally blood. In severe cases, collapse, coma, and convulsions may lead to death, which is usually due to paralysis of the respiratory centres.

When cantharides are criminally administered it is not with homicidal intent; the object is either to excite the sexual feeling or to procure abortion. In more than one instance death has accidentally resulted from a delirious patient eating a blister which was applied to his head. Cantharides are harmless to fowls; if, after being fed with them, a fowl is eaten by a human being, symptoms of cantharides poisoning are produced. Severe symptoms of poisoning have occurred from the external use of cantharides.

Fatal Dose.—The smallest recorded fatal dose is twenty-four grains of powdered cantharides; recovery has occurred after one drachm. One ounce of the tincture has caused death; recovery has followed after six ounces were swallowed. Very small doses may produce severe poisonous effects. Sedgwick[1] records the case of a girl, thirteen and a half years old, to whom one Spanish fly was given in a tart;

---

[1] *Med. Times and Gaz.*, 1864.

half an hour after giddiness, pain between the shoulders, and a burning sensation in the throat were experienced. The following morning, the abdomen was distended, there was stranguiy, and the vulva were swollen and irritable ; the patient vomited half a pint of blood, and complained of a strong disagreeable odour in the nostrils. For three days there was occasional vomiting of blood ; recovery took place. About seventy-five centigrammes (11½ grains) of cantharidin caused the death of a man of seventy in twelve or fourteen hours.[1]

**Treatment.**—Evacuate the stomach, and, if possible, wash it well out. Demulcents and morphine, with warm baths or fomentations, will be required. Fatty or oily substances must *not* be given.

**Post-mortem Appearances.**—Indications of inflammation are usually present in the mouth and along the digestive canal; they may diminish in intensity after the first part of the intestines is reached, or they may be continued as far as the rectum. Excoriation and ulceration of the mucous membrane, with swelling and softening, will probably be visible, producing in some cases the appearance of a raw blood-stained or purulent surface deprived of all trace of epithelium. If the powdered insect has been swallowed, bright, glistening particles are generally to be seen on the mucous or raw surface, especially of the intestines ; in such cases, examination of the digestive tract with a lens should never be omitted. If death has occurred very shortly after the poison was swallowed, the changes in the stomach and bowels may be less pronounced. The kidneys are usually large, red, and gorged with blood ; the epithelial cells of the glomeruli are swollen, softened and detached, frequently blocking up the tubules. The internal surface of the bladder is injected, and is often ecchymosed ; the mucous membrane of the urethra is also injected. The spleen has been found enlarged.

**Chemical Analysis.**—If the solid poison has been swallowed, the mucous membrane of the stomach and intestines should be scraped with the edge of a piece of glass and the scrapings distributed in water, by means of alternate agitation and decantation fragments of the shining wing-cases, which are easy of recognition, may be separated for microscopical and chemical examination. In order to obtain an extract of cantharidin from the tissues it will probably be necessary first to free it from combination, either by simply acidulating with sulphuric acid or by Dragendorff's method, after which it may be dissolved out by shaking with chloroform. Dragendorff's method consists in boiling the organic mixture with potash and water, filtering, adding sulphuric acid to the filtrate to liberate the cantharidin from the potash, and then boiling the filtrate with four times its volume of alcohol, after cooling, the alcoholic solution is filtered, the alcohol

[1] *Annales d'Hygiène* 1872.

evaporated, and the residue extracted with chloroform. On evaporation of the chloroform, a portion of the final residue may be taken up with a little oil

Tests —A morsel of cotton-wool saturated with the oily mixture obtained from the chloroform extract, and retained for some hours in contact with the skin on the arm or the breast, will raise a blister if even but a very minute quantity of cantharidin is present An aqueous solution of cantharidin in combination with potash or soda yields a green precipitate with copper sulphate, and a red precipitate with cobalt sulphate

Cantharides resist putrefaction for a long time

## PTOMAINES

The putrefactive processes by which complex animal tissues, step by step, are resolved into their primary elements, partake to some extent of a synthetical character The bacteria of putrefaction split up highly organised matter into primary constituents, and groups of primary constituents, at the same time that ammonia is being yielded by decomposing animal matter, temporary derivatives of ammonia are being formed, which possess special chemical and physiological properties It is characteristic of the mode in which these substances are formed that they are fugitive and are continually undergoing changes by which they are transformed into other bodies of an analogous constitution, but which may possess different properties a physiologically inert substance of definite chemical composition may give place to a toxine of equally definite but slightly dissimilar composition These changes vary not only according to the stage of putrefaction which the cadaver has reached, but also according to temperature, free or restricted access of air, with other conditions which are but imperfectly understood. Most of these new combinations are strongly basic, they have certain points of resemblance to the vegetable alkaloids, but they are of less complex constitution, being of the nature of amines (although some contain oxygen), whereas most of the vegetable alkaloids are to be regarded as derivatives of pyridine. To this group of basic substances the name Ptomaine (πτῶμα, a corpse) was applied by Selmi

Ptomaines may be isolated by Stas' process, described on p 401, or by Brieger's method —An alcoholic extract obtained from the organic matter which contains the ptomaine is precipitated with neutral lead acetate (in order to remove amorphous albuminoid and other inert matter), filtered, and the filtrate evaporated to a small bulk, the residue is dissolved in water through which $H_2S$ is passed until the lead is thrown down After filtration the solution is evaporated to a syrup, which, when cold, is extracted with alcohol, and the filtered extract precipitated with an alcoholic solution of $HgCl_2$. Advantage is taken of the varying solubility of the double salts formed by ptomaines with mercuric chloride to effect their separation by treatment with boiling water. The solutions thus obtained are severally decomposed by $H_2S$ and, after removal of the mercurous sulphide, are evaporated down so as to cause the ptomaine salts to crystallise out. Further separation is accomplished by forming double salts of the ptomaines with $PtCl_4$ and $AuCl_3$. During the various processes, especially in the early ones, the temperature should not exceed 40°, nor should the solutions be allowed to acquire more than a feebly acid reaction.

As free bases ptomaines are mostly liquid, some are crystallisable; some are volatile, others are not; they form salts, more or less easily crystallisable. Like vegetable alkaloids, ptomaines are precipitated by most of the alkaloidal group-tests. Some ptomaines are actively toxic, others are feebly so, and others again are devoid of toxic properties.

The study of ptomaines is a subject too extensive to be exhaustively dealt with in a text-book on Forensic Medicine; they will therefore be considered in two aspects only:—In relation to toxicological investigations made on the dead body, and to abnormal changes in food-stuffs which are thus rendered poisonous.

## CADAVERIC ALKALOIDS.

In the course of medico-legal investigations in cases of criminal poisoning a defence occasionally tendered is—that the poison found in the body of the deceased was a product of post-mortem changes undergone by the tissues themselves—a defence most commonly urged in cases of poisoning by one of the rarer alkaloids, which yields no special chemical reactions. In default of distinctive chemical reactions, the expert is obliged to rely on physiological tests; it becomes important therefore to ascertain the toxicity of those ptomaines that have been found in the human body after death, together with the symptoms they produce in animals to which they are experimentally administered. A recent tabulation by Brieger[1] of all ptomaines and toxines, which up to the present time have been isolated, enables this to be easily and reliably accomplished; toxines due to the presence of pathological micro-organisms in the body during life—such as those of tetanus, cholera, and typhoid fever—are obviously excluded. Of ptomaines that have been isolated from the cadaver, two only are actively poisonous—*neurin* and *mydalein*; others have toxic properties, but the lethal dose in relation to the body-weight is immeasurably greater

[1] Virchow's *Arch.*, 1889.

than that of the vegetable alkaloids for which it is alleged they might be mistaken. Neurin does not appear until five or six days after death, and mydalein not until seven days after, and then only in traces; it is not present in amount sufficient for analysis until after a lapse of two to three weeks. During the period after death, within which postmortem examinations are usually made, the only ptomaine present is cholin—a feebly poisonous substance probably derived from lecithin. Time and the access of air are required to develop actively toxic ptomaines, and when formed they exist in small amount, are very unstable and require special processes for their extraction.

Although cadaveric alkaloids respond to many of the alkaloidal group-tests, they do not respond to special tests like the vegetable alkaloids. If the reaction yielded by a cadaveric alkaloid to a special reagent somewhat resembles that produced by the same reagent with one of the vegetable alkaloids, it will behave differently towards a second special reagent; it will further have a different physiological effect to that of the vegetable alkaloid which, as regards one special chemical reaction, it may in a degree resemble. There is no test by which animal alkaloids, as a class, can be distinguished from vegetable alkaloids; on the other hand, no animal alkaloid has yet been discovered which yields the same chemical reactions, and possesses the same physiological properties, as any of the vegetable alkaloids.

According to Brieger[1] the **symptoms** in rabbits **produced by the subcutaneous injection of neurin hydrochlorate** are:—Moisture of the nostrils and upper lip, followed by movements as in the act of chewing, with the formation of drops of thick mucus at the angles of the mouth; profuse salivation then occurs, which continues to the end. The breathing is at first accelerated, it then becomes shallow and irregular, with marked symptoms of dyspnœa. The heart-beats much quickened at first are then slowed and enfeebled, becoming weaker and weaker until contractions finally cease, and the heart stops in diastole, respiration continuing for a time after the heart ceases to beat. Occasionally, but not constantly, the pupils are contracted after injection of the ptomaine; on the other hand, a concentrated solution of it dropped into the eye almost always produces narrowing of the pupil. Active peristalsis of the bowels comes on early. Clonic spasms, which are not altogether respiratory, and paralysis of the hind- and then of the fore-legs precede death. Five milligrammes produce symptoms of poisoning in, and four centigrammes constitute a lethal dose for, rabbits, weighing one kilogramme. The symptoms strongly resemble those produced by muscarine, and like them are combatted by atropine.

**Mydalein** produces the following symptoms in rabbits:—The secre-

[1] *Ueber Ptomaine, Theil, i. 11*

tion from the nostrils and the lacrymal glands is increased, the pupils are dilated and reactionless, and the vessels of the ears are injected, the temperature is elevated 1° to 2° C., the pulse and respirations at first increase in rapidity and then become slower, the heart ceasing in diastole. Peristalsis is increased, and there is diarrhœa and vomiting, clonic spasms and paralysis with a tendency to stupor precede death. Five milligrammes of mydaleïn hydrochlorate injected into a kitten caused rapid dilatation of the pupils, which were reactionless, diarrhœa, vomiting, salivation, sweating of the feet, stupor, muscular spasms, paralysis first of the hind- and subsequently of the fore-legs, slow laboured breathing and death. The heart was found in diastole, the mucous membrane of the bowels was somewhat injected, and they contained some thin fluid secretion.

### 2. PTOMAINES IN FOOD

Instances occur from time to time in which people, individually or collectively, are suddenly attacked with violent symptoms of poisoning shortly after partaking of food, examination of the remains of the food, and, in fatal cases, of the organs of the deceased and their contents, fails to afford evidence of the presence of an added poison. It has long been known that in certain stages of incipient putrefaction food is capable of acting as a poison, but it is only of late years that some knowledge has been obtained as to the nature of the toxines thus formed, so far, the information obtained is very imperfect, but the way has been opened out and the direction indicated by which a more exact knowledge of these decomposition products may be obtained.

Basic substances having toxic properties have been found in fish, in various kinds of animal food, in milk, cheese, and other food-stuffs. In some instances the changes which produce the toxine take place during life, more usually they are non-vital phenomena.

### Poisoning by Mussels

Mussel poisoning is due to the formation of a toxine whilst the fish (*mytilus edulis*) is still alive. It was formerly believed that mussels owed their poisonous properties to the presence in them of copper derived from ships' bottoms, or from copper-covered fixtures in harbours, to a special disease from which the fish laboured under, to the presence of specimens of a poisonous species along with the edible fish, to incipient putrefaction taking place after the harmless fish were removed from the water, and to various other conditions which were naturally assumed in default of positive knowledge. Brieger[1] was the first to succeed in isolating from poisonous mussels a basic product in a condition sufficiently pure to admit of ultimate analysis. A number of cases of mussel poisoning, several of which were fatal, occurred at Wilhelmshaven in 1885, from a quantity of the noxious mussels Brieger obtained a poisonous base which he called *mytilotoxin*, to which he ascribed the formula $C_6H_{15}NO_2$, other bases, among which is *betaine*, are also present.

The conditions which lead to the development of this toxine in mussels are:—stagnant water, or water which is not in free communication with the sea, or water which is contaminated with sewage, or other organic matter undergoing decomposition. It is not essential that the water should contain noxious matter; mere absence of freshness is sufficient to interfere with the metabolism of the mussels to such an extent as to lead to abnormal changes in their tissues, which result in the formation of a toxine during life. If mussels which have thus become poisonous are placed in water in free communication with the sea, they rapidly lose their poisonous properties. Poisonous mussels have invariably been obtained from harbours, docks, the mouths of rivers, and other places where either a deficiency of tidal interchange takes place, or where the water is contaminated with decomposing organic matter.

**Symptoms.**—The mild and common form of mussel poisoning is characterised by the appearance of an exanthematous, or urticarial eruption, all over the body, which may be associated with a feeling of oppression in the chest and difficulty of breathing. In the severer forms gastro-intestinal disturbance occurs, and in the most dangerous of all paralysis.

The following cases illustrate the etiology and the symptoms of fatal mussel poisoning. Permewan[2] relates the case of a man aged forty who ate uncooked a large quantity of mussels obtained from the bottom of a graving-dock. When seen a few hours after he was absolutely unconscious, the face was livid, the pulse almost imperceptible, and the pupils were widely dilated and inactive; he took gasping breaths about once or twice in the minute; there was no vomiting nor purging. The temperature did not materially fall until the circulation failed. The limbs were flaccid—there was complete paralysis and unconsciousness. Neither stimulants, atropine, strychnine, nor artificial respiration, evoked any attempts at natural respiration, and death took place in about twelve hours after the mussels were eaten; the heart continued to beat for many hours after voluntary

[1] *Ueber Ptomaine, Dritter Theil*, 1886.
[2] *The Lancet*, 1888.

respiration had ceased. In another case, reported by Cameron,[1] a woman and five children ate some mussels which had been gathered from a sheet of water to which the sea had access, fresh water and some sewage also flowed into it. In twenty minutes symptoms of poisoning commenced in the form of prickly pains in the hands; in less than an hour one child died, in two hours the mother and three other of the children were dead. They suffered from violent vomiting, dyspnœa, swelling and lividity of the face, and spasms; they appeared to have died asphyxiated. One child and a maid who ate but few of the fish recovered. Cameron found an alkaloidal substance, and McWeeney[2] found bacteria in some mussels from the same source.

Other shell fish besides mussels may develop toxines. Cameron relates a case in which ten out of twelve persons, who lunched together, ate of some oysters; nine out of the ten were attacked with nausea, vomiting, diarrhœa, abdominal pain, and prostration; they all recovered. The oysters had been grown in a place to which sewage had access.

**Treatment.**—Evacuate the stomach with an emetic and the bowels with an aperient, unless both vomiting and purging have already emptied the digestive canal; then give stimulants; apply external warmth and friction, and perform artificial respiration if required. Atropine has been recommended. Morphine may be advisable if the purging and abdominal pain are excessive.

**Post-mortem Appearances** are not characteristic; there may be indications of gastro-intestinal irritation.

## POISONOUS FOODS.

**Food-stuffs** which are undergoing chemical changes not unfrequently develop toxines. Poisoning from this source has followed the use of tinned meats and fish; sausages, black puddings, and liver, ham, veal, and other meats; milk, cheese, &c. From time to time large numbers of people are simultaneously attacked with symptoms of acute poisoning after partaking of a common meal.

**Symptoms.**—They comprise nausea, dryness in the mouth and throat, vomiting, diarrhœa, heaviness in the stomach, headache, giddiness, prostration, rigors, quick shallow breathing, feeble pulse, profuse sweating, dyspnœa, delirium, and coma. Dilatation of the pupils, paralysis of accommodation, ptosis, and paralysis of the organs of speech have been observed. The symptoms do not always run the same course even when produced in a number of people at the same time and by the same food—a condition closely resembling that due to a

[1] *Brit. Med. Journ.*, 1890. [2] *Ibid.*

metallic irritant may be produced in some, whilst in others the nervous system bears the brunt. The gastro-intestinal symptoms may be so intense as to resemble an attack of cholera, sometimes after profuse diarrhœa obstinate constipation occurs

In Germany where large quantities of sausages are eaten, poisoning from this cause is not uncommon, the term *botulismus* has been applied to it. Liver and blood enter into the composition of some of these sausages, which appear to be specially prone to develop toxic bases. Finely-divided meat is very liable to become toxic because of the large surface that is thus exposed to the air, as previously stated, the presence of oxygen appears to be necessary for the development of poisonous ptomaines

Instances have occurred in which poisoning has followed the use of perfectly fresh meat derived from cows that have recently calved, the toxic effects being presumably due to pathological changes taking place during life. In one or two such instances the cows were known to have had milk fever

**Tinned Food** may undergo toxic changes which do not affect its apparent freshness so far as taste and smell are concerned. Fish thus preserved appears specially liable to become toxic, the following is a case in point:—Six persons ate of tinned salmon to supper, early the following morning they were seized with violent pain in the stomach, vomiting, profuse diarrhœa, pain in the head, thirst, a temperature of $102°$-$103°$ F, and a pulse-rate from 110 to 160 in the minute. One patient became semi-unconscious, with a temperature of $104°$ F, the pulse was almost imperceptible, the skin was cold and clammy, and pupils were widely dilated; death ensued. At the necropsy the brain was found superficially congested, the stomach and the intestines were so deeply inflamed as to be almost gangrenous in parts.[1] Stevenson[2] records the case of a man, aged 21, who ate six sardines to breakfast, a few hours after he complained of feeling unwell, and vomited. Next morning there was slight pain in the stomach, the abdomen was tense, but not enlarged, and the patient was perspiring; shortly after noon collapse rapidly set in, and death occurred almost immediately. At the necropsy made the following day the features were found bloated so as to be unrecognisable, although the weather was cold ($47°$ F), blood-stained fluid exuded from mouth, nostrils, and ears; except the hands and feet the whole body was emphysematous, and there were large bullæ on the buttocks. The abdomen was distended with gas; the mucous membrane of the stomach and intestines was emphysematous, the liver was cavernous and friable, and along with the kidneys and bladder was hyperæmic, the

[1] *Brit. Med. Journ.*, 1891.    [2] *Brit. Med. Journ.*, 1892

bladder was distended with gas. The large intestine was normal and contained solid fæcal matter. Stevenson obtained alkaloidal extracts from four of the remaining sardines, from the contents of the stomach, and from a portion of the vomit, all of which were highly toxic and respectively killed three rats to which they were administered subcutaneously. From other experiments it was shown that the toxine was not present in all the fish, and that it was probably generated in the poisonous sardines before they were tinned.

**Milk** has caused severe poisoning owing to the occurrence in it of chemical changes. Newton and Wallace[1] give an instance in which a number of people living in two hotels were suddenly taken ill four hours after supper with symptoms of gastro-intestinal irritation—nausea, vomiting, cramps, and collapse; a few had diarrhœa. The following week a second series of cases, of precisely the same nature, occurred in another hotel. The symptoms were traced to the milk, but no added poison was found in it. Further investigation showed that the cows from whence the milk was derived were healthy, but that after milking, the milk was at once placed in cans and carted eight miles during the warmest part of the day and in a hot season of the year; the method usually adopted being to allow the milk to cool in shallow open vessels surrounded with cold water or ice previous to transport. Chemical examination of the suspected milk revealed the presence of a substance—identical with Vaughan's tyrotoxicon—which produced symptoms of poisoning in a cat; it is probably chemically allied to butyric acid.

**Cheese.**—Numerous instances of poisoning by cheese have occurred, especially in Germany and America. The symptoms which appeared in a number of cases (nearly three hundred) that happened in America in 1884 and 1885 were as follows:—Violent vomiting and diarrhœa, pain in the stomach, and cramps in the legs; the tongue at first coated white, was later red and dry; the pulse was weak and irregular, and the face pale and cyanotic. None of the cases were fatal. The cheese which caused the symptoms was not old nor decayed. Vaughan[2] found that it possessed the characteristic of instantly and intensely reddening litmus paper; good cheese when new slightly reddens litmus paper, but does not produce immediate and pronounced change of colour.

By extracting the poisonous cheese with water, alkalising, and shaking out with ether, Vaughan obtained needle-shaped crystals, which had a distinct toxic action, and to which he gave the name *tyrotoxicon*. The substance is not an alkaloid nor does it respond to the alkaloidal group-tests; it is soluble in water, alcohol, ether, and chloroform. It

[1] *Medical News,* 1886.    [2] *The Practitioner,* 1887.

appears to be due to the action of micro-organisms present in the milk from which the cheese is prepared. Subsequently Vaughan[1] found a toxalbumose in some cheese in which no tyrotoxicon was present. Old decayed cheese yields an alkaline reaction, and has frequently given rise to colic, diarrhœa, dizziness, diplopia, precordial pain, and collapse. Brieger obtained trimethylamine from decayed cheese.

[1] *Phil. Med. and Surg. Repr.*, 1890.

# INDEX.

ABDOMEN, Injuries of, 275.
Abortifaciants, 121.
Abortion, 119.
,,  Cause of death in, 126.
,,  Drugs used for procuring, 121.
,,  General violence as a cause of, 123.
,,  Law as regards, 120.
,,  Local violence as a cause of, 124.
,,  Modes of procuring, 121.
,,  Period when resorted to, 126.
,,  Signs of, 127.
Absorption and elimination of poisons, 384.
Acetylene and oxides of carbon, Poisoning by, 496.
Acid, arsenic, Poisoning by, 428.
,,  arsenious,  ,,  427.
,,  ,,  Tests for, 435.
,,  ,,  Treatment of poisoning by, 432.
,,  boric, Poisoning by, 490.
,,  carbolic,  ,,  534.
,,  ,,  Tests for, 537.
,,  ,,  Treatment of poisoning by, 536.
,,  hydrochloric, Poisoning by, 415.
,,  ,,  Tests for, 416.
,,  hydrocyanic, Poisoning by, 501.
,,  ,,  Tests for, 506.
,,  ,,  Treatment of poisoning by, 505.
,,  meconic, Tests for, 557.
,,  nitric, Poisoning by, 412.
,,  ,,  Tests for, 413.
,,  oxalic, Poisoning by, 416.
,,  ,,  Tests for, 418.
,,  ,,  Treatment of poisoning by, 417.
,,  picric, Poisoning by, 538.
,,  ,,  Tests for, 539.
,,  ,,  Treatment of poisoning by, 538.
,,  salicylic, Poisoning by, 533.
,,  ,,  Tests for, 534.
,,  sulphuric, Poisoning by, 407.
,,  ,,  Tests for, 411.
Acids, Burns by, 254.
,,  mineral, Treatment of poisoning by, 409.
Aconite, Poisoning by, 584.
,,  ,,  treatment, 587.
Aconitine,  ,,  585.

Aconitine, Properties and physiological action of, 584.
,,  Tests for, 587.
,,  Varieties of, 583.
Adipocere, 57.
Age, 21.
,,  in relation to power of procreation, 83-86.
,,  in relation to poisons, 383.
,,  Determination of, in new-born infant, 23.
,,  Marriageable, 22.
,,  Medico-legal bearings of, 21.
Air in stomach as sign of respiration, 141.
Alcohol, amyl, Poisoning by, 510.
,,  ethyl, Diagnosis of poisoning by, 507.
,,  ,,  Tests for, 510.
,,  ,,  Treatment of poisoning by, 509.
Alcoholic insanity, 334.
,,  paralysis, 336.
Alkalies, Burns by, 255.
Alkaloidal group reagents, 541.
Alkaloids, Characters of, 540.
,,  Isolation of, from organic matter, 401.
Almonds, bitter, Poisoning by, 502, 566.
,,  ,,  oil of,  ,,  501, 505.
Amanita muscaria, Poisoning by, 611.
,,  phalloides,  ,,  610.
Ammonia, Excess of, in urine in acute phosphorus poisoning, 481.
,,  Poisoning by, 420.
Ammonium carbonate, Poisoning by, 422.
Amyl alcohol, Poisoning by, 510.
,,  nitrite,  ,,  511.
Anæsthetics, Responsibility in death from, 305.
Aniline, Colour of surface in poisoning by, 528.
,,  Poisoning by, 527.
,,  Tests for, 529.
Antagonism of morphine and atropine, 391.
,,  of poisons, 391.
,,  Limited, 394.
Antidotes, 390.
Antifebrin, Poisoning by, 530.
,,  Tests for, 530.
Antimony, Acute poisoning by, 442.
,,  chloride,  ,,  444.
,,  Sub-acute  ,,  443.

Antimony, Tests for, 445
,, Treatment of poisoning by, 444
Antipyrin, Poisoning by, 531.
,, Tests for, 531
Aphasia in relation to testamentary capacity, 375
Aqua fortis, 412
Argyria, 467
Arsenetted hydrogen, 428
Arsenic, Acute poisoning by, 428
,, Chronic ,, 433.
,, Combinations of, 427
,, eaters, 434
,, Fatal dose of, 431
,, Poisoning by, post-mortem appearances of, 432
,, ,, Treatment of, 432
Arsenious sulphide, 428
Artificial inflation, 135
,, respiration, 232
Asphyxia, 63
,, Signs of death from, 34.
Assizes, 6
Atkinson's infant's preserver, 551
Atropine, Fatal dose of, 561
,, Poisoning by, 560
,, Properties of, 559
,, Tests for, 563
,, Treatment of poisoning by, 562

BACK, Wounds of, 292, 298
Baines, Reg r , 360
Banks e Goodfellow, 373
Barium, Poisoning by, 425.
,, Tests for, 426
,, Treatment of poisoning by, 425
Battle's vermin killer, 542
Belladonna, Fatal dose of, 561
,, Poisoning by, 560
,, Treatment of poisoning by, 562
Benzene and its derivatives, 522
,, Poisoning by, 522
,, ,, vapour of, 522
Berry, Reg r , 412
Bestiality, 109
Birth, Concealment of, 165
,, in relation to the civil law, 166
Birth-marks, 60
Bismuth, Poisoning by, 471.
,, Tests for, 472
,, Treatment of poisoning by, 471
Bisulphide of carbon, Acute poisoning by, 518
,, ,, Chronic poisoning by, 519
Bitter almonds, Oil of, Poisoning by, 501-505
,, Poisoning by, 502-506

Bittersweet, Poisoning by, 570
Blackening of hand by fire arms, 296.
,, wound ,, 296.
Bladder, Rupture of, 276
Bleaching fluid, Poisoning by, 490
Blood, Bright-red, after death from aconitine, 586.
,, ,, ,, exposure to cold, 234
,, ,, ,, CO, 497-499.
,, ,, ,, HCN, 503.
,, ,, ,, fire, 247.
,, Distinction of human, from animal, 64
,, -stains, 63
,, ,, Chemical examination of, 70
,, ,, Microscopical ,, 64
,, ,, Spectroscopical ,, 66
,, ,, in rape, 108
,, ,, on knives, 71, 295
Bodies, Exhumation of, 21.
Body, Cooling of, 38
,, Examination of, 17
,, ,, in cases of poisoning, 19
Bones, Fractures of, 279
,, in relation to identity of the dead, 74
,, Unnatural fragility of, 280
Boracic acid, Poisoning by, 490
,, Tests for, 491
Born alive, Legal definition of, 142.
Botulismus, 620
Brain, Concussion of, 265.
,, Contusion of, 266
Bromine, Poisoning by, 487.
,, Tests for, 489.
,, Treatment of poisoning by, 488
Brucine, Tests for, 548
,, Toxic action of, 548.
Bruises distinguished from post mortem stains, 42
Burns, Accidental, 249
,, and scalds, Cause of death from, 242
,, ,, Post-mortem appearances of death from, 245
,, by corrosive fluids, 254
,, Colour of blood after death from, 247
,, Homicide in relation to, 250
,, Identification of bodies after death from, 251
,, produced before and after death, 248
Burns, Reg., v 360
Butler's vermin-killer, 542
Butter of antimony, 444.

## INDEX.

Cadaveric alkaloids, 615
,, hypostases, 39
,, rigidity, 43
,, ,, Causation of, 44, 47
,, ,, Conditions which hasten, 44
,, ,, in respect to the heart, 45
,, spasm, or instantaneous rigor, 47
,, ,, Examples of, 48
Cadmium, Poisoning by, 470
Calabar bean Poisoning by, 600
,, Treatment of poisoning by, 602
Camphor, Poisoning by, 603
Cannabin, 566
Cannabinon, 566
Cannabis Indica Poisoning by, 566
Canonical impediment to marriage, 182
Cantharides, Poisoning by, 612
,, ,, Treatment of, 613
Cantharidin, Properties of, 612
,, Tests for, 614
Capacity of child's stomach, 27
,, ,, skull, 27
,, Testamentary, 373
Carbolic acid, Poisoning by, 535
,, Tests for, 537
,, Treatment of poisoning by, 336
Carbon bisulphide, Acute poisoning by, 518
,, ,, Chronic ,, 519
,, ,, Treatment of poisoning by, 519
,, dioxide, Air containing 494
,, ,, Chemical analysis of, 495
,, ,, Poisoning by, 494
,, monoxide, Acute poisoning by, 496
,, ,, Chronic ,, 500
,, ,, hæmoglobin, 497
,, ,, Intrinsic toxic action of, 497
,, ,, Sources of, 495
,, ,, Spectroscopic examination of the blood in poisoning by, 499
,, ,, Treatment of poisoning by, 497
Carburetted hydrogen, 495
Carnal knowledge, 89
Castor-oil seeds, Poisoning by, 606
Cathartics, Treatment of poisoning by, 606
Causes of death from wounds, 299
Cephalhæmatoma, 160
Certificates in lunacy, 361, 364, 367
,, ,, Responsibility as regards, 369

Chancery lunatics, 372
Cheese, Poisoning by, 621
,, Trimethylamine in decayed, 622
Chemical combination of poisons, Influence of, 385
,, evidence of poisoning, 399
Cherry laurel water, 502
Chest, Injuries of, 272, 291
Children, Suppositious, 176
Chloral hydrate, Poisoning by, 514
,, ,, Tests for, 516
,, ,, Treatment of poisoning by, 515
Chlorine, Poisoning by, 489
,, ,, treatment, 490
Chlorodyne, 551
Chloroform Poisoning by, 512
,, Tests for, 513
,, Treatment of poisoning by, 513
Choke-damp, 494
Chromate of lead, Poisoning by, 475
Chrome yellow, ,, 475
Chromic acid, ,, 473
,, ,, Treatment of, 474
Chromium, Tests for combinations of, 475
Chronic alcoholic insanity, 335
Cicatrices, 59
Circular insanity, 325
Circulation, Cessation of, 37
Civil disability as regards marriage, 182
,, rights, Deprivation of, in insanity, 372
Classification of poisons, 385
Clothing Blood stains on 65
Coal gas, Poisoning by, 495
Cocaine, Fatal dose of 569
,, Poisoning by, 568
,, Tests for, 569
,, Treatment of poisoning by, 569
Cocculus Indicus, Poisoning by, 549
,, ,, treatment of 550
Colchicine, Properties and physiological actions of, 579
,, Tests for, 581
Colchicum, Poisoning by, 579
,, ,, Treatment of, 580
Cold, Death from, 233
,, ,, Post mortem signs of, 234
Cole, Reg v, 352
Colocynth, Poisoning by, 605
Colostrum, 116
Coma, 35
Combustibility, Preternatural, 251
,, ,, medico legal bearing of, 254
Commission of inquiry in lunacy, 372
Common witness, 8

40

Concealment of birth, 165
,, pregnancy (Scotch law), 166
Concentration of poisons, Influence of, 385
Concussion of the brain, 265
Conine-methyl, 575
Coniine, Properties and physiological action of, 575
,, Poisoning by, 575
,, Tests for, 576
,, Treatment of poisoning by, 576
Conium maculatum, 574
Contusion of the brain, 266
Contusions, 256
Cooling of the body after death, 38
Copper, Acute poisoning by, 462
,, arsenite, 428
,, Constant presence of, in the body, 465
,, Chronic poisoning by, 463
,, in tinned green peas, 464
,, Tests for, 465
,, Treatment of poisoning by, 462
Cord, Mark of, in hanging, 191
,, ,, strangulation, 201
Coroner's act, 3
,, court, 2
Corpus luteum, 116
Corrosive fluids, Burns by 254
,, poisoning General symptoms of, 394
,, ,, Post mortem signs of, 396
,, sublimate, Poisoning by, 447
Corrosives, 407
Courtesy, Tenancy by, 167
Courts of Justiciary, 16
Creasote, Poisoning by, 539
,, Tests for, 540
Cretinism, 310
Criminal abortion, 119
,, ,, Modes of procuring 121
,, ,, Signs of, 127
, responsibility, 350
,, ,, plea of delirium tremens, 340
,, ,, delusional insanity, 356
,, ,, ,, drunkenness 359
,, ,, , impulsive insanity, 356
, ,, ,, moral insanity, 354
,, ,, ,, recurrent insanity, 354
Crockery-ware, Wounds from broken, 258

Cross examination, 7.
Cross, Reg v 435
Croton oil, Poisoning by, 605
Cryptorchids, Virility of, 82
Cut throat wounds, 289
Cyanogen, Compounds of, 501
Cyanide of potassium, Poisoning by, 505.
,, ,, Tests for, 506
Cytisine, Properties and physiological action of, 589
, Tests for, 590

Dally's carminative, 551
Daphne mezereon, Poisoning by, 590
Datura stramonium, ,, 565
Daturine, 565
Dead, Identity of the 72
Death of fœtus in utero, 175
,, of infant from accidental causes, 146
,, from anæsthetics, 305
,, ,, cold, 233
, ,, ,, Post mortem signs of, 234
, , hæmorrhage 299
,, . heat stroke, 236
,, , inflammation, 302.
,, , lightning, 236
,, , ,, Post mortem signs of, 240
, , psychical shock, 301
,, ,, septic processes, 303
,, ,, shock, 300
,, ,, tetanus 303
,, Molecular and somatic, 36
, Signs of, 36
Delirium ebriosum, 334
,, tremens, 335
Delivery, hasty, Death of infant from, 150
, Loss of consciousness during, 150
,, Prolonged, 118
,, Signs of, 116
,, ,, in the dead, 117.
,, ,, remote, 118
Delphinium staphisagria, Poisoning by, 588
Delusional insanity, 326, 356
Delusions, 319
,, and testamentary capacity, 373.
Dementia, Acute, 325
, Adventitia, 350
,, from coarse brain lesions, 342
,, naturalis, 370
,, Secondary, 342
, Senile, 341
Desquamation of the skin of new-born infant, 26
Detachment of funis, 27
Development of fœtus after five months, 23
,, ,, before ,, 128.

Development of fœtus, Table of, 26
Diagnosis of poisoning, 386
Diaphragm, Rupture of, 276
Discharge of lunatics, 364
Dichromate of Potassium, Poisoning by, 174
,, ,, Treatment of poisoning by, 174
Digitalin, Tests for, 579
Digitalis, Fatal dose of, 578
,, Poisoning by, 577
,, ,, Treatment of, 578
Dinitrobenzene, Acute poisoning by, 524
,, Chronic ,, 525
,, Tests for, 527
,, Treatment of poisoning by, 526
Dinitrotoluene, Poisoning by, 527
Dipsomania, 337
Disease as an impediment to procreation, 84
,, contrasted with the effects of poison, 386
Disposing mind, In testamentary capacity, 373
Divorce, Duties of medical inspectors in, 184
,, Incapacity as a plea for, 183
,, Insanity ,, 182
,, Medico-legal bearings of, 182
Documentary evidence, 13
Dodwell, Reg. c., 357
Doubtful sex, 79
Dover's powder, 551
Drowning, 215
,, and strangulation, 226
,, , wounds from firearms, 227
,, Artificial respiration in, 232
,, Condition of lungs in death from, 219
,, Death after recommencement of respiration, 232
,, Epitome of signs of death from, 224
,, Floatation of body after, 217
,, Hands and feet tied, 229
,, Importance of external relations in death from, 225
,, Inhibition of respiration in, 215
,, Injuries produced after death from, 227
,, ,, before death from, 226
,, in shallow water, 229
,, post mortem appearances, 217
,, Resuscitation from apparent, 230
,, Statistics of, 224
,, Water in intestines in, 223
,, ,, stomach in, 221

Drowning, wounds on body, 225
Drugs used to procure abortion, 121
Drunkards, Restraint of habitual, 378
Drunkenness, Criminal responsibility, plea of, 359
Dry method of destroying organic matter, 105
Dulcamara, Poisoning by, 565
Duration of gestation, 168
Dussart-Blondlot's test for phosphorus, 484
Dying declarations, 13
Dynamite, Gases produced by detonation of, 501
,, Poisoning by, 512
,, Suicide by detonation of, 288.

Ear, Injuries of, 271
Ecbolics, 121
Ecchymoses, 257
,, Colour changes in, 257
,, from slight pressure, 257
Edmunds, Reg. v., 355
Elaterium, Poisoning by, 605
Electricity, Death from, 212
Elevation of temperature, Post mortem, 38
Emetics in poisoning, 389
Emmenagogues, 121
Epileptic automaticity, 329
,, furor, 329
,, insanity, 328
Epispadias, 79
Epsom salts, Poisoning by, 426
Ergot, Acute poisoning by, 595
,, Chronic ,, 597
,, Nature and physiological action of, 595
,, Tests for, 598
,, Treatment of acute poisoning by, 596
Ergotism, Gangrenous, 597
,, Spasmodic, 597
Eserine, Poisoning by, 601
Ether, ,, 540
Evidence of poisoning from dead body, 396
Exalgin, Poisoning by, 530
Examination of lunatics, 306
,, dead body, 17
,, ,, in poisoning, 19
,, women, Precautions necessary in, 103
Examination-in-chief, 7
Excitement as a cause of death, 301
Exhumation, 21
Expert witness, 8
Exposure of person Indecent, 111
Eyes, Injuries of, 271

Face, Injuries of, 271
Fasting, Metabolism during, 311.

Fatty changes in poisoning by antimony, 441
,, ,, arsenic, 433
,, ,, copper, 465
,, ,, ergot, 596
,, ,, fungi, 611
,, ,, phosphorus, 479
Fees to medical witnesses, 12
,, ,, in Scotland, 17
Feigned delivery, 176
,, homicidal wounds, 308
,, ,, strangulation, 201
,, insanity, 370
Female organs, Abnormalities of, 82
Finger marks, Identification by, 294
Fire-arms, Multiple fatal wounds by, 297
,, Wounds produced by, 282
,, ,, Causal relation of, 296
Fish, Poisoning by tinned, 620
Fly-fungus, 609
,, papers, Use of, as toxic agents, 428
,, powder, 427
Fœtus at term, 24
,, Death of, in utero, 175
,, Development of, after five months, 23
,, ,, before ,, 128
Food, Symptoms of poisoning after, 386
,, poisonous, 619
Footprints, 62, 293
Foxglove, Poisoning by, 577
Fractures of bones, 279
,, ,, in the living and the dead, 282
,, from muscular contraction, 280
,, Delayed, 280
,, Previous, 281
,, Processes of union in, 281
,, of the skull, 266
,, ,, spine, 270
Fright, Death from, 301
Fruit, Poisoning by tinned, 470
,, stains, 72
Fungi, Causes of toxicity of edible, 607
,, Gastro-enteric symptoms due to, 608
,, Neurotic, ,, , 609
,, Poisoning by, 608
,, ,, Treatment of, 611
,, Varieties of poisonous, 607
Funis, Accidental injuries to, 159
,, in relation to live-birth, 144
,, Mummification of, 26
,, Neglect of tying, 158
,, Prolapse of, 146
,, Separation of, 27
,, strangulation of infant by, Accidental, 147, 157
,, ,, ,, Criminal, 158

Fusel oil, Poisoning by, 510
Gangrenous ergotism, 597
Gas, coal, Poisoning by, 493
,, water, ,, 493
Gaseous compounds, Poisoning by, 491.
Gases produced by explosives, 500
Gasoline-stoves, Poisoning by vapour from, 496
Gathercole, Reg. r., 349
Gaultheria, Poisoning by oil of, 594
Gelsemine and gelsemin, 567
,, Tests for, 568
Gelsemium, Poisoning by, 567
,, , Treatment of, 568
General paralysis of the insane, 331
,, ,, ,, Exceptional forms of, 333
,, symptoms of corrosive and irritant poisoning, 394
,, treatment of poisoning, 389
,, violence as a cause of abortion, 123
Genitals, Injuries of the, 278
Gestation, Abnormally prolonged, 169
,, ,, shortened, 171
,, normal, Duration of, 168
Giving evidence, 10
Glass, Wounds from broken, 258
Godfrey's cordial, 551
Gonococci in cases of rape, 99
Green hellebore, 581
Greened vegetables, 464
Group-reagents for alkaloids, 541
Guaiacum test for blood, 65
Gun cotton, Gases produced by explosion of, 501
,, powder, ,, ,, 501.
Gunshot wounds, 282
,, Causal relation of, 296

Habit, Influence of, as regards poisons, 383
Habitual drunkards, Placing under restraint, 378
Hæmatin, reduced, Spectrum of, 69
Hæmatoporphyrin in urine in poisoning by sulphonal, 518
Hæmatorrhachis, 269
Hæmin crystals, 70
Hæmatoma auris, 271
Hæmoglobin, Spectrum of, 67
Hæmorrhage as cause of death, 299.
,, from incised wounds, 259
Hair, Alteration in colour of, 61
Hairs, Source of, 62
Hallucinations, 319
Hanbury r. Hanbury, 183
Hand, Blackening of, by firearms, 296
,, Weapon in, after death, 292, 298.
Hanging, 183
,, Accidental, 193

Hanging, After effects of threatened death from, 200
," Cases of, 197
," compression of vessels in neck, 190
. Distinction of, before and after death, 194
," Experimental investigations as to, 186
.. Experimental investigations as to the condition of the lungs in, 188
," Homicidal, 194
," Mark of cord round neck in, 191
,, Modes of death in, 186
,, Post mortem appearances of death from, 190
,, Pressure on the vagi in, 189
,, Sudden loss of consciousness in suicidal, 190
Head Injuries of, 264, 286, 297
Health, State of, as to the effect of poisons, 353
Heart, Wounds of, 273, 297
Heat stiffening, 45
, stroke, Death from, 236
Hedeoma, Poisoning by, 593
Hellebore, Poisoning by, 588
,, ,, Treatment of, 588
Helleborin, Physiological action of, 587
,, Tests for, 588
Hemlock, Poisoning by, 571
Henbane, ,, 564
,, ,, Treatment of, 564
Hennah, Reg. v., 382
Hermaphrodism, 80
, Illustrations of varieties of, 81
Homicidal impulse, 346
Horse radish compared with aconite root, 583
Hunter v. Edney, 182
Hydrochloric acid, Poisoning by, 415
,, ,, Tests for, 416
Hydrocyanic acid, Fatal dose of, 504
, ,, Poisoning by, 501-2
, ,, Tests for, 506
, ,, Treatment of poisoning by, 505
Hydrostatic test, 134
,, ,, Inferences from, 140
,, ,, Possible fallacies of, 134
Hymen, Injuries of, 95
Hyoscine, 564
Hyoscyamine, Poisoning by, 564
Hyoscyamus, ,, 564
Hypospadias, 79

IDENTITY of the dead, 72
,, living, 59

Idiocy, 340
Idiosyncrasy as regards poisons, 383
Illusions, 349
Imbecility, 340
Immediate causes of death from wounds, 299
Impotence and sterility, 82
Impulse, Homicidal, 346
,, Suicidal, 347
Impulsive insanity, 345, 356
Incapacity a ground for nullity of marriage, 183
Incised wounds, 258
,, apparent from blunt weapons, 259
, of the abdomen, 278
Indecent exposure of the person, 111.
Indian hemp Poisoning by, 566
, tobacco , 572
Indications of poisoning 386, 388
Infanticide, 130
,, by drowning 162
,, , fracture of the skull, 159
,, ,, strangulation, 155
,, , ,, with the fingers, 158
,, ,, suffocation, 152
,, ,, wounding, 161
, causes of death of infant, 145
,, exposure of infant as a cause of death, 163
, hasty parturition ,, 150
,, prolonged ,, , 148
,, neglect of infant ,, 158
,, Hydrostatic test in cases of, 134
, Post mortem examination in cases of, 164
, Signs of respiration in cases of, 131
, Statistics of, 146
Inflation of lungs of infants, Artificial, 135
Injuries of the abdomen, 275
,, bladder, 276
,, cervical spine not immediately fatal, 270
,, chest, 272
,, diaphragm, 276
, ear, 271
,, face, 271
,, genital organs, 278.
,, head, 264
,, heart 274
,, intestines 275.
,, kidneys, 276
, liver, 275
,, neck, 272
,, skull, 264
,, spine, 269
, spleen 276
,, stomach, 275
, uterus, 279

Inorganic poisons, 407
„       Isolation of, 404
Inquests, Coroner s, 2
Inquisitions in lunacy, 371.
Insanity, 316
„   as a plea for divorce, 182
„   Certificates in, 361, 364
,   Circular, 325
„   Classification of forms of, 316
„   Criminal responsibility in, 350
„   Delusional, 326, 356
„   Deprivation of civil rights in, 372
„   Epileptic, 328.
„   Feigned, 376
„   from coarse brain-lesion, 312
„   general paralysis, 331.
„       „   exceptional forms of, 333
„   Hallucinations in, 319
„   Impulsive, 345, 356
„   Indications of, 317
„   in relation to child-bearing, 338
„   Legal terms used in, 350
,   Lucid intervals in, 326, 354
„   Moral, 342, 354
„   Medico legal relations of, 350
,   of lactation, 339
„   Plea of, in criminal cases, 359
„   in pregnancy, 338
„   Puerperal 338
„   Recurrent, 326, 354
„   Toxic, 334
Instantaneous rigor, 47
Insurance, Life, 178
Intervals, Lucid, in insanity 326, 354
Intestines, Punctured wounds of, 278
„   Rupture of, 275
„   Water in, after death from drowning, 223
Inverted sexual desire, 109
Iodine, Poisoning by, 485
„   Solution of, as a reagent for alkaloids, 541
„   Tests for, 487
„   Treatment of poisoning by, 487
Iodoform, Poisoning by, 486
Iron, Poisoning by, 472
„   Tests for, 473
„   Treatment of poisoning by, 472
Irritant poisoning, General symptoms of, 395
,   Post mortem signs of, 396
Isolation of alkaloids, 401
„   inorganic poisons, 404

JABORANDI, Poisoning by, 599
Jasmine, yellow, 567
Jaw, Changes in, from age 28
„   in old age, 29
Judicial inquisition as to lunacy, 371.
Juniperus sabina, 592

KIDNEYS, rupture of, 276
Kleptomania, 349
Knives, Blood stains on, 71, 295

LABOUR, Hasty, as a cause of infant's death, 150
„   Prolonged,    „   148
Laburnum, Poisoning by, 589
„       „       Treatment of, 590
Lacerated wounds 261
Laceration of the lungs, 273
Lactation, Insanity of, 339
Larynx, Death from spasm of, 210
Laudanum, 551, 554
Lead arthralgia, 457
,   Acute poisoning by, 454
„   Chronic    ,,   455
.   chromate, Poisoning by, 475
„   colic, 457
„   Elimination of, in chronic poisoning, 459
,   encephalopathy, 458
,   paralysis, 457
,   poisoning, Psychoses of chronic, 338
„   Tests for, 460
,   Treatment of acute poisoning by, 455
„   „   chronic   „   458
Legal procedure in Scotland, 15
„   Test of insanity as regards criminal responsibility, 351
Legitimacy, 168
„   Duration of gestation in relation to, 168
,   Laws of various countries with regard to, 173
„   Viability in relation to, 171
Leucin in the urine in acute phosphorus poisoning 481
Leucorrhoea in alleged rape, 99
Levant nut, Poisoning by, 549
Life assurance, 178
„   Form of medical report in, 181
Lightning, Death from, 236
,   „   Post mortem appearances of, 240
Lime-kilns, Vapours from, 494
Limits of age as regards procreative power, 83, 86
Liquids, corrosive, Burns by, 254
Live-birth, Changes in tunis as sign of, 144
„   Definition of, 142
„   in civil cases, 166
„   Signs of, 145
Liver, Rupture of, 275
Lobelia, Poisoning by, 572
„       „   Treatment of, 572.

Lobeline, Tests for, 572
Local violence as a cause of abortion, 124
Locomotion after fatal injuries from firearms, 297
,, ,, ,, of the bladder, 276
,, ,, , ,, head 269, 286
,, ,, ,, ,, heart 273
,, , ,, ,, large vessels, 280
,, ,, poisoning by hydrocyanic acid, 504
,, immediately after delivery, 155
Lockjaw after injury, 303
,, from tetanus and strychnine poisoning contrasted, 543
Lucid intervals in insanity, 326, 354
Lunacy certificates, 361, 364
,, , Legal responsibility as regards, 369
,, Judicial inquisition as to, 371
Lunatics, Discharge of, 364
,, Examination of, 366
,, Testamentary capacity of, 373
Lungs after death from drowning, 219
,, amount of blood in, before and after respiration 133
,, Artificial inflation of, 132
,, Colour of, before and after respiration 131
,, Consistence of, , 133
,, Foetal condition of, in infants that have breathed 138
, Hydrostatic test for, 131
,, ,, inferences from, 140
,, ,, possible fallacies of, 144
,, Laceration of, 273
,, Specific gravity of, before and after respiration, 131
,, ,, Effects of disease on, 137
,, ,, ,, imperfect respiration, 138
,, , putrefaction, 139

M'Gowan, Reg v, 360
M'Naughton, Reg v, 357
Magistrates court, 5
Magnesium sulphate, Poisoning by 426
Majority, Questions relating to attainment of, 22
Malapraxis, 306
Male organs, Abnormalities of, 82
,, fern, Danger of taking castor oil with, 571
,, ,, Poisoning by, 570
,, ,, , Treatment of, 571.
Mania, Acute delirious, 320
,, ,, ordinary, 321

Mania, Chronic, 322
Mark of finns round child's neck, 148, 156
Marriage, Grounds for nullity of, 183
, Impediments to, 182
Marsh's test for antimony, 445
,, ,, arsenic, 437
Mason v Marshall and others, 370
Matches, lucifer, Poisoning with, 476
Maturity of infant, Signs of, 24
Maybrick, Reg v, 430
Meat from diseased animals, Poisoning by, 620
Meconic acid, Tests for, 557
Meconium, 24
Medical certificates in lunacy, 364
, ,, examination of alleged lunatic, 366
,, evidence, Oral and documentary, 7
,, inspectors in divorce cases, 184.
,, responsibility 304
, as to giving evidence, 8
,, professional secrets, 9
, in cases of poisoning, 387
, in relation to lunacy certificates, 369
, ,, , examining women, 103
,, , patients with delirium tremens 379
, those criminally wounded, 304
, test of insanity as regards criminal responsibility, 352
witnesses, Fees to 12
Medico legal necropsies, 17
, , in cases of poisoning, 19
,, relations of insanity, 350,
, , suicide, 49
, reports, 14
Melancholy, 323
,, with agitation 325
,, , stupor 325
Menstruation Cessation of, 87
,, as evidence of pregnancy, 112, 168
, Commencement of, 86
,, Pregnancy without, 87,
Mercuric chloride Poisoned by, 447
, nitrate, ,, 449
Mercury, Acute poisoning by, 447
,, Chronic ,, 450
,, Tests for ,, 452
,, Treatment of acute poisoning by, 449

Metabolism during fasting, 311.
Metallic poisons, 427.
Methæmoglobin, Spectrum of, 68.
Mezereon, Poisoning by, 590.
Middle ear test of live-birth, 143.
Milk, Poisoning by, 621.
Mirbane, essence of, Poisoning by, 523.
Miscarriage, 119.
Mitscherlich's test for phosphorus, 484.
Modes of dying, 33.
Moist method of destroying organic matter, 404.
Molecular death, 36.
Moles, 115.
Monk's-hood, Poisoning by, 583.
Monomania, 326.
Monorchids, Virility of, 82.
Monsters cannot inherit, 78.
Moral insanity, 342, 354.
Morphine, Acute poisoning by, 552.
,, ,, ,, exceptional symptoms, 553.
,, ,, ,, Treatment of, 554.
,, Chronic ,, 558.
,, ,, ,, Treatment of, 559.
,, Elimination of, 558.
,, Fatal dose of, 554.
,, Properties of, 551.
,, Solvents for, 556.
,, Tests for, 557.
Morphinism, 337.
Muco-purulent discharge in cases of rape, 98.
Multiple suicidal wounding, 291.
Mummification, 57.
,, of funis, 26.
Muscarine, Properties and physiological action of, 609.
Mushrooms, Poisoning by, 607.
Mussels, Bacteria in, 619.
,, Cause of toxicity of, 618.
,, Poisoning by, 617.
,, ,, Treatment of, 619.
Mydalein (ptomaine), 616.
Mytilotoxin ,, 618.

NAPHTHALENE, Poisoning by, 531.
Neck, Injuries of, 272, 289.
Nepenthe, 551.
Neurin (ptomaine), 616.
Nicotine, Acute poisoning by, 573.
,, Chronic ,, 574.
,, Properties and physiological action of, 573.
,, Tests for, 574.
Nightshade, Deadly, 559.
Nitre, Poisoning by, 423.
Nitric acid, Poisoning by, 412.
,, fumes, ,, 414.
,, Tests for, 413.
Nitrite of amyl, Poisoning by, 511.

Nitrobenzene, Properties of, 523.
,, Tests for, 526.
,, Treatment of poisoning by, 524.
Nitroglycerine, Gases produced by detonation of, 501.
,, Poisoning by, 511.
Non compos mentis, 350.
Notes, must be the original copy, 9.
,, Reference to, when giving evidence, 9.
Noxious substances, 381.
Nullity, Suits for, 184.
Nutmeg, Poisoning by, 602.
Nux vomica, Poisoning by, 548.

OBLIGATION of medical witnesses, 8.
Œnanthe crocata, Poisoning by, 577.
Oil, croton, Poisoning by, 605.
,, of bitter almonds, Poisoning by, 501, 505.
,, ,, gaultheria, ,, 594.
,, ,, mirbane, ,, 523.
,, ,, pennyroyal, ,, 593.
,, ,, savin, ,, 592.
,, ,, tansy, ,, 594.
,, ,, turpentine, ,, 591.
,, ,, vitriol, ,, 407.
,, ,, wintergreen, ,, 594.
Opium and its alkaloids, 551.
,, Acute poisoning by, 552.
,, ,, ,, exceptional symptoms of, 553.
,, Chronic ,, 558.
,, eating, 558.
,, fatal dose, 554.
,, Treatment of acute poisoning by, 554.
,, ,, chronic ,, 559.
Orders for reception of lunatics, 361.
,, ,, Expiration of, 364.
,, ,, wandering at large, 363.
,, ,, pauper lunatics, 363.
,, Urgency for reception of lunatics, 362.
Orpiment, Poisoning by, 428, 431.
Ossification, Table of points of, 31.
Overlaying of infants, 212.
Oxalic acid, Poisoning by, 416.
,, Tests for, 418.
,, Treatment of poisoning by, 417.
Oxidicolchicine, 579.
Oysters, Poisoning by, 619.

PALMER, Reg. v., 544.
Paraffin oil, Poisoning by, 520.
Paraldehyde, 510.
Paranoia, 326.
Paregoric, 551.

Partial insanity, 329
Parton, Reg v, 515
Paternity, 168
  ,, and affiliation, 176
Peas greened with copper, 464
Pederastia, 109
Pelvis, Sexual characteristics of, 77
Penis, Malformation of, 85
Pennyroyal, oil of, Poisoning by, 593
Personal identity in the dead, 72
  ,,      ,,     living, 59
Person, Indecent exposure of the, 111
Petroleum oil, Characteristics of, 520
  ,       Poisoning by, 520
Phallin, Toxic action of, 610
Phenol, Poisoning by, 534
  ,    Tests for, 537
  ,,   Treatment of poisoning by, 536
Phosphomolybdic acid, 541
Phosphorus, Acute poisoning by, 476
  ,,       ,,        , Treatment of, 478
  ,      acute poisoning by, Changes in metabolism in, 481
  ,,     Chronic poisoning by, 483
  ,,     Fatal dose of, 478
  ,      Tests for, 483
Phosphotungstic acid, 541
Physical condition of poison, Influence of, 384
  ,,    signs of virginity, 97
Physostigmine Poisoning by, 601
  ,,        Properties and physiological action of, 600
  ,,        Tests for, 602
  ,        Treatment of poisoning by, 602
Picric acid, Poisoning by, 538
  ,,         , Treatment of, 538
  ,,       Properties of, 537
  ,,       Tests for, 539
Picrotoxin, 549
  ,,      Tests for, 551
Pilocarpine, Poisoning by, 599
  ,,         ,,        Treatment of, 600
  ,         Properties and physiological action of, 599
Placing habitual drunkards under restraint, 378
Plea of insanity in criminal cases, 350
Poisoning by acetylene and the oxides of carbon, 496
  ,,       aconite, 584
  ,,       alcohol amyl, 510
  ,         ,   ethyl, 507
  ,,       almonds, bitter, 506
  ,         ,,       ,,  oil of, 505
  ,,       amanita muscaria, 611
  ,,         ,,   phalloides, 610
  ,,       ammonia, 420
  ,,         ,    carbonate, 422
  ,,       amyl nitrite 511
  ,,       aniline, 527

Poisoning by antifebrin, 530
  ,,       antipyrin, 531
  ,        antimony, 442
  ,        arsenic (acute) 428
  ,          ,   (chronic), 433
  ,        atropine, 560
  ,,       barium, 425
  ,        Battle's vermin killer 546
  ,        belladonna, 560
  ,        benzene, 522
  ,        bismuth 474
  ,,       bisulphide of carbon (acute), 518
  ,          ,      ,    (chronic), 519
  ,        bitter almonds, 506
  ,         ,    ,   oil of, 505
  ,        bleaching fluid, 490
  ,        borax, 491
  ,        boracic acid 490
  ,        bromine, 487
  ,        cadmium, 470
  ,        calabar bean 600
  ,        camphor 603
  ,        cannabis Indica 566
  ,        cantharides, 612
  ,        carbolic acid, 535
  ,        carbon bisulphide (acute), 518
  ,          ,      ,      (chronic), 519
  ,          ,   dioxide 494
  ,          ,   monoxide (acute), 496
  ,,         ,       ,    (chronic), 500
  ,        castor oil seeds, 606
  ,        cheese 621
  ,        chloral hydrate, 514
  ,        chlorine, 489
  ,        chloroform, 512
  ,        chrome yellow 475
  ,        chromic acid, 473
  ,        coal-gas 495
  ,,       cocaine 568
  ,        cocculus Indicus, 549
  ,        colchicum, 579
  ,        colocynth 605
  ,        conium maculatum 574
  ,        copper (acute) 462
  ,          ,   (chronic), 463
  ,        corrosive sublimate 447
  ,,       creasote 539
  ,        croton oil, 605
  ,        cyanide of potassium, 505
  ,        daphne mezereon, 590
  ,,       datura stramonium 565
  ,,       delphinium staphisagria, 588
  ,,       dichromate of potassium, 474
  ,,       digitalis 577
  ,,       dinitrobenzene (acute), 524
  ,,         ,        (chronic), 525
  ,,       dinitrotoluene, 527

# 634 INDEX

Poisoning by duboisine, 565
,, dynamite, 512
,, elaterium, 605
,, Epsom salts, 426.
,, ergot (acute), 595
,, ,, (chronic), 597
,, eserine, 601.
,, ether, 510
,, exalgin, 530
,, fish, 620
,, fly-fungus, 609.
,, foxglove, 577
,, fruit, tinned, 470
,, fungi, 608
,, fusel oil, 510
,, gases produced by explosives, 500.
,, gaultheria, oil of, 594
,, gelseminum, 567
,, hellebore, 588.
,, hemlock, 574
,, henbane, 564
,, hydrochloric acid, 415
,, hydrocyanic ,, 502
,, hyoscyamus, 564
,, Indian hemp, 566
,, tobacco, 572.
,, iodine, 485
,, iodoform, 486.
,, iron 472
,, jaborandi, 599
,, laburnum 589
,, laudanum, 554
,, lead (acute), 454
,, ,, (chronic), 455
,, lobelia, 572
,, male fern, oil of, 570
,, meat from diseased animals 620
,, mercury (acute), 447.
,, ,, (chronic), 450
,, mezereon, 590.
,, milk, 624
,, mirbane, oil of, 523
,, morphine (acute), 552
,, ,, (chronic), 558
,, muscarine, 611
,, mushrooms, 607
,, mussels, 617.
,, naphthalene, 531
,, nicotine, 573
,, nitric acid, 412
,, nitrite of amyl, 511
,, nitrobenzene, 523
,, nitroglycerine, 511.
,, nutmeg, 602
,, nux vomica, 548
,, œnanthe crocata, 577
,, oil of bitter almonds, 505
,, ,, mirbane, 523
,, ,, pennyroyal, 595
,, ,, savin, 592
,, ,, tansy, 594
,, ,, turpentine, 591.

Poisoning by oil of vitriol, 407
,, ,, wintergreen, 594.
,, opium (acute), 552
,, ,, (chronic), 558
,, orpiment, 431
,, oxalic acid, 416
,, oysters, 619
,, parafin oil, 520
,, paraldehyde, 510
,, pennyroyal, 595
,, petroleum, 520
,, phenol, 534
,, phosphorus (acute), 476
,, ,, (chronic), 483.
,, physostigmine, 601
,, picric acid, 538
,, picrotoxin, 549.
,, pilocarpine, 599
,, poisonous foods, 619.
,, potassium bromide, 488
,, ,, chlorate, 423
,, ,, cyanide, 505
,, ,, dichromate, 474.
,, ,, hydrate, 419.
,, ,, iodide, 486
,, ,, nitrate, 423.
,, prussic acid, 502
,, ptomaines, 617
,, pyrogallol, 532
,, rat-paste, 476
,, red-precipitate, 448.
,, resorcin, 532
,, roburite, 526
,, salicylate of sodium, 533
,, santonin, 603
,, sardines, 620
,, sausages, 620
,, savin, 592
,, Schweinfurt green, 431.
,, sewer gas, 492
,, silver, 466
,, sodium borate, 491
,, ,, hydrate, 420
,, ,, salicylate, 533.
,, solanum dulcamara, 570.
,, spotted hemlock, 574.
,, stavesacre, 588
,, stramonium, 565
,, strychnine, 542
,, sugar of lead, 454.
,, sulphonal, 517
,, sulphuric acid, 407
,, sulphuretted hydrogen, 491.
,, tansy, 594
,, tartar emetic, 442.
,, taxus baccata, 592
,, tin, 470
,, tinned fish, 620
,, ,, foods, 620.
,, ,, fruit, 470
,, tobacco, 573
,, turpentine, 591.
,, vaseline, 521.
,, veratrine, 581.

Poisoning by water-gas, 496
,, white precipitate, 418
,, wintergreen, oil of, 594
,, yew, 592
,, zinc, 468
,, Chemical evidence of, 399
, Criminal law of, 382
, Diagnosis of, 386
, Evidence of, from dead body, 396
,, Examination of the dead body in, 19
, General treatment of, 389
,, Systematic chemical analysis in cases of, 400
Poisonous foods, 619
Poisons, Classification of, 385
,, Effect of, contrasted with those of disease, 397
,, ,, contrasted with post mortem changes, 398
,, in their general aspect 381
Position of the body in death from wounding, 293
,, ,, diaphragm in the newborn infant, 131
,, of wounds, 285
Post mortem coagulation of the blood, 39
, cooling, 38
,, elevation of temperature, 38
, examinations, Medico-legal, 17
, examination in cases of poisoning, 19
,, stains, 39
,, ,, distinguished from bruises, 41
,, ,, of internal organs, 42
Potash, Poisoning by, 419
,, Tests for 420
,, Treatment of poisoning by, 419
Potassium arsenate, ,, 428
,, binoxalate, ,, 418
,, bromide, ,, 488
,, chlorate, ,, 423
,, cyanide, ,, 502, 505
,, dichromate, ,, 474
,, iodide, ,, 486
,, nitrate, ,, 423
Precognitions (Scotch Law), 16
Pregnancy, Concealment of (Scotch law) 166
,, Duration of, 168
,, Earliest age for, 86
,, Insanity of, 338
,, Latest age for, 87
, Plea of, as bar to execution, 112
,, Post-mortem appearances of, 111

Pregnancy, Signs of, 112
Preternatural combustibility of the body, 251
Preternatural combustibility of the body, Medico legal bearings of, 254
Pritchard Reg v, 443
Procreative power, Age for, in the female, 89
, ,, ,, male, 83
Professional secrets in the witness box, 9
Prolapse of the funis, 149
Prolonged gestation, 169
Prostitutes Rape on, 90
Prussic acid, Fatal dose of, 504
,, Poisoning by, 502
,, ,, Treatment of, 505
,, Tests for, 506
Psychical impediment to sexual intercourse in the female, 88
, impediment to sexual intercourse in the male, 84
,, shock as a cause of sudden death, 301
Psychoses of chronic lead poisoning, 338
Ptomaines from the cadaver, 615
,, in food, 617
,, Isolation of, 614
,, Nature of, 614
Puberty in the female, 86
,, ,, male, 83
Puerperal insanity, 338
Punctured wounds, 279
Putrefaction in air, 50
,, in water, 52
,, Internal appearances produced by, 54
, Signs of, 51
Pyrogallol, Poisoning by 532
, , Treatment of, 533
, Tests for, 533

QUICKENING as an indication of pregnancy, 113
Quotations from books in the witness box, 10

RAPE, Blood stains in cases of, 108
,, Death from, 97
,, during abnormal sleep 91
, natural 90
,, an attack of hysteria 91
. insensibility due to anæsthetics and narcotics, 92
, , insensibility due to chloroform, 93
, Examination of females in cases of, 103
, ,, males in cases of, 105
,. ,, seminal stains in cases of, 106
, ,, the dead body in cases of, 104.

Rape, False accusations of, 95, 101.
,, Law in relation to, 89.
,, Signs of virginity in relation to, 97.
,, ,, loss of virginity in relation to, 98.
Recurrent insanity, 326, 354.
Red-precipitate, Poisoning by, 448.
Re-examination, 7.
Reinsch's test for antimony, 445.
,, ,, arsenic, 435.
Remote causes of death from wounds, 302.
Reports, Medico-legal, 14.
Resorcin, Poisoning by, 532.
,, Tests for, 532.
Respiration and circulation, Cessation of, 37.
,, Artificial, after immersion, 232.
,, before birth, 142.
,, Imperfect, in relation to infanticide, 138.
,, Signs of, 131.
Responsibility, Criminal, 350.
,, Medical, 304.
,, ,, as to death from anæsthetics, 305.
,, ,, in relation to lunacy certificates, 369.
,, ,, in the examination of women, 103.
Restraint, Placing habitual drunkards under, 378.
,, ,, lunatics under, 361.
Resuscitation from immersion, 230.
,, ,, modes of effecting, 232.
Revolver found in hand after death, 298.
,, Suicidal wounds with, not always blackened, 296.
,, wounds, 284, 298.
,, ,, of head and heart not immediately fatal, 297.
Rigidity. Cadaveric, 43.
Rigor mortis, 43.
,, Causation of, 43, 47.
,, Conditions which hasten, 44.
,, in respect to the heart, 45.
,, Instantaneous, 47.
,, ,, causation of, 47.
,, ,, examples of, 48.
Roburite, Acute poisoning by, 526.
,, Chronic ,, 526.
,, Gases produced by detonation of, 501.
Rupture of the bladder, 276.

Rupture of the bladder, Spontaneous, 277.
,, diaphragm, 276.
,, intestines, 275.
,, kidneys, 276.
,, spleen, 276.
,, stomach, 275.
SACRUM, Sexual characteristics of, 76.
Salicylic acid, Poisoning by, 533.
,, Tests for, 534.
Salt of sorrel, 418.
Saltpetre, Poisoning by, 423.
Sanguineous mole, 115.
Santonin, Poisoning by, 603.
,, ,, Treatment of, 604.
,, Tests for, 604.
Sardines. Poisoning by, 620.
Sausages, ,, 620.
Savin, ,, 592.
Scalds, 246.
,, and burns, Death from, 242.
Scalp-wounds, 264.
Scars, 59.
Scherer's test for phosphorus, 484.
Schultze's swinging, 133, 135.
Schweinfurt green, Poisoning by, 431.
Scot v. Wakem, 379.
Scotland, Legal procedure in, 15.
Secrets, Professional, 9.
Self-delivery, Alleged violence produced by, 156, 161.
Self-inflicted wounds feigning homicidal violence, 308.
Seminal stains, Examination of, 106.
Senile dementia. 341.
Separation of funis, 27.
Septic causes of death from wounds, 303.
Sewer-gas, Poisoning by, 492.
Sex, Determination of, 79.
,, Doubtful, 79.
Sexual abnormalities, 78.
,, characteristics of the skeleton, 75.
,, defects in females, 86.
,, ,, males, 83.
,, ,, Proof of, in divorce, 183.
Shell-fish. Poisoning by, 617.
Shock as cause of sudden death, 300.
Shortened gestation, 171.
Signs of abortion, 127.
,, death, 36.
,, delivery, 116.
,, live-birth, 145.
,, pregnancy, 112.
,, putrefaction, 51.
,, virginity, 97.
,, loss of virginity, 98.
Silver, Acute poisoning by, 466.
,, Chronic ,, 467.
,, Tests for, 467.
,, Treatment of poisoning by, 466.
Skeleton, Sexual characteristics of, 75.
Skull, Fractures of, 266.
,, Injuries of, 264.

Sleep, Rape during abnormal, 91
,, ,, natural, 90
Smothering, 213
Soda, Poisoning by, 420
Sodium salicylate, Poisoning by, 533
Sodomy, 109
Solanum dulcamara, Poisoning by, 570
Sorrel, Salt of, 418
Spanish-flies, Poisoning by, 612
Spasm, Cadaveric, 47
,, of the larynx, Death from, 210
Spasmodic ergotism, 597
Spectrum of hæmatin, Reduced, 69
,, hæmoglobin, 67
,, methæmoglobin, 68
,, phosphuretted hydrogen, 484
,, ergot, Solution of, 598
Spermatozoa, 107
Spine Fractures of, 270
,, Injuries of, 269
Spleen, Rupture of, 276
Spontaneous combustion, So-called, 251
Spotted hemlock, Poisoning by, 575
,, ,, Treatment of, 576
Stab wounds, 259
Stains, Post-mortem, 39
,, produced by aniline, 72
,, ,, blood, 63
,, ,, fruits, 72
,, ,, mineral salts, 72
,, on weapon, 71, 295
Starvation, 309
,, Diseases which may cause appearances resembling death from, 313
,, Duration of life in, 314
,, Effect of drinking water in, 314
,, Metabolism during, 311
,, Post-mortem appearances of, 312
Stas process, 400
,, Stevenson's modification of, 401
Statistics of deaths of legitimate and illegitimate children, 145
,, ,, from drowning, 224
,, ,, ,, suicidal hanging, 197
,, ,, ,, overlying of infants, 212
Stature, 73
Staunton, Reg. v., 313
Stavesacre, Poisoning by, 588
Sterility, 82
Stomach, Air in, as a sign of respiration, 141
,, Contents of, in new born infant, 145

Stomach, effects of poison, disease and post mortem changes contrasted, 397
,, Redness of, as a sign of poisoning, 396
,, Ulceration and perforation of, 397
,, Water in, after death from drowning, 221
Stomach-pump, Use of, in poisoning 389
Stones, Wounds from sharp-edged, 258
Strammonium, Poisoning by, 565
Strangulation, 201
,, Accidental, 202
,, by throttling, 207
,, ,, Position of marks in, 207
,, Homicidal, 202
,, indications from degree of violence, 206
,, mark of cord, 201
,, of infant with fumis, Accidental, 147
,, ,, Criminal 158
,, Post-mortem appearances of death from, 201
,, Suicidal, 205
Strontium, Salts of, not toxic 426
Strychnine, Fatal dose of, 544
,, Poisoning by, 542
,, ,, Treatment of 545
,, Properties of, 541
,, Tests for 547
,, Toxic action of, 542
Subjects involving sexual relations, 78
Subpœna, 6
Suffocation, 209
,, from compression of the chest, 211
,, ,, covering the mouth and nostrils, 212
,, ,, foreign bodies in the air passages, 209
,, ,, pathological causes, 209
,, ,, smothering, 213
,, Occasional absence of indications after death from, 209
,, Post-mortem signs of death from 214
Sugar in the urine in poisoning by carbon monoxide, 496
,, ,, phosphorus, 452
Suicidal impulse, 347
Suicide by cut throat, 289
,, ,, detonation of dynamite, 288
,, ,, drowning, 225
,, ,, electricity 242
,, ,, fire-arms 296
,, ,, foreign bodies in the air passages 211
,, ,, guillotine 288
,, ,, hanging, 197

Suicide by injuries to the head, 286.
,, ,, poisoning, see Poisoning.
,, ,, red-hot iron, 288.
,, ,, smothering, 213.
,, ,, stab-wounds, 291.
,, ,, strangulation, 205.
,, ,, throttling, 208.
,, ,, wounds of the head and heart, 297.
,, Medico-legal relations of, 349.
Sulphomolybdic acid, 548.
Sulphonal, Poisoning by, 517.
,, Tests for, 518.
Sulphuretted hydrogen, Poisoning by, 491.
,, ,, cause of death in 492.
,, ,, treatment of, 493.
Sulphuric acid, Poisoning by, 407.
,, ,, Treatment of, 409.
,, Tests for, 411.
,, Throwing of, 254.
Summary reception orders in lunacy, 362.
Superfœtation, 173.
Supposititious children, 176.
Survivorship, 177.
Symm v. Fraser and Andrews, 380.
Syncope, 34.
Systematic chemical analysis in poisoning, 400.

TABLE of development of fœtus, 26.
,, points of ossification, 31.
,, union of epiphyses and bones, 32.
Tanacetum vulgare, Poisoning by oil of, 594.
Tansy, Poisoning by, 594.
Tartar emetic, ,, 442.
Tattoo-marks, 60.
Taxus baccata, Poisoning by, 593.
Teeth, Development of, 29.
,, Permanent, 30.
,, Temporary, 29.
Tenancy by courtesy, 167.
Testamentary capacity, 373.
Tetanus as a cause of death from wounds, 303.
,, contrasted with the clonic spasms of strychnine poisoning, 543.
Throat, Wounds of, 289.
Throttling, 207.
Thymus gland, Hyperplasia of, in new-born infants, 149.
Tichborne, Reg. v., 61.
Tin, Poisoning by, 470.
,, ,, Treatment of, 471.
,, Tests for, 471.
Tinned foods, Poisoning by, 620.
,, fruit, ,, 470.
,, peas, Copper in, 464.

Tobacco, Acute poisoning by, 573.
,, ,, ,, Treatment of, 574.
,, Chronic ,, 574.
Tonite, Gases produced by detonation of, 501.
Toogood v. Wilkes, 370.
Townley, Reg. v., 357.
Toxic insanity, 334.
Toxicology, 381.
Tribadism, 109.
Tricomonas vaginæ, 108.
Triennial cohabitation, 183.
Trimethylamine in decayed cheese, 622.
Turpentine, oil of, Poisoning by, 591.
Tyrosin in the urine in acute phosphorus poisoning, 481.
Tyrotoxicon, 621.

ULCERATION and perforation of stomach, 397.
Umbilical cord, Hæmorrhage from, 158.
,, in relation to live-birth, 144.
,, Prolapse of, 146.
,, Separation of, 27.
,, Strangulation of infant with, 147, 156.
Unnatural sexual offences, 109.
Unconsciousness during delivery, 150.
,, ,, rape, 91.
Urgency orders in lunacy, 362.
Urochloral acid in poisoning by chloral hydrate, 517.
Uterus, Absence of, 88.
,, Injuries of, 279.

VAGINA, Injuries of, 278.
Vaginismus, 88.
Vaseline, Poisoning by, 521.
Venereal disease in cases of rape, 105.
Veratrine, Properties and physiological action of, 581.
,, Poisoning by, 582.
,, ,, Treatment of, 582.
,, Tests for, 583.
Verdigris, 462.
Vermin-killers, 542.
Vertebræ, Injuries of, 269.
,, ,, in hanging, 192.
Vesicular mole, 115.
Viability, 171.
Virginity, Physical signs of, 97.
,, ,, Loss of, 98.
Virility, Proof of absence of, in divorce cases, 183.
Vitriol throwing, 254.
Vulva, Injuries of, 278.
Vulval rape, 90.

WARE, Reg. v., 351.
Water in intestines after death from drowning, 223.
,, stomach ,, 221.

Water-gas, Poisoning by, 495
Weak-mindedness, 339
Weapon in the hand after death, 292, 298
— Stains on, 71, 245
Weight of child, Increase in, after birth, 27
Weldon v Winslow, 371
White arsenic, 427
, hellebore, 581
, precipitate, 448
Williams Reg v 359
Willis, Reg v, 121
Wills, Capacity to make 373
Wintergreen, Poisoning by oil of 594
Witness, Examination of, 7
,, Expert 8
,, Medical, 8
,, Obligations of, 8
Wolf's bane, Poisoning by, 583
Women Necessity for consent before examining, 103
Wounds, 258
, Blackening of, by fire arms 296
,, Causes of death from, 299
,, Extent and direction of, 288
,, fatal from anæsthetic during operation, 305
,, ,, improper treatment, 305
,, ,, negligent ,, 305
,, ,, septic processes, 303
,, ,, tetanus, 303
, Feigned homicidal, self inflicted, 308

Wounds, General causal indications after death from, 293
,, Incised, 258
,, indications from weapon, 261
,, in their causal relation 284
,, Lacerated, 261
,, made before and after death, 262
,, ,, by broken crockery-ware, &c, 258
, Multiple fatal 291, 299
, Nature of, 257
, of the back, 292, 298
,, chest, 272, 291
face, 271
,, genital organs 278, 287
,, ,, head, 264, 286, 297
,, ,, heart, 273, 297
neck, 272
throat, 289
,, Position of, 285
, Post-mortem examination of, 263
, produced by fire arms, 282
. causal relation of, 296
, Punctured 259

Yew Poisoning by, 592
Youth in relation to procreative power, 83, 86

Zinc, Acute poisoning by, 468
,, ,, Treatment of, 468
,, Chrome . 469
,, Tests for 470

PRIL AND BAIN, PRINTERS, TRINITY, MITCHELL STREET GLASGOW

A

# CATALOGUE

OF

# MEDICAL WORKS

PUBLISHED BY

CHARLES GRIFFIN & COMPANY.

LONDON:
12 EXETER STREET, STRAND.

MESSRS. CHARLES GRIFFIN & COMPANY'S PUBLICATIONS may be obtained through any Bookseller in the United Kingdom, or will be sent direct on receipt of a remittance to cover published price. To prevent delay, Orders must be accompanied by a Remittance. Postal Orders and Cheques to be crossed "SMITH, PAYNE & SMITHS."

LONDON
12 EXETER STREET, STRAND, W.C.

## INDEX TO AUTHORS.

| | PAGE |
|---|---|
| AITKEN (Sir W., M D.), Science and Practice of Medicine, | 18 |
| ——Outlines of, for Students, | 18 |
| ANDERSON (Prof. M'Call), Skin Diseases, | 16 |
| BLYTH (A W.), Hygiene, | 26 |
| ——Foods and Poisons, | 26 |
| BURNET (R., M D.), Foods and Dietaries, | 22 |
| BURY (Judson, M D.), Clinical Medicine, | 31 |
| CAIRD and CATHCART, Surgical Handbook, | 25 |
| CRIMP (W S.), Sewage Disposal Works, | 19 |
| CROOM (Halliday, M D.), Gynæcology, | 30 |
| DAVIS (Prof J R A.), Biology, | 29 |
| ——The Flowering Plant, | 29 |
| ——Zoological Pocket-book, | 29 |
| DUCKWORTH (Sir D., M D.), Gout, | 13 |
| DUPRÉ and HAKE, Manual of Chemistry, | 27 |
| ELBORNE (W.), Pharmacy and Materia Medica, | 27 |
| GARROD (A E., M D.), Rheumatism, | 14 |
| HADDON (Prof.), Embryology, | 8 |
| HORSLEY (Victor, F R S.), Surgery of the Brain, | 31 |
| ——Nervous System, | 31 |
| HUMPHRY (Laur.), Manual of Nursing, | 23 |
| JAKSCH (Prof v.) and CAGNEY, Clinical Diagnosis, | 12 |
| JAMIESON (Prof.), Electricity, | 28 |
| LANDIS (Dr.), Management of Labour, | 28 |
| LANDOIS and STIRLING'S Physiology, | 6, 7 |
| LEWIS (Bevan), Mental Diseases, | 9 |
| LONGMORE (Prof.), Sanitary Contrasts, | 28 |
| MACALISTER (Prof.), Human Anatomy, | 4, 5 |
| MEYER and FERGUS, Ophthalmology, | 15 |
| OBERSTEINER and HILL, Central Nervous Organs, | 10, 11 |
| PAGE (H W., F R C S.), Railway Injuries, | 17 |
| PARKER (Prof.), Mammalian Descent, | 28 |
| PORTER (Surg.-Major), Surgeon's Pocketbook, | 24 |
| SANSOM (A. E., M D.), Diseases of the Heart, | 30 |
| SEXTON (Prof.), Quantitative Analysis, | 27 |
| ——Qualitative Analysis, | 27 |
| STIRLING (Prof.), Human Physiology, | 6, 7 |
| ——Outlines of Practical Physiology, | 20 |
| ——Outlines of Practical Histology, | 21 |
| THORBURN (W., F R C S.), Surgery of Spine, | 17 |
| THORNTON (J., F R.C S.), Surgery of the Kidneys, | 17 |
| SCIENTIFIC SOCIETIES (Year-book of), | 32 |

## INDEX TO SUBJECTS.

| | PAGE |
|---|---|
| ANATOMY, Human, | 4, 5 |
| BIOLOGY, | 29 |
| BOTANY, | 29 |
| BRAIN, The, | 9, 14, 31 |
| CHEMISTRY, Inorganic, | 27 |
| ——Analysis, Qualitative and Quantitative, | 27 |
| CLINICAL Diagnosis, | 12 |
| ——Medicine, | 31 |
| DIETARIES for the Sick, | 22 |
| ELECTRICITY, | 28 |
| EMBRYOLOGY, | 8 |
| EYE, Diseases of the, | 15 |
| FOODS, Analysis of, | 26 |
| FOODS and Dietaries, | 22 |
| GOUT, | 13 |
| GYNÆCOLOGY, | 30 |
| HEART, Diseases of the, | 30 |
| HISTOLOGY, | 21 |
| HYGIENE and Public Health, | 19, 26 |
| KIDNEYS, Surgery of the, | 17 |
| LABORATORY Hand-books— | |
| Chemistry, | 27 |
| Histology, | 21 |
| Pharmacy, | 27 |
| Physiology, | 20 |
| MAMMALIAN DESCENT, | 28 |
| MEDICAL SOCIETIES, Papers read annually before, | 32 |
| MEDICINE, Science and Practice of, | 18 |
| ——Clinical, | 31 |
| MENTAL DISEASES, | 9 |
| NERVOUS ORGANS, Central, | 10, 11 |
| ——SYSTEM, | 31 |
| NURSING, Medical and Surgical, | 23 |
| OBSTETRICS, | 28 |
| PHARMACY, | 27 |
| PHYSIOLOGY, Human, | 6, 7 |
| ——Practical, | 20 |
| POCKET-BOOK, Surgical, | 24, 25 |
| ——Zoological, | 29 |
| POISONS, Detection of, | 26 |
| RAILWAY INJURIES, | 17 |
| RHEUMATISM, | 14 |
| SEWAGE Disposal Works, | 19 |
| SKIN, Diseases of the, | 16 |
| SPINAL Cord, | 17 |
| SURGERY, Civil, | 25 |
| ——Military, | 24 |
| ——of Kidneys, | 17 |
| ——of Spinal Cord, | 17 |
| ZOOLOGY, | 28, 29 |

FROM

## PROFESSOR MACALISTER'S

# TEXT-BOOK OF HUMAN ANATOMY.

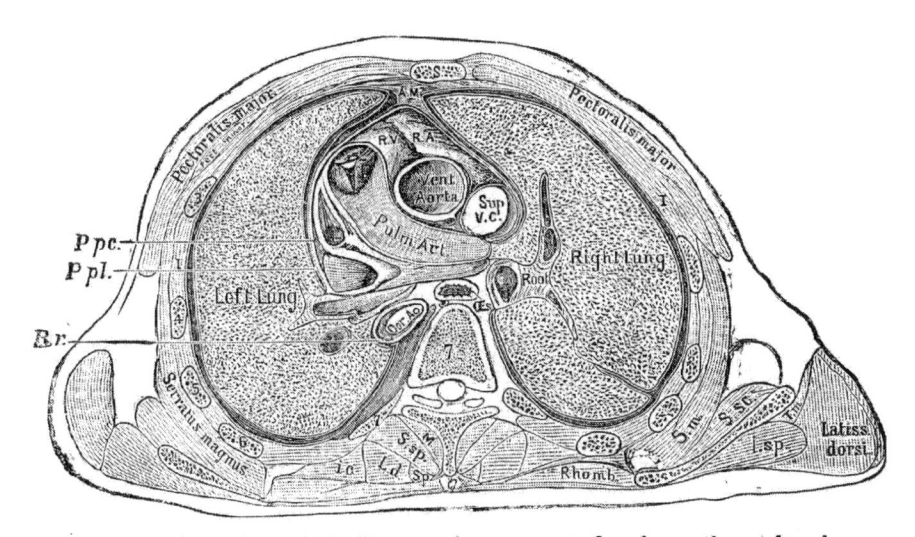

Fig. 452.—Section through the thorax at the uppermost edge of seventh vertebra along the line of the pulmonary artery and roots of the lungs.

LONDON: EXETER STREET, STRAND.

## By Prof. MACALISTER, M.D., F.R.S.

# HUMAN ANATOMY

(SYSTEMATIC AND TOPOGRAPHICAL),

A TEXT-BOOK OF:

INCLUDING THE EMBRYOLOGY, HISTOLOGY, AND MORPHOLOGY OF MAN, WITH SPECIAL REFERENCE TO THE REQUIREMENTS OF PRACTICAL SURGERY AND MEDICINE.

BY

ALEXANDER MACALISTER, M.A., M.D., F.R.S., F.S.A.,

Professor of Anatomy in the University of Cambridge, and Fellow of St. John's College; Examiner in Human Anatomy, University of London.

*In Large 8vo. With 816 Illustrations. Handsome Cloth, 36s.*

### OPINIONS OF THE PRESS.

"By far THE MOST IMPORTANT WORK ON THIS SUBJECT that has appeared in recent years, . . . treating its subject THOROUGHLY AND COMPREHENSIVELY. . . . The histology of the tissues is most ably and lucidly described."—*The Lancet.*

"THIS SPLENDID VOLUME fills up what was a great want in works on human anatomy. . . . We get morphology as a basis, and thread our way upwards."—*Saturday Review.*

"Contains an enormous amount of valuable matter. . . . A work which we feel sure will be a *main factor* in the *advancement* of *scientific anatomy*. In addition, we must mention the FINE COLLECTION OF ILLUSTRATIONS."—*Dublin Medical Journal.*

"Many of the figures are of great beauty. . . . The chapters on the brain and spinal cord, the ear, and the eye, contain *all that is really valuable in the most recent researches.*"—*Glasgow Medical Journal.*

"The book bears an unmistakable stamp of erudition and labour, and will be VALUED both by teachers and pupils AS A WORK OF REFERENCE."—*British Medical Journal.*

"Dr Macalister's extensive knowledge of comparative anatomy enables him to speak with authority on many interesting but difficult morphological problems. . . . A VERY ABLE and SCIENTIFIC treatise."—*Edinburgh Medical Journal.*

LONDON: EXETER STREET, STRAND.

CHARLES GRIFFIN & COMPANY'S

FROM
# LANDOIS & STIRLING'S HUMAN PHYSIOLOGY.

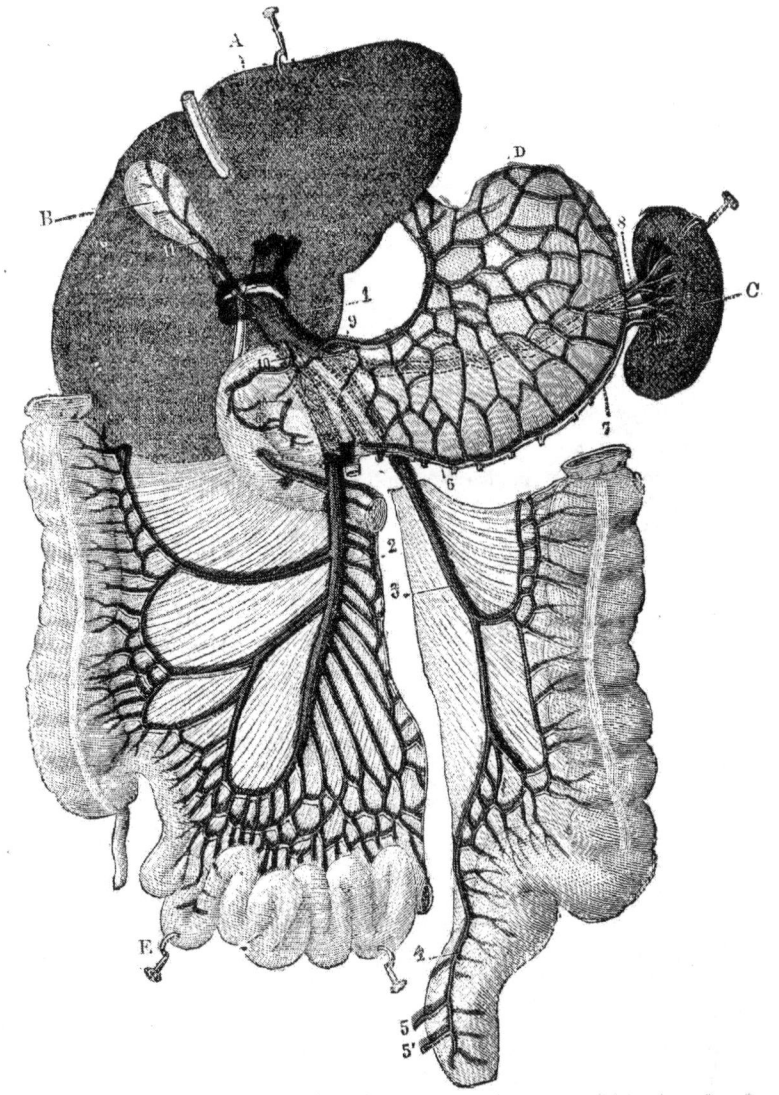

Fig. 224.—Portal vein and its branches of origin. A, liver; B, gall-bladder; C, spleen; D, stomach; E, part of the small intestine; 1, trunk of the portal vein; 2, superior, and 3, inferior mesenteric veins; 4, superior, 5, 5′, middle and inferior hæmorrhoidal veins; 6, right, and 7, left gastro-epiploic veins; 8, splenic vein; 9, gastric coronary vein; 10, pyloric vein; 11, cystic vein.

LONDON : EXETER STREET, STRAND.

Professors LANDOIS and STIRLING.

# HUMAN PHYSIOLOGY
(A TEXT-BOOK OF):
Including Histology and Microscopical Anatomy,
WITH SPECIAL REFERENCE TO PRACTICAL MEDICINE

By Dr L. LANDOIS,
PROFESSOR OF PHYSIOLOGY, UNIVERSITY OF GREIFSWALD

*Translated from the Seventh German Edition, with Annotations and Additions,*

By WM. STIRLING, M.D., Sc.D.,
BRACKENBURY PROFESSOR OF PHYSIOLOGY IN OWENS COLLEGE, AND VICTORIA UNIVERSITY, MANCHESTER
EXAMINER IN THE UNIVERSITY OF OXFORD

In Two Large 8vo Volumes, Handsome Cloth, 42s.
With 845 Illustrations (some in Colours).
FOURTH ENGLISH EDITION.

### GENERAL CONTENTS

PART I.—Physiology of the Blood, Circulation, Respiration, Digestion, Absorption, Animal Heat, Metabolic Phenomena of the Body, Secretion of Urine, Structure of the Skin.

PART II.—Physiology of the Motor Apparatus, the Voice and Speech, General Physiology of the Nerves Electro-Physiology, the Brain, Organs of Sight, Hearing, Smell, Taste, Touch, Physiology of Development

\*\*\* Since its first appearance in 1880, Prof LANDOIS' TEXT-BOOK OF PHYSIOLOGY has been translated into three Foreign languages, and passed through SEVEN LARGE EDITIONS

The Fourth English Edition has again been thoroughly revised, and a new feature introduced—that of printing some of the Illustrations in Colours The number of figures has also been largely increased, from 494 in the First, to 845 in the present Edition In order to do full justice to the coloured illustrations, and to admit of more of the text being printed in large type, it has been found necessary to put the work once again in two volumes.

### Opinions of the Press

"So great are the advantages offered by Prof LANDOIS' TEXT-BOOK, from the EXHAUSTIVE and EMINENTLY PRACTICAL manner in which the subject is treated, that it has passed through FOUR large editions in the same number of years . . Dr STIRLING'S annotations have materially added to the value of the work Admirably adapted for the PRACTITIONER . . With this Text-book at command, NO STUDENT COULD FAIL IN HIS EXAMINATION"—*The Lancet*

"One of the MOST PRACTICAL WORKS on Physiology ever written, forming a 'bridge' between Physiology and Practical Medicine. . Its chief merits are its completeness and conciseness . . . The additions by the Editor are able and judicious . . . EXCELLENTLY CLEAR, ATTRACTIVE, AND SUCCINCT '—*Brit Med Journal*

"The great subjects dealt with are treated in an admirably clear, terse, and happily-illustrated manner At every turn the doctrines laid down are illuminated by reference to facts of Clinical Medicine or Pathology "—*Practitioner*

"We have no hesitation in saying that THIS IS THE WORK to which the PRACTITIONER will turn whenever he desires light thrown upon, or information as to how he can best investigate, the phenomena of a COMPLICATED OR IMPORTANT CASE. To the STUDENT it will be EQUALLY VALUABLE "—*Edinburgh Medical Journal*

"LANDOIS and STIRLING's work cannot fail to establish itself as one of the most useful and popular works known to English readers "—*Manchester Medical Chronicle*

"As a work of reference, LANDOIS and STIRLING's Treatise OUGHT TO TAKE THE FOREMOST PLACE among the text-books in the English language The woodcuts are noticeable for their number and beauty "—*Glasgow Medical Journal*

"Unquestionably the most admirable exposition of the relations of Human Physiology to Practical Medicine that has ever been laid before English readers "—*Students' Journal.*

LONDON: EXETER STREET, STRAND.

By Prof. A. C. HADDON.

# EMBRYOLOGY

(AN INTRODUCTION TO THE STUDY OF).

BY

ALFRED C. HADDON, M.A., M.R.I.A.,

Professor of Zoology, Royal College of Science, Dublin.

*In Large 8vo, with 190 Illustrations. Handsome Cloth, 18s.*

*⁎⁎⁎* The main object of this work is to give a brief connected account of the principal organs by tracing the leading changes observed in the development of each organ from its initial to its mature stage. The elementary portion is printed in larger type than that which is more advanced, and the Illustrations are drawn so as to allow of their being uniformly coloured, whereby the memory is much assisted.

### OPINIONS OF THE PRESS.

"This work is a condensation of our present knowledge of embryology intelligently arranged and well adapted for self-study. The author *seems to have exhausted all the literature* of embryology since the date of Balfour's unfortunate death. . . . The reader will find REMARKABLY GOOD accounts of the different forms of placenta, of the development of the heart, &c., in which all recent work is included. The book is handsomely got up."—*Lancet.*

"WELL and CLEARLY WRITTEN. . . . Many important discoveries or theories are described, which are necessarily absent from Balfour's work."—*Nature.*

"Dr. Haddon has written the BEST of the three modern English works on the subject."—*Dublin Medical Journal.*

"The later chapters of Prof. Haddon's work ably demonstrate the development of organs from the mesoblast and epiblast."—*Brit. Med. Journal.*

"The zoological student, to whom as a text-book it is invaluable, will find it THOROUGH, TRUSTWORTHY, AND SOUND in all its teachings, and well up to date. . . . We specially commend the book to our readers."—*Nat. Monthly.*

LONDON : EXETER STREET, STRAND.

### By W. BEVAN LEWIS.

# MENTAL DISEASES

## (A TEXT-BOOK OF):

### Having Special Reference to the Pathological Aspects of Insanity.

BY

W. BEVAN LEWIS, L.R.C.P. Lond., M.R.C.S. Eng.,
Medical Director of the West Riding Asylum, Wakefield.

*In Large 8vo, with Eighteen Lithographic Plates and Illustrations in the Text. Handsome Cloth, 28s.*

---

#### OPINIONS OF THE PRESS.

"Will take the HIGHEST RANK as a Text-Book of Mental Diseases."—*British Medical Journal.*

"Without doubt the BEST BOOK in English of its kind. . . . The chapter on Epileptic Insanity and that on the Pathology of Insanity are perfect, and show a power of work and originality of thought which are admirable."—*Journal of Mental Science.*

"The work, all through, is the outcome of original observation and research."—*Mind.*

"A SPLENDID ADDITION to the literature of mental diseases. . . . The anatomical and histological section is ADMIRABLY DONE. . . . The clinical section is concise and tersely written. It is, however, to the pathological section that the work owes its chief merit. As a STANDARD WORK on the pathology of mental diseases this work should occupy a prominent place in the library of every alienist physician."—*Dublin Medical Journal.*

"Affords a fulness of information which it would be difficult to find in any other treatise in the English language."—*Edin. Medical Journal.*

"We record our conviction that the book is the best and most complete treatise upon the pathological aspect of the subject with which we are familiar. . . . An ABSOLUTELY INDISPENSABLE addition to every alienist's and neurologist's library."—*The Alienist and Neurologist.*

"It would be quite impossible to say too much in praise of the ILLUSTRATIONS."—*American Journal of Insanity.*

"The Section on Pathological Anatomy is UNRIVALLED in English literature."—*Bulletin de la Soc. Méd. Mentale de Belgique.*

---

LONDON: EXETER STREET, STRAND.

10 CHARLES GRIFFIN & COMPANY'S

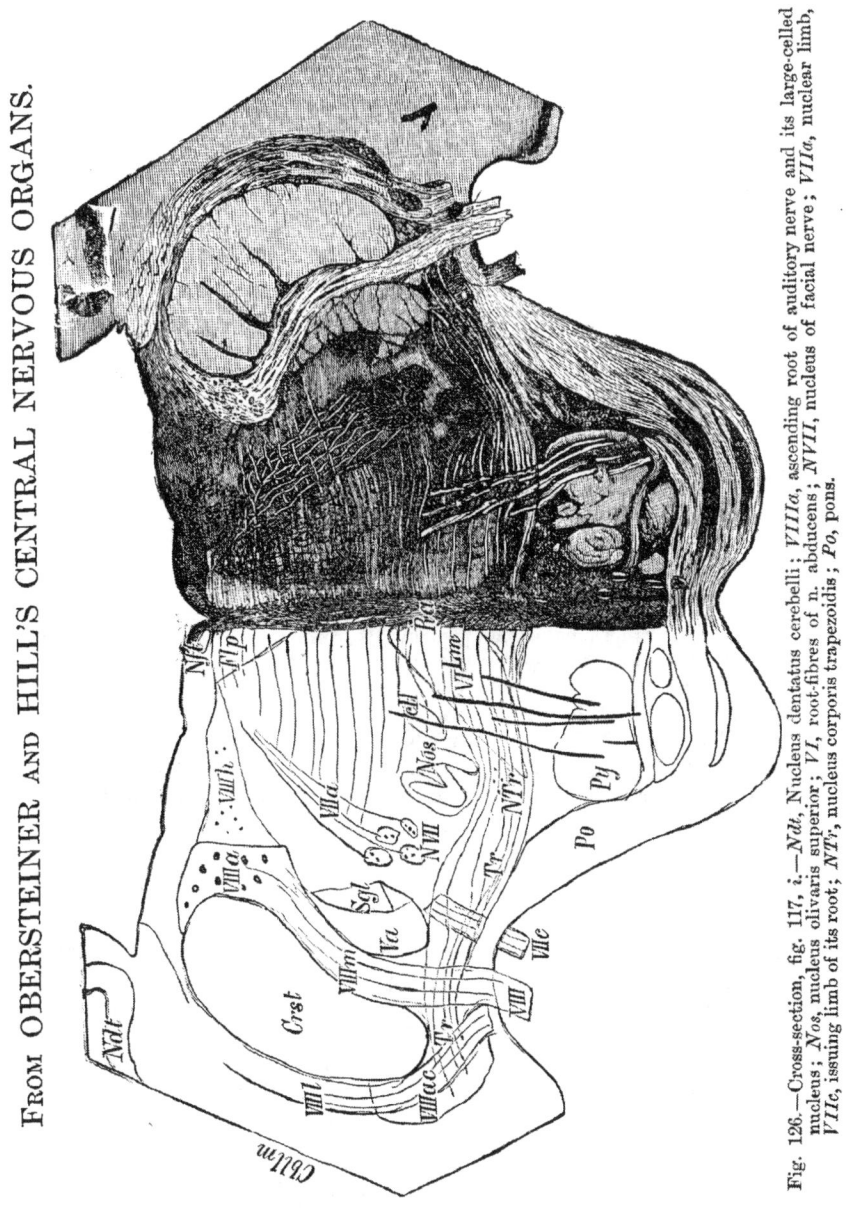

FROM OBERSTEINER AND HILL'S CENTRAL NERVOUS ORGANS.

Fig. 126.—Cross-section, fig. 117, i.—*Ndt*, Nucleus dentatus cerebelli; *VIIIa*, ascending root of auditory nerve and its large-celled nucleus; *Nos*, nucleus olivaris superior; *VI*, root-fibres of n. abducens; *NVII*, nucleus of facial nerve; *VIIa*, nuclear limb, *VIIc*, issuing limb of its root; *NTr*, nucleus corporis trapezoidis; *Po*, pons.

LONDON: EXETER STREET, STRAND.

By Drs. OBERSTEINER and HILL.

# THE
# CENTRAL NERVOUS ORGANS:

## A GUIDE TO THE STUDY OF THEIR STRUCTURE IN HEALTH AND DISEASE.

BY

PROFESSOR H. OBERSTEINER,
University of Vienna.

*TRANSLATED, WITH ANNOTATIONS AND ADDITIONS,*

BY

ALEX HILL, M.A., M.D.,
Master of Downing College, Cambridge.

*With all the Original Illustrations. Large 8vo, Handsome Cloth, 25s.*

*\*\** The Publishers have the pleasure to announce that to the English version of this important Treatise, numerous original ADDITIONS and a GLOSSARY of the subject have been contributed by the EDITOR, whose admirable work in this department of research is so well known. These Additions greatly increase the value of the book to students.

Special attention is also directed to the ILLUSTRATIONS. Many of these are on a plan peculiarly helpful to the student—the one-half being in outline, the other filled in. (See p. 10.)

### OPINIONS OF THE PRESS.

" Dr. Hill has enriched the work with many notes of his own. . . . Dr. Hill's translation is most accurate, the English is excellent, and the book is very readable. . . . Dr. Obersteiner's work is admirable. He has a marvellous power of marshalling together a large number of facts, all bearing on an extremely intricate subject, into a harmonious, clear, consecutive whole. . . . INVALUABLE as a text-book."—*British Medical Journal.*

" A MOST VALUABLE CONTRIBUTION to the Study of the Anatomy and Pathology of the Nervous System. We cannot speak too highly of the ability and skill which Prof. Obersteiner has brought to bear on this most difficult subject, and of the way in which the whole work is illustrated."—*Brain.*

" The FULLEST and MOST ACCURATE EXPOSITION now attainable of the results of anatomical inquiry. The Translation is done by one who is himself a Master of Anatomy, able not only to follow his author, but also to supplement him with the results of independent research. Dr. Hill's additions add materially to the value of the original. The work is specially commended to all students of mental science. . . . The illustrative figures are of particular excellence and admirably instructive."—*Mind.*

LONDON: EXETER STREET, STRAND.

By Prof. von JAKSCH.

## CLINICAL DIAGNOSIS:

THE

Bacteriological, Chemical, and Microscopical Evidence of Disease.

By Prof. R. v. JAKSCH,
Of the University of Prague.

Translated from the Third German Edition
and Enlarged

By JAMES CAGNEY, M.A., M.D.,
Phys. to the Hosp. for Epilepsy and Paralysis, Regent's Park.

With Additional Illustrations, many Coloured.

*In large 8vo, Handsome Cloth.*

**SECOND ENGLISH EDITION.**

### GENERAL CONTENTS.

The Blood — The Buccal Secretion — The Nasal Secretion — The Sputum — The Gastric Juice and Vomit — The Fæces — Examination of the Urine — Investigation of Exudations, Transudations, and Cystic Fluids — The Secretions of the Genital Organs — Methods of Bacteriological Research — Bibliography.

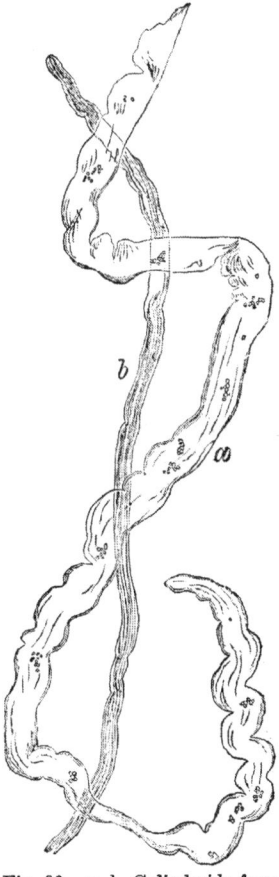

Fig. 86.—$a, b$. Cylindroids from the urine in congested kidney.

### OPINIONS OF THE PRESS.

"A striking example of the application of the Methods of Science to Medicine. . . . Stands almost alone amongst books of this class in the width of its range, the thoroughness of its exposition, and the clearness of its style. Its value has been recognised in many countries. . . . The translator has done his share of the work in an admirable manner. . . . A *standard work* . . . as trustworthy as it is scientific. . . . The numerous and artistic illustrations form a great feature of the work, and have been *admirably reproduced.*"—*Lancet.*

"Supplies a real want. . . . Rich in information, accurate in detail, lucid in style."—*Brit. Med. Journal.*

"Possesses a high value. . . . There is a most admirable bibliography."—*Edinburgh Med. Review.*

"A new and valuable work . . . worthy of a first place as a text-book. . . . Of great value both to medical practitioners and medical students."—*Journal of American Med. Association, Chicago.*

LONDON: EXETER STREET, STRAND.

*Now Ready. In Large 8vo, with Illustrations in the Text and 13 Folding-Plates, 28s.*

# DISEASES OF THE HEART AND THORACIC AORTA

## (THE DIAGNOSIS OF).

BY

### A. ERNEST SANSOM, M.D., F.R.C.P.,

Physician to the London Hospital; Consulting Physician, North-Eastern Hospital for Children; Examiner in Medicine, Royal College of Physicians (Conjoint Board for England), and University of Durham; Lecturer on Medical Jurisprudence and Public Health, London Hospital Medical College, &c.

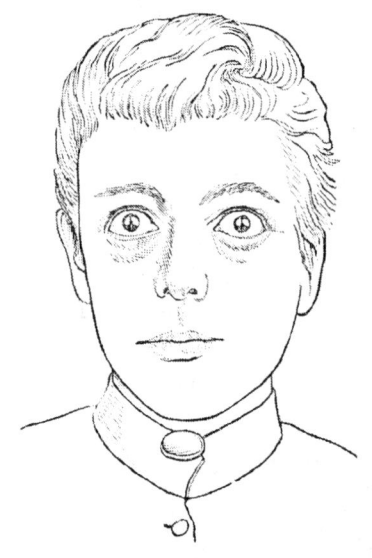

(From Chap. ix.—" The Observed Signs of Neuro-Cardiac Disease.')

FIG. 6.—Case of Grave's disease with well-marked retraction of upper eyelid (Stellway's sign). There was very little projection of the eyeball, though prominence appeared to be extreme. Patient aged twenty-four. (*From a photograph.*)

LONDON: EXETER STREET, STRAND.

## By SIR DYCE DUCKWORTH, M.D., F.R.C.P.

# GOUT

### (A TREATISE ON).

BY

### SIR DYCE DUCKWORTH,

M.D. Edin., LL.D., Hon. Physician to H.R.H. the Prince of Wales, Physician to, and Lecturer on Clinical Medicine in, St. Bartholomew's Hospital.

*In Large 8vo. With Chromo-Lithograph, Folding Plate, and Illustrations in the Text. Handsome Cloth, 25s.*

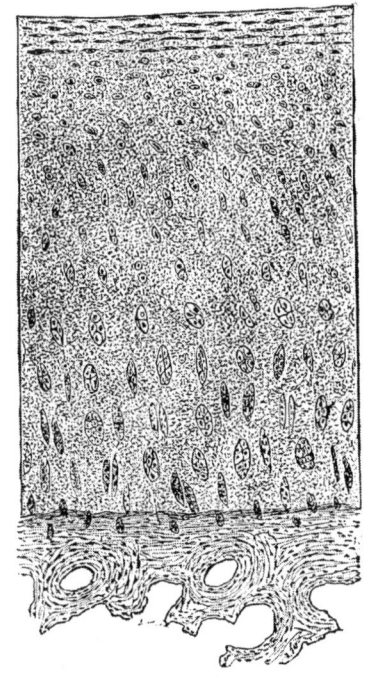

Fig. 1.—Human Articular Cartilage, from head of a metatarsal bone (Normal).

\*\*\* This work is the result of the special opportunities which London Practice affords as, probably, the largest field of observation for the study of Gout. It is based on the experience derived from both Hospital and Private Practice, each of which furnishes distinctive phases of the disease.

### OPINIONS OF THE PRESS.

"Thoroughly practical and highly philosophical. The practitioner will find in its pages an ENORMOUS AMOUNT OF INFORMATION. . . . A monument of clinical observation, of extensive reading, and of close and careful reasoning."—*Practitioner.*

"All the known facts of Gout are carefully passed in review. . . . We have chapters upon the clinical varieties of Gout, and the affections of special organs and textures. . . . A very VALUABLE STOREHOUSE of material on the nature, varieties, and treatment of Gout."—*Lancet.*

"A very well written, clear, and THOROUGHLY SATISFACTORY EPITOMÉ of our present knowledge upon the subject of Gout."—*Philadelphia Therapeutic Gazette.*

"Impartial in its discussion of theories, full and accurate in its description of clinical facts, and a TRUSTWORTHY GUIDE TO TREATMENT."—*British Medical Journal.*

LONDON: EXETER STREET, STRAND.

By A. E. GARROD, M.D., F.R.C.P.

# Rheumatism

AND

# Rheumatoid Arthritis

(A TREATISE ON).

BY

ARCHIBALD E. GARROD,

M.A., M.D. Oxon., F.R.C.P., Assistant-Physician to the West London Hospital, &c.

*In Large 8vo, with Charts and Illustrations. Handsome Cloth, 21s.*

---

*\*\** The author's aim is to give a consistent picture of Rheumatism as a systemic disease presenting one definite set of phenomena, the result, it is believed, of one single and specific morbid process.

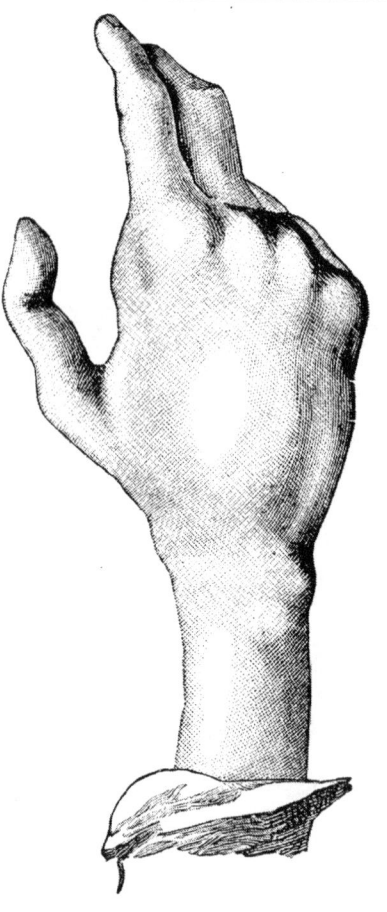

Fig. 1.—Gangliform Swelling on the Dorsum on the Hand of a Child aged Eight.

---

### OPINIONS OF THE PRESS.

"The wide subject of the etiology of rheumatism is *carefully treated*. . . . The discussion of etiology is completed by a *full analysis* of the conditions which determine individual attacks. . . . Dr. Garrod is to be congratulated on having put before the profession SO CLEAR AND COHERENT an account of the rheumatic diseases. The style of his work is eminently readable."—*Lancet.*

"Well written and reliable. . . . We have little doubt that this monograph *will take rank with the best treatises* on special medical subjects in the English language."—*Dublin Medical Journal.*

"An EXCELLENT ACCOUNT of the clinical features of the diseases in question. The chapters on treatment are THOROUGHLY PRACTICAL."—*Manchester Medical Chronicle.*

---

LONDON: EXETER STREET, STRAND.

By Drs MEYER and FERGUS

*Now Ready, with Three Coloured Plates and numerous Illustrations.*
*Royal 8vo, Handsome Cloth, 25s*

# DISEASES OF THE EYE

(A PRACTICAL TREATISE ON),

By EDOUARD MEYER,

*Prof. à l'Ecole Pratique de la Faculté de Médecine de Paris,*
*Chev. of the Leg. of Honour, &c.*

---

Translated from the Third French Edition, with Additions as
contained in the Fourth German Edition,
By F. FERGUS, M.B., Ophthalmic Surgeon, Glasgow Infirmary.

---

The particular features that will most commend Dr Meyer's work to English readers are—its CONCISENESS, its HELPFULNESS in explanation, and the PRACTICALITY of its directions. The best proof of its worth may, perhaps, be seen in the fact that it has now gone through *three* French and *four* German editions, and has been translated into most European languages—Italian, Spanish, Russian, and Polish—and even into Japanese.

---

### Opinions of the Press.

"A GOOD TRANSLATION OF A GOOD BOOK . . . A SOUND GUIDE in the diagnosis and treatment of the various diseases of the eye that are likely to fall under the notice of the general Practitioner. The Paper, Type, and Chromo-Lithographs are all that could be desired . . We know of no work in which the DISEASES and DEFORMITIES of the LIDS are more fully treated. Numerous figures illustrate almost every defect remediable by operation."—*Practitioner*

"A VERY TRUSTWORTHY GUIDE in all respects . . THOROUGHLY PRACTICAL. Excellently translated, and very well got up. Type, Woodcuts, and Chromo Lithographs are alike excellent."—*Lancet*

"Any Student will find this work of GREAT VALUE . The chapter on Cataract is excellent . . The Illustrations describing the various plastic operations are specially helpful."—*Brit Med Journal.*

"An EXCELLENT TRANSLATION of a standard French Text Book. We can cordially recommend Dr Meyer's work. It is essentially a PRACTICAL WORK. The Publishers have done their part in the TASTEFUL and SUBSTANTIAL MANNER CHARACTERISTIC OF THEIR MEDICAL PUBLICATIONS. The Type and the Illustrations are in marked contrast to most medical works."—*Ophthalmic Review*

---

LONDON. EXETER STREET, STRAND.

### By PROFESSOR T M'CALL ANDERSON, M D

*Now ready, with two Coloured Lithographs, Steel Plate, and numerous Woodcuts.
Royal 8vo, Handsome Cloth, 25s*

# DISEASES OF THE SKIN

(A TREATISE ON),

WITH SPECIAL REFERENCE TO DIAGNOSIS AND TREATMENT, INCLUDING AN ANALYSIS OF 11,000 CONSECUTIVE CASES.

### By T M'CALL ANDERSON, MD,
*Professor of Clinical Medicine, University of Glasgow*

The want of a manual embodying the most recent advances in the treatment of cutaneous affections has made itself much felt of late years PROFESSOR M'CALL ANDERSON'S Treatise, therefore, affording, as it does, a complete *résumé* of the best modern practice, will be doubly welcome It is written—not from the standpoint of the University Professor—but from that of one who, during upwards of a quarter of a century, has been actively engaged both in private and in hospital practice, with unusual opportunities for studying this class of disease, hence the PRACTICAL and CLINICAL directions given are of great value

Speaking of the practical aspects of Dr ANDERSON'S work, the *British Medical Journal* says —"Skin diseases are, as is well known, obstinate and troublesome, and the knowledge that there are ADDITIONAL RESOURCES besides those in ordinary use will give confidence to many a puzzled medical man, and enable him to encourage a doubting patient ALMOST ANY PAGE MIGHT BE USED TO ILLUSTRATE THE FULNESS OF THE WORK IN THIS RESPECT. . . . The chapter on Eczema, that universal and most troublesome ailment, describes in a comprehensive spirit, and with the greatest accuracy of detail, the various methods of treatment Dr Anderson writes with the authority of a man who has tried the remedies which he discusses, and the information and advice which he gives cannot fail to prove extremely valuable."

### Opinions of the Press.

"Beyond doubt, the MOST IMPORTANT WORK on Skin Diseases that has appeared in England for many years Conspicuous for the AMOUNT AND EXCELLENCE of the CLINICAL AND PRACTICAL information which it contains "—*British Medical Journal*

"Professor M'Call Anderson has produced a work likely to prove *very acceptable* to the busy practitioner The sections on treatment are very full For example, ECZEMA has 110 pages given to it, and 73 of these pages are devoted to treatment "—*Lancet*

### LONDON EXETER STREET, STRAND.

By Prof. A. C. HADDON.

# EMBRYOLOGY

(AN INTRODUCTION TO THE STUDY OF).

BY

ALFRED C. HADDON, M.A., M.R.I.A.,

Professor of Zoology, Royal College of Science, Dublin

*In Large 8vo, with 190 Illustrations. Handsome Cloth, 18s.*

### OPINIONS OF THE PRESS.

"WELL and CLEARLY WRITTEN . . . Many important discoveries or theories are described, which are necessarily absent from Balfour's work."—*Nature*

"Dr Haddon has written the BEST of the three modern English works on the subject."—*Dublin Medical Journal*

"The later chapters of Prof. Haddon's work ably demonstrate the development of organs from the mesoblast and epiblast."—*Brit Med Journal.*

"The zoological student, to whom as a text book it is invaluable, will find it THOROUGH, TRUSTWORTHY, AND SOUND in all its teachings, and well up to date .. We specially commend the book to our readers."—*Nat Monthly*

# THE JOURNAL

OF

# ANATOMY & PHYSIOLOGY:

## NORMAL AND PATHOLOGICAL.

CONDUCTED BY

SIR GEORGE MURRAY HUMPHRY, M D., LL D, F.R.S.,

Professor of Surgery, Late Professor of Anatomy in the University of Cambridge,

SIR WILLIAM TURNER, M B., LL D., D C L, F.R S,

Prof of Anatomy in the University of Edinburgh,

AND

J. G M'KENDRICK, M.D., F.R.S,

Prof of the Institutes of Medicine in the University of Glasgow

*Published Quarterly, Price 6s.   Annual Subscription, 20s ; Post Free, 21s.*
*Subscriptions payable in advance*

LONDON   EXETER STREET, STRAND.

### By W. THORBURN, F.R.C.S. Eng.

# THE SURGERY OF THE SPINAL CORD

(A Contribution to the Study of):

By WILLIAM THORBURN, B.S., B.Sc., M.D. Lond., F.R.C.S. Eng.,

Assistant Surgeon to the Manchester Royal Infirmary.

*In Large 8vo, with Illustrations and Tables. Handsome Cloth, 12s. 6d.*

"We congratulate Dr. Thorburn on his MASTERLY MONOGRAPH."—*Saturday Review.*
"A MOST VALUABLE CONTRIBUTION to the literature of a field of surgery which, although but recently brought under cultivation, is already yielding such brilliant results."—*Birmingham Medical Review.*
"Really the FULLEST RECORD we have of Spinal Surgery. . . . The work marks an important advance in modern Surgery."
"A most THOROUGH and EXHAUSTIVE work on Spinal Surgery."—*Bristol Medical Journal.*
"A MOST VALUABLE contribution both to Physiology and Surgery."—*Ophthalmic Review.*
"A VERY VALUABLE contribution to practical neurology. . . . This book is an excellent, clear, concise monograph."—*Philadelphia Therapeutic Gazette.*

---

### By J. KNOWSLEY THORNTON, M.B., M.C.

# THE SURGERY OF THE KIDNEYS,

Being the Harveian Lectures, 1889.

By J. KNOWSLEY THORNTON, M.B., M.C.,

Surgeon to the Samaritan Free Hospital, &c.

*In Demy 8vo, with Illustrations. Handsome Cloth, 5s.*

"The name and experience of the author confer on the Lectures the stamp of authority."—*British Medical Journal.*
"These Lectures are an exposition by the hand of an EXPERT of what is known and has been done, up to the present, in the Surgery of the Kidneys."—*Edinburgh Medical Journal.*
"The book will necessarily be widely read, and will have an important influence on the progress of this domain of Surgery."—*University Medical Magazine.*

---

### By H. W. PAGE, F.R.C.S.

# RAILWAY INJURIES:

*With Special Reference to those of the Back and Nervous System, in their Medico-Legal and Clinical Aspects.*

By HERBERT W. PAGE, M.A., M.C. (Cantab), F.R.C.S. (Eng.),

Surgeon to St. Mary's Hospital, Dean, St. Mary's Hospital Medical School, &c.

*In Large 8vo. Handsome Cloth, 6s.*

"A work INVALUABLE to those who have many railway cases under their care pending litigation. . . . A book which every lawyer as well as doctor should have on his shelves."—*British Medical Journal.*
"Deserves the most careful study. . . . A book which every medical man would do well to read before he presents himself for examination and cross-examination in the witness-box on a railway case."—*Dublin Med. Journal.*
"This book will undoubtedly be of great use to Lawyers."—*Law Times.*

---

LONDON: EXETER STREET, STRAND.

By Sir WILLIAM AITKEN, M.D. Edin., F.R.S.,

Late Professor of Pathology in the Army Medical School Examiner in Medicine for the Military Medical Services of the Queen, Fellow of the Sanitary Institute of Great Britain, Corresponding Member of the Royal Imperial Society of Physicians of Vienna, and of the Society of Medicine and Natural History of Dresden.

SEVENTH EDITION.

## THE SCIENCE AND PRACTICE OF MEDICINE.

*In Two Volumes, Royal 8vo, Cloth, 42s*

### OPINIONS OF THE PRESS.

"The work is an admirable one, and adapted to the requirements of the Student, Professor, and Practitioner of Medicine. The reader will find a large amount of information not to be met with in other books, epitomised for him in this. We know of no work that contains so much, or such full and varied information on all subjects connected with the Science and Practice of Medicine."—*Lancet*

"The STANDARD TEXT-BOOK in the English Language . . . There is, perhaps, no work more indispensable for the Practitioner and Student."—*Edin. Medical Journal.*

## OUTLINES OF THE SCIENCE AND PRACTICE OF MEDICINE.

A TEXT-BOOK FOR STUDENTS.

Second Edition. Crown 8vo, 12s 6d.

"Students preparing for examinations will hail it as a perfect godsend for its conciseness."—*Athenæum.*

## PRACTICAL SANITATION:

### A HANDBOOK FOR SANITARY INSPECTORS AND OTHERS INTERESTED IN SANITATION.

By GEORGE REID, MD, DPH,

Fellow of the Sanitary Institute of Great Britain, and Medical Officer, Staffordshire County Council

*WITH AN APPENDIX ON SANITARY LAW*

By HERBERT MANLEY, M.A, MB, DPH,

Medical Officer of Health for the County Borough of West Bromwich

*In Large Crown 8vo, with Illustrations. Price 6s*

### GENERAL CONTENTS.

Introduction—Water Supply: Drinking Water, Pollution of Water—Ventilation and Warming—Principles of Sewage Removal—Details of Drainage, Refuse Removal and Disposal—Sanitary and Insanitary Work and Appliances—Details of Plumbers' Work—House Construction—Infection and Disinfection—Food, Inspection of, Characteristics of Good Meat, Meat, Milk, Fish, &c, unfit for Human Food—Appendix, Sanitary Law, Model Bye Laws, &c

"A VERY USEFUL HANDBOOK with a very useful Appendix. We recommend it not only to SANITARY INSPECTORS, but to ALL interested in Sanitary matters."—*Sanitary Record*

LONDON EXETER STREET, STRAND.

# SEWAGE DISPOSAL WORKS:

A GUIDE TO THE

## Construction of Works for the Prevention of the Pollution by Sewage of Rivers and Estuaries.

BY

W. SANTO CRIMP, MEM INST C E, F G S.,

Assistant-Engineer, London County Council

With Tables, Illustrations in the Text, and 33 Lithographic Plates
Medium 8vo. Handsome Cloth, 25s

### PART I.—INTRODUCTORY

Introduction
Details of River Pollutions and Recommendations of Various Commissions
Hourly and Daily Flow of Sewage
The Pail System as Affecting Sewage
The Separation of Rain-water from the Sewage Proper

Settling Tanks
Chemical Processes
The Disposal of Sewage-sludge
The Preparation of Land for Sewage Disposal
Table of Sewage Farm Management

### PART II.—SEWAGE DISPOSAL WORKS IN OPERATION—THEIR CONSTRUCTION, MAINTENANCE, AND COST.

*Illustrated by Plates showing the General Plan and Arrangement adopted in each District*

1. Doncaster Irrigation Farm
2. Beddington Irrigation Farm, Borough of Croydon
3. Bedford Sewage Farm Irrigation
4. Dewsbury and Hitchin Intermittent Filtration
5. Merton, Croydon Rural Sanitary Authority
6. Swanwick, Derbyshire
7. The Ealing Sewage Works
8. Chiswick
9. Kingston on Thames, A B C. Process
10. Salford Sewage Works
11. Bradford, Precipitation
12. New Malden, Chemical Treatment and Small Filters.
13. Friern Barnet
14. Acton, Ferozone and Polarite Process.
15. Ilford, Chadwell, and Dagenham Sewage Disposal Works.
16. Coventry
17. Wimbledon
18. Birmingham
19. Newhaven
20. Portsmouth
21. Sewage Precipitation Works, Dortmund (Germany)
22. Treatment of Sewage by Electrolysis.

"All persons interested in Sanitary Science owe a debt of gratitude to Mr Crimp . . . His work will be especially useful to SANITARY AUTHORITIES and their advisers EMINENTLY PRACTICAL AND USEFUL . . . gives plans and descriptions of MANY OF THE MOST IMPORTANT SEWAGE WORKS of England with very valuable information as to the cost of construction and working of each The carefully-prepared drawings permit of an easy comparison between the different systems '—*Lancet*

"Probably the MOST COMPLETE AND BEST TREATISE on the subject which has appeared in our language . . . Will prove of the greatest use to all who have the problem of Sewage Disposal to face . . . The general construction, drawings, and type are all excellent "—*Edinburgh Medical Journal*

LONDON. EXETER STREET, STRAND.

By WILLIAM STIRLING, M.D., Sc.D.,
Professor in the Victoria University, Brackenbury Professor of Physiology and Histology in the Owens College, Manchester; and Examiner in the University of Oxford.

SECOND EDITION. *In Extra Crown 8vo, with 234 Illustrations. Cloth, 9s.*

# PRACTICAL PHYSIOLOGY (Outlines of):
## A Manual for the Physiological Laboratory,
INCLUDING
CHEMICAL AND EXPERIMENTAL PHYSIOLOGY, WITH REFERENCE TO PRACTICAL MEDICINE.

**Part I.—Chemical Physiology.**
**Part II.—Experimental Physiology.**

*\*\** *In the Second Edition, revised and enlarged, the number of Illustrations has been increased from 142 to 234.*

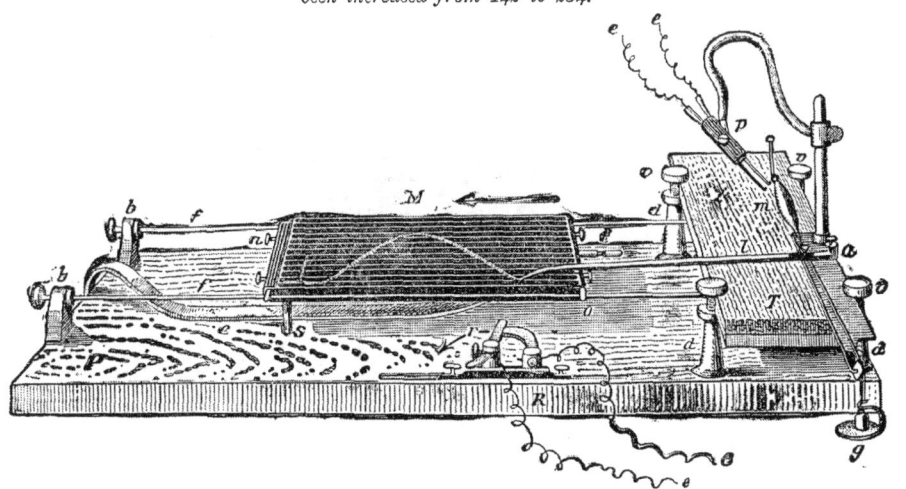

Fig. 118.—Horizontal Myograph of Frédéricq. *M*, Glass plate, moving on the guides *f, f*; *l*, Lever; *m*, Muscle; *p, e, e*, Electrodes; *T*, Cork plate; *a*, Counterpoise to lever; *R*, Key in primary circuit.

### OPINIONS OF THE PRESS.

" This valuable little manual. . . . The GENERAL CONCEPTION of the book is EXCELLENT; the arrangement of the exercises is all that can be desired; the descriptions of experiments are CLEAR, CONCISE, and to the point."—*British Medical Journal.*

" The Second Edition has been thoroughly worked up to date, and a large number of well-executed woodcuts added. It may be recommended to the student as one of the BEST MANUALS he can possess as a guide and companion in his Physiological Work, and as one that will usefully supplement the course given by a Physiological Teacher."—*Lancet.*

" The student is enabled to perform for himself most of the experiments usually shown in a systematic course of lectures on physiology, and the practice thus obtained must prove IN-VALUABLE. . . . May be confidently recommended as a guide to the student of physiology, and, we doubt not, will also find its way into the hands of many of our scientific and medical practitioners."—*Glasgow Medical Journal.*

" An exceedingly convenient Handbook of Experimental Physiology."—*Birmingham Medical Review.*

LONDON: EXETER STREET, STRAND.

## Companion Volume by Prof. Stirling.

SECOND EDITION. In Extra Crown 8vo, with 344 Illustrations. Cloth, 12s. 6d.

# PRACTICAL HISTOLOGY (Outlines of):
## A MANUAL FOR STUDENTS.

*⁎* Dr. Stirling's "Outlines of Practical Histology" is a compact Handbook for students, providing a COMPLETE LABORATORY COURSE, in which almost every exercise is accompanied by a drawing. Very many of the Illustrations have been prepared expressly for the work.

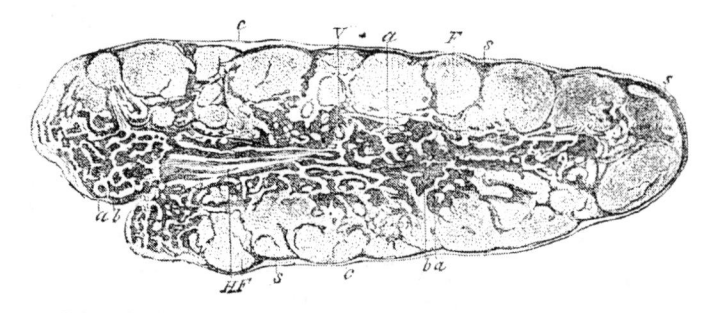

Fig. 200.—L.S., Cervical Ganglion of Dog.  c, Capsule ; s, Lymph sinus ; F, Follicle ; a, Medullary cord ; b, Lymph paths of the medulla ; V, Section of a blood-vessel ; HF, Fibrous part of the hilum, × 10.

---

### OPINIONS OF THE PRESS.

"The general plan of the work is ADMIRABLE. . . . It is very evident that the suggestions given are the outcome of a PROLONGED EXPERIENCE in teaching Practical Histology, combined with a REMARKABLE JUDGMENT in the selection of METHODS. . . . Merits the highest praise for the ILLUSTRATIONS, which are at once clear and faithful."—*British Medical Journal.*

"We can confidently recommend this small but CONCISELY-WRITTEN and ADMIRABLY ILLUSTRATED work to students. They will find it to be a VERY USEFUL and RELIABLE GUIDE in the laboratory, or in their own room. All the principal METHODS of preparing tissues for section are given, with such precise directions that little or no difficulty can be felt in following them in their most minute details. . . . The volume proceeds from a MASTER in his craft."—*Lancet.*

"We have no doubt the OUTLINES will meet with most favourable acceptance among workers in Histology."—*Glasgow Medical Journal.*

---

LONDON: EXETER STREET, STRAND.

### By Dr. BURNET, M.R.C.P.

SECOND EDITION.   *Handsome Cloth*, 4s.

# FOODS AND DIETARIES:
## A Manual of Clinical Dietetics.

BY

### R. W. BURNET, M.D.,

Member of the Royal College of Physicians of London, Physician to the
Great Northern Central Hospital, &c.

---

In Dr Burnet's "Foods and Dietaries," the *rationale* of the special dietary recommended is briefly stated at the beginning of each section. To give definiteness to the directions, the HOURS of taking food and the QUANTITIES to be given at each time are stated, as well as the KINDS of food most suitable. In many instances there is also added a list of foods and dishes that are UNSUITABLE to the special case. References are given, where required, to the RECIPES for Invalid Cookery, which form the Appendix, and which have all been very carefully selected.

---

### GENERAL CONTENTS.

DIET in Diseases of the Stomach, Intestinal Tract, Liver, Lungs and Pleuræ, Heart, Kidneys, &c., in Diabetes, Scurvy, Anæmia, Scrofula, Gout (Chronic and Acute), Obesity, Acute and Chronic Rheumatism, Alcoholism, Nervous Disorders, Diathetic Diseases, Diseases of Children, with a Section on Prepared and Predigested Foods, and Appendix on Invalid Cookery.

---

"The directions given are UNIFORMLY JUDICIOUS and characterised by good sense . . . May be confidently taken as a RELIABLE GUIDE in the art of feeding the sick."—*Brit. Med. Journal.*

"To all who have much to do with Invalids, Dr Burnet's book will be of great use. . . . It will be found all the more valuable in that it deals with BROAD and ACCEPTED VIEWS. There are large classes of disease which, if not caused solely by errors of diet, have a principal cause in such errors, and can only be removed by an intelligent apprehension of their relation to such. Gout, Scurvy, Rickets, and Alcoholism are instances in point, and they are all TREATED with ADMIRABLE SENSE and JUDGMENT by Dr Burnet. He shows a desire to allow as much range and VARIETY as possible. The careful study of such books as this will very much help the Practitioner in the Treatment of cases, and powerfully aid the action of remedies."—*Lancet.*

"Dr Burnet's work is intended to meet a want which is evident to all those who have to do with nursing the sick. The plan is METHODICAL, SIMPLE, and PRACTICAL. . . . Dr Burnet takes the important diseases *seriatim* . . . and gives a Time table of Diet, with Bill of Fare for each meal, quantities, and beverages. An appendix of cookery for invalids is given, which will help the nurse when at her wits' end for a change of diet to meet the urgency of the moment, or tempt the capricious appetite of the patient."—*Glasgow Herald.*

LONDON: EXETER STREET, STRAND.

## By Drs. CAIRD and CATHCART.

FOURTH EDITION, Revised. Pocket-Size, Leather, 8s. 6d.
With very Numerous Illustrations.

# A SURGICAL HANDBOOK,

FOR

Practitioners, Students, House-Surgeons, and Dressers.

BY

F. M. CAIRD, M.B., F.R.C.S.,

AND

C. W. CATHCART, M.B., F.R.C.S.,
Assistant-Surgeons, Royal Infirmary, Edinburgh.

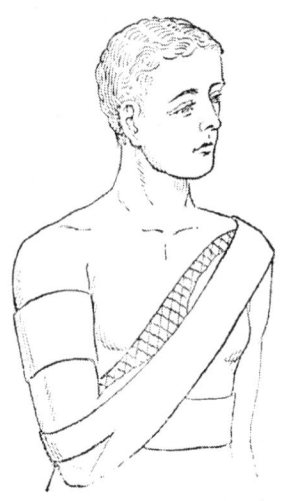

Fig. 85.—Sayre's Treatment for Fracture of Clavicle, Front View.

### GENERAL CONTENTS.

Case-Taking—Treatment of Patients before and after Operation—Anæsthetics: General and Local—Antiseptics and Wound-Treatment—Arrest of Hæmorrhage—Shock and Wound-Fever—Emergency Cases—Tracheotomy: Minor Surgical Operations—Bandaging—Fractures—Dislocations, Sprains, and Bruises—Extemporary Appliances and Civil Ambulance Work—Massage—Surgical Applications of Electricity—Joint-Fixation and Fixed Apparatus—The Urine—The Syphon and its Uses—Trusses and Artificial Limbs—Plaster-Casting—Post-Mortem Examination—Appendix: Various Useful Hints, Suggestions, and Recipes.

### OPINIONS OF THE PRESS.

"THOROUGHLY PRACTICAL AND TRUSTWORTHY, well up to date, CLEAR, ACCURATE, AND SUCCINCT. The book is handy, and very well got up."—*Lancet.*

"ADMIRABLY ARRANGED. The best practical little work we have seen. The matter is as good as the manner."—*Edinburgh Medical Journal.*

"Will prove of real service to the Practitioner who wants a useful *vade mecum.*"—*British Medical Journal.*

"Fulfils admirably the objects with which it has been written."—*Glasgow Medical Journal.*

"THIS EXCELLENT LITTLE WORK. Clear, concise, and very readable. Gives attention to important details, often omitted, but ABSOLUTELY NECESSARY TO SUCCESS."—*Athenæum.*

"A dainty volume."—*Manchester Medical Chronicle.*

LONDON: EXETER STREET, STRAND.

## WORKS by A. WYNTER BLYTH, M.R.C.S., F.C.S.,

Public Analyst for the County of Devon, and Medical Officer of Health for St Marylebone

*NEW EDITION   Revised and partly Rewritten*

### FOODS: THEIR COMPOSITION AND ANALYSIS.

*In Crown 8vo, Cloth, with Elaborate Tables Folding Litho-Plate, and Photographic Frontispiece*
*THIRD EDITION   Price 10s*

GENERAL CONTENTS

History of Adulteration—Legislation, Past and Present—Apparatus useful to the Food-Analyst—"Ash"—Sugar—Confectionery—Honey—Treacle—Jams and Preserved Fruits—Starches—Wheaten-Flour—Bread—Oats—Barley—Rye—Rice—Maize—Millet—Potato—Peas—Chinese Peas—Lentils—Beans—MILK—Cream—Butter—Cheese—Tea—Coffee—Cocoa and Chocolate—Alcohol—Brandy—Rum—Whisky—Gin—Arrack—Liqueurs—Beer—Wine—Vinegar—Lemon and Lime Juice—Mustard—Pepper—Sweet and Bitter Almond—Annatto—Olive Oil—Water. *Appendix*   Text of English and American Adulteration Acts

"Thoroughly practical .    Should be in the hands of every medical practitioner"—*Lancet*

"An admirable digest of the most recent state of knowledge    Interesting even to lay readers"—*Chemical News*

"STANDS UNRIVALLED for completeness of information"—*Sanitary Record*

\*\*\* The new Edition contains many Notable Additions, especially on the subject of **MILK and its relation to FEVER EPIDEMICS, the PURITY of WATER-SUPPLY, the New MARGARINE ACT, &c &c**

### POISONS: THEIR EFFECTS AND DETECTION.

*With Tables and Illustrations   Price 16s*
GENERAL CONTENTS

Historical Introduction—Statistics—General Methods of Procedure—Life Tests—Special Apparatus—Classification   I.—ORGANIC POISONS (*a*) Sulphuric, Hydrochloric, and Nitric Acids, Potash, Soda, Ammonia, &c ; (*b*) Petroleum, Benzene Camphor, Alcohols, Chloroform, Carbolic Acid, Prussic Acid, Phosphorus, &c , (*c*) Hemlock, Nicotine, Opium, Strychnine, Aconite, Atropine, Digitalis, &c ; (*d*) Poisons derived from Animal Substances, (*e*) The Oxalic Acid Group   II—INORGANIC POISONS. Arsenic, Antimony, Lead, Copper, Bismuth, Silver, Mercury, Zinc, Nickel, Iron, Chromium, Alkaline Earths, &c   *Appendix* (A) Examination of Blood and Blood-Spots, (B) Hints for Emergencies

"One of the best and most comprehensive works on the subject"—*Saturday Review*

"A sound and Practical Manual of Toxicology, which cannot be too warmly recommended   One of its chief merits is that it discusses substances which have been overlooked"—*Chemical News*

### HYGIÈNE AND PUBLIC HEALTH (A Dictionary of):

Embracing the following subjects —

I —SANITARY CHEMISTRY   the Composition and Dietetic Value of Foods, with the Detection of Adulterations

II —SANITARY ENGINEERING   Sewage, Drainage, Storage of Water, Ventilation, Warming, &c

III —SANITARY LEGISLATION   the whole of the PUBLIC HEALTH ACT, together with portions of other Sanitary Statutes, in a form admitting of easy and rapid Reference

IV —EPIDEMIC AND EPIZOOTIC DISEASES   their History and Propagation, with the Measures for Disinfection

V —HYGIÈNE—MILITARY, NAVAL, PRIVATE, PUBLIC, SCHOOL

*Royal 8vo, 672 pp , Cloth, with Map and 140 Illustrations, 28s*

"A work that must have entailed a vast amount of labour and research. . . . Will become a STANDARD WORK IN PUBLIC HEALTH"—*Medical Times and Gazette.*

"Contains a great mass of information of easy reference"—*Sanitary Record*

LONDON · EXETER STREET, STRAND.

## By W. ELBORNE, F.L.S.

*In Extra Crown 8vo, with Litho-plates and Numerous Illustrations. Cloth, 3s. 6d.*

# PHARMACY AND MATERIA MEDICA

(A LABORATORY COURSE OF):

Including the Principles and Practice of Dispensing.

ADAPTED TO THE STUDY OF THE BRITISH PHARMACOPŒIA AND THE REQUIREMENTS OF THE PRIVATE STUDENT.

By W. ELBORNE, F.L.S., F.C.S.,

Late Assistant-Lecturer in Materia Medica and Pharmacy in the Owens College, Manchester.

"A work which we can very highly recommend to the perusal of all Students of Medicine. . . . ADMIRABLY ADAPTED to their requirements."—*Edinburgh Medical Journal*.

"Mr. Elborne evidently appreciates the Requirements of Medical Students, and there can be no doubt that any one who works through this Course will obtain an excellent insight into Chemical Pharmacy."—*British Medical Journal*.

"The system . . . which Mr. Elborne here sketches is thoroughly sound."—*Chemist and Druggist*.

---

## By Drs. DUPRÉ AND HAKE.

*With Coloured Plate of Spectra. Crown 8vo. Cloth, 7s. 6d.*

# INORGANIC CHEMISTRY (A Short Manual of).

By A. DUPRÉ, Ph.D., F.R.S., AND WILSON HAKE,

Ph.D., F.I.C., F.C.S., of the Westminster Hospital Medical School.

"A well-written, clear, and accurate Elementary Manual of Inorganic Chemistry. . . . We agree heartily in the system adopted by Drs. Dupré and Hake. WILL MAKE EXPERIMENTAL WORK TREBLY INTERESTING BECAUSE INTELLIGIBLE."—*Saturday Review*.

---

## WORKS by Prof. HUMBOLDT SEXTON, F.I.C., F.C.S., F.R.S.E.,

Glasgow and West of Scotland Technical College.

# OUTLINES OF QUANTITATIVE ANALYSIS.

*With Illustrations. THIRD EDITION. Crown 8vo, Cloth, 3s.*

"A practical work by a practical man . . . will further the attainment of accuracy and method."—*Journal of Education*.

"An ADMIRABLE little volume . . . well fulfils its purpose."—*Schoolmaster*.

"A COMPACT LABORATORY GUIDE for beginners was wanted, and the want has been WELL SUPPLIED. . . . A good and useful book."—*Lancet*.

### BY THE SAME AUTHOR.

# OUTLINES OF QUALITATIVE ANALYSIS.

*With Illustrations. SECOND EDITION. Crown 8vo, Cloth, 3s. 6d.*

"The work of a thoroughly practical chemist . . . and one which may be unhesitatingly recommended."—*British Medical Journal*.

"Compiled with great care, and will supply a want."—*Journal of Education*.

---

LONDON: EXETER STREET, STRAND.

### By Prof. A. JAMIESON, M.I.E.E., F.R.S.E.

# MAGNETISM AND ELECTRICITY
### (An Elementary Manual on):
WITH NUMEROUS ILLUSTRATIONS AND EXAMINATION QUESTIONS.

PART I.—MAGNETISM, 1s.    PART II.—VOLTAIC ELECTRICITY, 1s. 6d.
PART III.—ELECTRO-STATICS, or FRICTIONAL ELECTRICITY, 1s. 6d.
*Or, the 3 Parts, bound, in One Volume, 3s. 6d.*

"An ADMIRABLE Introduction to Magnetism and Electricity . . . the production of a skilled and experienced Teacher . . . explained at every point by simple experiments, rendered easier by admirable Illustrations."—*British Med. Journal.*

"Teachers are to be congratulated on having such a THOROUGHLY TRUSTWORTHY Text-Book at their disposal."—*Nature.*

---

### By Prof. H. G. LANDIS, M.D., Starling Medical College.

# THE MANAGEMENT OF LABOUR AND OF THE LYING-IN PERIOD.
*In 8vo, with Illustrations. Cloth, 7s. 6d.*

"Fully accomplishes the object kept in view by its author. . . . Will be found of GREAT VALUE by the young practitioner."—*Glasgow Medical Journal.*

---

### By Surgeon-General Sir THOMAS LONGMORE, C.B.

# THE SANITARY CONTRASTS OF THE CRIMEAN WAR.
*Demy 8vo. Cloth limp, 1s. 6d.*

"A most valuable contribution to Military Medicine."—*British Medical Journal.*
"A most concise and interesting Review."—*Lancet.*

---

### By Prof. W. KITCHEN PARKER, F.R.S.

# MAMMALIAN DESCENT:
### Being the Hunterian Lectures for 1884.
*Adapted for General Readers. With Illustrations. In 8vo, cloth, 10s. 6d.*

"The smallest details of science catch a LIVING GLOW from the ardour of the author's imagination, . . . we are led to compare it to some quickening spirit which makes all the dry bones of skulls and skeletons stand up around him as an exceeding great army."—Prof. Romanes in *Nature.*

"A very striking book . . . as readable as a book of travels. Prof. PARKER is no Materialist."—*Leicester Post.*

---

LONDON: EXETER STREET, STRAND.

## WORKS
### By J. R. AINSWORTH DAVIS, B.A.,
PROFESSOR OF BIOLOGY, UNIVERSITY COLLEGE, ABERYSTWYTH.

## BIOLOGY (A TEXT-BOOK OF):
Comprising Vegetable and Animal Morphology and Physiology.

In Large Crown 8vo, with 158 Illustrations. Cloth, 12s 6d.

**GENERAL CONTENTS**

PART I. VEGETABLE MORPHOLOGY AND PHYSIOLOGY —Fungi—Algæ—The Moss—The Fern—Gymnosperms—Angiosperms

Comparative Vegetable Morphology and Physiology—Classification of Plants

PART II ANIMAL MORPHOLOGY AND PHYSIOLOGY —Protozoa—Cœlenterata—Vermes-- Arthropoda—Mollusca—Amphibia—Aves—Mammalia

Comparative Animal Morphology and Physiology—Classification of Animals

*With Bibliography, Exam -Questions, Complete Glossary, and 158 Illustrations*

"As a general work of reference, Mr Davis's manual will be HIGHLY SERVICEABLE to medical men "—*British Medical Journal*

"Furnishes a clear and comprehensive exposition of the subject in a systematic form "—*Saturday Review*

"Literally PACKED with information "—*Glasgow Medical Journal*

## THE FLOWERING PLANT,
### AS ILLUSTRATING THE FIRST PRINCIPLES OF BOTANY.

Specially adapted for London Matriculation, S Kensington, and University Local Examinations in Botany Large Crown 8vo, with numerous Illustrations 3s 6d

"It would be hard to find a Text book which would better guide the student to an accurate knowledge of modern discoveries in Botany The SCIENTIFIC ACCURACY of statement, and the concise exposition of FIRST PRINCIPLES make it valuable for educational purposes In the chapter on the Physiology of Flowers, an *admirable resumé* is given, drawn from Darwin, Hermann Muller, Kerner, and Lubbock, of what is known of the Fertilization of Flowers — *Journal of the Linnean Society*

"We are much pleased with this volume . . the author's style is MOST CLEAR, and his treatment that of a PRACTISED INSTRUCTOR The Illustrations are very good, suitable, and helpful The Appendix on Practical Work will be INVALUABLE to the private student We heartily commend the work "—*Schoolmaster*

\*<sub>\*</sub>\* Recommended by the National Home-Reading Union ; and also for use in the University Correspondence Classes

## A ZOOLOGICAL POCKET-BOOK:
### or, Synopsis of Animal Classification.

*Comprising Definitions of the Phyla, Classes, and Orders, with explanatory Remarks and Tables*

### By Dr. EMIL SELENKA,
Professor in the University of Erlangen

Authorised English translation from the Third German Edition.

In Small Post 8vo, Interleaved for the use of Students Limp Covers, 4s.

"Dr Selenka's Manual will be found useful by all Students of Zoology It is a COMPREHENSIVE and SUCCESSFUL attempt to present us with a scheme of the natural arrangement of the animal world "—*Edin Med Journal*

"Will prove very serviceable to those who are attending Biology Lectures. . . The translation is accurate and clear "—*Lancet*

LONDON: EXETER STREET, STRAND.

# FORTHCOMING WORKS.

*In Preparation. In Large 8vo, with Plates and Illustrations.*

## DISEASES OF THE HEART
### (THE DIAGNOSIS OF).

BY

### A. ERNEST SANSOM, M.D., F.R.C.P.,

Physician to the London Hospital; Consulting Physician, North-Eastern Hospital for Children;
Examiner in Medicine, Royal College of Physicians (Conjoint Board for England), and
University of Durham; Lecturer on Medical Jurisprudence and Public Health,
London Hospital Medical College, &c.

---

*In Preparation. In Large 8vo, with Chromo-Lithographs and Numerous Illustrations in the Text.*

## GYNÆCOLOGY (A Practical Treatise on).

BY

### JOHN HALLIDAY CROOM, M.D., F.R.C.P.E., F.R.C.S.E.,

Physician to, and Clinical Lecturer on Diseases of Women at, the Royal Infirmary, Edinburgh;
Physician Royal Maternity Hospital, Edinburgh; Examiner in Midwifery, R.C.P.,
Edinburgh; Lecturer on Midwifery and Diseases of Women,
Edinburgh School of Medicine, &c., &c.,

WITH THE COLLABORATION OF

### MM. JOHNSON SYMINGTON, M.D., F.R.C.S.E.,

AND

### MILNE MURRAY, M.A., M.B., F.R.C.P.E.

LONDON : EXETER STREET, STRAND.

# FORTHCOMING WORKS.

*In Preparation.   In Large 8vo, with Numerous Illustrations*

# THE SURGERY OF THE BRAIN
## (A TREATISE ON)
### BY
### VICTOR A. HORSLEY, M.B, F R S, &c,
Assistant-Surgeon, University College Hospital   Professor of Pathology, University College, &c, &c

By the same Author.

*Shortly.   In Demy 8vo, with Numerous Illustrations*

# THE NERVOUS SYSTEM:
## ITS STRUCTURE AND FUNCTIONS.
### BEING
### THE FULLERIAN LECTURES ON PHYSIOLOGY FOR 1891.

---

*Shortly   In Large Crown 8vo   Fully Illustrated*

# CLINICAL MEDICINE (A Manual of).
## FOR THE USE OF STUDENTS
### By JUDSON BURY, M D, M R C P,
Assistant Physician, Royal Manchester Infirmary

LONDON . EXETER STREET, STRAND.

**Eighth Annual Issue, now Ready.**

☞ For a COMPLETE RECORD of the PAPERS read before the MEDICAL SOCIETIES throughout the United Kingdom during each Year, *vide*

# THE OFFICIAL YEAR-BOOK
### OF THE
# SCIENTIFIC AND LEARNED SOCIETIES
## OF GREAT BRITAIN AND IRELAND.
### Price 7s. 6d.
#### COMPILED FROM OFFICIAL SOURCES.

*Comprising (together with other Official Information) LISTS of the PAPERS read during 1890 before the ROYAL SOCIETIES of LONDON and EDINBURGH, the ROYAL DUBLIN SOCIETY, the BRITISH ASSOCIATION, and all the LEADING SOCIETIES throughout the Kingdom engaged in the following Departments of Research:—*

§ 1. Science Generally: *i.e.*, Societies occupying themselves with several Branches of Science, or with Science and Literature jointly.
§ 2. Mathematics and Physics.
§ 3. Chemistry and Photography.
§ 4. Geology, Geography, and Mineralogy.
§ 5. Biology, including Microscopy and Anthropology.
§ 6. Economic Science and Statistics.
§ 7. Mechanical Science and Architecture.
§ 8. Naval and Military Science.
§ 9. Agriculture and Horticulture.
§ 10. Law.
§ 11. MEDICINE.
§ 12. Literature.
§ 13. Psychology.
§ 14. Archæology.

"The YEAR-BOOK OF SOCIETIES is a Record which ought to be of the greatest use for the progress of science."—*Sir Lyon Playfair, F.R.S., K.C.B., M.P., Past-President of the British Association.*

"It goes almost without saying that a Handbook of this subject will be in time one of the most generally useful works for the library or the desk."—*The Times.*

"The YEAR-BOOK OF SOCIETIES meets an obvious want, and promises to be a valuable work of reference."—*Athenæum.*

"The YEAR-BOOK OF SCIENTIFIC AND LEARNED SOCIETIES meets a want, and is therefore sure of a welcome."—*Westminster Review.*

"AS A BOOK OF REFERENCE, WE HAVE EVER FOUND IT TRUSTWORTHY."—*Lancet.*

"Remarkably full and accurate."—*British Medical Journal.*

"An exceedingly well drawn up volume, compiled with great accuracy, and indispensable to any one who may wish to keep himself abreast of the scientific work of the day."—*Edin. Medical Journal.*

Copies of the FIRST ISSUE, giving an account of the History, Organisation, and Conditions of Membership of the various Societies [with Appendix on the Leading Scientific Societies throughout the world], and forming the groundwork of the Series, may still be had, price 7s. 6d. *Also Copies of the following Issues.*

The YEAR-BOOK OF SOCIETIES forms a complete INDEX TO THE SCIENTIFIC WORK of the year in the various Departments. It is used as a ready HANDBOOK in all our great SCIENTIFIC CENTRES, MUSEUMS, and LIBRARIES throughout the Kingdom, and will, without doubt, become an INDISPENSABLE BOOK OF REFERENCE to every one engaged in Scientific Work.

---

LONDON: CHARLES GRIFFIN & COMPANY, EXETER STREET, STRAND.

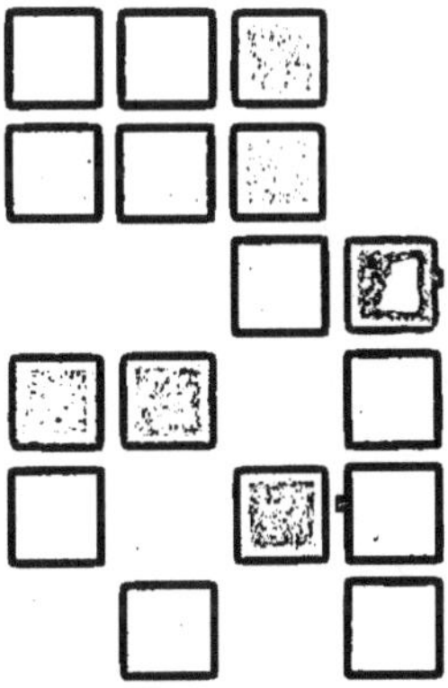

CPSIA information can be obtained
at www.ICGtesting.com
Printed in the USA
LVHW080953050622
720537LV00024B/76